I0822223

EPHESIANS

EVANGELICAL EXEGETICAL COMMENTARY

EPHESIANS

S. M. Baugh

Ephesians
Evangelical Exegetical Commentary

Lexham Academic, an imprint of Lexham Press
1313 Commercial St., Bellingham, WA 98225
LexhamPress.com

English quotations from Ephesians are the author's own translation.

ISBN 9781577996569

Lexham Editorial Team: Claire Brubaker, Lynnea Fraser, Elliot Ritzema, Elizabeth Vince
Cover Design: Brittany Schrock
Typesetting: ProjectLuz.com

24 25 26 27 28 29 30 / IN / 12 11 10 9 8

This work is dedicated to my fathers and brothers of the
Presbytery of Southern California of the Orthodox Presbyterian Church,
with thanks for the honor of ministering among you
and with good hope that you will continue to
stand fast in the Lord's strong armor.

Contents

Commentary Editors

General Editor
H. Wayne House

Old Testament Editor
William D. Barrick

Assistant Old Testament Editor
JoAnna M. Hoyt

New Testament Editor
W. Hall Harris

Assistant New Testament Editor
Andrew W. Pitts

Preface

With all the commentaries on this brief book, what more can be said to justify a new offering? In one sense, I am happy to simply reaffirm much that has already been said in the superb commentaries, monographs, and articles related to Ephesians. My method when dealing with biblical texts is always to do my own work before consulting others, and it was with gratitude that some of my conclusions that cut against the grain of most interpreters were also supported by competent authorities (e.g., Eph 4:20–24). My purpose was not to come up with novel insights but to apply my particular areas of study and expertise to the interpretive task.

That being said, my particular interests and areas of study are fairly broad across the range of classics, ancient history (with particular interest in Ephesus), Greek grammar, and biblical theology. In the years working on this commentary, I have also developed my interests in text criticism and Greek literary composition and rhetoric. I think these various interests will show up clearly in the course of the comments, which I hope will augment the current literature in helpful ways.

In light of what has just been said, the reader who wants a comprehensive review of all recent thought on Ephesians will no doubt be disappointed. I have tried to deal with most major works in the secondary literature and in the translations, but to do that comprehensively would require a commentary far larger than this one, and we already have some fine, recent examples of such large works. I have to confess that the reading and study of ancient books and of other primary sources like inscriptions and papyri has always been more of a priority for me throughout my academic career. I can only hope that this enthusiasm for primary sources and their study will make up for my many deficiencies by offering the reader a first-century perspective insofar as I have been able to acquire one over the last four decades or so.

I wish to thank the many people who gave me assistance and encouragement on this project, including John Terrell and my daughter, Leah, and son, Isaac. The support and generous study leave provided by the Trustees of Westminster Seminary California gave me the needed time to wrap up this project. I am particularly grateful to Wayne House, Hall Harris, and to the people of Lexham Press for their patience and for the opportunity to pursue this work. Εὐλογητὸς ὁ θεὸς καὶ πατὴρ τοῦ κυρίου ἡμῶν Ἰησοῦ Χριστοῦ (Eph 1:3).

—S. M. Baugh

Editors' Preface

We are happy to present the Evangelical Exegetical Commentary (EEC) series on the Bible. Though there are many excellent commentaries that have been produced in recent years, the EEC is a needed addition for scholars, pastors, and students of the Bible. As the title of the series indicates, the authors of this series are committed to both the evangelical faith and a careful exegesis of the biblical text. Each of the authors affirms historic, orthodox Christianity and the inspiration and inerrancy of the Holy Scriptures. In this series, the biblical books are studied with the tested tools of biblical scholarship, keeping in mind that these books, produced by human authors, come from the very mouth of God (2 Tim 3:16). The EEC reflects the important interpretative principles of the Reformation, while utilizing historical-grammatical and contextual interpretative methods.

Each part of the biblical text—as reflected in the original reading—has something to teach us about God, his world, and how we should relate to him and to others. Thus in this series, each biblical unit is analyzed and interpreted. Then recommendations for application to everyday life and biblical theology are offered. This last step will aid pastors and teachers in their ministry of God's Word.

We hope that you will have greater appreciation for the Word of God and the ability to better share it because of reading the EEC.

For us, the EEC is an offering of praise to the great Triune God, who is our Creator, Savior, and Sustainer, and who, through Jesus the Messiah and Lord, dwelled among humanity to bring us salvation and gifts of His grace.

ὅτι ἐξ αὐτοῦ καὶ δι' αὐτοῦ καὶ εἰς αὐτὸν τὰ πάντα·
αὐτῷ ἡ δόξα εἰς τοὺς αἰῶνας, ἀμήν. (Rom 11:36)

Because out of him and through him and unto him are all things; To him be the glory unto all the ages, amen. (Rom 11:36)

H. Wayne House, General Editor
William D. Barrick, Old Testament Editor
JoAnna M. Hoyt, Assistant Old Testament Editor
W. Hall Harris, New Testament Editor
Andrew W. Pitts, New Testament Editor

Abbreviations

AB	Anchor Bible
ABD	*Anchor Bible Dictionary*. Edited by D. N. Freedman. 6 vols. New York, 1992.
ABR	*Australian Biblical Review*
ACCS	Edwards, Mark J. *Galatians, Ephesians, Philippians*. Ancient Christian Commentary on Scripture. 2nd ed. Downers Grove, IL: InterVarsity Press, 2005.
AD	anno Domini
AGJU	Arbeiten zur Geschichte des antiken Judentums und des Urchistentums
AJP	*American Journal of Philology*
AnBib	Analecta biblica
ANRW	*Aufstieg und Niedergang der römischen Welt*
ANTF	Arbeiten zur neutestamentlichen Textforschung
ATJ	*Ashland Theological Journal*
AUSS	Andrews University Seminary Studies
BAGL	*Biblical and Ancient Greek Linguistics*
BBR	*Bulletin for Biblical Research*
BC	before Christ
BDAG	Bauer, W., F. W. Danker, W. F. Arndt, and F. W. Gingrich. *Greek-English Lexicon of the New Testament and Other Early Christian Literature*, 3rd ed. Chicago, 2000
BDF	Blass, F., A. Debrunner, and R. W. Funk. *A Greek Grammar of the New Testament and Other Early Christian Literature*. Chicago, 1961
BETS	*Bulletin of the Evangelical Theological Society*
BHS4	Biblia Hebraica Stuttgartensia
BHT	Beiträge zur historischen Theologie
Bib	*Biblica*
BJRL	*Bulletin of the John Rylands University Library of Manchester*
BNTC	Black's New Testament Commentaries
BR	*Biblical Research*

BRS	Biblical Resource Series
BSac	*Bibliotheca Sacra*
BTS	Biblical Tools and Studies
BU	Biblische Untersuchungen
BZ	Biblische Zeitschrift
BZNW	Beihefte zur Zeitschrift für die neutestamentliche Wissenschaft und die Kunde der älteren Kirche
ca.	circa
CBQ	*Catholic Biblical Quarterly*
cf.	*confer,* compare
chap(s).	chapter(s)
CJ	*Classical Journal*
ConBNT	Coniectanea neotestamentica
ed(s).	edition; edited by; editor(s)
e.g.	*exempli gratia*, for example
esp.	especially
etc.	*et cetera*, and the rest (Greek: κτλ., καὶ τὰ λοίπα)
CPhil	*Classical Philology*
CQ	*Classical Quarterly*
CTJ	*Calvin Theological Journal*
CTQ	*Concordia Theological Quarterly*
CTR	*Criswell Theological Review*
CurBS	*Currents in Research: Biblical Studies*
DJD	Discoveries in the Judean Desert
DPL	*Dictionary of Paul and His Letters.* Edited by G. F. Hawthorne and R. P. Martin. Leicester, UK, 1993
EDNT	*Exegetical Dictionary of the New Testament.* Edited by H. Balz and G. Schneider. Grand Rapids, 1990–93
EKKNT	*Evangelisch-katholischer Kommentar zum Neuen Testament*
Ep.	*Epistle(s)*
esp.	especially
ET	English translation
ESV	English Standard Version
EV	English Version(s)
EvQ	*Evangelical Quarterly*
FS	*Festschrift*
GNCNT	Good News Commentary New Testament
GNS	Good News Studies
GRBS	Greek, Roman, and Byzantine Studies

GTJ	*Grace Theological Journal*
HNT	Handbuch zum Neuen Testament
HTKNT	Herders theologischer Kommentar zum Neuen Testament
HTR	*Harvard Theological Review*
HUT	Hermeneutische Untersuchungen zur Theologie
IBS	*Irish Biblical Studies*
ICC	International Critical Commentary
i.e.	*id est*, that is
Int	*Interpretation*
IvE	*Die Inschriften von Ephesos*. Edited by R. Meriç, R. Merkelbach, J. Nollé, and S. Sahin. Bonn: Rudolph Habelt, 1979–84
JAC	*Jahrbuch für Antike und Christentum*
JÖAI	*Jahreshefte des östereichischen archäologischen Institutes in Wien*
JB	Jerusalem Bible
JBL	*Journal of Biblical Literature*
JETS	*Journal of the Evangelical Theological Society*
JGRChJ	*Journal of Greco-Roman Christianity and Judaism*
JQR	*Jewish Quarterly Review*
JSNT	*Journal for the Study of the New Testament*
JSNTSup	Journal for the Study of the New Testament: Supplement Series
JSOTSup	Journal for the Study of the Old Testament: Supplement Series
JTS	*Journal of Theological Studies*
KEK	Kritisch-exegetischer Kommentar über das Neue Testament (Meyer-Kommentar)
KJV	King James Version
κτλ.	Καὶ τὰ λοίπα ("and the rest" = etc.)
LBL	Library of Biblical Theology
LCL	Loeb Classical Library
lit.	literally
l(l).	line(s)
L&N	*Greek-English Lexicon of the New Testament Based on Semantic Domains*. 2 vols. Edited by Johannes P. Louw and Eugene A. Nida. New York, 1988
LNTS	Library of New Testament Studies
LSJ	Liddell, H. G., R. Scott, and H. S. Jones. *A Greek-English Lexicon*. 9th ed. with revised supplement. Oxford, 1996

LXX	Septuagint version(s)
MHT	*A Grammar of New Testament Greek*, by J. H. Moulton, W. F. Howard, and N. Turner. 4 vols. Edinburgh: T&T Clark, 2006.
MS(S)	manuscript(s)
MT	Masoretic Text
NA[28]	Nestle-Aland: Novum Testamentum Graece, 28th ed.
NAB	New American Bible
NASB	New American Standard Bible
NCB	New Century Bible
n.d.	no date
Neot	*Neotestamentica*
New Docs	*New Documents Illustrating Early Christianity*. Edited by G. H. R. Horsley and S. Llewelyn. North Ryde: N. S. W., 1981–
NICNT	New International Commentary on the New Testament
NIGTC	New International Greek Testament Commentary
NIV	New International Version (1984 ed.)
NKJV	New King James Version
NLT	New Living Translation
NovT	*Novum Testamentum*
NovTSup	Novum Testamentum Supplements
NPNF[1]	*A Select Library of the Nicene and Post-Nicene Fathers of the Christian Church*. First series. Edited by P. Schaff et al.
NRSV	New Revised Standard Version
n.s.	new series
NSBT	New Studies in Biblical Theology
NT	New Testament
NTC	New Testament Commentary
NTD	Das Neue Testament Deutsch
NTL	New Testament Library
NTM	New Testament Monographs
NTS	*New Testament Studies*
OCD	*The Oxford Classical Dictionary*. Edited by Simon Hornblower, Antony Spawforth, and Esther Eidinow. 4th ed. Oxford: Clarendon, 2012
OL	Old Latin
Or.	*Oration(s)*
OT	Old Testament
p(p).	page(s)

P.Amh.	*Amherst Papyri*
P.Oxy.	*Oxyrhynchus Papyri*
P.Par	*Paris Papyri*
P.Ryl.	*Rylands Papyri*
P.Tebt.	*Tebtunis Papyri*
PBM	Paternoster Biblical Monographs
PGM	Papyri graecae magicae: Die griechischen Zauberpapyri. Edited by K. Preisendanz. Berlin, 1928
PNTC	Pillar New Testament Commentary
Presb	*Presbyterion*
RB	*Revue biblique*
RelSBul	*Religious Studies Bulletin*
ResQ	*Restoration Quarterly*
RevExp	*Review and Expositor*
RGRW	Religions in the Graeco-Roman World
RRBS	*Recent Research in Biblical Studies*
RSV	Revised Standard Version
SANT	Studien zum Alten und Neuen Testaments
SBG	Studies in Biblical Greek
SBLDS	Society of Biblical Literature Dissertation Series
SBLGNT	Society of Biblical Literature Greek New Testament
SBLSBS	Society of Biblical Literature Sources for Biblical Study
SCHT	Studia ad corpus hellenisticum Novi Testamenti
SEG	*Supplementum Epigraphicum Graecum*
SJT	*Scottish Journal of Theology*
SNT	Studien zum Neuen Testament
SNTSMS	Society of New Testament Studies Monograph Series
SP	Sacra pagina
SIG	Sylloge Inscriptionum Graecarum
Sup	Supplement
TANTZ	Texte und Arbeiten zum neutestamentlichen Zeitalter
TDNT	*Theological Dictionary of the New Testament.* Edited by G. Kittel and G. Friedrich. Translated by G. W. Bromiley. 10 vols. Grand Rapids: 1964–76
TDOT	*Theological Dictionary of the Old Testament.* Edited by G. J. Botterweck and H. Ringgren. Translated by J. T. Willis, G. W. Bromiley, and D. E. Green. 8 vols. Grand Rapids: 1974–
TheolZeit	*Theologische Zeitschrift*
TLG	Thesaurus Lingua Graeca

TNTC	Tyndale New Testament Commentary
trans.	translator(s); translation
TrinJ	*Trinity Journal*
TynB	*Tyndale Bulletin*
UBS[4]	United Bible Society *Greek New Testament*. 4th ed.
v(v).	verse(s)
VC	*Vigiliae christianae*
VE	*Vox evangelica*
Vg.	Vulgate
WBC	Word Biblical Commentary
WTJ	*Westminster Theological Journal*
WUNT	Wissenschaftliche Untersuchungen zum Neuen Testament
ZNW	*Zeitschrift für die neutestamentliche Wissenschaft und die Kunde der älteren Kirche*
ZPE	*Zeitschrift für Papyrologie und Epigraphik*
ZTK	*Zeitschrift für Theologie und Kirche*
§	section/paragraph
[…]	Indicates places where the stone is broken on inscriptions with only conjectural readings

Grammatical Abbreviations

acc.	accusative
adj.	adjective
adv.	adverb, adverbial
aor.	aorist
conj.	conjunction
fem.	feminine
gen.	genitive
impv.	imperative
indic.	indicative
inf.	infinitive
masc.	masculine
obj.	object
pass.	passive
pl.	plural
poss.	possessive
prep.	preposition
pres.	present

ptc(s).	participle
sg.	singular
voc.	vocative

Ancient Sources

Old Testament

Gen	Genesis
Exod	Exodus
Lev	Leviticus
Num	Numbers
Deut	Deuteronomy
Josh	Joshua
Judg	Judges
1–2 Sam	1–2 Samuel
1–2 Kgs	1–1 Kings
1–2 Chr	1–2 Chronicles
Neh	Nehemiah
Esth	Esther
Psa/Pss	Psalm/Psalms
Prov	Proverbs
Eccl	Ecclesiastes
Song	Song of Songs
Isa	Isaiah
Jer	Jeremiah
Lam	Lamentations
Ezek	Ezekiel
Dan	Daniel
Hos	Hosea
Obad	Obadiah
Mic	Micah
Nah	Nahum
Hab	Habakkuk
Zeph	Zephaniah
Hag	Haggai
Zech	Zechariah
Mal	Malachi

New Testament

Matt	Matthew
Rom	Romans
1–2 Cor	1–2 Corinthians
Gal	Galatians
Eph	Ephesians
Phil	Philippians
Col	Colossians
1–2 Thess	1–2 Thessalonians
1–2 Tim	1–2 Timothy
Phlm	Philemon
Heb	Hebrews
Jas	James
1–2 Pet	1–2 Peter
Rev	Revelation

Apocrypha and Pseudepigrapha

1 Bar.	*1 Baruch*
2 Bar.	*2 Baruch*
1 Esd	1 Esdras
1 Macc	1 Maccabees
2 Macc	2 Maccabees
3 Macc	*3 Maccabees*
4 Macc	*4 Maccabees*
Bar	Baruch
Jdt	Judith
Jub.	*Jubilees*
Pss. Sol.	*Psalms of Solomon*
Sir	Sirach/Ecclesiasticus
T. Benj.	*Testament of Benjamin*
T. Jos.	*Testament of Joseph*
T. Nap.	*Testament of Naphtali*
T. Reu.	*Testament of Reuben*
T. Sim.	*Testament of Simeon*
T. Sol.	*Testament of Solomon*
T. Zeb.	*Testament of Zebulun*
Tob	Tobit
Wis	Wisdom of Solomon

Classical Writings

Aen.	Virgil, *Aeneid*
Anab.	Xenophon, *Anabasis*
Anach.	Lucian, *Anacharsis*
Ann.	Tacitus, *Annales*
Argon.	Apollonius of Rhodes, *Argonautica*
Brut.	Cicero, *Brutus or De claris oratoribus*
Char.	Theophrastus, *Characteres*
Claud.	Suetonius, *Divus Claudius*
Comp.	Dionysius of Halicarnassus, *De compositione verborum* ("On the Composition of Speeches" or *The Art of Composition*)
Conj. praec.	Plutarch, *Conjugalia Praecepta*
Cons. ux.	Plutarch, *Consolatio ad uxorem*
Cor.	Demosthenes, *De corona (On the Crown)*
Dial.	Tacitus, *Dialogus de oratoribus*
Diatr.	Epictetus, *Diatribai (Dissertationes)*
Din.	Dionysius of Halicarnassus, *De Dinarcho*
Dom.	Suetonius, *Domitianus*
Eloc.	Demetrius, *On Style (Elocution)*
Ep.	Pliny the Younger, *Epistulae*
Fort. Rom.	Plutarch, *De fortuna Romanorum*
Geog.	Strabo, *Geographica (Geography)*
Hist.	Polybius, *The Histories*
Id.	Hermogenes, *On Types of Style*
Il.	Homer, *Iliad*
Inst.	Quintilian, *Institutio oratoria*
Ira	Seneca, *De ira*
Jul.	Suetonius, *Divus Julius*
Leuc. Clit.	Achilles Tatius, *Leucippe et Clitophon (The Adventures of Leucippe and Cleitophon)*
Lib. ed.	Pseudo-Plutarch, *De liberis educandis*
Mem.	Xenophon, *Memorabilia*
Mor.	Plutarch, *Moralia*
Nat.	Pliny the Elder, *Naturalis historia (Natural History)*
Nat. d.	Cicero, *De natura deorum*
Nav.	Lucian, *The Ship, or The Wishes*
Od.	Homer, *Odyssey*
Oec.	Xenophon, *Oeconomicus*
Op.	Hesiod, *Opera et dies*

Or. Brut.	Cicero, *Orator ad M. Brutum*
Plutarch, *Ant.*	Plutarch, *Antonius*
Pomp.	Plutarch, *Pompeius*
Protr.	Epictetus, *Exhortation to the Greeks*
Rhet.	Aristotle, *Rhetorica*
Satyr.	Petronius, *Satyricon*
Theog.	Hesiod, *Theogonia (Theogony)*
Thuc.	Dionysius of Halicarnassus, *De Thucydide*
Vit. soph.	Philostratus, *Vitae sophistarum*
Vit. Apoll.	Philostratus, *Vita Apollonii*

Dead Sea Scrolls

1QH[a]	Hodayot[a] or Thanksgiving Hymns[a]
11Q5	Psalms Scroll
1QS	Serekh ha-Yaḥad or Rule of the Community (formerly called Manual of Discipline)

Early Christian and Related Writings

1 Clem.	*1 Clement*
2 Clem.	*2 Clement*
Ap. John	*Apocryphon of John*
Apol.	Tertullian, *Apologeticus*
Barn.	*Barnabas*
Did.	*Didache*
Eph.	Ignatius, *To the Ephesians*
Gos. Thom.	*Gospel of Thomas*
Hist. eccl.	Eusebius, *Ecclesiastical Histories*
Hom. Col.	John Chrysostom, *Homilies on Colossians*
Hom. Eph.	John Chrysostom, *Homilies on Ephesians*
Magn.	Ignatius, *To the Magnesians*
Marc.	Tertullian, *Against Marcion*
Mart. Pol.	*Martyrdom of Polycarp*
Odes. Sol.	*Odes of Solomon*
Phld.	Ignatius, *To the Philadelphians*
Pol.	Ignatius, *To Polycarp*
Pol. Phil.	Polycarp, *To the Philippians*
Smyrn.	Ignatius, *To the Smyrnaeans*

Josephus

Ant.	*Jewish Antiquities*
J.W.	*Jewish War*

Philo

Alleg. Interp.	*Allegorical Interpretation*
Embassy	*On the Embassy to Gaius*
Migr.	*On the Migration of Abraham*
Spec. Laws	*On the Special Laws*
Virtues	*On the Virtues*

Introduction

Authorship

Anyone writing on Ephesians today must deal with the issue of the denial of Pauline authorship by a significant number of scholars. Skepticism that Paul wrote this epistle was first raised by a few lone voices in the seventeenth century, but became more widespread in the mid-nineteenth century after F. C. Baur proposed that Ephesians originated in the second century. Before the critical period, there had never been any question about Pauline authorship or the canonical identity of this epistle, including its acceptance in the early church among even the earliest apostolic fathers.[1]

Generally, there are five issues raised to deny Pauline authorship:

1. the vocabulary
2. the epistle's theological interests
3. the impersonal tone of the epistle
4. the relationship of Ephesians to Colossians
5. the Greek style of Ephesians versus the other Pauline Epistles

All of these issues and more have been discussed at great length and have been countered in equal length by various writers and commentators, such that a full review of all of them is not necessary here.[2] It is safe to say that among some scholars, non-Pauline authorship of Ephesians has reached the status of unquestioned dogma (O'Brien, 46) denied by only a few "cranky

1. See esp. Hoehner, 2–6, and Clinton Arnold, "Ephesians, Letter to the," in *DPL*, 238–53 (esp. 240–42).

2. The introductory comments in O'Brien, 4–47; Hoehner, 2–61 (who includes a very extensive review of scholars and bibliography); and Barth, 36–50, are particularly helpful and full. *Contra* Pauline authorship, see esp. Lincoln, xlvii–lxxiii (though he accepts the authority and canonicity of Ephesians); Best, 6–36.

obscurantists."[3] Indeed, even the repeated scholarly defense of its Pauline authorship has been said to indicate its untenability (Lincoln, lxix). This is a very dubious argument, but it does show that some scholars will probably not be persuaded on the issue no matter what evidence is adduced.

How does one offer something new and worthwhile in such a situation? In my opinion, there was a significant advance in the discussion made by Randolph Richards in his examination of the role of secretaries and cosenders in ancient compositions, which must be reckoned with by anyone examining Pauline authorship of his epistles, including the issue of the relationship of Ephesians to Colossians, which directly affects issues one, four, and five above.[4] Furthermore, the alleged impersonal character of the epistle (issue three) will be addressed below under "Recipients," since it can be informed by research into the history of Ephesus through its material remains.[5] As for the theological interests in Ephesians (issue two), this epistle has seemed to countless generations of readers to represent a Pauline expression of apostolic teaching. The hundreds of cross-references to other passages in the course of my comments below will allow the reader to see this quite clearly.[6]

I will be offering a somewhat new contribution as regards the Greek style of Ephesians (issue five), though "I am aware that I often seem to be making original remarks when what I am saying is very old but generally unknown" (Cicero, *Or. Brut.* 3.12). In particular, though there has been some valuable work of late on rhetoric and its influence on NT epistles, one area that has not been fully attended to is the related issue of literary composition and its bearing on Greek style. The starting point for my inquiry into these issues was and is: How would an ancient Greek reader have analyzed the style of Ephesians in relation to, for example, Romans? I think the answer might surprise us and need some explanation to be

3. Cf. Luke Timothy Johnson, review of Michael Prior, *Paul the Letter-Writer and the Second Letter to Timothy*, *CBQ* 53 (1991): 339.

4. E. Randolph Richards, *The Secretary in the Letters of Paul*, WUNT 2.42 (Tübingen: Mohr Siebeck, 1991); and in popular form: E. Randolph Richards, *Paul and First-Century Letter Writing: Secretaries, Composition and Collection* (Downers Grove, IL: InterVarsity Press, 2004).

5. This commentary includes epigraphical evidence (inscriptions) from Ephesus to illumine how the epistle relates to its audience.

6. See esp. O'Brien, 21–33, for a lucid discussion.

appreciated. For example, was Paul's style a "monocolon" style (μονόκωλος), which (Pseudo-)Plutarch found disagreeable and monotonous?[7] Or would Jerome have complained about Paul's style in Romans (as he does about Ephesians; see comment on 3:1) that Paul does not "render a hyperbaton" or "round his periods"? These are the sorts of critical issues related to ancient Greek style that will be discussed briefly below (and brought up throughout the comments where relevant).

Finally, the issue of pseudonymity in Christian circles is currently being researched and addressed in helpful ways. There are actually very few pseudepigraphical (forged) epistles from early Christianity (cf. comments on 6:21–24), but recent research has shown that there is reason to believe that the early church opposed this practice and would have been ready to reject Ephesians if it were suspicious.[8] If the recipients had received this epistle from anyone beside Tychicus in Paul's day, suspicions would have been confirmed (see again comments on 6:21–22). I think we underestimate the ancient interest in this issue and the discernment of ancient Christians on this score (cf. Rev 2:2).

For example, it is not as if ancient authors did not consider or discuss matters of style affecting authorship in works that were suspicious. They did, as when Dionysius of Halicarnassus desired to distinguish genuine from spurious speeches of the orator Dinarchus of Corinth, who lived roughly two centuries earlier, and noted regarding Dinarchus' style: "It is

---

7. "While I am still dwelling upon my own opinion in regard to education, I desire to say that in the first place a discourse composed of a series of short sentences (τὸν μονόκωλον λόγον) I regard as no small proof of lack of culture; in the second place I think that in practice such discourse soon palls, and in every case it causes impatience; for monotony is in everything tiresome and repellent, but variety is agreeable, as it is in everything else, as, for example, in entertainments that appeal to the eye or the ear" (*Lib. ed.* 7B–D; LCL trans.). Hence, each colon* is a "period" (see below). The idea of a "sentence" is a more modern concept than the colon*.

8. See Richard Bauckham, "Pseudo-Apostolic Letters," *JBL* 107 (1988): 469–94, for discussion of other pseudoapostolic letters; and more recently Terry L. Wilder, *Pseudonymity, the New Testament, and Deception: An Inquiry into Intention and Reception* (Lanham, MD: University Press of America, 2004). Pseudonymous literary works with no author's name attached (cf. Eph 1:1; 3:1) might come about innocently enough. An author sometimes shared his work(s) with a friend without title or signature. When the friend died, this work by another was found in his library by his heirs and assumed to be his work and distributed as such; cf. D. A. Russell, *Plutarch* (New York: Scribner's, 1973), 19.

difficult to define, for he possessed no quality common to all his oratory, or any individual characteristic, either in his private or in his public speeches" (*Din.* 5). It seems to me that Paul had a flexible style of this sort, exacerbated by free involvement of his secretarial assistants (below).

Paul the Author

Dio Chrysostom advises: "Writing, however, I do not advise you to engage in with your own hand, or only very rarely, but rather to dictate to a secretary" (*Or.* 18.18). John Calvin followed this advice in the formation of his commentary on Isaiah, which he explains in a letter to Francis Dryander:

> You say that you are waiting for my meditations on Isaiah. They will come out soon. But they were written by des Gallars; for I do not have much time for writing. He takes down what I dictate to him, and later arranges it at home. Then I read it over again, and if anywhere he has not followed my meaning, I restore the sense.[9]

Writing in antiquity was a particularly arduous business. It was done while seated on the ground with the tablet or papyrus suspended on one's garment between crossed legs. The reed pen had to be sharpened just so and the ink made by hand. It is no wonder that secretaries (γραμματεῖς) with specialized knowledge of the mechanics of writing were usually employed in drafting one's writings.

For some time, scholars have proposed that the differences of style between Paul's Epistles were caused by the influence of different secretaries in their composition, which accounts for differences between Ephesians and the other Pauline Epistles.[10] This was sound conjecture, but what was needed was a thorough study of the whole role of secretaries in ancient compositions to compare with Paul, which was finally pursued in notably helpful

---

9. From *Opera Calvini* XIII, 536, as cited and translated by T. H. L. Parker, *Calvin's New Testament Commentaries* (Grand Rapids: Eerdmans, 1971), 20. Calvin also acknowleges that this commentary was "drawn up by another person" from his lectures in the preface to its first edition in 1550.

10. E.g., A. Van Roon, *The Authenticity of Ephesians*, NovTSup 39 (Leiden: Brill, 1974), 91–94.

doctoral research by E. Randolph Richards, published as *The Secretary in the Letters of Paul.*

I will not rehearse all of Richards' points, but the impact of his study for the flexibility of style in the Pauline Letters cannot be underestimated. He shows that the secretary might have had a significant role in the Greek style of the composition, much as de Gallars had with Calvin's Isaiah commentary. "It has been noted repeatedly that another effect of using a secretary (in any manner except as a recorder) is variation in the language, style, or content of the letter. The more freedom that the secretary was given, the more variance that was possible."[11] Yet Paul thoroughly controlled the meaning, content, and style by following up the secretary's work—also as Calvin notes with his Isaiah commentary. "Irrespective of any secretarial influence, the author assumed complete responsibility for the content, including the subtle nuances. Because of his accountability, he checked the final draft."[12] But this means that the elements of the composition that are Paul's and that are the secretary's will be almost impossible to distinguish for certain.

This situation is further complicated by an unusual feature of the Pauline Epistles in that they were not all sent by him alone: He names three cosenders—Sosthenes, Silvanus (Silas), and Timothy—in his epistles, with only six (including Ephesians) having Paul's name alone as the sender.[13] These cosenders (such as Timothy for Colossians but not Ephesians) might very well have been coauthors. Richards states:

---

11. Richards, *Secretary*, 115. For a study that posits a significant contribution by Tertius (Rom 16:22) as the secretary of Romans see Ian J. Elmer, "I, Tertius: Secretary or Co-author of Romans," *ABR* 56 (2008): 45–60.

12. Richards, *Secretary*, 127.

13. Only Romans, Galatians, Ephesians, and the Pastorals were sent by Paul without mention of a cosender (cf. Gal 1:2, "all the brothers who are with me"): Sosthenes (1 Corinthians), Silvanus (1–2 Thessalonians), and Timothy (2 Corinthians, Philippians, Colossians, 1–2 Thessalonians, and Philemon). Cf. Richards, *Secretaries*, 153–58; Samuel Byrskog, "Co-Senders, Co-Authors and Paul's Use of the First Person Plural," *ZNW* 87 (1996): 230–50. Both Richards and Byrskog remark at how few other letters from antiquity have a cosender (or coauthor) named. However, they both reference primarily literary sources like Cicero and Egyptian papyri letters, not the many extant letters on inscriptions. Discovery and analysis of those epigraphical letters would be a worthwhile doctoral dissertation (see the introduction to Eph 6:21–24 below for one such letter [*IvE* 2121]).

> It is quite unlikely, though, that Paul's references to others *by name* in his address was intended to indicate anything *less* than an *active* role in the composition of the letter. A practice of including others in the address as a "nicety" is not supported by the evidence. What constitutes an active role is more debatable. The co-authors apparently were not full contributors on an equal level with Paul. On the other hand, they must have some role in the writing of the letter.[14]

One model for Paul in this regard may have been the letter arising out of the Jerusalem council in Acts 15:23–29, sent to the churches in Syria and Cilicia from "the brothers, both the apostles and elders" (Acts 15:23). In many epistles where Paul had cosenders, he signs the letter himself (1 Cor 16:21; Col 4:18; 1 Thess 5:27; 2 Thess 3:17; Phlm 19; cf. Rom 16:22; Gal 6:11; and comments on Eph 6:21–24). Paul is obviously the senior, apostolic sender of the letter and presumably reserved final control over its contents.

That being the case, however, it is interesting that scholars speculate that Ephesians was copied by a forger who was a careful student of Paul, especially utilizing Colossians as a model (e.g., Lincoln). Yet, as a cosender, Timothy contributed to Colossians but not to Ephesians. This means that the similarities between the two epistles can most easily be traced to a common Pauline authorship, and any differences between the two possibly came from Timothy in Colossians. It would be more credible, then, to posit that it was Colossians, not Ephesians, that shows the marks of a student of Paul, Timothy.[15]

For example, here is a sample of three verses in Colossians compared with three in Ephesians.[16] I have put common words in bold (not includ-

---

14. Richards, *Secretaries*, 154 (emphasis original). See also Jerome Murphy-O'Connor, *Paul the Letter-Writer: His World, His Options, His Skills*, GNS 41 (Collegeville, MN: Liturgical Press, 1995), 16–19. Byrskog agrees that cosenders should often be regarded as coauthors, but adds that he thinks Richards' statement is "too categorical" ("Co-Senders," 249). Byrskog does not examine ancient letter writing per se but uses only the 1 pl. pronominal references in Paul's letters as a somewhat arbitrarily applied criterion for his analysis.

15. Note that the late, pseudepigraphical *Letter to the Laodiceans* contains phrases lifted directly out of Pauline works. See introduction to 6:21–24.

16. Cf. Lincoln, 228, who states, "The Colossians passage has been condensed and its key words taken over in this writer's own composition." This begs the question of literary dependence, since some see Colossians as dependent on Ephesians, and

ing cognates ἐκλεκτός, κλῆσις, and καλέω ["elect," "calling," "call"]) in both passages, with division of the text into cola* and periodic groupings (see "Greek Style" below):

Colossians 3:12–14:
Ἐνδύσασθε οὖν
ὡς ἐκλεκτοὶ τοῦ θεοῦ ἅγιοι καὶ ἠγαπημένοι
σπλάγχνα οἰκτιρμοῦ χρηστότητα
ταπεινοφροσύνην πραΰτητα μακροθυμίαν

ἀνεχόμενοι ἀλλήλων
καὶ χαριζόμενοι ἑαυτοῖς ἐάν τις πρός τινα ἔχῃ μομφήν
καθὼς καὶ ὁ κύριος ἐχαρίσατο ὑμῖν
οὕτως καὶ ὑμεῖς
ἐπὶ πᾶσιν δὲ τούτοις τὴν **ἀγάπην**
ὅ ἐστιν **σύνδεσμος** τῆς τελειότητος.[17]

Ephesians 4:1–3:
Παρακαλῶ οὖν ὑμᾶς
ἐγὼ ὁ δέσμιος ἐν κυρίῳ
ἀξίως περιπατῆσαι τῆς κλήσεως ἧς ἐκλήθητε
μετὰ πάσης **ταπεινοφροσύνης** καὶ **πραΰτητος**

μετὰ **μακροθυμίας ἀνεχόμενοι ἀλλήλων** ἐν **ἀγάπῃ**
σπουδάζοντες τηρεῖν τὴν ἑνότητα τοῦ πνεύματος
ἐν τῷ **συνδέσμῳ** τῆς εἰρήνης.[18]

Although there are seven words used between the two passages (which are both exhortations), the constructions of the statements are quite different.

---

others see simply two products of one author (with few or none taking into account Timothy's involvement in the writing of one of these texts).

17. "Put on then, as God's chosen ones, holy and beloved, compassion, kindness, humility, meekness, and patience, bearing with one another and, if one has a complaint against another, forgiving each other; as the Lord has forgiven you, so you also must forgive. And above all these put on love, which binds everything together in perfect harmony" (Col 3:12–15).

18. "I therefore, the prisoner in the Lord, strongly urge you to set out in a manner worthy of the calling with which you have been called, accompanied with all humility and gentleness, and with patience to bear with one another in love, and to take pains to maintain the unity of the Spirit in the bond of peace" (my trans.).

For example, Colossians 3:13, with its trailing οὕτως καὶ ὑμεῖς ("so also you as well"), is without parallel in Ephesians (cf. 1 Cor 14:12; 16:1; 2 Cor 10:7). While asyndeton* (lack of joining conjs.) is present throughout Ephesians—usually with prepositional phrases—the string of five accusative nouns without conjunctions in Col 3:12 also has no parallel in Ephesians.

The conclusion is that scholars who discuss literary matters to decide the authorship of Ephesians or the other Pauline Epistles need to take into account both the involvement of secretaries and cosenders. Failure to consider this factor seriously is failure to treat the Pauline Epistles in their historical context. It is true that we will probably never know the exact extent of secretarial involvement in particular passages or epistles, but this should lead to a heavier dose of caution about making firm conclusions than is often done. Accordingly, although I will occasionally bring up texts from Colossians or other Pauline texts for comparison with an Ephesians passage, it will not be a major factor shaping my comments. Neither will I use such parallels for speculation about priority of one text over another.

The Greek Style

When it comes to matters of style as it affects Pauline authorship of Ephesians, usually three issues are brought up: (1) the heavy use of prepositional phrases and genitive modifiers in interesting ways; (2) the "solemnity" and "rhythm" of the language found in Ephesians; and (3) the long "sentences," particularly at the beginning of the epistle.[19] Others have sufficiently addressed the first issue.[20] The second and third issues, though, need more careful qualification and discussion for ancient Greek. This will afford the opportunity to survey certain basic elements of ancient literary composition that bear on the Greek style in Ephesians and guide many of my comments.

---

19. Cf. Van Roon, *Authenticity*; Anthony Kenny, *A Stylometric Study of the New Testament* (Oxford: Clarendon, 1986); Kenneth J. Neumann, *The Authenticity of the Pauline Epistles in the Light of Stylostatistical Analysis*, SBLDS 120 (Atlanta: Scholars Press, 1990); C. Leslie Mitton, *The Epistle to the Ephesians: Its Authorship, Origin and Purpose* (Oxford: Clarendon, 1951). I wonder whether a computer could ever analyze whether a Greek period is rounded—a key factor of ancient Greek style (see below).

20. E.g., Van Roon, *Authenticity*, 121–28; Hoehner, 24–29.

In 1986 Charles J. Robbins published an important article on the compositional style of the opening long grammatical sentence of Eph 1:3–14, in which he demonstrated that "the length of the sentence and the manner of its composition are not unique but are in accord with the principles of Greek rhetoric as explained by the ancient rhetoricians themselves and exemplified in classical literature."[21] His judgment differs markedly from that of several others who regard Paul's Ephesians sentences as "infinitely long, heavy, and clumsy" (Barth, 77). Although I believe that Robbins' analysis needs some qualification, he has set us on the right path by pointing to distinctive features of ancient Greek literary composition and style.

To orient to this topic, I am in agreement with Martin Hengel that Paul was a native Greek speaker from Tarsus, trained at some point in Jerusalem, whose undoubted inspiration was the LXX rather than Homer.[22] While it is probable that Paul did not have advanced rhetorical training, all ancient liberal arts education from the beginning focused on public oral presentation.[23] At the first phases of his education, a young boy learned to breathe, to enunciate properly, and to scan the quantity of syllables for metrical awareness in order to lay a foundation for public speaking, the epicenter of a liberal education.[24] From the beginning of his schooling, every boy learned certain features of Greek composition for oral public presentation.[25]

21. Charles J. Robbins, "The Composition of Eph 1:3–14," *JBL* 105 (1986): 677–87 (quote from 677); cf. Robbins, "Rhetorical Structure of Philippians 2:6–11," *CBQ* 42 (1980): 73–82.
22. Martin Hengel, *The Pre-Christian Paul* (Philadelphia: Trinity Press International, 1991), 34–35.
23. For the probable limits on Paul's rhetorical training with references to the literature, see Andrew W. Pitts, "Hellenistic Schools in Jerusalem and Paul's Rhetorical Education," in *Paul's World*, ed. Stanley E. Porter (Boston: Brill, 2008), 19–50.
24. Two modern surveys of Graeco-Roman education that cover this and more are: Teresa Morgan, *Literate Education in the Hellenistic and Roman Worlds* (Cambridge: Cambridge University Press, 1998; repr., 2007); and Raffaella Cribiore, *Gymnastics of the Mind: Greek Education in Hellenistic and Roman Egypt* (Princeton: Princeton University Press, 2001). The classic work by H. I. Marrou (*A History of Education in Antiquity* [New York: Sheed and Ward, 1956]) is still very valuable.
25. The classic ancient handbooks on rhetoric by authors such as Aristotle, Cicero, and Quintilian have sections on the various elements of delivery. Pliny the Younger has several comments on both Greek and Latin rhetorical style and delivery of various contemporaries he has heard; e.g., *Ep.* 1.16 ("weighty and elegant periods"); 2.3

Furthermore, any lower-level education Paul received in Greek literature and rhetoric would have been refined both through hearing others and through his own practice "daily in the school (σχολή) of Tyrannus" during his extended residence in Ephesus (Acts 19:9).[26] While this building, home, or portico area cannot now be identified, it was likely on the "Embolos" street near the city center and the theater.[27] It is impossible to imagine someone totally inept at public speaking finding an audience in such a venue with the outcome that "all Asia" heard his message (Acts 19:10).

Paul's own downplaying of his oratorical skills (2 Cor 10:10; 11:6) should probably be seen over against the background of excessively elaborate sophistic adornment prevalent in the rhetorical schools of the time. Certainly the Ephesians would have known of Paul's unconcern for the infinite crafting of pyrotechnic speeches in contrast with various sophists who shook Ephesus "with a chorus of rhetoricians and their noisy applause" (Tacitus, *Dial.* 16.14).[28] Yet, as we will see below and in the commentary, Paul's compositional style did have its own strengths and character and is impressive in its own way. Paul's letters were "weighty and strong" (βαρεῖαι καὶ ἰσχυραί) in compositional style (2 Cor 10:10).

Granted that Ephesians is not a Pauline oration, nevertheless the oral character of all ancient writings must be stressed. These were documents

("the genuine Attic"); 4.16 (Pliny's seven-hour speech!); 9.22 (versatile style); for Pliny on Greek literature and the use of Greek among the Romans see also *Ep.* 4.3, 18; 7.4, 9, 25 ("you would think the man lived at Athens"); 8.24.

26. Note that Thucydides, Pericles, Plato, Xenophon, Aristotle, and many other important Greek speakers and authors also did not have advanced rhetorical training.

27. A σχολή was a place for rhetorical and philosophical instruction, according to Cribiore, *Gymnastics,* 20–21. Note that some current archaeologists of Ephesus see the σχολή of Acts 19:9 as a private dwelling, such as one of the terrace houses (per private conversations at the conference on Ephesus at the Harding School of Theology in honor of Richard Oster, May 18–19, 2012). The standard overview of archaeology and topography of Ephesus is Peter Scherrer, *Ephesus: The New Guide* (Turkey: Zero, 2000).

28. Ephesus was home to an important school of rhetoric centered on certain members of the Second Sophistic; e.g., sophist and local benefactor T. Flavius Domitianus, who was the "panegyriarch" for Emperor Verus at the Great Epheseia festival in AD 166 (*IvE* 672).

to be *heard*, as NT scholars are increasingly recognizing.[29] The evidence for this is extensive and impressive. For example, it is interesting to read that Thucydides wrote his history for posterity rather than for a "one-time *hearing*" (*History of the Peloponnesian War* 1.22.4; emphasis added), while a couple of centuries later Dionysius of Halicarnassus analyzed the aural effects Thucydides' composition had on "his audience" (τοῖς ἀκούουσι; *Comp.* 376–77).[30] Demetrius gives an offhand remark that repetition helps a prose composition to be properly heard and that one should use the nominative or accusative case to begin a period because "[u]se of the other cases will cause some obscurity and torture for the actual speaker and also the listener" (*Eloc.* 196–97, 201).

Nevertheless, Ephesians is an *epistle* and not a written version of an oration. We can utilize ancient rhetorical and literary treatises as guides for the Greek compositional elements of Ephesians, but we recognize that they were usually guiding and analyzing the composition of orations or of other kinds of prose texts, not of letters. When we do get advice for writing ancient letters, it sometimes seems rather dull. For example, Demetrius writes: "The length of a letter, no less than its style, must be kept within due bounds. ... It is absurd to build up periods, as if you were writing not a letter

29. For interesting discussion and references see two essays by Pieter J. J. Botha: "New Testament Texts in the Context of Reading Practices of the Roman Period," *Scriptura* 90 (2005): 621–40; and "The Verbal Art of the Pauline Letters: Rhetoric, Performance and Presence," in *Rhetoric and the New Testament*, ed. Stanley E. Porter and Thomas H. Olbricht, JSNTSup 90 (Sheffield: JSOT, 1993), 409–28; cf. Sam Tsang, "Are We 'Misreading' Paul?: Oral Phenomena and Their Implication for the Exegesis of Paul's Letters," *Oral Tradition* 24 (2009): 205–25; John D. Harvey, *Listening to the Text: Oral Patterning in Paul's Letters* (Grand Rapids: Baker, 1998); see also earlier Paul Achtemeier, "*Omne verbum sonat*: The New Testament and the Oral Environment of Late Western Antiquity," *JBL* 109 (1990): 3–27, with qualifications by Frank D. Gilliard, "More on Silent Reading in Antiquity: *Non Omne Verbum Sonabat*," *JBL* 112 (1993): 689–96 ("Although ancient texts were most often read aloud, there was nothing astonishing or difficult about reading letters and other short documents silently," p. 691). Also Raymond J. Starr, "Reading Aloud: *Lectores* and Roman Reading," *CJ* 86 (1990): 337–43.

30. Similarly, the Greek historian Polybius advised that Roman political institutions should not be "followed inattentively" by his "hearers" (τοῖς ἀκούουσιν, rendered "by the reader" in the LCL; Polybius, *Hist.* 1.64.3). References to Dionysius, "On Literary Composition" (*Comp.*), will be to both the Greek and English page numbers of the Loeb edition. All English translations from this and other classical works will be that of the LCL series unless otherwise indicated.

but a speech for the law courts" (*Eloc.* 4.228–29). However, the context for Demetrius' statement is that a letter to a friend or circle of friends should not become a "treatise" (συγγράμμα) with the heading "My dear So-and-So." The Pauline epistle, though, is much more like a treatise than a personal letter in many ways, so perhaps we can see some value in treating Ephesians in light of ancient instruction in literary prose.

To summarize this point, Ephesians is not an oration, yet it does show itself to be a literary composition with certain oral features from someone with both a fair degree of Greek literary and presentational training and a good deal of native ability. Ephesians is not a pure essay or a speech, but neither is it an informal letter. As a result, I will not analyze the epistle along the lines of rhetorical divisions of a speech, as found in Witherington and others (see below). Instead I will be pointing out the features of Greek literary compositional elements and their analysis as found in Greek authors who discuss such things in antiquity.

Rhythm

This leads now to the "rhythm" of Ephesians, mentioned above (point two) and used from time to time to determine Pauline authorship of this epistle. For example, Nigel Turner notes that Ephesians shares "a simple rhythm" with the other Pauline Epistles and sees this as evidence that Ephesians is Pauline.[31] Others see "rhythm" in sections of Ephesians as evidence of a post-Pauline author adapting hymnic or kinds of poetic or confessional sources in his pseudepigraphical work.[32]

I will address this issue of "rhythm" in Ephesians in various places as it comes up in the comments, but it should be noted here that NT scholars far too frequently speak of "rhythm" (and sometimes "lilt") in the Greek text of Ephesians and of other NT works in vague or improperly defined ways. The fact is that *rhythm* for ancient Greek and Latin texts means

---

31. Nigel Turner, *A Grammar of New Testament Greek*, vol. 4, *Style* (Edinburgh: T&T Clark, 1976), 84–85.

32. E.g., Ralph P. Martin, *Reconciliation: A Study of Paul's Theology* (Atlanta: John Knox, 1981), 157–98, repr. in "Reconciliation and Unity in Ephesians," *RevExp* 93 (1996): 203–35, who takes the (post-Pauline) Ephesians to be a theological "tract" or "liturgical document" with a "solemn, elevated, and rhythmic style" (203).

quantitative metrical patterns of long and short syllables.[33] I have yet to see scansion of the meter of these supposed "rhythmic" sections in Ephesians, but that is what is needed to find rhythm in Greek.[34] Furthermore, while metrical scansion is usually studied and applied to Greek poetry, it should be emphasized that Greek and Latin authors *did* use metrical patterns in their prose also, particularly in the final handful of syllables at the end of their cola* and periods (below), known as *clausulae*.[35] When ancient authors discussed Greek style, they did often speak of rhythm, but that meant *meter* to them (dactyls, anapests, paeans, and the rest).[36]

Because of ancient literary analysis of meter, I will show the prose scansion occasionally in the comments. However, let me admit up front that

---

33. E.g., Dionysius of Halicarnassus, *Comp.* 124–25, who equates ῥυθμός ("rhythm) with πούς (metrical foot). I am aware of discussions of a transition from quantitative to stress meter sometime in the first or second centuries AD in Greek texts, but from what I can gather, this seems to have arisen due to the influence of Latin authors in Greek and is irrelevant for Pauline texts. See, for example, the first-century Greek metrical fables of Babrius, who shows his Latin origin by having an accent on the penultimate syllable at the end of each colon*. Similar accentual rhythm has been traced in the work of (Roman) *1 Clement*, for which see G. L. Hendrickson, "Accentual Clausulae in Greek Prose of the First and Second Centuries of Our Era," *AJP* 29 (1908): 280–302. For "clausulae" see next note.

34. *Scansion* refers to the analysis and presentation of syllables being either long or short. Metrical feet are known by various terms such as the Homeric *dactyl* (¯ ˘ ˘ [οὐ μόνον; Eph 1:21]), the *anapest* (˘ ˘ ¯ [κατὰ τὴν; Eph 1:5]), the *spondee* (¯ ¯ [Χριστῷ; Eph 1:3]), or the *paean* (either ¯ ˘ ˘ ˘ [τῆς χάριτος; Eph 2:7] or ˘ ˘ ˘ ¯ [ἐν ἐλέει; Eph 2:4]), the latter of which Aristotle says is the meter of conversation and therefore should mark well-crafted prose. Cf. Barbara Eckman, "A Quantitative Metrical Analysis of the Philippians Hymn," *NTS* 26 (1980): 258–66 (which does not work without alteration of the Philippians text); S. M. Baugh, "The Poetic Form of Col 1:15-20," *WTJ* 47 (1985): 230–32.

35. Singular "clausula"; usually three to seven final syllables of a colon* or period, often marked by a few favorite, distinctive rhythms by Greek and Latin prose authors; see the standard work on various such literary issues, now happily available in English as Henrich Lausberg, *Handbook of Literary Rhetoric: A Foundation for Literary Study*, ed. David E. Orton and R. Dean Anderson (Boston: Brill, 1998), §§985–1054; cf. A. W. de Groot, *A Handbook of Antique Prose-Rhythm* (Groningen and The Hague: J. B. Wolters, 1919); and H. J. Rose, "The Clausulae of the Pauline Corpus," *JTS* 25 (1924): 17–43, who does not recognize the probable role of secretaries and coauthors in the Pauline texts and so labels Ephesians as "spurious."

36. Cf. Richard Graff, "Prose versus Poetry in Early Greek Theories of Style," *Rhetorica* 23 (2005): 303–35. There are not many metrical texts in the NT, including the so-called hymns (see "Excursus: Hymns" below).

my scansion of Greek prose meter is simplified.[37] I am aware of some of the more complex rules governing this process, but ancient Greek prose scansion does not seem to be as complex as that for poetry and seems to allow for a simpler and more consistent method.[38] I will only scan small portions of Ephesians from time to time when it might provide some interest for exegesis.[39]

Related to this issue of rhythm is the description of Ephesians as having a "solemn" character in its prose. I agree for some passages (e.g., 2:1–3; cf. 2:4), but, again, what makes up this solemnity is often not explained by commentators. If an ancient Greek text is truly solemn (σεμνός, or "somber"), it has a predominance of long versus short syllables: "As for the other rhythms, the heroic [dactyls and spondees] is solemn and not suitable for prose. It is too sonorous (ἠχώδης). ... [T]he accumulation of long syllables goes beyond the limits of prose (meter; ὑπερπίπτει τοῦ λογικοῦ μέτρου)" (Demetrius, *Eloc.* 42); "The diction that is appropriate for Solemnity

37. For example, we will ignore the fact that speakers in antiquity did not treat all long or short syllables equally, as Dionysius notes: "There is more than one kind of length and shortness of syllables: some are actually longer than the long and some shorter than the short" (Dionysius, *Comp.* 104–5). Furthermore, elision was undoubtedly more common in ancient pronunciation than our written texts indicate. The editors of our modern Greek New Testaments spell out forms that may have been elided (or spelled with crasis) in ancient oral reading. Hence ἵνα ἐνδείξηται in 2:7 is six syllables but may have been pronounced as five (ἵν' ἐνδείξηται [cf. ἵν' ἔχῃ in P[46] at 4:28 or ἵν' ἐκ in *IvE* 18c, line 20]), but I will not scan the words as elided for simplicity's sake.

38. Here are just three reasons I say this: (1) Note the many times that Rose ("Clausulae") introduces crasis and ellipsis (he even drops articles) in his scansion of Pauline texts where the critical Greek editions do not. I will not do this with my scansion; (2) James Moffatt (*A Critical and Exegetical Commentary on the Epistle to the Hebrews*, ICC [Edinburgh: T&T Clark, 1924], lvi–lix) discusses favorite meters in the book of Hebrews but scans καί as long in some places and short in others without any reason that I can discern. I know about the short, poetic scansion of diphthongs like -αι (and crasis κἀγώ), and I have seen this conj. spelled as (short) κέ in the Ephesian inscriptions, but I scan καί and other forms of this diphthong (also -οι) as long just to be consistent. Finally, (3) note how the ancient rhetorician Dionysius of Halicarnassus scans Greek prose in *Comp.* 134–41, but the editor of the LCL volume (Stephen Usher) in various footnotes finds his scansion irregular.

39. The standard work in English is M. L. West, *Introduction to Greek Metre* (Oxford: Clarendon, 1987); however, this work is on poetics, and neither West nor anyone I could find discusses prose scansion, which must be discerned from scattered ancient and modern sources.

(σεμνότης) consists of broad sounds that make us open our mouth wide when we pronounce them. … There are other possibilities, but long *a*'s and *o*'s especially produce this effect."[40] According to ancient sources, word order, word choice, and other variables play a part in solemnity, but scansion for meter is also necessary to accurately describe this and other stylistic characteristics of Greek prose.[41]

The Periodic Sentence

We turn now to the issue of the long "sentences" in Ephesians (e.g., Eph 1:3–14) as one reason some scholars reject Pauline authorship of this epistle (issue three above). This actually raises an important question from the start and explains why I spend a considerable time in the introduction to each passage showing a suggested division of the text as it would have been perceived by the ancient audience and readers.[42]

To anticipate my conclusion on this point, I believe this discussion of "sentences" in Paul or other ancient Greek authors is misleading and anachronistically uses a modern conception of discourse for the ancient text.[43] To say, for example, that Eph 1:3–14 is one sentence makes it seem like there would have been no break for the hearer or reader in their experience of the text. Yet when ancient authorities spoke about division of a Greek text, they did not usually speak of grammatical "sentences" (Latin *sententia*, "thought"), but rather of the colon* and the period as the essential building blocks of discourse.[44] In light of this ancient analysis, Eph 1:3–14 would

---

40. Hermogenes, *Hermogenes' On Types of Style*, trans. Cecil W. Wooten (Chapel Hill: University of North Carolina Press, 1987), 22 (§247).

41. This is normally described under either "rhythm" (ῥυθμός) or "diction" (φράσις) in the rhetorical treatises.

42. See Robbins, "Composition of Eph 1:3–14"; "Rhetorical Structure of Philippians 2:6–11."

43. For example, Van Roon does speak a few times about long syllables and isocola but relies too heavily on the punctuation by Nestle (*Authenticity*, 105–6) for defining Ephesian long "sentences." The punctuation of the NA[28], in fact, breaks Eph 1:3–14 into four sentences.

44. The smallest logical unit that will not come up often in my analysis is the comma (κόμμα; pl., κόμματα), which corresponds roughly to a syntactical phrase or even to a single word. This may be the unit of division of lines in a MS like Codex Claromontanus (D 06), where single words like νεκρούς (Eph 2:1), πάντες (Eph 2:3), a gen. phrase like τῆς σαρκός (Eph 2:3), or a prepositional phrase like ἐν ἐλέει (Eph 2:4) occupy one line. Ancient authors consulted for the discussion of

not appear to be one long sentence but an interconnected "paragraph" of nine easily manageable periods—as I suggest the text be arranged—with an unfolding unity of thought. In fact, given the nature of Pauline style along these lines, Ephesians looks very similar to other such periodic sentences in Romans and elsewhere, since longer units (sometimes called a "periodic sentence") might be composed of more than one grammatical sentence.

A Greek colon* (κῶλον; pl. κῶλα, "cola"*) was originally modeled on the dactylic hexameter of epic poetry, and thus was approximately twelve to seventeen syllables in length. In practice, the colon* could be only a word or two (e.g., Eph 4:5) or quite longer.[45] Some orators ("rhetors") sought roughly equal length of cola* ("isocola"), but some found this monotonous and taught and practiced writing cola* of varying length for variety and to hold the audience's interest (Dionysius, *Comp.* 152–55). Without doubt, though, the colon* was the essential element of discourse, though one did not want to present a μονόκωλος λόγος ("monocolon discourse") stringing together ideas in a series of discrete and unconnected cola*.[46]

Hence, the well-ordered discourse consisted of a series of succeeding, unfolding cola*, usually between two and six, into the period (ἡ περίοδος; pl., περίοδοι). The period was the subject of much discussion in antiquity and the backbone of two primarily different styles: the "periodic" or "turned down" (λέξις κατεστραμμένη), and the "spare," "loose," or "strung-together"

---

cola* and periods to follow include Aristotle, Cicero, Dionysius of Halicarnassus, Quintilian, a writer known as Demetrius (*On Style* esp.), and writings under the name of Hermogenes.

45. Cf. Toivo Viljamaa, "*Colon* and *Comma*, Dionysius of Halicarnassus on the Sentence Structure," in *Syntax in Antiquity*, ed. Pierre Swiggers and Alfons Wouters, Orbis Supplementa 23 (Dudley, MA: Peeters, 2003), 163–78; Lausberg, *Handbook*, §§924–34. One of the more helpful discussions I have found on these matters is still Charles Darwin Adams, *Lysias: Selected Speeches* (New York: American Book Co., 1905; repr., Norman: University of Oklahoma Press, 1970), 344–52; cf. Demetrius, *Eloc.* 1–35.

46. So Pseudo-Plutarch: "While I am still dwelling upon my own opinion in regard to education, I desire to say that in the first place a discourse composed of a series of short sentences (τὸν μονόκωλον λόγον) I regard as no small proof of lack of culture; in the second place I think that in practice such discourse soon palls, and in every case it causes impatience; for monotony is in everything tiresome and repellent, but variety is agreeable, as it is in everything else, as, for example, in entertainments that appeal to the eye or the ear" (*Lib. ed.* 7B–D).

style (λέξις εἰρομένη; Aristotle, *Rhet.* 3.9).[47] However, I am not always using the term *period* technically, particularly for the more conversational latter chapters of Ephesians where the "period" is simply a grouping of cola* with a unity of thought. Technically, a period was a grouping of cola* that a trained speaker could present in one breath and had a certain "rounded" character.[48] Hence, the end of the period was a place of particular focus and emphasis since there was a pause while the speaker or reader took a breath and left the last few words in the audience's mind before starting up again (see discussion on the end of periods in 1:3–14 in particular in the comments). The correct pauses at the end of cola* and periods in delivery and reading was part of elementary education in antiquity (e.g., Quintilian, *Inst.* 1.8; 11.3.10–60).

Aldo Scaglione explains further that delivery is important even for understanding the division of a text:

> The difference between a non-periodic sequence and a periodic one is that, in the former, all units are "pronounced with the same expression," while in the latter "the *membra* [= κῶλα] are held suspended by the speaker's voice until the last one is completed." ... In other words, the difference is one of musical movement or rhythm, and the manner of definition throws the emphasis on delivery.[49]

Hence, division of texts into cola* is something of an art that even the ancients would not necessarily have agreed on for someone else's written text when there was no original presentation of the work by its author to serve as a guide.[50] Scaglione again writes:

47. For an introduction to discussions on the period among classicists see: Tamá Adamik, "Aristotle's Theory of the Period," *Philologus* 168 (1984); 184–201; R. L. Fowler, "Aristotle on the Period (Rhet. 3.9)," *CQ* 32 (1982): 89–99, esp. 89n1, "In practice rhythms and cohesive syntax both characterize the period." Cf. Lausberg, *Handbook,* §§923–24; 941–47.
48. See particularly the comment on Eph 3:1 below, where Jerome states that Paul does not "round" his periods.
49. Aldo Scaglione, *The Classical Theory of Composition from Its Origins to the Present* (Chapel Hill: University of North Carolina Press, 1972), 73.
50. Cf. Dioysius' uncertainty on the exact division of Thucydides, discussed below.

> Elements of rhythm, formal arrangement, and physiological division (on the basis of delivery according to breathing capacity) remained, to ancient ears, more basic than considerations of logical content and organization. Thus, for instance, both complete periods and parts therefore (mainly cola) are sometimes hard for us to reconstruct, because they do not necessarily correspond to our sentences and clauses or even phrases—which are essentially logical and, concurrently, syntactic units.[51]

Nevertheless, most of the cola* in Ephesians do probably open with items like conjunctions, adverbial participles, or repeated prepositions. Where these kinds of words are not found, one may have a colon* like θεοῦ τὸ δῶρον ("the gift is from God") in Eph 2:8, where the fronted, anarthrous θεοῦ is strikingly prominent because the colon* starts in an unusual way.

Let me repeat that the division into cola* and periods I provide for Ephesians is a suggestion.[52] To know the exact division of a text like this would require one to hear it read from the original author or his reader. This became clear to me when Dionysius of Halicarnassus, an expert teacher of rhetoric, divided the beginning of Thucydides' *History of the Peloponnesian War*, written some four centuries earlier, and says he cannot be absolutely certain of his division: "To summarize, I have adduced some twelve periods, *if the breathing-space be taken as the unit of division*, and these comprise no fewer than thirty clauses (κῶλα)" (*Comp.* 190–91; emphasis added). Most of these periods in Thucydides are in the range of thirty-six to forty syllables long, which compare well to the length of periods in Ephesians. What is notable is that Dionysius evaluates the third period in Thucydides as being sixty-one syllables in length, which requires substantial lung power to

51. Scaglione, *Classical Theory*, 38.

52. Classical scholars have been working on the linguistic markers for inception of the colon* in Greek and Latin for a considerable amount of time, though they often use the term *colon** (German *Kolon*) to reference a smaller unit more like the Greek *comma*; see esp. Eric Laughton, "Review of Eduard Fraenkel, *Leseproben aus Reden Ciceros und Catos*," *Journal of Roman Studies* 60 (1970): 188–94; Frank Scheppers, *The Colon Hypothesis: Word Order, Discourse Segmentation and Discourse Coherence in Ancient Greek* (Brussels: VUBPRESS, 2011). Unfortunately, I came across this research after finishing the manuscript for the commentary, but it is valuable for further work on the topic.

pronounce in one breath, but this does not draw his comment as being particularly troublesome.[53]

The conclusion to draw from this is that the "periodic sentence" as found, for example, in Eph 1:3–14, with over two hundred Greek words, is really the equivalent of an English *paragraph*, while the nine periods comprising this section are more like English sentences.[54] While *periodic sentence* is used to describe these long divisions of the text, it will be noted in the analysis of the Greek composition throughout the comments that we are dealing with something here that is more akin to a long paragraph than a modern sentence.

In the course of this analysis, we will gain greater appreciation for Paul's expressive abilities—even though his epistolary style might not have matched an oration by a sophistic rhetor. Our concern, however, in this analysis is not exclusively literary but literary for the sake of exegesis. For example, this analysis centers on the flow, divisions, focus, and unity of these texts—a subject that is drawing more attention lately as scholars think of the nature of ancient pericopes and their rhetorical background.[55]

On the latter, rhetorical background, Ben Witherington in particular has done much to emphasize this avenue of study for Ephesians in his recent rhetorical commentary on Ephesians, which he identifies as a written form of a homily and "large-scale example of epideictic rhetoric" (Witherington, 219; see 217–23). The model for this kind of speech is the panegyric, which involved "eloquence for its own sake, or for the sake of flattering a governor

53. This third period in Thucydides consists of four cola* of seventeen, eleven, twenty, and thirteen syllables (sixty-one total), while a similar long period of four cola* in Eph 1:13 has seventeen, thirteen, seven, and nineteen syllables for fifty-six total.

54. See also the analysis of Manuel Alexandre Jr., "The Art of Periodic Composition in Philo of Alexandria," *Studia Philonica* 3 (1991): 135–50. In his first example from Philo's embassy to Gaius (Philo, *Embassy*), Alexandre finds four sentences "divided into two periodic units in which the ideal tetracolon prevails" (142). The modern sentence and the ancient period do not always coincide. Cf. the long "sentence" in Xenophon's *Hellenica* (6.4.2–3), with some 226 words.

55. E.g., Simon Crisp, "Scribal Marks and Logical Paragraphs," *UBS Bulletin* 198/99 (2005): 77–87; Simon Wong, "Ancient Windows to the NT Text," *UBS Bulletin* 198/99 (2005): 67–76. For the older, Euthalian division of the NT, see the 1970 dissertation recently published: Louis Charles Willard, *A Critical Study of the Euthalian Apparatus*, ANTF 41 (New York: Walter de Gruyter, 2009).

or a group of citizens," or praise of benefactors (Witherington, 219, 228–30). Interestingly, Witherington believes that Ephesians represents an "Asiatic" versus an "Attic" (or "spare") rhetorical style, and he believes it indicates Pauline authorship of the book and explains the "extravagant" nature of its style, which, he thinks, Paul adopted for the sake of his audience. Hence, the "one long sentence" in Eph 1:3–14 "is a classic example of Asiatic rhetoric in its epideictic form, where amplification is accomplished by repetition of both content and form" (Witherington, 228–29).[56]

I think there is merit to using rhetorical analysis for the Pauline Epistles, and it may be that there are some "Asiatic" characteristics of Ephesians in its use of unusual, expressive vocabulary (e.g., ἐπουράνιοι, "high-heavenlies") and some sections with flowing periods—though they are not "rounded."[57] However, Witherington's evaluation that this epistle is a homily and Asiatic epideictic oration is stated too strongly. He says, for instance, that such epideictic rhetoric is found in praise of emperors and other benefactors, but he gives no examples from Ephesus for comparison, when it turns out that we have many such pieces inscribed in the epigraphical remains from Ephesus he could have used (e.g., *IvE* 22). This issue of whether Ephesus itself was a center of the "Asiatic" style of rhetoric deserves more attention, but there

56. Cf. Michael Winterbotom, "Asianism and Atticism," *OCD*, 184; and Eduard Norden, *Die Antike Kunstprosa* (Stuttgart and Leipzig: Teubner, 1995; repr. of 1915 ed.), 1:251–99 (*Der Kampf des alten und des neuen Stils. Attizismus und Asianismus*). More directly, Cicero's essay *De Oratore* is a defense of his more ornamental style versus the *Attici*, though he criticizes the Asianism of Caria, Phrygia, and Mysia (but not *Ephesian* Asia per se) for poor refinement and taste with their "rich and unctuous diction," for they "sing in the Asiatic manner, in a whining voice with violent modulations" (*Or.* 8.25, 27).

57. Stanley E. Porter and Bryan R. Dyer ("Oral Texts? A Reassessment of the Oral and Rhetorical Nature of Paul's Letters in Light of Recent Studies," *JETS* 55 [2012]: 323–41) critique Witherington's views in particular—with some justification—yet they undervalue oral training in elementary and intermediate levels of all ancient education and what Paul may have picked up through experience and extensive knowledge of ancient texts. Cf. earlier Stanley E. Porter, "The Theoretical Justification for Application of Rhetorical Categories to Pauline Epistolary Literature," in *Rhetoric and the New Testament*, 100–122.

may be some slight indication that at least some Ephesian rhetors and sophists in its schools also had a more "Attic" flavor.[58]

Furthermore, Asiatic rhetoric relates in large part to its performance through "extravagant" oral devices, frequent use of mythology, "far-fetched metaphors," and cola* of equal length that frequently end with similar sounds (Cicero, *Or. Brut.* 19.65). In particular, it was marked by "rhythmical rounding out" of its periods (Cicero, *Brut.* 8.33), which Ephesians does not exhibit (as Jerome noted on Eph 3:1). Furthermore, Asianism was marked by use of regular meters, which were regarded as more appropriate for songs and poetry. Quintilian says of Asiatic oratory: "For what can be less becoming to an orator than modulations that recall the stage and a sing-song utterance which at times resembles the maudlin utterance of drunken revelers? (*et nonunquam ebriorum aut comissantium licentiae similis*)" (*Inst.* 11.3.57). Quintilian's student, Pliny the Younger, speaks of hearing "sing-song oratory" (*fracta pronuntiatio*) as Asiatic and a "grave and deliberate manner" as Attic (*Ep.* 2.14). There are no regular metrical sections in Ephesians that I could find, and there certainly are "grave and deliberate" sections in this Pauline epistle comparable to sections of other Pauline epistles; for example, compare Rom 1:21–24 with Eph 4:17–24, discussed in the latter's introduction below.

When it comes, then, to the style of the Ephesian cola* and periods, we are dealing with someone who has a certain rugged power at times, but is also unconcerned with the smoothness that marked the work of a contemporary orator. For example, Dionysius critiques the opening colon* of Thucydides as having two sounds in conjunction that create an unwelcome pause before it ends as follows: Θουκυδίδης Ἀθηναῖος ξυνέγραψε τὸν πόλεμον ("Thucydides the Athenian wrote this history on the war"). He writes:

> At the very beginning the verb ξυνέγραψε, being appended to the appellative Ἀθηναῖος, makes a considerable break in the structure,

58. It is only circumstantial, but we have the case of P. Hordeonius Lollianus. Philostratus (*Vit. soph.* 1.23) notes that this second-century Ephesian became the holder of the first official chair of rhetoric at Athens—i.e., the center of revivied Attic style ("Atticism") in competition with Asianism. Either the father or grandfather of this Lollianus (also named P. Hordeonius Lollianus) was engaged in the fishing trade in Ephesus and appears as the first and most important donor for the Ephesian fishery toll house under Nero (*IvE* 20).

> since σ is never placed before ξ with a view to being pronounced with it in the same syllable: the sound of the σ must be arrested by a pause of silence before the ξ is heard, and the impression created by this is one of *roughness and dissonance.* (*Comp.* 186–87; emphasis added)

Dionysius continues by pointing to the juxtaposition of a ν-τ in the phrase τὸν πόλεμον and elsewhere, which he says lead to "clashes of sound ... *[that] grate upon the ear very violently* and break up the rhythm of the sentence considerably" (*Comp.* 188–89; emphasis added).[59] The point is that this kind of arrangement of words does not interrupt the meter of the line per se but introduces unwelcome pauses before the end of the colon* and makes the delivery "choppy" and "grate on the ears."[60]

Like Thucydides, Paul throughout his compositions, including Ephesians, shows little interest in this kind of "smoothness" to his cola* that Dionysius or other rhetors would demand of an agonistic or other kind of oratory. In the words of Jerome, "As a Hebrew of the Hebrews," he lacked "the polish of rhetorical speech, the knowledge of the proper arrangement of words and the grace of eloquence."[61] Hence the ν-π combination in τὸ ὑπερβάλλον πλοῦτος (Eph 2:7) creates an unwelcome pause in midcolon that τὸ πλοῦτος τὸ ὑπερβάλλον would have avoided. Yet there are some fine features to Paul's prose, even though these seem to be more a matter of feel and intuited good taste rather than what Paul would probably have regarded

59. Generally a liquid (λ, μ, ν, and ρ) followed by a plosive (or "stop," e.g., ν-β, ν-γ, ν-δ, ν-κ, ν-π, and ν-τ) would cause this pause. Quintilian echoes this thought: "Further, we avoid placing two consonants near each other when their juxtaposition would cause a harsh sound" (*Inst.* 11.3.35; cf. 9.4.37–40).

60. It is easy to find the ν-τ combination in the middle of Paul's cola* throughout his epistles, whereas it is notably more rare in, say, Hebrews, which shows a smoother style (e.g., Heb 9:15, where such combinations of sounds fall at the end rather than in the middle of cola*). In just one example from Demosthenes, whom many Greeks regarded as their greatest orator, we find the following phrase at the opening of his speech "On the Crown" (*Cor.* 226.1): εἰς τουτονὶ τὸν ἀγῶνα ("in this trial"). Here Demosthenes uses the emphatic demonstrative pronoun form with its added *iota* (τουτονί) in order to avoid the ν-τ "violence" in midcolon (τουτονὶ τὸν rather than τοῦτον τὸν), even though the demonstrative is not emphatic in meaning here.

61. Origen and Jerome, 143.

as the pointless preoccupation of the flamboyant showmen (sophists) he undoubtedly encountered in places like Ephesus, Athens, or Corinth.[62]

For fine instances of style, consider these two small examples from Ephesians and Romans. The first is called "tricolon crescendo" or "rising cola," where parallel cola* increase in size, creating a kind of swelling effect to conclude the period. The second example from Romans includes the preceding three cola,* which have "falling cola," where the cola* get increasingly smaller. The examples are presented with syllable counts in parentheses:

Ephesians 1:17–19 (see also 6:12):
τίς ἐστιν ἡ ἐλπὶς τῆς κλήσεως αὐτοῦ (12)
τίς ὁ πλοῦτος τῆς δόξης τῆς κληρονομίας αὐτοῦ ἐν τοῖς ἁγίοις (20)
19 καὶ τί τὸ ὑπερβάλλον μέγεθος τῆς δυνάμεως αὐτοῦ εἰς ἡμᾶς τοὺς πιστεύοντας κατὰ τὴν ἐνέργειαν τοῦ κράτους τῆς ἰσχύος αὐτοῦ (41)

v. 18c	*what* (τίς) is the hope of his calling
v. 18d	*what* (τίς) is the glorious wealth of his inheritance among the saints
v. 19	and *what* (τί) is the supreme greatness of his power toward us who believe in accordance with the effectiveness of the strength of his might

Romans 11:33–35 (cf. 2 Cor 6:14–16)
33 Ὦ βάθος πλούτου καὶ σοφίας καὶ γνώσεως θεοῦ (15)
ὡς ἀνεξεραύνητα τὰ κρίματα αὐτοῦ (13)
καὶ ἀνεξιχνίαστοι αἱ ὁδοὶ αὐτοῦ (12)

34 τίς γὰρ ἔγνω νοῦν κυρίου; (8)
ἢ τίς σύμβουλος αὐτοῦ ἐγένετο; (11)
35 ἢ τίς προέδωκεν αὐτῷ καὶ ἀνταποδοθήσεται αὐτῷ; (18)

62. Bowersock, in his classic work, defines the sophist as "a virtuoso rhetor with a big public reputation" (G. W. Bowersock, *Greek Sophists in the Roman Empire* [Oxford: Oxford University Press, 1969], 13; cf. more recently Bruce W. Winter, *Philo and Paul among the Sophists,* 2nd ed. [Grand Rapids: Eerdmans, 2002]). Although one can distinguish a "sophist" from a "rhetor," the terms are also interchangeable; e.g., on an honorary Ephesian inscription to "Dionysius, the rhetor and sophist" (*IvE* 3047).

v. 33a O the depth of the riches and of the wisdom and of the knowledge of God
v. 33b How inscrutable are his judgments
v. 33c and how untraceable are his ways!

v. 34a For *who* has known the mind of the Lord?
v. 34b Or *who* has been his counselor?

v. 35 Or *who* has first given him anything and then received payment in return?

The second example is of a "falling bicolon," where one or more pairs of cola* have a long first member and a shorter second one.[63] In both the Ephesians and Romans passages, Paul uses this device as he draws a long digression to a close:

Ephesians 3:12–13
[12]ἐν ᾧ ἔχομεν τὴν παρρησίαν καὶ προσαγωγὴν ἐν πεποιθήσει (20)
διὰ τῆς πίστεως αὐτοῦ (8)
[13]διὸ αἰτοῦμαι μὴ ἐγκακεῖν ἐν ταῖς θλίψεσίν μου ὑπὲρ ὑμῶν (19)
ἥτις ἐστὶν δόξα ὑμῶν (8)

v. 12a in whom we have bold access with confidence
v. 12b through our faith in him

v. 13a Wherefore, I ask you not to lose heart at my tribulations on your behalf
v. 13b which is your glory.

Romans 7:25b–c
Ἄρα οὖν αὐτὸς ἐγὼ τῷ μὲν νοῒ δουλεύω νόμῳ θεοῦ (18)
τῇ δὲ σαρκὶ νόμῳ ἁμαρτίας (10)

v. 25b So then I am myself in my mind, on the one hand, slave to the law of God
v. 25c but on the other, in my flesh to the law of sin.

63. Contrast the "rising bicolon," where the first member is shorter than the second, and the "isocolon," where both pairs are either exactly or very close to equal in length.

Many more examples from Ephesians and Romans and the other Pauline texts could be given of the habits of literary composition of the same writer (even given secretarial mediation). One further factor that needs discussion is the Semitic character of some aspects of this composition, but that must be mentioned in the comments.

To summarize, then, modern scholars dealing with the Greek style of Ephesians have focused on the grammatical sentence length and other traits that are more appropriate to a modern work than to an ancient Greek one. Cola* and periods are the foundational elements of Greek prose composition, and they many times transcend the boundaries of the grammatical sentence.[64] For example, Romans provides four long "periodic sentences" in Rom 5:1–11, 12–21; 6:1–11, 12–23 that share compositional features with Ephesians. To provide a compelling case that Paul (with or without secretarial assistance) did not write Ephesians, one would have to compare certain literary elements of ancient style that usually go unnoticed today but will receive some attention throughout the commentary to follow.

Sectioning

Readers of the NT rely on chapter and verse divisions that were set up by a book publisher in 1551 to facilitate the sale of a planned Bible concordance.[65] Unfortunately, these divisions may not always correspond to the actual contours of the biblical text, as, for example, in the division that spans Eph 4:25–5:2. Yet these divisions do aid modern readers and were not new in 1551.[66] Copies of Old Greek translations of the OT (antedating our modern LXX) often contained divisions into sections and "verses" using spacing,

---

64. For example, see the unity of Eph 2:1–10 and its constituent periods, which the NA[28] divides into *four* sentences with period marks at the end of vv. 3, 7, 9, and 10 (which cuts off the main verbs in vv. 5–6 from the beginning of the sentence).

65. William P. Weaver, "The Verse Divisions of the New Testament and the Literary Culture of the Reformation," *Reformation* 16 (2011): 161–77; Nicholas J. Zola, "Why Are There Verses Missing from My Bible? The Emergence of Verse Numbers in the New Testament," *ResQ* 54 (2012): 241–53; cf. Elizabeth Armstrong, *Robert Estienne, Royal Printer: An Historical Study of the Elder Stephanus* (Cambridge: Cambridge University Press, 1954).

66. Apparently Stephanus was using the verse number to mark out Greek periods. Many times there is no dispute about his accuracy in doing so. In other cases, it is simply a matter of difference of opinion.

paragraphoi lines between lines of text, and enlarged initial letters, which sometimes extended in the margins (*ekthesis*).[67] Texts originating in Greek documentary papyri discovered in Egypt—letters, wills, contracts, etc., as opposed to copies of Greek literature—were frequently written with sense divisions marked primarily by spacing. Colin Roberts believes these kinds of texts formed the background to copies of Christian Scriptures by scribes employing a "reformed documentary" style.[68]

For our purposes, it will inform our own analysis of the text to consult ancient scribes of Ephesians to see how they read the sense of the text. One proviso, however, as Emanuel Tov has noted regarding sectioning in both Hebrew and Greek OT MSS: These divisions of the text are too often "individualistic" or "impressionistic" by scribes who were not active in literary analysis as they wrote.[69] Yet perhaps they do preserve some sense of how these texts were read in antiquity and have the advantage of text division based on Greek rather than on the conventions of other languages.

The following table shows various section divisions in four key early MSS of Ephesians: Vaticanus (B), Sinaiticus (א), Alexandrinus (A), and the partial Codex Ephraemi Rescriptus (C).[70] These four MSS mark sec-

67. In general see C. H. Roberts, *Manuscript, Society and Belief in Early Christian Egypt* (London: Oxford University Press, 1979), 1–25, esp. 16–18; Emanuel Tov, *Scribal Practices and Approaches Reflected in the Texts Found in the Judean Desert* (Atlanta: SBL, 2004), 139, 299–315, for Greek texts. For discussion of sectioning in one important Greek MS of the Minor Prophets from the Dead Sea area see Emanuel Tov, *The Greek Minor Prophets Scroll from Nahal Hever (8HevXIIgr)*, DJD 8 (Oxford: Clarendon, 1990), 9–12. For *paragraphoi* see William A. Johnson, "The Function of the Paragrapus in Greek Literary Prose Texts," *ZPE* 100 (1994): 65–68; and Simon Crisp, "Scribal Marks and Logical Paragraphs," *UBS Bulletin* 198/99 (2005): 77–87.

68. Roberts, *Manuscript*, 14.

69. Tov, *Scribal Practices*, 144, 149. Often scribes were copying syllable by syllable rather than word for word, which also accounts for variations in analysis. Cf. Dirk Jongkind, *Scribal Habits of Codex Sinaiticus* (Piscataway, NJ; Gorgias, 2007); see especially 95–107 for discussion on "paragraphing." Jongkind suggests that scribes followed individual habits rather than a long tradition and may have used key conjs. as signals of section divisions in Sinaiticus. For other recent discussion see M. C. A. Korpel and J. M. Oesch, eds., *Delimitation Criticism: A New Tool in Biblical Scholarship* (Assen: Van Gorcum, 2000); and Korpel and Oesch, *Studies in Scriptural Unit Division* (Assen: Van Gorcum, 2002).

70. P^{46} has no such sense divisions and only slight spacing after the abbreviations of *nomina sacra**.

tions to varying degrees of detail, with devices that include spacing, some punctuation dots (στιγμαί), *ekthesis*, and *paragraphoi* lines.[71]

Ephesians Sense Division in Four Ancient MSS

B	א	A	C
1:1–2	1:1–2	1:1	vacant to 2:19
		1:2	
1:3–14	1:3–10	1:3–9a	
		1:9b–12	
	1:11–14	1:13–14	
1:15–23	1:15–23	1:15–2:3	
2:1–3	2:1–3		
2:4–7	2:4–7	2:4–5b	
		2:5c–10	
2:8–10	2:8–10(?)		
2:11–18	2:11–12	2:11–12	
	2:13–16	2:13–18	
	2:17–18		
2:19–22	2:19–22	2:19–22	2:19–22
3:1–13	3:1–4	3:1–12	3:1–3
			3:4–7
	3:5–7		
	3:8–12		3:8–9
			3:10–12
	3:13	3:13	3:13
3:14–19	3:14–19	3:14–19	3:14–19
3:20–21	3:20–21	3:20–21	3:20–21

71. A series of dots (στιγμαί) were developed in Alexandria for marking the conclusion of a thought (στιγμὴ τελεία, high dot), the place to draw breath (στιγμὴ μέση, middle dot), and the place for pause with more thought remaining (στιγμὴ ὑποστιγμῆς, the underdot dot [i.e., on the line like our period but functioning like a modern semicolon]); so Dionysius Thrax, *Ars Grammatica* 1.1.7–8, ca. 100 BC. The difference between the the first two and the underdot was in the length of the pause in presentation. This system was not followed universally or consistently in the MSS.

B	א	A	C
4:1–16	4:1–6	4:1–3	4:1–4
		4:4	
		4:5–6	4:5–6
	4:7–10	4:7–10	4:7–8
			4:9–10
	4:11–13	4:11–14	4:11–12
			4:13–14
	4:14–16		
		4:15–16	4:15–16
4:17–28	4:17–18	4:17	vacant to end
		4:18–19	
	4:19		
	4:20–24	4:20–24	
	4:25	4:25–27	
	4:26–27		
	4:28	4:28	
	4:28	4:28	
4:29–30	4:29	4:29–30	
	4:30		
4:31–32	4:31	4:31–32 (?)	
	4:32–5:2		
5:1–2		5:1(?)–2	
5:3–5	5:3	5:3–5	
	5:4		
	5:5		
5:6–14	5:6	5:6–14a	
	5:7–10		
	5:11–14a		
	5:14b–14e	5:14b–17	
5:15–21	5:15–17		
	5:18–19	5:18–21	
	5:20(?)		
	5:21		

B	א	A	C
5:22–24	5:22–24	5:22–24	
5:25–33	5:25–28c	5:25–30	
	5:28d–31		
		5:31	
	5:32	5:32–33	
	5:33		
6:1–3	6:1–3	6:1–4	
6:4	6:4		
6:5–8	6:5–8	6:5–8	
6:9	6:9	6:9	
6:10–13	6:10–12	6:10	
		6:11–12	
	6:13	6:13	
6:14–20	6:14–18a	6:14–20	
	6:18b–20		
6:21–23	6:21–23	6:21–23	
6:24	6:24	6:24	

If we were to add the later, more standardized "Euthalian Apparatus," Ephesians is divided into two lectionary divisions of Eph 1–3 and 4–6, which are then subdivided into ten "chapters" (κεφάλαια) at: 1:3–14; 1:15–2:10; 2:11–22; 3:1–13; 3:14–21; 4:1–16; 4:17–5:2; 5:3–21; 5:22–6:9; 6:10–20.[72]

The first point to notice is trends among the four MSS. Vaticanus (B) is happy to divide the text into larger units (e.g., 1:3–14; 1:15–23; 2:11–18; 3:1–13; 4:1–16; 5:6–14), while the other MSS usually divide these into two or three shorter sections (e.g., א divides 1:3–14 into two between vv. 10 and 11, and 2:11–18 into three at 2:11–12; 2:13–16; 2:17–18, yet it agrees with B in having 1:15–23 as one periodic sentence).

Despite the differences here, though, the four MSS surveyed do show agreement on certain boundaries of our text. For instance, all see a

72. From N. Dahl, "The 'Euthalian Apparatus' and the Affiliated 'Argumenta,'" *Studies in Ephesians*, WUNT 131 (Tübingen: Mohr Siebeck, 2000), 231–75; cf. Willard, *Euthalian Apparatus*.

boundary between 1:14 and 1:15, 2:3 and 2:4, 2:10 and 2:11, etc.[73] It seems that these ancient divisions of the text may have generally set the tone for later divisions as found in the Euthalian material and modern paragraph and chapter divisions.

My own analysis on the best way to divide Ephesians into pericopes is to favor the longer types as found in Vaticanus.[74] This is partly due to the oral nature of these texts and the character of flowing periodic sentences, which favor longer units of discourse. The benefit of this approach is both to read the text in a way closer to how it was intended to be heard and to see the larger unity of thought that is too often broken up and missed by focusing on individual verses.

Date and Place of Writing

Paul mentions that he is a "prisoner of Christ" (3:1), a "prisoner in the Lord" (4:1), and "an emissary in chains" (6:20), which is not merely a metaphor (cf. 2 Cor 11:23; Phil 1:7, 13, 17; Col 4:3, 10, 18). This suggests that Paul was actually being detained when he wrote this epistle. He had spent a little more than two years at Ephesus in the early to mid-50s (Acts 18:18–19:20). Later he was detained in Caesarea, from ca. AD 57–59 (Acts 21:17–24:27), and after a trial before Festus (ca. AD 58–60) he was sent to Rome to be held in house arrest while awaiting trial before Caesar, sometime ca. AD 59–62 (Acts 25:1–28:31).[75] This puts Paul in Roman custody for roughly four years in the range of AD 57–62, or anywhere from five to ten years after he was in Ephesus. Usually people who hold to Pauline authorship place the writing

73. Both B and ℵ have 1:15–23 as one unit, but A curiously continues the passage into 2:3, which divides the direct obj. in 2:1 from its verbs in 2:5–6.

74. T. C. Skeat has made a convincing case that this MS was one of those commissioned by Constantine in the mid-fourth century AD, and it eventually found its way into the Vatican; see Skeat, "The Codex Sinaiticus, the Codex Vaticanus and Constantine," *JTS* ns 50 (1999): 583–625, repr. in *The Collected Biblical Writings of T. C. Skeat*, ed. J. K. Elliott (Leiden: Brill, 2004), 193–237; cf. Elliott, "T. C. Skeat on the Dating and Origin of Codex Vaticanus," *Collected Biblical Writings*, 281–94.

75. Cf. L. C. A. Alexander, "Chronology of Paul," in *DPL*, 115–23 ; cf. Paul Barnett, *Paul: Missionary of Jesus* (Grand Rapids: Eerdmans, 2008), 136–37 (Barnett has Ephesians written in Ephesus [?] around AD 57); Robert Jewett, *A Chronology of Paul's Life* (Philadelphia: Fortress, 1979).

of Ephesians toward the end of that period (AD 60–62), when Paul was being detained in Rome before his first trial.[76]

Occasion

There seem to be no serious problems or concerns with his addressees that led Paul to write Ephesians. This gives this epistle somewhat of a "generic" character and sets it off from most of his other letters to churches, such as those at Corinth, Galatia, and even Colossae, where problems can be discerned in the congregations that led to Paul's writings. This more neutral and less polemic tone of Ephesians has supported the notion that it was a circular epistle.

Nevertheless, Paul is interested that his audience hear about his affairs (see on 6:21–22), and he wants them to pray for him (6:19) as he is praying for them (1:15–23). In particular, he is most concerned that his imprisonment may not upset their faith or cause them to doubt that, as Gentiles (2:11; 3:1), their status as "fellow citizens with the saints" (2:19) was somehow unfounded or in jeopardy (see 3:1–19). Hence, the tone of the epistle is positive and opens with a somewhat lengthy explanation of the eternal council of God behind their election, calling, and salvation in the disclosed mystery in Christ Jesus and the unity of the whole church, occupying Eph 1–4 in particular.

---

76. The concluding note in Codex Angelicus (L) represents the consensus of ancient opinions when it states: "This epistle was written to the Ephesians from Rome [and sent] through Tychicus." This appears to be around the same time and place for the writing of Colossians; "It is probable that Ephesians, Colossians, and Philemon were written from the same place" (with Rome being the most likely place), according to D. A. Carson and Douglas J. Moo, *An Introduction to the New Testament*, 2nd ed. (Grand Rapids: Zondervan, 2005), 521. There is good reason to suppose that Paul was released from this first Roman imprisonment and afterward active in Greece and Asia Minor again before his final imprisonment and death; see Harry W. Tajra, *The Martyrdom of St. Paul*, WUNT 2.67 (Tübingen: Mohr Siebeck, 1994), who dates Paul's martyrdom to AD 63/4 after a second imprisonment; cf. S. M. Baugh, "1 Timothy," in *Zondervan Illustrated Bible Backgrounds Commentary*, ed. Clinton E. Arnold (Grand Rapids: Zondervan, 2002), 3:446–48.

Recipients

Some early and important MSS lack the phrase "in Ephesus" (ἐν Ἐφέσῳ) in the opening address or give it as a correction, giving rise to a number of hypotheses about the original recipients of the epistle by those who think this phrase is missing in the autographa.[77] One early opinion is that of Marcion (Tertullian, *Marc.* 5.17), who proposed that this epistle is that of Paul to the Laodiceans mentioned in Col 4:16; however, there is no MSS evidence at all for this suggestion, so it must remain mere speculation.

A second important hypothesis is that this epistle was a circular letter and the blank space found in some MSS ("to the saints who are ______"; Eph 1:1) was left out of the autograph intentionally in order to be filled in by the reader wherever the epistle was read. This is thought to account for what is regarded as the impersonal nature of the letter and the lack of personal greetings at its conclusion.

This is a popular position among modern scholars (e.g., O'Brien and Bruce). Unfortunately, we have no evidence from antiquity that people left a blank spot in a circular letter for the addressees.[78] In the NT, when more than one church is addressed, they are all identified (Rev 1:4, 11), or their region or province is given in the address (Gal 1:2). Even multiple provinces may be mentioned (1 Pet 1:1). Paul wrote to both a city and to a province in 2 Corinthians, but he identifies them in his address: "to the church of God in Corinth along with all the saints who are in the whole of Achaia" (2 Cor 1:1). Circular letters may simply make general reference to believers in general as their audience (Jas 1:1; Jude 1; 2 Pet 1:1) or make no reference at all (Hebrews, 1 John). The notion that Ephesians is circular is an attractive idea, but the evidence from antiquity does not support it.

As I discuss in the note on Eph 1:1, it is probable that "in Ephesus" dropped out of a very early copy of the epistle and was omitted by a few later copyists and then reinserted by correctors. There is early and widespread attestation among the MSS and early church fathers (e.g., Irenaeus,

---

77. See the long text-critical note on Eph 1:1 in the commentary for discussion of the MSS evidence. The earliest witness is P[46], which lacks ἐν Ἐφέσῳ but has the heading ΠΡΟΣ ΕΦΕΣΙΟΥΣ ("To the Ephesians") as a prescript in the same hand. Hence, to say that this MS has no place name in it (O'Brien, 49) is not accurate.

78. Note also that "in Rome" is missing from some MSS and fathers at Rom 1:7. See discussion in the textual comment on Eph 1:1.

Origen, the Muratorian Canon, Clement of Alexandria) that this epistle was sent to the Ephesians, and so it seems best to accept this testimony. Furthermore, more precise discussion of Ephesus and its history (as well as careful examination of the passages in the comments) helps account for the supposed impersonal character of the letter. In the meantime, let us assume Ephesian identity of the original recipients due to the nearly unanimous early testimony to it.[79]

The city of Ephesus is one of the more interesting and important ancient cities, in part because of its state of preservation and the indefatigable efforts of modern archaeologists to uncover and restore it.[80] That search began in 1863 by John Turtle Wood, who concentrated on the Artemisium area, the huge temple of the city goddess, Artemis Ephesia, which he uncovered below more than twenty-five feet of soil in 1870.[81] Since 1896, the Austrian Archaeological Institute in Vienna (Österreichische Archäologische Institut in Wien) has been actively excavating Ephesus in conjunction with Turkish officials and has led the way in widespread publishing efforts of important archaeological studies and of the city's recovered inscriptions, coins, and other artifacts, which is still ongoing.

In antiquity, the settlement of Ephesus traditionally began in the Mycenaean period with an Athenian prince named Androclos. Many of the famous kings and generals of antiquity, such as Croesus, Xerxes, Alexander, Lysimachus, Mithridates, Sulla, and Julius Caesar, ruled, fought over, or spent time in Ephesus in their day. In the time closer to Paul's interactions with Ephesus (ca. AD 50–62), the city had shown its propensity to pick the losing side in fights by welcoming Mark Antony and Cleopatra in 33 BC.

79. Cf. Clinton Arnold, "Ephesians, Letter to the," in *DPL*, 243–45; Gnilka, 1–7.

80. General introductions to the city are provided by Jerome Murphy-O'Connor, *St. Paul's Ephesus: Texts and Archaeology* (Collegeville, MN: Liturgical, 2008); Paul Trebilco, *The Early Christians in Ephesus from Paul to Ignatius* (Grand Rapids: Eerdmans, 2008; first published 2004); cf. Dieter Knibbe, *Ephesus = Ephesos: Geschichte einer bedeutenden antiken Stadt und Portrait einer modernen Großgrabung im 102. Jahr der Wiederkehr des Beginnes österreichischer Forschungen (1895–1997)* (New York: Peter Lang, 1998); Stefan Karwiese, *Groß ist die Artemis von Ephesos: die Geschichte einer der großen Städte der Antike* (Vienna: Phoibos, 1995); Winfried Elliger, *Ephesos: Geschichte einer Antiken Weltstadt* (Stuttgart, Berlin, Cologne, and Mainz: Kohlhammer, 1985). See Scherrer, *Ephesus: The New Guide* for an overview of the archaeology of the city.

81. The Artemisium is about a mile outside the city center of Ephesus in Paul's day.

Antony promptly looted Ephesus and the other Asian cities in order to lavish their treasures on his followers and to prepare for his upcoming (losing) battle against Octavian at Actium (Plutarch, *Ant.* 24). The victorious Octavian, now the Emperor Augustus, treated the city mildly despite its association with Antony by restoring some of Artemis Ephesia's ancient lands and making it the administrative center of the province of Asia.

The rule of Augustus launched the great Ephesian building program and civic growth that was to last close to three hundred years. A devastating earthquake in AD 23 stunted the growth for a while, and the effects of Mark Antony's pillaging of the city also continued to cause the growth to be slow in the first half of the first century AD, when Paul was present in the city. The year AD 82 was an important one as Ephesus, while vying with its bitter rival Smyrna for imperial honors, won the honor of building an imperial temple and the right to proclaim that it was "The Emperor-Loving Council of the Ephesians and Temple-Warden People" (*IvE* 266). This right as "temple-warden" (νεωκόρος; cf. Acts 19:35) of the emperor cult* carried with it significant financial benefits connected with the regular festivals of this temple.[82] The boom in building and population increase in Ephesus followed this jump start in the Flavian period with the erection of the Celsus Library and other great buildings marking the modern site, many of which were built in the second to early third centuries.

While one encounters the population estimate of Pauline Ephesus at around a quarter of a million people (e.g., O'Brien, 48), this is a better figure for the second century after the great building boom began under the Flavians (i.e., starting over twenty years after Ephesians was written). The population in the mid-first century was more likely about half that or less (see comment on 2:19 and the 1,040 citizens). In the period of Paul's residence in the city (ca. AD 50–54), the growth and recovery of Ephesus from the devastation from the previous earthquake and Roman civil war was starting to gain momentum, so that by the time Ephesians was written possibly ten years later, the city and its population may have grown considerably. It is entirely possible that the effect Paul's ministry had in Ephesus and on "all Asia" (Acts 19:10) was that the church experienced a

82. Imagine a modern city winning the right to host the Olympic games every four years. The games connected to imperial worship were comparable even if on a smaller scale than today's Olympics.

considerable growth and personnel turnover from the time he resided in the city to the time he wrote Ephesians. Perhaps this explains some "impersonal" elements in the epistle and why he wants to catch the audience up on his affairs through Tychicus (Eph 6:21–22). Further details about the city and its life will be noted as background to the comments below.

Theological Emphases

The main theme of Ephesians is easy to summarize with the phrase "unity in the inaugurated new creation." Paul starts out teaching at some length on the church's unity as it is rooted in God's counsel and then in his redemptive accomplishment in the incarnate Son sealed to believers in the Holy Spirit. We see throughout Ephesians the rich, biblical teaching of a full and free salvation accomplished by the Triune God and received by faith alone. But biblical faith is a living faith, which necessarily manifests its presence through love. In Ephesians, Paul elicits this love in his audience by encouraging them to "thoughts, words, and deeds" that concretely accomplish the "unity of the Spirit in the bond of peace" (4:3).

Paul expresses the notion of the inaugurated new creation in distinctive ways that are appropriate to his ancient audience and to their world. In particular, Ephesians expresses the absolute sovereignty of the ascended Messiah over the old powers that used to keep them captive in pagan beliefs and "magical" practices. This latter issue will be addressed particularly in the exposition of Eph 1:15–23. While the commentary will elaborate on details flowing out of these central issues, it is important to keep the theological center of "unity in the inaugurated new creation" in view throughout elaboration of these details. The trees are beautiful in themselves, but the whole forest is where the vision of majesty dwells.

A Note on Greek Verbs and Syntax

While I normally cite NT Greek grammars, I also utilize references for Greek of the earlier, classical period. The syntax of any language, in contrast with the meaning of its lexemes* or its morphology, changes very slowly over time, and there are many things about classical Greek and all the modern work done on it that we in NT studies would do well to learn from. My own work in classics and in the thousands of Greek Ephesian inscriptions has influenced my discussion, for example, on the use of some participles and in the meaning of Greek verbal aspect.

Furthermore, throughout the writing of this commentary, I refer to *tense form choice* and to other related terms that may be unfamiliar to many readers. Happily, now that the commentary is written, a new intermediate Greek grammar that presents a very similar viewpoint on Greek verbs and their distinctives of aspect, and on the factors in the use of the language that guided an author to choose one tense form over another in a particular situation, will hopefully soon see publication.[83] Therefore, only the briefest introduction to the viewpoint represented in the comments will be given here.[84]

First, the indicative mood and only some uses of other moods (e.g., infinitives in indirect discourse) often communicate both tense and aspect in their tense forms, sometimes just one or the other. Tense communicates time and answers the question: "When does the event occur?" Aspect communicates the author or speaker's description of the manner in which the event occurs—whether it is attempted (conative*), finished (resultative), begun (inceptive), repeated (iterative or customary), etc.—and answers the question: "How does the event occur?" My term *event* is used for anything to which a verb or verb phrase refers.[85]

Most uses of the non-indicative moods do not convey tense. For example, an aorist imperative refers to a future event the speaker wishes or

---

83. The grammar is: Andreas J. Köstenberger, Benjamin L. Merkle, and Robert L. Plummer, *Going Deeper with New Testament Greek: An Intermediate Study of the Grammar and Syntax of the New Testament* (forthcoming). My own views have floated around the Internet in a freely available PDF titled "Introduction to Greek Tense Form Choice in the Non-Indicative Moods" (2009).

84. Among the authors on Greek verbal aspect that I have particularly profited from are: Buist M. Fanning, *Verbal Aspect in New Testament Greek* (Oxford: Clarendon, 1990); Stanley Porter, *Verbal Aspect in the Greek of the New Testament*, SBG 1 (New York: Peter Lang, 1989); Kenneth L. McKay, *A New Syntax of the Verb in New Testament Greek: An Aspectual Approach*, SBG 5 (New York: Peter Lang, 1994). For classical Greek: Albert Rijksbaron, *The Syntax and Semantics of the Verb in Classical Greek: An Introduction*, 3rd ed. (Chicago: University of Chicago Press, 2002); Peter Stork, *The Aspectual Usage of the Dynamic Infinitive in Herodotus* (Groningen: Bouma's Boekhuis, 1982); and C. M. J. Sicking and Peter Stork, "The Synthetic Perfect in Classical Greek," in *Two Studies in the Semantics of the Verb in Classical Greek* (New York: E. J. Brill, 1996), 119–298.

85. Some Greek scholars and linguists use "states of affairs" for this idea.

commands someone to perform from the time frame of utterance. It cannot refer to a past event. Because of this, we in the NT student community often have thought that these non-indicative forms always therefore communicate aspect. Hence, the present imperative is always "progressive," and the aorist is always "punctiliar" (or worse, "one-time") and the like.

The mitigating factor that is not always appreciated is that the Greek language very frequently has what can be called *default* forms in many situations. In the language of the linguists, these forms are semantically "unmarked" rather than "marked." This means that the default tense form carries no (or little) semantic value; it simply is the form in that situation that the community of Greek speakers expects as "normal" or "proper." The corollary to this is that when a speaker or author uses the form that is *not* default and is therefore marked, one can then confidently interpret that verb tense form as having aspectual value (see, e.g., περιπατῆσαι as inceptive "set out" in 4:1).

The exact factors governing default forms is a very large and involved study, particularly since, I believe, each mood has its own rules governing the default situation for that particular mood. Nevertheless, two recurring factors particularly involving infinitive and subjunctive verb forms are: (1) the construction the form is found in, and (2) what is termed the *telic* or *atelic* nature of the event itself. As for the constructions, there are some constructions that are somewhat rigid, and to use the "wrong" tense form might have been considered a mistake of usage. For example, after οὐ μή, the aorist, not the present subjunctive, is normally expected in Greek, whereas an infinitive complement for ἄρχομαι expects that the present, not the aorist, form be used.[86] Hence, forms that conform to the expected pattern in those constructions are default, and their tense form carries no particular semantic value.

Students familiar with the work of Buist Fanning know that he divides the nature of events into a number of subgroups. This is very valuable work. However, for the sake of simplicity, I divide them into just two groups: telic and atelic.[87] Atelic events are a state of being, a condition, a relationship, or

---

86. Cf. Fanning, *Verbal Aspect*, 389–400.

87. Other scholars use the terms *bounded* and *unbounded* for this idea. We are talking here about what Buist Fanning calls "the nature of the action or the procedural character of the verb or verb-phrase," Fanning, *Verbal Aspect*, 85.

even a certain kind of action that has no natural terminus implied in its being or accomplishment. On the other hand, a telic event—always an action, never a state—refers to an action that does have an understood terminus, whether or not it takes some discernible amount of time.[88] This is a very large topic, but it is important to emphasize that we are talking here about the nature of events in the world and how they naturally occur, or at least how they were perceived by the ancient Greeks, not of verbs themselves.[89] In the end, this whole matter is easier to see in actual use and exegesis of Greek texts, so I refer the matter to the comments and some occasional excurses as they come up in Ephesians.

Outline

Pauline texts are typically divided into two parts: (1) an indicative opening that concentrates on an exposition of various aspects of the Christian faith, and (2) a closing imperative section with exhortations to live a Christian lifestyle based on those truths. In Ephesians, one can see the transition to the second section begin in chapter 4. We would expect a simple division of Eph 1–3 as indicatives and Eph 4–6 as imperatives, yet the transition to the second section is not seamless, as Paul elaborates further on the basis of the inaugurated new creation life of Christians in this age in the victorious ascent of the Messiah to his throne and its results. Accordingly, the exhortations proper do not begin until 4:25, with much foundational teaching ("indicatives") sprinkled throughout the second part of the epistle as well. Here is the structure and development of the epistle:

- I. Letter Opening (1:1–2)
    - A. Author and audience (1:1)
    - B. Apostolic benediction (1:2)

---

88. Of particular note here are Fanning, *Verbal Aspect*, and Rijksbaron, *Syntax and Semantics.*

89. I.e., some Greek lexemes* can have both telic and atelic meanings, which are clarified by contextual elements. So Sicking and Stork: "One and the same verb, according to its context, can refer to Situations of a different type: e.g., drank in he drank water refers to a durative [=atelic] Situation, in he drank a glass of water to a terminative [= telic] Situation"; Sicking and Stork, "Synthetic Perfect in Classical Greek," 124.

- II. Opening Benediction (1:3–14)
    - A. For the Father's eternal, gracious purpose (1:3–6a)
    - B. For the Son's climactic, redemptive accomplishment (1:6b–10)
    - C. For the Spirit's down payment of the new creation (1:11–14)
- III. Paul Reports on His Prayer for Insight (1:15–23)
    - A. When and how Paul is praying (1:15–16)
    - B. Object of this prayer for the audience (1:17–18b)
    - C. Content of the insight for which Paul prays (1:18c–19)
    - D. Expansion on Christ's exaltation in power over creation (1:20–21)
    - E. Christ's exaltation and the church (1:22–23)
- IV. Deliverance from Death to Life in Christ (2:1–10)
    - A. The old life in death (2:1–3)
    - B. Even while dead, believers are made alive in Christ's life (2:4–7)
    - C. Expansion on this new life as a divine work leading to new obedience (2:8–10)
- V. The Unified New Creation Inaugurated (2:11–22)
    - A. Gentile separation from Israel and from God (2:11–12)
    - B. Christ has united Gentiles with the saints into a new human race (2:13–18)
    - C. The unified church household as new creation temple (2:19–22)
- VI. The Mystery of Redemption and Its Revelation (3:1–13)
    - A. Opening to (delayed) prayer (3:1)
    - B. Redemptive revelation as a mystery (3:2–7)
    - C. The revelation of this mystery (3:8–12)
    - D. Conclusion not to grow disheartened (3:13)
- VII. Paul's Resumed Prayer (3:14–21)
    - A. Posture of prayer before the Father (3:14–15)
    - B. Report of content of intercession for audience (3:16–19)
        1. For divine indwelling and love (3:16–17)
        2. For understanding (3:18–19)
    - C. Concluding blessing of God (3:20–21)
- VIII. Paul's Exhortation to Unity in Love (4:1–6)
    - A. The exhortation proper (4:1–3)
        1. The worthy walk (4:1c–2a)
        2. Patient endurance in love (4:2b)
        3. Zeal for the church's unity in peace (4:3)
    - B. The basis of the exhortation (4:4–6)

IX. Gifts from the Ascended Messiah to Unify His Church (4:7–16)
  A. Gifts from Christ's triumphant victory and ascent (4:7–10)
    1. Gifts of grace (4:7)
    2. Psalm 68:18 (4:8)
    3. Gifts given to loyal subjects after Christ's victory in death (4:9–10)
  B. Word-based church officers as gifts for edification (4:11–13)
  C. The outcome of the gifts in operation (4:14–16)
    1. Protection from error and deceit (4:14)
    2. Doctrinal maturity in love (4:15)
    3. Ecclesiastical unity in love (4:16)
X. The New Way of Life versus the Old (4:17–24)
  A. Solemn exhortation to turn away from the old life (4:17)
  B. The old life is futility, ignorance, and impurity (4:17–19)
  C. Converts to Christ have made a definitive break with the past (4:20–24)
XI. The New Creation Walk in Love (4:25–5:2)
  A. In word (4:25)
  B. In thought (4:26–27)
  C. In deed (4:28)
  D. In word again (4:29)
  E. In thought and word (4:31–5:2)
XII. The Saints and the Sinful World (5:3–14)
  A. The sinful world's practices (5:3–5)
  B. Exhortation to resist enticements of the world (5:6)
  C. Central exhortation (5:7)
  D. Walk wisely in the light and bear its fruit (5:8–14)
XIII. Summarizing Exhortation to the Whole Church (5:15–21)
  A. Walk in wisdom, not folly (5:15–17)
  B. Not in drunken excess and license (5:18a)
  C. The church in God's presence in the Spirit as the new temple and priesthood (5:18b)
  D. Service in song (5:19)
  E. Service in thanksgiving (5:20)
  F. Service in submission (5:21)

XIV. Exhortations to Christian Households: Wives and Husbands (5:22–33)
- A. Exhortation to wives (5:22–24)
  - 1. First manner and motive (5:22)
  - 2. Rationale (5:23)
  - 3. Second manner and motive (5:24)
- B. Exhortation to husbands (5:25–32)
  - 1. Manner and rationale (5:25–27)
  - 2. Exhortation repeated with stress on union (5:28)
  - 3. Rationale in archetype of Christ and the church (5:29–32)
- C. Final exhortation to both husband and wife (5:33)

XV. Exhortations to Christian Households: Children and Parents in the Lord (6:1–4)
- A. Children to be obedient, as is right (6:1)
- B. OT justification (6:2–3)
- C. Parents' nurture of children in the Lord (6:4)

XVI. Exhortations to Christian Households: Slaves and Masters in the Lord (6:5–9)
- A. Slaves obey their masters (6:5–8)
  - 1. With sincerity of heart (6:5)
  - 2. As to the Lord (6:6–7)
  - 3. Mindful of their eternal inheritance (6:8)
- B. Masters' mild treatment of their slaves (6:9)

XVII. The Church Equipped for Its Struggle (6:10–20)
- A. Urged to stand fast in the spiritual struggle (6:10–13)
- B. Urged to stand fast in the Lord's battle armor (6:14–17)
- C. Urged to persevering prayer (6:18–20)

XVIII. Concluding Thoughts and Benediction (6:21–24)
- A. The ministry of Tychicus (6:21–22)
- B. The closing apostolic blessing (6:23–24)

Selected Bibliography

Alexander, L. "Chronology of Paul." In *DPL*, 115–23.

Arnold, C. "Ephesians, Letter to the." In *DPL*, 238–49.

Barnett, P. *Paul: Missionary of Jesus.* Grand Rapids: Eerdmans, 2008.

Bauckham, R. "Pseudo-Apostolic Letters." *JBL* 107 (1988): 469–94.

Byrskog, S. "Co-Senders, Co-Authors and Paul's Use of the First Person Plural." *ZNW* 87 (1996): 230–50.

Carson, D. A., and D. J. Moo. *An Introduction to the New Testament.* 2nd ed. Grand Rapids: Zondervan, 2005.

Cribiore, R. *Gymnastics of the Mind: Greek Education in Hellenistic and Roman Egypt.* Princeton: Princeton University Press, 2001.

Elliger, W. *Ephesos: Geschichte einer Antiken Weltstadt.* Stuttgart, Berlin, Cologne, and Mainz: Kohlhammer, 1985.

Elmer, I. "I, Tertius: Secretary or Co-author of Romans." *ABR* 56 (2008): 45–60.

Fanning, B. *Verbal Aspect in New Testament Greek.* Oxford: Clarendon, 1990.

Hengel, M. *The Pre-Christian Paul.* Philadelphia: Trinity Press International, 1991.

Jewett, R. *A Chronology of Paul's Life.* Philadelphia: Fortress, 1979.

Karwiese, S. *Gross ist die Artemis von Ephesos: die Geschichte einer der grossen Städt der Antike.* Vienna: Phoibos, 1995.

Kenny, A. *A Stylometric Study of the New Testament.* Oxford: Clarendon, 1986.

Knibbe, D. *Ephesus = Ephesos: Geschichte einer bedeutenden antiken Stadt und Portrait einer modernen Großgrabung im 102.* Jahr der Wiederkehr des Beginnes österreichischer Forschungen (1895–1997). New York: Peter Lang, 1998.

Koester, H., ed. *Ephesos, Metropolis of Asia.* Valley Forge, PA: Harvard Divinity School Press, 1995.

Lausberg, H. *Handbook of Literary Rhetoric: A Foundation for Literary Study.* Edited by D. Orton and R. D. Anderson. Boston: Brill, 1998.

McKay, K. L. *A New Syntax of the Verb in New Testament Greek.* SBG 5. New York: Peter Lang, 1994.

Mitton, C. L. *The Epistle to the Ephesians: Its Authorship, Origin and Purpose.* Oxford: Clarendon, 1951.

Morgan, T. *Literate Education in the Hellenistic and Roman Worlds.* Cambridge: Cambridge University Press, 1998. Repr., 2007.

Murphy-O'Connor, J. *Paul the Letter-Writer: His World, His Options, His Skills.* GNS 41. Collegeville, MN: Liturgical Press, 1995.

Murphy-O'Connor, J. *St. Paul's Ephesus: Texts and Archaeology.* Collegeville, MN: Liturgical Press, 2008.

Neumann, K. *The Authenticity of the Pauline Epistles in the Light of Stylostatistical Analysis.* SBLDS 120. Atlanta: Scholars Press, 1990.

Pitts, A. "Hellenistic Schools in Jerusalem and Paul's Rhetorical Education." In *Paul's World*, ed. S. Porter, 19–50. Boston: Brill, 2008.

Porter, S. *Verbal Aspect in the Greek of the New Testament.* SBG 1. New York: Peter Lang, 1989.

Richards, E. R. *Paul and First-Century Letter Writing: Secretaries, Composition and Collection.* Downers Grove, IL: InterVarsity Press, 2004.

———. *The Secretary in the Letters of Paul.* WUNT 2.42. Tübingen: Mohr Siebeck, 1991.

Rijksbaron, A. *The Syntax and Semantics of the Verb in Classical Greek: An Introduction*. 3rd ed. Chicago: University of Chicago Press, 2002.

Robbins, C. J. "The Composition of Eph. 1:3–14." *JBL* 105 (1986): 677–87.

Scaglione, A. *The Classical Theory of Composition from its Origins to the Present.* Chapel Hill: University of North Carolina Press, 1972.

Scheppers, F. *The Colon Hypothesis: Word Order, Discourse Segmentation and Discourse Coherence in Ancient Greek*. Brussels: VUBPRESS, 2011.

Scherrer, P. *Ephesus: The New Guide.* Turkey: Zero, 2000.

Sicking, C., and P. Stork. "The Synthetic Perfect in Classical Greek." In *Two Studies in the Semantics of the Verb in Classical Greek*, 119–298. New York: Brill, 1996.

Stork, P. *The Aspectual Usage of the Dynamic Infinitive in Herodotus*. Groningen: Bouma's Boekhuis, 1982.

Tajra, H. *The Martyrdom of St. Paul.* WUNT 2.67. Tübingen: Mohr Siebeck, 1994.

Trebilco, P. *The Early Christians in Ephesus from Paul to Ignatius.* Grand Rapids: Eerdmans, 2008. First published 2004.

van Roon, A. *The Authenticity of Ephesians.* NovTSup 39. Leiden: Brill, 1974.

West, M. *Introduction to Greek Metre.* Oxford: Clarendon, 1987.

Wilder, T. *Pseudonymity, the New Testament, and Deception: An Inquiry into Intention and Reception*. Lanham, MD: University Press of America, 2004.

Commentary Bibliography

Abbott, Thomas. *A Critical and Exegetical Commentary on the Epistles to the Ephesians and to the Colossians*. Edinburgh: T&T Clark, 1985.

Aletti, Jean. *Saint Paul, Épître aux Éphésiens*. Paris: J. Gabalda, 2001.

Ambrosiaster. *In epistolam Beati Pauli ad Ephesios*. Paris: Excudebatur et Venit Apud J.-P. Migne Editorem, 1845.

Aquinas, Thomas. *Commentary of Saint Paul's Epistle to the Ephesians*. Albany, NY: Magi Books, 1966.

Arnold, Clinton E., Frank Thielman, and S. M. Baugh. *Ephesians, Philippians, Colossians, Philemon: Zondervan illustrated Bible Backgrounds Commentary*. Softcover ed. Grand Rapids: Zondervan, 2002.

Arnold, Clinton. *Ephesians*. Grand Rapids: Zondervan, 2010.

Barclay, William. *The Letters to the Galatians and Ephesians*. Rev. ed. The Daily Study Bible. Philadelphia: Westminster John Knox, 2002.

Barth, Markus. *Ephesians*. 2 vols. AB. Garden City, NY: Doubleday, 1974.

Becker, Jürgen. *Die Briefe an die Galater, Epheser und Kolosser*. 18th ed. Göttingen: Vandenhoeck & Ruprecht, 1998.

Beet, Joseph Agar. *A Commentary on St. Paul's Epistle to the Ephesians, Philippians, Colossians, and to Philemon*. London: Hodder and Stoughton, 1890.

Belser, Johannes Evang. *Der Epheserbrief des Apostles Paulus*. Freiburg im Breisgau: Herdersche Verlagshandlung, 1908.

Best, Ernest. *A Critical and Exegetical Commentary on Ephesians*. ICC. Edinburgh: T&T Clark, 1998.

Bouttier, Michel. *L'Épître de saint Paul aux Éphésiens*. Geneve: Labor et Fides, 1991.

Bruce, Frederick Fyvie. *The Epistles to the Colossians, to Philemon, and to the Ephesians*. 2nd ed. NICNT. Grand Rapids: Eerdmans, 1984.

Caird, G. B. *Paul's Letters from Prison: Ephesians, Philippians, Colossians, Philemon, in the Revised Standard Version*. New Clarendon Bible. Oxford: Oxford University Press, 1976.

Calvin, John. *Calvin's New Testament Commentaries: The Epistles of Paul The Apostle to the Galatians, Ephesians, Philippians and Colossians*. Grand Rapids: Eerdmans, 1965.

Chrysostom, John. *In epistulam ad Ephesios* (homiliae 1–24). Thesaurus Linguae Graecae of the University California, Irvine.

Conzelmann, Hans. *Die Briefe an die Galater, Epheser, Philipper, Kolosser, Thessalonicher und Philemon*. 15th ed. NTD 8. Göttingen: Vandenhoeck & Ruprecht, 1981.

Dale, R. W. *The Epistle to the Ephesians. Its Doctrine and Ethics*. London: Hodder and Stoughton, 1883.

Davies, J. Llewelyn. *The Epistles of St. Paul to the Ephesians, the Colossians, and Philemon*. 2nd ed. London: Macmillan, 1884.

Dibelius, Martin. *An die Kolosser, Epheser, an Philemon*. HNT. Tübingen: Mohr, 1953.

Donelson, Lewis R. *Colossians, Ephesians, First and Second Timothy, and Titus*. Louisville: Westminster John Knox, 1996.

Eadie, John. *A Commentary on the Greek Text of the Epistle of Paul to the Ephesians*. 3rd ed. Edinburgh: T&T Clark, 1883 (1st ed., 1854).

Edwards, Mark J. *Galatians, Ephesians, Philippians.* Ancient Christian Commentary on Scripture. 2nd ed. Downers Grove, IL: InterVarsity Press, 2005.

Ellicott, Charles J. *A Critical and Grammatical Commentary on St. Paul's Epistle to the Ephesians: With a Revised Translation*. 5th ed. London: Longmans, Green, 1884 (1st ed., 1855).

Ernst, Josef. *Die Briefe an die Philipper, an Philemon, an die Kolosser, an die Epheser*. Regensburg: Pustet, 1974.

Ewald, Paul. *Die Briefe des Paulus an die Epheser, Kolosser und Philemon*. 10 vols. Leipzig: A. Deichertische Verlagsbuchhandlung, 1905.

Foulkes, Francis. *Ephesians: An Introduction and Commentary*. TNTC. Repr. Downers Grove, IL: InterVarsity Press, 2008.

Gaugler, Ernst. *Der Epheserbrief*. Zürich: EVZ-Verlag, 1966.

Gnilka, Joachim. *Der Epheserbrief*. HTKNT. Freiburg: Herder, 1971.

Hendriksen, William. *Ephesians*. NTC. Grand Rapids: Baker, 1967.

Hodge, Charles. *A Commentary on the Epistle to the Ephesians*. Grand Rapids: Eerdmans, 1994 (1st ed., 1856).

Hoehner, Harold W. *Ephesians: An Exegetical Commentary*. Grand Rapids: Baker, 2002.

Houlden, J. L. *Paul's Letters from Prison: Philippians, Colossians, Philemon, and Ephesians*. Baltimore: Penguin, 1970.

Hubner, Hans. *An Philemon. An die Kolosser. An die Epheser*. HNT. Tübingen: Mohr, 1997.

Hugede, Norbert. *L'Épître aux Éphésiens*. Geneve: Labor et Fides, 1973.

Jerome. *The Commentaries of Origen and Jerome on St. Paul's Epistle to the Ephesians*. Translated by R. Heine. Oxford and New York: Oxford, 2002.

Kitchen, Martin. *Ephesians*. New Testament Readings. New York: Routledge, 1994.

Kreitzer, Larry J. *The Epistle to the Ephesians*. Peterborough: Epworth, 1998.

Lenski, R. C. H. *The Interpretation of St. Paul's Epistles to the Galatians, to the Ephesians and to the Philippians*. Repr. Minneapolis: Augsburg, 1961 (First published 1937).

Lincoln, Andrew T. *Ephesians*. WBC 42. Dallas: Word, 1990.

Lindemann, Andreas. *Der Epheserbrief*. Zürich: Theologischer Verlag, 1985.

Luther, Martin. *Die Briefe an die Epheser, Philipper und Kolosser*. Vol. 3. Göttingen: Vandenhoeck & Ruprecht, 1973.

Luz, Ulrich. *Die Briefe an die Galater, Epheser und Kolosser*. 18th ed. NTD. Göttingen: Vandenhoeck & Ruprecht, 1998.

MacDonald, Margaret. *Colossians and Ephesians*. Sacra Pagina. Collegeville, MN: Liturgical, 2000.

Mackay, John A. *God's Order. The Ephesian Letter and This Present Time*. New York: Macmillan, 1953.

Macpherson, John. *Commentary on St. Paul's Epistle to the Ephesians*. Edinburgh: T&T Clark, 1892.

Martin, Ralph. *Ephesians, Colossians, and Philemon*. Atlanta: John Knox, 1991.

Masson, Charles. *L'Épître de saint Paul aux Éphésiens*. Neuchatel: Delachaux & Niestle, 1953.

Maxwell, Marcus. *Ephesians to Colossians and Philemon*. Peabody, MA: Hendrickson, 2007.

Meinertz, Max, and Fritz Tillmann. *Die Gefangenschaftsbriefe des Heilgen Paulus.* Bonn: Peter Hanstein, 1931.

Meyer, Heinrich A. W. *Critical and Exegetical Handbook to the Epistle to the Ephesians and the Epistle to Philemon.* Edinburgh: T&T Clark, 1880 (German ed., 1843).

Mitton, C. Leslie. *Ephesians.* NCB. London: Oliphants, 1976.

Morris, Leon. *Expository Reflections on the Letter to the Ephesians.* Grand Rapids: Baker, 1994.

Moule, H. C. G. *The Epistle to the Ephesians.* Cambridge: Cambridge University Press, 1886.

Muddiman, John. *A Commentary on the Epistle to the Ephesians.* BNTC. New York: Continuum, 2001.

Murray, J. O. F. *The Epistle of Paul the Apostle to the Ephesians.* Cambridge: Cambridge University Press, 1914.

Mussner, Franz. *Der Brief an die Epheser.* Gütersloh: Gütersloher Verlagshaus, 1982.

O'Brien, Peter. *The Letter to the Ephesians.* PNTC. Grand Rapids: Eerdmans, 1999.

Olshausen, Hermann. *Biblical Commentary on St Paul's Epistles to the Galatians, Ephesians, Colossians, and Thessalonians.* Edinburgh: T&T Clark, 1851.

Origen. *Fragmenta ex commentariis in epistulam ad Ephesios.* Thesaurus Linguae Graecae of the University California, Irvine.

———. *The Commentaries of Origen and Jerome on St. Paul's Epistle to the Ephesians.* Translated by R. Heine. New York: Oxford University Press, 2002.

Patzia, Arthur. *Ephesians, Colossians, Philemon.* GNCNT. San Francisco: Harper & Row, 1984.

Perkins, Pheme. *Ephesians.* ANTC. Nashville: Abingdon, 1997.

Phillips, Richard. *Saved by Grace: The Glory of Salvation in Ephesians 2.* Phillipsburg, NJ: P&R, 2009.

Pokorný, Petr. *Der Brief des Paulus an die Epheser.* Leipzig: Evangelische Verlagsanstalt, 1992.

Rendtorff, Heinrich. *Die kleineren Briefe des Apostels Paulus.* 6th ed. Göttingen: Vandenhoeck & Ruprecht, 1953 (1st ed., 1933).

Rienecker, Fritz. *Der Brief des Paulus an die Epheser.* Wuppertal: Brockhaus, 1961.

Robinson, J. Armitage. *St Paul's Epistle to the Ephesians: An Exposition.* London: Macmillan, 1903.

Salmond, S. D. F. "Ephesians." In *The Expositor's Greek Testament.* London: Hodder and Stoughton, 1903.

Sampley, J. Paul. "The Letter to the Ephesians." In *The Deutero-Pauline Letters: Ephesians, Colossians, 2 Thessalonians, 1–2 Timothy, Titus.* Rev. ed. Philadelphia: Fortress, 1993.

Schlatter, Adolf. "Der Brief an die Epheser." In *Erlauterungen zum Neuen Testament*. Stuttgart: Calwer, 1963.

Schlier, Heinrich. *Der Brief an die Epheser: Ein Kommentar*. 7th ed. Dusseldorf: Patmos, 1971 (1st ed., 1957).

Schmid, J. *Der Epheserbrief des Apostels Paulus: Seine Adresse, Sprache und literarischen Beziehungen*. Freiburg: Herder, 1928.

Schnackenburg, Rudolf. *Ephesians: A Commentary*. Translated by Helen Heron. Edinburgh: T&T Clark, 1991 (German ed., 1982).

Scott, E. F. *The Epistles of Paul to the Colossians, to Philemon and to the Ephesians*. London: Hodder and Stoughton, 1930.

Sellin, Gerhard. *Der Brief an die Epheser*. 9th ed. Göttingen: Vandenhoeck & Ruprecht, 2008.

Simpson, E. K. *The Epistles of Paul to the Colossians, to Philemon and to the Ephesians*. NICNT. Grand Rapids: Eerdmans, 1957.

Snodgrass, Klyne. *Ephesians*. Grand Rapids: Zondervan, 1996.

Soden, H. von. *Die Briefe an die Kolosser, Epheser, Philemon, die Pastoral Briefe*. 2nd ed. Freiburg: Akademische Verlagsburchhandlung von Mohr, 1893 (1st ed., 1891).

Speyr, Adrienne von. *The Letter to the Ephesians*. San Francisco: Ignatius, 1996 (German ed., 1983).

Staab, Karl. *Die Thessalonicherbriefe, die Gefangenschaftsbriefe*. 3rd ed. Regensburg: Friedrich Pustet, 1959 (1st ed., 1950).

Stadelmann, Helge. *Der Epheserbrief*. Neuhausen-Stuttgart: Hansler, 1993.

Stott, John. *The Message of Ephesians*. Downers Grove, IL: InterVarsity Press, 1979.

Swain, Lionel. *Ephesians*. Wilmington, DE: Michael Glazier, 1980.

Synge, F. C. *St. Paul's Epistle to the Ephesians: A Theological Commentary*. London: SPCK, 1941.

Talbert, Charles. *Ephesians and Colossians*. Grand Rapids: Baker, 2007.

Tanzer, Sarah J. "Ephesians." In *Searching the Scriptures: A Feminist Commentary*, edited by Elisabeth Schüssler Fiorenza, vol. 2, 325–48. New York: Crossroad, 1994.

Taylor, Walter F., Jr. *Ephesians*. Minneapolis: Augsburg, 1985.

Theodore of Mopsuestia. *Commentary on the Minor Pauline Epistles*. Translated by Rowan A. Greer. WGRW. Atlanta: SBL, 2010.

Thielman, Frank. *Ephesians*. Grand Rapids: Baker, 2010.

Thompson, G. H. P. *The Letters of Paul to the Ephesians, to the Colossians and to Philemon*. Cambridge: Cambridge University Press, 1967.

Thurston, Bonnie. *Reading Colossians, Ephesians, and 2 Thessalonians: A Literary and Theological Commentary*. New York: Crossroad, 1995.

Turner, Max. "Ephesians." In *New Bible Commentary: 21st Century Edition*, ed. D. A. Carson, R. T. France, J. A. Motyer, and G. J. Wenham, 1222–44. 4th ed. Downers Grove, IL: InterVarsity Press, 1994.

Turner, Samuel H. *The Epistle to the Ephesians in Greek and English*. New York: Dana, 1856.

Verhey, Allen, and Joseph Harvard. *Ephesians: A Theological Commentary on the Bible*. Louisville: Westminster John Knox, 2011.

Westcott, Brooke Foss. *Saint Paul's Epistle to the Ephesians: The Greek Text with Notes and Addenda*. London: Macmillan, 1906.

Wette, W. M. L. *Kurze Erklarung der Briefe an die Colosser, an Philemon, an die Ephesier und Philipper*. 2nd ed. Leipzig: Weidmann'sche Buchhandlung, 1847 (1st ed., 1843).

Williamson, Peter S. *Ephesians*. Grand Rapids: Baker, 2009.

Witherington, Ben III. *The Letters to Philemon, the Colossians, and the Ephesians: A Socio-Rhetorical Commentary on the Captivity Epistles*. Grand Rapids: Eerdmans, 2007.

Wood, A. Skevington. "Ephesians." In *The Expositor's Bible Commentary: Ephesians through Philemon,* ed. Frank E. Gabelein, 1–92. Grand Rapids: Zondervan, 1978.

Wright, N. T. *Paul for Everyone: The Prison Letters: Ephesians, Philippians, Colossians, and Philemon*. 2nd ed. Louisville: Westminster John Knox, 2004.

Letter Opening (1:1–2)

Introduction

Paul opens his letter by identifying himself and his addressees, and then pronouncing an apostolic benediction for "grace and peace." These elements are standard for the Pauline Epistles. The one thing that makes the opening of Ephesians distinctive and controversial is that the words that identify the audience as ἐν Ἐφέσῳ ("in Ephesus") are missing in some key early MSS (discussed at length below). Otherwise the opening of Ephesians is unremarkable.

As noted in the introduction and defended below, I am taking the reading "in Ephesus" in v. 1 as original and therefore the epistle as indeed addressed to the Ephesian church. The main implication of this is that the physical remains of this ancient city—which has been excavated for more than a century—can illumine certain aspects of the people and society relative to the epistle. It should be noted, however, that if this identification of the epistle with Ephesus is wrong, the background material from Ephesus will still be illuminating since ancient cities in the eastern Roman provinces have many things in common despite any individual distinctions.[1] There are certainly differences between cities, of course, yet the core similarities still outnumber the differences.

---

1. For example, Corinth and Philippi were Roman colonies, and Ephesus was an historic Greek colony. Ephesus was, however, the provincial capital of Asia in the first century, which brought increasing Roman involvement in its civic affairs. This involvement is evidenced most notably in *IvE* 17–19, the edict of the Roman provincial governor Paullus Fabius Persicus in AD 44, who objected to certain local practices such as purchase of priesthoods and public slaves buying and raising (at public expense) foundlings to serve as their own slaves. Cf. Beate Dignas, *Economy of the Sacred in Hellenistic and Roman Asia Minor* (Oxford: Oxford University Press, 2002), 141–56, 238–39.

In all later sections, I will be providing a division of the Greek text into cola* and periods in addition to the modern format and punctuation provided in critical texts. The explanation and discussion of this issue is addressed in the book's introduction and the introduction to 1:3–14 below.

Outline

I. Letter Opening (1:1–2)
  A. Author and audience (1:1)
  B. Apostolic benediction (1:2)

Original Text[2]

1 Παῦλος ἀπόστολος Χριστοῦ Ἰησοῦ[a] διὰ θελήματος θεοῦ τοῖς ἁγίοις [b]τοῖς οὖσιν ἐν Ἐφέσῳ[c] καὶ πιστοῖς ἐν Χριστῷ Ἰησοῦ, **2** χάρις ὑμῖν καὶ εἰρήνη ἀπὸ θεοῦ πατρὸς ἡμῶν καὶ κυρίου Ἰησοῦ Χριστοῦ.

Textual Notes

1.a. ℵ, A, F, G, Ψ, 1739, 1881, M, and a few other MSS invert the name here from Χριστοῦ Ἰησοῦ to Ἰησοῦ Χριστοῦ, which is probably to conform to the word order at the end of v. 2. P[46], B, and many other MSS have the word order as given in our text and major editions.

1.b. A few MSS (e.g., the second hand of ℵ as well as A, P, 81, 326, and 629) add πᾶσιν here ("to *all* the saints"), which conforms the reading to the opening of Romans (**πᾶσιν** τοῖς οὖσιν ἐν Ῥώμῃ, "to *all* those who are in Rome"; Rom 1:7) and Philippians (**πᾶσιν** τοῖς ἁγίοις … τοῖς οὖσιν ἐν Φιλίπποις, "to **all** the saints … who are among the Philippians"; Phil 1:1). If this reading were original, we would expect πᾶσιν to come in front of τοῖς ἁγίοις as in Phil 1:1, not after it (i.e., πᾶσιν τοῖς ἁγίοις τοῖς οὖσιν, not τοῖς ἁγίοις πᾶσιν τοῖς οὖσιν as in the MSS). In ℵ the words are added after ἁγίοις, which occurs at the end of the line and is a more convenient place to add the correction (i.e., ΑΓΙΟΙσπασι, where the last five letters extend into the right margin).

---

2. The text used in this section of the commentary is based on the NA[28], with just a few changes defended in the notes.

1.c. The textual variants here are the most important in the epistle and require extended discussion.[3] There are three primary readings:

1. τοῖς ἁγίοις οὖσιν καὶ πιστοῖς ἐν Χριστῷ Ἰησοῦ—P[46]
2. τοῖς ἁγίοις τοῖς οὖσιν καὶ πιστοῖς ἐν Χριστῷ Ἰησοῦ—א*, B*, 6, 424[c], 1739, and Origen[4]
3. τοῖς ἁγίοις τοῖς οὖσιν ἐν Ἐφέσῳ καὶ πιστοῖς ἐν Χριστῷ Ἰησοῦ—א[c2], A, B[2], D, F, G, Ψ, 0278, 33, 1881, M, and all ancient versions

Because P[46], א* (Sinaiticus), and B* (Vaticanus) in particular do not have "in Ephesus," many scholars since the time that these MSS were discovered have doubted that the epistle was originally addressed to the Ephesians.[5] This has led to three notable textual emendation proposals: (1) that there were originally two churches addressed ("to the saints in … and in …"); (2) that οὖσιν should be dropped and the phrase be read "to saints and believers in Christ Jesus"; and (3) that the original text had a blank space for the location of the addressees because the epistle was a circular and the copyist would write in the appropriate city name of the copy sent to

3. For survey of scholarly discussion see: J. Schmid, *Der Epheserbrief des Apostels Paulus: Seine Adresse, Sprache und literarischen Beziehungen* (Freiburg: Herder, 1928), 37–129; Ernest Best, "Ephesians i.1," in *Text and Interpretation*, ed. E. Best and R. McL. Wilson (Cambridge: Cambridge University Press, 1979), 29–41; Best, "Ephesians i.1 Again," in *Paul and Paulinism*, ed. M. D. Hooker and S. G. Wilson (London: SPCK, 1982), 273–79; David Alan Black, "The Peculiarities of Ephesians and the Ephesian Address," *GTJ* 2 (1981): 59–73.

4. א and B have οὖσι καί without the movable *nu* (it is added in the margin in B), as is appropriate when the next word begins with a consonant (καί), whereas P[46] has the *nu*, which may suggest that the next word in this MS originally had a vowel (i.e., οὖσι**ν ἐν** Ἐφέσῳ), although admittedly the use of this final *nu* in the ancient period did not conform to any strict rules; see Wilbert F. Howard, *A Grammar of New Testament Greek*, vol. 2, *Accidence and Word-Formation* (Edinburgh: T&T Clark, 1929), 113.

5. Marcion identified the epistle as addressed to the Laodiceans, probably because of reference to an epistle addressed to them in Col 4:16 rather than because of any manuscript evidence. The later MSS 6, 424, and 1739 come from the tenth to thirteenth centuries and will not receive further attention in my discussion.

different cities. None of these proposals has MS evidence, and neither have they received universal support among scholars.[6]

Many generally propose that the original text was that of the second proposal and means something like "to the saints who are also faithful" (e.g., margins of ESV and NRSV), but if this were intended, *οὖσιν* would not be present in the text. As is often pointed out, when Paul addresses churches, this participle of *εἰμί* is used with locative *ἐν* and the city name:[7]

---

6. The first emendation is from A. van Roon, *The Authenticity of Ephesians*, NovTSup 39 (Leiden: Brill, 1974), 72–85, followed for the most part by Lincoln, 1–4; few others are convinced of this view. The second emendation is from J. Schmid, *Der Epheserbrief des Apostels Paulus: Seine Adresse, Sprache und literarischen Beziehungen* (Freiburg: Herder, 1928), 125–29; and Best, 95–99, yet it is contradictory. If the reading *τοῖς ἁγίοις* [*τοῖς*] *οὖσιν καὶ πιστοῖς ἐν Χριστῷ Ἰησοῦ* is accepted on the strength of three early MSS, why delete *οὖσιν*, which is present in *all* MSS and early versions, including those three early MSS? Best in particular overstresses the difficulty of the grammar of the second clause in the phrase *τοῖς ἁγίοις τοῖς οὖσιν ἐν Ἐφέσῳ καὶ πιστοῖς ἐν Χριστῷ Ἰησοῦ* (see below). The third emendation (e.g., Brooke F. Westcott and F. J. A. Hort, *The New Testament in the Original Greek* [Cambridge and London: Macmillan, 1881], 2:123–24; and Bruce, 240) also has little to commend it, since epistles aimed at multiple cities simply addressed them all (Rev 1:4, 11) or referenced churches in a provincial region (Gal 1:2) or regions (1 Pet 1:1). Or they may simply make general reference to believers as their audience (Jude 1; 2 Pet 1:1). It would have been expected that the author would have keep copies of important epistles for wider distribution beyond the original recipients; see E. Randolph Richards, *The Secretary in the Letters of Paul*, WUNT 2.42 (Tübingen: Mohr Siebeck, 1991), 6–7. Prominent evidence of this is found in Polycarp: "We send you, as you asked, the letters of Ignatius, which were sent to us by him, and others which we had by us. These are subjoined to this letter" (Polycarp, *Phil.* 13.2).

7. For other constructions with the attributive or substantive ptc. of *εἰμί* followed by a prepositional phrase in Paul see: Rom 4:10; 7:23; 8:23; 9:5; 12:3; 13:1; 16:11; 2 Cor 5:4; Eph 4:18 (*διὰ τὴν ἄγνοιαν τὴνοὖσαν ἐν αὐτοῖς*); Col 4:11; 1 Thess 2:14 (*τῶν ἐκκλησιῶν τοῦ θεοῦ τῶνοὐσῶνἐντῇ Ἰουδαίᾳ ἐν Χριστῷ Ἰησοῦ*). Note that "in Rome" is missing in some MSS and fathers at Rom 1:7, leading Bruce Metzger and the majority of the UBS committee to suggest that this was "a deliberate excision, made in order to show that the letter is of general, not local, application," Bruce M. Metzger, *A Textual Commentary on the Greek New Testament*, 2nd ed. (New York: United Bible Societies, 1994), 446.

πᾶσιν **τοῖς οὖσιν ἐν Ῥώμῃ** ἀγαπητοῖς θεοῦ (Rom 1:7)
τῇ ἐκκλησίᾳ τοῦ θεοῦ **τῇ οὔσῃ ἐν Κορίνθῳ** (1 Cor 1:2)
τῇ ἐκκλησίᾳ τοῦ θεοῦ τῇ οὔσῃ ἐν Κορίνθῳ σὺν **τοῖς ἁγίοις πᾶσιν τοῖς οὖσιν ἐν ὅλῃ τῇ Ἀχαΐᾳ** (2 Cor 1:1)
τοῖς ἁγίοις ἐν Χριστῷ Ἰησοῦ **τοῖς οὖσιν ἐν Φιλίπποις** (Phil 1:1).

What this shows is that we certainly expect specification of a location such as ἐν Ἐφέσῳ in Eph 1:1 because of the participle οὖσιν. Without the location phrase, we are left with a very strange—indeed, an "impossible"—reading (BDF §413 [3]).[8] That "in Ephesus" should be found in the bulk of the MS witnesses conforms to the superscript and/or to the postscript reference of "To the Ephesians" in all MSS, even in those early three where "in Ephesus" is missing in 1:1 or added by a corrector (P[46], ℵ, and B). Except for Marcion and a few other MSS that have "To the Laodiceans," these superscriptions and postscripts in the early MSS testify to a widespread church tradition that this epistle was sent to Ephesus.

A number of good arguments have been made in favor of accepting ἐν Ἐφέσῳ as the reading of the autograph (esp. Gnilka, 1–7; Arnold, 23–29; Hoehner, 78–79, 144–48). For example, we could point out that the critical editions do not accept readings and omissions from P[46], ℵ, and/or B elsewhere in Ephesians, variants I discuss in the textual notes on 1:15 (2x), 18; 2:5; 3:1, 3, 9, 18, 19; 4:4, 18, 23–24; 5:2 (2x), 19; 6:1, 16, 19, 20. However, I would like to add some observations on P[46] in particular, since it antedates both Sinaiticus (ℵ) and Vaticanus (B) by 150-plus years and is our only extensive papyrus witness for Ephesians.

First, as can be seen in the first proposal above, P[46] drops the article in front of οὖσιν, which turns ἁγίοις into a predicate and makes the participle function as a substantive to read: "to those who exist as saints and as

---

8. I.e., that of Origen: "In the case of Ephesians alone we find the phrase, 'to the saints who are.' We ask what the phrase 'who are' can mean, if it is not redundant when added to 'the saints.' Consider, then if not as in Exodus he who utters the words 'he who is' to Moses speaks his own name (Exod. 3:14), so those who participate in 'the one who is' become those 'who are,' called, as it were, from 'not being' into 'being.' " Jerome demurs from Origen here and says, "Others, however, think it has been written straightforwardly not to those 'who are,' but 'who are the saints and faithful in Ephesus' " (Origen and Jerome, 80). Note that Origen here and, e.g., on Eph 4:3 or 4:28 regards this book as addressed to the Ephesians, "those even in Ephesus" (Origen and Jerome, 197).

faithful ..." This reading makes even less sense than the reading of א* and B*, which have the article but not "in Ephesus." Even if the papyrus had "in Ephesus," the reading without this article would still be most unlikely and in need of correction.

Second, P[46] deletes ten words in v. 3 (εὐλογητὸς ὁ θεὸς καὶ πατὴρ τοῦ κυρίου ἡμῶν Ἰησοῦ Χριστοῦ) to read χάρις ὑμῖν καὶ εἰρήνη ἀπὸ θεοῦ πατρὸς ἡμῶν καὶ κυρίου Ἰησοῦ Χριστοῦ [...] ὁ εὐλογήσας ἡμᾶς. ... This yields an ungrammatical reading where the nominative participle ὁ εὐλογήσας must rather be expressed as a genitive to agree with either ἀπὸ θεοῦ πατρὸς or κυρίου Ἰησοῦ Χριστοῦ. The scribe's eye obviously skipped from εὐλογητός to εὐλογήσας, yet this simple copyist mistake was not corrected.

And, third, the original text of the second colon* of Eph 4:9 is εἰ μὴ **ὅτι** καὶ κατέβη ("but that he had also descended," ESV), yet P[46] inexplicably has a dative participle of εἰμί here to read εἰ μὴ **ὄντι** καὶ κατέβη ("except *for the one who exists* he also descended"). Again, this nonsensical reading should have been corrected but was not.

Although it must be stressed that P[46] is our earliest and among our most important witnesses to the text of Ephesians, it seems quite likely that ἐν Ἐφέσῳ was accidentally left out of this MS and that the mistake was not corrected, even though the resultant reading made poor sense. The omission of ἐν Ἐφέσῳ created just one of many eccentric readings in this early papyrus MS, which contains few corrections for Ephesians (e.g., at 2:12). The conclusion one can most plausibly draw, therefore, is that the omission of ἐν Ἐφέσῳ in P[46] or an early relative stands behind those few other MSS that do not include the epistle's destination in 1:1. We are on solid ground to accept the overwhelming testimony of our Greek MSS, the prescripts and postscript references to Ephesus, and of all early versions that ἐν Ἐφέσῳ is part of the original text of the epistle.

Translation

1 Paul, an apostle of Christ Jesus through the will of God, to the saints[9] who are in Ephesus, even[10] those who believe[11] in Christ Jesus, **2** grace to you and peace from God our Father and from Jesus Christ.

Commentary

1:1 Παῦλος ἀπόστολος Χριστοῦ Ἰησοῦ διὰ θελήματος θεοῦ, "Paul, an apostle of Christ Jesus through the will of God." It is normal for the author of a letter to identify himself by name to his addressee(s). Although Paul was known to have been born a Roman citizen (Acts 16:37–38; 22:25–29; 23:17) and therefore would have possessed a full name (in the Latin *tria nomina* style), such as C. Julius Paulus or Gn. Cornelius Paulus, it was fairly normal for people to use just one name among friends and acquaintances and even among others if he was well known.[12] For example, Pilate (Acts 3:13), Felix

---

9. Ἅγιοι, rendered "saints," has an OT ancestry (Heb. קדשים, e.g., Deut 7:6; 26:19; Exod 19:6; Pss 16:3; 34:9) to refer to covenant members who are committed to the Lord. Cf. Otto Procksch, *TDNT*, 1:88–110, esp. 105–10. It is used here to refer to members of the visible church to whom Paul is writing, and there is no idea of a select group within the church.

10. Καί is best taken here as expressing "a limiting or defining expression" (LSJ, 857; "even" or "namely") since the same group of people are addressed with two qualifying attributes; i.e., they are "saints" and "in Ephesus" (cf. BDAG, 494–96; esp. 495 for the "explicative" use).

11. Cf. Col 1:2. While the adj. πιστός in Greek at large usually refers to someone who is "reliable," "faithful," or "trustworthy" to some office, obligation, or standard of conduct (e.g., "God is faithful" in 1 Cor 1:9; 10:13; 2 Cor 1:18; cf. Eph 6:21; LSJ, 1408; BDAG, 820–21), here in Eph 1:1 the reference is clearly to people who believe in Christ, a meaning found most notably in Gal 3:9, "Abraham, the believer" (NASB; cf. similar in ESV, NIV, and NRSV; cf. 1 Tim 4:3, 10, 12; Titus 1:6) and contrasts with the adj. ἄπιστος, "unbelieving" person (e.g., 1 Cor 14:22; 2 Cor 6:15; cf. BDAG, 103–4).

12. For general treatment see A. N. Sherwin-White, *Roman Citizenship*, 2nd ed. (Oxford: Oxford University Press, 1973); cf. Colin J. Hemer, "The Name of Paul," *TynB* 36 (1985): 179–83. The *tria nomina* gives the praenomen, nomen, and cognomen (with a man's fuller filiation and *tribus* identity for census lists and other formal occasions; e.g., *IvE* 684A–B). It is possible (though unprovable) that Paul's family had received their citizenship under Pompey the Great (Gn. Pompeius Paulus) or under Julius Caesar or Augustus (C. Julius Paulus) for service to prominent Romans who had a number of conflicts in the eastern Mediterranean region.

(e.g., Acts 23:26), and Gallio (Acts 18:12, 14, 17) were all Roman citizens with *tria nomina* but are referenced in Acts only with their cognomen.[13]

While the identification of an author by name is normal in a letter, this letter opening is more formal than an ordinary letter between friends or acquaintances in that Paul includes a reference to his office, "an apostle of Christ Jesus through the will of God," rather than simply saying something like "Paul, to the saints in Ephesus, greetings" (e.g., Acts 23:26) as one might expect.[14] Yet this more formal tone is customary for Paul, who references his apostolate at the opening of his correspondence nine times (in Romans, 1–2 Corinthians, Galatians, Ephesians, Colossians, 1–2 Timothy, and Titus).[15]

The formality of Paul's opening is carried further when he adds that he is ἀπόστολος **Χριστοῦ Ἰησοῦ** ("an apostle *of Christ Jesus*"). Grammatically

---

We know of many Ephesians whose families may have had a similar experience of Roman citizenship; e.g., Cn. Pompeius Berantianus and C. Julius Cosinnius Tryphon, who both appear on a second-century AD list of Ephesian religious officials (*IvE* 1044). (The first two names are Roman and derive from the patrons whence Roman citizenship was derived; the cognomens are Greek.) Furthermore, there are a number of Ephesians attested with the cognomen of "Paul"; e.g., C. Geminius Paulus (*IvE* 1017), L. Flaminius Paulus (*IvE* 1047), and T. Flavius Savinianus Paulus (*IvE* 2260A), as well as a man simply called "Paulos" like our Paul (*IvE* 3224).

13. E.g., Pliny the Younger in his letters typically refers to people with only one or two of their names but never with their full *tria nomina*. E.g., Gavius Bassus (*Ep.* 10.21, 86a), who is also known from an Ephesian bilingual inscription with his full name "M. Gavius P. filius Palatina Bassus" (*IvE* 680); cf. (Tib.) Claudius Aristion (Pliny, *Ep.* 6:31; and *IvE* 424-5, 27, et al.).

14. The many papyrus letters from Egypt and the famous ones of Cicero or Pliny the Younger serve as contrasts for their openings; cf. Klaus Berger, "Apostelbrief und apostolische Rede / Zum Formulae frühchristlicher Briefe," *ZNW* 65 (1975): 190–231. Citing Pseudo-Libanius, Sean Adams notes that "So-and-so to So-and-so, greetings" is a recommended letter address; see Sean A. Adams, "Paul's Letter Opening and Greek Epistolography: A Matter of Relationship," in *Paul and the Ancient Letter Form*, ed. Stanley E. Porter and Sean A. Adams (Boston: Brill, 2010), 35 (see also 39–40).

15. Paul identifies himself in seven of these letters as an "apostle of Christ Jesus" (1–2 Corinthians, Ephesians, Colossians, 1–2 Timothy, Titus ["of Jesus Christ"]), and four of these also have "through the will of God," as in Eph 1:1 (1–2 Corinthians, Colossians, 2 Timothy). The other four Pauline letters have cosenders (Philippians, 1–2 Thessalonians, Philemon [which resembles Eph 3:1 as "prisoner of Christ Jesus"]) and do not mention Paul's apostolate in the address.

speaking, the genitive Χριστοῦ Ἰησοῦ is possessive, but the idea should be refined to say that Paul is an apostolic *representative* of Christ, much like an ambassador (cf. 6:20; Best, 90–91; O'Brien, 84), and that this epistle is an important correspondence.[16] As such, Paul proclaims his message on behalf of Christ and of God (esp. 2 Cor 5:20) as one sent for this purpose (cf. Rom 10:15; 1 Cor 1:17; 9:16–18; Eph 2:17; 3:8; 4:1). Rengstorf helpfully observes: "Paul stresses in his salutations his apostolic authorisation by Christ. What is at issue is not his own person but the cause for which he stands. Like the prophet, Paul as an apostle serves only his message"[17] (cf. "Excursus: Apostle").

Paul highlights his divine appointment to the apostolic office by saying that it was "by the will of God" (also Eph 4:11; 1 Cor 12:28; 1 Tim 2:7; 2 Tim 1:11), and elsewhere in Ephesians he expresses his personal unworthiness to this grace (3:8). Paul views his specific appointment as apostle to the Gentiles (Rom 11:13; Gal 2:2, 7) to be divine testimony to their inclusion into God's salvation in Christ (1 Tim 2:3–7).[18] Hence, he mentions God's will behind his appointment, for he knows that to make a false claim to the apostolate was to risk shameful exposure by a vigilant church such as that of the Ephesians (Rev 2:2; cf. Heb 5:4; 1 Cor 9:1–2; 2 Cor 11:4–6).

τοῖς ἁγίοις τοῖς οὖσιν ἐν Ἐφέσῳ καὶ πιστοῖς ἐν Χριστῷ Ἰησοῦ, "to the saints who are in Ephesus, even those who believe in Christ Jesus." The saints ("consecrated people") are the faithful members of God's covenant people, as the qualifier that they are *πιστοί ἐν* Χριστῷ Ἰησοῦ makes clear.[19] Calvin expresses this admirably: "No man, therefore, is a believer who is not also a saint; and on the other hand, no man is a saint who is not a believer" (Calvin, 123). In Ephesians itself Paul clearly uses the term *saint* for members of the

16. Cf. Adams, "Paul's Letter Opening," 51. See also Philip L. Tite, "How to Begin, and Why? Diverse Functions of the Pauline Prescript within a Greco-Roman Context," in *Paul and the Ancient Letter Form*, 57–99, where the prescript sets the "tone and perspective" (98) of the whole epistle.

17. Rengstorf, *TDNT*, 1:441.

18. Cf. Philip H. Towner, *The Letters of Timothy and Titus*, NICNT (Grand Rapids: Eerdmans, 2006), 186.

19. For discussion and review of literature see Procksch, *TDNT*, 1:88–115. While the use of the one article with two substantive adjs. (**τοῖς** *ἁγίοις ... καὶ πιστοῖς*) may indicate that both adjs. refer to one group of people (Best, 101; cf. discussion at 2:20), this meaning is more properly conveyed by the "explicative" use of *καί* ("even, that is") here, as defended in the translation section above.

church (vv. 15, 18; 2:19; 3:18; 4:12; 6:18), who are specially called to be holy (v. 4; 5:3). Acts 26:10 is particularly interesting in this connection because Luke represents Paul's usage of ἅγιοι ("saints") for Christians in his defense before Agrippa in contrast with "the Jews."

Without denying the need for personal sanctity (esp. v. 4; 5:3 again), there is an objective side to being among the ἅγιοι. Believers are members of Christ's body, the church, and belong to God's own household (vv. 22–23; 2:19; 3:6; 4:12, 16; 5:23, 30) and thereby participate already in the inaugurated glories and power of the new creation (vv. 13–14; 2:10; cf. Heb 6:5). The foundation of this objectivity is the consecration (ἁγιωσύνη, ἁγιασμός, ἁγιάζω) of Christ through his self-sacrifice, which purified his covenant people that they may be οἱ ἅγιοι (5:26–27; cf. 1 Cor 1:2; Heb 9:13–15; 10:10; 13:12).

In the Greek world it was quite common to refer to the people of a city in the addresses of formal documents: τῇ ἐπιφανεστάτῃ **Ἐφεσίων** πόλει, "for the most distinguished city of the Ephesians" (*IvE* 23.26); τοῖς ἁγίοις ... τοῖς οὖσιν ἐν **Φιλίπποις**, "to the saints ... who are *among the Philippians*" (Phil 1:1). Hence, we could expect in Eph 1:1 ἐν Ἐφεσίοις ("among the *Ephesians*") rather than the city name ἐν Ἐφέσῳ, "in Ephesus." This focus on citizens rather than location comes across even with the word rendered "Ephesus" (Ἔφεσος), which is feminine despite the masculine ending (e.g., **τὴν** Ἔφεσον, Acts 20:16) because it may originally have been an adjective; i.e., ἡ Ἔφεσος [πόλις], meaning "the Ephesian [city]" (the adjectival form Ἐφέσιος would have come to prominence later); cf. *IvE* 2, where Ἔφεσος occurs with names meaning "[So and So] the Ephesian." Yet the city name ἡ Ἔφεσος is used frequently by Paul and others in the NT (1 Cor 15:32; 16:8; 1 Tim 1:3; 2 Tim 1:18; 4:12; Rev 2:1; cf. Rev 2:18 and 3:1), and ἐν Ἐφέσῳ does appear in the Ephesian inscriptions; e.g., *IvE* 18a.3 (AD 44).

The phrase πιστοὶ ἐν Χριστῷ Ἰησοῦ can refer to people who are faithful or reliable in union with Christ, but I have already defended the common rendering "those who believe in Christ Jesus." One could expect the participle πιστευόντες for this meaning (e.g., 1:13, 19), but the adjective πιστός was preferred here simply because it is balanced in series with another adjective (τοῖς ἁγίοις ... καὶ πιστοῖς).

There are two options for understanding the function of the prepositional phrase in the reference to πιστοὶ ἐν Χριστῷ Ἰησοῦ. The first takes ἐν Χριστῷ Ἰησοῦ as describing believers' union "with Christ Jesus," a very rich and multiplex concept that has drawn considerable and sustained attention through the years.[20] This specifies that *πιστοί* are members of Christ's body and participants in all the benefits of his substitutionary work.[21]

The second option for *πιστοὶ ἐν Χριστῷ Ἰησοῦ* is to take the prepositional phrase as expressing the object of the believers' faith, the person in whom they entrust themselves: "and to those who believe in Christ Jesus." This view was recently defended by Constantine Campbell, who points to this meaning in equivalent noun phrases such as *διὰ τῆς πίστεως ἐν Χριστῷ Ἰησοῦ* (Gal 3:26; "through faith *in Christ Jesus*"; cf. Col 1:4; 1 Tim 3:13; 2 Tim 3:15).[22]

It is tempting to take the first view (union with Christ) here and see *ἐν Χριστῷ Ἰησοῦ* as qualifying both substantive adjs. *ἅγιοι* and *πιστοί*: "to the saints ... even those who believe [who are] in Christ Jesus." But this is unlikely, since *ἅγιοι* is distant and already qualified by *ἐν Ἐφέσῳ* with the participle *οὖσιν*.[23] Hence, we should prefer the second view that "in Christ Jesus" specifies the person in whom the *πιστοί* have placed their faith. Either view is biblical and Pauline.[24]

1:2 *χάρις ὑμῖν καὶ εἰρήνη*, "grace to you and peace." Ancient Greek letters normally opened with *χαίρειν*, "greetings" (e.g., Acts 15:23; 23:26; Jas 1:1), but Paul and other NT authors typically open theirs with a benediction that has

---

20. E.g., cf. the older work of Albert Schweitzer, *The Mysticism of Paul the Apostle*, trans. William Montgomery (London: A. & C. Black, 1931; repr., Baltimore: Johns Hopkins University Press, 1998), to the recent thorough treatment by Constantine R. Campbell, *Paul and Union with Christ: An Exegetical and Theological Study* (Grand Rapids: Zondervan, 2012); cf. Hoehner, 170–74 (who lists all the various expressions in Ephesians for this and related concepts).

21. "In Christ," "in him," and "in whom" are central aspects of the benediction of vv. 3–14 and are discussed below; and see 4:17, where Paul testifies "in the Lord" (cf. 6:1). The "union" view is accepted by Best, 101, 153–54; Hoehner, 142–43; O'Brien, 87; and Lincoln, 6; cf. Barth, 1:68–69.

22. Campbell, *Union*, 111–14; cf. Arnold, 69.

23. The other understanding would be likely if Paul had written *τοῖς ἁγίοις καὶ πιστοῖς ἐν Χριστῷ Ἰησοῦ*.

24. The prep. *ἐν* is less common with this meaning than *εἰς* or *ἐπί*. For instance, in Rom 4:24 *ἐπί* specifies the obj. of faith with the ptc. of *πιστεύω* (also Rom 9:33; 10:11, quoting the LXX of Isa 28:16). The whole phrase in Eph 1:1c with its *ἐν*, however, consists of four spondees (– –), and *ἐπί* here would add an extra syllable and spoil the sonorous rhythm of the spondees.

the similar-sounding χάρις, as here (cf. Rom 1:7; 1 Cor 1:3; 2 Cor 1:2; Gal 1:3; Eph 6:24; Phil 1:2; Col 1:2; 1 Thess 1:1; 2 Thess 1:2; 1 Tim 1:2; 2 Tim 1:2; Titus 1:4; Phlm 3; Rev 1:4–5). Both *grace* and *peace* are frequent terms in Ephesians and other Pauline works; see especially comments on Eph 2:8 and 2:14–17. The inspiration for pronouncing such a benediction on the audience is undoubtedly the great Aaronic benediction in Num 6:22–27.[25] As such, it is not the expression of a wish or of a prayer but the priestly conveyance of blessing based on the Lord's promise: "So shall they put my name upon the people of Israel, and I will bless them" (Num 6:27).

ἀπὸ θεοῦ πατρὸς ἡμῶν καὶ κυρίου Ἰησοῦ Χριστοῦ, "from God our Father and from the Lord Jesus Christ." We might expect the source of all blessings to be identified by a first-century Jew steeped in the OT to be "the Lord God" or "the Lord our God." Instead the fatherhood of God is referenced and the full title of the Messiah as "the Lord Jesus Christ" is used.[26]

Application and Devotional Implications

In a phrase we have grown used to, Paul pronounces a blessing on his audience "from God our Father." That God the Father is *our* Father should be seen as the most extraordinary privilege imaginable. Both the OT and NT testify that God acts as a Father to his people in the most persistently loving fashion: "For as high as the heavens are above the earth, so great is his steadfast love toward those who fear him; ... As a father shows compassion to his children, so the LORD shows compassion to those who fear him" (Psa 103:11–13). The Sovereign God of the universe intimately and tenderly identifies with us, his adopted children, who were once "children of wrath" (2:3). This is all brought about through the mediation of the second person named in the benediction: "grace to you and peace from God our Father *and from Jesus Christ.*"

25. Best (102) also points to "equivalent greetings" in *2 Bar.* 78:2 ("Grace and peace be with you" in a letter opening) and *Jub.* 12:29; 22:8–9 (yet these latter two are blessings of a father on a son, like Gen 27:28–29, not letter openings to a group). One can also point out that this apostolic benediction was picked up in the early fathers; e.g., Clement (*1 Clem.* prologue) and Polycarp (Polycarp, *Phil.* prologue).

26. See comments on v. 3 and the excursus "Articular Χριστός as Messianic Title" below.

Selected Bibliography

Agnew, F. "On the Origin of the Term *Apostolos.*" *CBQ* 38 (1976): 49–53.
———. "The Origin of the NT Apostle-Concept: A Review of Research." *JBL* 105 (1986): 75–96.
Berger, K. "Apostelbrief und apostolische Rede / Zum Formulae frühchristlicher Briefe." *ZNW* 65 (1975): 190–231.
Best, E. "Ephesians i.1." In *Text and Interpretation*, ed. E. Best and R. McL. Wilson, 29–41. Cambridge: Cambridge University Press, 1979.
———. "Ephesians i.1 Again." In *Paul and Paulinism*, ed. M. D. Hooker and S. G. Wilson, 273–79. London: SPCK, 1982.
———. "Paul's Apostolic Authority—?" *JSNT* 27 (1986): 3–25.
Black, D. "The Peculiarities of Ephesians and the Ephesian Address." *GTJ* 2 (1981): 59–73.
Campbell, C. *Paul and Union with Christ: An Exegetical and Theological Study.* Grand Rapids: Zondervan, 2012.
Dunn, J. *The Theology of Paul the Apostle.* Grand Rapids: Eerdmans, 1998.
Hemer, C. "The Name of Paul." *TynB* 36 (1985): 179–83.
Porter, S., and S. Adams. *Paul and the Ancient Letter Form.* Boston: Brill, 2010.
Purvo, R. I. *The Making of Paul: Constructions of the Apostle in Early Christianity.* Minneapolis: Fortress, 2010.
Richards, E. *The Secretary in the Letters of Paul.* WUNT 2.42. Tübingen: Mohr Siebeck, 1991.
Schreiner, T. *Paul, Apostle of God's Glory in Christ: A Pauline Theology.* Downers Grove, IL: InterVarsity Press, 2001.
Schweitzer, A. *The Mysticism of Paul the Apostle.* Translated by W. Montgomery. London: A&C Black, 1931. Repr., Baltimore: Johns Hopkins University Press, 1998.
Sherwin-White, A. *Roman Citizenship.* 2nd ed. Oxford: Oxford University Press, 1973.
van Roon, A. *The Authenticity of Ephesians.* NovTSup 39. Leiden: Brill, 1974.

Opening Benediction (1:3–14)

Introduction

In Ephesians 1:3–14 Paul blesses the Father for his eternally planned and graciously executed redemption on behalf of all his elect in his Son, sealed to them through the Holy Spirit. The context here is that Paul is opening his epistle with genuine praise and wonder at God's lavish grace. The subtext is that this praise teaches us these things and how we should overflow with praise as well.[1]

As explained in the commentary's introduction, we analyze the text of Ephesians as containing flowing periodic sentences with some literary features, granting the less demanding features of epistolary prose on Greek authors. We are doing this because that is how *everyone* learned to compose Greek from grammar school onward. Pauline texts overtly exhibit this periodic style to varying degrees, in contrast to the simpler, more Semitic style of works like Mark or the Johannine Epistles. One key to this compositional style is that Ephesians and the other epistles were written to be *heard* by the church rather than to be read silently and piecemeal by individuals.

As a result, the periods, which are indicated in the organization below with indents and spacing, are suggested divisions where the presenter of the text would pause (at the end of a colon*) or take a breath (at the end of a period). As Quintilian notes, in the first stages in learning, instruction was given on "when the boy (*puer*) should take breath, at what point he should introduce a pause into a line, [and] where the sense ends or begins" (*Inst.* 1.8.1). Even if Paul did not have advanced rhetorical training, he shows facility with reading and composition that characterized instruction

1. "Eph 1:3–14 is a digest of the whole epistle and replete with key terms and topics that anticipate the contents of what follows" (Barth, 1:97); also J. Cambier, "La Bénédiction D'Eph 1 3–14," *ZNW* 54 (1963): 58–104, esp. 58.

among the Greeks at the least in the elementary and intermediate levels of school (Quintilian, *Inst.* 2.5.3). His native genius was not hampered from lack of advanced study under a famous rhetor or sophist; Sophocles, Herodotus, Socrates, Xenophon, and innumerable other famous Greek authors did not have this advanced study in rhetoric and composition either.[2]

For this reason, each section of the commentary from this point will open with a suggested periodic division in which the English-style punctuation and markings found in our modern editions are removed and verse numbers are minimized.[3] This organization will form the basis of my interpretation of different points, not the verse division or English-like punctuation in our editions, in order to take us back more closely to how an ancient text actually worked. The NA[28] text is given later for the purpose of the presentation of text-critical issues.

A ³Εὐλογητὸς ὁ θεὸς καὶ πατὴρ τοῦ κυρίου ἡμῶν
Ἰησοῦ Χριστοῦ
ὁ εὐλογήσας ἡμᾶς
ἐν πάσῃ εὐλογίᾳ πνευματικῇ
ἐν τοῖς ἐπουρανίοις ἐν Χριστῷ

B ⁴καθὼς ἐξελέξατο ἡμᾶς ἐν αὐτῷ
πρὸ καταβολῆς κόσμου
εἶναι ἡμᾶς ἁγίους καὶ ἀμώμους
κατενώπιον αὐτοῦ

2. All levels of ancient education had a focus on speaking well in public. Cf. Ryan S. Schellenberg, "Rhetorical Terminology in Paul: A Critical Reappraisal," *ZNW* 104 (2013): 153–76, who analyzes a few terms in the "authentic" Pauline Epistles, and, finding that they are not rhetorical technical terms, concludes that Paul did not have training in rhetoric. This is a curious method for such a conclusion at best.

3. See *MHT*, 2:48, for a reminder that modern punctuation of the ancient Greek text is simply a form of commentary. Furthermore, modern punctuation is so inconsistent that it can actually get in the way of seeing the original contours of the text; cf. remarks to this effect in G. L. Hendrickson, "Accentual Clausulae in Greek Prose of the First and Second Centuries of our Era," *AJP* 29 (1908): 280–302 (esp. 284n1), remarking on editions of *1 Clement* for "superfluous" punctuation and places where it was missing where desirable to mark cola* and clauses.

C ἐν ἀγάπῃ
5προορίσας ἡμᾶς εἰς υἱοθεσίαν
διὰ Ἰησοῦ Χριστοῦ εἰς αὐτόν
κατὰ τὴν εὐδοκίαν τοῦ θελήματος αὐτοῦ
6εἰς ἔπαινον δόξης τῆς χάριτος αὐτοῦ

D ἧς ἐχαρίτωσεν ἡμᾶς ἐν τῷ ἠγαπημένῳ
7ἐν ᾧ ἔχομεν τὴν ἀπολύτρωσιν διὰ τοῦ αἵματος αὐτοῦ
τὴν ἄφεσιν τῶν παραπτωμάτων
κατὰ τὸ πλοῦτος τῆς χάριτος αὐτοῦ

E 8ἧς ἐπερίσσευσεν εἰς ἡμᾶς
ἐν πάσῃ σοφίᾳ καὶ φρονήσει
9γνωρίσας ἡμῖν τὸ μυστήριον τοῦ θελήματος αὐτοῦ
κατὰ τὴν εὐδοκίαν αὐτοῦ

F ἣν προέθετο ἐν αὐτῷ
10εἰς οἰκονομίαν τοῦ πληρώματος τῶν καιρῶν
ἀνακεφαλαιώσασθαι τὰ πάντα ἐν τῷ Χριστῷ
τὰ ἐπὶ τοῖς οὐρανοῖς καὶ τὰ ἐπὶ τῆς γῆς ἐν αὐτῷ

G 11ἐν ᾧ καὶ ἐκληρώθημεν προορισθέντες
κατὰ πρόθεσιν τοῦ τὰ πάντα ἐνεργοῦντος
κατὰ τὴν βουλὴν τοῦ θελήματος αὐτοῦ
12εἰς τὸ εἶναι ἡμᾶς εἰς ἔπαινον δόξης αὐτοῦ
τοὺς προηλπικότας ἐν τῷ Χριστῷ

H 13ἐν ᾧ καὶ ὑμεῖς ἀκούσαντες τὸν λόγον τῆς ἀληθείας
τὸ εὐαγγέλιον τῆς σωτηρίας ὑμῶν
ἐν ᾧ καὶ πιστεύσαντες
ἐσφραγίσθητε τῷ πνεύματι τῆς ἐπαγγελίας τῷ ἁγίῳ

I 14ὅ ἐστιν ἀρραβὼν τῆς κληρονομίας ἡμῶν
εἰς ἀπολύτρωσιν τῆς περιποιήσεως
εἰς ἔπαινον τῆς δόξης αὐτοῦ.

To describe Ephesians 1:3–14 as a long Greek "sentence," as is often done, is misleading to a modern English reader.[4] It makes it seem that Paul is writing an undifferentiated stream of text that gives a silent reader no break in thought. Our analysis—based on that of ancient Greek and Roman authors who discuss these things—shows that the *hearer* does get breaks after each period, where a pause is taken when the presenter would take a breath. Even when an individual read a text privately, he would quite often read it audibly this way. In consequence, it is better to call each of the nine periods of Eph 1:3–14 the equivalent of English "sentences" and the whole "periodic sentence" as the rough equivalent of our paragraph.

Even though we can take each period as the equivalent of one of our sentences, the translation cannot really present each one as a sentence, since too much transformation of the original form must be performed on the text. I hope, then, that you the reader will treat the translation of this and the following sections in Ephesians more as a transcript of an oral presentation and read each period out loud, with a breath taken at the end of each period (and better yet, read the Greek out loud as well if you can). Only then will this text live again and be understood better for what it is: a powerful oral presentation of a master teacher and preacher.

One important consequence of what we have just noted is that the beginning and end of each period are places of particular focus on the hearers. For this reason, Demetrius, an (unknown) ancient author, in a work titled "On Style" remarks that long syllables at the beginning and end of periods lend grandeur to one's style and stir the audience to attend to them and remember those points in particular (Demetrius, "On Style," 39). As a result, notice how throughout this composition in Eph 1:3–14 the attention is relentlessly focused on what God has done in Christ at the beginning of the periods: "insofar as he chose us. ... In love he predestined us ... which he bestowed on us ... which he lavished upon us," etc., and at the end of the periods: "in Christ ... before him ... glory of his grace ... with the promised

---

4. E.g., Lincoln, 9, note a; O'Brien, 90; Best, 107–8. See esp. Hoehner, 153 ("a long sentence of 202 words"), who continues: "It is not unusual to have lengthy sentences for praise and prayer: Even in our present day it is not uncommon to have long sentences in prayers and doxologies." While this shows unawareness of common Greek periodic style, it does highlight that moderns may do a similar thing in (oral) praise and prayers, whereas it is usually avoided in our written style. Ancient Greek written style should be regarded as an oral style.

Holy Spirit ... to the praise of his glory." The ending words in particular (e.g., Χριστῷ twice and αὐτοῦ five times) normally end with two long syllables (a spondee). This makes these phrases in particular stand out to the listeners and was part of Paul's intentional compositional strategy.

As one confirmation of the point just made, look at the last two cola* in v. 10: ἀνακεφαλαιώσασθαι τὰ πάντα **ἐν τῷ Χριστῷ** / τὰ ἐπὶ τοῖς οὐρανοῖς καὶ τὰ ἐπὶ τῆς γῆς **ἐν αὐτῷ**, "to summarize all things *in Christ* / the things in heaven and things on earth *in him*." The phrase "in him" is not needed since it duplicates "in Christ" here, but it was included in order to have Christ appear at the end and focus of the period (rather than the less fitting "on the earth").[5] This opening blessing of Ephesians in particular was very carefully composed.

As several times with Paul's periodic sentences, Eph 1:3–14 opens and closes with the same element—and in this case, there are two opening and closing elements. The first unifying feature is brought out in our translation of εὐλογία πνευματικῇ as "blessing of the Spirit," instead of the more common "spiritual blessing" (ESV, NASB, NIV, NRSV, etc.), which connects the opening period with the end of the period of 1:13 and its focus on "the promised Holy Spirit."

The second unifying element is seen in the very last phrase of the periodic sentence, "for the praise of his glory," found earlier in v. 12 and a little more fully in v. 6 ("for the praise of the glory of his grace"). While the unifying theme here may seem subtle at first glance, it is actually rather obvious: This passage repeats throughout that God's stupendous work in Christ redounds to the praise of his glory, which is exactly what Paul is doing, praising his glory: "Blessed be the God and Father of our Lord Jesus Christ ..."

What we are terming the "benediction" form of Eph 1:3–14 comes from the opening word of our passage, εὐλογητός ("blessed [be]"), which was a common form of prayer in Judaism, reaching back as far as Gen 9:26, "Blessed be the LORD, the God of Shem," and the notable

5. While this can be considered a Semitic ("pleonastic") use of the personal pronoun, common in the LXX, its function here is rather a feature of Paul's compositional style to end the period with reference to Christ.

blessing of Abraham by Melchizedek in Gen 14:19–20 (cf. Heb 7:1–10).[6] Ephesians 1:3–14 is rather longer than most OT and other Jewish benedictions (though not Tob 13). That and various other features have made it subject to repeated scrutiny as an adapted early Christian hymn or other form of composition such as a homily or baptismal liturgy.[7]

The opening words of Eph 1:3 are found verbatim in 1 Pet 1:3 ("Blessed be the God and Father of our Lord Jesus Christ") and in 2 Cor 1:3. John Coutts proposes that the benedictions of Ephesians and 1 Peter originated in a common baptismal prayer that survives not in content but in form. Yet his analysis concentrates on linguistic ties between the two passages—i.e., content—and relies on words found in both places that are often etymologically related but different (e.g., ἐπουράνιος ["high-heavenly"] in Eph 1:3 and οὐρανός ["heaven"] in 1 Pet 1:4), and common Christian words like *God* and *salvation*. The two texts are actually quite different in rhythm and other marks of style.[8] While one can easily imagine both texts (and other por-

---

6. This is sometimes called a *eulogy*, transliterated from the Greek term εὐλογητός, or a *berakah*, from the Hebrew term for a blessing (בְּרָכָה), originating from the verb's Qal pass. ptc. בָּרוּךְ (*barukh*, "blessed") used in this form of prayer. The LXX renders *barukh* with either the adj. εὐλογητός (e.g., Gen 14:20) or pass. ptc. εὐλογημένος (e.g., Gen 14:19). Philo distinguishes between the Greek adj. and the ptc., saying that the latter simply refers to "the opinions and report of the many," but the former refers to blessing in reality (*Migr.* 107). Jews typically recited *berakot* at various times throughout the day; the Talmudic tractate *Berakot* is devoted to discussion of times, occasions, and exceptions to this duty. Thomas Talley ("The Literary Structure of the Eucharistic Prayer," *Worship* 58 [1984]: 404–20, esp. 406) notes that Joseph Heinemann has shown that "the *berakah* which would become so central a prayer form in the Amoraic period had been, in its biblical background, not a prayer addressed to God at all, but a praise of God stated in the third person" (406), as in Eph 1:3–14 and NT parallels.

7. The latter two are the opinion of John Coutts, "Ephesians 1:3–14 and 1 Peter 1:3–12," *NTS* 3 (1957): 115–27. J. H. Barkhuizen ("The Strophic Structure of the Eulogy of Ephesians 1:3–14," *Hervormde teologiese studies* 46 [1990]: 390–413) thinks 1:3–14 is "most probably related to a baptismal ritual" (391) but describes it as originating as a hymn.

8. First Peter 1:3–12 can be divided into six periods of four cola* each (1 Pet 1:6–7 forms one period with five cola*); for the first two see Charles J. Robbins, "Rhetorical Structure of Philippians 2:6–11," *CBQ* 42 (1980): 79. Peter's periods are generally longer than Paul's in either Eph 1:3–14 or 2 Cor 1:3–7 and contain more cases of piling up nouns ("for praise and glory and honor"; v. 7) or modifiers ("imperishable and spotless and unfading, kept"; v. 4) and show less interest in repeated words as structural focus words than does Paul.

tions of both epistles) as part of a baptism rite, they merely present basic Christian teaching that is appropriate in many contexts. Unless we were to find concrete evidence of such an early, original liturgical form, it remains an imaginary source at best.

A hymnic background to Eph 1:3–14 has also been proposed.[9] What is most interesting about this idea is how it connects to Eph 5:19, where we are told to address "one another with psalms and hymns and songs of the Spirit"; perhaps Paul is doing just that in 1:3–14. Problems come in the details, however. To make a prose hymn out of Eph 1:3–14, we have to remove important strands of the text (e.g., vv. 12b and 13) and combine large chunks of text into three or four long and unwieldy strophes* that undercut the periodic structure that the unaltered text naturally exhibits.[10]

Edgar Krentz has recently provided a well-researched investigation into ancient Greek hymnody in prose, and Paul possibly may have known about such prose hymns.[11] The Greeks, however, still preferred metrical forms for hymns and other types of poetry (see the remarks on 5:14 and "Excursus: Hymns"). Granting that Paul's benediction in Eph 1:3–14 is a form of "praise" (ἔπαινος), as I believe (see vv. 6, 12, 14), here is an example of "praise" in more traditional Greek form (elegiac couplets) inscribed on an Ephesian building roughly thirty years after Ephesians was written:

> Κλαυδία Τροφίμη ἱερῆ ἡ πρύτανις Ἑστίῃ ἔπαινον ἔγραψε·
> Αὕτα καὶ μακάρεσσιν ἐπήρκεσ' ἐν εὐφροσύναισιν,
> αὕτη καὶ θαλερὸν φῶς κατέχει πατρίδος·

9. Cf. Jack T. Sanders, "Hymnic Elements in Ephesians 1–3," *ZNW* 56 (1965): 214–32 (but only hymnic fragments); H. Krämer, "Zur sprachliche Form der Eulogie Eph. 1, 3–14," *Wort und Dienst* 9 (1967): 34–46; Barth, 1:97–101; Barkhuizen, "Srophic Structure."

10. For discussion and bibliography on the various strophic arrangements see esp. Barkhuizen, "Srophic Structure"; and Hoehner, 153–61, who reports on more than forty scholarly treatments. For a periodic analysis see Charles J. Robbins, "The Composition of Eph. 1:3–14," *JBL* 105 (1986): 677–87; and the discussion in the introduction above. For compelling critique of the failed search for an original hymn behind Eph 1:3–14 see Chrys Caragounis, *The Ephesian* Mysterion: *Meaning and Context*, ConBNT 8 (Lund: GWK Gleerup, 1977), 41–45; also Lincoln, 10–19, and O'Brien, 89–91.

11. E. M. Krentz, "Epideiktik and Hymnody: The New Testament and Its World," *BR* 40 (1995): 50–97; cf. Matthew E. Gordley, *Teaching through Song in Antiquity*, WUNT 2.302 (Tübingen: Mohr Siebeck, 2011).

ἁδυτάτα δαῖμον, κόσμου θάλος, ἀέναον φῶς
ἃδκατέχεις βωμοῖς δαλὸν ἀπ' οὐρανόθεν.

Claudia Trophime, the priestess (and) Prytanis, composed this praise (ἔπαινος) to Hestia:
She (Hestia) both helps the Blessed Ones in their festivities,
And she maintains the blooming fire of our fatherland;
Sweetest Divine, blossom of the cosmos, everlasting fire,
You who maintain the thunderbolt from heaven on your altars.[12]

In form, the meter (a dactylic hexameter line followed by a pentameter), the poetic language (i.e., *μακάρεσσιν* with the extra *sigma*; ἁδυτάτα, superlative of ἡδύς; ἀέναος [= "ever-flowing" light]; etc.), the lack of articles, and the elision (ἐπήρκεσ' ἐν) are all things missing in the benediction of Eph 1:3–14 or other NT poetic-type passages (e.g., John 1:1–18; Rom 8:31–39; 1 Cor 13:1–13; Col 1:15–20). In other words, if a Greek person wrote a hymn of praise that is behind Paul's text, we would expect to see some residual marks of Greek poetry like Claudia's in metrical form and language at the least.[13]

---

12. *IvE* 1062.1–5, my translation (another poem from Claudia follows in *IvE* 1062.6–10). Cf. a slightly different translation in Mary R. Lefkowitz and Maureen B. Fant, *Women's Life in Greece and Rome: A Source Book in Translation*, 3rd ed. (Baltimore: Johns Hopkins University Press, 2005), 302. Claudia Trophime was *prytanis* around AD 93 (cf. *IvE* 508 and 1012); Hestia was the goddess of the hearth at home, and the *prytaneis* tended the hearth for the city. Young girls were typically charged with making sure the hearth fire did not go out in the Greek *oikos* ("household," "estate"), and Claudia was undoubtedly unmarried during her time as *prytanis* (i.e., not yet past puberty; cf. comments on 5:22–24 below).

13. Again, Krentz has shown that prose hymns were known to the Greeks, but it does not mean that they were common when poetry appears to be the norm for Greek song known from everyday life in a city like Ephesus that had active groups of *rhapsodes* (composers and performers of heroic poems), poets, lyric musicians (μελοποιοί), *theologoi* (rhetors connected with temples and their festivals, not to be confused with the ἱεροκῆρυξ ["sacred-herald"]), *hymnodoi* (often singing tributes to emperors; cf. *IvE* 973 for a *hymnologos* and *IvE* 1149 for a *hymnographos*), and other kinds of public poetic performers (*IvE* 22, 27, 645, 892, 1002, 1004, 1023, etc.). These singers were engaged in creating as well as preserving and performing ancient poems and hymns; e.g., Philostratus (*Vit. Apoll.* 3.17) mentions that a paean of Sophocles was still sung at Athens to Asclepius nearly six hundred years after

A more fruitful line of inquiry would be to compare the benediction of Eph 1:3–14 with other such *berakot*. Most of our other examples are rather brief; e.g., "Blessed be the Lord for he has attended to the voice of my petition" (Psa 27:6 LXX) or "Blessed be the Lord God, the God of Israel who alone performs wonders, and blessed be his glorious name forever and forever and ever, and his glory will fill all the earth, may it be so (γένοιτο), may it be so" (Psa 71:18–19 LXX). But besides 2 Cor 1:3–7 or 1 Pet 1:3–12, we do have two interesting longer ones that are instructive for comparison with our passage: Tob 13:1–18 and Luke 1:67–79.[14] Tobit explicitly calls his composition "a prayer of jubilation" (προσευχὴν εἰς ἀγαλλίασιν) rather than a hymn (Tob 13:1), and in Luke 1:67 Zachariah is said to prophesy, not to sing.

The conclusion, then, is that efforts to divine liturgical forms or hymns behind Eph 1:3–14 have not succeeded.[15] If the passage looks like a hymn, it is because hymns can be prayers of praise, and our passage is a prose composition of prayer "to the praise of the glory of his grace" (v. 6). The text divides itself naturally into a succession of normal Greek periods, not strophes* or stanzas*, despite some repeated words or phrases (found also in other benedictions like Tob 13 or Luke 1:67–78). On the other hand, the search for baptismal liturgy in the background has produced some interesting ideas that are worth further reflection.

---

his death. We possess ancient metrical works with musical notation; see Giovanni Comotti, *Music in Greek and Roman Culture* (Baltimore: Johns Hopkins University Press, 1989), 99–120; M. L. West, *Ancient Greek Music* (Oxford: Clarendon, 1992); cf. Johannes Quasten, *Music & Worship in Pagan & Christian Antiquity*, trans. Boniface Ramsey (Washington, D.C.: National Association of Pastoral Musicians, 1983). The best we can say about the meter of Eph 1:3–14 is that one can find the paean (˘ ˘ ˘ ¯ ˘ or ¯ ˘ ˘ ˘) and spondee (¯ ¯) meters fairly often, but the paean meter (not to be confused with the song of that name) was considered by ancient Greeks to be the meter of ordinary speech, not of poetry.

14. Cf. Gordley, *Teaching through Song*, 215–17.

15. So also Michael Peppard, " 'Poetry,' 'Hymns' and 'Traditional Material' in New Testament Epistles or How to Do Things with Indentations," *JSNT* 30 (2008): 319–42.

Outline

II. Opening Benediction (1:3–14)
- A. For the Father's eternal, gracious purpose (1:3–6a)
- B. For the Son's climactic, redemptive accomplishment (1:6b–10)
- C. For the Spirit's down payment of the new creation (1:11–14)

Original Text

3 Εὐλογητὸς ὁ θεὸς καὶ πατὴρ τοῦ κυρίου ἡμῶν Ἰησοῦ Χριστοῦ,[a] ὁ εὐλογήσας
ἡμᾶς ἐν πάσῃ εὐλογίᾳ πνευματικῇ ἐν τοῖς ἐπουρανίοις ἐν Χριστῷ, **4** καθὼς
ἐξελέξατο ἡμᾶς ἐν αὐτῷ πρὸ καταβολῆς κόσμου εἶναι ἡμᾶς ἁγίους καὶ ἀμώμους
κατενώπιον αὐτοῦ ἐν ἀγάπῃ, **5** προορίσας ἡμᾶς εἰς υἱοθεσίαν διὰ Ἰησοῦ Χριστοῦ
εἰς αὐτόν, κατὰ τὴν εὐδοκίαν τοῦ θελήματος αὐτοῦ, **6** εἰς ἔπαινον δόξης τῆς
χάριτος αὐτοῦ ἧς[b] ἐχαρίτωσεν ἡμᾶς ἐν τῷ ἠγαπημένῳ. **7** Ἐν ᾧ ἔχομεν[c] τὴν
ἀπολύτρωσιν διὰ τοῦ αἵματος αὐτοῦ, τὴν ἄφεσιν τῶν παραπτωμάτων, κατὰ τὸ
πλοῦτος τῆς χάριτος αὐτοῦ **8** ἧς ἐπερίσσευσεν εἰς ἡμᾶς, ἐν πάσῃ σοφίᾳ καὶ φρονήσει, **9** γνωρίσας ἡμῖν τὸ μυστήριον τοῦ θελήματος αὐτοῦ, κατὰ τὴν εὐδοκίαν
αὐτοῦ ἣν προέθετο ἐν αὐτῷ **10** εἰς οἰκονομίαν τοῦ πληρώματος τῶν καιρῶν, ἀνακεφαλαιώσασθαι τὰ πάντα ἐν τῷ Χριστῷ, τὰ ἐπὶ τοῖς οὐρανοῖς[d] καὶ τὰ ἐπὶ τῆς
γῆς ἐν αὐτῷ. **11** Ἐν ᾧ καὶ ἐκληρώθημεν[e] προορισθέντες κατὰ πρόθεσιν τοῦ τὰ
πάντα ἐνεργοῦντος κατὰ τὴν βουλὴν τοῦ θελήματος αὐτοῦ **12** εἰς τὸ εἶναι ἡμᾶς
εἰς ἔπαινον δόξης αὐτοῦ τοὺς προηλπικότας ἐν τῷ Χριστῷ. **13** Ἐν ᾧ καὶ ὑμεῖς
ἀκούσαντες τὸν λόγον τῆς ἀληθείας, τὸ εὐαγγέλιον τῆς σωτηρίας ὑμῶν, ἐν ᾧ καὶ
πιστεύσαντες ἐσφραγίσθητε τῷ πνεύματι τῆς ἐπαγγελίας τῷ ἁγίῳ, **14** ὅ[f] ἐστιν
ἀρραβὼν τῆς κληρονομίας ἡμῶν, εἰς ἀπολύτρωσιν τῆς περιποιήσεως, εἰς ἔπαινον
τῆς δόξης αὐτοῦ.

Textual Notes

3.a. P^{46} omits ten words: Εὐλογητὸς ὁ θεὸς καὶ πατὴρ τοῦ κυρίου ἡμῶν Ἰησοῦ Χριστοῦ. By having the nominative ὁ εὐλογήσας immediately after Χριστοῦ at the end of v. 2, the participle εὐλογήσας now modifies Christ rather than the Father, as in v. 3a, and creates a grammatical solecism. This is one of the many places in this early MS where lack of careful proofreading is evident. In some cases these eccentric readings early on may have influenced later copies (e.g., the missing "in Ephesus" in 1:1).

6.b. Some later MSS have ἐν ᾗ for ἧς, including D, G, Ψ, and M, which smooth up the meaning with the pronoun attracted to the case of its antecedent (χάριτος). ἐν τῷ ἠγαπημένῳ **υἱῷαὐτοῦ** in some later MSS (D*, F, G, 629, et al.) conforms the statement to the divine testimony at Jesus' baptism (Matt 3:17 and par.; cf. 2 Pet 1:17).

7.c. ℵ*, D*, Ψ, 104, 1505, and a few other MSS have aorist ἔσχομεν ("in whom we have acquired our redemption") for present ἔχομεν ("we have"). Either reading makes good sense in context, but the present-tense form has better MS witnesses through wider geographical distribution and is found in the earliest witnesses, outside ℵ. The MSS A, 365, and a few others have χρηστοτητος ("of his *kindness*") for χάριτος ("of his grace"), which was clearly influenced by this phrase in Rom 2:4 (cf. Eph 2:7).

10.d. Quite a few good MSS including A, 33, 1739, and 1881 smooth up ἐπὶ τοῖς οὐρανοῖς, which might be read as "*upon* the heavens," with ἐν, "in." Reading ἐπί here has the colon* open with a nice paean meter: τὰ ἐπὶ τοῖς (˘ ˘ ˘ ¯), which the stylists recommended in prose and marks the other many short syllables in vv. 9c–10.

11.e. The verb ἐκληρώθημεν, rendered "we have been appointed," is a difficult one in context, so it is not surprising that a few MSS (A, D, F, and G) read ἐκλήθημεν, "we were called," in an attempt—whether deliberate or not—to make an easier reading. The principle of *lectio difficilior** applies here with the preferred UBS/NA reading.

14.f. ℵ, D, Ψ, 33, and M have masculine ὅς in place of neuter ὅ (which agrees with its neuter antecedent πνεῦμα). Bruce Metzger notes that the masculine may be influenced by the (masc.) gender of the predicate noun ἀρραβών, "guarantee," but it may also be the case that either Paul or the scribes used the masculine because of the natural (versus grammatical) gender of the Holy Spirit (which also happens in Greek generally).[16]

16. Bruce M. Metzger, *A Textual Commentary on the Greek New Testament*, 2nd ed. (New York: United Bible Societies, 1994), 533.

Translation

3 Blessed be the God and Father of our Lord Jesus Christ, who has blessed us with every blessing of the Spirit[17] in the high-heavenlies[18] in Christ, 4 insofar as[19] he chose us in him before the foundation of the world that we should be holy and blameless before him. In love 5 he predestined us for adoption to himself[20] through Jesus Christ according to the good pleasure of his will 6 for praise of the glory of his grace,[21] which[22] he bestowed[23] on us in his[24] Beloved, 7 in whom we have our redemption through his blood,

---

17. The adj. πνευματικός in the phrase ἐν πάσῃ εὐλογίᾳς πνευματικῇ has been rendered here "(with every blessing) of the Spirit" because in modern American English the adj. *spiritual* would not convey Paul's meaning. *Spiritual* is frequently used in the present culture to refer to someone or something with any sort of religious sense, but for Paul it most often points to something related to the Holy Spirit. In the case of people, they are filled, gifted, or enabled by the Spirit in some way (e.g., 1 Cor 2:14, 15; 14:37). Here the blessings are conveyed to believers through the Holy Spirit, and v. 3 is connected to and rounds out the periodic paragraph down to vv. 13–14, where the Spirit appears again.

18. The translation "high-heavenlies" is used for the phrase ἐν τοῖς ἐπουρανίοις because the substantive adj. here has a slightly different "feel" from the more common noun οὐρανός (cf. 1:10; 3:15; 4:10; 6:9).

19. Καθώς normally introduces a close comparison between two things, as in Eph 4:17 ("you no longer walk, just as the Gentiles walk") or 4:32 ("forgive one another, just as God in Christ forgave you"), but here its meaning refers to the basis of a previous assertion or fact and is a logical cause or reason: God is worthy of praise insofar as he chose us (BDAG, 494; cf. Rom 1:28; 1 Cor 5:7; Phil 1:7).

20. The simple pronoun form in the phrase εἰς αὐτός often functions as a reflective pronoun, as here; cf. BDF §283.

21. The meaning could also be "for praise of his glorious grace" if one were to attach δόξα to χάρις, which follows; cf. BDF §168 (2); 1:13–14; Phil 1:11.

22. The relative pronoun ἧς in v. 6b would normally be acc., but it is attracted into the gen. case of its antecedent: χάριτος, "of grace," in v. 6a (BDF §294 [2]). See also below on v. 8 and 4:1.

23. The rare verb χαριτόω ("bestow favor on"; LSJ, 1980; BDAG, 1081) was obviously chosen because of its etymological relation to χάρις, since it only occurs here and in one other NT place (Luke 1:28; cf. Sir 18:17). The more common synonyms δίδωμι ("give") or even χαρίζομαι ("grant," "bestow") would have been chosen if the etymology were not a factor in the use of χαριτόω here.

24. I take the article in the phrase ἐν τῷ ἠγαπημένῳ as a poss. pronoun ("his"): "The article often takes the place of an unemphatic possessive pronoun when there is no doubt as to the possessor," Herbert Wier Smyth, *Greek Grammar*, rev. Gordon M. Messing (Cambridge, MA: Harvard University Press, 1956; original ed., 1920),

the forgiveness of our[25] transgressions, according to the riches of his grace,
8 which[26] he lavished[27] upon us in all wisdom and insight **9** when he made
known to us the mystery of his will according to his good pleasure, which
he purposed in him **10** for the administration[28] of the fullness of (all) eras
to sum up[29] all things in the Messiah,[30] the things in heaven and things on
earth in him, **11–12** in whom also we who had hoped beforehand[31] in the
Messiah[32] were apportioned to be for the praise of his glory, since[33] we were

---

§1121. The scribes who wrote the variant "in his beloved Son" (ἐν τῷ ἠγαπημένῳ υἱῷαὐτοῦ) agreed with this interpretation (see textual note above). The more common rendering is "in the Beloved" (e.g., NASB, NKJV, ESV; cf. NIV, "the One he loves"). "Beloved" here in v. 6b is the perf. ptc. ἠγαπημένος, which Paul uses only a few times elsewhere (Col 3:12; 1 Thess 1:4; 2 Thess 2:13), but the reference there is to the saints rather than to Christ (cf. Rom 9:25). The equivalent adj. ἀγαπητός is more common in Paul's writings (twenty-six occurrences, including Eph 5:1 and 6:21). It could be that the perf. ptc., which has one more syllable and a different scansion than the adj., fit the desired rhythm of this colon* better; cf. Col 1:13, ὁ υἱὸς τῆς ἀγάπης αὐτοῦ, "his beloved Son," which would have added three syllables to the expression in Eph 1:6b.

25. Again, taking the article alone (τῶν παραπτωμάτων) as conveying a poss. idea.

26. The relative pronoun ἧς is attracted into the gen. case of its antecedent, χάριτος, in v. 7c. See also on v. 6 above, where the same attraction with the same antecedent appears.

27. The verb περισσεύω is normally intransitive ("to increase," "abound") but is causative here, "which he caused to abound toward us," and has been smoothed in English as "which he lavished upon us" (as ESV). The thought is that God's grace is given to his people in great abundance. For the causative use of περισσεύω see also 2 Cor 9:8 ("God is able to make all grace abound to you") and 1 Thess 3:12.

28. As NASB; possibly "plan" (ESV), "scheme," or "design"; cf. "dispensation" (NKJV); cf. BDAG, 869; LSJ, 1480–81; Hoehner, 216–18; and the translation note on Eph 3:9.

29. See comment for the verb ἀνακεφαλαιόω ("sum up") here.

30. For ἐν τῷ Χριστῷ as "in *the Messiah*" as a title, see excursus below.

31. The perf. ptc. here (τοὺς προηλπικότας) has the force of a pluperfect, which "denote[s] a state existing antecedent to the time of the principal verb" (E. Burton, *Syntax of the Moods and Tenses in New Testament Greek* [Edinburgh: T&T Clark, 1898], §156), which is "we ... were apportioned" (ἐκληρώθημεν).

32. See translation note on v. 10 above and excursus.

33. Taking the adv. ptc. προορισθέντες as having a causal sense; cf. Burton, *Moods*, §439.

predestined according to his plan who brings all things into effect[34] in accordance with the counsel of his will,[35] **13** in whom you[36] as well, when you heard the word of truth,[37] the gospel of your salvation, in whom also when you believed, you were sealed with the promised Holy Spirit, **14** who is a down payment of our inheritance for redemption of his[38] prized possession for the praise of his glory.

Commentary

1:3 Εὐλογητὸς ὁ θεὸς καὶ πατὴρ τοῦ κυρίου ἡμῶν Ἰησοῦ Χριστοῦ, "Blessed be the God and Father of our Lord Jesus Christ."[39] As shown in the periodic

---

34. The ptc. in the phrase τοῦ ... ἐνεργοῦντος is rendered "of the one who brings into effect" in order to express this verb's idea of actual production of some object in mind; so also 1:20 (cf. LSJ, 564; BDAG, 335).

35. The two κατά clauses in v. 11 could be read as parallel with asyndeton*: "predestined according to his purpose ... [and] according to the counsel of his will." But it reads more smoothly to see the second clause as expanding on the substantive ptc. τοῦ ... ἐνεργοῦντος from v. 11b: "who brings all things into effect in accordance with the counsel of his will."

36. The pronoun ὑμεῖς here is not emphatic, as one might expect with a personal pronoun in the nominative, but is required to clarify the subject of the ptc. ἀκούσαντες.

37. The phrase "the word of truth" (τὸν λόγον τῆς ἀληθείας; v. 13b) could be read as "the true word" (adj. gen.), but more likely the truth is the content of the discourse (λόγος) of the preaching (εὐαγγέλιον; v. 13c) that they heard. This is what Smyth, *Greek Grammar*, §1380 calls the "gen. of connection" (unfortunately not discussed in Daniel B. Wallace, *Greek Grammar beyond the Basics* [Grand Rapids: Zondervan, 1997]).

38. I render the article with "prized possession" (εἰς ἀπολύτρωσιν τῆς περιποιήσεως) as equivalent to a poss. pronoun, "his," as is common in Greek usage. One normally expects both nouns in a gen. sequence to be either articular or anarthrous (i.e., Apollonius' Canon), but here "redemption" in anarthrous and "prized possession" is articular (εἰς ἀπολύτρωσιν τῆς περιποιήσεως). "Redemption" can be either indefinite or definite because anarthrous nouns operating as objs. of preps. might be definite. Here and throughout vv. 3–14, the lack of articles in certain phrases is also due to rhythmical considerations. Cf. Sanford D. Hull, "Exceptions to Apollonius' Canon in the New Testament: A Grammatical Study," *TrinJ* NS (1986): 3–16.

39. The words of 1:3a are found verbatim in 2 Cor 1:3 and 1 Pet 1:3. The former is not a problem granting Pauline authorship of Ephesians, but the 1 Peter use shows that this particular identity of God in a benediction was perhaps used generally in the early church. Paul expresses praise to God with the adj. εὐλογητός also in Rom 1:25; 9:5; 2 Cor 11:31.

division given in the introduction, this period consists of four cola*, with a trinitarian focus on God the Father, the Spirit (through the adjective "spiritual"), and the incarnate Son, "our Lord Jesus Christ" (v. 3a) and "in Christ" (v. 3d). The passage is filled with long syllables, which are appropriate for the majesty of the subject and the solemnity of God's glorious praise.

"Blessed (be) ..." (εὐλογητός) introduces a common form of Hebraic prayer of praise recited throughout the day by Jews in Paul's day. This form of prayer is very ancient and common in the OT: "Blessed be the LORD, the God of Shem" (Gen 9:26); "[B]lessed be God Most High" (Gen 14:20); "Blessed be the LORD" (Gen 24:31; cf. Gen 24:27; Exod 18:10; Pss 18:47; 31:22; 41:14; 124:6; Zech 11:5). It is also common in various extrabiblical sources (e.g., *Pss. Sol.* 6:6; *3 Macc* 7:23; Jdt 13:17; 1QH[a] 8.16; 11Q5 19.7–8).[40] The verb "blessed *be*" is implied rather than expressed in this form of prayer, as in Eph 1:3.

In the OT, the covenant name of God (יהוה, usually rendered κύριος ["Lord"] in the LXX and NT) is often expressed in these benedictions along with reference to the bond between God and his covenant people as: "Blessed be the LORD God of Israel" (1 Sam 25:32; 1 Kgs 1:48; 8:15; 1 Chr 16:36; 29:10 ["Blessed are you, LORD God of Israel"]; 2 Chr 2:11; 6:4; Pss 41:14; 72:18 ["Blessed be the LORD God, the God of Israel"]; 106:48; cf. Tob 13:18 [Sinaiticus ending]; *Odes. Sol.* 9:68; 1 Macc 4:30 ["Blessed are you, the Savior of Israel"]; *3 Macc* 7:23 ["Blessed is the Deliverer of Israel"]).

In what is essentially a final moment of OT revelation just before the dawn of the new, Zachariah opens his benedictus with "Blessed be the Lord God of Israel" (Luke 1:68). However, in Ephesians 1:3 (with 2 Cor 1:3 and 1 Pet 1:3) and other post-Pentecost references (Rom 15:6; 2 Cor 11:31; Rev 1:6 ["his God and Father"]; cf. 1 Thess 3:11; Eph 4:6; 5:20), the name of God has been updated from his identity with theocratic Israel to "the God and Father of our Lord Jesus Christ" to signal the international character of the new covenant in contrast with the old. God is no longer exclusively the God of Israel but through the one mediator, Jesus Christ, is now the God of Jews and "Greeks" from all nations (Rom 1:16; 2:9; 3:29–30; 1 Tim 2:1–8). Israel, whose were the "covenants of promise" (Eph 2:12; cf. Rom 9:4), and

40. Hoehner, 162–63. For study of the Dead Sea Scroll hymns see Bonnie Pedrotti Kittel, *The Hymns of Qumran*, SBLDS 50 (Atlanta: Scholars Press, 1981).

Gentiles, who were formerly "far off" (Eph 2:13), can know and have access to the living God through Christ Jesus.

To say that God the Father is the God of Jesus (also 1:17) is not to deny the incarnate Son's true divinity but to express his true humanity and that through him God is also our God and Father (see esp. John 20:17). To ancient pagan peoples like the Ephesians, the appearance of a god in human *form* was fairly common in their literature and religious festivals.[41] The language of this is ἐπιφάνεια, "manifestation" or "appearance" (whence English "epiphany"), and cognates like ἐπιφανής ("manifest"; cf. Acts 2:20), which was sometimes used to express a divine appearance. For example, in *IvE* 251 Julius Caesar is honored as "the manifest god (τὸν ἀπὸ Ἄρεως καὶ Ἀφροδε[ί]της θεὸν ἐπιφανῆ) [sprung] from Ares and Aphrodite," and in *IvE* 27 Artemis Ephesia is called a goddess ἐπιφανεστάτη ("most manifest"), while coins from Ephesus depict doorways in the pediment of her temple where it is thought that Artemis or a priestess made an appearance during festivals.[42]

There is, however, no parallel for a Greek or Roman god to appear among us as *a true human*. The NT authors have to work hard to clarify to their contemporaries that the Son of God made his "appearance" (2 Thess 2:8; 1 Tim 6:14; 2 Tim 1:10; 4:1, 8; Titus 2:13) as a *man* in the flesh (e.g., John 1:14; 6:51; 1 John 4:2–3; Acts 17:31; 1 Tim 2:5; Heb 2:14).

41. One does not have to go far in ancient literature to find Greek and Roman gods making various appearances. For example, in Homer flashing-eyed Athena Pallas appears as both Mentes and Mentor to Telemachus (*Od.* 1.96–112; 2.267–69) or as herself (*Od.* 15.7–9) and transforms Odysseus so that Telemachus takes him to be a god (*Od.* 16.172–89). Such ideas were deeply rooted in the pagan world, so it is perfectly understandable that the Lystrans would take Paul and Barnabas as the appearance of Olympian gods in their midst (Acts 14:8–18). See Clinton E. Arnold, "Acts," in in *Zondervan Illustrated Bible Backgrounds Commentary*, ed. Clinton E. Arnold (Grand Rapids: Zondervan, 2002), 2:349, for nice discussion of a similar episode in Ovid; cf. Heb 13:2.

42. Cf. Paul Trebilco, *The Early Christians in Ephesus from Paul to Ignatius* (Grand Rapids: Eerdmans, 2008; first published 2004), 356. For divine epiphanies in art from the earliest times in Greece see Walter Burkert, *Greek Religion* (Cambridge, MA: Harvard University Press, 1985), 40–44; for general treatments on Artemis Ephesia and her worship see Richard Oster, "Ephesus as a Religious Center under the Principate," *ANRW* 2.18.3 (1990): 1661–1728; and Oster, "The Ephesian Artemis as an Opponent of Early Christianity," *JAC* 19 (1976): 24–44; cf. Guy MacLean Rogers, *The Sacred Identiy of Ephesos* (New York: Routledge, 1991).

So Paul's reference to the Father as the God of "our Lord Jesus" in Eph 1:3 was to bring out Christ's human identity as the one true mediator (1 Tim 2:5; Heb 2:14 again), expressed further in the passage with the many references to the redemptive benefits lavished on his people "in" or "through" Christ (vv. 3d, 4a, 5b, 6b, 7a, 9b, 10b–c, 11a, 13c).

ὁ εὐλογήσας ἡμᾶς ἐν πάσῃ εὐλογίᾳ πνευματικῇ ἐν τοῖς ἐπουρανίοις ἐν Χριστῷ, "who has blessed us with every blessing of the Spirit in the high-heavenlies in Christ." It is common in benedictions and other forms of praise to specify the basis for this praise. The most overt way to signal this is with ὅτι, "for" or "because," as here:

> Εὐλογητὸς κύριος ὁ θεὸς τοῦ Ἰσραήλ,
> **ὅτι** τπεσκέψατο καὶ ἐποίησεν λύτρωσιν τῷ λαῷ αὐτοῦ
>
> Blessed be the Lord, the God of Israel,
> *for* he has had regard for and rendered redemption for his people. (Luke 1:68)

In more Hebrew-inspired form, the specification can be given as a qualification in a relative clause:

> εὐλογητὸς κύριος ὁ θεὸς Ισραηλ
> **ὃς** ςδωκεν σήμερον ἐκ τοῦ σπέρματός μου καθήμενον ἐπὶ τοῦ θρόνου μου
>
> Blessed be the Lord, the God of Israel,
> who today has granted that one from my line should sit on my throne. (1 Kgs 1:48)

The attributive participle ὁ εὐλογήσας ("who has blessed") in Eph 1:3 (also 2 Cor 1:4; 1 Pet 1:3) identifies something God has done and is semantically the equivalent of a relative pronoun clause. The LXX translators also used this construction:

> εὐλογητὸς κύριος ὁ θεὸς ὁ θεὸς Ισραηλ
> **ὁὖποιῶν** θαυμάσια μόνος
>
> Blessed be the Lord God, the God of Israel,
> who alone performs wonderful deeds. (Psa 71:18 LXX; 72:18 MT)

It seems clear that both the relative pronoun and participle clauses are specifying the reason(s) for praise and are similar in meaning, if not overt form, to a clause with ὅτι.

The blessings God has lavished on his people in Eph 1:3 are πνευματικός ("of the Spirit") because they have their origin and ultimate fulfillment in the "high-heavenlies," which were obtained by the Last Adam, the "life-giving spirit" who is "from heaven," and in the likeness of whose resurrection body believers will be conformed in resurrection into "spiritual bodies" (see esp. 1 Cor 10:3; 15:40, 44–50).[43] The Holy Spirit is himself the link between this world and the new creation so that his presence with the elect is the ultimate blessing and the guarantee of future heavenly blessings (see on vv. 13–14; so also 2 Cor 5:5 and Rom 8:23).[44] Geerhardus Vos writes:

> In this instance, therefore, the Spirit is viewed as pertaining specifically to the future life, nay as constituting the substantial make-up of this life, and the present possession of the Spirit by the believer is regarded in the light of an anticipation. The Spirit's proper sphere is according to this the world to come; from there He projects Himself into the present.[45]

The spiritual blessings of God in Christ are ἐν τοῖς ἐπουρανίοις ("in the high-heavenlies"), which is this realm of the Spirit and of the world to come (cf. esp. O'Brien, 96–97).[46] While the prepositional prefix ἐπί (**ἐπ**ουρανίοις) can intensify the simple adjective οὐράνιος (found only in Matthew and

43. Cf. the parallelism in Isa 44:3: "I will pour my *Spirit* upon your offspring, and my *blessing* on your descendants" (emphasis added). Sinclair B. Ferguson's little book is particularly helpful on this and other related issues: *The Holy Spirit* (Downers Grove, IL: InterVarsity Press, 1996).

44. This is the reality of "inaugurated eschatology" seen throughout the NT and particularly in Ephesians; cf. Geerhardus Vos, "The Eschatological Aspect of the Pauline Conception of the Spirit," in *Redemptive History and Biblical Interpretation: The Shorter Writings of Geerhardus Vos*, ed. R. B. Gaffin Jr. (Phillipsburg, NJ: P&R, 1980; repr. of 1912 essay), 91–125; and more recently Michael Horton, *Covenant and Eschatology: The Divine Drama* (Louisville: Westminster John Knox, 2002); Andrew T. Lincoln, *Paradise Now and Not Yet*, SNTSMS (Cambridge: Cambridge University Press, 1981).

45. Vos, "Eschatological Aspect," 103; cf. G. Vos, *Pauline Eschatology* (Grand Rapids: Eerdmans, 1952), 160–71.

46. The same phrase appears five times in Ephesians at 1:3, 20; 2:6; 3:10; 6:12.

Luke/Acts), with my translation "*high*-heavenlies" I am not suggesting a gradation of realms within heaven.[47] Instead, it is an attempt to capture the more grand and exalted or even semipoetic sound of this phrase in English, in contrast with the more common "in heaven" (ἐν οὐρανοῖς), which itself is used in Ephesians (3:15; 6:9; cf. 1:10; 4:10). The grander-sounding phrase ἐν τοῖς ἐπουρανίοις demands more attention, with almost twice the syllables of ἐν οὐρανοῖς (˘ ¯ ˘ ¯), with an interesting rhythm (¯ ¯ ˘ ¯ ˘ ˘ ¯). This exalted "feel" comes out especially well in the next use of the phrase in the royal language of 1:20 ("seating him at his right hand *in the high-heavenlies*") and compares favorably with the similarly grand statement in Hebrews: "he has taken his seat at the right hand of the Majesty on High" (Heb 1:3; my trans.).

1:4 *καθὼς ἐξελέξατο ἡμᾶς ἐν αὐτῷ πρὸ καταβολῆς κόσμου εἶναι ἡμᾶς ἁγίους καὶ ἀμώμους κατενώπιον αὐτοῦ*, "insofar as he chose us in him before the foundation of the world that we should be holy and blameless before him." The second period—which comprises most of v. 4—ends with κατενώπιον αὐτοῦ ("before him") to continue Paul's focus on the Lord in this long passage of praise (1:3–14). It specifies a further reason for blessing "the God and Father of our Lord Jesus Christ" with the opening conjunction καθώς, "insofar as" or "because."

The verb rendered "he chose" (ἐκλέγομαι) is an ordinary term for "choosing" or "selecting" something or someone. For example, Jesus "chose" certain men as the Twelve (e.g., Luke 6:13; John 6:70); they did not "choose" him (John 15:16; cf. 1 Cor 1:27–28; cf. Acts 15:7; Jas 2:5). Throughout Ephesians 1:3–14, Paul emphasizes God's initiative in redeeming his people from transgressions (v. 7) and that this is only accomplished in union with Christ, i.e., "in him." The mediation of Christ is essential for any benefit from God and was planned by him (vv. 5, 9, 11) "before the foundation of the world" (v. 4b). (See discussion in "Biblical Theological Comments" at Eph 2:1–10 for other views.)

God's selection of particular believers has a definite goal: to be "holy and blameless before him" as a result of the redemptive work of Christ (see esp. comments on 5:25–27). Holiness expresses moral purity and is in

---

47. Cf. W. Hall Harris III, "'The Heavenlies' Reconsidered: Οὐρανός and Ἐπουράνιος in Ephesians," *BSac* 148 (1991): 72–89; M. Jeff Brannon, *The Heavenlies in Ephesians: A Lexical, Exegetical, and Conceptual Analysis*, LNTS (London: T&T Clark, 2011).

contrast with being sinful, while blamelessness is freedom from the guilt incurred by transgressions of God's law (v. 7; cf. 2:1, 5; Col 1:22; Phil 2:15).

Ephesian Christians would understand the notion of purity before God from their prior lives. Artemis Ephesia was portrayed in antiquity as a virgin huntress (despite erroneous modern conceptions of her as a mother goddess).[48] Sexual purity of some form was required of Artemis' followers; for example, there is a report that married women could not enter the temple of Artemis at Ephesus (the "Artemisium").[49] There is also the interesting temporary religious office held by certain men who were called "Essenes," which required some sort of purity, most likely sexual abstinence during their time of office. For example, a first- or second-century AD inscription by C. Scaptius Frontinus says: "I completed a term as Essene purely and piously."[50] The purity and blamelessness before the living God, however, is not completed during a temporary term of office but has its beginning in this life and its consummate perfection at the believer's resurrection. Christians have been chosen for this great inheritance and given the Spirit of holiness, through whom Christ was raised (Rom 1:4) as its guarantee (Eph 1:14).

The God whom the Ephesian Christians now worship is far more exalted and divine than Artemis (whose worship and temple have fallen into a boggy ruin).[51] She was thought to have been born in time from Leto and Zeus, but the living God ("I AM WHO I AM," Exod 3:14) exists before all time and chose his people πρὸ καταβολῆς κόσμου ("before the foundation of the world"). Paul adds this qualification in v. 4 to further stress God's initiative in redemption. Paul's hearers are hereby enjoined to join him in

48. Cf. S. M. Baugh, "A Foreign World: Ephesus in the First Century," in *Women in the Church*, 2nd ed., ed. A. J. Köstenberger and T. R. Schreiner (Grand Rapids: Baker, 2005), 13–38, 181–95, with discussion on Artemis and literature cited on 23–26 and 187–88.

49. Achilles Tatius, *Leuc. Clit.* 7.13.

50. "(I) completed a term as Essene purely and piously" (Ἐσσηνεύσας ἁγνῶς καὶ εὐσεβῶς, *IvE* 1578B); cf. Baugh, "Foreign World," 23–26, 186n57.

51. The Artemisium is in a low, marshy area, "and the whole area is often under water" (Peter Scherrer, ed., *Ephesus: The New Guide* [Turkey: Zero, 2000], 55). The worship of Artemis Ephesia suffered serious decline toward the end of the second century after a major earthquake, and the temple itself was plundered by invading Goths in AD 262/3; cf. Guy Maclean Rogers, *The Mysteries of Artemus of Ephesos: Cult, Polis, and Change in the Graeco-Roman World* (New Haven, CT: Yale University Press, 2012), 251–56.

praise as a result, which is why he leads off the epistle in this way and leads naturally to a report of his prayers on their behalf in vv. 15–23.

1:4–6 *ἐν ἀγάπῃ, προορίσας ἡμᾶς εἰς υἱοθεσίαν διὰ Ἰησοῦ Χριστοῦ εἰς αὐτόν, κατὰ τὴν εὐδοκίαν τοῦ θελήματος αὐτοῦ, εἰς ἔπαινον δόξης τῆς χάριτος αὐτοῦ,* "In love he predestined us for adoption to himself through Jesus Christ according to the good pleasure of his will for praise of the glory of his grace." There are three options for the placement and understanding of *ἐν ἀγάπῃ* ("in love"). The first two attach it to v. 4 rather than prefixed to vv. 5–6a, as I have (cf. KJV, NKJV, NRSV, UBS[4], NA[27], Vg.).[52] The first view takes "in love" with the main indicative verb in v. 4a, *ἐξελέξατο ... ἐν ἀγάπῃ*, "he chose us ... in [his] love." While this is possible, it is very distant from that verb, and the seven-word infinitive clause with *εἶναι* (vv. 4c–d) intervenes, making it difficult at best. The second view attaches the phrase to the end of the infinitive clause ("that we may be holy and blameless before him [which is characterized by our] love") and refers not to God's love but to the believer's (e.g., Calvin, 126; Hodge, 35; Hoehner, 182–85). Lincoln makes a good case for this structurally by showing the parallelism of *ἐν ἀγάπῃ* with *ἐν Χριστῷ* in v. 3d (Lincoln, 15–16). There is no problem grammatically or theologically with this view, but it does not fit the emphasis at the end of each period in vv. 3–14 on the Triune God rather than on the believer. Furthermore, being "holy and blameless" here does not refer to moral growth but to an objective state of purification achieved through atonement and forgiveness (e.g., v. 7; Col 1:14; cf. 5:27; Col 1:22; Heb 9:11–15).

The third option, represented in NASB, NIV, and ESV, is to take *ἐν ἀγάπῃ* with the participle *προορίσας* ("he predestined") in v. 5a, as I have (also Arnold, 81). This preserves the focus on God at the end of each period and also shows how the participle *προορίσας* acts as the centerpiece of vv. 4e–6a.

---

52. Origen writes: "One must join the 'in love' either with 'having predestined,' or with 'he chose us in him in love before the foundation of the world, having predestined us' in adoption '[through] Jesus Christ unto himself' so that 'we might be holy and blameless before him' (Eph. 1:4)" (Origen and Jerome, 87). The Vg. connects "in love" with v. 4, *ut essemus sancti et immaculati in conspectu eius in charitate,* "that we may be holy and spotless in his sight in love," but the Latin version (and the comments) of the roughly contemporary Theodore of Mopsuestia connects it with predestined in v. 5: *in caritate praeordinans nos*, "in love he predestinated us" (Theodore, 186–89). See also the phrase *μετὰ χαρᾶς* ("with joy") at the end of Col 1:11, which many see as actually the beginning of the next verse.

However, Greek cola* and periods frequently open with an adverbial participle like προορίσας, so the unusually placed "in love" here is "fronted" and draws particular attention to itself.[53] It is tempting to regard this as a "swing phrase" that qualifies *both* statements in vv. 4 and 5, but it is probably better to regard this as belonging with the participle προορίσας because it is closer. Predestination to adoption is not some cold, abstract act of an impersonal God, but an act of *love* of an inexpressibly gracious kind "for the praise of the glory of his *grace*."

The grammar of the participle προορίσας here can be analyzed in two ways. It can be substantive and in parallel with ὁ εὐλογήσας in v. 3 above ("who blessed [and] who predestined"). This meaning, though, would expect καί to join the latter with the former. More likely, προορίσας acts in parallel with indicative ἐξελέξατο in v. 4 as simply another statement: "Insofar as he chose us ... [and] he predestined us."[54] The conjunction καί is not used in this construction, and use of participles in periodic style such as we find in Ephesians has many of these participles marking the beginning of periods.[55]

The meaning of the verb προορίζω is to make a previous determination about something or someone and is closely related to "choose" in v. 4 (see

53. Separation of elements that belong together (*hyperbaton*) as well as unusual word order for the sake of focus, stress, or simply to mark out cola* is a common feature of Greek. For the function of *hyperbaton* within the Greek colon* see esp. Daniel Markovic, "Hyperbaton in the Greek Literary Sentence," *GRBS* 46 (2006): 127–46; and with a focus on smaller units see A. M. Devine and Laurence D. Stephens, *Discontinous Syntax: Hyperbaton in Greek* (New York: Oxford, 2000) (see note on 3:10).

54. The Vg. has *qui praedestinavit,* "who predestined," which would substantially agree with this analysis and also means that "in love" (*in caritate*) is taken with v. 4. The aor. tense form of προορίσας and of indic. ἐξελέξατο both communicate the "simple" idea that the event is asserted as occuring beforehand "as a complete and undifferentiated process" (Stanley E. Porter, *Idioms of the Greek New Testament*, Biblical Languages: Greek 2 [Sheffield, UK: JSOT, 1992], §2.2) or "a mere event" (Albert Rijksbaron, *The Syntax and Semantics of the Verb in Classical Greek*, 2nd ed. [Amsterdam: J. C. Gieben, 1994], §6.1).

55. In some grammars, this use of the ptc. is labeled "attendant circumstances" (Smyth, *Greek Grammar,* §§2068–69; Burton, *Moods*, §§449–50; Wallace, *Greek Grammar*, 640–45), but I prefer the term *parallel ptc.*, since the ptc. takes on the function of the mood of the main verb form with which it acts in concert; discussed briefly in S. M. Baugh, *A First John Reader: Intermediate Greek Reading Notes and Grammar* (Phillipsburg, NJ: P&R, 1999), 115–16, and in the excursus below.

also v. 11; cf. Acts 4:28; Rom 8:29–30; 1 Cor 2:7). While one must be particularly cautious about using etymology to understand a word's meaning, the etymology of ὁρίζω is instructive. It is derived from the noun ὅρος (or Ionic, οὖρος), which refers to a marker used to mark out one's property.[56] Hence, ὁρίζω can be rendered "to mark out" or "determine." From there, the meaning when people are the objects of the action is closer to "appoint," as in 1:5, since the elect are "predetermined" (i.e., "preappointed") to the position of υἱοθεσίαρ (below).

What is most remarkable about the period of 1:4e–6a is that it consists entirely of six prepositional phrases qualifying προορίσας. This is a very high number and shows the focus here on the act of predestination. The logical relations of these phrases can be sketched out as follows:

Predestined:
God's motive: ἐν ἀγάπῃ, "in love"
Goal: εἰς υἱοθεσίαν, "for adoption"
Mediation: διὰ Ἰησοῦ Χριστοῦ, "through Jesus Christ"
Interrelation of adoption: εἰς αὐτόν, "to himself"
Standard governing the act: κατὰ τὴν εὐδοκίαν τοῦ θελήματος αὐτοῦ, "according to the good pleasure of his will"
Result: εἰς ἔπαινον δόξης τῆς χάριτος αὐτοῦ, "for the praise of the glory of his grace."

εἰς υἱοθεσίαν, "for adoption." While English "adoption" is the best rendering for υἱοθεσία, this term does not convey the same connotations today as it did in a Graeco-Roman city like Ephesus.[57] The first part of the etymology of **υἱο**θεσία ("appoint as son") was still active in its meaning, as also in the rarer terms **θυγατρο**θεσία ("adopt as daughter") or **τεκνο**θεσία

56. Such boundary stones marking the property of the Artemisium have been found up to thirty miles away in the region of Ephesus, leading to the rough estimate that some 77,000 acres of rich farm lands were controlled by the temple bureaucracy (cf. *IvE* 3501–12). This kind of land control is necessary to support the population of any ancient city. Cf. Dieter Knibbe, Recep Meric, and Reinhold Merkelbach, "Der Grundbesitz der ephesischen Artemis im Kaystrostal," *ZPE* 33 (1979): 139–46.

57. I.e., ancient adoption focused on the needs of the adopter and the *oikos/familia* rather than the adoptee; interests in the latter are better termed "fosterage" for antiquity; see 1 Thess 2:7; cf. Eph 5:29; *IvE* 660.

("adopt as child").[58] This is important because of the importance of sons in the Greek οἶκος ("family, household") or Roman *familia* (also "family, household").[59]

The primary connection between ancient adoption and the son(s) was inheritance.[60] One Roman form is particularly instructive. The *paterfamili-*

58. Θυγατροθεσία ("adopt as daughter") occurs in only a few sources from a few locations, though the exact reason for this rare practice is not fully understood; cf. A. V. Walser, "ΘΥΓΑΤΡΟΘΕΣΙΑ—Ein neues Zeugnis aus Kaunos für die Adoption von Frauen," *Epigraphica Anatolica* 37 (2004): 101–6; and see *P.Oxy.* 3271 for τεκνοθεσία used for an adopted woman (*New Docs,* 3.16–17). A more generic Greek term for "adoption" is εἰσποίησις (not found in the NT or LXX; cf. LSJ, 496). Interestingly, the Vg. includes "sons" in its rendering of Eph 1:5a: *in adoptionem filiorum*, "for the adoption *of sons*," where *adoptio* or similar *adrogatio* without reference to *filii* ("sons") would have sufficed.

59. Both *oikos/oikia* and *familia* are broader than the modern "nuclear family," with extended relatives, freedmen, and slaves. The practice and implications of adoption in the Greek and Roman world must be pieced together from a large number of scattered sources and references; one of the best modern studies is Jane F. Gardner, *Family and* Familia *in Roman Law and Life* (Oxford: Clarendon, 1998); cf. Hugh Lindsay, *Adoption in the Roman World* (Cambridge: Cambridge University Press, 2009); and briefer S. M. Baugh, "Marriage and Family in Ancient Greek Society," in *Marriage and Family in the Biblical World,* ed. K. M. Campbell (Downers Grove, IL: InterVarsity Press, 2003), 103–31; and Susan Treggiari, "Marriage and Family in Roman Society," in *Marriage and Family*, 132–82. The difficulty of tracing adoption among peoples in the Greek East in Paul's day is that most of our sources for the Greek world on adoption relate to Athens from several centuries earlier. Yet Roman adoption practices can be assumed to have had some influence in a place like first-century Ephesus (even as some believe earlier Greek adoption had influence on early Roman practice). For Ephesus, see, for example, P. Vedius Antoninus Sabinus (originally M. Claudius Sabinus), asiarch (Acts 19:31), who was adopted by one of wealthiest and most prominent second-century Ephesians, P. Vedius Antoninus (cf. *IvE* 728–29, 1017, 1491–93, 2029); see *IvE* 8.88–91 for the family tree ("stemma"). See discussion below on 2:3 for a Greek man from Kyme who was adopted son of one man and son "by nature" (φύσει) of another.

60. Note how the terms for adoption (υἱοθεσία and εἰσποιητός) occur in connection with terms relating to inheritance in Ammonius Grammaticus (possibly AD 1–2): "A 'disinherited' [son] and 'alienated' [one] are different. For the disinherited is ejected from the family by his father because of wrongs done, but the alienated is one who is given by his father to another for adoption as son (εἰς υἱοθεσίαν), for which they say, 'He is adopted' (εἰσποιητὸς γέγονεν)" (*On the Differences of Synonymous Expressions* 61); virtually the same discussion is also attributed to Ptolemaeus Grammaticus, *On the Differences of Synonymous Expressions* 390.11 and 32.3 (*TLG*).

as (i.e., head of the family) held *patria potestas* (i.e., paternal legal authority) over all members of his *familia,* including sons of whatever age, unless he were to release them from his *potestas* through *mancipatio* ("emancipation") or possibly give them through *adoptio* into the *patria potestas* and *familia* of a new *paterfamilias*. If the son had already been emancipated, the procedure was *adrogatio* and was considered more serious because the son held his own *patria potestas* and his *familia* was thus terminated.[61]

Such an adopted son, then, was no longer a member of his old *familia/oikos* but the heir to become *paterfamilias* of the property and persons of the new *familia*: "If a son, then an heir" (Gal 4:7). Behind adoption was *continuity* of the *familia/oikos* and of its external relations, in particular if the *paterfamilias* was patron of a town or of soldiers; the son inherited that position as part of his patrimony.[62]

The adoption of P. Cornelius Scipio Aemilianus Africanus (Numantius) (185/4–129 BC) is just one instructive example.[63] Diodorus Siculus writes: "Now Publius Scipio was the natural son (κατὰ φύσιν υἱός) of Aemilus who had triumphed over Perseus ... and he was given in adoption (δοθεὶς δὲ εἰς υἱοθεσίαν) to Scipio ... succeeding to a family (οἰκία) and clan (γένος) of such importance" (31.26.4; also Velleius Paterculus, 1.10.3–6; 1.11.2–3).

With this (too) brief sketch of adoption background, we can return to Eph 1:4–5 and hopefully see its implications more clearly, as well as the

61. "The initial purpose of the institution of adoption, therefore, like that of will-making, appears to have been to allow people without *sui heredes* of their own to acquire someone to inherit their patrimonies—and, initially at least, it was possible to adopt ... only someone capable of carrying on the *familia* in the sense of the agnatic line, i.e., only a male" (Gardner, *Family*, 202).

62. E.g., Pompey the Great recruited an army from among his father's clients in the region of Picenum (a northwest Italian coastal area; *Velleius Paterculus* 2.29), and likewise, through his adoption by Julius Caesar, Octavian (Augustus) inherited the allegiance of his "father's" (his great-uncle by birth) soldiers, which gave him immediate resources to prosecute his bid to "save" the Roman Republic by transforming it into an empire; cf. the classic work of Ronald Syme, *The Roman Revolution* (Oxford: Clarendon, 1939; rev. ed., 2002). As an example of municipal patronage see Pliny, *Ep.* 4.1 ("Tifernum on Tiber which adopted me as its patron"; cf. *Ep.* 3.4); cf. the work of my esteemed former professor, John Nicols, *Civic Patronage in the Roman Empire* (Leiden: Brill, forthcoming).

63. For the families and men involved see John Briscoe, "Aemilius Paullus, Lucius (2)," *OCD*, 21, and Ernst Badian, "Cornelius Scipio Aemilianus Africanus (Numantinus), Publius," *OCD*, 381–82.

connection of sonship and inheritance in vv. 13–14. Paul declares that *all* believers ("us"; Jew and Greek, male and female, slave and free) have been transferred by the *fiat* ("according to the good pleasure of his will"; v. 5) of the Father of the whole of his *familia/oikos* in heaven and earth (see on 3:15) as sons into his own *oikos* ("to himself"; v. 5b; also 2:19) through the redeeming act of his own beloved Son (v. 5b; i.e., a Son "by nature"). And this act was motivated by *love*, not self-interest.

Graeco-Roman adoptees were often members of the father's extended relations.[64] In the case of believers, God has taken the most distant foreigners to be his kin for inheritance of his whole estate. Not the deserving or good (Rom 5:7), not many well-born, powerful, or wise (1 Cor 1:26–30), but those who were "by nature" (φύσει) not of his kin at all but "children of wrath" (Eph 2:3) and darkened "sons of disobedience" (Eph 5:6, 8; also 4:17–24)—his helpless, wicked, sinful enemies (Rom 5:6–10) under thrall to the realm of darkness (Eph 2:1–3; Col 1:13; John 8:44; etc.). God does not place these new sons into a subordinate, inferior family; he appoints them all to become coheirs with his natural, firstborn Son, in whom the whole creation is "summarized" (v. 10) for corule over all things with him as those who have been coseated with him in the high-heavenlies (2:6; Rom 8:14–17, 29–32; cf. Gal 3:26–4:7; Col 1:12–14; 2 Tim 2:12; Rev 3:21).[65] These stupendous acts of divine grace have no parallel in Graeco-Roman society. It surpasses even the unthinkable idea of the Roman emperor adopting a slave from the most barbaric hinterlands to be the next emperor. It is no wonder that Paul exults in "praise of the glory of his grace, which he bestowed on us in his Beloved" (1:6).

It is worth stressing that the inheritance to the highly exalted position as sons is not restricted to males, or to Jews ("Israel is my firstborn son,"

---

64. "Close kin were commonly chosen for adoption in both communities [i.e., Greece and Rome] to shore up a deficit of immediate family" (Lindsay, *Adoption*, 34).

65. Cf. Trevor J. Burke, *Adopted into God's Family*, NSBT 22 (Downers Grove, IL: InterVarsity Press, 2006); James M. Scott, *Adoption as Sons of God: An Exegetical Investigation into the Background of* Huiothesia *in the Pauline Corpus*, WUNT 2/48 (Tübingen: Mohr Siebeck, 1992), the latter of which stresses the Jewish background of adoption (as, e.g., in 2 Sam 7:14) and virtually ignores Ephesians. Interesting analysis of adoption in Ephesians that stresses the sanctifying effects of adoption is in David B. Garner, "Adoption in Christ" (PhD diss., Westminster Theological Seminary, 2002), 56–69.

Exod 4:22), or even to free persons, but to all to whom the Lord extends his grace (cf. Gal 3:28–29). We have lost the momentous impact Paul's statement would have had in its original setting. Slaves in Graeco-Roman antiquity were legally not human persons (even if they were treated as such by kindly masters; see comments on 6:5–9). For the Christians at Ephesus who were or had been slaves, to hear that God had predestined them not just to become God's freedmen (1 Cor 7:22) or free children (John 1:12) but through υἱοθεσία to become ruling *sons* (whether male or female) was an astoundingly magnificent statement of God's lavish grace, poured out upon the objects of his eternal love.

κατὰ τὴν εὐδοκίαν τοῦ θελήματος αὐτοῦ, "according to the good pleasure of his will." This unusual phrase is redundant, since εὐδοκία and θέλημα are synonyms and do not occur together elsewhere in the NT (or LXX). The redundancy stresses here that God's gracious bestowal of the believer's position as son-heir is entirely due to the Father's own will and grace, independent of any sort of qualifications or attractiveness inherent in him or her (cf. Deut 7:6–8).

1:6b–7 ἧς ἐχαρίτωσεν ἡμᾶς ἐν τῷ ἠγαπημένῳ. Ἐν ᾧ ἔχομεν τὴν ἀπολύτρωσιν διὰ τοῦ αἵματος αὐτοῦ, τὴν ἄφεσιν τῶν παραπτωμάτων, κατὰ τὸ πλοῦτος τῆς χάριτος αὐτοῦ, "which he bestowed on us in his Beloved, in whom we have our redemption through his blood, the forgiveness of our transgressions, according to the riches of his grace." The remaining periods to the end of the "paragraph" (v. 14) all begin with relative pronouns (ἧς [twice], ἐν ᾧ [twice], and ὅ), which is common in periodic sentences, even though relative pronouns are otherwise not as frequent in Greek as they are, for example, in Latin or in English. In the case of vv. 6b–7, notice the clear parallelism with the next period (vv. 8–9b). Both begin with ἧς ("which"), and both end with a colon* that begins with κατά ("according to") and ends with αὐτοῦ ("his"). This kind of repeated structure of periods is also found, for example, in Rom 5:15–17 (look for repeated ἀλλ' οὐχ ὡς ... εἰ γὰρ ... and πολλῷ μᾶλλον) and should be taken into account in discussions of Greek style and the Pauline authorship of Ephesians. Finally, the period of vv. 6b–7 opens and closes with a verb and noun that are etymologically related as an inclusio*: ἐχαρίτωσεν ... χάριτος ("he bestowed" ... "grace").

With the phrase "in his Beloved" (cf. Isa 42:1; Matt 12:18), Paul links vv. 6b–7 with earlier vv. 4e–6a, where believers are predestined "in love" to adopted sonship—here we are told that this grace is bestowed "in his Beloved."[66] Paul does not normally use this title for Christ.[67] Here it probably references the sonship of the incarnate, beloved Son (e.g., Matt 3:17; Col 1:13), whose great love led him to intervene by sacrificing his own life (i.e., "his blood" in v. 7a) in exchange for his sheep: "I lay down my life for the [better: *my*] sheep. ... For this reason the Father loves me, because I lay down my life that I may take it up again" (John 10:15, 17; cf. John 3:35).

In his recitation of the blessings of God bestowed on the church so far, Paul has hinted at the center of these great gifts in the gospel, but now, in a few short lines, he zeroes in on the heart of the gospel and what makes it gracious: the substitutionary mediation of Christ (cf. comments on 2:1–10). "For Paul, God's love is not found in the philosopher's detachment from the world. Rather grace, motivated and empowered by God's love and mercy (Eph 2:4; 2 Thess 2:16; cf. 1 Tim 1:14), assumes a cruciform shape in a broken and suffering world."[68]

The heart of Christ's mediation is expressed in v. 7 with "redemption" (ἀπολύτρωσις), which was most commonly used in the Ephesians' world either for redemption of kidnapped people or of slaves into the status of freedmen through payment of a λύτρον (or pl. λύτρα), "ransom."[69] In both the slavery and kidnapping contexts of ἀπολύτρωσις there is an assumption that one's family was obligated to pay the ransom. The same is true in the OT world, and the preeminent case of redemption is the exodus from Egypt at Israel's founding as a nation:

> Say therefore to the people of Israel, "I am the LORD, and I will bring you out from under the burdens of the Egyptians, and I will deliver you from slavery to them, and I will *redeem* (גאל,

---

66. As noted above, adding υἱός αὐτοῦ to this phrase ("in his beloved Son"), as found in variant readings, does not change the referent. This is clearly Jesus Christ, since the benediction in 1:3 begins by identifying God as his God and Father.
67. See the translation note and variant reading noted above.
68. James R. Harrison, *Paul's Language of Grace in Its Graeco-Roman Context*, WUNT 2.172 (Tübingen: Mohr Siebeck, 2003), 268.
69. BDAG, 605–6. A classic work on redemption and its related concepts that still repays reading is Leon Morris, *The Apostolic Preaching of the Cross*, 3rd ed. (London: Tyndale, 1965; 1st ed., 1955), 11–64. For background on slavery and manumission see Henrik Mouritsen, *The Freedman in the Roman World* (Cambridge, Cambridge University Press, 2011).

> LXX λυτρόω) you with an outstretched arm and with great acts of judgment." (Exod 6:6, emphasis added; cf. Exod 15:13; Deut 7:8; 2 Sam 7:23; Mic 6:4)

Here and as also expressed in Eph 1:7, it is the Lord himself who acts as the great Kinsman to redeem his people (cf. 1:14; Col 1:13–14). In the case of Israel, redemption was from slavery in Egypt, but in the gospel for God's new covenant people drawn from all the clans of the earth (3:15), it is slavery to the guilt of sin and transgressions from which he eternally redeems all his people (cf. Rom 3:24–25; Heb 9:11–15).

The phrase "the forgiveness of our transgressions" in v. 7b is in apposition to "redemption through his blood."[70] Appositional phrases explain something further, but it would be inaccurate to think that a phrase in apposition must explain *everything*. What is said is that forgiveness from "our transgressions" (or "our sins," as Col 1:14) is integral to redemption because the bondage in transgressions and sins (Eph 2:1, 5) is the tyrannical rule of death from which humans cannot free themselves without God's initiative and grace (cf. Rom 8:23; Hodge, 41). While we may want Paul to explain the mechanics of the interrelation of redemption through Christ's blood and forgiveness more fully (as in the Epistle to the Hebrews), we must recall that this part of Ephesians is not an expansive discussion of these themes but a recounting in outline of God's magnificent works in praise of his grace.

1:8–9b *ἧς ἐπερίσσευσεν εἰς ἡμᾶς, ἐν πάσῃ σοφίᾳ καὶ φρονήσει, γνωρίσας ἡμῖν τὸ μυστήριον τοῦ θελήματος αὐτοῦ*, "which he lavished upon us in all wisdom and insight when he made known to us the mystery of his will." As noted under the previous section, this period, comprising vv. 8–9b, is structurally linked by identical words with the previous one. We will find this kind of repetition in other places as well (e.g., vv. 11–13). By this Paul develops what has just been said at greater length. Here, the link with the relative pronoun ἧς is to divine grace, expressed in the last colon* of v. 7. Once more, it is critical to grasp the nature of this material as a flow of oral utterances that are interrelated rather than a series of pithy statements meant to stand on their own.

70. Paul uses the noun ἄφεσις only here and in parallel Col 1:14; cf. πάρεσις, "passing over" of sins in Rom 3:25; cf. Eph 4:32.

The phrase "in all wisdom and insight"—like "in love" at the end of v. 4—may be taken either with the previous verb (ἐπερίσσευσεν, "he lavished") or with the participle that follows (γνωρίσας, "he made known"). The parallelism between vv. 4d–5a and v. 8b–9a is impressive:

ἐν ἀγάπῃ
  προορίσας
ἐν πάσῃ σοφίᾳ καὶ φρονήσει
  γνωρίσας

Hence, I am taking "wisdom and insight" to be how God reveals his gift of grace and further expresses that grace by making known to his people "the mystery of his will" (cf. Col 1:9; Prov 3:19; 8:1; Hodge, 42–45; Lincoln, 15–16, 29–30; Hoehner, 210–13). These terms all pile up to designate a divine revelation and acts that are definitive markers in redemptive history.

The term *mystery* has been taken down all sorts of winding paths (including the Graeco-Roman mystery religions).[71] There is nothing here to suggest that God is making known mysterious rites or rituals or is granting secrets to a select few, but rather he is broadcasting what he had eternally planned about the extravagant largesse of grace in the present time "to sum up all things in [Christ]" (v. 10b). Redemption in Christ had been prophesied earlier, but in such a way that its exact character was hidden until its historical fulfillment (see esp. 1 Cor 2:6–11; and "Excursus: The Mystery of Christ"). This idea rests on the fact that God has definitely moved to make himself the God of all nations at this stage in redemptive history. This was something he had always planned to do, but now in Christ he has inaugurated its expanding glory in Paul's ministry as apostle to the Gentiles "according to his good pleasure" (v. 9b; cf. 1 Tim 2:3–7). This is something more fully developed as Ephesians unfolds and will be dealt with in those places (including in the next period and esp. on 3:3–11).

---

71. Particularly by Rudolf Bultmann in a previous generation; for full discussion and survey of literature see Caragounis, *Ephesian* Mysterion; Markus N. A. Bockmuehl, *Revelation and Mystery in Ancient Judaism and Pauline Christianity* (Grand Rapids: Eerdmans, 1997; repr. of 1990 ed.). The term μυστήρια has the meaning "rituals" or "sacred rites" in the Ephesian inscriptions. These were not part of mystery religions per se but elements of public worship; e.g., τὰ μυστήρια τῆς θεοῦ [= Artemis] (*IvE* 3059; AD 2); and see the excursus below. Cf. Rogers, *Mysteries of Artemus of Ephesos.*

1:9c–10 *κατὰ τὴν εὐδοκίαν αὐτοῦ ἣν προέθετο ἐν αὐτῷ εἰς οἰκονομίαν τοῦ πληρώματος τῶν καιρῶν, ἀνακεφαλαιώσασθαι τὰ πάντα ἐν τῷ Χριστῷ, τὰ ἐπὶ τοῖς οὐρανοῖς καὶ τὰ ἐπὶ τῆς γῆς ἐν αὐτῷ*, "according to his good pleasure, which he purposed in him for the administration of the fullness of (all) eras to sum up all things in the Messiah, the things in heaven and things on earth in him." This period opens and closes with cola* ending in the phrase ἐν αὐτῷ ("in him"; vv. 9c and 10c). In the fourth colon* in particular (v. 10c), the phrase is redundant and unnecessary, since Paul had just said "in the Messiah" in v. 10b (see "Excursus: Articular Χριστός as Messianic Title"). Redundancy of this kind shows that Paul is interested in leaving the effect of "in him" on his hearers at the end of cola* and periods (instead of ἐπὶ τῆς γῆς, "on the earth," in v. 10c).

Verses 1:9c–10c contain one of the central statements of the opening benediction and of the epistle as a whole.[72] The incarnate Son as Messiah is the center of the Trinitarian God's redemptive work. This is what Paul means when he says that God's disclosed will and good pleasure (vv. 9a–b) was "to sum up all things in the Messiah" (ἀνακεφαλαιώσασθαι τὰ πάντα ἐν τῷ Χριστῷ, v. 10b).[73] The prophecies of Pss 2; 110 and elsewhere lead us

---

72. Caragounis sees the redemptive, cosmic "summing up" (ἀνακεφαλαίωσις) in Christ and in the church as the central theme of Ephesians and its unveiled mystery (*Ephesian* Mysterion, esp. 143–46).

73. The verb ἀνακεφαλαιόω appears here and in Rom 13:9 for the "summing up" of the whole law as love for one's neighber (see also a variant at Gal 5:14 for πληρόω, which parallels Rom 13:9; cf. BDAG, 65; Lincoln, 32–34). The term appears in literature and rhetoric for summaries (κεφάλαια) of one's point (Heb 8:1), but more commonly in daily life as a banking term (cf. Acts 22:28 for κεφάλαιον as a *sum* of money). Origen comments: "Bankers and similar people use the noun 'summation' (κεφάλαιον) when they add up accounts, and when they bring payments and expenses or receipts together in one sum total. I think the apostle drew on this source when he used the expression here" (Origen and Jerome, 97). It is natural to imagine that the Ephesians would also take ἀνακεφαλαιόω as a financial term, since the Ephesian Artemisium was well known as one of the biggest banking establishments in the province and its bankers guild was one of the largest and most powerful in the city. Temples ordinarily acted as banks or, more properly, depositories in antiquity, but the Artemisium was a central bank not only for private citizens but also for city-states for the province of Asia; cf. *IvE* 3065 and 454; Dio Chrysostom (*Or.* 31) and Aristides (*Or.* 23); discussion in Jerome Murphy-O'Connor, *St. Paul's Ephesus* (Collegeville, MN: Liturgical Press, 2008), 64–66; Paul Trebilco, *The Early Christians in Ephesus from Paul to Ignatius* (Grand Rapids: Eerdmans, 2008; first published 2004), 25–26.

here.[74] Christ's messianic work is a royal, forceful conquest over all "the things in heaven and things on earth in him" (v. 10c), "not only in this age but also in the age to come" (1:21), and thus God has acted definitively in the Messiah to bring world history to a climax in "the fullness of (all) eras" (v. 10a). Paul uses a more philosophical term than ἀνακεφαλαιόω in Col 1:17 for the same idea when he says that all things of the first creation and of the new creation "subsist" in Christ.[75] The work of Christ on the cross is the central axis for the history of all creation, whether in heaven or on earth (v. 10c), since he has redeemed his people with his blood (1:7) and silenced all hostile powers (cf. 1:19–23; 3:10; Hodge, 48–55; Hoehner, 219–22).

Christ's work as the central act in all history is also implied in the reference in v. 10 to the "fullness of (all) eras" (καιροί), which is tantamount to saying "the fulfillment of all time" (cf. Rom 5:6; Gal 4:4; Hoehner, 218–19, 301–4; Barth, 1:128–30). In some Greek conceptions—most notably that of Plato—time was regarded as a great cycle that kept revolving back on itself. But the Judaeo-Christian view expressed here is that history has an ultimate, cosmic goal, when all things will be consummated into a new creation (cf. on 2:10). Christ's coming has inaugurated that great event in ways that are still veiled yet irrevocably present.

1:11–12 Ἐν ᾧ καὶ ἐκληρώθημεν προορισθέντες κατὰ πρόθεσιν τοῦ τὰ πάντα ἐνεργοῦντος κατὰ τὴν βουλὴν τοῦ θελήματος αὐτοῦ εἰς τὸ εἶναι ἡμᾶς εἰς ἔπαινον δόξης αὐτοῦ τοὺς προηλπικότας ἐν τῷ Χριστῷ, "in whom also we who had hoped beforehand in the Messiah were apportioned to be for the praise of his glory, since we were predestined according to his plan who brings all things into effect in accordance with the counsel of his will." This period,

74. Cf. Nils A. Dahl, "The Messiahship of Jesus in Paul," in *The Crucified Messiah and Other Essays* (Minneapolis: Augsburg, 1974), 39.

75. πάντα ἐν αὐτῷ **συνέστηκεν**, "all things *subsist* in him" (emphasis added). Fittingly, this statement is the very center of the chiastic poem of Col 1:15–20; cf. S. M. Baugh, "The Poetic Form of Col 1:15-20," *WTJ* 47 (1985): 227–44. Markus Barth helpfully renders the phrase with ἀνακεφαλαιώσασθαι as "All things are to be comprehended under one head, the Messiah" (Barth, 1:76), and see Barth, 1:89–92, for discussion of various options in history for ἀνακεφαλαιόω here as well as my translation note on it above. See also Lincoln, 32–33, though note his statement: "The divine purpose is to sum up all things ἐν Χριστῷ" (Lincoln, 33), which is good, but he misquotes the text without the article in the phrase ἐν **τῷ** Χριστῷ; cf. the excursus below on articular Χριστός as the royal title "Messiah."

like the previous two, opens with a relative pronoun phrase that is repeated in the next one (ἐν ᾧ; vv. 11a and 13a). There is striking repetition of the *κατά* phrases in the second and third cola* (v. 11b–c), which emphasize God's will as the ultimate basis of his people's inheritance and the extension of his grace to those whom he predestines (προορισθέντες; v. 11a) for glory.

The verb ἐκληρώθημεν, rendered "we have been apportioned," is difficult here (hence the variant in a few early MSS, ἐκλήθημεν, "we were called"). The term normally refers to appointing someone to some office or function by drawing lots (κλῆρος).[76] The only LXX use of the term is in 1 Sam 14:41, where Jonathan and Saul are "taken by lot" through Urim and Thummim. Foerster takes the infinitive clause as referring to "those who had hoped beforehand in Christ" in v. 12a–b and as dependent on ἐκληρώθημεν as follows:

> It is an "appointment" or "determination" which affects men in their being. It is also the goal which is assigned to them in their calling. Materially, then, it is related to ἐκλήθημεν, but with the nuance, implicit in κλῆρος, that the call imparts something to the called, namely, a life's goal. (Foerster, *TDNT*, 3:765).

The idea is that the earliest, Jewish converts to the Messiah (τοὺς προηλπικότας), among whom Paul includes himself, were apportioned "to be for the praise of his glory."[77] This glory was advanced as they fulfilled their

---

76. See κλῆρος and κληρόω in Foerster, *TDNT*, 3:758–65. The κλῆρος can also refer to an inherited property assigned to one; hence it could be synonymous with κληρονομία (v. 14) and derived from this. The verb κληρόω might conceivably be rendered in v. 11 as "in whom *we have obtained an inheritance*" (BDAG, 548–49; though the meaning given above is seen as possible).

77. Cf. Col 1:12; O'Brien, 116–17. The substantive substantive ptc. τοὺς προηλπικότας is in apposition to ἡμᾶς in v. 12a. ("we ... [namely] who had hoped beforehand"). Its prepositional prefix (**προ**ηλπικότας) is simply temporal ("beforehand"), rather than the most unlikely interpretation of Halter that it relates to the church's preexistence (so Lincoln, 37). The perf. tense form of the ptc. is either the equivalent of a pluperfect idea (and hence strengthened by the temporal prefix πρό): "we who *had* hoped" (Burton, *Moods*, §156; cf. John 11:44; 1 Cor 15:19). The other way to take the force of the perf. tense here is intensive: "we who had earlier *fixed our hope* in the Messiah"; see K. L. McKay, *A New Syntax of the Verb in New Testament Greek*, SBG 5 (New York: Peter Lang, 1994), §3.4.6; cf. John 5:45; 2 Cor 1:10; 1 Tim 4:10; 5:5; 6:17.

appointed task of extending the gospel to the Gentiles (vv. 13–14), so that all together, both Jew and Greek, might be to the praise of God's glory (v. 14c).[78]

The participle προορισθέντες ("since we were predestined") is added to underline once again God's initiative in redeeming his people (also vv. 4–5, 9). The adverbial participle here explains that the apportioning (ἐκληρώθημεν) to serve God's glory in the gospel was determined by God before all time and is taken as explanatory in meaning here.[79]

The second and third cola* build to a crescendo the idea that God's actions in redemptive history are not haphazard, whimsical, or arbitrary but are the execution of his purpose in Christ, which he has fixed by his own council.[80] Three terms for God's will—πρόθεσις, βουλή, and θέλημα—are all used here in v. 11 to show that God's own will and that of no other directs his actions: "[H]e does according to his will among the host of heaven and among the inhabitants of the earth; and none can stay his hand or say to him, 'What have you done?' " (Dan 4:35).

The truth of God's omnipotence and independence from his creation stands in sharp contrast with the old pagan beliefs of the Ephesian audience, for whom even Zeus, "the father of the gods and of men," bowed to the inevitable will of the inscrutable fates (μοῖραι). One of the more memorable examples of this was when Zeus held up the golden scales and sorrowfully acknowledged that the death of his hero, Hector of Troy, at the hand of Achilles was sealed by the fates (Homer, *Il.* 22.207–13). The Ephesians themselves bowed to "Lady Luck" (or Fate) in their affairs by prefacing their many public actions with a dedication to the goddess Τυχή ("Luck"),

---

78. Alternatively, Hodge writes: "In either case it [τοὺς προηλπικότας] designates not the first converts to Christianity, but the Jews who, before the Gentiles, had the Messiah as the object of their hopes" (59); cf. Barth, 130–33; cf. Lincoln, 37; Hoehner, 231–33.

79. This is a type of causation; cf. Burton, *Moods*, §§439–40; Wallace, *Greek Grammar*, 662. Hoehner (228) takes the aor. ptc. as causal but makes it contemporaneous with the main verb because of its word order. Yet a cause must, at least logically, *precede* its effect, hence the aor. is previous in relative time. Word order does not determine semantic value of the aor. in this case; cf. Rom 5:1, 9–10; 6:18.

80. In classic Reformed theology, this divine council, termed in Latin *pactum salutis,* is the archetype of all subsequent divine covenants with mankind; cf. John V. Fesko, *Eternal Love: The Doctrine of the Covenant of Redemption* (forthcoming).

or more commonly Ἀγαθὴ Τυχή ("Good Luck").[81] In Paul's gospel there is no competing, arbitrary Luck, but an omnipotent God who has graciously revealed "the mystery of his will" in Christ (v. 9; cf. 2:8–10).

The phrase *κατὰ πρόθεσιν* can be rendered "by the design," expressing that God, who "brings all things into effect" (*τοῦ … ἐνεργοῦντος*), is acting out of a plan he has conceived of himself. The focus of this plan is seen especially in redemption revealed in Christ (so 3:10–11; cf. Rom 8:28; 9:11; 2 Tim 1:9). With *ἐνεργέω* ("effect"or "produce") here, Paul expresses the idea that God actually brings his designs into historical effect, whereas the rendering "who *works* all things" (e.g., NASB, NKJV, ESV) is not as clear because it may be taken as a project that is never quite finished. Especially when this verb is joined with the cognate noun *ἐνέργεια* ("effectiveness"), used in Eph 1:19 (cf. 3:7 and 4:16) for the manifestation of God's effective power, one sees the contrast with the attempts at power through magic, which permeated the culture of Ephesus and of many other places in antiquity (see comments on 1:19–23).

1:13 *Ἐν ᾧ καὶ ὑμεῖς ἀκούσαντες τὸν λόγον τῆς ἀληθείας, τὸ εὐαγγέλιον τῆς σωτηρίας ὑμῶν, ἐν ᾧ καὶ πιστεύσαντες ἐσφραγίσθητε τῷ πνεύματι τῆς ἐπαγγελίας τῷ ἁγίῳ*, "in whom you as well, when you heard the word of truth, the gospel of your salvation, in whom also when you believed, you were sealed with the promised Holy Spirit." The opening of this period with *ἐν ᾧ* (v. 13a; cf. v. 13c) matches that of the previous one (v. 11a), and both refer to Christ ("in him," v. 10c, and "in the Messiah," v. 12b). This kind of repetition marks the periods of this longer section (vv. 3–14). In the original setting, the centrality of Christ in all of God's working is reinforced time and again by all these repeated phrases when they were heard in an oral stream. There is also repetition of participles between v. 13a and v. 13c: *ἐν ᾧ καὶ ὑμεῖς ἀκούσαντες … ἐν ᾧ καὶ πιστεύσαντες* ("in whom you as well, when you heard … in whom also when you believed"), which further unifies the period.

By starting with a shift of focus to "you" in the opening phrase, with its nominative pronoun, the apostle moves from "*we* who had hoped beforehand" (v. 12b) to his audience (*ἐν ᾧ καὶ ὑμεῖς*, "in whom also *you*"),

81. Just a few of many dozens of examples are *IvE* 27, 269, 273, and 301, which span two centuries. The letter carrier of Ephesians, Tychicus ("Lucky," "Fortunate"; Eph 6:21), is named for this goddess; cf. Eutychus, "Good Luck" in Acts 20:9.

who are at least predominantly Gentiles (2:11–12; see also 2:22 for ἐν ᾧ καὶ ὑμεῖς). Paul is concerned in this verse to show that Gentile Christians are full members of the covenant community in Christ, which he will develop much more fully in Eph 2. Much of what Paul says in 1:3–14 foreshadows themes he will develop later in the epistle.

The aorist tense form of the two adverbial participles ἀκούσαντες (v. 13a) and πιστεύσαντες (v. 13c) would normally communicate that their events are temporally prior to that of the main verb in v. 13d, ἐσφραγίσθητε, "you were sealed." This temporal priority, though, may give way to logical priority, as is the case with the second participle, "when you believed" (πιστεύσαντες). Faith is required for this sealing of the Spirit, but the sealing and faith may occur simultaneously since the Holy Spirit is the one who works faith in the believer as a divine gift (see on 2:8; cf. Phil 1:29).[82]

The phrase "you were sealed *with* the Spirit" (τῷ πνεύματι) rather than "*by* the Spirit" (which would be expressed as ὑπὸ τοῦ πνεύματος), in which the Spirit would be the agent of the sealing, expresses the idea that God the Father (v. 3a)—who is the subject of the central verbs in vv. 3–14—has performed the sealing and that the Spirit is himself the seal (see also 4:30). This is fitting with v. 14, where the Spirit is himself the ἀρραβών ("guarantee") of the Christian's full inheritance.[83]

Sealing in the NT has the function of closing up an enclosure (Matt 27:66; Rev 20:3) or a scroll (e.g., Rev 5:1; 10:4; 22:10), or it acts to authenticate something (John 3:33; 6:27; 1 Cor 9:2; 2 Cor 1:22; 2 Tim 2:19; Rev 7:2), to mark ownership, or to provide protection from harm (Rev 7:3–5; cf. Ezek 9:3–6). In Ephesians 1:13, because it is joined with the notion of "a guarantee of our inheritance" in v. 14, the sealing certifies the reality of "your salvation" through faith (v. 13). By receiving the promised

82. It is possible to read the two aor. ptcs. in v. 13 as "parallel" with the indic. ἐσφραγίσθητε, which means that they are the equivalent of saying all three with indics. joined by καί or another conj. The logical interrelations of the events are still only understood from context.

83. See esp. 2 Cor 1:22: ὁ καὶ σφραγισάμενος ἡμᾶς καὶ δοὺς τὸν ἀρραβῶνα τοῦ πνεύματος ἐν ταῖς καρδίαις ἡμῶν, "and who has also put his seal on us and given us his Spirit in our hearts as a guarantee." It is possible to read the dative τῷ πνεύματι in Eph 1:13d as a dative of agency, but it is not preferred; cf. Wallace, *Greek Grammar*, 373–74; Eph 4:30, τὸ πνεῦμα τὸ ἅγιον τοῦ θεοῦ **ἐν ᾧ** ἐσφραγίσθητε, "the Holy Spirit of God, *in whom* you were sealed."

Holy Spirit (see esp. Gal 3:14), Gentiles can know without doubt that God's salvation has extended not only to Abraham's natural children but to all his children in Christ, who share Abraham's faith (e.g., Acts 10:44–48; Rom 4:16–18; Gal 3:8–9, 29).

From very early times, sealing with the Spirit here was identified as a reference to Christian baptism.[84] While it is true that baptism, like circumcision, is a "seal of the righteousness of faith" (Rom 4:11; as well as a "sign"), the sealing in Eph 1:13 is not itself the sacrament of baptism. It is the reception of the Holy Spirit through faith, even though in Acts overt signs of the Spirit's presence accompanied Christian baptism (e.g., Acts 19:1–7 at Ephesus).[85] This is part of the reality to which baptism connects the believer.

A further notion defended recently by Rodney Thomas understands the sealing here as providing protection from harmful spirits.[86] This interpretation conforms well with the magical background behind much of Ephesians, which will be examined especially under 1:15–23 and also fits well with Paul's concern for Christian assurance here. Thomas concludes:

> By linking the Holy Spirit so closely with the inheritance promised to Christians, the writer is able to bolster very powerfully the confidence of his audience. They, as believers, share Christ's position of heavenly authority over the "powers." This counters, in a very potent way, the fear and the temptations of the magical influences of their environment, in western Asia Minor. The seat [*sic* for "seal"] of the Holy Spirit then becomes for them the talisman above all other talismans and the protection from all forms of magical influence and the temptation of reliance upon magic.[87]

While this is an attractive and well-argued position, it fits the context of Eph 1:13–14 better to see this seal as a certification of the reality that salvation has now extended to the Gentiles as an inbreaking of the eschaton

84. Cf. G. W. H. Lampe, *The Seal of the Spirit* (New York: Longmans, Green, 1951).
85. Cf. excellent brief discussion in Ferguson, *Holy Spirit,* 162, 180–82.
86. Rodney Thomas, "The Seal of the Spirit and the Religious Climate of Ephesus," *ResQ* 43 (2001): 155–66; cf. E. Woodcock, "The Seal of the Holy Spirit," *BSac* 155 (1998): 139–63.
87. Thomas, "Seal of the Spirit," 166.

(see summary comments below), rather than having a protective function (cf. Arnold, 92–93; Hoehner, 238–39).

The Holy Spirit is presented in v. 13 as "promised" (τῆς ἐπαγγελίας), or even more strongly in Gal 3:14 with the epexegetical genitive τὴν ἐπαγγελίαν τοῦ πνεύματος, "the promise of the Spirit" (cf. Acts 1:4–5). The Spirit himself as the believer's "seal" is the eschatological fulfillment of the divine promise of a new creation (cf. Isa 32:15; 44:3; Ezek 36:26–28; 37:14; Joel 2:28–31), which is inaugurated at the first advent of the Messiah and is projected into the life of the believer through the Holy Spirit (see on 2:10, 21–22).

1:14 ὅ ἐστιν ἀρραβὼν τῆς κληρονομίας ἡμῶν, εἰς ἀπολύτρωσιν τῆς περιποιήσεως, εἰς ἔπαινον τῆς δόξης αὐτοῦ, "who is a down payment of our inheritance for redemption of his prized possession for the praise of his glory." The long paragraph of vv. 3–14 concludes with its shortest period, which has only three cola*, whereas the earlier ones consist of four or five cola*. The presenter of the material would give a longer pause at the end of the periodic sentence, and this shorter period moves into the break a little quicker. However, the period ends with a colon* that has only one short syllable with eight long, ending with dignity appropriate for divine praise.[88] Furthermore, the whole piece ends with αὐτοῦ (as also in four previous periods, vv. 4–9), continuing the focus throughout on God in Christ. Finally, it should not be lost on us that the whole praise of God in this benediction in vv. 3–14 concludes with the words "for the praise of his glory" as a kind of refrain echoing vv. 6a and 12a.

Ephesians 1:14 opens with an expansion on the previous phrase, "Holy Spirit of promise" (v. 13d), who is the "seal" of the Father on these Gentile believers (and by implication on all believers). In the expansion Paul notes that this sealing by the Spirit constitutes a "down payment" or "guarantee" of the believer's inheritance. Much work has been done on ἀρραβών, rendered here as "down payment." There are two main ideas possible: deposit of some object to guarantee payment, which is returned when payment is made ("pledge"; e.g., Judah's possessions used as pledge for payment of a child to Tamar in Gen 38:16–18), or partial payment of the obligation, which might constitute a significant portion of the whole that would be

88. Two syllables with otherwise short omicrons are long by position: εις επαινον της δοξης αυτου.

retained against the debt when the remainder is paid.[89] Jerome understands the second meaning in our passage and is followed by many other early fathers; it is the preferred meaning in Eph 1:14, as explained in the discussion below.[90]

In v. 7, Paul had expressed that ἀπολύτρωσις was "redemption" from bondage to the guilt of transgressions through Christ's mediatorial death. Here in v. 14, the apostle calls those who are redeemed ἡ περιποιήσις, rendered "his prized possession."[91] While this unusual word may refer to the act of "preservation" (e.g., Heb 10:39) and thus be understood as something like "redemption of those who are to be preserved" (cf. LSJ, 1384), it makes better sense because of the connection with "inheritance" in v. 14a to understand it as referring to the redeemed as the Lord's unique and prized possession (as 1 Pet 2:9; cf. 1 Thess 5:9; 2 Thess 2:14; Titus 2:14), "which he obtained with his own blood" (Acts 20:28). "Paul speaks of believers as God's possession. ... [H]ere the thought ties back with 1:5, where Paul says that God has chosen and predestined believers to adoption *for himself*" (Arnold, 93; emphasis original). All believers are *his* inheritance, as were the Levites under the old covenant in fulfillment of his promise: "They shall be mine, says the LORD of hosts, in the day when I make up my treasured possession" (Mal 3:17).[92]

By being sealed with the Holy Spirit, believers come to possess by faith *now* the "down payment of our inheritance" (v. 14), which will be consummated in the future. This inheritance centers on his people's resurrection in the new creation, of which the Spirit is the mediating agent (Rom 1:4; 8:11;

89. LSJ, 246, and supplement, 52; BDAG, 134; "first installment," in A. J. Kerr, "*ARRABŌN*," *JTS* 39 (1988): 92–97.
90. Jerome writes: "The Latin word *pignus* has been used to translate the Greek ἀρραβων. But *pignus* does not signify precisely that which *arrhabon* does. For an *arrhabon* is given for a future purchase, as if it were some proof and obligation. Security, on the other hand, that is ἐνέχυρον, is pledged for a loan so that when the loan has been repaid the security owed to the borrower is returned by the creditor" (Origen and Jerome, 104). Cf. Barnabas Ahern, "The Indwelling Spirit, Pledge of Our Inheritance (Eph 1:14)," *CBQ* 9 (1947): 179–89.
91. BDAG, 804; cf. Barth, 1:97; Gnilka, 87; Lincoln, 41–42; O'Brien, 121–23; Hoehner, 244; cf. Schnackenburg, 67. See also translation note on this phrase above.
92. Heb. סגלה; LXX: ἐγὼ ποιῶ εἰς περιποίησιν; cf. Exod 19:5; Psa 135:4; Deut 7:6; 14:2; 26:18; Num 3:12, 45; 8:14; Josh 14:3–4; 18:7. In 1 Chr 29:3 and Eccl 2:8 this Hebrew word refers to royal treasure; see Lipiński, *TDOT*, 10.144–48.

cf. 1 Cor 15:35–50).[93] Finally, in v. 14b, having this inheritance confirmed in believers through the Spirit leads to "redemption" and a "sealing" for a (future) "day of redemption" (4:30), which is the day of the church's "adoption, the redemption of our bodies" (Rom 8:23; cf. Eph 1:5a).

Biblical Theology Comments

The teaching on the Holy Spirit in the whole of Eph 1:3–14 is more fully expressed in 1 Cor 15 and the interconnections that center on the resurrection of Christ as "firstfruits," that is, as the inauguration of the general resurrection (1 Cor 15:20, 23). There in 1 Corinthians and here in Ephesians, the Spirit is the intrusion of the new creation into this age, signaled by his being *promised* and now given because the victorious Messiah dispenses the Spirit as part of the largesse of his great victory on the cross (cf. 4:8; John 16:7). Moreover, Christ himself, because he is "from heaven" (1 Cor 15:47) and therefore "high-heavenly" (ὁ ἐπουράνιος; 1 Cor 15:48; see Eph 1:3e), has become the "life-giving spirit" (πνεῦμα ζῳοποιοῦν; 1 Cor 15:45) of a new human race as Last Adam. Therefore, those who are united to him by faith are "the high-heavenly ones" (οἱ ἐπουράνιοι; 1 Cor 15:48) who will be raised with bodies that are "high-heavenly" (σώματα ἐπουράνια; 1 Cor 15:40) through the operation of the Spirit, so that this resurrected body can be called "spiritual" (σῶμα πνευματικόν; 1 Cor 15:44; cf. "spiritual blessings" in Eph 1:3d). The believer's inheritance, then, is fulfilled in the kingdom of God with eternal incorruptibility (1 Cor 15:50; Eph 5:5).[94]

Application and Devotional Implications

Paul recounts three times in 1:3–14 how God's incredible redemption, revealed and accomplished in Christ, redounds "for the praise of the glory of his grace" (v. 6) and "for praise of his glory" (vv. 12, 14). For this reason, Paul not only recounts these as facts, but he is here *praising* the glory of his grace in the benediction form: "Blessed (be) the God and Father of our

---

93. See also Eph 3:6, where inheritance and entering into the promise are associated.

94. Obviously, Paul's teaching in 1 Cor 15:20–58 is especially important for these connections; cf. Peter Jones, "Paul Confronts Paganism in the Church: A Case Study of First Corinthians 15:45," *JETS* 49 (2006): 713–37; Vos, "Eschatological Aspect," 91–125.

Lord Jesus Christ …" Here doctrine and practice meet in sweet fellowship of grateful praise.

Ephesians 1:3–14 is a very full passage with many other recurring themes: "[E]very blessing of the Spirit … you were sealed with the promised Holy Spirit," "In love he predestined us … we were predestined according to his plan," and "according to the good pleasure of his will … according to his good pleasure which he purposed … according to his plan … in accordance with the counsel of his will." The most prominent recurrence occurs at the end of each of the periods: "In Christ … before him … his grace … his grace … his good pleasure … in him … in Christ … the promised Holy Spirit … his glory." Each of these words ends with one or more long syllable, mirroring the divine dignity of the subject matter.[95] In this passage, all focus of praise is on God in Christ through the Spirit.

Time and again, Paul emphasizes God's initiative in planning, ordaining, executing, and then revealing our redemption. In fact, the only thing we contribute is hearing and believing (v. 13), and these are themselves the reception of grace, not initiatory or meritorious actions (cf. 2:8–10). In all other cases, the Father is the subject of the other acts: He blesses, chooses, predestines, purposes, forgives (v. 7), lavishes grace, seals, and redeems his treasured possession, among the many other things given here. The monergism of redemption cannot be expressed any more clearly (cf. 1 Cor 1:26–31; Hodge, 38).

To make the initiative of God even more profoundly understood, Paul expresses in v. 4 that this was "before the foundation of the world." There can be no mistaking that God originates his grace from his eternally conceived plan (vv. 9, 11). And Paul emphasizes, again through repetition, that this plan conforms only to God's "good pleasure" (εὐδοκία; vv. 5, 9), "will" (v. 5; cf. v. 9a), and "the council of his will" (v. 11) rather than to any external forces or other considerations. This is a large part of how we are to understand grace.

Grace is certainly at the heart of our passage, as can be seen in these interlocking phrases: "for praise of the glory of his *grace* which he bestowed on us in his Beloved … according to the riches of his *grace* which he lavished

---

95. See the introduction for Greek compositional style features in which long syllables were used to convey the related effects of "dignity" (ἀξίωμα), "grandeur" (μέγεθος), and "solemnity" (σεμνότης); see Hermogenes, *Style* 1.5–6.

upon us" (vv. 6–8). The interconnectedness of this section can be seen more clearly in the periodic structure, where a period ending in *grace* is advanced with a relative pronoun at the start of the next one:

C	…
	εἰς ἔπαινον δόξης **τῆς χάριτος αὐτοῦ**
D	ἧς ἐχαρίτωσεν ἡμᾶς ἐν τῷ ἠγαπημένῳ
	…
	κατὰ τὸ πλοῦτος **τῆς χάριτος αὐτοῦ**
E	ἧς ἐπερίσσευσεν εἰς ἡμᾶς …

The exact character of grace is seen in the divine initiation and grant: he "bestows" it and "lavishes" it on us in accordance with his eternal plan; it is not something we stumble across or attain to on our own or through our own efforts.[96] This comes out within Eph 1:6–7 by clear implication: Grace is bestowed "in his Beloved." In keeping with the repeated theme that all the benefits of redemption are mediated through the incarnate Son, Paul names and refers to him in various ways in vv. 3–14 a total of thirteen times. Indeed, mediation is the critical component in Paul's conception of "grace," a term he uses technically at times.[97] The necessity of mediation is implicit in 1:7 in the statement that we need "redemption" through Christ's blood and "forgiveness of our transgressions." It is common for one to hear that grace is "God's unmerited favor" (e.g., Hoehner, 149). But this and other passages in Paul clearly show that grace is better understood as God's favor lavished on those who deserve his wrath. We were "dead in our sins and transgressions" as "sons of wrath" and willing allies in the devil's militant army (2:2–3), but God out of his pure grace rescued us out of those

---

96. Contrasting the medieval dictum: *Facientibus quod in se est, Deus non denegat gratiam* ("God does not withhold grace to those who do what is in them" [i.e., "do their best"]). This does not diminish the necessity of faith in the process or the fact that we truly believe of our own volition through God's gift, but rather the divine initiative is the source of faith's objective reality. For grace and its covenantal foundations see Michael Horton, *Covenant and Salvation* (Louisville: Westminster John Knox, 2007), 130–39.

97. This was discussed briefly in S. M. Baugh, "Galatians 5:1–6 and Personal Obligation: Reflections on Paul and the Law," in *The Law Is Not of Faith: Essays on Works and Grace in the Mosaic Covenant*, ed. Bryan D. Estelle, John V. Fesko, and David VanDrunen (Phillipsburg, NJ: P&R, 2009), 262–63.

foul ranks into newness of life in his Son. This is grace indeed—and love (v. 4e; 2:4).

The obvious result of Paul's lavish paean of praise to our Triune God is that we should join him in praise as well. Too often we focus our prayers on requests from the Father. Here and many places elsewhere we are shown how to simply focus our praises on God. While there is repetition here, this is not mere restatement of bare phrases, but the unfolding of a rich tapestry of praise. We would do well to memorize Eph 1:3–14, recite it frequently, and then adapt and expand on it as we join the worldwide chorus of the saints "for praise of the glory of his grace, which he bestowed on us in his Beloved."

Additional Exegetical Comments: Redemption

In our world, "redemption" (ἀπολύτρωσις, 1:7) refers most often to the exchange of coupons for discounts on goods in a store, but to the Ephesians and to other contemporaries of Paul, "redemption" would have been used most frequently to buy someone out of slavery through payment (λύτρον or pl. λύτρα, "ransom"). In the first century BC, because of the dominance of pirates in the eastern Mediterranean at that time, "redemption" often occurred in payment of ransom for someone who had been kidnapped.[98] The most famous example of this was the kidnapping of a young Julius Caesar off the island of Pharmacusa; he avenged himself on his captors after his redemption by returning and crucifying them to the last man.[99]

Though pirates were no longer such a large threat in Paul's day, he does mention elsewhere "enslavers" as among "the lawless and disobedient ... the ungodly and sinners" (1 Tim 1:9–10). This word "enslaver" (ἀνδραποδιστής) may better refer to a "slave-dealer" or "kidnapper" (LSJ, 128; BDAG, 76),

98. As, e.g., Joseph (Gen 37:28). Origen writes: " 'Redemption' [or] deliverance has to do with prisoners and those who have come under the power of enemies. And we had come under the power of enemies, namely 'the ruler of this world' and the evil powers under him (2 Cor 4:4; Eph 2:2) and for this reason were in need of redemption and of him who purchased us, that he might receive us back who were alienated from him" (Origen and Jerome, 91).

99. Plutarch, *Caesar* 1.4–2.4; cf. Velleius Paterculus, 2.42; Suetonius, *Jul.* 4. Caesar had the help of supporters and ships from Miletus, a near neighbor of Ephesus (Acts 20:17).

something the Ephesians were well familiar with, since their city was home to a Roman slave wholesale market (see comment on 6:5). Some of these slaves may have been kidnapped in the inland areas of Asia Minor (cf. possibly 2 Cor 11:26).

Where the everyday background of ἀπολύτρωσις in antiquity breaks down as an analogy for Christ's redemption of his people is in the nonmonetary price of the believer's redemption: "knowing that you were ransomed from the futile ways inherited from your forefathers, not with perishable things such as silver or gold, but with the precious blood of Christ, like that of a lamb without blemish or spot" (1 Pet 1:18–19); "in whom we have our redemption through his blood" (Eph 1:7). "Blood" here refers to the cross (Col 1:20, "through the blood of his cross") and is a synecdoche* for Christ's death on the believer's behalf.

The mention of redemption "through his blood" shows that the instrument of the believer's purchase from "transgressions" (1:7) was accomplished through Christ's substitutionary, priestly mediation as an ἱλαστήριον ("propitiatory sacrifice"; Rom 3:25, and see esp. Rom 3:23–26; cf. Eph 1:14; 2:13; 4:30; Heb 9:11–15). Christ intervened on our behalf and stood in our place so that his death is our death and his life becomes our life (Gal 2:19–20) to deliver us from divine wrath (Rom 5:9). Hence, Christ's blood brings believers near to God and makes peace with him (see 2:13–14).

Selected Bibliography

Ahern, B. "The Indwelling Spirit, Pledge of Our Inheritance (Eph 1:14)." *CBQ* 9 (1947): 179–89.

Barkhuizen, J. H. "The Strophic Structure of the Eulogy of Ephesians 1:3–14." *Hormormde Teologiese Studies* 46 (1990): 390–413.

Baugh, S. M. "A Foreign World: Ephesus in the First Century." In *Women in the Church*, 2nd ed., ed. A. Kostenberger and T. Schreiner, 13–38. Grand Rapids: Baker, 2005.

Bockmuehl, M. *Revelation and Mystery in Ancient Judaism and Pauline Christianity*. Grand Rapids: Eerdmans, 1997. Repr. of 1990 ed.

Brannon, M. *The Heavenlies in Ephesians: A Lexical, Exegetical, and Conceptual Analysis*. LNTS. London: T&T Clark, 2011.

Burke, T. J. *Adopted into God's Family*. NSBT 22. Downers Grove, IL: InterVarsity Press, 2006.

Cambier, J. "La Bénédiction D'Eph 1 3–14." *ZNW* 54 (1963): 58–104.

Caragounis, C. C. *The Ephesian* Mysterion: *Meaning and Context.* Lund: CWK Gleerup, 1977.

Coutts, J. "Ephesians 1:3–14 and 1 Peter 1:3–12." *NTS* 3 (1957): 115–27.

Ferguson, S. *The Holy Spirit.* Downers Grove, IL: InterVarsity Press, 1996.

Gardner, J. *Family and* Familia *in Roman Law and Life.* Oxford: Clarendon, 1998.

Gordley, M. *Teaching through Song in Antiquity.* WUNT 2.302. Tübingen: Mohr Siebeck, 2011.

Harris, H., III. "'The Heavenlies' Reconsidered: Οὐρανός and Ἐπουράνιος in Ephesians." *BSac* 148 (1991): 72–89.

Harrison, J. *Paul's Language of Grace in Its Graeco-Roman Context.* WUNT 2.172. Tübingen: Mohr Siebeck, 2003.

Head, P. M. "Named Letter-Carriers among the Oxyrhynchus Papyri." *JSNT* 31 (2009): 279–99.

Horton, M. *Covenant and Eschatology: The Divine Drama.* Louisville: Westminster John Knox, 2002.

———. *Covenant and Salvation.* Louisville: Westminster John Knox, 2007.

Kerr, A. J. "*ARRABŌN.*" *JTS* 39 (1988): 92–97.

Krentz, E. "Epideiktik and Hymnody: The New Testament and Its World." *BR* 40 (1995): 50–97.

Lampe, G. W. H. *The Seal of the Spirit.* New York: Longmans, Green, 1951.

Lincoln, A. T. *Paradise Now and Not Yet.* SNTSMS. Cambridge: Cambridge University Press, 1981.

Lindsay, H. *Adoption in the Roman World.* Cambridge: Cambridge University Press, 2009.

Morris, L. *The Apostolic Preaching of the Cross.* 3rd ed. London: Tyndale, 1965. 1st ed., 1955.

Mouritsen, H. *The Freedman in the Roman World.* Cambridge: Cambridge University Press, 2011.

Oster, R. "Ephesus as a Religious Center under the Principate." *ANRW* 2.18.3 (1990): 1661–1728.

———. "The Ephesian Artemis as an Opponent of Early Christianity." *JAC* 19 (1976): 24–44.

Peppard, M. " 'Poetry', 'Hymns' and 'Traditional Material' in New Testament Epistles or How to Do Things with Indentations." *JSNT* 30 (2008): 319–42.

Robbins, C. J. "The Composition of Eph. 1:3–14." *JBL* 105 (1986): 677–87.

Rogers, G. M. *The Mysteries of Artemis of Ephesos: Cult, Polis, and Change in the Graeco-Roman World.* New Haven, CT: Yale University Press, 2012.

———. *The Sacred Identiy of Ephesos.* New York: Routledge, 1991.

Scott, J. M. *Adoption as Sons of God: An Exegetical Investigation into the Background of Huiothesia in the Pauline Corpus.* WUNT 2.48. Tübingen: Mohr Siebeck, 1992.

Smith, J. *Christ the Ideal King*. WUNT 2.313. Tübingen: Mohr Siebeck, 2011.

Thomas, R. "The Seal of the Spirit and the Religious Climate of Ephesus." *ResQ* 43 (2001): 155–66.

Trebilco, P. *The Early Christians in Ephesus from Paul to Ignatius*. Grand Rapids: Eerdmans, 2008. First published 2004.

Vos, G. "The Eschatological Aspect of the Pauline Conception of the Spirit." In *Redemptive History and Biblical Interpretation: The Shorter Writings of Geerhardus Vos*, ed. R. Gaffin Jr., 91–125. Phillipsburg, NJ: P&R, 1980. Repr. of 1912 essay.

Woodcock, E. "The Seal of the Holy Spirit." *BSac* 155 (1998): 139–63.

Paul Reports on His Prayer for Insight (1:15–23)

Introduction

In Epheisans 1:15–23 Paul reports on his prayers for the recipients' deeper understanding of their God himself and of his redemptive gifts and power for his people in Christ. This passage is itself not a prayer but a report of his intercession on the Ephesians' behalf. In the opening of his other epistles Paul often mentions that he is praying for his correspondents and gives some indication of the content of those prayers (Rom 1:9–10; 1 Cor 1:4; Phil 1:3–4; Col 1:3–4; 1 Thess 1:2–3; 2 Tim 1:3; Phlm 4–5). In Ephesians 1:15–23 Paul subtly turns this prayer report into a vehicle to partially accomplish his prayer by offering instruction on some of the profound truths he hopes his audience will grow to see with "the eyes of your heart" (v. 18); in particular, he helps them to grasp the sovereign power of God applied to them in the exalted Messiah, in vv. 18–23.

Ephesians 1:15–23 picks up certain threads from vv. 3–14 about believers' redemptive inheritance (vv. 3, 14, 18), the revelation of the knowledge of God (8–9, 17), and the all-encompassing sovereign centrality of Christ in this age (vv. 10, 20–22) and develops them further. Paul is also laying the basis here for certain themes to be developed as the epistle unfolds, especially in the next section (2:1–10).

As in the previous section, vv. 15–23 consists of a long periodic "sentence" that spans the whole of these verses, which can be divided into six periods that are close in their function to English sentences.[1] As a reminder,

1. See the introduction for periodic analysis, including the necessity to cross "verse" boundaries at times. Even ancient readers were not always certain of the exact division of periods and cola* of someone else's work that they had not heard presented

a Greek period is not a grammatically self-contained unit like an English sentence but a division of an oral presentation marked by some "rounding off" before the reader/presenter takes a breath.[2]

Ephesians 1:15–23 was not composed quite as elaborately as the previous section (vv. 3–14), which is understandable given their different functions in the epistle. Verses 3–14 represent a form of prayer and act as an introduction to themes to be developed as the epistle unfolds—these verses were obviously composed very carefully. The current section moves into Paul's report of his prayers for the audience and, as such, he reveals his desire for their stronger grasp of the truths of God's working in Christ. It is a more prosaic elaboration of his desires for their own deeper understanding, although it has some nice stylistic features, which will be observed in the course of the comments below.

Ephesians 1:15–23 is divisible into six periods, as follows:

A
15 Διὰ τοῦτο κἀγὼ ἀκούσας
τὴν καθ' ὑμᾶς πίστιν ἐν τῷ κυρίῳ Ἰησοῦ
καὶ τὴν ἀγάπην τὴν εἰς πάντας τοὺς ἁγίους
16 οὐ παύομαι εὐχαριστῶν ὑπὲρ ὑμῶν
μνείαν ποιούμενος ἐπὶ τῶν προσευχῶν μου

B
17 ἵνα ὁ θεὸς τοῦ κυρίου ἡμῶν Ἰησοῦ Χριστοῦ, ὁ πατὴρ τῆς δόξης
δώῃ ὑμῖν πνεῦμα σοφίας καὶ ἀποκαλύψεως εν επιγνώσει αὐτοῦ
18 πεφωτισμένους τοὺς οφθαλμοὺς τῆς καρδίας
εἰς τὸ εἰδέναι ὑμᾶς

C
τίς ἐστιν ἡ ἐλπὶς τῆς κλήσεως αὐτοῦ
τίς ὁ πλοῦτος τῆς δόξης τῆς κληρονομίας αὐτοῦ ἐν τοῖς ἁγίοις
19 καὶ τί τὸ ὑπερβάλλον μέγεθος τῆς δυνάμεως αὐτοῦ
εἰς ἡμᾶς τοὺς πιστεύοντας
κατὰ τὴν ἐνέργειαν τοῦ κράτους τῆς ἰσχύος αὐτοῦ

by the author, but the analysis given here makes better sense for the division of the text than the too-often-whimsical modern versification and punctuation.

2. This is explained in the introduction under compositional analysis.

D 20 Ἣν ἐνήργησεν ἐν τῷ Χριστῷ
ἐγείρας αὐτὸν ἐκ νεκρῶν καὶ καθίσας ἐν δεξιᾷ αὐτοῦ
ἐν τοῖς οπουρανίοις

E 21 ὑπεράνω πάσης ἀρχῆς καὶ ἐξουσίας
καὶ δυνάμεως καὶ κυριότητος
καὶ παντὸς ὀνόματος ὀνομαζομένου
οὐ μόνον ἐν τῷ αἰῶνι τούτῳ ἀλλὰ καὶ ἐν τῷ μέλλοντι

F 22 καὶ πάντα ὑπέταξεν ὑπὸ τοὺς πόδας αὐτοῦ
καὶ αὐτὸν ἔδωκεν κεφαλὴν ὑπὲρ πάντα τῇ ἐκκλησίᾳ
23 ἥτις ἐστὶν τὸ σῶμα αὐτοῦ
τὸ πλήρωμα τοῦ τὰ πάντα ἐν πᾶσιν πληρουμένου.

While we do not have the kind of repetitions "in Christ," "in him," etc., as found in vv. 3–14, the composition of this larger section (vv. 15–23) develops from seemingly ordinary epistolary reporting about Paul's concern for his audience (vv. 15–16) and then deftly builds up to greater and greater magnification on the workings of the "Father of glory" (v. 17), whose overwhelming power in the resurrection and glorification of his Son is described with an imposing string of synonyms to bring out "the superabundant greatness of his power toward us who believe in accordance with the effectiveness of the strength of his might" (v. 19). This leads to lavish statements about Christ's ultimate suzerainty over all things in this age and in the next (v. 21; cf. v. 10).

Paul expresses excitement about the truth of Christ's rule "far above all rule and authority and power and lordship" in v. 21a–b by increasing the speed of his diction in the next colon* (v. 21c), where the participle is not strictly necessary. The "rapidity" (γοργότης; Lat. *velocitas*; Hermogenes, *Id.* 2.1) is communicated by the notable predominance of short syllables here, καὶ παντὸς ὀνόματος ὀνομαζομένου ("and every name that can be named," v. 21c), which has nine short syllables compared with only four long. The culmination of the whole periodic sentence is an explosive last colon*, where all words but one begin with a plosive *tau* or *pi*: **τὸ πλήρωμα τοῦ τὰ πάντα** ἐν **πᾶσιν πληρουμένου** ("the fullness of him who fills everything entirely," v. 23b; with predominance of long syllables here lending the statement dignity—see comment).

Outline

III. Paul Reports on His Prayer for Insight (1:15–23)
- A. When and how Paul is praying (1:15–16)
- B. Object of this prayer for the audience (1:17–18b)
- C. Content of insight for which Paul prays (1:18c–19)
- D. Expansion on Christ's exaltation in power over creation (1:20–21)
- E. Christ's exaltation and the church (1:22–23)

Original Text

15 Διὰ τοῦτο κἀγὼ ἀκούσας τὴν καθ' ὑμᾶς πίστιν ἐν τῷ κυρίῳ[a] Ἰησοῦ καὶ τὴν
ἀγάπην[b] τὴν εἰς πάντας τοὺς ἁγίους **16** οὐ παύομαι εὐχαριστῶν ὑπὲρ ὑμῶν
μνείαν ποιούμενος ἐπὶ τῶν προσευχῶν μου, **17** ἵνα ὁ θεὸς τοῦ κυρίου ἡμῶν Ἰησοῦ
Χριστοῦ, ὁ πατὴρ τῆς δόξης, δώῃ ὑμῖν πνεῦμα σοφίας καὶ ἀποκαλύψεως ἐν
ἐπιγνώσει αὐτοῦ, **18** πεφωτισμένους τοὺς ὀφθαλμοὺς τῆς καρδίας[c] εἰς τὸ εἰδέναι
ὑμᾶς τίς ἐστιν ἡ ἐλπὶς τῆς κλήσεως αὐτοῦ, τίς ὁ πλοῦτος τῆς δόξης τῆς κληρονομίας αὐτοῦ ἐν τοῖς ἁγίοις, **19** καὶ τί τὸ ὑπερβάλλον μέγεθος τῆς δυνάμεως αὐτοῦ
εἰς ἡμᾶς τοὺς πιστεύοντας κατὰ τὴν ἐνέργειαν τοῦ κράτους τῆς ἰσχύος αὐτοῦ.
20 Ἣν ἐνήργησεν ἐν τῷ Χριστῷ ἐγείρας αὐτὸν ἐκ νεκρῶν καὶ καθίσας ἐν δεξιᾷ
αὐτοῦ ἐν τοῖς ἐπουρανίοις **21** ὑπεράνω πάσης ἀρχῆς καὶ ἐξουσίας καὶ δυνάμεως
καὶ κυριότητος καὶ παντὸς ὀνόματος ὀνομαζομένου, οὐ μόνον ἐν τῷ αἰῶνι τούτῳ
ἀλλὰ καὶ ἐν τῷ μέλλοντι· **22** καὶ πάντα ὑπέταξεν ὑπὸ τοὺς πόδας αὐτοῦ καὶ
αὐτὸν ἔδωκεν κεφαλὴν ὑπὲρ πάντα τῇ ἐκκλησίᾳ, **23** ἥτις ἐστὶν τὸ σῶμα αὐτοῦ,
τὸ πλήρωμα τοῦ τὰ πάντα ἐν πᾶσιν πληρουμένου.

Textual Notes

15.a. P^{46} adds a personal pronoun in the phrase: ἐν τῷ κυρίῳ **ἡμῶν** Ἰησοῦ. This kind of variant occurs frequently in the MSS where the article (ἐν **τῷ** κυρίῳ) already implies possession, made explicit with the pronoun.

15.b. P^{46}, ℵ*, B, P, 33, 1739, et al., drop the article and noun τὴν ἀγάπην in the phrase **τὴν** ἀγάπην **τὴν** εἰς πάντας τοὺς ἁγίους. As Metzger points out, this was possibly because the scribe skipped ahead to the second occurrence of the same article: τὴν ἀγάπην τὴν (*homoeoarcton*).[3] The longer reading is no doubt original since the article in the shorter reading would refer to the previous πίστιν and have Paul say that he heard of their "*faith* in all the saints." A later variant adds ἀγάπην later in the clause τὴν εἰς πάντας τοὺς ἁγίους ἀγάπην, mirroring the structure of the previous colon* and trying to fix the discrepancy.

18.c. A personal pronoun brings out the obvious meaning of the second article in the phrase τοὺς ὀφθαλμοὺς τῆς καρδίας **ὑμῶν** in many MSS, such as א, A, D, F, G, Ψ, and M. For this reason the UBS/NA editions include ὑμῶν in brackets, though the meaning is unchanged, since the possessive meaning of the article (**τῆς** καρδίας, "*your* heart") is clear from context.

Translation

15 For this reason, when I received word of your faith[4] in the Lord Jesus and of your love[5] for all the saints, **16** I have not ceased[6] giving thanks[7] for

3. Bruce M. Metzger, *A Textual Commentary on the Greek New Testament*, 2nd ed. (New York: United Bible Societies, 1994), 533.
4. The phrase τὴν καθ' ὑμᾶς πίστιν is a circumlocution for the poss. τὴν πίστιν ὑμῶν (as Col 1:4); see also Acts 17:28; 18:15 (νόμου τοῦ καθ' ὑμᾶς, "your own law"); 25:27; 26:3; Rom 1:15 (cf. BDF §224 [1], who say it is Hellenistic; e.g., Polybius, 1.55.8 [τῶν κατὰ τὴν Σικελίαν ἱερῶν, "of the Sicilian shrines"]). The same construction is also represented in the phrase τὰ κατ' ἐμέ, "my affairs" (Eph 6:21; cf. Acts 24:22; Phil 1:12; Col 4:7). Technically the prepositional phrase κατά + acc. is a form of "specification" that qualifies or restricts the reference of the noun (cf. 6:5).
5. Both πίστιν ("faith") and ἀγάπην ("love") are acc., as the things heard or learned about with ἀκούω ("I hear"); the gen. is normally used when one listens to a person (LSJ, 54; BDAG, 38).
6. The verb παύομαι is a pres. tense, properly rendered with an English perf. ("I have not ceased") when the idea is that the event was begun in the past and continues into the present. E. Burton, *Syntax of the Moods and Tenses in New Testament Greek* (Edinburgh: T&T Clark, 1898), §17.
7. The lead verb παύομαι ("I have not ceased") regularly takes a ptc. rather than an inf. complement, as here with εὐχαριστῶν ("giving thanks"; BDAG, 790; BDF §414 [2]).

you, and I have been making mention[8] of you in my prayers, **17** that[9] the God of our Lord Jesus Christ, the Father of glory, may grant you a spirit of wisdom and of revelation in the knowledge of him, **18** and that the eyes of your heart be enlightened,[10] so that you may understand[11] what[12] is the hope of his calling, what is the glorious wealth[13] of his inheritance among the saints,[14] **19** and what is the superabundant[15] magnitude of his power

---

8. See note above for rendering the Greek pres. tense of the ptc. ποιούμενος ("I have been making") with an English perf. here (cf. Burton, *Moods*, §17). This ptc. is middle voice as part of an idiom with μνεία ("mention") for "make mention" (BDAG, 841, meaning 7a). It is a minor point, but I am taking μνείαν ποιούμενος ("making mention [of you]") as parallel with the main verb παύομαι ("I have not ceased") and not with the ptc. complement εὐχαριστῶν ("giving thanks"). The statement is: "I have not ceased ... [and I] make mention" (the conj. and pronoun are supplied by context). *Parallel* is my preferred term for certain adv. ptcs. in place of "attendant circumstances" (e.g., Herbert Wier Smyth, *Greek Grammar*, rev. Gordon M. Messing [Cambridge, MA: Harvard University Press, 1956; original ed., 1920], §§2068–69; Burton, *Moods*, §§449–50); see note on προορίσας ("predestined") in 1:5 above and the excursus below. If ποιούμενος were a complement of παύομαι alongside εὐχαριστῶν, the conj. καί ("and") would have been used to join the two ptc. complements together. See Col 1:9 for such a construction: οὐ παυόμεθα ὑπὲρ ὑμῶν προσευχόμενοι **καὶαἰτούμενοι**, "We have not ceased praying for you *and (we have not ceased) asking.*"

9. The ἵνα clause here is the obj. of the prayers; i.e., this is that for which Paul prays. Normally ὅτι has this function, but ἵνα can have this meaning too, especially after verbs of prayer; cf. Burton, *Moods*, §203 (also in 3:14–16); Daniel B. Wallace, *Greek Grammar beyond the Basics* (Grand Rapids: Zondervan, 1997), 475.

10. See comment for discussion of the translation and possibilities here.

11. The inf. phrase εἰς τὸ εἰδέναι expresses the result of the grant of a "spirit of wisdom and of revelation" and of the enlightenment of "the eyes of your heart *so that [as a result]* you may understand."

12. The three interrogative pronouns (τίς, τίς, and τί, all rendered "what") in 1:18–19 are used to mark indirect questions introduced in the phrase εἰς τὸ εἰδέναι ὑμᾶς, "so that you may understand" (cf. Burton, *Moods*, §340).

13. For ὁ πλοῦτος τῆς δόξης as meaning "glorious wealth" or "riches" see the comment; cf. BDAG, 832.

14. See the comment for "among the saints"; cf. "in the saints" (ESV; NASB; NIV).

15. The adj. ptc. ὑπερβάλλον ("superabundant"; or "exceeding" [KJV, NKJV], "immeasurable" [ESV, NRSV], "surpassing" [NASB], "incomparably great" [NIV]; cf. Vg., *supereminens magnitudo,* "pre-eminent in greatness") is found five times in 1 Corinthians and Ephesians (also as adj. ptcs.). In its finite form the verb may mean "to surpass" or "exceed" something (e.g., Sir 25:11), but here and in the other places in Paul it marks the divinely supreme expression of the noun's quality. Hence it is used with nouns whose referents can exist in different degrees: "superabundant glory"

toward us who believe in accordance with the effectiveness of the strength of his might, **20** which he effected[16] in the Messiah[17] by raising him from the dead and seating him at his right hand in the high-heavenlies,[18] **21** far above[19] all rule and authority and power and lordship and every name that can be named,[20] not only in this age but also in the age to come, **22** and "he put everything under his feet" and gave him as head over and above[21] everything in the church, **23** which is his body, the fullness of him who fills[22] everything entirely.[23]

(1 Cor 3:10); "superabundant grace" (1 Cor 9:14); "superabundant wealth of his grace" (Eph 2:7); and "superabundant love" (Eph 3:19); cf. LSJ, 1860; BDAG, 1032.

16. Ἐνεργέω ("he effected") can refer to an activity that is in process, "be active," or "be in operation" (e.g., Eph 2:2; 3:20; Gal 3:5), or, as here, to bring one's will or power into effect (or "to produce"); cf. note on v. 11 above; 1 Cor 12:6; 1 Thess 2:13; Jas 5:16; LSJ, 564; BDAG, 335.

17. See translation note for v. 10 and "Excursus: Articular Χριστός as Messianic Title" below for the rendering "in the Messiah" rather than "in Christ," encountered more often in English versions (e.g., ESV, NASB, NIV). We could also take the article in this phrase as substituting for a poss. pronoun: "in *his* Messiah" to bring out a connection with Psa 2:2, "against the LORD and against his Messiah."

18. See on v. 3 for the rendering "in the high-heavenlies" for ἐν τοῖς ἐπουρανίοις.

19. The improper prep. ὑπεράνω ("far above") occurs three times in the NT. In Heb 9:5 it simply means "above," but here and in Eph 4:10 it refers to Christ's ascendancy "*far* above" to a supreme position of authority. The ὑπέρ component of the phrase, then, functions as a marker for a degree "beyond that of a compared scale of extent" (BDAG, 1031 [meaning B]). See also the note on the phrase ὑπὲρ πάντα in v. 22 and ὑπερεκπερισσοῦ ("far more exceedingly" or "quite beyond all measure" [BDAG, 1033]) in Eph 3:20.

20. The simple attributive ptc. ὀνομαζόμενος is rendered as "name that *can be named*" rather than the bare "every name *that is named*" (e.g., ESV, NASB, NKJV); cf. NIV, "every title that can be given." This is not a meaning of the ptc. mood itself, but it is a way to bring out a conative* pres.-tense meaning, as one can see in this paraphrase: "name that someone may attempt to name" = "that *can be named* by anyone." For the conative* aspectual nuance see Burton, *Moods*, §11; BDF §319; Wallace, *Greek Grammar*, 534–35.

21. For the rendering "over and above everything" for ὑπέρ in the phrase ὑπὲρ πάντα, see BDAG, 1031 (meaning B).

22. The middle/pass. ptc. τοῦ ... πληρουμένου is taken here not as pass. ("of him who is being filled"; e.g., Hoehner, 294–301) but as a middle with act. meaning (BDAG, 828; BDF §316 [1]); cf. 4:10. See comment.

23. For ἐν πᾶσιν, "entirely," "in every way," or "in all respects" (also 6:16), see BDAG, 783 (meaning 1dβ); ἵνα ᾖ ὁ θεὸς τὰ πάντα **ἐνπᾶσιν** (1 Cor 15:28); cf. Col 1:18; 1 Tim 3:11; Titus 2:9.

Commentary

1:15–16 Διὰ τοῦτο, "For this reason." The first period opens with a connector, διὰ τοῦτο, that normally introduces an inference from a previous foundation or a real or hypothetical question.[24] Here the connection is rather looser, as Paul develops his own response to the faith in the gospel of his recipients (ἀκούσαντες ... πιστεύσαντες, v. 13) that was corroborated by a report to him (ἀκούσας, "when I received word," v. 15; O'Brien, 127).

ἀκούσας τὴν καθ' ὑμᾶς πίστιν ἐν τῷ κυρίῳ Ἰησοῦ καὶ τὴν ἀγάπην τὴν εἰς πάντας τοὺς ἁγίους, "when I received word of your faith in the Lord Jesus and your love for all the saints." The "saints" here are the whole church, both Jews and Gentiles, as in 1:18 ("among the saints"; cf. 3:8, 18; 6:18; Col 1:12; O'Brien, 128), not angels (Schlier, 82–84; cf. Brown, 1:151 and note 38) or Israel. At first glance, when Paul says that he has "received word of" the faith of those at Ephesus, it appears that he does not know them.[25] However, he says the same thing to Philemon, someone he knows well, in the context of reporting his prayer on Philemon's behalf: "I thank my God always when I remember you in my prayers, *because I hear of your love and of the faith that you have toward the Lord Jesus and all the saints* ..." (Phlm 4–5; emphasis added). In other words, Paul has "received word" as *evidence* of the Ephesians' faith in the acts of love they have shown the saints (cf. Col 1:3–4), which has continued after his departure (Hodge, 69; cf. Best, 158–59). He has been away from them for some time and can only have contact with them indirectly through reports from others—Tychicus, perhaps?

μνείαν ποιούμενος ἐπὶ τῶν προσευχῶν μου, "and I have been making mention of you in my prayers." It is a distinctive idiom of Paul to say that he has been "making mention" of his audience in his prayers (1:16; so also Rom 1:9; Phil 1:3; 1 Thess 1:2; 2 Tim 1:3; Phlm 4). His point is that he is interceding for these churches by name and not simply offering generic prayers for the church at large.

1:17–18b ἵνα ὁ θεὸς τοῦ κυρίου ἡμῶν Ἰησοῦ Χριστοῦ ... δώῃ ὑμῖν, "that the God of our Lord Jesus Christ ... may grant you." The ἵνα ("that") clause

---

24. See BDAG, 225 (meaning B2b).

25. Theodore of Mopsuestia takes this to mean that Paul is writing before his trip to Ephesus in Acts 19; Theodore of Mopsuestia, *Commentary on the Minor Pauline Epistles*, trans. Rowan A Greer (Atlanta: SBL, 2010), 171–79.

opening v. 17 expresses the content of Paul's prayers in the previous verse and is the equivalent of a clause begun with ὅτι.[26] The subjunctive verb (δώῃ, "may grant") is suspended slightly until v. 17b because of the rather lengthy reference to the Father.

As we saw in v. 3, Paul and the other biblical writers express the genuine humanity of Christ by speaking of God the Father as *his* God (see esp. John 20:17), though this does not deny that the incarnate Son has true "equality with God" (Phil 2:6). The humanity of the Son is stated for two reasons. The first and most important is that it expresses the exclusive *human* mediation of Christ Jesus as the only way to the Father. There is no other (e.g., John 14:6; 1 Tim 2:5). God is no longer known as "the God of Israel" (e.g., Pss 41:13; 59:5; Isa 17:6; Ezek 11:22; Luke 1:68) or "the God of Abraham" (e.g., 1 Kgs 18:36; Psa 47:9; Acts 3:13) but as "the God and Father of our Lord Jesus Christ" (Eph 1:3; also Rom 15:5; 2 Cor 1:3; 11:31; Col 1:3; 1 Pet 1:3) as his covenant name, because God is no longer a national God but the God of all nations (including Israelites) who come to the Father through the incarnate Son.

The second reason NT authors stress Christ's humanity is particularly because of the pagan Hellenistic climate into which they were writing. The ancient Greek gods were thought to appear on earth in human guise (Acts 14:11–12). Among the more famous of these was the appearance of Athena as trusted old Mentor to Odysseus's son, Telemachos, in the *Odyssey* (*Od.* 2.255–68). More apropos for Ephesians is the evidence that Artemis Ephesia was thought to manifest her appearance to her worshipers in the Ephesian Artemisium.[27] In none of these pagan instances, though, is this a true *incarnation*, as was the appearance of Emmanuel (see esp. 1 John 4:1–3).

ὁ πατὴρ τῆς δόξης, "the Father of glory." The genitive δόξης functions as an adjectival genitive and is the equivalent of the "glorious Father."[28]

26. For the "content" use of ἵνα with verbs meaning "request" or "demand" see BDAG, 476 (meaning 2aγ) and note above.

27. Artemis of Ephesus and other gods and deified humans (e.g., Julius Caesar, *IvE* 251) were described in Ephesus as "manifest" (ἐπιφανῆς), and the Artemisium had "epiphany windows" for the goddess to appear; see Paul Trebilco, *The Early Christians in Ephesus from Paul to Ignatius* (Grand Rapids: Eerdmans, 2008; first published 2004), 356–57; cf. S. M. Baugh, " 'Savior of All People': 1 Tim 4:10 in Context," *WTJ* 54 (1992): 331–40 (on *IvE* 251).

28. BDF, §164; Wallace, *Greek Grammar*, 78–81.

As Paul stated it in its own colon*, though, the phrase has more charm with its stress on the Father's glory than a more prosaic adjective ὁ ἔνδοξος πατὴρ ("the glorious Father"; see 5:27) would have.

πνεῦμα σοφίας καὶ ἀποκαλύψεως ἐν ἐπιγνώσει αὐτοῦ, "a spirit of wisdom and of revelation in the knowledge of him."[29] The human spirit is the seat of the inner life, which enables perception and discernment and is therefore related to "the eyes of the heart" (i.e., the "mind's eye"; v. 18). We would not want to dissociate this divine gift here from the Holy Spirit and the wisdom "from above" (Jas 3:17), who enables believers' spirits to have true wisdom and insight (see Deut 34:9; Acts 6:3; 1 Cor 2:6–13). There may also be a connection with a messianic prophecy in Isaiah here: "And the Spirit of the LORD shall rest upon him, the Spirit of wisdom and understanding, the Spirit of counsel and might, the Spirit of knowledge and the fear of the LORD. And his delight shall be in the fear of the LORD" (Isa 11:2–3).

In Ephesians 1:17 the "wisdom and revelation" leads to "knowledge of him" because all true wisdom has its foundation in the fear of the Lord (Prov 1:7), and the knowledge of the Most Holy is true understanding (Prov 9:10; cf. Prov 15:33; Job 28:28). The noun ἐπίγνωσις, with its prefix (**ἐπί**γνωσις), can connote that the knowledge (γνῶσις) is genuine or perceptive of something transcendent.[30] Here the object of knowledge is God the Father himself, facilitated through the mediation of the incarnate Christ. "He who has seen me has seen the Father" (John 14:9).

πεφωτισμένους τοὺς ὀφθαλμοὺς τῆς καρδίας εἰς τὸ εἰδέναι ὑμᾶς, "and that the eyes of your heart be enlightened, so that you may understand." This accusative phrase appears "awkward syntactically" (O'Brien, 133n167), primarily because it is parallel in meaning with πνεῦμα ("spirit") as the object of "give," as follows: Ἵνα ... δώῃ ὑμῖν (1) πνεῦμα σοφίας ... (2) πεφωτισμένους τοὺς ὀφθαλμοὺς τῆς καρδίας, "that (he) may grant you (1) a spirit of wisdom ...

29. The NIV has "the Spirit of wisdom" here, with an obvious direct reference to the Holy Spirit. There is no grammatical reason to take anarthrous πνεῦμα here as definite ("the" versus "a" in English), and it is not likely that Paul would ask that these "saints ... who believe in Christ Jesus" (v. 1) and who have already been sealed by the Holy Spirit (v. 13) to receive when they already had. That being said, there is a distinct link between the "spirit of wisdom" and the Holy Spirit, as explained in the comment.

30. See also Eph 3:19 (γνῶσις) and 4:13 (ἐπίγνωσις); cf. BDAG, 203–4, 369.

(and grant that) (2) the eyes of your heart be enlightened."[31] The meaning in English requires the conjunction *and* be supplied to bring out the parallelism. That the two ideas are "parallel" can and does here also show that they explain each other: To receive a spirit of wisdom means to see with the heart. The participle is accusative because the word to which it connects (ὀφθαλμοὺς) is itself accusative; cf. Lincoln, 47. The idea of the perfect tense of πεφωτισμένους here is that the light puts believers' eyes into a state of illumination—that is, their hearts can "see" now because the darkness has been dispelled by God (cf. 5:8; 2 Cor 4:6).

"Eyes of the heart" is a unique expression in the Scriptures.[32] However, Cicero uses a similar phrase in his essay *The Nature of the Gods*: "It remains for us to consider the qualities of the divine nature; and on this subject nothing is more difficult than to divert *the eye of the mind* (*oculi mentis*) from following the practice of bodily sight" (Cicero, *Nat. d.* 2.17; emphasis added).

The impact of the "enlightenment" Paul wishes for his audience is a little diminished in the modern world. Today we rarely experience life without street lamps or even the ambient light of a city affecting even rural areas. In Paul's day, where torches or bonfires were the biggest lights available, normal illumination was provided by the tiny, flickering flames of lamps. Deep darkness was the norm at night. In such a world, Paul prays that God would cast his piercing spotlight for the Ephesians' mind's eyes and then would rise the messianic morning star in their hearts (2 Pet 1:9; cf. Amos 5:8; Matt 4:16; Acts 26:18; 2 Cor 4:6; Heb 10:32).

1:18c–19 τίς ἐστιν ἡ ἐλπὶς τῆς κλήσεως αὐτοῦ, τίς ὁ πλοῦτος τῆς δόξης τῆς κληρονομίας αὐτοῦ ἐν τοῖς ἁγίοις, καὶ τί τὸ ὑπερβάλλον μέγεθος τῆς δυνάμεως αὐτοῦ εἰς ἡμᾶς τοὺς πιστεύοντας κατὰ τὴν ἐνέργειαν τοῦ κράτους τῆς ἰσχύος αὐτοῦ, "what is the hope of his calling, what is the glorious wealth of his inheritance among the saints, and what is the superabundant magnitude of his power toward us who believe in accordance with the effectiveness

31. Cf. Hoehner, 261–62, for the main alternative, which takes this phrase as a kind of acc. abs. This would function to expand on what it means that God grant to the Ephesians a spirit of wisdom and revelation. The outcome is similar to the interpretation given above.

32. *Contra* O'Brien, 133, who cites two places in the Psalms, though they are are not the same expression.

of the strength of his might." This period has what is called "tricolon crescendo," a technique whereby three parallel statements grow both in length and magnitude of meaning to form a climax.[33] In this case, the repeated elements are introduced by the interrogative pronouns τίς ("what"; twice) and τί ("what") as follows (the numbers at the end are the number of syllables in the Greek cola*):

v. 18c *what* (τίς) is the hope of his calling (12)

v. 18d *what* (τίς) is the glorious wealth of his inheritance among the saints (20)

v. 19 and *what* (τί) is the supreme greatness of his power toward us who believe in accordance with the effectiveness of the strength of his might (41)

Notice how each clause gets longer as it builds to the climax. As will be noted, this makes the last element on "power" gain the focus, and it is the subject of elaboration in the succeeding periods.

The beginning element of the tricolon is "what is the hope of his calling." Paul wants his audience to understand the hope and its object, which God's call has provided them, as he also says later: "[J]ust as also you were called to the one hope from your calling" (Eph 4:4; cf. 4:1).[34] Formerly Paul's audience had no such hope because they were ἄθεοι ἐν τῷ κόσμῳ, "without God in the world" (2:12). "The writer believes it is essential that the addressees be aware of the hope they can enjoy as a result of the fact that God has called them" (Lincoln, 59; cf. Brown, 1:150–51).

---

33. Latin *tricolon crescens*; this device is rather widespread in Greek and Latin prose and poetry. The pattern is nicely reversed ("tricolon descendo"?) in John the Baptist's increasingly agitated reply to his questioners regarding his identity: ἐγὼ οὐκ εἰμὶ ὁ χριστός … οὐκ εἰμί … οὔ (John 1:20–21).

34. The ESV, NIV, and NRSV all bring this out for v. 18 with the rendering "the hope to which he has called you." Hence, ἐλπίς probably points not to the obj. for which one hopes but to the subjective expectation of something, though either meaning is possible here (BDAG, 319–20).

The second colon* is "what is the glorious wealth of his inheritance among the saints."[35] The first part (ὁ πλοῦτος τῆς δόξης τῆς κληρονομίας αὐτοῦ) consists of a lead noun ("wealth" or "riches") and three connected gens., "of the glory," "of the inheritance," and "his." There are a variety of ways to put these together. Several English versions attach *glory* as an adjective to *the inheritance*: "the riches of his *glorious* inheritance" (NIV, ESV, NRSV; Lincoln, 59; Hoehner, 265–67; emphasis added). I have attached glory to the wealth: "the glorious wealth of his inheritance" (cf. Barth, 151), but we could also read it as "rich glory of his inheritance" in line with "riches of his grace" (2:7) or "riches of his glory" (3:16 and Rom 9:23; cf. Col 1:27; Eph 3:8; Phil 4:19).[36] It makes little real difference which option we choose here since the idea is that the inheritance is rich and full of glory.[37]

Where our interpretation of v. 18d does make a difference is how we understand the relation of God's inheritance and the saints. The first idea is that God's own heritage is the saints themselves, which he will consummately gain in the glory of the new creation.[38] This is in line with my interpretation of v. 14 above, where we saw that believers are God's "prized possession." The second option is that the inheritance is something God dispenses freely to his children (as v. 14), and Christians will receive its glorious riches "among the saints" (NRSV; cf. NAB), i.e., in the same inherited

35. See also κατὰ τὸ πλοῦτος τῆς δόξης in 3:16. Similar strings with three or more nouns connected by at least two in the gen. can be found in Rom 4:11; 5:2; 8:2–3, 21; 2 Cor 4:4, 6; Col 1:27; 2:2, 12; Eph 1:6; 6:15.

36. *Wealth* and *glory* appear together as twins frequently in the OT; e.g., LXX Gen 31:16; 1 Kgs 3:13; 1 Chr 29:12; Esth 5:11; Psa 111:3 [= MT 112:3]; Prov 3:16. Both are also quite common in Ephesians (1:6–7, 12, 14, 17; 2:7; 3:8, 13, 16, 21).

37. Some interpreters have seen a difference in the conception of inheritance in Ephesians and the other Paulines as part of the authorship issue (e.g., P. L. Hammer, "A Comparison of *KLĒRONOMIA* in Paul and Ephesians," *JBL* 79 [1960]: 267–72), but they sometimes accomplish this by dismissing some of the passages that show harmony of thought; see D. R. Denton, "Inheritance in Paul and Ephesians," *EvQ* 54 (1982): 157–62. Cf. esp. Eph 5:5 with 1 Cor 6:9–10 and Gal 5:21. Cf. James D. Hester, *Paul's Concept of Inheritance: A Contribution to the Understanding of Heilsgeschichte* (Edinburgh and London: Oliver & Boyd, 1968); James A. Meek, "The Riches of His Inheritance," *Presbyterion* 28 (2002): 34–46.

38. O'Brien, 133 ("the rich inheritance which he possesses in them"), 135–36; cf. Hoehner, 265–67; Lincoln, 59–60; Arnold, 108–9. This view is brought out in the versions by their rendering of ἐν τοῖς ἁγίοις that his inheritance "[consists] *in* the saints" (KJV, NIV, NASB, ESV; emphasis added).

glory alongside all God's perfected saints through the ages in the kingdom of God (5:5; cf. Heb 12:22–23, 28).[39] I prefer this second view. "Glory" does not reside essentially in the saints, but in the "Father of glory" (v. 17) who dispenses it to believers out of mere grace. Furthermore, v. 18d is parallel with the hope (v. 18c) and abundant power (v. 19) that God bestows on and for believers in Christ, not things God himself receives.

As often, the two options just discussed present a choice between two biblical truths, and we must merely determine the meaning uttered here in this place. Both are true because the heart of biblical religion is the covenant bond that God is the God of his people and they are his people (see on 2:12). Believers are God's heritage, and he and all that he possesses belongs to them through their elder brother, the incarnate Son, who purchased this rare privilege for them (e.g., Rom 8:29; see on Eph 3:6). The concept of inheritance here also relates directly to adoption as sons, discussed above on v. 5.

Paul does not expand on the content of the inheritance here except to say that it is marked by "glorious wealth" and is "among the saints." The latter is particularly important for Paul's Gentile audience, since they were decidedly *not* heirs previously, as those alienated from Israel and its covenant promises of inheritance (2:11–13; Gal 3:18), which have now been extended to them and to believers from all other nations in Christ (2:13–22; Gal 3:26–29) and sealed by the Holy Spirit (1:13–14; Gal 3:14). Hence, the audience members are fellow heirs with the saints and inherit alongside them (3:6; Col 1:12).

Some scholars understand the ἅγιοι ("saints"; see on vv. 1, 15) as a reference to either angels or to Israel (cf. Barth, 151–52; Gnilka, 91). In Hebrews 12:22–23, NT believers have joined with angels and believers from past ages in an approach to God in the "heavenly Jerusalem" through the Holy Spirit. If this conception can be extended to Paul, then he is referencing in 1:18 an inheritance as broad as the new creation in which both the holy angels and the saints of all generations have a share (cf. Rom 4:13–17; Gal 3:9).

---

39. Cf. Barth, 151–52; Best, 167–68; Gnilka, 91–92. This heritage is the benefit of believers' adoption as sons; see comment on v. 5. The prep. in the phrase **ἐν τοῖς** ἁγίοις as "*among* the saints" has many parallels in the LXX either as inheritance "in the midst (ἐν μέσῳ) of the sons of Israel" (Num 18:20, 23; cf. Num 27:7; 36:2; Judg 18:1),"in the house of our father" (Gen 31:14), "among them" (Num 32:19), or "alongside (ἐν) their brothers" (Job 42:15).

However, it seems that the reference in v. 18 is to an inheritance granted to the church consisting of both Jew and Gentile (cf. Acts 20:32; 26:18) in light of Paul's interest in context to stress Christ's destruction of the barrier between the two (esp. 2:19; cf. Lincoln, 59–60; O'Brien, 136).

Verse 19 begins with a generic word for "power" (δύναμις), but Paul modifies it with a superlative phrase: "the *superabundant magnitude* of his power." As if that were not enough, he piles up three synonyms for power—ἐνέργεια ("effectiveness"), κράτος ("strength"), and ἰσχύς ("might")—in the last colon* in an elaborate description of the display of omnipotence by the Lord of Hosts in Christ. The use of all four of these synonyms together is notable and unique.[40]

Why all the language of power in v. 19? Clinton Arnold has convincingly shown that Paul's extravagant focus on God's power unleashed on behalf of believers in Christ and of Christ's supreme place in the cosmos and in the church in vv. 20–23 is set over against the preoccupation with supernatural forces manipulated through magic and the occult in antiquity, and especially in ancient Ephesus.[41] It is not difficult for people from some parts of the modern world to understand this, since similar practices continue. Ephesian converts, whose whole lives had been steeped in attempts to placate unseen, hostile powers, could not easily and quickly shake these old beliefs and patterns of thought (witness Acts 19:19–20). Hence, Paul looks to God in prayer that his audience would be convinced of Christ's supremacy over any supposed demonic competitor.

The articular participle (πιστεύοντας) in the phrase εἰς ἡμᾶς τοὺς πιστεύοντας ("toward us who believe") is attributive, modifying ἡμᾶς. The present-tense form conveys that these people are characterized by faith and is

---

40. See 3:7; 6:10; Col 1:11, 29; 2 Thess 2:9; 2 Pet 2:11; Rev 5:12; 7:12 for the few places where two of these terms appear together, but nowhere else do three or four appear in one place; cf. Deut 3:24; 8:17–18 in the LXX.

41. Arnold, 109–20; Clinton E. Arnold, *Ephesians: Power and Magic; The Concept of Power in Ephesians in Light of Its Historical Setting*, SNTSMS 63 (New York: Cambridge University Press, 1989), 70–85. He understands the false teaching at Colossae as a blend of Judaism and folk magic ideas in Clinton E. Arnold, *The Colossian Syncretism: The Interface between Christianity and Folk Belief at Colossae* (Grand Rapids: Baker, 1996). See discussion on ancient magic under "Additional Exegetical Comments" below.

the equivalent of saying "toward us believers."[42] Of note here is how faith is the *sine qua non* of Christian identity, experience, and divine blessing.

The final colon* in v. 19 (κατὰ τὴν ἐνέργειαν τοῦ κράτους τῆς ἰσχύος αὐτοῦ, "in accordance with the effectiveness of the strength of his might") belongs conceptually to both vv. 18c–9b and to v. 20 as a transition between the two periods.[43] The connection is made explicit by the opening relative pronoun ἥν in v. 20, where this colon* will be discussed.

1:20 Ἣν ἐνήργησεν ἐν τῷ Χριστῷ ἐγείρας αὐτὸν ἐκ νεκρῶν καὶ καθίσας ἐν δεξιᾷ αὐτοῦ ἐν τοῖς ἐπουρανίοις, "which he effected in the Messiah by raising him from the dead and seating him at his right hand in the high-heavenlies." The opening feminine relative pronoun ἥν ("which") refers either to ἐνέργεια ("effectiveness") or to the closer ἰσχύς ("strength") from v. 19c, though the exact assignment makes little difference since the phrase "the effectiveness of the strength of his might" forms a whole concept for God's overwhelming, sovereign power to bring his redemption to pass.

God "effects" his supreme power toward believers "by raising" and "by seating" Christ at the place of rule at his right hand.[44] Although it is not quoted directly, Psa 110:1–2 stands behind the statement that Christ has been seated at God's right hand: "The Lord says to my Lord: 'Sit at my right hand, until I make your enemies your footstool.' The Lord sends

42. This is sometimes referred to as the "gnomic" meaning, but it can more precisely be called "characteristic" or "general" (Burton, *Moods*, §12; Wallace, *Greek Grammar*, 521–25) in meaning and is common with pres.-tense-form substantive or attributive ptcs.; e.g., ὁ κλέπτων, "the thief" (4:28); ὁ καθεύδων, "O sleeper" (5:14); μετὰ πάντων τῶν ἀγαπώντων, "with all those who love" (6:24). Context or a helping adv. needs to indicate that the event is currently in process of fulfillment; e.g., τοῦ πνεύματος τοῦ **νῦν** ἐνεργοῦντος ("the spirit who is *now* at work"; 2:2) ("progressive"; Burton, *Moods*, §8).

43. There are other examples of such swing or transitional statements in Paul; for example, 5:7 and 21; cf. Gal 5:1, which belongs equally with the material in Gal 4 and transitions into Gal 5:2–6.

44. This anticipates what Paul will shortly say in 2:1–6; see Thomas G. Allen, "Exaltation and Solidarity with Christ: Ephesians 1:20 and 2:6," *JSNT* 28 (1986): 103–20. The two ptcs. ἐγείρας ("raising") and καθίσας ("seating") express the manner of *how* the Father brought his power into effect (cf. Burton, *Moods*, §444). The aor.-tense form of these ptcs. expresses not antecedent action, as is common for aor. adv. ptcs., but that the two events are described as simply occurring rather than as processes (cf. Burton, *Moods*, §35; Wallace, *Greek Grammar*, 557–58).

forth from Zion your mighty scepter. Rule in the midst of your enemies!" At Christ's ascent to the Father's right hand, Christ's messianic reign has been initiated "in the midst of his enemies" until the ultimate enemy, death, is destroyed for his people at their future resurrection at his Parousia (1 Cor 15:23–26).[45]

To take one's seat rather than to be standing was a sign of royal enthronement (e.g., 1 Kgs 1:46; Pss 9:7, 11; 29:10; 47:8; 99:1; Matt 23:22; Heb 12:2; Rev 5:13; 7:10, 15), often after winning a great victory (Psa 110:1–5; cf. Heb 1:3–4). And to be at God's right hand was to be at the place of power over one's enemies (e.g., Psa 17:7; Matt 26:64; Luke 22:69; Acts 2:33; 1 Pet 3:22) and of privilege (Psa 45:6–9; Acts 5:31; Rom 8:34; Heb 8:1).[46] Frank Thielman notes: "Jesus' resurrection led to his exaltation to a place of equal regal authority with the king of the universe, just as the psalm [110] implies that Yahweh shares his authority with the king at his right hand."[47]

Believers experience this effect of power through union with Christ in his death and exaltation.[48] Paul does not elaborate here on either the exact nature of this union or on the specifics of the application of this power

---

45. Psalm 110 is often quoted or referenced in the NT, including by Jesus himself, to explain Christ's inaugurated reign in this age; e.g., Matt 22:44; 26:64; Acts 2:34; 1 Cor 15:25; Heb 1:3, 13. Cf. Frank S. Thielman in *Commentary on the New Testament Use of the Old Testament*, ed. G. K. Beale and D. A Carson (Grand Rapids: Baker Academic, 2007), 814–17. See also the quotation of Psa 8 in v. 22 below.

46. See Timothy G. Gombis, "Ephesians 2 as a Narrative of Divine Warfare," *JSNT* 26 (2004): 403–18 (who spends much time on this section of Ephesians); cf. Tremper Longman III, "The Divine Warrior: The New Testament Use of an Old Testament Motif," *WTJ* 44 (1982): 290–307; and more fully: Tremper Longman III, Daniel G. Reid, and Willem A. Van Gemeren, *God Is a Warrior* (Grand Rapids: Zondervan, 1995); O'Brien, 140–41.

47. Thielman, in *New Testament Use of the Old Testament*, 815.

48. Cf. Constantine R. Campbell, *Paul and Union with Christ: An Exegetical and Theological Study* (Grand Rapids: Zondervan, 2012); Robert Letham, *Union with Christ: In Scripture, History, and Theology* (Phillipsburg, NJ: P&R, 2011); Michael S. Horton, *Covenant and Salvation: Union with Christ* (Louisville: Westminster John Knox, 2007); focusing more on history of the doctrine is John V. Fesko, *Beyond Calvin: Union with Christ and Justification in Early Modern Reformed Theology (1517–1700)* (Bristol, CT: Vandenhoeck & Ruprecht, 2012). Cf. Juraj Fenik, "Enthroned with Christ: An Exegetical and Theological Study of Eph 1:20–23 and 2:5–6" (STD diss., Catholic University of America, 2008).

toward believers; it is simply stated to have occurred.[49] To have said more would have led to an exceedingly long digression, since union with the Mediator and identification with his death, resurrection, and exaltation is the nexus for all spiritual benefits a Christian experiences. The believer died when Christ died, was buried with him, was raised with him, and is seated with him in the heavens (Rom 6:3–11; Gal 2:20; Eph 2:1–6; Col 2:12; 3:1–4). All of this is inaugurated now in the believer's life through the Holy Spirit, the guarantee of the full, new creation inheritance in resurrection (see on 1:13–14; cf. 1 Cor 6:14; O'Brien, 139–40). The Messiah's own resurrection and exaltation over all competing powers (see v. 21) brings this into effect: "But our citizenship is in heaven, and from it we await a Savior, the Lord Jesus Christ, who will transform our lowly body to be like his glorious body, by the power that enables him even to subject all things to himself" (Phil 3:20–21).

1:21 ὑπεράνω πάσης ἀρχῆς καὶ ἐξουσίας καὶ δυνάμεως καὶ κυριότητος καὶ παντὸς ὀνόματος ὀνομαζομένου, "far above all rule and authority and power and lordship and every name that can be named." The pace is quickened in this period with the use of many short syllables, as noted in the introduction above. The effect reduces the time to move through the period as we head to the end of the whole periodic sentence and expresses excitement at the ascendancy of Christ.

The supremacy of the risen Christ's ascent comes out with the piling up of four synonyms for authorities (ἀρχή, ἐξουσία, δύναμις, and κυριότης), over which he has been installed by the Father.[50] The fourfold list of nouns is designed to underline the comprehensive suzerainty of Christ, which is further strengthened by the use of πᾶς at the beginning of the list and at the beginning of the add-on phrase of "*all* rule ... and *every* name that can

49. When Paul does elaborate on the nature of the union of Christ and his people, he either resorts to metaphor (e.g., the body/head in Ephesians [v. 23]; or "firstfruits" in 1 Cor 15:20, 23) or the Adam analogy with Christ as "Last Adam" (1 Cor 15:21–22, 45–47; Rom 5:12–21) and believers being re-created in his likeness (1 Cor 15:48–49; cf. Eph 2:10). Cf. C. K. Barrett, *From First Adam to Last: A Study in Pauline Theology* (London: Adam & Charles Black, 1962); Robin Scroggs, *The Last Adam: A Study in Pauline Anthropology* (Philadelphia: Fortress, 1966).

50. Κυριότης (4x in the NT) in particular points to the majesty of angelic beings (cf. Col 1:16; 2 Pet 2:10; Jude 8); cf. Arnold, 112–14.

be named" (**πάσηςἀρχῆς** ... καὶ **παντὸςὀνόματος**).[51] The terminology of rulers is rather general and is probably meant to be comprehensive for both earthly and heavenly powers: "all creation ... in heaven and on earth, things visible and invisible, whether thrones or lordships or rulers or authorities" (Col 1:15–16).[52]

The clause "and every name that can be named" signals more than simply rounding off the comprehensive list. It points to the idea mentioned above (v. 19) that Paul has in mind the audience's previous preoccupation with manipulation of unseen spiritual forces in what is commonly called magic or occult practices. Acquisition and use of a spirit's or demon's name was thought to give one control over it.[53] For example, the Romans apparently kept the name of their tutelary god secret so that enemies could not gain power over their city through use of the name (Pliny the Elder, *Nat.* 28.4). And while it may be a much later document than Ephesians, King Solomon throughout the pseudepigraphical *Testament of Solomon* shows a great concern to acquire the names of the many demons he brings under his sway to build the temple. All of this is part of his authority and power, for which he blesses the Lord in terms familiar from Ephesians:

> Εὐλογητὸς εἶ, κύριε ὁ θεός, ὁ δοὺς τῷ Σολομῶντι τὴν ἐξουσίαν ταύτην· σοὶ δόξα καὶ κράτος εἰς τοὺς αἰῶνας· ἀμήν.

---

51. Cf., for example, Col 1:16, εἴτε θρόνοι εἴτε κυριότητες εἴτε ἀρχαὶ εἴτε ἐξουσίαι ("whether thrones, whether lordships, whether rulers, whether authorities").

52. See also on 6:10–18. For the spirit world in Paul see in general: Martin Dibelius, *Die Geisterwelt im Glauben des Paulus* (Göttingen: Vandenhoeck & Ruprecht, 1909); G. B. Caird, *Principalities and Powers: A Study in Pauline Theology* (New York: Oxford University Press, 1956); Pierre Benoit, "Pauline Angelology and Demonology: Reflexions on Designations of Heavenly Powers and on Origin of Angelic Evil according to Paul," *RelSBul* 3 (1983): 1–18; Chris Forbes, "Paul's Principalities and Powers: Demythologizing Apocalyptic?" *JSNT* 82 (2001): 61–88; Barth, 170–83; O'Brien, 143–44.

53. In general see: Georg Luck, *Arcana Mundi: Magic and the Occult in the Greek and Roman Worlds* (Baltimore: Johns Hopkins University Press, 1985); Hans Dieter Betz, "Secrecy in the Greek Magical Papyri," in *Antike und Christentum* (Tübingen: Mohr Siebeck, 1998), 4:152–74; and Fritz Graf, *Magic in the Ancient World* (Cambridge, MA: Harvard University Press, 1999), 218–20; cf. John M. Dillon, "The Magical Power of Names," in *Origeniana Tertia: The Third International Colloquium for Origen Studies*, ed. R. P. C. Hanson and Henri Crouzel (Rome: Edizioni dell' Ateneo, 1985), 203–16.

> Blessed are you, O Lord God, who has given to Solomon this authority. To you be glory and might forever, amen. (*T. Sol.* 1.1; my trans.)
>
> Εὐλογητὸς εἶ, κύριε ὁ θεὸς ὁ παντακράτωρ ὁ δοὺς τῷ παιδί σου Σολομῶντι τὴν τῶν σῶν θρόνων πάρεδρον σοφίαν καὶ ὑποτάξας εἰς ἐμὲ πᾶσαν τὴν τῶν δαιμόνων δύναμιν.
>
> Blessed are you, O Lord God Almighty, who has given to your servant Solomon, wisdom, the lieutenant of your thrones, and you have subjected all the power of the demons to me. (*T. Sol.* 3.5; my trans.)

Hence, Paul qualifies πᾶν ὄνομα ("every name) with the cognate participle ὀνομαζόμενον ("that can be named") to underline to the Ephesians that in Christ there is no power whatsoever—seen or unseen—that has escaped subjection to Christ at his exaltation and enthronement and that they must still fear.

οὐ μόνον ἐν τῷ αἰῶνι τούτῳ ἀλλὰ καὶ ἐν τῷ μέλλοντι, "not only in this age but also in the age to come." As if the extent of Christ's preeminent kingship were not sufficiently expressed already, Paul adds that it covers not only "this age" but also "the age to come." While "age to come" is itself not a common phrase (only here; Matt 12:32; Heb 6:5), it communicates the common biblical conception that this era will be displaced by the new creation (e.g., Rev 21:1–7; cf. note on 2:7).[54] That Christ has already been placed into supreme authority in both this age and the coming one expresses the notion of inaugurated eschatology (e.g., Matt 28:18).[55]

These statements of Christ's comprehensive suzerainty in this age stand in clear contrast to the external political viewpoint of the period. For by

---

54. The phrase ὁ αἴων ὁ ἐρχόμενος found in Mark 10:30, and parallel Luke 18:30 is synonymous.

55. The notion of inaugurated versus consummated eschatology in Paul (and in the Scriptures at large) has been observed for quite some time (e.g., Geerhardus Vos, *The Pauline Eschatology* [Grand Rapids: Eerdmans, 1953]) and more recently, Andrew T. Lincoln, *Paradise Now and Not Yet*, SNTSMS (Cambridge: Cambridge University Press, 1981); and G. K. Beale, *A New Testament Biblical Theology: The Unfolding of the Old Testament in the New* (Grand Rapids: Baker Academic, 2011), where the "now and not yet" motif is a central theme.

that time, as Polybius notes, "The Romans have brought the whole world into subjection to themselves."[56] Hence, Paul's words could easily have been taken by the Roman authorities to be "provocative and seditious." As John Lotz observes:

> That Christ reigned in heaven at God's right hand, and that his power extended not only into the next age, but was rooted in the present one, could hardly have failed to escape comparison with the governors of provinces, or even the emperor, whose power and rule offered only timid promises of peace and empty slogans of harmony and concord.[57]

1:22 καὶ πάντα ὑπέταξεν ὑπὸ τοὺς πόδας αὐτοῦ, "and 'He put everything under his feet.' " This first colon* is a quote of Psa 8:6 (without citation notice) and is the first direct quotation of the OT in Ephesians.[58] Paul has already stressed Christ's exaltation emphatically in the previous two verses: He has been placed at God's right hand, far above every conceivable authority in this age and the next. Why add this quoted text? The context of Psa 8 is humankind's placement over the first creation. By citing this text here, Paul expresses his Second Adam theology here in brief (also 1 Cor 15:20–28; cf. Heb 2:5–9). As in the carefully crafted poetic passage in Col 1:15–20, the exalted Son—who already has all things under his feet by virtue of being the agent of creation—is supreme over the new creation as well (cf. 4:8–16) as its firstfruits (1 Cor 15:20–23).[59]

καὶ αὐτὸν ἔδωκεν κεφαλὴν ὑπὲρ πάντα τῇ ἐκκλησίᾳ, "and gave him as head over and above everything in the church." The second colon* has a double accusative construction: **αὐτὸν** ἔδωκεν **κεφαλὴν**, which is not common with δίδωμι but seems straightforward enough.[60] The pronoun αὐτόν

56. Ῥωμαῖοι πᾶσαν ἐποιήσαντο τὴν οἰκουμένην ὑπήκοον αὐτοῖς (Polybius, 3.3.9).

57. John Paul Lotz, "The *Homonoia* Coins of Asia Minor and Ephesians 1:21," *TynB* 50 (1999): 173–88 (quotes from 187–88); cf. Nijay K. Gupta and Fredrick J. Long, "The Politics of Ephesians and the Empire: Accommodation or Resistance?" *JGRChJ* 7 (2010): 112–36.

58. Cf. 5:24; Rom 8:20; 1 Cor 15:27–28; Phil 3:21; Heb 2:8; 1 Pet 3:22.

59. Cf. S. M. Baugh, "The Poetic Form of Col 1:15–20," *WTJ* 47 (1985): 227–44.

60. Only at Matt 20:28 (and parallel Mark 10:45); 2 Thess. 3:9; 1 Tim. 2:6; cf. Hoehner, 287–90, for other options.

is placed first in the series and in front of the verb for slight emphasis. The verb ἔδωκεν, rendered "he gave," may have the meaning "appoint" here, which is picked up from the LXX (LSJ, 423 [meaning II.5]; BDAG, 242; e.g., Exod 31:6; Num 14:4). Hence, "head" is an office like "king," which is suggested by Paul's use of "body" for the church in the next verse (cf. 5:23; Col 1:18; 2:10).[61] Christ is so identified with the church that believers are said to be his very body, much as Adam described Eve as "bone of my bones and flesh of my flesh" (Gen 2:23; see on 5:30–32).

There is a connection between Christ as supreme ruler over the new creation with all things subjected to him and his position as head of the church in that the church itself is the embassy of the inaugurated new creation (see on 2:10; cf. Rom 8:23; Jas 1:18; Rev 14:4). Its members are citizens of a heavenly city (see on 2:11–22; cf. Gal 4:26–31; Phil 3:20; Heb 12:22; 13:14), with the power of the age to come unleashed on them in regeneration and sanctification (again, see on 2:10; cf. Rom 8:11; Heb 6:5).[62]

1:23 ἥτις ἐστὶν τὸ σῶμα αὐτοῦ, "which is his body." The metaphor of the body was used by other authors in Graeco-Roman antiquity, especially to explain the relation of the state to the individual (see Lincoln, 70–71; Hoehner,

61. The metaphor of Christ's "headship" obviously refers to his authority, especially in this context led off with the quote of Psa 8. Subjection of all things under Christ's feet makes him "head." This contrasts with modern views that "head" here means "source" or "origin" (e.g., Berkeley and Alvera Michelsen, "What Does *Kephalē* Mean in the New Testament?" in *Women, Authority & the Bible*, ed. Alvera Mickelsen [Downers Grove, IL: InterVarsity Press, 1986], 97–110). See fuller discussion of this in comments on 5:22–24. Some people find a medical background in the image; cf. Hoehner, 285–89; Lincoln, 67–72; Arnold, 80–82; Barth, 190 (cf. "Head, Body, and Fullness" on 183–210); O'Brien, 146–48.

62. Recent monographs on the new creation in Paul (though usually omitting use of Ephesians) include: T. Ryan Jackson, *New Creation in Paul's Letters: A Study of the Historical and Social Setting of a Pauline Concept*, WUNT 2.272 (Tübingen: Mohr Siebeck, 2010); cf. Ulrich Meli, *Neue Schöpfung: Eine traditionsgeschichtliche und exegetische Studie zu einem soteriologischen Grundsatz paulinischer Theologie*, BZNW 56 (New York: de Gruyter, 1989); Moyer V. Hubbard, *New Creation in Paul's Letters and Thought*, SNTSMS 119 (Cambridge: Cambridge University Press, 2002); and Rodrigo J. Morales, *The Spirit and the Restoration of Israel: New Exodus and New Creation Motifs in Gaiatians*, WUNT 2.282 (Tübingen: Mohr Siebeck, 2010); and earlier: Paul S. Minear, *Christians and the New Creation: Genesis Motifs in the New Testament* (Louisville: Westminster John Knox, 1994).

290–94).[63] The church as Christ's unified body appears elsewhere in Paul's writings (4:12, 16; 5:30; cf. Rom 12:4–5; 1 Cor 12:12–27; Col 1:18, 24; 2:10) and has been frequently discussed in scholarly literature.[64]

Given the context, and especially the fact that v. 23a appears as the third colon* of a unified period, why does Paul state that the church is Christ's body *here*?[65] This is not an isolated ecclesiological statement but something Paul felt needed to be added in the flow of his presentation. Rereading especially from v. 19, we see that God has exerted his sovereign power toward believers by raising Christ, though this was not explained or developed fully there (see comment above). Then the focus in vv. 20–21 expands on the Messiah's own exaltation to comprehensive sovereign authority, culminating in v. 22 (the first half of this last period) with the quote from Psa 8 that everything has been brought into subjection under Christ's feet and that he has been appointed as "head over and above everything in the church."

To this point, it is not exactly clear where the church stands. Does Christ have his foot on the necks of the Ephesians and of other believers (v. 22a)? He may be their head, but where do they stand relative to this conquest? For believers in Asia Minor, currently under the dominion of Rome and with extensive domination from Pergamum or the Persians (Parthia) in the not-too-distant past, the idea of Christ as Supreme Head needed a little qualification.[66] Paul provides the qualification with a succinct statement.

---

63. For discussion of metaphors in general and specifically as used in Ephesians see Gerald A. Klingbeil, "Metaphors and Pragmatics: An Introduction to the Hermeneutics of Metaphors in the Epistle to the Ephesians," *BBR* 16 (2006): 273–93.

64. E.g., Ernest Best, *One Body in Christ* (London: SPCK, 1955); Robert H. Gundry, *Soma in Biblical Theology* (Cambridge: Cambridge University Press, 1976); George E. Howard, "The Head/Body Metaphors of Ephesians," *NTS* 20 (1974): 350–56; G. M. M. Pelser, "Once More the Body of Christ in Paul," *Neot* 32 (1998): 525–45; Best, 189–96.

65. The periodic division was presented in the introduction for 1:15–23 above. Here is the last period again for convenience:

[22] καὶ πάντα ὑπέταξεν ὑπὸ τοὺς πόδας αὐτοῦ
καὶ αὐτὸν ἔδωκεν κεφαλὴν ὑπὲρ πάντα τῇ ἐκκλησίᾳ
[23] ἥτις ἐστὶν τὸ σῶμα αὐτοῦ
τὸ πλήρωμα τοῦ τὰ πάντα ἐν πᾶσιν πληρουμένου.

66. The grandparents of those living at the time of this epistle would have experienced the particularly deleterious effects of the Roman civil war of the second triumvirate. Mark Anthony had his headquarters at Ephesus at one point and ravaged the city to fund his campaigns (Plutarch, *Antonius* 24). There were grave fears that

The church is Christ's body—not a subject enemy under his feet. The next colon*, expressing particularly the church as Christ's "fullness," adds even more to assure the Ephesians that Christ's great ascent and exaltation to glory and power was for their benefit and that they share in its bounty.

τὸ πλήρωμα τοῦ τὰ πάντα ἐν πᾶσιν πληρουμένου, "the fullness of him who fills everything entirely." Like the previous colon* (v. 23a), this statement has drawn much discussion, particularly whether there may be some sort of (proto-)gnostic influence on the author in describing the church as τὸ πλήρωμα (see also 3:19 and 4:10; cf. Jer 23:24; John 1:16; Col 3:11).[67] Besides being anachronistic for Gnosticism, which was a later development, there seems to be no polemics or borrowing here but an interest in explaining the tremendously privileged position accorded to church members, who are united to the triumphantly sovereign Messiah (as just seen on v. 23a; cf. O'Brien, 151). Given that Christ is exalted to the heavenly realm over every other conceivable power (vv. 20–21), he nevertheless fills all of creation ("everything entirely"; so also 4:10; Col 2:10) with his sovereign presence in and through the church, his body and fullness, in this age (e.g., Matt 28:20; 2 Cor 4:7–12; Col 1:27; Heb 13:5).

This interpretation has been supported recently by Roy Jeal, who has pointed to the oral/aural character of v. 23b and its rhetorical character.[68] In particular, he points out the important parallelism between v. 23a and 23b, with two nouns ending in -μα, and connecting gens. that have rhyming endings (*homoeoteleuton*): τὸ σῶμα αὐτοῦ / τὸ πλήρωμα τοῦ ... πληρουμένου. Jeal concludes: "The rhetorical and practical function of 1:23 is to point out that the church is the «body» and the «fulness» on whose behalf

---

Octavian/Augustus would punish the city because of this and great relief when he did not; Strabo, *Geog.* 14.1.23; Cassius Dio, 51.20.6. Ephesus was still in process of economic recovery from that war in Paul's day.

67. Cf. C. F. D. Moule, " 'Fulness' and 'Fill' in the New Testament," *SJT* 4 (1951): 79–86; Josef Ernst, *Pleroma und Pleroma Christi: Geschichte und Deutung eines Begriffs der paulinischen Antilegomena*, BU 5 (Regensburg: Pustet, 1970); P. D. Overfield, "*Pleroma*: A Study in Context and Content," *NTS* 25 (1979): 384–96; Craig A. Evans, "The Meaning of *Pleroma* in Nag Hammadi," *Bib* 65 (1984): 254–65; John M. Dillon, "*Pleroma* and Noetic Cosmos: A Comparative Study," in *Neoplatonism and Gnosticism* (Albany: State University of New York, 1992), 99–110; Hoehner, 301–4.

68. Roy R. Jeal, "A Strange Style of Expression: Ephesians 1:23," *Filologia Neotestamentaria* 10 (1997): 129–38.

the sovereign Christ «fills», i.e., rules, the cosmos."[69] This is a very helpful approach, particularly since *πλήρωμα* was meant to parallel and further explicate the church as Christ's *σῶμα* (Barth, 158).

If I were to add anything to Jeal's treatment and to those of others, it would be in relation to their describing the wordplay in v. 23 as "poetic" or even "sonorous."[70] Their focus has been on rhyming endings and use of cognates. These are important elements of composition, but the key element that defines Greek poetry and the "feel" of Greek to the hearers is syllable length and meter, which is missing from most modern examinations of our text. The meter of this colon* is: ¯ ¯ | ¯ ˘ ¯ | ˘ ¯ ¯ ˘ | ¯ ¯ | ¯ ¯ | ¯ ˘ ¯ (*τὸ πλήρωμα τοῦ τὰ πάντα ἐν πᾶσιν πληρουμένου*). This is not metrical poetry, but the two cretic feet (¯ ˘ ¯) and the predominance of long syllables (eleven out of fifteen) give this colon* a clear dignity of tone (see the introduction). Add to that the use of plosive sounds (*pi* and *tau*) opening each word but one, **τὸ** *πλήρωμα* **τοῦ** **τὰ** *πάντα ἐν πᾶσιν πληρουμένου*, and the effect is a dramatic punctuation to the end of the periodic sentence begun in v. 15.[71]

Application and Devotional Implications

In Ephesians 6:18 Paul exhorts his audience to pray for all the saints; it is an exhortation he models in this passage. While 1:15–23 is not itself a prayer, Paul reports on his prayers for the recipients and aids them in gaining a deeper understanding of God himself and of his redemptive gifts and power for his people in Christ. Christ himself, the head of the church, is presented as supreme over every conceivable competing power in the universe. This latter point would be particularly striking for people whose lives had been dominated by various magical practices designed to protect one from dangerous unseen forces. All those forces have been put under his feet: "He [God] disarmed the rulers and authorities and put them to open shame, by triumphing over them in him" (Col 2:15; cf. Eph 4:8). So also today, believers have no reason to fear any unseen spiritual forces in their lives.

---

69. Ibid., 137–38; cf. Lincoln, 77–78; O'Brien, 151–52.

70. See Jeal, "Strange Style," 136; Lincoln, 72.

71. Plosive *pi* stands out in the first colon* of this period also: *καὶ πάντα ὑπέταξεν ὑπὸ τοὺς πόδας αὐτοῦ* (v. 22a); cf. 3:19; 4:6, 10; esp. Heb 1:1.

In 1:18–19 Paul explains that the knowledge he prays his audience will gain centers on the truths of God's redemptive accomplishment on their behalf rather than on their duties. They have evidenced the reality of their faith in "love toward the saints" (v. 16) in fulfillment of the "royal law" (Jas 2:8; cf. 1 Tim 1:5; 1 Pet 1:22). Paul will not withhold any exhortation to holy living as the epistle continues, but he knows that sustained and greater holiness in love arises out of deeper knowledge of the gospel of God's lavish gifts of hope, redemption, and powerful salvation rather than endlessly bludgeoning Christians with demands for fulfilling the law's duties.

Additional Exegetical Comments: Magic

Magical practices of various sorts (divination, incantations, theurgy, charms, amulets, astrology, etc.) were an important part of daily affairs everywhere and at all times in antiquity, but especially at Ephesus (Acts 19:19; cf. Acts 8:9; 13:6, 8).[72] It is sometimes hard to imagine how much of daily life was engaged in warding off dangers from dark, unseen forces. "Take nothing to eat or to wash with from uncharmed pots," advises one of Greece's earliest poets, Hesiod, "for in them there is mischief" (Hesiod, *Op.* 748–49). The superstitious man does not stop with pots, but "is apt to purify his house frequently, claiming Hekate has bewitched it" (Theophrastus, *Char.* 16.7). And discovery of a tortoise is particularly lucky, for this animal was "a bulwark against baneful spells" (Homeric Hymns, "To Hermes," 37–38; my trans.). Famous witches like Circe or Medea dot Hellenistic literature with

72. See esp. the work of Clinton Arnold noted in comments on v. 19 above. Mention can be made particularly of the well-known Ἐφεσήϊα γράμματα, Ephesian "letters" (e.g., λιξ, τετραξ, and δαμναμενευς); cf. Arnold, *Power and Magic*, 15–16. These were particularly powerful elements in spells and charms; see Roy Kotansky, "Incantations and Prayers for Salvation on Inscribed Greek Amulets," in *Magika Hiera: Ancient Greek Magic and Religion*, ed. Christopher A. Faraone and Dirk Obbink (New York: Oxford University Press, 1991), 107–37; esp. 110–12; 121–22; and Kotansky, "Greek Exorcistic Amulets," in *Ancient Magic and Ritual Power*, ed. Marvin W. Meyer and Paul Allan Mirecki, RGRW 129 (Leiden: Brill, 1995), 243–77, esp. 253–57, for discussion of an incantation amulet that contains the Ephesian letters. It is thought that Artemis Ephesia herself rivaled Hekate as a mistress of the dark arts and was possibly connected with the power of astrology; cf. Elma Heinzel, "Zum Kult der Artemis von Ephesos," *JAÖI* 50 (1970): 243–51. For recent analysis of Artemis and magic see J. R. Harrison, in *New Docs*, 10:37–47.

their use of "noxious roots of the earth," the evil eye, and mystic incantations and rites too fearful even to recount (e.g., Apollonius, *Argon.* 4.50–65; 4.123–61; 4.247–50). These were devotees of night-stalking Hekate (or Lat. Hecate), "the only-begotten Maiden" (Κούρη μουνογένεια) (*Argon.* 3:846), "Lovely Hecate ... reveling in the souls of the dead ... monstrous queen ... of repelling countenance" (*Hymn to Hecate*) and fierce mistress of the black arts who had an active cult* throughout Asia Minor, including many references in the remains from Ephesus (e.g., *IvE* 567).[73]

The early Christians lived in a world where syncretism of Christianity with magical practices and beliefs of various sorts was still a live temptation, such that the early postbiblical writers repeatedly warned their flocks away from the black arts.[74] In the *Epistle of Barnabas* and the *Didache* (*Barn.* 20.1 and *Did.* 2.2; 3.4, 5.1) we read that the way of the Black One lies in sorcery (φαρμακεία; cf. Rev 9:21; 18:23; Gal 5:20) and magic (μαγεία; cf. Acts 8:11). Ignatius of Antioch encourages the Ephesians by saying that the incarnation of Christ has dissolved all magic practices (μαγεία) and the bondage of evil and ignorance; the old kingdom of the prince of this age has been destroyed (Ignatius, *Eph.* 19.3; cf. Ignatius, *Pol.* 5.1).

Clinton Arnold concludes on the teaching of Ephesians related to its background in a world of ritual power and magic:

> God's superior power is available to believers and is working for their best interest—he desires to mediate it to his people for their protection and growth. Believers are depicted as having been transplanted from one sphere of power (kingdom, or dominion) and placed in another. This transfer forms the basis for their access to the power of God. There is therefore no need for believers to seek any additional protection from the "powers" by

73. The hymn to Hekate and translation above is from Apostolos N. Athanassakis, *The Orphic Hymns: Text, Translation and Notes* (Atlanta: Scholars Press, 1977; repr., 1988), 4–7. Shakespeare gives Hekate a speaking role in *Macbeth* connected with the famous chant of the three witches: "Double, double toil and trouble; Fire burn, and cauldron bubble. Fillet of a fenny snake, in the cauldron boil and bake. ... For a charm of powerful trouble, Like a hell-broth boil and bubble" (*Macbeth* IV.1).

74. Cf. Marvin Meyer and Richard Smith, eds., *Ancient Christian Magic: Coptic Texts of Ritual Power* (San Francisco: HarperCollins, 1994).

any means. This would include the devising of ways to manipulate the demons or the invoking of angelic assistance.[75]

The revolutionary teaching that Paul impresses on his audience in 1:15–23 is that these marvelous realities are appropriated in their fullness by faith in Christ alone.

Selected Bibliography

Allen, T. "Exaltation and Solidarity with Christ. Ephesians 1:20 and 2:6." *JSNT* 28 (1986): 103–20.

Arnold, C. *Ephesians: Power and Magic: The Concept of Power in Ephesians in Light of Its Historical Setting*. SNTSMS 63. New York: Cambridge University Press, 1989.

Barrett, C. *From First Adam to Last: A Study in Pauline Theology*. London: Adam & Charles Black, 1962.

Beale, G. *A New Testament Biblical Theology: The Unfolding of the Old Testament in the New*. Grand Rapids: Baker Academic, 2011.

Benoit, P. "Pauline Angelology and Demonology: Reflexions on Designations of Heavenly Powers and on Origin of Angelic Evil according to Paul." *RelSBul* 3 (1983): 1–18.

Best, E. *One Body in Christ*. London: SPCK, 1955.

Betz, H. "Secrecy in the Greek Magical Papyri." In *Antike und Christentum* 4, 152–74. Tübingen: Mohr Siebeck, 1998.

Caird, G. *Principalities and Powers: A Study in Pauline Theology*. New York: Oxford University Press, 1956.

Campbell, C. *Paul and Union with Christ: An Exegetical and Theological Study*. Grand Rapids: Zondervan, 2012.

Denton, D. "Inheritance in Paul and Ephesians." *EvQ* 54 (1982): 157–62.

Dibelius, M. *Die Geisterwelt im Glauben des Paulus*. Göttingen: Vandenhoeck & Ruprecht, 1909.

Dillon, J. "*Pleroma* and Noetic Cosmos: A Comparative Study." In *Neoplatonism and Gnosticism*, 99–110. Albany: State University of New York Press, 1992.

Ernst, J. *Pleroma und Pleroma Christi: Geschichte und Deutung eines Begriffs der paulinischen Antilegomena*. BU 5. Regensburg: Pustet, 1970.

Evans, C. "The Meaning of *Pleroma* in Nag Hammadi." *Biblica* 65 (1984): 254–65.

Fenik, J. "Enthroned with Christ: An Exegetical and Theological Study of Eph 1:20–23 and 2:5–6." STD diss., Catholic University of America, 2008.

75. Arnold, *Power and Magic*, 169.

Fesko, J. *Beyond Calvin: Union with Christ and Justification in Early Modern Reformed Theology (1517–1700)*. Bristol, CT: Vandenhoeck & Ruprecht, 2012.

Forbes, C. "Paul's Principalities and Powers: Demythologizing Apocalyptic?" *JSNT* 82 (2001): 61–88.

Gombis, T. "Ephesians 2 as a Narrative of Divine Warfare." *JSNT* 26 (2004): 403–18.

Graf, F. *Magic in the Ancient World*. Cambridge, MA: Harvard University Press, 1999.

Gundry, R. *Soma in Biblical Theology*. Cambridge: Cambridge University Press, 1976.

Gupta, N., and F. Long. "The Politics of Ephesians and the Empire: Accommodation or Resistance?" *JGRChJ* 7 (2010): 112–36.

Hammer, P. "A Comparison of *KLĒRONOMI* in Paul and Ephesians." *JBL* 79 (1960): 267–72.

Heinzel, E. "Zum Kult der Artemis von Ephesos." *JAÖI* 50 (1970): 243–51.

Hester, J. *Paul's Concept of Inheritance: A Contribution to the Understanding of Heilsgeschichte*. Edinburgh and London: Oliver & Boyd, 1968.

Horton, M. *Covenant and Salvation: Union with Christ*. Louisville: Westminster John Knox, 2007.

Howard, G. "The Head/Body Metaphors of Ephesians." *NTS* 20 (1974): 350–56.

Hubbard, M. *New Creation in Paul's Letters and Thought*. SNTSMS 119. Cambridge: Cambridge University Press, 2002.

Jackson, T. *New Creation in Paul's Letters: A Study of the Historical and Social Setting of a Pauline Concept*. WUNT 2.272. Tübingen: Mohr Siebeck, 2010.

Jeal, R. "A Strange Style of Expression: Ephesians 1:23." *Filologia Neotestamentaria* 10 (1997): 129–38.

Klingbeil, G. "Metaphors and Pragmatics: An Introduction to the Hermeneutics of Metaphors in the Epistle to the Ephesians." *BBR* 16 (2006): 273–93.

Kotansky, R. "Greek Exorcistic Amulets." In *Ancient Magic and Ritual Power*, ed. M. Meyer and P. Mirecki, 243–77. RGRW 129. Leiden: Brill, 1995.

———. "Incantations and Prayers for Salvation on Inscribed Greek Amulets." In *Magika Hiera: Ancient Greek Magic and Religion*, ed. C. Faraone and D. Obbink, 107–37. New York: Oxford University Press, 1991.

Letham, R. *Union with Christ: In Scripture, History, and Theology*. Phillipsburg, NJ: P&R, 2011.

Longman, T. "The Divine Warrior: The New Testament Use of an Old Testament Motif." *WTJ* 44 (1982): 290–307.

Lotz, J. "The Homonoia Coins of Asia Minor and Ephesians 1:21." *TynB* 50 (1999): 173–88.

Luck, G. *Arcana Mundi: Magic and the Occult in the Greek and Roman Worlds.* Baltimore: Johns Hopkins University Press, 1985.

Meli, U. *Neue Schöpfung: Eine traditionsgeschichtliche und exegetische Studie zu einem soteriologischen Grundsatz paulinischer Theologie.* BZNW 56. New York: de Gruyter, 1989.

Meyer, M., and R. Smith, eds. *Ancient Christian Magic: Coptic Texts of Ritual Power.* San Francisco: HarperCollins, 1994.

Michelsen, B., and A. Michelsen. "What Does *Kephalē* Mean in the New Testament?" In *Women, Authority & the Bible*, ed. A. Mickelsen, 97–110. Downers Grove, IL: InterVarsity Press, 1986.

Minear, P. *Christians and the New Creation: Genesis Motifs in the New Testament.* Louisville: Westminster John Knox, 1994.

Morales, R. *The Spirit and the Restoration of Israel: New Exodus and New Creation Motifs in Galatians.* WUNT 2.282. Tübingen: Mohr Siebeck, 2010.

Moule, C. " 'Fulness' and 'Fill' in the New Testament." *SJT* 4 (1951): 79–86.

Overfield, P. "Pleroma: A Study in Context and Content." *NTS* 25 (1979): 384–96.

Pelser, G. "Once More the Body of Christ in Paul." *Neot* 32 (1998): 525–45.

Scroggs, R. *The Last Adam: A Study in Pauline Anthropology.* Philadelphia: Fortress, 1966.

Vos, G. *The Pauline Eschatology.* Grand Rapids: Eerdmans, 1953.

Deliverance from Death to Life in Christ (2:1–10)

Introduction

In Ephesians 2:1–10 Paul instructs his audience regarding their former utter hopelessness and guilt under the evil inclinations of this age and then expands on the entirely gracious intervention of God on their behalf when he raised and exalted Christ and freed them for grateful obedience as part of the new creation in Christ for his glory. In the previous section (1:15–23) Paul reported on his prayers for the Ephesians' understanding of God's work on their behalf in Christ. There the exaltation of Christ to supreme power over all competing cosmic forces was emphasized, along with its benefits for the church. As Ephesians 2:1–10 opens, though, Paul dwells briefly on the fact that this work was accomplished for God's people at the very time when they were God's vile, willing enemies ("dead in transgressions and sins ... performing the will of the flesh"). Because of this initial focus, we can see that Paul's overarching concern here is to stress that believers' deliverance is entirely a divine act of grace. Furthermore, we see particularly in the verbs in 2:5–6 a development of the idea of believers' union with Christ, which Paul had been working with in 1:19–20.

Ephesians 2:1–10 is an extraordinarily powerful and complex passage—probably the most powerful in this rich book. Many features of its composition go into making it so forceful: the opening direct object clauses with suspension of the main verbs until vv. 5–6; the use of long syllables in the opening (vv. 1–3), along with the switch to predominantly short syllables when the news gets better (esp. v. 4a); and, most of all, the incredible content conveyed in Paul's instruction here. An ancient sophist would undoubtedly find many objectionable features in the language and form of the passage—it is by no means smooth and elegant—but Paul's style overall is rugged and powerful, not elegant. To blaze a trail through Gentile pretension and pride called for a bulldozer, not an ornamental hoe.

The grammatical and rhetorical complexity of 2:1–10 makes it exceedingly hard to render into smooth English. English versions typically break this passage into multiple sentences and turn the accusative participle phrases in vv. 1 and 5 (ὑμᾶς ὄντας νεκροὺς … ὄντας ἡμᾶς νεκροὺς, "and you—even though you were dead … even though we were dead") into independent statements.[1] However, the accusative pronouns in these phrases are true direct objects of the main verbs of vv. 5–6 (συνεζωοποίησεν … καὶ συνήγειρεν καὶ συνεκάθισεν, "co-made alive … and co-raised and co-seated"). As a result, the opening accusative clause in v. 1 creates a most notable tension as one awaits resolution of the suspended subject and verbs. In an oral presentation, this resolution does not take long, but it does require concentration from the hearers and fine oral skill from the presenter (Tychicus?).

It is common to break Eph 2:1–10 into two or more sections, especially with vv. 8–10 treated as a separate short section picking up and explaining the parenthetical remark (χάριτί ἐστε σεσῳσμένοι, "by grace are you saved") from v. 5.[2] While this is possible because of the syntax, it is better to preserve the unity of the whole section from v. 1 all the way to v. 10 based on an inclusio* from *walking* in evil works of the old creation in the last colon* of the first period (v. 2a, ἐν αἷς ποτε περιεπατήσατε, "in which you formerly walked") to *walking* in good works in the new creation in the last colon* of the last period (v. 10, ἵνα ἐν αὐτοῖς περιπατήσωμεν, "that we should start walking in them"; cf. O'Brien, 154–55).[3] This overarching unity of vv. 1–10 overrides the temptation to cut the pericope short at v. 7.

---

1. The Vg.—since Latin allows periodic composition much the same as Greek—has vv. 1–7 as one sentence.
2. Codex Alexandrinus (A) divides the text (with *paragraphus* marks and a high dot [*stigme teleia*] "·" at the end of v. 7) into vv. 1–3, 4–7, 8–10, while Codex Claromontanus (D) divides it into vv. 1–3, 4–7, 8–12. Cf. William A. Johnson, "The Function of the Paragrapus in Greek Literary Prose Texts," *ZPE* 100 (1994): 65–68.
3. Best writes that this inclusio* "would be easier to accept if the first occurrence of the verb had been at the beginning of the passage" (Best, 199). However, this shows the weakness of relying on modern versification for structuring the text rather than the way ancient Greek was actually organized. (E.g., Eph 2:9 is strangely just one colon* and belongs with the material of v. 8!) Both occurrences of περιπατέω appear as the last word in their respective periods (vv. 2a and 10d), which is a place of focus as the presenter paused for breath there. Hence, the first occurrence of περιπατέω

The periodic sentence structure of Eph 2:1–10 was presented in the introduction with some observations on its composition. Here is the suggested periodic division again:

A	[1] καὶ ὑμᾶς ὄντας νεκροὺς τοῖς παραπτώμασιν καὶ ταῖς ἁμαρτίαις ὑμῶν [2] ἐν αἷς ποτε περιεπατήσατε
B	κατὰ τὸν αἰῶνα τοῦ κόσμου τούτου κατὰ τὸν ἄρχοντα τῆς ἐξουσίας τοῦ ἀέρος τοῦ πνεύματος τοῦ νῦν ἐνεργοῦντος ἐν τοῖς υἱοῖς τῆς ἀπειθείας
C	[3] ἐν οἷς καὶ ἡμεῖς πάντες ἀνεστράφημέν ποτε ἐν ταῖς ἐπιθυμίαις τῆς σαρκὸς ἡμῶν ποιοῦντες τὰ θελήματα τῆς σαρκὸς καὶ τῶν διανοιῶν καὶ ἤμεθα τέκνα φύσει ὀργῆς ὡς καὶ οἱ λοιποί
D	[4] ὁ δὲ θεὸς πλούσιος ὢν ἐν ἐλέει διὰ τὴν πολλὴν ἀγάπην αὐτοῦ ἣν ἠγάπησεν ἡμᾶς
E	[5] καὶ ὄντας ἡμᾶς νεκροὺς τοῖς παραπτώμασιν συνεζωοποίησεν τῷ Χριστῷ χάριτί ἐστε σεσῳσμένοι
F	[6] καὶ συνήγειρεν καὶ συνεκάθισεν ἐν τοῖς ἐπουρανίοις ἐν Χριστῷ Ἰησοῦ
G	[7] ἵνα ἐνδείξηται ἐν τοῖς αἰῶσιν τοῖς ἐπερχομένοις τὸ ὑπερβάλλον πλοῦτος τῆς χάριτος αὐτοῦ ἐν χρηστότητι ἐφ᾽ ἡμᾶς ἐν Χριστῷ Ἰησοῦ

---

in fact appears in a prominent place at the beginning of the passage, clearly parallel with the second usage. What shows that this was intentional is that Paul chose a synonym for περιπατέω in v. 3 (ἀναστρέφω) to avoid spoiling the inclusio*.

H [8] τῇ γὰρ χάριτί ἐστε σεσῳσμένοι διὰ πίστεως
καὶ τοῦτο οὐκ ἐξ ὑμῶν
θεοῦ τὸ δῶρον
[9] οὐκ ἐξ ἔργων ἵνα μή τις καυχήσηται

I [10] αὐτοῦ γάρ ἐσμεν ποίημα
κτισθέντες ἐν Χριστῷ Ἰησοῦ ἐπὶ ἔργοις ἀγαθοῖς
οἷς προητοίμασεν ὁ θεὸς
ἵνα ἐν αὐτοῖς περιπατήσωμεν

The overall flow of this passage can be divided into three seamless sections: (1) the opening, with its dismal rehearsal of human failure (vv. 1–3, 5a); (2) the thrilling central section announcing the gracious intervention of God to save his elect in Christ Jesus (vv. 4, 5b–7); and (3) the concluding restatement that all of this is by God's grace alone and produces a new life of obedience in Christ (vv. 8–10; cf. Lincoln, 84). All of these sections are interlocked with one another but clearly mark the development of Paul's instruction.[4]

The somber material in vv. 1–3 is marked appropriately by the heavy use of long syllables. The statements plod along as the grim rehearsal of the audience's former lostness is unfolded. For example, in the last colon* (v. 3d) there are only four short syllables, compared to eleven long (καὶ ἤμεθα τέκνα φύσει ὀργῆς ὡς καὶ οἱ λοιποί, ¯ ¯ ˘ ˘ | ¯ ˘ ˘ | ¯ ¯ | ¯ ¯ | ¯ ¯ | ¯ ¯). But then the story shifts with a striking suddenness to the stupendous intervention of God on behalf of his enemies with the greatest short statement in the history of human language: "But God, because he is rich in mercy ..." (v. 4). The rhythm speeds up dramatically here in v. 4 with opening and closing paeans and many other short syllables (ὁ δὲ θεὸς πλούσιος ὢν ἐν ἐλέει, ˘ ˘ ˘ ¯ | ¯ ˘ ˘ ¯ | ˘ ˘ ˘ ¯). While this is not poetic or studied use of meter, it is obvious that Paul has an intuitive ear for rhythms that match his subject matter and his argument's development at times like this.

4. The various (unpersuasive) ideas about this passage's background as a hymn, (baptismal) confession, or other kind of liturgical unit are discussed in Lincoln, 85–91. Lincoln's own idea that this forms a *narratio* section of an oration is possible, but this epistle is not a speech, where such analysis provides helpful insight into its function (so also O'Brien, 155; cf. Lincoln, 91; Witherington, 250–51).

At the most basic level, the main syntactical components spanning vv. 1–6 consist of the direct object, subject, restatement of the direct object, and the three main verbs: καὶ ὑμᾶς ... ὁ δὲ θεὸς ... καὶ ... ἡμᾶς ... συνεζωοποίησεν ... καὶ συνήγειρεν καὶ συνεκάθισεν. The restatement of the direct object changes from ὑμᾶς ("you") to ἡμᾶς ("us"), making it appear to be different, but the repetition of the concessive phrase ("even though you/we were dead in transgressions," καὶ ὑμᾶς ὄντας νεκροὺς τοῖς παραπτώμασιν ... καὶ ὄντας ἡμᾶς νεκροὺς τοῖς παραπτώμασιν) in the restatement in v. 5 shows that it is resuming the point broken off from v. 1. The switch from "you" to "us" is an important part of the development of Paul's argument, as will be addressed in the comments.[5]

The restatement of salvation by grace in vv. 5 and 8 is a noteworthy case of anaphoric* framing.[6] Except for the addition of an article to the noun and use of the conjunction γάρ in the restatement, otherwise the wording is identical: χάριτί ἐστε σεσῳσμένοι ... τῇ γὰρ χάριτί ἐστε σεσῳσμένοι ("by grace you are saved ... for by grace you are saved"). In this case, however, the first mention of the idea acts not as an idea broken off to be resumed later, but as a *preview* in v. 5 of what is to be developed later in vv. 8–10.[7] As such, the restatement serves as an expansion of an idea that connects to the main verbs of vv. 5–6 ("co-made alive ... co-raised and co-seated").

---

5. The same shift in person of the pronoun is found in Col 2:13: καὶ **ὑμᾶς** νεκροὺς ὄντας ἐν τοῖς παραπτώμασιν καὶ τῇ ἀκροβυστίᾳ τῆς σαρκὸς ὑμῶν, συνεζωοποίησεν **ὑμᾶς** σὺν αὐτῷ, χαρισάμενος **ἡμῖν** πάντα τὰ παραπτώματα, "And even though *you* were dead in your transgressions and in the uncircumcision of your flesh, he made *you* alive together with him and forgave *us* all our transgressions" (emphasis added).

6. The term *anaphora* is used loosely here for repetition of several words rather than being more strictly related to the first word of successive cola*; Heinrich Lausberg, *Handbook of Literary Rhetoric: A Foundation for Literary Study*, ed. David E. Orton and R. Dean Anderson (Boston: Brill, 1998), §629. John Harvey calls the phenomenon found in Eph 2:5 and 8 "ring composition" in *Listening to the Text: Oral Patterning in Paul's Letters* (Grand Rapids: Baker, 1998), esp. 65–82, 103, 126–27 (for Rom 5:12, 18). For example, Harvey notes: " 'Anaphoric' framing sentences are used to resume a narrative or an argument that has been interrupted by a digression" (81). For anaphora in general see BDF §§489, 491; for various types of repetition in ancient literature see Lausberg, *Handbook*, §§608–64.

7. See Rom 5:12, 18, when Paul breaks off his thought in v. 12 for critical digression and explanation of premises to his argument only to resume the suspended thought in 5:18 with nearly identical wording, signaled by ἄρα οὖν (cf. Rom 7:25 [resuming 7:15–18] and 8:12 [resuming 8:4–5]).

Once again, in an oral setting, anaphora serves to bring the hearers back to a point introduced earlier and to underline the repeated words. Repetition of this sort is a vital part of the aural experience in order to track the flow of any presentation, especially one as dense and complex as the theological material in Ephesians.

Outline

IV. Deliverance from Death to Life in Christ (2:1–10)
- A. The old life in death (2:1–3)
- B. Even while dead, believers are made alive in Christ's life (2:4–7)
- C. Expansion on this new life as a divine work leading to new obedience (2:8–10)

Original Text

1 Καὶ ὑμᾶς ὄντας νεκροὺς τοῖς παραπτώμασιν καὶ ταῖς ἁμαρτίαις[a] ὑμῶν, **2** ἐν
αἷς ποτε περιεπατήσατε[b] κατὰ τὸν αἰῶνα τοῦ κόσμου τούτου, κατὰ τὸν ἄρχοντα
τῆς ἐξουσίας τοῦ ἀέρος, τοῦ πνεύματος τοῦ νῦν ἐνεργοῦντος ἐν τοῖς υἱοῖς τῆς
ἀπειθείας· **3** ἐν οἷς καὶ ἡμεῖς πάντες ἀνεστράφημέν ποτε ἐν ταῖς ἐπιθυμίαις τῆς
σαρκὸς ἡμῶν ποιοῦντες τὰ θελήματα τῆς σαρκὸς καὶ τῶν διανοιῶν, καὶ ἤμεθα
τέκνα φύσει ὀργῆς ὡς καὶ οἱ λοιποί· **4** ὁ δὲ θεὸς πλούσιος ὢν ἐν ἐλέει, διὰ τὴν
πολλὴν ἀγάπην αὐτοῦ ἣν ἠγάπησεν[c] ἡμᾶς, **5** καὶ ὄντας ἡμᾶς νεκροὺς τοῖς παραπτώμασιν[d] συνεζωοποίησεν τῷ Χριστῷ[e],—χάριτί[f] ἐστε σεσῳσμένοι— **6** καὶ
συνήγειρεν καὶ συνεκάθισεν ἐν τοῖς ἐπουρανίοις ἐν Χριστῷ Ἰησοῦ, **7** ἵνα ἐνδείξηται ἐν τοῖς αἰῶσιν τοῖς ἐπερχομένοις τὸ ὑπερβάλλον πλοῦτος τῆς χάριτος αὐτοῦ
ἐν χρηστότητι ἐφ᾽ ἡμᾶς ἐν Χριστῷ Ἰησοῦ. **8** Τῇ γὰρ χάριτί ἐστε σεσῳσμένοι διὰ
πίστεως· καὶ τοῦτο οὐκ ἐξ ὑμῶν, θεοῦ τὸ δῶρον· **9** οὐκ ἐξ ἔργων, ἵνα μή τις καυχήσηται. **10** αὐτοῦ γάρ ἐσμεν ποίημα, κτισθέντες ἐν Χριστῷ Ἰησοῦ ἐπὶ ἔργοις
ἀγαθοῖς οἷς προητοίμασεν ὁ θεός, ἵνα ἐν αὐτοῖς περιπατήσωμεν.

Textual Notes

1.a. Vaticanus (B) has ἐπιθυμίαις ("passions") for ἁμαρτίαις ("sins"), picked up from v. 3.

2.b. P[46] has a double augment with this word (ἐπεριεπατήσατε). There are many such minor matters in this, our earliest papyrus witness for Ephesians, as also, for example, a dropped *omicron* in συνεζω[ο]ποί[ησεν] in v. 5.

4.c. P[46] and a few Latin MSS have ἠλεήσεν ("he showed mercy") for ἠγάπησεν ("he loved").

5.d. P[46] has the curious σώμασιν ("[we were dead] *in our bodies*") for παραπτώμασιν ("in our trespasses"), while D* has ἁμαρτίαις ("sins"). B, Ψ, and a few other witnesses combine the variants with (ἐν) τοῖς παραπτώμασιν καὶ ταῖς ἁμαρτίαις. The reading accepted by the UBS/NA editions with τοῖς παραπτώμασιν is widely attested and doubtlessly original.

5.e. P[46], B, 33, and other MSS add the preposition ἐν to τῷ Χριστῷ, which seems to be an accident or assimilation to the same phrase in v. 6.[8] The simple dative is obviously governed by the preposition συν in the compound verb συνεζωοποίησεν.

5.f. Some Western witnesses (D*, F, G, and various Latin MSS) add οὗ to make the phrase οὗ χάριτι and therefore more specific: "by *whose* grace."[9] Other later witnesses remove the asyndeton* by adding γάρ (or δέ), conforming to v. 8. The reading of the critical text is clearly original and makes for a strikingly strong parenthetical statement at this point in the period.

---

8. Cf. Bruce M. Metzger, *A Textual Commentary on the Greek New Testament*, 2nd ed. (New York: United Bible Societies, 1994), 533.
9. Cf. ibid.

Translation

1 And you—even though you were dead in your transgressions and sins,[10]
2 in which you formerly walked in accordance with the age[11] of this world,
in accordance with the ruler of the realm[12] of the air[13], the spirit who is now
at work in the sons of disobedience— **3** among whom we all formerly also
conducted our lives in the lusts of our flesh, performing the will of the flesh
and of our rationalizations,[14] and we were by nature children of wrath, as
also the others[15]— **4** but God, because he is rich in mercy, on account of the
abundant love with which[16] he loved us, **5** and even though we were dead

---

10. The near synonyms παράπτωμα ("transgression") and ἁμαρτία ("sin") may have slightly different meanings. A transgression implies a law code that is violated, while sin is a personal affront to the holy God (so Rom 5:12–14, where transgression exists only when sin is counted under covenant law; cf. "all sin is lawlessness" [1 John 5:17]). Here in Eph 2:1, the two terms seem to be used as synonyms, and use of both is pleonastic to underline the comprehensiveness of guilt; cf. 1:7 and 2:5; Gen 50:17; BDAG, 50–51, 770.

11. Some take αἰών here as a personal reference to a spiritual being, "the Aeon" (also at 3:9 and Col 1:26). While this is possible linguistically, it seems more likely to see a contrast here between "this age" and the "age to come" as in 1:21 (also 2:7; Matt 12:32; Heb 6:5); cf. BDAG, 32–33.

12. I take ἐξουσία ("realm" or "domain") as a synonym of βασιλεία ("kingdom") here, as also in Col 1:13 (cf. Luke 4:6; 22:53 ["domain of darkness"]; 23:7), which denotes the territory over which one holds ruling power and authority; BDAG, 352–53; not reported in LSJ, 599.

13. Cf. BDAG, 23, on ἀήρ as "space as [the] locale of celestial bodies or phenomenon ... the political domain of transcendent beings or powers."

14. The term διάνοια here refers to a thinking process that has become "darkened" (4:18) and leads to rationalizing evil actions that are hostile to God and to his truth (Col 1:21). See comment.

15. ὡς καὶ οἱ λοιποί, "as also the others" or "as also the rest" (BDAG, 602), refers back to the previous people who were dead and fallen. The reason he adds this qualifying phrase is to clearly assert the universal corruption of the human race outside Christ.

16. The acc. relative pronoun ἥν was attracted to the case of its antecedent (ἀγάπην), but its function is like a Greek dative of means to accentuate the enormity of God's love; i.e., God loved his people *with* abundant love. BDF §153 (2) take the acc. relative pronoun as the equivalent of a cognate acc. noun, citing the same phrase in John 17:26 in particular (though note the variant dative form ᾗ in Codex Bezae in this Johannine text).

in our transgressions—it was *us* he co-made alive[17] with the Messiah—by
grace you are saved— **6** and co-raised us and co-seated us in the high-heavenlies[18] in Christ Jesus, **7** so that in the ages to come he might show the surpassing wealth of his grace in kindness toward us in Christ Jesus— **8** for by
grace you are saved[19] through faith, and this does not originate from[20] you,
it is God's[21] gift, **9** not from works, so that no one may boast— **10** for we are
his creation[22], created in Christ Jesus for good works, which[23] God prepared
beforehand, that we should start walking[24] in them.

---

17. The συν- prefix in the three main verbs in this passage, συνεζωοποίησεν ... συνήγειρεν ... συνεκάθισεν, is normally rendered as "with" or "together with." By rendering these verbs with neologisms "**co**-made alive" ... "**co**-raised" ... "**co**-seated" I am trying to bring out the close bond between these events in Christ and for his people.

18. For the rendering "in the high-heavenlies" for ἐν τοῖς ἐπουρανίοις see the note on 1:3.

19. The periphrastic perf. ἐστε σεσῳσμένοι (E. Burton, *Syntax of the Moods and Tenses in New Testament Greek* [Edinburgh: T&T Clark, 1898], §84) focuses on the state resulting from a completed event, hence the use of the English pres. tense in translation is most appropriate: "you *are saved*"; cf. Burton, *Moods*, §75; K. L. McKay, *A New Syntax of the Verb in New Testament Greek: An Aspectual Approach*, SBG 5 (New York: Peter Lang, 1994), 31 (§3.4).

20. Ἐκ expresses origin here, hence "originate from" in translation (cf. BDAG, 296–97).

21. The gen. of origin with θεοῦ as previously expressed with the prep. **ἐξ** ὑμῶν is brought forward into a position of emphasis without an expected article (**θεοῦ** τὸ δῶρον). Hence, this is an example of "fronting" and breaking of Apollonius' canon that the translation tries to bring out (without complete success) by putting "God's" before "gift."

22. For the gloss "creation" for ποίημα ('the product of labor') see BDAG, 842. This noun is only used elsewhere in the NT with the same meaning in Rom 1:20 (cf. LXX Psa 142:5 [English 143:5]). Some English versions opt for the older term "workmanship," as KJV (ESV, NASB, NIV; cf. NRSV, "what he has made us").

23. The relative pronoun οἷς is attracted to the dative case of its antecedent, ἔργοις ("works"). The acc. (ἅ) is expected.

24. I take the aor. subjunctive περιπατήσωμεν as inceptive in meaning here (cf. Burton, *Moods*, §§41, 98; BDF §331). The meaning of περιπατέω ("walk") is inherently "atelic" or "unbounded," and so an aor. with this verb and meaning typically carried an inceptive nuance. It is clear from this context that we were *not* walking in these good works previously. The parallel in Rom 6:4 with the same inceptive idea is instructive: "in order that ... we may *start walking* (ἵνα ... περιπατήσωμεν) in newness of life."

Commentary

2:1 καὶ ὑμᾶς ὄντας νεκροὺς, "And you—even though you were dead." It is possible to take this participle clause as an accusative absolute, but this is entirely unnecessary and doesn't fit the mold of other biblical and extrabiblical examples of accusative abs.[25] One could also view this clause as a "hanging accusative" (*accusativus pendens*), in which the need for the accusative is broken off and the statement is incomplete in itself (*anacoluthon*; BDF §§466–69). This latter is the notion of many interpreters, such as Barth (212), who takes v. 1 as "a broken sentence containing no subject and no verb" (cf. Lincoln, 84; Best, 198). Yet this is not the case here, since the subject (ὁ θεὸς, v. 4) and verbs (συνεζωοποίησεν τῷ Χριστῷ ... καὶ συνήγειρεν καὶ συνεκάθισεν, vv. 5–6) controlling this accusative phrase (later expressed with ἡμᾶς in v. 5) are stated later in the passage (cf. Col 2:13).[26] While the delay in expressing the subject and verbs lacks the smoothness and clarity recommended by the ancient stylists, it does have particularly compelling and forceful features (see introduction above). Furthermore, the concessive force of the participle only becomes clear as the sentence unfolds ("*even though* you were dead"). The tension of the audience grows as their former, futile life apart from Christ (cf. 4:17–19) is ponderously sounded in their ears, awaiting the resolution that only begins eleven cola* later.[27]

νεκροὺς τοῖς παραπτώμασιν καὶ ταῖς ἁμαρτίαις ὑμῶν, "dead in your transgressions and sins." The dative in the statement "*in* your transgressions and sins" (restated in v. 5) designates the *sphere* (i.e., locative dative) where this

25. BDF §§137 (3), 424–25; Smyth, *Greek Grammar*, §§2059, 2076–78, but the ptc. is usually impersonal with no subject supplied, whereas Eph 2:1 is a complete predication. Colossians has καὶ ὑμᾶς ποτε ὄντας (1:21) governed by an indic. verb (ἀποκατήλλαξεν) a little later (1:22). Cf. Polybius 2.4.5 and 2.7.1 with ἀνθρώπους ὄντας as part of inf. constructions ("We are but men" in LCL trans.).

26. In true *anacoluthon,* the syntax would change and there would be no expressed verb(s) controlling these accs. A more prosaic statement of the skeleton of the sentence would be something like: Καὶ ὑμᾶς ὁ θεὸς συνεζωοποίησεν τῷ Χριστῷ ὄντας νεκροὺς τοῖς παραπτώμασιν ("And *you* God made alive with Christ, even though [you] were dead in your transgressions").

27. For the concessive ptc. see Burton, *Moods*, §437; BDF §425. One use of humor by the rhetors was to relieve "strained and gloomy pathos" as found in Eph 2:1–3 (Lausberg, *Handbook*, §257), though granted our few periods of vv. 1–3 are nothing like a long speech filled with the πάθος of tragedy (Quintilian, *Inst.* 6.2.20–36).

was true. A dative of reference or respect, "dead *with regard* to transgressions," is not possible, since believers before their conversion were in fact alive to transgressions, not dead to them.[28] This interpretation is confirmed further by the prepositional phrase "*in which* (ἐν αἷς) you formerly walked," where sins (the direct antecedent of the feminine relative pronoun—but the farther [neuter] transgressions are also included here) are the sphere where the audience formerly conducted their life (i.e., walked).

A "transgression" (παραπτώμα) is generally the violation of a sanctioned statute or law (1:7; Ezek 3:19–20 LXX; Rom 5:15–20; BDAG, 770). The focus is on the act as bringing consequences of curse and punishment, which are absent when there is no law (so Rom 4:15; 5:13–14; cf. Eph 1:7; 2:5; Col 2:13). "Sin," on the other hand, is an act of traitorous rebellion (1 John 3:4; 5:17) and particularly offends God (BDAG, 50–51). In both cases, death is the consequence (Rom 6:23), and hence these Ephesians were the walking dead "in transgressions and sins," not those who made an unintended mistake or error of judgment (cf. ἁμαρτία; LSJ, 77) like Actaeon or Oedipus with terrible consequences in Greek mythology and tragedy.[29]

2:2 ἐν αἷς ποτε περιεπατήσατε, "in which you formerly walked." "Walking in" something (περιπατέω ἐν) is a common OT metaphor for the conduct of one's life (e.g., Exod 16:4; 1 Kgs 3:14; Neh 10:29; Psa 1:1) and, as mentioned above, is found at the beginning and end of Eph 2:1–10 to unify the passage as an inclusio* (cf. 4:1; 5:2). A more common verb among the Greeks to communicate the conduct of life is ἀναστρέφω, which Paul uses in v. 3, and he thereby avoids using περιπατέω again so as not to interfere with the inclusio* of vv. 1 and 10. The point is that Paul's audience before their conversion were willingly engaged in *lifestyles* devoted to rebelliously violating God's holy law, not merely occasional mistakes or foibles (cf. 4:17; Rom 7:12; 11:30; Col 3:7; 1 John 1:6–10).

---

28. I.e., as implied in Rom 6:2. For the locative use of the dative see Daniel B. Wallace, *Greek Grammar beyond the Basics* (Grand Rapids: Zondervan, 1997), 153–55; *contra* BDF §199.

29. The Theban hunter Actaeon accidentally stumbled on Artemis while she was bathing in a pool; as punishment he was turned into a stag by the goddess and torn to pieces by his hunting dogs. The more familiar Oedipus unknowingly married his mother and fell under a curse for incest, as presented in the famous Oedipus trilogy of plays by Sophocles.

κατὰ τὸν αἰῶνα τοῦ κόσμου τούτου, "in accordance with the age of this world." We have already seen "this age" contrasted with the future "age to come" (Eph 1:21; cf. Matt 12:32; Luke 18:30), but in v. 2 we have a unique pleonasm (i.e., the use of more words than those necessary) with "the age of this world." The closest parallel in Pauline thought to this is a series about the wise "of this age" who possess the "wisdom of this world" (1 Cor 3:18–19). In our passage, "the age of this world" clearly has a negative reference, as it is not only a time reference but refers to the fallen world system. As such it is dominated by "fleshly lusts" (v. 3) and is a system to which Christians must not be conformed (Rom 12:2). Its rulers are doomed to pass away (1 Cor 2:6–8), along with "the god of this age," who has blinded the minds of unbelievers (2 Cor 4:4), "sons of this age" (Luke 16:8; cf. Luke 20:34), who are accordingly called here "sons of disobedience" (v. 2), the objects of God's wrath (5:6).

As mentioned in the translation note, some scholars take αἰών in the phrase "the age of this world" as referring to a personal, spiritual being; i.e., "the *Aeon* of this world." This makes the colon* in v. 2b virtually synonymous with the next one as a reference to "the ruler of the realm of the air." This is possible and an attractive possibility, especially since ancient peoples like the Ephesians were absorbed in ideas associated with "magic arts" (Acts 19:19), which included a healthy dose of astrology and animism, in which world forces were considered to be powerful beings that could be alternately placated or manipulated (e.g., Acts 8:9, 14–19). However, Paul, as already stated, seems more likely to be referencing the whole complex of this age in contrast with "the age to come" (cf. v. 7). He is showing throughout this epistle that when one strips away the veil hiding the heavens from human gaze, only the ascended, exalted Messiah dominates the view (e.g., 1:20–21). And Paul does not seem to be much influenced by pagan cosmology.

κατὰ τὸν ἄρχοντα τῆς ἐξουσίας τοῦ ἀέρος, "in accordance with the ruler of the realm of the air." This colon* is presented in parallel with the previous one without a conjunction (asyndeton*).[30] The meaning of "air" (ἀήρ) here connects with pagan notions of spirits and powers inhabiting the "airy"

30. Cf. Witherington, 254, who identifies the two κατά-initiated cola* (vv. 2b and 2c) as isocola with "nearly the same number of syllables" (11 and 15 respectively; cf. Lausberg, *Handbook*, §§719–54, who discusses various kinds of parallel cola* and

realms (BDAG, 23) and is therefore meaningful to Paul's audience as a description of Satan. Paul has just summarily stated that Christ has ascended as sovereign conqueror over all spiritual forces (1:20–22; cf. John 12:31; 16:33; Heb 2:14; Rev 12:7–12). Now he identifies his audience as formerly marching in line (i.e., walked *according to*) with the black prince of those defeated foes. Ἐξουσία more often points to right of command or governance, "authority," but here and in a few other places it points to the "realm" where that authority is exercised (cf. Luke 22:53; BDAG, 352–53 [meaning 6]). The statement in Col 1:13 is notably germane here: "He has delivered us from the domain of darkness (ἐκ τῆς ἐξουσίας τοῦ σκότους) and transferred us to the kingdom of his beloved Son."

τοῦ πνεύματος τοῦ νῦν ἐνεργοῦντος ἐν τοῖς υἱοῖς τῆς ἀπειθείας, "the spirit who is now at work in the sons of disobedience." Paul dispels any triumphalist notion that the ascent of Christ over all cosmic forces means that evil in this age is completely powerless. Instead, "the spirit who is now at work" is surely active, but his reach extends over "the sons of disobedience" (see 5:6)—no longer over Paul's Christian audience (cf. 1 John 4:4), even if they must engage his forces in conflict (Eph 6:10–17). This idea expresses the heart of the NT's inaugurated eschatology: The exalted Christ rules in the midst of his enemies (Psa 110:1–2; cf. Psa 2).[31] Paul is most concerned in these early chapters to drive home this truth to his Ephesian audience, with their former devotion to the magical arts, whose primary objective was the control of semiunderstood, hostile forces in the airy world.

2:3 ἐν οἷς καὶ ἡμεῖς πάντες ἀνεστράφημέν ποτε ἐν ταῖς ἐπιθυμίαις τῆς σαρκὸς ἡμῶν, "among whom we all formerly also conducted our lives in the lusts of our flesh." So far Paul has been talking to the Gentile Ephesians about their lostness before Christ brought them near through his blood (v. 13). Verse 3 begins an important transition to show that Christ's redemptive work was needed for the whole human race, both Jew and Greek (cf. Rom 1:16; 2:9–10; 1 Cor 1:24; Gal 3:28; Col 3:11). Here nominative ἡμεῖς πάντες ("we all") are not needed by the verb and are therefore emphatic. The "we" here signals Paul, as a representative of the Jews, alongside his Gentile audience

---

other sentence units). Parallel cola* opening with preps. and no conj. are common in Ephesians; see esp. comment on 4:12 (cf. Phil 3:6 and Col 2:8 with κατά also).

31. For a survey of eschatology related to Ephesians see the excursus in Gnilka, 122–28.

in a life of sin (cf. 3:8; 1 Tim 1:13). The "conduct of life" (ἀναστρέφω) in "the lusts of our flesh" (see Gal 5:16) shows that this lostness is not a passing error, lack of education, or a low social position—it is a life-dominating force from which no one can escape on his own. "Flesh" here and in the next colon* (v. 3d) has the meaning of the fallen system of this age, which is distinctive of Pauline usage.[32]

It is possible to take "flesh" (σάρξ) in some places in Paul as simply referring to the corporeal side of human existence (e.g., 6:12; 1 Cor 15:50), or even in the sense of בָּשָׂר in Hebrew, as the equivalent of "human" (Rom 3:20; 1 Cor 1:29; Gal 2:16), but as noted under v. 3, Paul also uses this term to signify our endemic fallenness in this age, which must be transformed in resurrection in order to acquire eternal life in "incorruptibility" (1 Cor 15:35–50; cf. Rom 8:3). As such, the flesh is opposed to the Spirit (e.g., Rom 8:3–5; Gal 3:3; 5:16–17). Christians are therefore no longer "in the flesh" anymore (Rom 8:9) in this sense. This latter sense of "flesh" is clearly the meaning in our phrase, "performing the *will of the flesh*," where "flesh" leads to evil impulses that lead to "walking in transgressions and sins" (v. 1; cf. v. 5) and to enmity with God and to death (Rom 8:6–7).

ποιοῦντες τὰ θελήματα τῆς σαρκὸς καὶ τῶν διανοιῶν, "performing the will of the flesh and of our rationalizations." The phrase τῶν διανοιῶν ("our rationalizations") is presented in apposition with τὰ θελήματα τῆς σαρκὸς ("the will of the flesh"). While διάνοια can refer more generally to "thought" or "intent," it has a negative meaning here, as in the other two places of its appearance in Paul, where non-Christian διάνοιαι are "darkened" (4:18) and full of enmity with God (Col 1:21; cf. BDAG, 234). This is part of the evidence that "flesh" is used in this passage with reference to the fallenness of humans' whole inner self, including their intellectual side: "for the intention of man's heart (ἡ διάνοια τοῦ ἀνθρώπου in LXX) is evil from his youth" (Gen 8:21). This is not a passing phase or event, but "every intention of the thoughts of his heart was only evil continually" (Gen 6:5; cf. Jer 17:9;

32. Herman Ridderbos, *Paul: An Outline of His Theology*, trans. John De Witt (Grand Rapids: Eerdmans, 1975), 93–114; cf. Schweizer, Baumgärtel, and Meyer, *TDNT*, 7:98–151; R. J. Erickson, "Flesh," in *DPL*, 303–6.

Titus 1:15; Rom 3:10–19). Sin before a holy God is the willing fruit of a fallen heart (Eph 4:22; Mark 7:23; Jas 1:14–15).[33]

καὶ ἤμεθα τέκνα φύσει ὀργῆς ὡς καὶ οἱ λοιποί, "and we were by nature children of wrath, as also the others." As if Paul's judgment on his and his audience's former selves were not enough, he proceeds even further down the gloomy, Stygian path. The fallen condition of all humankind in Adam is not the result of mere social conditioning but is such "by nature" (φύσει).[34] We have lost the appreciation of just how shocking v. 3f would have been. Paul the Pharisee undoubtedly believed that because he was a Jew "by nature" (Gal 2:15; cf. Rom 2:14, 27) he was in consequence a son of Abraham (Luke 19:9), a "son of the kingdom" (cf. Matt 8:12; 13:38), not a "son of destruction" (John 17:12) or "of Gehenna" (Matt 23:15), and therefore he was by birth a child of God (John 8:39–44), unlike the polluted Gentiles (e.g., Gal 2:15 again). Now Paul rightly understands that nature does not convey right standing before God, but instead the whole world, both Jew and Gentile, stands condemned before God apart from Christ (esp. Rom 3:9), and therefore "we all [both Jew and Greek] were by nature children of [God's] wrath." If he had simply said that "we were children of wrath," it might be supposed that this was a state humans happened to fall into or could climb out of themselves. But when Paul says that this state belongs to all "by nature," he is saying that all—excepting only Christ Jesus (e.g., Heb 4:15; 1 John 3:5)—were conceived in sin (Gen 5:3; Psa 51:5; Job 15:14; cf. John 3:6; Rom 5:12; Lincoln, 99).

Furthermore, there is a striking parallel with Paul's statement that all are by nature (φύσει) children of wrath in the documentary material, the kind of which both Paul and his audience would see every day. An honorary inscription from Kyme in Asia Minor lauds a local benefactor as follows: Κλεάναξ Σαραπίωνος φύσει δὲ Φιλοδάμω, ὁ πρύτανις, ἀμφιθάλεα τὰν ἐκ πατέρων ἔχων εὐγένηαν, "Kleanax, (adopted son) of Sarapion and natural

---

33. Henri Blocher, *Original Sin: Illuminating the Riddle*, NSBT 5 (Downers Grove, IL: InterVarsity Press, 1997).

34. The Greeks had centuries-old deliberations on whether justice and social norms are embedded in nature (φύσις) or are variable societal customs (νόμος); for example, this is a theme in tragedies of Sophocles as well as in various philosophers. This is discussed in Christian literature under the rubric of natural law; cf. David VanDrunen, *Divine Covenants and Moral Order: A Biblical Theology of Natural Law* (Grand Rapids: Eerdmans, 2014).

(son) of Philodemos, the *prytanis,* who holds nobility of birth from both his fathers."[35] The Christian is an adopted son of God (see discussion above on 1:4–5) and natural (φύσει) son of divine wrath; he or she derives "nobility of birth" from only the one Father (cf. 1 Cor 1:26 and below on 3:14–15).

2:4 ὁ δὲ θεὸς, "but God." The grim, plodding, hopeless, long-syllabled announcement of human lostness—dead in trespasses and sins, children of wrath by nature—is shattered by a lightning bolt from heaven; not in judgment but with intervening mercy—and love beyond all reckoning. The flash of Paul's message is mirrored by the speed of the short syllables in the line ὁ δὲ θεὸς πλούσιος ὢν ἐν ἐλέει, "but God, since he is rich in mercy." Paul had kept his hearers waiting for the nominative subject and the main verbs with the long recital of grave news in vv. 1–3, but here the subject, God, bursts on the scene, and one can hear the explosion with two plosive sounds strategically placed in the middle of the first two cola: **π**λούσιος ... **π**ολλὴν.

πλούσιος ὢν ἐν ἐλέει, διὰ τὴν πολλὴν ἀγάπην αὐτοῦ ἣν ἠγάπησεν ἡμᾶς, "because he is rich in mercy, on account of the abundant love with which he loved us." God's motivation for reaching down to deliver his enemies from their hell-bound course of life is explicable—but not for anything found in them. It was mercy according to his love (cf. 1:4 and esp. Rom 9:22–24). It is therefore inexplicable except that it was "on account of the abundant love with which he loved us." The phrase "abundant love" (πολλὴν ἀγάπην) expresses either an abundant measure (e.g., Rom 9:22 or 2 Cor 8:4) or abundant in profundity (i.e., "deep love"; cf. Col 4:13 or 1 Thess 2:17).

---

35. Kyme was an Aeolian city on the coast of Asia Minor between Pergamum and Smyrna. The inscription is in the Aeolian dialect (e.g., τὰν ... εὐγένηαν for τὴν εὐγένειαν), with a "high-flown rhetorical style and elaborate and circuitous patterns of praise typical of the *koine* in the early imperial period" (R. A. Kearsley in *New Docs*, 7:236). The inscription is dated between 2 BC and AD 2 and is reproduced in *New Docs*, 7:233–36, with helpful discussion of ancient benefactors (233–41); my translation of the cited portion. The *prytanis* was a civic official in Greek city-states that usually involved large outlays of cash for sacrifices and festivals. Cf. further Polybius, 1.64.6, where Hamilcar is noted to be the "natural" (κατὰ φύσιν) father of Hannibal.

2:5 καὶ ὄντας ἡμᾶς νεκροὺς τοῖς παραπτώμασιν, "and even though we were dead in our transgressions."[36] Paul resumes the line that began this periodic paragraph in v. 1, but with the change from ὑμᾶς, "you," to ἡμᾶς, "us," as already noted. The repetition of most of the phrase in v. 5a is part of an oral strategy to return the hearers to where the periodic sentence began and reorient to stress exactly who it is and in what condition his people were in when God intervened with his saving love: They were the walking dead.

συνεζωοποίησεν τῷ Χριστῷ, "it was *us* he co-made alive with the Messiah." I have rendered συνεζωοποίησεν in v. 5b, along with its companions συνήγειρεν καὶ συνεκάθισεν in v. 6, as "co-made alive ... co-raised ... and co-seated" in a rough attempt to bring out the force of these compound verbs with their συν- prefix.[37] As is often discussed, Paul coins these terms here and similar συν- prefixed words elsewhere to bring out the fact that when God was acting to raise and exalt Christ, he was concurrently acting on his people (e.g., 2:21–22; 4:16; Rom 6:4; 8:17; Gal 2:19; Col 2:12; 3:1).[38] See comment in v. 6 for more on these verbs.

As noted in "Excursus: Articular Χριστός as Messianic Title," articular τῷ Χριστῷ can be rendered "with *the Messiah*" here in v. 5, though "with *Christ*" is chosen in nearly all English versions (e.g., KJV, NASB, NIV, ESV). The presence of the article with **τῷ** Χριστῷ is an important, possible signal that Paul intends to use Χριστός as a title here. In any case, ὁ Χριστός should be understood to refer to Jesus in his royal office as one who has a

36. Hodge remarks that *καί* here "belongs to the participle" and renders it as bringing out the concessive idea: "even when we were dead in trespasses" (Hodge, 112; emphasis removed). He further notes: "Notwithstanding our low, and apparently helpless condition, God interfered for our recovery."
37. The English prefix *co-* is based on Latin *com-/cum* and is cognate with Greek σύν (ξύν); e.g., "codefendant," "co-sign," "coexist"; it is etymologically parallel in English to the Greek idiom of attaching σύν to the verbs.
38. E.g., Carl B. Hoch Jr., "The Significance of the *Syn-* Compounds for Jew-Gentile Relationships in the Body of Christ," *JETS* 25 (1982): 175–83; Brendan McGrath, " 'SYN' Words in Saint Paul," *CBQ* 14 (1952): 219–26, both of whom include noun and adj. compounds with συν- in their discussions. Paul is not doing anything unusual by coining words with the συν- prefix, since this compound was very popular in Greek. LSJ includes forty densely packed pages of συν-prefixed words alone (LSJ, 1690–1730), which does not include the words with the phonetic shift of συγ-, συλ-, or συμ-.

kingdom (5:5) and who has been raised to an exalted cosmic kingship (see on 1:20–22 above).

χάριτί ἐστε σεσῳσμένοι, "by grace you are saved." This phrase is inserted here as a preview of a point to be developed further in vv. 8–9, where it will be discussed again. In many ways, "grace" is the key idea of this passage.[39] Yet why does Paul give this phrase here, if he intends to develop it in vv. 8–9? The answer cuts to the heart of the gospel and of grace. As vv. 1–3 and 5a have made abundantly clear, Christ died for God's people *at the time* when they were his helpless—even *dead*—sinful, enemies (cf. Rom 5:6, 8, 10). Hence, Paul clarifies that it was *grace* behind God's saving action. As noted after the comments on 1:3–14 above and below on v. 8, grace should be understood here and elsewhere in Paul's writings as God's favor despite the demerits of its undeserving recipients. God forgives and imputes righteousness to those who had earlier rejected his rule as their Creator and treacherously fought against him. Note in connection with this grace as well as other echoes of Ephesians in this passage from Titus:

> For we ourselves were once foolish, disobedient, led astray, slaves to various passions and pleasures, passing our days in malice and envy, hated by others and hating one another. But when the goodness and loving kindness of God our Savior appeared, he saved us, not because of works done by us in righteousness, but according to his own mercy, by the washing of regeneration and renewal of the Holy Spirit, whom he poured out on us richly through Jesus Christ our Savior, so that being justified by his grace we might become heirs according to the hope of eternal life. (Titus 3:3–7)

2:6 καὶ συνήγειρεν καὶ συνεκάθισεν ἐν τοῖς ἐπουρανίοις, "and co-raised us and co-seated us in the high heavenlies." The verbs here are parallel with "co-made alive" (συνεζωοποίησεν) in v. 5b. This is the only time in Ephesians where we have three indicative mood verbs joined by καί. This is not a common feature of Paul's style; he prefers a less "monocolon" style with variation provided by participles or other subordinate constructions (cf. LSJ,

39. Cf. James R. Harrison, *Paul's Language of Grace in Its Graeco-Roman Context*, WUNT 2.172 (Tübingen: Mohr Siebeck, 2003), who discusses grace against its contemporary uses.

1144 [μονόκωλος]). In some of the few places where such a string of indicatives does appear, the apostle is putting stress on the actions: "For [the trumpet] *will indeed sound* and the dead *will indeed be raised* incorruptible and we *will indeed be changed*" (1 Cor 15:52; cf. Phil 4:9; Col 1:16–17). As Lausberg notes: "The concatenation of independent cola is also used for emotive insistence" as well as for "a linearly progressing sequence of cola."[40] Hence, we can understand the concatenated verbs in this passage to have a note of "emotive insistence," with a possible paraphrase of "Yes, it was indeed *us* he has most certainly co-made alive with the Messiah—by grace you are saved—and he most certainly co-raised and co-seated even *us* in the high heavenlies in Christ Jesus."

ἐν Χριστῷ Ἰησοῦ, "in Christ Jesus." This phrase seems out of place, since the συν- verbs in v. 6a would seem to demand a simple dative as object of this prepositional prefix (as in v. 5b): "co-raised and co-seated *together with* Christ Jesus." But as we have seen already in Ephesians, Paul likes to end his periods with "in Christ," "in Christ Jesus," or "in him" as the place of focus as the presenter pauses for breath. This is why the prepositional phrase is added here. The same phrase appears at the end of the next period as well (v. 7d) for further emphasis, and see also v. 10b.

The teaching to this point in vv. 4–6 may be summarized as focused on the believer's union with Christ.[41] Before conversion, believers were "dead in your/our transgressions and sins" (vv. 1, 5). Yet in the eternal council of God, those who were chosen before the foundation of the world (1:4) were thus predestined for redemption and forgiveness (1:7, 11), bringing eternal life and consequent holiness (1:4; Rom 8:29–30). All of this is inaugurated in this life by an operation of the Holy Spirit (see on 1:13–14), who somehow mysteriously brings the believer into fellowship with the death, burial, resurrection, and ascension of Christ such that Paul can say that the believer is "co-made alive," "co-raised," and "co-seated" with Christ Jesus in the heavenly realms (cf. Rom 6:3–11; Gal 2:20; Col 2:12; 3:1–4). It is a mysterious, monergistic divine operation.

2:7 ἵνα ἐνδείξηται ἐν τοῖς αἰῶσιν τοῖς ἐπερχομένοις τὸ ὑπερβάλλον πλοῦτος τῆς χάριτος αὐτοῦ ἐν χρηστότητι ἐφ' ἡμᾶς ἐν Χριστῷ Ἰησοῦ, "so that in the ages

40. Lausberg, *Handbook*, §932 (2).

41. See comments and literature cited on 1:20 above.

to come he might show the surpassing wealth of his grace in kindness toward us in Christ Jesus."[42] One practice common throughout the ancient pagan world was to dedicate statues and trophies won in battle to the gods. Thus, to enter a temple in antiquity (assuming it had not been plundered at some earlier point) was like entering a museum displaying various dedications and spoils of victory from old battles. For example, the oracle center, Delphi, was filled with treasuries that housed gold and silver objects and various weapons and other spoils of victories.[43]

This period flows out of what was said before and anticipates what will be said shortly. The church is God's redeemed, prized possession (1:14), rescued out of thrall to the prince of the power of the air (2:2–3) and included in the host-given gifts out of the bounty of Christ's victorious ascent to heaven (1:20–23; 3:10; 4:7–10). Hence, in v. 7 Paul says that the *church* will be the trophies of battle on display "in the ages to come." For example, God remarks before the heavenly court: "Have you considered my servant Job, that there is none like him on the earth" (Job 1:8). But by being a *redeemed* and *washed,* resplendent church (5:27), Paul says more particularly that God's heavenly sacred treasury will be filled with the "surpassing wealth of his grace in kindness toward us in Christ Jesus."[44]

This is the only occurrence of the phrase "ages to come" with ἐπέρχομαι and plural αἰῶνες. The meaning is obvious as a future time reference and as a near equivalent of αἰών in the singular with μέλλω, as earlier in Ephesians: ἐν τῷ αἰῶνι τούτῳ ἀλλὰ καὶ ἐν τῷ μέλλοντι [αἰῶνι] ("in this age and in the [age] to come"; 1:21; cf. Matt 12:32; Heb 6:5).[45] While it is tempting to take

---

42. The apostle employs a nice alliteration here with χάριτος ... χρηστότητι ... Χριστῷ (vv. 7b–d).

43. Cf. Pausanias, book 10. Temples in Graeco-Roman antiquity typically acted as banks and depositories for precious objects, and the Artemesium of Ephesus was well known as the largest and wealthiest deposit bank in all Asia, serviced by a large guild of bankers; cf. Dio Chrysostom, *Or.* 31; Aristides, *Or.* 23; *IvE* 454, 3065.

44. The phrase "wealth of grace" is also at 1:7. God's remark to Satan about Job is a display before the heavenly court: "Have you considered my servant Job, that there is none like him on the earth" (Job 1:8).

45. Cf. the common rabbinic phrase "world to come" (e.g., *Berakhot* 8a, where "world to come" is contrasted with "this world"); Sasse, *TDNT*, 1:197–209 (esp. 204–7). The more common Greek term where a Jewish background is not influential on the idiom for "eternity" is ὁ ἀεί [χρόνος] (LSJ, 26). The idea that αἰῶνες here are personal powers is not at all likely (cf. O'Brien, 173).

the time reference as the "age to come" (after Christ's Parousia), the use of the plural *αἰῶνες* underlines the endless extent of unfolding eras and refers simply to all future time, both in this age and in the age to come (cf. Hodge, 117; O'Brien, 173; Best, 223; Hoehner, 337–38).

The final colon* of the period (v. 7d) ends in five long syllables, adding a note of dignity in sound as well as content (ἐν Χριστῷ Ἰησοῦ, "in Christ Jesus"). The same phrase is found at the end of the previous period (v. 6c) and underlines the fact that every benefit the believer enjoys from God is mediated exclusively through the incarnate Messiah (e.g., Matt 11:25–27; John 14:6; 15:4–5; 2 Cor 1:20). "[F]or we must expect no grace, no love, from God, except through His mediation" (Calvin, 144). The theme of divine grace and love in vv. 4–7 is well expressed by Peter O'Brien:

> The apostle's thought in vv. 4–7 has gone full circle: he began by speaking of God's mercy and love as the motivation for his initiative in saving his people (v. 4); Paul then drew the readers' attention to the mighty rescue which arose out of God's gracious action (v. 5), and he concludes by declaring that God's lavishing his mercy on rebels is to serve as a demonstration of his grace for all succeeding ages. (O'Brien, 173)

2:8 Τῇ *γὰρ χάριτί ἐστε σεσῳσμένοι διὰ πίστεως*, "for by grace you are saved through faith." Paul resumes the line previewed in v. 5 with the addition of the explanatory *γάρ*, "[F]or by grace you are saved through faith." The verb is a periphrastic perfect, in which the perfect tense form converts a verb that denotes a telic ("bounded") action ("save" or "deliver") into a virtual stative event: "you are saved (or delivered)."[46] This presents the salvation as completed and the Christian as enjoying the benefits of that deliverance.[47]

---

46. See the introduction on verb tense analysis for brief discussion and general bibliography on Greek verb analysis. See Hoehner (332–33) for use of *σῴζω* in Paul (cf. Lincoln, 104–5). Romans 5:9–10 is especially interesting in connection with Eph 2:3, 5, 8, where believers are explicitly said to be saved from divine wrath (cf. Matt 19:15 and parallels).

47. It is analogous to "you are healed" (θεραπεύω, of which *σῴζω* is a synonym sometimes as, e.g., Matt 9:22; Luke 18:42; Acts 4:9), where the healing is completed and the person is in a state of good health (e.g., Luke 8:2; John 5:10; Acts 4:14). In contrast the Greek pres. tense would express the event as continuing and not necessarily completed yet: "you are being saved" (cf. 15:2; 2 Tim 1:9).

The terms σῴζω ("save") and σώτηρ ("savior," "benefactor") were quite familiar to the Ephesians, and the latter σώτηρ appeared on an important statue honoring Julius Caesar that was possibly still standing at the time when Ephesians was written. The inscription reads:

> αἱ πόλεις αἱ ἐν τῆι Ἀσίαι καὶ οἱ [δῆμοι]
> καὶ τὰ ἔθνη Γάϊον Ἰούλιον Γαΐο[υ υἱ-]
> ὸν Καίσαρα, τὸν ἀρχιερέα καὶ αὐτο-
> κράτορα καὶ τὸ δεύτερον ὕπα-
> τον, τὸν ἀπὸ Ἄρεως καὶ Ἀφροδε[ί-]
> της θεὸν ἐπιφανῆ καὶ κοινὸν τοῦ
> ἀνθρωπίνου βίου σωτῆρα

> The cities of Asia, along with the [citizen-bodies] and the nations, (honor) Gaius Julius Caesar, son of Gaius, the High Priest, Imperator, and twice Consul, the manifest god (sprung) from Ares and Aphrodite, and *universal savior of human life*. (*IvE* 251; my trans.; emphasis added)[48]

The "salvation" accomplished by Caesar was from confiscation of Ephesian treasures in the civil war during the first Roman triumvirate.[49]

It is typical to hear divine grace defined as "God's undeserved favor," but this does not capture the idea communicated here in Eph 2 or in other places in Paul's writings.[50] As this whole passage shows, God's grace, which is emphasized here by putting it first in the colon* (v. 8a), is actually God's favor granted to those who deserve his wrath (v. 3). It is not just undeserved, as if the people whom God befriends were neutral. It is an act of immense favor bestowed on those who lie under God's just condemnation

48. The rather bulky official name spelled out on the inscription ("Gaius Julius Caesar, son of Gaius") would normally be abbreviated in Latin as "C. Iulius C. f. Caesar" (where "f." abbreviates "filius"). "Imperator" (αὐτοκράτωρ; i.e., "emperor") was a technical Latin title at the time of Julius Caesar for a special, supreme military command.

49. For discussion see S. M. Baugh, " 'Savior of All People': 1 Tim 4:10 in Context," *WTJ* 54 (1992): 331–40.

50. Cf. the overview of scholarly discussion in Lincoln, 102–4, and more recently Harrison, *Paul's Language of Grace*.

as transgressors and sinners. Hence, a better quick definition is: "God's favor despite human demerit."

καὶ τοῦτο οὐκ ἐξ ὑμῶν, "and this does not originate from you." There is much popular discussion about the word τοῦτο ("this") and its antecedent in v. 8b. It is tempting to take the antecedent as "faith" (i.e., "this *faith* is not from you"; as Hodge, 119–20), even though πίστις ("faith") is feminine and the demonstrative pronoun is neuter. Grammatically, one could suppose that an abstract idea like "faith" or "believing" could be referenced as neuter, but that would make this rather common construction unnecessarily complicated (cf. BDF §131). In Greek, events as a whole are treated as neuter singular things with neuter articles (e.g., τὸ πιστεύειν, "believing"), neuter relative pronouns (e.g., Eph 5:5), or neuter demonstrative pronouns, as in v. 8b (also, for example: 6:1; 1 Cor 6:6, 8; Phil 1:22, 28; Col 3:20; 1 Thess 5:18; 1 Tim 2:1–3).[51] Hence, the antecedent of τοῦτο is the whole event: "being saved by grace through faith."[52]

One implication of this proper understanding of τοῦτο ("this") is that all the components of the event are also referenced as originating not from human capacity or exertion but as God's gift. This means that even the believer's act of believing comes from God, as is said more explicitly by Paul elsewhere: "For it has been granted to you that for the sake of Christ you should not only believe in him (τὸ εἰς αὐτὸν πιστεύειν) but also suffer

---

51. This is a very common use of the neuter demonstrative pronoun in Greek; e.g., καὶ **τοῦτο** μεῖζον τῆς ἀληθείας κακόν, ὅστις τὰ μὴ προσόντα κέκτηται κακά, "and *this* is a misfortune exceeding the reality, if a man incurs the blame for evils that are not his doing" (Euripedes, *Helen* 271; as cited in Herbert Wier Smyth, *Greek Grammar*, rev. Gordon M. Messing [Cambridge, MA: Harvard University Press, 1956; original ed., 1920], §2510 [cf. §1248], emphasis added). English has precisely the same idiom: "To be, or not to be: *that* is the question" (Shakespeare, *Hamlet,* act 3, scene 1), or, "A mind always employed is always happy. *This* is the true secret, the grand recipe, for felicity" (Thomas Jefferson in a letter to Martha Jefferson dated May 21, 1787).

52. So Gnilka, 129; Lincoln, 111–12; O'Brien, 175; Hoehner, 342–43; and many others. Cf. Barth, 224–25, 347, who takes "faith" here as "the obedience and love of Christ toward God and man," which may be biblically true but not what is being said in Eph 2:8. It is possible to take neuter τοῦτο as referring to δῶρον ("gift") as a postcedent, but this still leaves the question, What is the gift from God? The answer would be the same as above: the gift is being saved by grace through faith. BDF §442 (9) takes καὶ τοῦτο as emphatic and "used to particularize," though it is not clear how this helps with the meaning.

for his sake" (Phil 1:29). This is part of the evidence of Protestantism's historic position that salvation is *sola gratia* and *sola fide* (e.g., Calvin, 144–45). Humans contribute nothing of their own to this salvation, since even believing (which the elect are indeed enabled to do) is a divine gift (cf. Rom 3:24–25).[53] In the context of Eph 2:8, the key to this is what Paul had been driving home so forcefully up until now: Before God's gracious intervention, believers were hopelessly *dead*, with their wills imprisoned by nature (φύσει) in acts that led only to transgression and sin (2:1–5a, 12).

θεοῦ τὸ δῶρον, "it is God's gift." This short predicate statement (v. 8c) comes across as abrupt (with only five syllables) and has clear stress on the first word: θεοῦ.[54] It is clear that the meaning of this genitive is source ("from God") in parallel with the preposition ἐκ in the previous colon* (οὐκ ἐξ ὑμῶν), because gifts come "from" someone, but Paul left out this second use of the preposition and a conjunction such as δέ or ἀλλά as part of the abrupt emphasis on θεοῦ expressed here.[55]

2:9 οὐκ ἐξ ἔργων, "not from works." There are two important elements to v. 9. The first is another abrupt statement: "not from works" (also Rom 9:12 and Titus 3:5; cf. Rom 11:6). This shows the fundamental Pauline opposition of works with faith (e.g., Rom 3:27–28 [with "boasting" also as v. 9]; 9:32; Gal 2:16; 3:1–10; 2 Tim 1:9).[56] Notice that he did not say "Not from *good*

53. This is what makes grace "free." The historic Westminster Larger Catechism expresses this in a classic question and answer (#71): "Q. How is justification an act of God's free grace? A. Although Christ, by his obedience and death, did make a proper, real, and full satisfaction to God's justice in the behalf of them that are justified; yet inasmuch as God accepteth the satisfaction from a surety, which he might have demanded of them, and did provide this surety, his own only Son, imputing his righteousness to them, and requiring nothing of them for their justification but faith,which also is his gift, their justification is to them of free grace."

54. Exact parallels with this syntax and word order (a gen. predicate noun followed by a subject nominative) are not common in Paul's writings. The only ones I have found are in Rom 13:4 (twice: θεοῦ γὰρ διάκονός ἐστιν) and 1 Cor 14:37 (κυρίου ἐστὶν ἐντολή), where the gen. predicates may also be seen to have the primary focus; cf. similar but not exactly parallel grammar in 1 Cor 3:9; 14:33; Gal 1:10.

55. I.e., τὸ δὲ δῶρον ἐκ θεοῦ [ἐστιν] could be expected as in ἡ ἀγάπη ἐκ τοῦ θεοῦ ἐστιν ("Love is from God"; 1 John 4:7; cf. John 4:22).

56. An opposition that needs careful qualifications; cf. Ridderbos, *Paul*, 170–74. Ridderbos concludes: "Faith represents a new mode of existence that has been given with Christ's advent; it 'comes' with the coming of the fullness of the time (Gal.

works" or the like, but "Not from works (at all)." *Works* for Paul implies human effort and use of human resources (i.e., σάρξ), and these have no value for the acquisition of human standing before God (e.g., Rom 3:20–28; 4:2–6; Gal 3:10–12; Titus 3:4–5; cf. John 6:29; O'Brien, 176–77). Paul is not opposed to good deeds (see v. 10; "zealous for good works," Titus 2:14), but for him they flow from a renewed heart as the outcome and result of God's freeing justification and deliverance from bondage to sin by the substitutionary sacrifice and obedience of Christ (e.g., Rom 6:1–14; Titus 2:14; cf. Heb 9:14).

ἵνα μή τις καυχήσηται, "so that no one may boast." The second element in v. 9 is that if humans contributed any element in salvation, this would leave room for "boasting." This refers to people conceivably making a claim on God as reward for their efforts (see esp. Rom 4:1–5). One can boast *in* the Lord (Rom 5:11; Gal 6:14 [in the cross]), but not *before* him (Rom 4:2; 1 Cor 1:29; cf. Rom 3:27; Phil 3:3; Judg 7:2).[57] This connects directly to those in Graeco-Roman Ephesus, where the buildings were replete with notices (i.e., "boasts" to Paul) of the lavish deeds of various benefactors, which in Greek are one's φιλοτιμ(ε)ία.[58] In Paul's Ephesus, one of the most impressive examples of such a benefaction was a grand archway entrance to the central market (*agora*) funded by two imperial freedmen of Augustus named Mazaeus and Mithridates.[59]

Jerome brings the theology of Eph 2:8–9 to conclusion for us:

3:23; 4:4), and with the manifestation of the grace of God in the death and resurrection of Christ" (174).

57. Cf. ibid., 140–41.

58. The term does not appear in the NT. It is normally rendered "generosity," but it is hard to resist the temptation to note its etymology as "love of honor." Certainly public honors were expected as a consequence of generosity for the public good. This is nowhere more evident than from a second-century Ephesian inscription (*IvE* 1491) in which the emperor Antoninus Pius chides the city for failing to properly honor his client, Vedius Antoninus, for all his munificence (φιλοτιμεία) to the city. Vedius had the emperor's letter chiseled onto one of his buildings for all to see. Cf. Dio Chrysostom, *Or.* 45–47; Pliny, *Ep.* 6.31; F. W. Danker, *Benefactor: Epigraphic Study of a Graeco-Roman and New Testament Semantic Field* (St. Louis: Clayton, 1982); Bruce W. Winter, *Seek the Welfare of the City: Christians as Benefactors and Citizens* (Grand Rapids: Eerdmans, 1994).

59. See *IvE* 3006 for discussion and literature; cf. *IvE* 851.

> He says, therefore, that he will show the abundant riches of his grace in kindness in the ages to come because you have been saved by grace by means of faith, not by means of works. And this faith itself is not from yourselves but is from him who has called you. Now so that the secret thought, "If we have not been saved by means of our works, perhaps we have been saved by means of faith, and it is in another manner that we are saved of ourselves," not sneak into our thinking by chance in reference to this, he thus goes on and says that faith itself is also not of our will but is the gift of God. It is not that human free will is removed. In accordance with what the apostle says to the Romans, "It is not of him who runs, or of him who wills, but of God who shows mercy" (Rom. 9:16), the very freedom of the will has God as its author, and all things are referred to his benefaction, since it is he himself who permits us even to will the good. But all of this has been said so that no one might glory as if he has been saved by himself and not by God. (Jerome and Origen, 129)

2:10 αὐτοῦ γάρ ἐσμεν ποίημα, κτισθέντες ἐν Χριστῷ Ἰησοῦ, "for we are his creation, created in Christ Jesus." With αὐτοῦ γάρ ἐσμεν ποίημα, as we also saw in v. 8c with θεοῦ τὸ δῶρον, the genitive is brought forward for the sake of stress: "For we are *his* creation."[60] The word ποίημα occurs only here and in Rom 1:20 in the NT. In the latter passage it occurs in the plural for the elements of God's creation that evidence his divine attributes even to unbelievers ("things which God has created"; also a LXX usage, see note above; O'Brien, 178). In our passage it is a little unusual to have ποίημα in the singular with the plural "we are," unless it is collective with the meaning "the product of his creative work." Of course, all human beings are God's creatures, but Paul is here talking about Christians being the product of God's act of *new* creation in Christ, as he states in the next colon*: "created in Christ Jesus" (cf. 2 Cor 5:17; Gal 6:15; Rom 6:4; cf. Eph 3:9; 4:24). There is

60. For alternative word orders with similar constructions see Rom 8:16; 2 Cor 1:14; 6:16 [2x]; Phil 3:3. With our phrase, ἐσμεν τὸ ποίημα αὐτοῦ or τὸ ποίημα αὐτοῦ ἐσμεν would be more normal word order. Cf. Matt 5:3, 10, where similar stress is communicated: **αὐτῶν** ἐστιν ἡ βασιλεία τῶν οὐρανῶν, "*Theirs* is the kingdom of heaven."

a little wordplay in that believers are God's *work* (ποίημα) created for good *works* (ἔργα).[61]

ἐπὶ ἔργοις ἀγαθοῖς, "for good works." The word order in the phrase ἐπὶ ἔργοις ἀγαθοῖς, with the attributive adjective trailing the noun, is found often in Paul's writings, especially where the noun is anarthrous in a prepositional phrase (e.g., 2:21; 4:13; 5:31). And in Paul's writings, "good work(s)" occurs eleven times with ἀγαθός in the trailing position and only once with the word order reversed (Rom 13:3). The point is that there is no emphasis here on "good"; it simply seemed to have a better rhythm with this phrase to put the adjective after its noun even though that is not the most common position for an attributive adjective.[62] (The rhythm of ἐπὶ ἔργοις ἀγαθοῖς is ˘ ˘ ¯ ¯ | ˘ ˘ ¯, whereas the more common attributive position [ἐπὶ ἀγαθοῖς ἔργοις] would have an unpleasant four short syllables in a row followed by three longs: ˘ ˘ ˘ ˘ ¯ ¯ ¯.) Rhythm and feel in Greek word order would have been a clear signal of an author's style in antiquity.

οἷς προητοίμασεν ὁ θεὸς, "which God prepared beforehand." The prefix προ- here is redundant, "prepared *beforehand*" (all preparation occurs beforehand). Perhaps Paul wished to stress again that God had determined to include Gentiles in his redemption in Christ before the world's foundation (as 1:3–14).[63] We should not, however, skip over the fact that earlier Paul had focused on his audience's predestination, election, and redemption, but here the *outcome* and *effect* of that redemption in their life of grateful service to God are also part of what God has prepared for them. Good works in the life of the believer are not incidental or optional. They are the necessary outcome of their election to holiness and blamelessness (1:4; cf. Lincoln, 115–16).

ἵνα ἐν αὐτοῖς περιπατήσωμεν, "that we should start walking in them." Finally, the long section running from v. 1 to v. 10 ends as it opened: with the Gentile Ephesians "walking." Formerly they walked in transgressions and sins; now they begin their steps in newness of life in a new creation in

---

61. In the LXX, see Pss 63:10 (English 64:9); 91:5 (English 92:4); 142:5 (English 143:5) for ποίημα parallel with pl. ἔργα ("works"), found also in Eph 2:10.

62. See also the phrase πνεῦμα ἅγιον in Paul (e.g., Eph 1:13; 4:30).

63. The verb προετοιμάζω occurs only at Rom 9:23 in the NT and ἑτοιμάζω only at 1 Cor 2:9; 2 Tim 2:21; Phlm 22 in Paul. Lincoln notes that the majority of commentators hold that the prefix προ- here "indicates that God's preparation precedes not simply the believer's work but also the foundation of the world" (Lincoln, 115).

the good works that God has set out for them long ago. I take the aorist subjunctive ἵνα … περιπατήσωμεν as inceptive, which is normal for an aorist of an atelic meaning such as "walk."[64] The same meaning is conveyed, for example, in Rom 6:4, which has several key parallel elements with Eph 2:1–10; it reads: "We were buried therefore with him by baptism into death, in order that, just as Christ was raised from the dead by the glory of the Father, we too may *start walking* in newness of life (ἵνα … οὕτως καὶ ἡμεῖς ἐν καινότητι ζωῆς περιπατήσωμεν)." The qualification "newness" shows that the Christian was not walking in life before Christ's intervention on his behalf, so we should see that good works in a new lifestyle in both Rom 6 and Eph 2 flow out of regeneration and faith in Christ.

Biblical Theology Comments

The Augustinian view of election of believers outlined in the comments on Eph 1:4 in particular has come under challenge recently from scholars who defend a view they term "corporate election."[65] Brian J. Abasciano explains:

> Most simply, corporate election refers to the choice of a group, which entails the choice of its individual members by virtue of their membership in the group. Thus, individuals are not elected as individuals directly, but secondarily as members of the elect group. … Individuals are elect as a consequence of their membership in the group. … On both the individual and the corporate level, election is contingent on faith in Christ.[66]

64. So also BDF §337 (1) and Hoehner, 349; cf. pres. subjunctive ἵνα περιπατῆτε in 1 Thess 4:12, which would be the default tense form.

65. For Augustine in particular, see his "The Predestination of the Saints," in *The Works of Saint Augustine: A Translation for the 21st Century*, 1/26, trans. R. J. Teske (New York: New City, 1999), 149–90; and for Calvin see John Calvin, *Institutes of the Christian Religion*, trans. Ford Lewis Battles, 2 vols. (Philadelphia: Westminster, 1960), 920–87; for a modern treatment see Michael Horton, *The Christian Faith: A Systematic Theology for Pilgrims On the Way* (Grand Rapids: Zondervan, 2011), 560–72. Cf. Hoehner, 185–93, for a helpful excursus on election and a critique of Markus Barth's unhelpful caricature of Augustinianism (Barth, 105–9).

66. Brian J. Abasciano, "Clearing Up Misconceptions about Corporate Election," *ATJ* 41 (2009): 59–90 (quotes from 60 and 80). See also the recent interchange between Abasciano and Thomas Schreiner over the interpretation of Rom 9: Thomas R. Schreiner, "Corporate and Individual Election in Romans 9: A Response to

This view is proposed over against the historic Augustinian/Calvinist view, which, we are told, "refers to the direct choice of individuals as autonomous entities" and leads to a "maverick Christianity" of isolated individuals rather than to a healthy, unified church.[67]

Furthermore, we are told, the insights of the "new perspective on Paul" (NPP) have bolstered this corporate view of election as consistent with E. P. Sanders' homogenized view of Second Temple Judaism, in which corporate Israel was elected gratuitously and individuals enjoyed this election and predestination only insofar as they maintained their status within the group through personal covenant fidelity, i.e., obedience to the law.[68] It should be noted that not everyone agrees that the radically diverse groups in Second Temple Judaism can be homogenized quite so easily.[69]

The argument for corporate election as it relates to Ephesians concentrates on Eph 1:4a (καθὼς ἐξελέξατο ἡμᾶς ἐν αὐτῷ, "insofar as he chose us in him"), where ἡμᾶς ("us") is said to refer not to individuals but to "the church as a whole, especially as it was uttered in a collectivist cultural milieu in which the group was seen as primary and the individual as secondary, embedded in the group to which he belonged and referred to as a result of his membership in the group."[70] Furthermore, the phrase ἐν αὐτῷ ("in

---

Brian Abasciano," *JETS* 49 (2006): 373–86; and Brian J. Abasciano, "Corporate Election in Romans 9: A Reply to Thomas Schreiner," *JETS* 49 (2006): 351–71. Cf. William W. Klein, *The New Chosen People: A Corporate View of Election* (Grand Rapids: Zondervan, 1990).

67. Abasciano, "Clearing Up," 60; Klein, *Chosen People,* 265. Abasciano's "autonomous entities," of course, is not a phrase any Augustinian would use to describe humans made in the image of God, and no human is truly autonomous or independent from the sovereignty of the Creator despite having genuine free will (see below).

68. "Righteousness in Judaism is a term which implies the *maintenance of status* among the group of the elect," E. P. Sanders, *Paul and Palestinian Judaism* (Philadelphia: Fortress, 1977), 544 (emphasis original); cf. 85–87; 257–70; 422. Also see James D. G. Dunn, *The Theology of Paul the Apostle* (Grand Rapids: Eerdmans, 1998), 509–19; 534–52; cf. N. T. Wright, *The New Testament and the People of God* (Minneapolis: Fortress, 1992), 259–79; founded on earlier ideas by Krister Stendahl, "The Apostle Paul and the Introspective Conscience of the West," *HTR* 56 (1963): 199–215.

69. See most notably D. A. Carson, Peter T. O'Brien, and Mark A Seifrid, eds., *Justification and Variegated Nomism*, vol. 1 (Grand Rapids: Baker Academic, 2001).

70. Abasciano, "Clearing Up," 86n30; cf. Klein, *Chosen People*, 179–80.

him") in the corporate election view refers to the election of Christ as "the sphere of election" of individuals as they (voluntarily) unite to him by faith and become elect in consequence.[71] Hence election is contingent on faith, which itself is not a divine gift but solely a human act to which God responds by choosing that individual. He has chosen the group before human history, but not people directly.

Let me merely mention initially in response that the description of the cultures of the NT as "collectivist," where the group was "primary" and the individual "secondary," begs the question on a number of fronts and certainly needs careful, extended qualifications at the least to fit the world both of Paul and of the Ephesians. Unfortunately, the corporate election position seems to rest at this point on H. Wheeler Robinson's notion of "corporate personality," in which ancient peoples were conceptually unable to distinguish themselves from groups of which they were a part ("psychical unity").[72] This unsatisfactory notion still plays a role in exegesis of Paul, but it needs to be recast into something more fitting for ancient peoples and the biblical text. The first-century people whom I have studied for well over thirty years do not strike me as "collectivist" in Robinson's or Abasciano's sense.[73]

---

71. Abasciano, "Clearing Up," 66–72. Abasciano remarks: "In the case of Eph. 1:4, Christ is presented as existing before the foundation of the world and chosen by God as the head of his people and the heir to all of his blessings. All those who come to be in Christ then necessarily come to share in his election, identity, and inheritance" (69). Note, however, that Eph 1:4 does not say the God chose Christ (a position that marked the theology of Karl Barth in the last century) but that he chose *us* in Christ, the mediator of all redemptive benefits, before the world's foundation. Cf. Isa 62:1, quoted in Matt 12:18.

72. H. Wheeler Robinson, *Corporate Personality in Ancient Israel* (Philadelphia: Fortress, 1964).

73. As just one indication of this, notice that the corporate concepts Paul relates to his individual audience members in the next section are citizenship and covenant (Eph 2:12). For a fine review of the issues and literature on these matters see Andrew Perriman, "The Corporate Christ: Re-Assessing the Jewish Background," *TynB* 50 (1999): 239–63. For example, Perriman notes: "Not only biological descent but also covenant determines the proper basis for the perceived unity of the people of Israel with their forebears and descendants: God shows favour to Israel because of the covenant established with the patriarchs rather than because the group is included in the individual (cf. Rom. 11:28)" (252).

Yet it should be noted that some of the interests of defenders of the corporate election view can be appreciated by anyone. For instance, concern to guard against "maverick Christianity" is well taken, and NT scholars are helpfully prompted to explore more accurately how election is "in Christ" and the biblical issues of covenant mediation and representation.[74] Be that as it may, it should be emphasized that the "corporate election" view (i.e., historically Arminian or semi-Pelagian) is an issue of systematic theology involving careful examination and integration of a whole host of biblical texts and conceptions into a coherent network of truths. In other words, it cannot be established or refuted by simply examining ἡμᾶς ("us") or ἐν Χριστῷ ("in Christ") in Eph 1:4. This latter point is why the issue is being discussed here after Eph 2:1–10 and not earlier in the commentary. The Augustinian view of election is interconnected with certain other key biblical notions that clearly arise from Eph 2:1–10 and are not satisfactorily addressed by defenders of the corporate election view.

In particular, in the passage quoted from Abasciano above, he says that "Individuals are elect as a consequence of their membership in the group. ... On both the individual and the corporate level, election is contingent on faith in Christ." This establishes a cause-effect relationship in election resting on the faith of the believer as the prime cause. God may have chosen "us" (i.e., the church) before the foundation of the world, yet members of this collective must choose to join this group voluntarily by believing in Christ to enjoy this election: "election is contingent on faith." To the Augustinian, redemption (salvation, resurrection, eternal life, etc.) is contingent on faith, but election is the cause of faith.[75] Here is why.

In Ephesians 2:1, 5, Paul has identified his audience as "dead" in transgressions. Even more damning, humans were universally ("we" and "the rest") identified as "by nature children of wrath" (v. 3). There is no escaping nature. Humans are born in transgressions and are dead in them

74. It should be noted, though, that most confessional Augustinians (Calvinists) are *presbyterian* in church government, or they practice some other form of real ecclesiastical connectionalism that extends beyond the local congregation. Isolated individualism is antithetical to Reformed ecclesiology; cf. Edmund P. Clowney, *The Church* (Downers Grove, IL: InterVarsity Press, 1995).

75. "God chose you to be saved through sanctification of the Spirit and belief in the truth" (2 Thess 2:13). Faith (and the Holy Spirit's work) here is the means for being saved, which is a consequence of divine election.

(see comments above). The dead cannot choose to believe and enter into election in consequence. They are "without hope and without God in the world" (2:12). Who, then, will deliver the lost human race from bondage to this death?

The answer, of course, is that even faith—the capacity to believe in Christ—is itself a gift originating from God, mediated by his incarnate Son, and effected in them through the Holy Spirit through the secondary means of gospel proclamation ("faith comes by hearing"; Rom 10:17) as an act of new creation.[76] God's gracious salvation through faith does not originate from humans themselves, and neither is it given in response to human efforts making them worthy of the gift (2:8–9; see comments). It is certainly true that believers do themselves believe (1:13) and confess Christ for salvation through gospel preaching (Rom 10:8–15), and they do so of their own volition, but all this is in consequence of the divine gift to them given solely out of "the good pleasure of his will" (Eph 1:5), "according to the riches of his grace" (1:7), in "his good pleasure" (1:9), "according to his plan who brings all things into effect in accordance with the counsel of his will" (1:11–12).[77] It runs counter to the clear teaching of Eph 2:1–10 to propose that humans acquire the benefits of election by believing. It is a gift to those who are by nature dead and therefore must first be enlivened and raised in their Mediator before exercising this faith and enjoying its benefits (2:5–6). Believers believe and live because they were elected and predestined to faith and all of its consequences out of God's grace and good pleasure alone. As Augustine observes:

> God, therefore, chose believers, but in order that they might be believers, not because they already were (citing Jas 2:5). ... Faith, then, both in its beginning and in its completeness, is a gift of God, and let absolutely no one who does not want to be

---

76. "The new creation is not first of all the new birth of individuals, but the dawn of the age to come in this present age [inaugurated at the resurrection of Christ]. Individuals are swept into it by the Spirit. Nevertheless, the renewal of all things begins with the Spirit's regeneration of sinners, effectually calling them into union with the Son, through the faith that the Spirit gives through the preaching of the gospel" (Horton, *Christian Faith*, 561).

77. See chap. 9 of the Augustinian/Calvinist *Westminster Confession of Faith*, titled "Of Free Will."

> opposed to the perfectly clear sacred writings deny that this gift is given to some and not given to others.[78]

In summary, the Father and the Son choose people to whom the Father will be revealed (Matt 11:25–27), according to the divine purpose, independent of human effort (Rom 9:11, 16). It was the Father's good pleasure to grant his kingdom as a covenantal inheritance to his Son and from his Son to his people (Luke 12:32); to accomplish this end, God sent his Son as mediator (Isa 42:1; 1 Pet 1:20; John 3:16) out of his originating love. They did not love him first, but he did love them first (1 John 4:10). In consequence of this love, Christ gave himself for his sheep (John 10:11, 15; Matt 1:21; Eph 5:25), his friends (John 15:13–14), whom the Father had given him before the world existed (John 17:5–12, 20) and whom he calls "by name" (John 10:3) rather than as a nameless collective.

Application and Devotional Implications

As discussed above, the composition of vv. 1–10 consists of three interlocked sections that move from the depths of human hopelessness in rebellion and death to the heights of believers being raised and seated with Christ in the high-heavenlies. The movement of this instruction and the way Paul has composed the whole together leave one clear conclusion: Believers had and have no contribution to offer for their salvation but faith in their substitutionary mediator (cf. Hodge, 113–14). Further, Witherington remarks that the focus on the wholly divine gift of an accomplished salvation makes "a deep emotional impact on the audience ... which prepares them to be receptive to the exhortations that follow" (Witherington, 256).

We should not overlook the fact that Paul opens Eph 2:1–10 with the bad news of human sin, misery, and death. He knows that the gospel of God's grace in Christ Jesus can only be properly understood after first rightly seeing our hopeless state without Christ. It was not after we had

---

78. Augustine, "Predestination," §34 and §16. Augustine quotes Eph 1:3–12 at length here and feels that this text is clear enough in itself to substantiate his position on election and predestination (§§35–36). "He chose us, therefore, not because we were going to be, but in order that we might be holy and spotless. It is, of course, certain; it is, of course, clear; we were going to be such precisely because he chose us, predestining us to be such by his grace" (§36).

renovated ourselves even fractionally that God showed us mercy. We were sinners, transgressors, engaged in lusts and the will of the prince of darkness along with other "sons of disobedience," and all this "by nature," and hence we were willing objects of divine wrath. Dead. But that was precisely when God, out of the boundless treasury of his mercy and kindness, came to our aid and lifted us out of his own righteous fury. He made us alive together with Christ and seated us in great glory and exaltation along with our Savior.

Yet all this ends with a note about good works in which we must surely walk. After all, we were elected to "be holy and blameless before him" (1:4), and so we must walk in good works (2:10). But there is no exhortation at this point in Ephesians, since that comes later in the epistle. Even when Paul mentions our engaging ("walking") in good works (v. 10), he is teaching us about how these arise as the result of God's work of new creation in us, not exhorting us to good works at this point. He does this because he knows that once we truly understand and appreciate the wealth of the glory of God's grace, only then are we free to love and serve him with grateful hearts as his children and heirs.

Selected Bibliography

Abasciano, B. "Clearing Up Misconceptions about Corporate Election." *ATJ* 41 (2009): 59–90.

Augustine. "The Predestination of the Saints." In *The Works of Saint Augustine: A Translation for the 21st Century*, trans. R. Teske, 149–90. 1/26. New York: New City, 1999.

Blocher, H. *Original Sin: Illuminating the Riddle.* NSBT 5. Downers Grove, IL: InterVarsity Press, 1997.

Calvin, J. *Institutes of the Christian Religion.* 2 Vols. Translated by L. F. Battles. Philadelphia: Westminster, 1960.

Carson, D., P. O'Brien, and M. Seifrid, eds. *Justification and Variegated Nomism.* Vol. 1. Grand Rapids: Baker Academic, 2001.

Clowney, E. *The Church.* Downers Grove, IL: InterVarsity Press, 1995.

Danker, F. *Benefactor: Epigraphic Study of a Graeco-Roman and New Testament Semantic Field.* St. Louis: Clayton, 1982.

Dunn, J. *The Theology of Paul the Apostle.* Grand Rapids: Eerdmans, 1998.

Gombis, T. "Ephesians 2 as a Narrative of Divine Warfare." *JSNT* 26 (2004): 403–18.

Harvey, J. *Listening to the Text: Oral Patterning in Paul's Letters*. Grand Rapids: Baker, 1998.

Hock, C. "The Significance of the *Syn*- Compounds for Jew-Gentile Relationships in the Body of Christ." *JETS* 25 (1982): 175–83.

Horton, M. *The Christian Faith: A Systematic Theology for Pilgrims On the Way*. Grand Rapids: Zondervan, 2011.

Klein, W. *The New Chosen People: A Corporate View of Election*. Grand Rapids: Zondervan, 1990.

Llewelyn, S. *New Documents Illustrating Early Christianity*. Vol. 7. Sydney: Macquarie University Press, 1994.

McGrath, B. " 'SYN' Words in Saint Paul." *CBQ* 14 (1952): 219–26.

Perriman, A. "The Corporate Christ: Re-Assessing the Jewish Background." *TynB* 50 (1999): 239–63.

Robinson, H. W. *Corporate Personality in Ancient Israel*. Philadelphia: Fortress, 1964.

Sanders, E. *Paul and Palestinian Judaism*. Philadelphia: Fortress, 1977.

Suh, R. "The Use of Ezekiel 37 in Ephesians 2." *JETS* 50 (2007): 715–33.

Winter, B. *Seek the Welfare of the City: Christians as Benefactors and Citizens*. Grand Rapids: Eerdmans, 1994.

Wright, N. T. *The New Testament and the People of God*. Minneapolis: Fortress, 1992.

The Unified New Creation Inaugurated (2:11–22)

Introduction

In Ephesians 2:11–22 Paul asks his Gentile audience to recall their prior lost condition, then he teaches about how Christ has brought them peace and unified them with the saints as a new, eschatological human race and is building them up in an inaugurated new creation household and temple. The theme of new creation had been introduced in v. 10 but is expanded on here, where the church is εἷς καινὸς ἄνθρωπος ("one new human race" or "new man"). Earlier in Ephesians God had been the main performer of the action, but now the focus falls on Christ Jesus and his redemption as the one performing his unifying work in the church. Several interpreters see this section as "the key and high point of the whole epistle" (Barth, 275; cf. O'Brien, 182).

The whole section running from vv. 11–22 has an essential unity but is divided grammatically and thematically into three "movements." In them Paul moves from reminder of Gentile separation from Israel and thereby separation from God (vv. 11–12) to the work of Christ to unite these estranged Gentiles with the OT and newly emerging NT saints in a new creation (vv. 13–18). He concludes by teaching that the new, united church is growing into a new creation temple and household (vv. 19–22). This last section is treated as a separate unit in the four early MSS reviewed in the introduction (B, ℵ, A, and C) but is treated here as part of the larger unit beginning in v. 11, to which it belongs thematically.[1]

1. Codex Vaticanus (B) treats 2:11–18 as one unit, followed by vv. 19–22 as the next unit (with minor divisions marked with the high dot [·] in vv. 12 and 20 and between vv. 13 and 14 and vv. 21 and 22). Sinaiticus (ℵ) has demarcations at vv. 11–12, 13–16, 17–18, 19–22; Alexandrinus (A) has three divisions (vv. 11–12; 13–18, 19–22);

We do not have repeated catchwords at the beginning and end of this long unit as we did in 2:1–10 with περιπατέω ("walk"). However, we may possibly see two interesting elements of contrast between the opening and close of vv. 11–22. The first is the simple focus of circumcision "in the flesh" (v. 11) contrasted with the last phrase "in the Spirit" (v. 22b), which are juxtaposed elsewhere in Paul's writings (esp. Rom 8:3–13; Gal 5:16–19). These two elements correspond here in Ephesians in that the opening (vv. 11–16) concentrates on the old enmity and division between Jew and Gentile resolved through Christ in an interconnected temple made up of both groups "in the Spirit" (vv. 21–22).[2]

The exact division of individual periods throughout this section is not certain, and I have used the verse numbers as a guide for the units in some cases (e.g., vv. 17–20) even though the periods may have been intended to be longer (i.e., vv. 17–18 may be one period). This creates some relatively short periods of three cola* and speeds things up slightly until the last long period at the end of the chapter (vv. 21–22). Here is my suggested organization into cola* and periods:

A	11 Διὸ μνημονεύετε ὅτι ποτὲ ὑμεῖς τὰ ἔθνη ἐν σαρκί
οἱ λεγόμενοι ἀκροβυστία
ὑπὸ τῆς λεγομένης περιτομῆς
ἐν σαρκὶ χειροποιήτου

B	12 ὅτι ἦτε τῷ καιρῷ ἐκείνῳ χωρὶς Χριστοῦ
ἀπηλλοτριωμένοι τῆς πολιτείας τοῦ Ἰσραὴλ
καὶ ξένοι τῶν διαθηκῶν τῆς ἐπαγγελίας
ἐλπίδα μὴ ἔχοντες
καὶ ἄθεοι ἐν τῷ κόσμῳ

C	13 νυνὶ δὲ ἐν Χριστῷ Ἰησοῦ
ὑμεῖς οἵ ποτε ὄντες μακρὰν
ἐγενήθητε ἐγγὺς

---

and Ephraemi Rescriptus (C) is vacant to v. 19 but has vv. 19–22 as one section. Many commentators (Gnilka, Best, Lincoln, O'Brien, etc.) treat vv. 11–22 as one block of text.

2. Some interpreters (e.g., I. H. Thomson) have seen a more detailed chiasm* in 2:11–22, but the interrelations within the passage are not that elaborately structured (cf. Best, 236; O'Brien, 184).

ἐν τῷ αἵματι τοῦ Χριστοῦ

D [14] αὐτὸς γάρ ἐστιν ἡ εἰρήνη ἡμῶν
ὁ ποιήσας τὰ ἀμφότερα ἓν
καὶ τὸ μεσότοιχον τοῦ φραγμοῦ λύσας
τὴν ἔχθραν ἐν τῇ σαρκὶ αὐτοῦ

E [15] τὸν νόμον τῶν ἐντολῶν ἐν δόγμασιν καταργήσας
ἵνα τοὺς δύο κτίσῃ ἐν αὐτῷ
εἰς ἕνα καινὸν ἄνθρωπον ποιῶν εἰρήνην

F [16] καὶ ἀποκαταλλάξῃ τοὺς ἀμφοτέρους
ἐν ἑνὶ σώματι τῷ θεῷ
διὰ τοῦ σταυροῦ
ἀποκτείνας τὴν ἔχθραν ἐν αὐτῷ

G [17] καὶ ἐλθὼν εὐηγγελίσατο
εἰρήνην ὑμῖν τοῖς μακρὰν
καὶ εἰρήνην τοῖς ἐγγύς

H [18] ὅτι δι᾽ αὐτοῦ ἔχομεν τὴν προσαγωγὴν
οἱ ἀμφότεροι ἐν ἑνὶ πνεύματι
πρὸς τὸν πατέρα

I [19] ἄρα οὖν οὐκέτι ἐστὲ ξένοι καὶ πάροικοι
ἀλλὰ ἐστὲ συμπολῖται τῶν ἁγίων
καὶ οἰκεῖοι τοῦ θεοῦ

J [20] ἐποικοδομηθέντες ἐπὶ τῷ θεμελίῳ
τῶν ἀποστόλων καὶ προφητῶν
ὄντος ἀκρογωνιαίου αὐτοῦ Χριστοῦ Ἰησοῦ

K [21] ἐν ᾧ πᾶσα οἰκοδομὴ συναρμολογουμένη
αὔξει εἰς ναὸν ἅγιον ἐν κυρίῳ
[22] ἐν ᾧ καὶ ὑμεῖς συνοικοδομεῖσθε
εἰς κατοικητήριον τοῦ θεοῦ ἐν πνεύματι

The opening at v. 11 introduces the content of what the Gentiles are to recall (ὅτι ποτὲ ὑμεῖς), which is suspended until v. 12, where Paul repeats the ὅτι in order to return to the suspended point. This is quite similar to what was seen earlier in 2:1–10 and other places in Paul (e.g., Rom 5:12, 18).

Also, as we have already seen in Paul's periodic style, he likes to end his periods—the place of stress—with focus on God and Christ, so also in vv. 11–22: "the blood of Christ" (v. 13); "in his flesh" (v. 14); "in him" (v. 16); "to the Father" (v. 18); "of God" (v. 19); "Christ Jesus" (v. 20); and "in the Spirit" (v. 22). This emphasis, as heretofore throughout Ephesians, stresses that deliverance of fallen humans is entirely a divine work.

There are a few more compositional elements of interest in vv. 11–22. In v. 12, for example, the whole period is balanced with alternating elements as follows:

> 12 ὅτι **ἦτε** τῷ καιρῷ ἐκείνῳ χωρὶς Χριστοῦ
> ἀπηλλοτριωμένοι τῆς πολιτείας τοῦ Ἰσραὴλ (ptc. clause)
> καὶ (**ἦτε**) ξένοι τῶν διαθηκῶν τῆς ἐπαγγελίας
> ἐλπίδα μὴ ἔχοντες (ptc. clause)
> καὶ (**ἦτε**) ἄθεοι ἐν τῷ κόσμῳ.

Likewise, there is a balance and alternation of elements in the final period comprising vv. 21–22, with the repeated elements emphasized below in bold:

> 21 **ἐν ᾧ** πᾶσα οἰκοδομὴ **συν**αρμολογουμένη
> αὔξει εἰς ναὸν ἅγιον ἐν κυρίῳ
> 22 **ἐν ᾧ** καὶ ὑμεῖς **συν**οικοδομεῖσθε
> εἰς κατοικητήριον τοῦ θεοῦ ἐν πνεύματι.

This repetition of words is part of the indication that vv. 21–22 form one period, not two, as the modern versification would have us believe.

Finally, vv. 15 and 16 are parallel in form, with leading purpose clauses followed by adverbial participles that explain how the subjunctive events were accomplished (means): ἵνα … κτίσῃ … ποιῶν εἰρήνην … καὶ [ἵνα] ἀποκαταλλάξῃ … ἀποκτείνας τὴν ἔχθραν, "in order to create … by making peace … and [in order to] reconcile … by putting to death the enmity." Both purpose clauses explain the reason why Christ annulled "the law of commandments in its ordinances" (v. 15a).

Nigel Turner points out that a particular kind of wordplay using words that have shared roots ("paronomasia") is a mark of Pauline style.[3] This comes out particularly in Rom 12:3, where we read: "For by the grace given to me I say to everyone among you not to think of himself more highly (ὑπερ**φρονεῖν**) than he ought to think (φρονεῖν), but to think (φρονεῖν) with sober judgment (σω**φρονεῖν**)." We have the same kind of wordplay in Eph 2:19–22 as well, with words built on οἶκος ("house"): πάρ**οικοι** ("resident aliens") … **οἰκ**εῖοι ("family members"; v. 19), ἐπ**οικο**δομηθέντες ("built on"; v. 20) **οἰκο**δομή ("building"; v. 21), συν**οικο**δομεῖσθε ("built up together"), and κατ**οικ**ητήριον ("dwelling"; v. 22).[4] Perhaps this kind of subtle stylistic feature of Ephesians bears on its Pauline authorship?

Outline

V. The Unified New Creation Inaugurated (2:11–22)
- A. Gentile separation from Israel and from God (2:11–12)
- B. Christ has united Gentiles with the saints into a new human race (2:13–18)
- C. The unified church household as new creation temple (2:19–22)

Original Text

11 Διὸ μνημονεύετε ὅτι ποτὲ ὑμεῖς τὰ ἔθνη ἐν σαρκί, οἱ λεγόμενοι ἀκροβυστία ὑπὸ τῆς λεγομένης περιτομῆς ἐν σαρκὶ χειροποιήτου, **12** ὅτι ἦτε τῷ καιρῷ
ἐκείνῳ[a] χωρὶς Χριστοῦ, ἀπηλλοτριωμένοι τῆς πολιτείας τοῦ Ἰσραὴλ καὶ ξένοι
τῶν διαθηκῶν τῆς ἐπαγγελίας, ἐλπίδα μὴ ἔχοντες καὶ ἄθεοι ἐν τῷ κόσμῳ. **13** νυνὶ
δὲ ἐν Χριστῷ Ἰησοῦ ὑμεῖς οἵ ποτε ὄντες μακρὰν ἐγενήθητε ἐγγὺς ἐν τῷ αἵματι
τοῦ Χριστοῦ. **14** Αὐτὸς γάρ ἐστιν ἡ εἰρήνη ἡμῶν, ὁ ποιήσας τὰ ἀμφότερα ἓν
καὶ τὸ μεσότοιχον τοῦ φραγμοῦ λύσας, τὴν ἔχθραν ἐν τῇ σαρκὶ αὐτοῦ, **15** τὸν
νόμον τῶν ἐντολῶν ἐν δόγμασιν καταργήσας, ἵνα τοὺς δύο κτίσῃ ἐν αὐτῷ εἰς ἕνα
καινὸν[b] ἄνθρωπον ποιῶν εἰρήνην **16** καὶ ἀποκαταλλάξῃ τοὺς ἀμφοτέρους ἐν ἑνὶ
σώματι τῷ θεῷ διὰ τοῦ σταυροῦ, ἀποκτείνας τὴν ἔχθραν ἐν αὐτῷ. **17** καὶ ἐλθὼν
εὐηγγελίσατο εἰρήνην ὑμῖν τοῖς μακρὰν καὶ εἰρήνην[c] τοῖς ἐγγύς· **18** ὅτι δι᾽ αὐτοῦ
ἔχομεν τὴν προσαγωγὴν οἱ ἀμφότεροι ἐν ἑνὶ πνεύματι πρὸς τὸν πατέρα. **19** Ἄρα

3. Turner, *MHT*, vol. 4, *Style*, 84–85.
4. See also the note on οἰκονομία ("[household] management") at 3:2 below.

οὖν οὐκέτι ἐστὲ ξένοι καὶ πάροικοι ἀλλὰ ἐστὲ συμπολῖται τῶν ἁγίων καὶ οἰκεῖοι τοῦ θεοῦ, **20** ἐποικοδομηθέντες ἐπὶ τῷ θεμελίῳ τῶν ἀποστόλων καὶ προφητῶν, ὄντος ἀκρογωνιαίου αὐτοῦ Χριστοῦ Ἰησοῦ, **21** ἐν ᾧ πᾶσα[d] οἰκοδομὴ συναρμολογουμένη αὔξει εἰς ναὸν ἅγιον ἐν κυρίῳ, **22** ἐν ᾧ καὶ ὑμεῖς συνοικοδομεῖσθε εἰς κατοικητήριον τοῦ θεοῦ ἐν πνεύματι.

Textual Notes

12.a. The reading of P[46] is of some slight interest; it reads ἐν τῷ καιρῷ ἐκείνῳ ("at that time"). Yet the preposition ἐν is clearly crossed out, with two dots above both characters, signifying a correction deleting this word and thereby conforming to the critical edition's reading. This is noteworthy because P[46] in Ephesians manifests few and only haphazard corrections and a tolerance for several surprising blunders (e.g., at 1:1, 3; 4:15, 30). Another such example in our passage would be a stray *alpha* found in P[46] between v. 15 and v. 16 (ποιῶν εἰρήνην **α** καὶ ἀποκαταλλάξῃ), though I'm not sure what that would be except a neuter plural relative pronoun that would have no clear antecedent and creates some slight nonsense in the text. This is important to note particularly in light of my comments above regarding the lack of ἐν Ἐφέσῳ in this early papyrus witness.

15.b. Instead of εἰς ἕνα καινὸν ἄνθρωπον ("into one new human race" or "man"), P[46], F, and G read εἰς ἕνα **κο**ινὸν ἄνθρωπον, "one common [or 'profane'!] man," while K muddles it further with καὶ μόνον ("even one man alone"). Perhaps this is a case where αι and οι were sounding alike and we have a simple spelling error or itacism rather than some sort of gnostic teaching making its way into our text.

17.c. This second occurrence of εἰρήνην in this verse is not found in several later MSS (e.g., K, L, Ψ, 81, 104, 630, M) and therefore was omitted in the Textus Receptus, as Metzger says, "probably because it seemed redundant and therefore superfluous."[5] The far better attested reading, which has this second instance of εἰρήνην, also makes a more powerful statement rhetorically.

---

5. Bruce M. Metzger, *A Textual Commentary on the Greek New Testament*, 2nd ed. (New York: United Bible Societies, 1994), 534.

21.d. The correctors of א and 1739, along with some other MSS (A, C, 81, 326, 1881, et al.), have an article in the phrase *πᾶσα ἡ οἰκοδομὴ* ("the whole building"). As Metzger says, copyists would have been tempted to add an article to clarify the meaning and so, combined with its good early attestation, the anarthrous text is probably original.[6] It is not definitive, but it is worth noting that the meter of the line reads evenly without the article with five trimeters: *ἐν ᾧ πᾶσα οἰκοδομὴ συναρμολογουμένη* is: ˘ ¯ ¯| ˘ ¯ ˘ | ˘ ¯ ˘ | ¯ ˘ ˘ | ¯ ˘ ¯. The section in question has two amphibrachs (˘ ¯ ˘), which would be interrupted with the expression of the article.

Translation

11 Therefore recall that you, formerly fleshly[7] Gentiles, the so-called uncircumcision by the so-called circumcision, which is in the flesh, made by hands— **12** (recall) that you were at that time apart from Christ, alienated from the citizenship of Israel and strangers from the covenants of promise, without hope and without God in the world, **13** whereas now in Christ you who were formerly far off were brought near by the blood of Christ, **14** for he himself is our peace, who made the two one and destroyed the dividing wall,[8] the enmity, in his flesh **15** by invalidating[9] the law of commandments in its ordinances, in order that he might create the two in himself into one new human race[10] by making peace **16** and reconcile both in one body to God through the cross by putting to death the enmity in himself, **17** and

---

6. Ibid.
7. Or "in the flesh" for the prepositional phrase *ἐν σαρκί*. The adjs. *σαρκινός* or *σαρκικός* could also have been used, though they only appear in Romans and the Corinthian correspondence (Rom 7:14; 15:27; 1 Cor 3:1, 3; 9:11; 2 Cor 1:12; 3:3; 10:4) and may have simply been preferred by Paul's secretary (Tertius) or collaborators (Sosthenes and Timothy) in those places.
8. The gen. in the phrase *τὸ μεσότοιχον τοῦ φραγμοῦ* is appositional; BDF §167 (cf. on 4:9).
9. The term *καταργέω* can have a general sense of "destroy," but here it carries a legal sense of "invalidate" or "annul." Cf. BDAG, 525: "to cause something to lose its power or effectiveness, *invalidate, make powerless*" with citation of Rom 3:3, 31; 4:14; Gal 3:17; 1 Cor 1:28. The aor. ptc. conveys the means whereby Christ made the two peoples one: *καταργήσας*, "by invalidating" (cf. Burton, *Moods*, §443).
10. Ἄνθρωπος here has generic reference to the human race or "humankind" (cf. BDAG, 81–82).

now that he has come[11] he has proclaimed[12] peace to you who were far off and peace to those nearby, **18** for through him we both have access in one Spirit to the Father. **2:19** So then you are no longer strangers and resident aliens,[13] but you are fellow citizens with the saints and members of God's family, **20** built on the foundation of the apostles and prophets, and its cornerstone[14] is Christ Jesus, **21** in whom the whole building[15] is interconnected[16] and grows together into a holy temple[17] in the Lord, **22** in whom you as well are being built up together into a dwelling of God in the Spirit.

11. The aor. adv. ptc. ἐλθών here has a simple temporal reference to an event preceding the main verb (εὐηγγελίσατο), which is best captured by the English perf. verb because it conveys that there is no specified interval between the two events (cf. Burton, *Moods*, §§52 and 88).

12. Because εὐαγγελίζω has a direct obj. here (εἰρήνην, "peace") it would be more proper yet bulky to render "proclaim peace as good news," which is the significance of the εὐ- prefix (cf. BDAG, 402). The aor. tense is rendered with the English perf. here ("he has proclaimed"), for which see the previous note.

13. πάροικος (an adj. used as a substantive) is a technical term for "resident foreigner[s]" (BDAG, 779) from the Greek *polis*, as explained in the comment on v. 19.

14. See BDAG, 39–40. The other option is "capstone"; cf. 1 Pet 2:6 for the only other NT use.

15. The phrase πᾶσα οἰκοδομὴ ("the whole building") refers to "completeness or wholeness" (BDAG, 783) even without an article, though there is a variant where the article is included (see "Textual Notes" above).

16. This rendering takes the ptc. in the phrase πᾶσα οἰκοδομὴ συναρμολογουμένη as adv. and forming a parallel clause with the main verb αὔξει (cf. NIV and NRSV). The other, equally likely way to take it is as an attributive ptc.: "the whole, *interconnected* building grows" (cf. ESV and NASB). The verb συναρμολογέω is used only here and in 4:16, where it occurs alongside συμβιβάζω, "unite" (cf. Col 2:2, 19). See LSJ, 1699, who only cite Ephesians for this form of the verb; cf. συναρμόζω/-όττω or adj. σύναρμος, which could have been used to the same effect. The verb is derived from and carries the idea of ἁρμός, which refers to a masonry, stone, or metal-working "joint" or "fastening" (LSJ, 244; BDAG, 132). Hence, συναρμολογουμένη communicates the strong bond that results from all the original, disperate groups of people brought together in the church through Christ.

17. The ναός of a Greek temple complex (ἱερόν) contained the cult* statue and refers to the inner "shrine" where the god or goddess was thought to reside (LSJ, 1160), though it can be used by synecdoche* for the whole temple (as Acts 19:24 for the Artemisium; cf. BDAG, 665–66).

Commentary

2:11 Διὸ μνημονεύετε ὅτι ποτὲ ὑμεῖς τὰ ἔθνη ἐν σαρκί, "Therefore recall that you, formerly fleshly Gentiles." Paul opens with a call for his audience to recall their former life apart from Christ and explains that they were actually hopeless and devoid of fellowship with the living God (v. 12). This call extends to v. 12. The whole of vv. 11–22 mirrors the earlier focus in 2:1–3, with its contrast between the audience's former life (vv. 1–3 and 11–12), then moves to their current enjoyment of God's free and effective deliverance in Christ (vv. 4–10 and vv. 13–22; cf. O'Brien, 183).

While it may be tempting to see the present-tense form of the imperative μνημονεύετε, "recall," as conveying some sort of constant or continuous notion, this verb only appears as a present imperative in the NT even when the item to be remembered is a specific thing on a specific occasion (e.g., Luke 17:32; John 15:20; Col 4:18).[18] Hence, Paul is not calling on the Ephesians here (and thereby others) to keep their former lives in mind as a general practice, but he asks them to recall that earlier life in preparation for the teaching that is to follow (cf. 5:8; 1 Cor 12:2; Col 2:11; 3:7; cf. Phil 3:13, "forgetting what lies behind").[19]

The phrase ἐν σαρκί ("fleshly," "in the flesh") may possibly have a double meaning here. The first is that the audience members were ethnic Gentiles simply because they had not undergone the physical ("in the flesh") rite of circumcision and the conversion to Judaism it represented. This is also the meaning of the "made-by-hands" circumcision with regard to the Jews in v. 11d (Rom 2:28; 2 Cor 10:3; Gal 2:20; Col 2:11, 13; Phil 1:22, 24; etc.). The second side to the phrase ἐν σαρκί is that the Gentile audience members were formerly lost in sin and in their deadly allegiance to the "lusts of the flesh" (v. 3; cf. Rom 7:5, 18, 25; 8:8–9; Gal 2:15). Here "flesh" refers to the fallen and corrupted character of human nature. One cannot always

---

18. In the LXX there are five pres. impv. uses of μνημονεύω and one in the aor. (2 Sam 14:11; rendered in the ESV as "invoke"). For a helpful survey of impvs. and tense usage see Stanley E. Porter, *Idioms of the Greek New Testament*, Biblical Languages: Greek 2 (Sheffield, UK: JSOT, 1992), 220–29.

19. In this instance, a different lexeme* at Paul's disposal, φρονέω, could also have conveyed a call for a more general and enduring recollection of some point of fact: "*Set your minds* (φρονεῖτε) on things that are above" (Col 3:2, emphasis added).

assume double meaning in words and phrases, but it is possible here in v. 11 given the context of v. 3 and general Pauline usage of *σάρξ*.

οἱ λεγόμενοι ἀκροβυστία ὑπὸ τῆς λεγομένης περιτομῆς ἐν σαρκὶ χειροποιήτου, "the so-called uncircumcision by the so-called circumcision, which is in the flesh, made by hands." The expression "so-called" (for *λεγόμενοι* here) is not necessarily pejorative; it can simply mean "who are called" (as the major versions here), "who are known as," or "who are designated as." For example, "Jesus, who is known as 'Justus' " (Col 4:11; *Ἰησοῦς ὁ λεγόμενος Ἰοῦστος*; cf. Matt 1:16; 4:18; 10:2; John 11:16; 21:2). However, there are two places in Paul's writings with this expression where "so-called" is found in some versions: "there may be so-called gods" (1 Cor 8:5; ESV, NASB, NIV, NRSV) and "every so-called god" (2 Thess 2:4; ESV, NASB, NRSV). In these cases, Paul is distancing himself from labels other people use. That seems to be the case here in Eph 2:11 because Paul does not use derogatory labels for his audience; he calls them "saints" (e.g., 1:1; 5:3).

What is said in Eph 2:11 with the phrase "the so-called *uncircumcision*" appears to show that hostility between the two groups has come from the Jewish side, since *uncircumcised* was a term of derision for a long time (e.g., 1 Sam 17:26).[20] In Paul's view, circumcision, if it was only "in the flesh" or "made by hands," was in itself of no value but had always been a matter of purifying one's heart before God (Deut 10:16; 30:6; Rom 2:25–29). This is particularly true now that Christians have been circumcised in Christ (Col 2:11; cf. Phil 3:3), making both circumcision and uncircumcision obsolete as a sacrament of the righteousness of faith (Rom 4:11; 1 Cor 7:1). There is also some irony here in the repetition of the phrase *ἐν σαρκί*. If the audience members were Gentiles "in the flesh," then so also the Jews were only circumcised "in the flesh," neither of which matters for covenant standing after the first advent and work of Christ.

2:12 *ὅτι ἦτε τῷ καιρῷ ἐκείνῳ χωρὶς Χριστοῦ*, "(recall) that you were at that time apart from Christ." By repeating *ὅτι* at the opening of v. 12, Paul resumes his point begun in v. 11 with what his audience was to recall. This

---

20. And see esp. Gal 2:14–15, contrasting Gentiles who were regarded as sinners by nature. This does not necessarily mean that there was a particular conflict between Jews and Gentiles at Ephesus behind these statements (cf. Lincoln, 132–33; O'Brien, 183).

recollection consists of five things true of their former pagan state, and these are articulated in each of the five cola* in this period:

> [12] ὅτι ἦτε τῷ καιρῷ ἐκείνῳ χωρὶς Χριστοῦ
> ἀπηλλοτριωμένοι τῆς πολιτείας τοῦ Ἰσραὴλ
> καὶ ξένοι τῶν διαθηκῶν τῆς ἐπαγγελίας
> ἐλπίδα μὴ ἔχοντες
> καὶ ἄθεοι ἐν τῷ κόσμῳ

To say that a person in his or her pre-Christian life was "apart from Christ" (χωρὶς Χριστοῦ, v. 12a) seems rather obvious and unnecessary. But Paul's point is covenantal and therefore objective: Gentiles, by virtue of being separated from Israel, did not have the hope of the messianic promise and the privileged status with God that Israel's covenant relationship with him brought. This is really a combination of Paul's points made, for example, in Romans: Jews had the advantage of possessing the oracles of God (Rom 3:1–2); they had pride of place in the proclamation of the gospel (Rom 1:16; cf. Matt 15:21–8); and they had the adoption, the covenants, the promises, and the patriarchs (Rom 9:4–5). And, what is all-important, they had the Messiah "according to the flesh" (Rom 9:5), which is what Paul is saying about the Gentiles in Eph 2:12: *Gentiles* prior to Christ's advent and prior to their faith in him did not have the Messiah as their inheritance; they were "apart from Christ."[21] For the divine covenant of promise was not made with the nations at large but with national and ethnic Israel:

> The LORD your God has chosen you to be a people for his treasured possession, out of all the peoples who are on the face of the earth. It was not because you were more in number than any other people that the LORD set his love on you and chose you, for you were the fewest of all peoples, but it is because the LORD loves you and is keeping the oath that he swore to your fathers. (Deut 7:6b–8a; cf. Exod 34:10; Deut 4:7, 32–34)

ἀπηλλοτριωμένοι τῆς πολιτείας τοῦ Ἰσραήλ, "alienated from the citizenship of Israel." It seems unusual in English to say "alienated" (ἀπαλλοτριόω)

---

21. Cf. Gal 5:4, where apostasy in the form of accepting circumcision and the law's demand to personally fulfill all of its stipulations for righteousness leads Paul to say κατηργήθητε ἀπὸ Χριστοῦ, "you have been severed from Christ."

from citizenship (v. 12b; cf. Col 1:21; Ezek 14:5). Why not say "outside the state (πόλις)" or "political institutions (πολιτεία)" of Israel, or more simply "outside Israel" (ἔξω [or χωρὶς] τοῦ 'Ισραήλ)? BDAG, 96, takes the phrase to mean various things; for example, as "*excluded* from the corporate life of Israel." In the Hippocratic writings this verb is used more generally when the author states that one cannot *separate* (ἀπαλλοτριωθῆναι) consideration of leg joints that can and cannot be cured.[22] More interesting for our context in Eph 2:12 is Diodorus Siculus' statement that after some intercity wars of Sicily (fifth century BC), the cities drove out "the forms of government which *aliens* had introduced (τὰς ἀπαλλοτρίους πολιτείας ἀποβαλοῦσαι)" and divided the lands up by lot among all the citizens.[23] The adjective ἀπαλλότριος here in Diodorus is etymologically related to our verb ἀπαλλοτριόω and may show that it could have a sense of being an alien to civic institutions (i.e., πολιτεία, the same word in Eph 2:12b; cf. LSJ, 176). In other words, the verb too might have legal usage in the semantic realm of citizenship in the Greek city-states.

In any case, Paul's point in v. 12b is that Gentiles were not a part of the citizen-body, the city-state institutions, or better, the citizen rights (πολιτεία) of ancient Israel.[24] The tribune who arrested Paul purchased his Roman πολιτεία ("citizenship"), no doubt under Claudius (Acts 22:28), and the meaning "citizenship" or "citizen rights" makes the best sense in Eph 2:12b. This meaning would be familiar to Ephesians who were living where some old inscriptions may have still been legible that granted "citizenship" (πολιτεία) to various individuals.[25] Paul is hereby accenting that

22. Hippocrates, *On Joints* 58. Cf. G. H. R. Horsley, *New Docs,* 3:62, no. 24.
23. Diodorus Siculus, 11.76; LCL trans.; emphasis added.
24. The English versions predominantly have "commonwealth" (KJV; NASB; ESV; NRSV) or "community" (NAB); cf. "state, people, body politic" (BDAG, 845) rather than "citizenship" (NIV) for πολιτεία. The term can refer to a citizen-body and by transferred meaning to a city or government or to a state's "political institutions" (e.g., Polybius, 2.38.4, yet later, in 2.57.2, πολιτεία means "citizenship"), so these renderings are possible if not preferred here in Eph 2:12. If Paul had wanted to refer to the "commonwealth" of Israel in v. 12, πολίτευμα would have been a clearer term to use as in Phil 3:20. The LXX uses πολιτεία only in the Maccabean literature (8x), probably because of these distinctly Hellenic writings. The only other NT use of this noun is in Acts 22:28 ("citizenship"). Cf. LSJ, 1434.
25. E.g., δοῦναι πολιτείαν αὐτῷ καὶ ἐκγόνοις, "to grant citizenship to him and to his descendants" (*IvE* 1409, line 3).

the Gentiles lacked Israel's covenant rights and privileges under the theocracy as the nation God distinctly possessed as his prized possession (1:14 and Deut 7:6–8 quoted above). See on v. 19 for more on citizenship in an Ephesian context.

καὶ ξένοι τῶν διαθηκῶν τῆς ἐπαγγελίας, "and strangers from the covenants of promise." With v. 12c, Paul shows that he is at heart a systematic theologian of the first order.[26] This may seem obvious, but the contrast with thinkers with which his audience were familiar is quite pronounced. Philosophies sometimes tried to come up with coherent explanations of reality (especially the "pre-Socratics"), but none of them really took history very seriously (e.g., Platonism or the skeptical Academics). With the phrase "strangers from the covenants of promise," Paul systematizes the historical divine-human covenants of the OT as being unified in that they were "promissory."[27] These covenants looked forward to their messianic fulfillment, which was the impulse for God making them with his ancient people to begin with.[28] This is the basis of Paul saying that the Gentile Christians were formerly "apart from Christ"; they were aliens to the divine covenants with Israel, with their messianic core (i.e., "the seed is Christ," Gal 3:16;

26. *Contra* Martin Rese ("Die Vorzüge Israels in Röm 9,4f und Eph 2,12: exegetische Anmerkungen zum Thema Kirche und Israel," *TheolZeit* 31 [1975]: 211–22), who sees nothing but contrast between Paul's statements on Israel and the Gentiles in Rom 9:4–5 and Eph 2:12, which leads him to conclude that Ephesians is pseudepigraphical. Scholars often do not allow for the subtlety, nuance, and complexity one finds in Paul's theology, which, even from our rather spartan remains in his epistles, is impressively evident.

27. This takes the gen. "of promise" as adj. (Daniel B. Wallace, *Greek Grammar beyond the Basics* [Grand Rapids: Zondervan, 1997], 78). The NIV takes the article with "promise" (τῶν διαθηκῶν **τῆς** ἐπαγγελίας) as conveying a definite idea: "foreigners to the covenants of *the* promise" (NIV, emphasis added; also Hodge, 127), but it is more likely that this article was used because "covenants" is also articular, an example of Apollonius' canon (Wallace, *Greek Grammar*, 239–40) (with ξένοι τῶν διαθηκῶν being an exception to the same canon; Wallace, *Greek Grammar*, 239n60).

28. So explicitly Gal 3:8 and context. The interrelations of redemptive history, revelation, covenant, and eschatology are the main focus of Michael Horton's *Covenant and Eschatology: The Divine Drama* (Louisville: Westminster John Knox, 2002). That Paul unifies the previous divine covenants under the heading "of promise" is one of the bases for Reformed theology speaking of an overarching, postlapsis "covenant of grace" (e.g., *Westminster Confession of Faith* 7.3–6).

cf. 2 Cor 1:20; Heb 7:20–22; 8:6; 9:15), through "the promised Spirit" (1:13; Gal 3:14; Acts 2:33).

The junction of ἀπαλλοτριόω ("alienate") in v. 12b and ξένος ("stranger," "alien") in v. 12c finds an interesting parallel in the LXX of Psa 69:8 (68:9): **ἀπηλλοτριωμένος** ἐγενήθην τοῖς ἀδελφοῖς μου καὶ **ξένος** τοῖς υἱοῖς τῆς μητρός μου, "I have become one alienated with my brothers, and a stranger to the sons of my mother." Perhaps Paul also saw these terms as interrelated in Eph 2:12 as in this psalm, though a direct allusion to Psa 69 is admittedly tenuous.

ἐλπίδα μὴ ἔχοντες καὶ ἄθεοι ἐν τῷ κόσμῳ, "without hope and without God in the world." The adjective ἄθεος occurs only here in the NT (and not in the LXX), and in secular Greek it could refer to an "atheist" or one who denies the gods.[29] The Ephesians, though, had been very "religious," with a full panoply of deities and others worshiped there alongside the state goddess, Artemis Ephesia, which Paul had seen for himself.[30] Before their conversion, the Ephesians were undoubtedly not atheists.

The term ἄθεος, however, does not mean "atheist" in v. 12 but "without a relationship to God" (BDAG, 24). God was not committed to them: Not only did they not acknowledge the true and living God, but he did not "know" them in the sense of entering into a covenant relationship with them (so Gal 4:8–9; 1 Thess 4:5; cf. Hos 2:20; Isa 19:21; Jer 31:34). With ἄθεοι ἐν τῷ κόσμῳ ("without God in the world"), Paul connects his thought with the mainstream of biblical revelation. If the "covenants of promise" are a systematic summary of God's redemptive words and acts, then to belong to God as his people is the heartbeat of those covenants and of the Scriptures: "I am your God and you are my people" has been identified for centuries as the "covenant formula" (Latin *formula foederis* or German

---

29. This, of course, was the main charge against Socrates at Athens, though he denied that he was τὸ παράπαν ἄθεος, "a complete atheist" (Plato, *Apologia* 26C); cf. *Mart. Pol.* 3:2.

30. Epigraphical remains for worship of various deities at Ephesus are collected in *IvE* 1201–71. Ephesians also venerated a full range of demigods or personifications (e.g., [ἀγαθὴ] τυχή, "[Good] Fortune"), emperors, and heroes as well. Cf. Dieter Knibbe, "Ephesos—Nicht nur die Stadt der Artemis: die 'anderen' ephesischen Götter," in *Studien zur Religion und Kultur Kleinasiens II. Festschrift für Friedrich Karl Dörner zum 65. Geburtstag am 28. Februar 1976*, ed. S. Şahin, E. Schwertheim, and J. Wagner (Leiden: Brill, 1978), 489–503. For focus on Artemis, the emperor cult*, and Judaism see Paul Trebilco, *The Early Christians in Ephesus from Paul to Ignatius* (Grand Rapids: Eerdmans, 2008; first published 2004), 19–52.

Bundesformel). As Otto Kaiser has noted, "[T]he covenantal formula is anything but an empty predicate. It is in fact the chief thread through the labyrinth of the Bible."[31] Hence, the audience may formerly have had hope of some sort, but not a true hope based on the rich inheritance of free grace (cf. 1:18; 1 Thess 4:13).

2:13 νυνὶ δὲ ἐν Χριστῷ Ἰησοῦ ὑμεῖς οἵ ποτε ὄντες μακρὰν, "whereas now in Christ you who were formerly far off." Paul turns from his hearers' old, Gentile state to their new state in Christ. Ironically, they may still be "fleshly Gentiles" (v. 11) in their ethnic origin, but these believers are no longer "far off" Gentiles since they are "now in Christ" (see esp. on 4:17). The issue is not only that they were pagans but that they were outside God's covenants of promise. This is the second of three movements in the larger section of Eph 2:11–22. The opening has some stress with νυνὶ δέ ("whereas now"; "but at present") because of the *iota* with νυνί (cf. Rom 3:21; 6:22: 7:6; 1 Cor 12:18; 13:13; Col 1:22).[32]

What follows in vv. 13–18 prepares for what Paul is about to say later in the epistle about the unity of the church (esp. 4:4–7). The focus at this earlier stage stands in contrast to the former separation of the Gentiles through Israel's regulations in the Mosaic covenant, which kept the Gentiles at a distance from its blessings, especially the blessing of divine fellowship (vv. 11–12; 14–15). These theocratic, national covenant stipulations were annulled by God in Christ as part of his work to create one new, international "church of God" (1 Cor 10:32) as one inseparable household

31. Otto Kaiser, "The Law as Center of the Hebrew Bible," in *"Sha'arei Talmon" Studies in the Bible, Qumran, and the Ancient Near East Presented to Shemaryahu Talmon*, ed. M. Fishbane and E. Tov (Winona Lake, IN: Eisenbrauns, 1992), 96; and more than two centuries earlier by Francis Turretin, *Institutes of Elenctic Theology*, trans. George Musgrave Giger (Phillipsburg, NJ: P&R, 1992), 2:179–80, 232.

32. The stress comes from pronunciation; the phrase νυνὶ δέ would have been pronounced as two words, while νῦν δέ would have been combined into one (i.e., νῦνδε; cf. καίγε, καίτοιγε, κἀγώ, and the like). Both νῦν and νυνί are used with δέ by Paul, with either a temporal ("whereas now," "but at present") or logical meaning ("but the fact is"; especially in contrast with a preceding contrary statement). For example: ἦτε γάρ ποτε σκότος, **νῦνδὲ** φῶς ἐν κυρίῳ, "for you were formerly darkness, *but now* you are light in the Lord" (Eph 5:8); and ἐπεὶ ἄρα τὰ τέκνα ὑμῶν ἀκάθαρτά ἐστιν, **νῦνδὲ** ἅγιά ἐστιν, "For then your children would be unclean, *but the fact is,* they are indeed holy" (1 Cor 7:14). Cf. BDAG, 681–82.

and temple (vv. 19–22).[33] In Ephesians, Paul had earlier stated (esp. 1:3–14) and will stress again throughout chaps. 3 and 4 that this movement in redemptive history was not some ad hoc divine act but part of God's predetermined plan all along, even though he had earlier held it in suspense as a "mystery" until Christ should come in the "fullness of all eras" (1:10; cf. Gal 4:4) at the "consummation of the ages" (Heb 9:26) to bring that plan into its inaugurated effect. Its consummation awaits fulfillment in the future at Christ's return.

ἐγενήθητε ἐγγὺς ἐν τῷ αἵματι τοῦ Χριστοῦ, "were brought near by the blood of Christ."[34] That the Gentiles are brought "near" means that they now have access (προσαγωγή; see v. 18) to God through Christ's blood, which refers to his death on the cross (v. 16; Phil 2:8) for all his sheep (John 10:16), even for those who were formerly "far off" (Acts 2:39). By referring to Christ's "blood," Paul combines the ideas of both purification from the guilt of sin (Heb 9:22; cf. Eph 1:7; 5:26) and of substitutionary atonement, which itself includes both paying the price for sins (1:7; Col 1:20) and propitiating the wrath of God against sinners (2:3; Rom 3:25; 5:9).[35] Hence, Christ is their peace, as is stated next (v. 14).

Some scholars see that the mediation of Christ was through his blood here in v. 13 and combine it with ἐν τῇ σαρκὶ αὐτοῦ ("in his flesh") in the next verse to argue that Christ's work was accomplished through his

33. OT separation laws distinguishing Jews from Gentiles regulated diet (e.g., Lev 11:1–8), dress (e.g., Lev 19:19; Deut 22:11), and especially worship (e.g., Deut 12:29–31). For "Jew and Gentile" or "Jew and Greek" as the two main classes of people from the Jewish perspective see, for example, John 7:35; Acts 14:1, 5; Rom 2:9; 3:9, 29; 9:24; 1 Cor 1:22–24; 10:32; 12:13; Gal 3:28; Col 3:11. The implication is, as Gnilka (137) notes, "The universal Church is the true Israel, the Israel of God" (my trans.).

34. Markus Barth makes a case for rendering this phrase as "in the Messiah" (Barth, 260, 292–93).

35. Cf. Brian Vickers, *Jesus' Blood and Righteousness: Paul's Theology of Imputation* (Wheaton, IL: Crossway, 2006). Colossians 1:20–22 has several terms and ideas that are parallel to this section in Ephesians, including: εἰρηνοποιήσας διὰ τοῦ αἵματος τοῦ σταυροῦ αὐτοῦ, "by making peace by the blood of his cross" (Col 1:20; cf. Eph 2:16) and ἐν τῷ σώματι τῆς σαρκὸς αὐτοῦ (Col 1:22; cf. Eph 1:14; Rom 7:4). "Like the cross (σταυρός), the 'blood of Christ' is simply another and even more graphic phrase for the death of Christ in its soteriological significance," Johannes Behm, *TDNT*, 1:174; cf. J. Schneider, *TDNT*, 7:572–84.

incarnation rather than through his high-priestly sacrifice.[36] While it is true that Christ's incarnation and true humanity is an essential part of his mediatorial work on the cross (v. 16), it would be difficult for any ancient person to hear about "blood" in this context and *not* think about blood sacrifices. They were an ordinary part of life in antiquity. It would be highly unusual to eat meat that was *not* offered in sacrifice at some point.[37] Ephesus was filled with shrines as well as the largest temple in the ancient world, the Artemisium of Artemis Ephesia, with its large, enclosed altar nearby, where regular animal sacrifices took place.[38]

2:14 Αὐτὸς γάρ ἐστιν ἡ εἰρήνη ἡμῶν, "for he himself is our peace." With this verse we start a section of text (vv. 14–18) that has inspired many attempts to find alleged sources for the author's statements from Colossians, from hymns or liturgical material, or even from gnostic (or protognostic) myths.[39] Resistance to Roman imperial propaganda for their rule and *Pax Romana*

---

36. I.e., "blood and flesh" as reference to human bodily existence (as 6:12; 1 Cor 15:50; Heb 2:14). For thorough treatment and response see Barth, 298–305; cf. Markus Barth, *The Broken Wall: A Study of the Epistle to the Ephesians* (Valley Forge, PA: Judson, 1959).

37. E.g., *IvE* 10 enumerates the main daily sacrifices and portions at Ephesus. The inscription is third century AD but says it is recording the "traditional law" (νόμος πατρίος) of the city. The well-known decree of the Roman governor Paullus Fabius Persicus (*IvE* 17–9) in AD 44 chided the Ephesians for selling municipal priesthoods "as if at auction" rather than keeping them in well-bred families. An ancient priesthood could be quite lucrative. See also most of Menander's extant plays, where fowl or other meats were sacrificed in shrines as part of what seems to be otherwise ordinary family meals (Menander, *Dyskolos* [Sykon), *Epitrepontes* [Karion], *Samia* [unnamed]). Portions of meat sold in the *agora* were typically sold there by priests from the parts of sacrificial animals they received as fees for their services; cf. Walter Burkert, *Greek Religion*, trans. John Raffan (Cambridge, MA: Harvard University Press, 1985), 96–97; E. Ferguson, *Backgrounds of Early Christianity*, 3rd ed. (Grand Rapids: Eerdmans, 2003), 188–92; S. M. Baugh, "A Foreign World: Ephesus in the First Century," in *Women in the Church*, 2nd ed., ed. A. J. Köstenberger and T. R. Schreiner (Grand Rapids: Baker, 2005), 20–23.

38. See Peter Scherrer, ed., *Ephesus: The New Guide* (Turkey: Zero, 2000), 53, for a plan of the Artemisium and the main altar to its west; cf. below on 5:2.

39. For an older but still helpful review see Michael S. Moore, "Ephesians 2:14–16: A History of Recent Interpretation," *EvQ* 54 (1982): 163–68. For the supposed background in hymnic material see discussion and sources under 1:3–14 above (cf. Gnilka, 147–52). The gnostic myth source was championed by Heinrich Schlier in *Christus und die Kirche im Epheserbrief*, BHT 6 (Tübingen: Mohr Siebeck, 1930)

(which the Ephesian elites in particular seem to have readily embraced) is also seen as the background to the statements here.[40] Far more likely, as with all the Pauline Epistles, there are significant OT influences on our passage, especially since Paul sees Christ bringing all the promises of the previous covenant administrations (v. 12) into their complete fulfillment (e.g., 2 Cor 1:20).[41]

For Paul, Christ represents the sum total of all God's blessings and grace for his people, and so he says here that Christ Jesus is the church's peace, both with one another (2:14–15, 19) and with God (2:16–17; cf. Psa 72:7; Mic 5:5; Zech 9:10; Col 3:15). This metaphorical manner of speaking is used elsewhere, for example, in 1 Corinthians, where Christ is wisdom, righteousness, sanctification, and redemption (1 Cor 1:30), the church's foundation (1 Cor 3:11), the following rock (1 Cor 10:4), the head (1 Cor 11:3; cf. Eph 4:15; 5:23), and the resurrection firstfruits of those who belong to him (1 Cor 15:23).

ὁ ποιήσας τὰ ἀμφότερα ἓν καὶ τὸ μεσότοιχον τοῦ φραγμοῦ λύσας, τὴν ἔχθραν ἐν τῇ σαρκὶ αὐτοῦ, "who made the two one and destroyed the dividing wall,

---

and advanced in evangelical circles by Ralph P. Martin, *Reconciliation: A Study of Paul's Theology* (Atlanta: John Knox, 1981), 157–98.

40. Some scholars have seen Ephesians as presenting Paul as accommodating to Roman imperial claims, but see Nijay K. Gupta and Fredrick J. Long, "The Politics of Ephesians and the Empire: Accommodation or Resistance?" *JGRChJ* 7 (2010): 112–36, who persuasively show that, "In fact, the particular language of Ephesians shows many signs of counter-imperial resistance by affirming the establishment of an alternative political identity in the church assembly around Jesus Christ as the one Lord (4.5). ... Ephesians often confronts and trumps imperial prerogatives and titles while also subverting conventional wisdom about household relations. This is achieved by featuring as the head of the church body a political leader and ruler, Jesus Messiah Lord, who himself modeled sacrificial love (1.4–8; 3.15–19; 5.2, 25, 29) and expects such from his followers (4.20–24; 4.32–5.2; 5.25–29)" (115, 135); see also the comments on 1:21 above. Cf. Margaret Y. MacDonald, "The Politics of Identity in Ephesians," *JSNT* 26 (2004): 419–44; Peter Stuhlmacher, " 'He Is Our Peace' (Eph 2:14)—On the Exegesis and Significance of Eph 2:14-18," in *Reconciliation, Law, & Righteousness: Essays in Biblical Theology* (Philadelphia: Fortress, 1986), 182–200. Ephesus seemed to welcome Roman influence and its peace after suffering several centuries of war and financial ruin before the principate of Augustus.

41. See comment on v. 17 below and cf. esp. Robert H. Suh, "The Use of Ezekiel 37 in Ephesians 2," *JETS* 50 (2007): 715–33; Thorsten Moritz, *A Profound Mystery: The Use of the Old Testament in Ephesians* (New York: Brill, 1996), 23–55.

the enmity, in his flesh." The stress in v. 14 is on the "hostility" or "enmity" (ἔχθρα) between Jews and Greeks through the separation provisions of the law (see above on v. 13). The one constant in human experience since the Adamic fall is enmity (Gen 3:15), which was exacerbated by division of humans through language barriers (Gen 11:7–9) and by the "dividing wall" of the law's separation doctrines (v. 15), keeping Jews and Gentiles ("both" in v. 14) at odds.[42] On the Graeco-Roman side, these laws created for the Jews a "misanthropic and inhospitable way of life" that sometimes created anti-Jewish attitudes.[43] Cutting through all this, Christ has created a unified new people from the old hostile camps (Col 3:15; John 17:20–21) and made them at peace.[44]

A famous wall inscription that faced the outer courtyard of the Jerusalem temple is extant; it warned Gentiles that they would have only themselves to blame for their death if they passed into the inner courts.[45] Hence, it was a "dividing wall" or "a wall that separates."[46] Paul may or may not be alluding to this wall in v. 14, but it well illustrates Jesus Christ's reconciliation of all peoples by tearing down this wall and building up both Jews and Gentiles into a new humanity (v. 15). It is ironic that in his early

---

42. A classic anthology of sources on this topic is Margaret Williams, *The Jews among the Greeks and Romans: A Diaspora Sourcebook* (Baltimore: Johns Hopkins University Press, 1998); for the search for Jews in Asia in particular see Paul Trebilco, *Jewish Communities in Asia Minor*, SNTSMS 69 (Cambridge: Cambridge University Press, 1991). The Jewish community left very little physical evidence behind in Ephesus, though they had lived there for many centuries by the time of Paul.

43. Hecataeus of Abdera as quoted in Katell Berthelot, "Hécatée d'Abdère et la « misanthropie » juive," *Bulletin du Centre de recherche français à Jérusalem* 19 (2008): n.p., also available in English as "Hecataeus of Abdera and Jewish 'Misanthropy,'" from http://bcrfj.revues.org/5968 (accessed September 2013). For a Roman view see Juvenal's biting comments on exclusive Jewish rites and customs in *Satires* 14.96–106.

44. BDAG, 419, says that the opposite of ἔχθρα ("enmity") is φιλία, "friendship" (e.g., Polybius, 3.12.5, for "reconciliation of enmities [ἔχθραι]" and "formation of friendships [φιλίαι]"), but here in Eph 2:14 the antonym of ἔχθρα is εἰρήνη ("peace"), which is objective and stronger than φιλία. Cf. Cilliers Breytenbach, *Grace, Reconciliation, Concord: The Death of Christ in Graeco-Roman Metaphors*, NovTSup 135 (Leiden: Brill, 2010).

45. Cf. Elias J. Bickerman, "The Warning Inscriptions of Herod's Temple," *Jewish Quarterly Review* 37 (1947): 387–405.

46. Cf. BDAG, 625, 1064, for μεσότοιχον (1x) and φραγμός (4x).

life, Jesus probably worked as a "builder" (τέκτων; Matt 13:55; Mark 6:3) or building contractor who would have torn down and built up, and that as the divine Son he built all creation (1 Cor 8:6; Col 1:15–20), and now through his mediatorial, incarnate work he has inaugurated God's new creation in a unified, universal church.[47]

The unity of the church is a central concern of this epistle, and its objective basis is expressed here in that Christ has "made the two (into) one." By using the neuter ἕν ("one thing") rather than masculine εἷς ("one person"), Paul expresses that the two are "unified" in one corporate body (so v. 16) through the Spirit (v. 18). The similarity of this statement of unity to the Son's prayer in John 17:11, 21–22, should not be missed: ἵνα πάντες **ἓν** ὦσιν, "in order that all (of them) may be one," John 17:21 (cf. John 10:30 and 1 Cor 3:8).[48]

2:15 τὸν νόμον τῶν ἐντολῶν ἐν δόγμασιν καταργήσας, "by invalidating the law of commandments in its ordinances." While Paul does not specify it here, it is clear that the commandments Christ "invalidated" are those that kept Jew and Gentile apart—the teachings on purity and separation (cf. Col 2:14).[49] These particular commandments were tied to Israel's theocracy and were part of that typological purity legislation that led God to command Israel to exterminate the Canaanites from the holy land in preliminary judgment.[50]

47. For τέκτων see BDAG, 995; cf. Ken M. Campbell, "What Was Jesus' Occupation?" *JETS* 48 (2005): 501–19.

48. In Gal 3:28 Paul says that in Christ there is no more "Jew nor Greek, slave nor free, male and female, for you are all one (εἷς) in Christ Jesus." By using masc. εἷς in this context instead of neuter ἕν, as in Eph 2, Paul focuses on the church's legal status for the purpose of inheritance; in Christ they are one (legal) person and coheirs. In Ephesians, the focus is on believers' unity together in the new creation. The difference is subtle but communicated by the gender form of *one*. Masc. *one* is used in Eph 2:15b only because it modifies masc. ἄνθρωπος and therefore does not alter this interpretation.

49. This has often (since the church's earliest days) been labeled the "ceremonial" law, but that category is broader than the separation laws that separated Israel from its neighbors and defined it holiness in various practical ways; e.g., Exod 23:31–33; Lev 19:19; 20:25–26; Deut 7:1–11; 22:9–11; cf. Ezra 6:21; Neh 9:2; 10:28–31. In general see Peter D. Myers, "Cognitive Linguistics and the Tripartite Division of the Law," *WTJ* 74 (2012): 387–415.

50. M. G. Kline labeled this "intrusion ethics" in that the final judgment had "intruded" prolepticly into this age; see *The Structure of Biblical Authority*, 2nd ed. (Grand Rapids; Eerdmans, 1975), 154–71. The kingdom work that Christ

This whole body of "legislation" or "ordinances," the referent of δόγμα here, was invalidated by Christ as part of his work of new creation.[51]

ἵνα τοὺς δύο κτίσῃ ἐν αὐτῷ εἰς ἕνα καινὸν ἄνθρωπον ποιῶν εἰρήνην, "in order that he might create the two in himself into one new human race by making peace." Christ invalidated the typological separation regulations both by fulfilling them and by removing believers from the law's condemnation (see Matt 5:17; Rom 8:1; Heb 9:11–14; 10:1–10). The result is a "new man," i.e., a new human race. Paul could have said, "new people" (καινοὶ ἄνθρωποι or καινὸς λαός), but the focus here is on a new human race that is *unified* as "*one* new man."[52] This "single new man" is the bride of Christ (e.g., 5:23–32; 2 Cor 11:2), created out of both Jews and Gentiles who were formerly dead (vv. 1, 5) and at war with each other (v. 16; cf. Barth, 309–10). The new creation "man" is both corporate and individual, as the church as "one person" (εἷς; Gal 3:28) has been created anew in Christ in one body on the cross (again v. 16 and on 4:22–24), while individual believers experience this corporate reality in the church spanning regeneration (above 1:13–14) to resurrection (Phil 3:21) through renewal day by day (2 Cor 4:16) from glory to glory (2 Cor 3:18).[53]

The consequence of this new human race in Christ is that any sort of segregation or exclusion of any human being who professes Christ from full membership in his church is in direct odds with the church's very reality as a work of inaugurated new creation and defies the Lord who founded it (v. 20; cf. Gal 2:11–14). This Lord was constituted as a Second Adam as head of the new humanity, and in his image believers are being re-created (1 Cor 15:45, 49; Col 3:10–11) as members of his "body" (v. 16).

---

inaugurated and will continue until his Parousia in this age specifically introduced grace and reconciliation until his "coming again in glory and to judge both the living and the dead" (Nicene Creed); cf. John 12:47; Luke 9:54–55; Rev 6:16.

51. For δόγμα (5x) see BDAG, 254: "a formal statement concerning rules or regulations that are to be observed."

52. This line of reasoning is confirmed by the use of κτίζω, "create," here rather than more generic words for "make" (like ποιέω as in v. 14). The human race is re-created in Christ. Cf. Ignatius (*Eph.* 20.1), who sees Christ as the "new man" (καινὸς ἄνθρωπος).

53. See esp. Herman Ridderbos, *Paul: An Outline of His Theology*, trans. John De Witt (Grand Rapids: Eerdmans, 1975), 57–64, 223–31; and Barth, 308–11.

2:16 καὶ ἀποκαταλλάξῃ τοὺς ἀμφοτέρους ἐν ἑνὶ σώματι τῷ θεῷ διὰ τοῦ σταυροῦ, "and reconcile both in one body to God through the cross." Christ reconciled all his people, but the foundation is stated here in that believers are reconciled together "to God" (also 2 Cor 5:18).[54] As Paul explains in Rom 5:1–11, this reconciliation involved Christ satisfying God's wrath against his enemies and turning them into his friends (cf. John 15:13–15). While the "enmity" in Eph 2:14 refers to the enmity between Jew and Gentile, now in v. 16 the enmity that was destroyed was the enmity between God and his rebellious creatures (so vv. 1–3). Hence, Christ's enemies used the cross (v. 16c) to put him to death (Matt 21:38–39), but God used the cross to destroy his own wrath against people on whom he had set his eternal, electing love (so 1:3–14), and through this new-creation work in Christ reconciled the former hostile groups of Jew and Gentile to each other.

An interesting addition in v. 16b was necessary for Paul's continuing interest in church unity in this larger passage. He could have said "to reconcile both parties to God," but this might imply that Jews and Gentiles are reconciled in different ways or separately.[55] Instead he adds, "to reconcile both *in one body* (ἐν ἑνὶ σώματι) to God."[56] While it is tempting to understand "body" here as the equivalent of "group," Paul is simply using his favorite metaphor of a human body to bring out the organic unity among all believers in the church to one another and to Christ (see esp. Rom 12:5; 1 Cor 10:17; Col 3:11; Eph 4:4–5).[57]

ἀποκτείνας τὴν ἔχθραν ἐν αὐτῷ, "by putting to death the enmity in himself." As we saw before in Eph 1:10, the phrase "in him" (ἐν αὐτῷ) is not really necessary for the sense in v. 16d, but Paul wanted to end the period with Christ as the focus of attention (cf. 2:15b). Otherwise the reader would pause for breath and leave "enmity" in the place of stress before moving

54. Cf. Leon Morris, *The Apostolic Preaching of the Cross* (Grand Rapids: Eerdmans, 1965), 214–50; Barth, *Broken Wall.*

55. See esp. Rom 3:30, where God's being one (from the Shema of Deut 6:1–4) is used to show that there is only one way for Jews and Gentiles to be saved (cf. 1 Tim 2:5–6 for virtually the same argument).

56. "For in one Spirit we were all baptized into one body—Jews or Greeks, slaves or free—and all were made to drink of one Spirit" (1 Cor 12:13).

57. Cf. Corneliu Constantineanu, *The Social Significance of Reconciliation in Paul's Theology: Narrative Readings in Romans* (New York: T&T Clark, 2010), which has ideas of value for Ephesians also.

on. These are the sorts of stylistic concerns brought out at early educational levels in antiquity for both training in composition and literary analysis and appreciation.

The notion of "killing" (ἀποκτείνω) enmity states the matter rather strongly. Yet it was simply a development from διὰ τοῦ σταυροῦ ("through the cross") in the previous colon*, which was a well-known instrument of execution.[58] Remarkably, as Christ was executed on the cross, God was "executing" enmity with himself and his elect enemies.

2:17 καὶ ἐλθὼν εὐηγγελίσατο εἰρήνην ὑμῖν τοῖς μακρὰν καὶ εἰρήνην τοῖς ἐγγύς, "and now that he has come he has proclaimed peace to you who were far off and peace to those nearby." The language of far and near used earlier (v. 13) is now used in a more direct allusion to its sources in Isa 52:7; 57:19. In particular, Paul taps into the verb εὐαγγελίζομαι from the first passage in Isa 52.[59] And as we read further in Isaiah, we can see a prophecy of Christ as the Lord's Servant proclaiming peace and the Lord's favor (Isa 61:1–3; cf. Luke 4:16–21). The LXX of Isa 18b–9 reads: ἔδωκα αὐτῷ παράκλησιν ἀληθινή εἰρήνην ἐπ' εἰρήνην τοῖς μακρὰν καὶ τοῖς ἐγγὺς οὖσιν καὶ εἶπεν κύριος ἰάσομαι αὐτούς, "I have given him genuine consolation, peace upon peace to those far off as well as to those who are near, and the Lord said, 'I will heal them.' "[60] Paul is obviously not directly quoting the Greek (or Hebrew) text of either Isa 52:7 or Isa 57:19, but he is alluding to these texts to bring out

---

58. Cf. Martin Hengel, *Crucifixion*, trans. John Bowden (Philadelphia: Fortress, 1977); John Granger Cook, "Roman Crucifixions: From the Second Punic War to Constantine," *ZNW* 104 (2013): 1–32.

59. The LXX of Isa 52:7 reads: ὡς πόδες εὐαγγελιζομένου ἀκοὴν εἰρήνης ὡς εὐαγγελιζόμενος ἀγαθά ὅτι ἀκουστὴν ποιήσω τὴν σωτηρίαν σου λέγων Σιων βασιλεύσει σου ὁ θεός, "Like the feet of the one who announces the good news of the report of peace, like one who spreads glad tidings of good things, for I will make your salvation heard, and say to Zion, 'Your God will reign.' " The LXX varies quite a bit here from the Hebrew (and English versions).

60. The Hebrew reads somewhat differently: " 'I have seen his ways, but I will heal him; I will lead him and restore comfort to him and his mourners, creating the fruit of the lips. Peace, peace, to the far and to the near,' says the LORD, 'and I will heal him' " (ESV).

the ministry of God's peace through the message of the prophet Isaiah, who acted along with the apostles as foundation layers for the church (v. 20).[61]

What is most notable here in Eph 2:17 is that Christ Jesus is said to have proclaimed peace to far and near. This, of course, is after his resurrection and displays the apostle's conviction that through his own ministry and that of the other apostles, Christ himself speaks and acts: "preaching peace (εὐαγγελιζόμενος εἰρήνην) through Jesus Christ" (Acts 10:36; cf. Rom 10:14–17; Col 1:24–29; 1 Tim 2:4–7; Acts 1:1).

The people who were "near" (ἐγγύς) are "the sons of the prophets and of the [old] covenant" (Acts 3:25), Israel. They were "near" to God (Psa 148:14) because God was "near" to them (Deut 4:7). This expresses the essence of the covenant bond: "And I will establish my covenant between me and you and your offspring after you throughout their generations for an everlasting covenant, to be God to you and to your offspring after you" (Gen 17:7); "I will take you to be my people, and I will be your God" (Exod 6:7). This same bond is now opened up to all the peoples of the earth through faith in the one mediator of all: "'Behold, the dwelling place of God is with man. He will dwell with them, and they will be his peoples, and God himself will be with them as their God' " (Rev 21:3; cf. Rom 3:29–30; 1 Tim 2:5–7). This mediation of the incarnate Son is secured in the eternal, intratrinitarian counsel of God and cannot be altered or amended by others.[62]

2:18 ὅτι δι' αὐτοῦ ἔχομεν τὴν προσαγωγὴν, "for through him we both have access." While ὅτι here is rendered as "for" (along with KJV, NASB, NIV, NRSV,

61. It is probable that Paul had these passages memorized in Hebrew, though he would have been familiar with a Greek version. Cf. Frank S. Thielman in *Commentary on the New Testament Use of the Old Testament*, ed. G. K. Beale and D. A Carson (Grand Rapids: Baker Academic, 2007), 817–18, for a helpful discussion. Interestingly, in the context of Isa 52, Zion is assured that "the uncircumcised and the unclean" will no more enter into Jerusalem (Isa 52:1; yet see vv. 13–15), and in Isa 57, "drawing near" refers to approaching God, even if those who do so are apostate "sons of the sorceress" and "children of transgression" (Isa 57:3–4). And the passage contains a warning: " 'There is no peace for the wicked,' says my God" (Isa 57:21). Yet Paul sees the restoration of the remnant of Israel to divine peace and forgiveness as blossoming into a dwelling place in "the tents of Shem" for the Gentiles (Gen 9:27).

62. Paul makes a very careful and rich argument to this effect in Gal 3:15–22; see S. M. Baugh, "Galatians 3:20 and the Covenant of Redemption," *WTJ* 66 (2004): 49–70.

ESV), this conjunction can also communicate the content of Christ's proclamation in v. 17: "He proclaimed peace … *that* through him we have access …" (i.e., peace that consists of access; so also Rom 5:1–2). This makes sense if we see the content clause as expanding on "peace": to have peace with God means to have access into his presence, much like the high priest had access into the holy of holies after establishing peace through propitiatory and expiatory sacrifice (cf. Exod 30; Lev 16; Num 29; cf. Heb 9:11–15, 22). Though taking ὅτι as conveying content is possible, it makes slightly better sense to take it as explanatory or causal ("for"), indicating the underlying basis for Christ's proclamation of peace. He proclaims peace because access to the Father has been brought into effect "through him" (so John 14:6). If there were no accomplishment of redemption, its proclamation would be an empty promise and devoid of all value (similar to Paul's point in 1 Cor 15:12–19).

The idea of access in v. 18 connects with Paul's earlier point that the Gentiles who were formerly "far off" have been brought "near" (vv. 13, 17). The language is a graphic description for approaching God in worship. The book of Hebrews in particular accents this language of "approaching" (προσέρχομαι) or "drawing near" (ἐγγίζω) to God and having access into the most holy place through the high-priestly sacrifice of Jesus (Heb 4:16; 7:19, 25; 10:1, 19–22; 11:6; 12:18).

οἱ ἀμφότεροι ἐν ἑνὶ πνεύματι πρὸς τὸν πατέρα, "both [have access] in one Spirit to the Father." By placing οἱ ἀμφότεροι ("both") in the colon* after the verb (ἔχομεν) and expressing it after the direct object (τὴν προσαγωγὴν), Paul puts some stress on it: "we have access, *both* of us do." The point is once again to highlight that there is complete and equal access for anyone who is in Christ, without any sort of distinction. Faith alone in Christ is the single requirement for entrance into the Father's presence.

Access to the Father is "in one Spirit" (see 4:3–4). While it is possible to read this as referring to the union together of believers "in [our] one spirit," this idea is rather vague, and that concept would have been expressed as "in one *mind*" (νοῦς; cf. 4:23) rather than in one πνεῦμα ("spirit"). With "in" (ἐν), the Spirit is presented as the sphere of the Christian's new-creation existence in the presence of God (see below on 2:22 and 5:18). "Access" (προσαγωγή, cf. 3:12; Rom 5:2) means to draw near to God and to enjoy him forever, which is the greatest good for his creatures and is the ultimate accomplishment of Jesus Christ's earthly work of redemption (cf. Heb 10:19–22). This reality is portrayed in visionary form in Rev 21:22; 22:4 as a perfect city in the new creation where there is no need of a temple with a walled-off holy of holies to separate God from his people, because he will dwell in their midst and they will see his face.

We should not overlook that Paul is expressing a trinitarian accomplishment of redemption here in v. 18: the incarnate Son's cross work brings his people to the Father in the Holy Spirit (see also Heb 9:14). The opening benediction had the same Trinitarian focus (see on 1:3–14; cf. Hoehner, 389).

2:19 Ἄρα οὖν, "So then." Paul concludes the long section beginning with v. 11 with this final "movement" of vv. 19–22. Believing Gentiles have been united "in one body to God" (v. 16b), along with believing Jews of both the OT and NT periods (see below), through Christ's substitutionary mediation. In this last section, the focus is on the unity of this merged group into one household (v. 19) and then into a building (v. 20) that turns out to be a temple building filled with the divine presence through the Spirit (vv. 21–22; cf. 3:19, 20–21).[63]

The two conjunctions *ἄρα οὖν* are synonyms, and when Paul uses them together they communicate either resumption of a point broken off earlier (e.g., Rom 5:18) or, as here, an important elucidation of a conclusion to be drawn from previous argumentation. Paul uses this combination frequently in Romans, and he is the only author in the NT and the LXX to use both

63. For supposed Qumran background for the NT imagery of the church as a temple, particularly in Eph 2:19–22, see Derwood C. Smith, "Cultic Language in Ephesians 2:19–22: A Test Case," *ResQ* 34 (1989): 207–17. How Paul could have had access to or interest in these documents from a small, remote group of sectarians remains a complete mystery. Unless, of course, recent opinions are correct that the Qumran cave texts actually may have come from Jerusalem libraries and have had no relation with "Essene" sectarians of the nearby building site that some now view as either a pottery factory, an agricultural *latifundia* ("investment farm") complex, or some other kind of outpost; cf. Yizhak Magen and Yuval Peleg, "Back to Qumran: Ten Years of Excavation and Research, 1993–2004," in *Qumran the Site of the Dead Sea Scrolls: Archaeological Interpretations and Debates* (Boston: Brill, 2006), 55–113; Yizhar Hirschfeld, *Qumran in Context: Reassessing the Archaeological Evidence* (Peabody, MA: Hendrickson, 2004). Interestingly, Ephesian "Essenes" were worshipers of Artemis Ephesia, who devoted a term of Essene service to her (ἐσσηνεύσας) "purely [through sexual abstinence] and piously (ἁγνῶς καὶ εὐσεβῶς)" (*IvE* 1578B; cf. *IvE* 1447).

conjunctions together like this.[64] Here is a distinctive mark of Pauline style that an imitator would easily overlook.

οὐκέτι ἐστὲ ξένοι καὶ πάροικοι ἀλλὰ ἐστὲ συμπολῖται τῶν ἁγίων καὶ οἰκεῖοι τοῦ θεοῦ, "you are no longer strangers and resident aliens, but you are fellow citizens with the saints and members of God's family."[65] In v. 12 Paul used distinctively Graeco-Roman citizenship categories to interpret his audience's separation from Israel, and here in v. 19 he resumes the point with three Graeco-Roman categories most familiar to his Ephesian audience: ξένοι, πάροικοι, and (συμ)πολῖται.[66] Strangers (ξένοι) were foreigners in the city with no guaranteed civil rights or privileges (see Acts 16:20–23; cf. Acts 21:39). Usually such persons were only passing through or staying temporarily in the city (like Paul had been) and would only be accorded such protections that local business associates, patrons, and friends may provide through personal influence.[67] "Sojourners," or better, "resident free aliens" (πάροικοι), may have been born in and lived in the city for generations but were not citizens with full access to legal privileges and protections (cf. Heb 11:13; 13:14; 1 Pet 2:11). Most of the residents of Ephesus had this resident alien status, while exceedingly few who lived in Ephesus were citizens either of Ephesus or of other cities like Tarsus or Rome

64. In fact, I could find no other first-century author who used ἄρα οὖν via searches in the *TLG*. For ἄρα οὖν see Rom 5:18; 7:3, 25; 8:12; 9:16, 18; 14:12 (possibly), 19; Gal 6:10; 1 Thess 5:6; 2 Thess 2:15; and second-century *2 Clem.* 2.15; 14.3; *Barn.* 9.6. Cf. J. D. Denniston, *The Greek Particles*, 2nd ed. (Oxford: Clarendon, 1978), 32–43 (οὖν ἄρα, p. 43), 50–51 (ἄρα οὖν in questions in Plato).

65. I am taking "saints" (ἅγιοι) here as believers of both the OT period and contemporaries of Paul—almost exclusively Jewish—who believed in Christ prior to the great blossoming of faith among the Gentiles. Ephesian believers, then, are also now ἅγιοι; see esp. on 1:1, 15, 18.

66. Cf. Benjamin H. Dunning, "Strangers and Aliens No Longer: Negotiating Identity and Difference in Ephesians 2," *HTR* 99 (2006): 1–16.

67. E.g., Paul's friends the asiarchs of Ephesus were the most powerful and influential provincials at the time; they would, for example, undoubtedly have influenced the positive view of the secretary of the people (γραμματεύς) toward Paul and his associates in Acts 19:31, 35–41.

(cf. Acts 21:39).[68] A few people, such as Paul, possessed dual citizenship of their home city and of Rome.[69]

In Ephesus, a late second- to early third-century AD inscription (*IvE* 951) praises the magnificent generosity of one Aurelius Barenus, who put on an eleven-day banquet for the city leaders and its *1,040 citizens*.[70] Ephesus had grown quite dramatically by this time so that more than a century earlier, in Paul's first-century time period, the citizen body was undoubtedly smaller than one thousand. Hence, for Paul to say that his Christian Gentile audience (which included slaves [6:5–6]) were *fellow-citizens* with the saints would have communicated what a stunningly elite privilege God has bestowed on his people in Christ. What is far more stunning is when Paul shifts from the political metaphor to say that God has included believers in his very family as his "family members" (οἰκεῖοι; cf. Gal 6:10).[71] Graeco-Roman families included widowed or orphaned relations, one's freedmen and slaves, and were therefore often quite large.[72] Believers, however, are not included in God's family as slaves or even freedmen, but have all been

---

68. Greek (as similarly Roman) citizenship was conveyed by birth to a citizen by honorary grant or through (under the table) purchase. Records of grant of citizenship make up a sizable number of the extant inscriptions from Ephesus and elsewhere (e.g., a number of citizenship grant inscriptions can be found in *IvE* 1405–73).

69. For overview of Graeco-Roman citizenship see James S. Jeffers, *The Greco-Roman World of the New Testament Era: Exploring the Background of Early Christianity* (Downers Grove, IL: InterVarsity Press, 1999). The classic work on Roman citizenship is still valuable: A. N. Sherwin-White, *Roman Citizenship*, 2nd ed. (Oxford: Clarendon, 1973; 1st ed., 1939); cf. S. M. Baugh, "Paul and Ephesus: The Apostle among His Contemporaries" (PhD diss., University of California, Irvine, 1990), 165–93, for discussion of Paul's Roman citizenship in relation to Ephesus.

70. The inscription has been mistakenly thought to read *forty thousand* Ephesian citizens (even by the *IvE* editors) rather than 1,040. For discussion of the number (πολείτας χειλίους τεσσαράκοντα, "1,000 [and] 40 citizens") see Preston Duane Warden and Roger S. Bagnall, "The Forty Thousand Citizens of Ephesus," *CPhil* 83 (1988): 220–23; cf. Pliny, *Ep.* 10.116–17.

71. BDAG, 694: "persons who are related by kinship or circumstances and form a closely knit group." Cf. 1 Tim 5:8; Gal 6:10; and similar οἱ ἴδιοι in John 1:11 (and 1 Tim 5:8) over against a lord's domain and possessions, expressed as neuter τὰ ἴδια in in John 1:11 also.

72. For resources on the Greek and Roman family, see comment on 1:5 (on υἱοθεσία).

adopted into the household as sons and therefore as his heirs and coheirs with the eternal Son (see on 1:5).

2:20 ἐποικοδομηθέντες ἐπὶ τῷ θεμελίῳ τῶν ἀποστόλων καὶ προφητῶν, "built on the foundation of the apostles and prophets." Paul moves deftly from Christians being members of God's house to being also the material from which it is built (cf. 1 Cor 3:9; Matt 16:18; Rev 21:14). It is not until the next verse (v. 21) that he reveals that believers are a temple rather than a simple house, but we are moving there quickly with a period (v. 20) of only three cola*.

When we take the participle ἐποικοδομηθέντες as parallel with indicative ἐστέ ("you are"; v. 19), it resolves to being the equivalent of indicative ἐπῳκοδομήθητε, "you were built upon."[73] The point is that the Ephesian congregation has already been laid down as a first layer of stone upon the temple's foundation. From here the building will continue to be erected (αὔξω, "grow," v. 21), but the foundation and the initial level had already been laid down when Paul wrote this epistle (cf. Rom 15:20; 1 Cor 3:10–14). In the background is the notion that there is no going back to a Mosaic theocracy that excluded Gentiles from full membership in "the covenants of promise" (cf. Gal 2:18). The Mosaic "old covenant" has been displaced by its fulfillment in the "new covenant" definitively and permanently instituted by the once-for-all, high-priestly sacrifice of Christ (e.g., 2 Cor 3:7–11; Heb 7:12; 8:13; 9:15–18; 10:8–12).

The foundation (θεμέλιος) on which the Ephesian saints are built up (cf. 1 Cor 3:11) is the (ministry) "of the apostles and prophets" (τῶν ἀποστόλων καὶ προφητῶν), which is a word-based ministry (cf. 4:11).[74] It is possible to take "prophets" here as a reference to those of the OT era whose ministry and writings particularly formed the background to the apostolic message (Rom 1:1–2; cf. Calvin, 154–55). Paul has just alluded to one of the main OT prophets, Isaiah (v. 17), and his frequent citation of the OT

---

73. My term *parallel ptc.* is a simpler label than more common "attendant circumstances" (Burton, *Moods*, §§449–50), but the idea is the same; see discussion in excursus below.

74. In the OT, priests were charged with instruction in God's revelation, and elders with giving counsel and judgment (see esp. Ezek 7:26; Mal 2:7), but it was to prophets that revelation was given, even if normally by way of symbolic visions and "dark sayings" (see esp. Num 12:6–8).

prophetic writings testifies to the rightful place of OT revelation as support for the Gentiles' faith in the new covenant era, which has been cemented in its final form through the apostles (see on 3:2–12).[75]

More likely, however, is that προφῆται ("prophets") here in v. 20 (as in 3:5 and 4:11) refers to prophets like Agabus (Acts 11:28; 21:10) or the four daughters of Philip (Acts 21:9; cf. Acts 2:17) in the apostolic era (cf. Hoehner, 397–404; Lincoln, 153–54; Barth, 314–17; O'Brien, 214–15). These prophets gave inspired revelation to the NT communities, which lacked written, apostolic revelation such as the one we are now reading (see on vv. 3:5 and 4:11; cf. 1 Cor 12:28–29). The word order here ("apostles and prophets," not vice versa) supports this view, and both apostles and prophets carry forward Christ's proclamation of peace, mentioned in v. 17 (cf. Heb 2:1–4).[76]

ὄντος ἀκρογωνιαίου αὐτοῦ Χριστοῦ Ἰησοῦ, "and its cornerstone is Christ Jesus." Paul's casual metaphors on elements of building construction are interesting given that Ephesus was in early phases of a building boom that lasted into the next century (cf. 1 Cor 3:9–12). When this epistle was written, one would undoubtedly see new construction sites throughout the

---

75. There are helpful observations to this effect in Ignatius of Antioch, writing only a few decades afterward (e.g., *Phld.* 5.2; *Magn.* 8.2, 9.2; *Smyrn.* 5.1). Ignatius does not mention or know of prophets active in his day in place of the regular ministry of overseers, elders, and deacons.

76. Wayne Grudem's interpretation that the apostles and prophets are identical here is based on the use of one article with the two pl. nouns (invoking Granville-Sharp's rule) and on his conviction that NT prophets in contrast to the OT ones give messages mixed with truth and error; Grudem, *The Gift of Prophecy in the New Testament and Today* (Wheaton, IL: Crossway, 2000; rev. of 1988 ed.). For more accurate description of Greek article usage here see the long and detailed discussion in Wallace, *Greek Grammar*, 270–90 (esp. 284–86); and more fully in Daniel B. Wallace, *Granville Sharp's Canon and Its Kin: Semantics and Significance*, SBG 14 (New York: Peter Lang, 2009). Cf. Karl Olav Sandnes, *Paul—One of the Prophets?* WUNT 2.43 (Tübingen: Mohr Siebeck, 1991), 224–46 (Sandnes suggests hendiadys* here: "the apostles who are also prophets" [233–24], with cross-references to Luke 14:3; Mark 15:1; 2 Pet 1:10, or possibly that at least the apostles and prophets form a unity because of the single "foundation"); R. Fowler White, "Gaffin and Grudem on Eph 2:20: in Defense of Gaffin's Cessationist Exegesis," *WTJ* 54 (1992): 303–20; O'Brien, 215–16. I may add that if Paul had used a second article in this colon* (τῶν ἀποστόλων καὶ **τῶν** προφητῶν) it would have added an unwanted syllable in the last foot and changed the nice repeating rhythm: ¯ ˘ ¯ | ˘ ¯ ¯ | [¯] ˘ ¯ ¯.

city with foundations and stones being brought in from quarries (or reused from earlier buildings). Christ forms the "cornerstone" (ἀκρογωνιαῖον—a substantive adj.), which ensures that the whole building is square and stable. Both 1 Peter 2:6 and *Barn.* 6.2, derived from Isa 28:16 (cf. Luke 20:17), may use ἀκρογωνιαῖον to refer to a "capstone," and some read the word this way in Eph 2:20. While both the cap and foundation stones were crucial elements for a stone building, it fits best to see Christ as the central element in the foundation of the church of the new covenant era (cf. 1 Cor 3:11; 1 Pet 2:4–8).[77]

2:21 ἐν ᾧ πᾶσα οἰκοδομὴ συναρμολογουμένη αὔξει εἰς ναὸν ἅγιον ἐν κυρίῳ, ἐν ᾧ καὶ ὑμεῖς συνοικοδομεῖσθε εἰς κατοικητήριον τοῦ θεοῦ ἐν πνεύματι, "in whom the whole building is interconnected and grows together into a holy temple in the Lord, in whom you as well are being built up together into a dwelling of God in the Spirit." Verses 21–22 form one period. This is confirmed by the repetition of phrases, prefixes, and prepositions in each verse that give the period balance and symmetry as follows:

21 **ἐν ᾧ** πᾶσα οἰκοδομὴ **συν**αρμολογουμένη
αὔξει **εἰς ναὸν** ἅγιον
ἐν κυρίῳ
22 **ἐν ᾧ** καὶ ὑμεῖς **συν**οικοδομεῖσθε
εἰς κατοικητήριον τοῦ θεοῦ
ἐν πνεύματι.

Both vv. 21–22 clarify that the building whose foundation and cornerstone was addressed in v. 20 is actually a temple (ναός; v. 21) and therefore a "dwelling of God" (κατοικητήριον τοῦ θεοῦ; v. 22). The word for *temple* (ναός, in contrast to more generic ἱερόν) refers particularly to that inner housing of a temple where the deity dwelt (BDAG, 665–66; LSJ, 1160).[78] Formerly God "lived among" his OT people and was seated on the ark (e.g., 2 Sam 15:25) in the tabernacle and then in Solomon's temple (e.g., Ezra 7:15), but now the international church, composed

77. Cf. R. J. McKelvey, "Christ the Cornerstone," *NTS* 8 (1962): 352–59; Hoehner, 404–7; Lincoln 154–56; Barth 271, 317–19; O'Brien, 216.
78. Cf. Ignatius, who calls the Ephesians ναοφόροι ("those who bear the temple"; *Eph.* 9.2) and says, "we are his temples" (*Eph.* 15.3); cf. *Phld.* 7.2.

of reconciled Jews and Gentiles, houses the Lord's presence in the Spirit (also 1 Cor 3:16–17; 6:16, 19; 2 Cor 6:16; 1 Tim 3:15; 1 Pet 2:5; cf. Ignatius, *Eph.* 9.1; Ignatius, *Magn.* 7.2).[79]

That God dwells with his people *ἐν πνεύματι* ("in the Spirit") is not a throwaway phrase but a key, eschatological idea in Paul.[80] The Holy Spirit's presence in the original garden of Eden shows it to be a sanctuary and proto-temple; so also his presence with his people transforms them into a new creation garden and temple imbued with inaugurated resurrection life through regeneration even in this age.[81]

No Ephesian could hear vv. 21–22 without thinking immediately of the great Temple of Artemis Ephesia (the Artemisium), one of the seven wonders of the ancient world and the largest building in the Greek world.[82] It made Ephesus an important tourist attraction and formed a large part of its economy (Acts 19:24–27, 35).[83] But the temple of which these Christian Ephesians are now a part is "growing" into a cosmic temple that will transcend all human buildings in magnificence and variegated beauty: the worldwide church of Christ Jesus. The verb *αὐξάνω/αὔξω* ("grow") is normally used for plants (Matt 6:28) or people (Luke 1:80; Eph 4:15), but Paul adapts it here for the new temple because he wants his audience to know that the building project has only begun. He himself wanted to see the church planted at the far-flung western edge of his world, Spain (Rom 15:24, 28), and he expected more stones from every nationality

---

79. R. J. McKelvey, *The New Temple: The Church in the New Testament* (New York: Oxford University Press, 1969); and more broadly G. K. Beale, *The Temple and the Church's Mission*, NSBT 17 (Downers Grove, IL: InterVarsity Press, 2004), esp. 259–63 for Eph 2:19–22.

80. Cf. Geerhardus Vos, "The Eschatological Aspect of the Pauline Conception of the Spirit," in *Redemptive History and Biblical Interpretation: The Shorter Writings of Geerhardus Vos*, ed. R. B. Gaffin Jr. (Phillipsburg, NJ: P&R, 1980; repr. of 1912 essay), 91–125, and comment on *πνευματικός* in 1:3 above and on *ἐν πνεύματι* in 5:18 below.

81. See M. G. Kline, *Images of the Spirit* (Grand Rapids: Baker, 1980).

82. The Artemisium was about four times larger than the Athenian Parthenon (cf. Pliny, *Nat.* 16.213–14; 35.92–93; 36.95–97; Pausanias, 6.3.15–16).

83. For discussion and references see Baugh, "Foreign World," 19–26; Trebilco, *Early Christians*, 25–26.

imaginable—even the notoriously savage Scythians (Col 3:11)—to to be added to this new, "interconnected" (συναρμολογουμένη) temple.[84]

> Paul, indeed, believes not merely that the church is "like" the temple but that it is the actual beginning fulfillment of the latter-day temple prophecies from the Old Testament. ... As a result of Christ's resurrection, the Spirit continued building the end-time temple, the building materials of which are God's people, thus extending the temple into the new creation in the new age. This building process will culminate in the eternal new heavens and earth as a paradisal city-temple.[85]

Biblical Theology Comments

Throughout Ephesians 2:11–22 the focus is on unity. Formerly Gentiles were separated and alienated from God's covenant promises to Israel. Now, in the new human race of believers, Gentiles and Jews reside together in peace in the church brought about for them by God by means of the blood and cross of Christ, and God now resides with his united people in a new temple through the Spirit (vv. 19–22).

This passage rehearses biblical history relating to the Gentiles in outline form. As the uncircumcised and therefore polluted outsiders to God's covenant blessings with OT Israel, Gentiles were separated from Christ and therefore without hope and without God. But Christ has intervened and acted without any contribution from the Gentiles' own efforts to reconcile them to himself and to his Father through his cross work and fulfillment of the promissory covenants in a new covenant, in which believers from all nations, both Jew and Greek, now stream in together as an indivisibly unified human race into new-creation existence. Both groups now reside in peace with God and with each other because Christ is "our peace."

The implications of the foregoing relating to OT theocratic Israel should not be overlooked. National Israelites were formerly *not* separated

---

84. Συναρμολογέω occurs only here and in 4:16 (for a body). BDAG, 966, gives: "to join together so as to form a coherent entity, *fit/join together.*" Paul's point in 2:21 seals his focus on the unity of the church throughout 2:11–22.

85. Beale, *Temple*, 259–60, 393.

from Christ because the benefits of his redemption to be accomplished had been administered to them via the promissory covenants and its sacrificial sacraments. Christ was from them according to the flesh (Rom 9:5), salvation originated from them (John 4:22), and Christ and his deliverance were their unique heritage as sons and daughters of Abraham, of the covenant, and of the kingdom (Luke 1:46–55, 67–79; 13:16; Acts 3:25; 13:26; Matt 8:12; 13:38). Yet Christ's triumphant conquest of the world (so 1:18–23) released his elect from every nation under the sun from their willing slavery to the prince of this age (2:2) and those things that are not gods (Gal 4:8), and called these faraway peoples to come near in peace with God and with the saints as fellow citizens (2:19).

There are two interconnected implications of the foregoing outline Paul provides in 2:11–22 that must be briefly discussed. These points flow out of what Paul has said in this section and provide further understanding for the theological framework for his continued teaching in Ephesians and for biblical teaching in general.

First is what we can call the organic development of redemptive revelation in the Scriptures. The writings of the biblical books themselves are the written, inerrant expression of this revelation so that what Scripture declares and does is a divine act (e.g., Gal 3:8, 22; cf. Heb 4:12–13). But the revelation of God is an unfolding story from Genesis to Revelation; hence, it *develops* through different administrations of God's redemption. Under the Israelite theocracy and the promissory covenants undergirding it, redemption was restricted to ethnic descendants of Abraham and to proselytes who entered into the theocracy's citizenship through circumcision and adoption of the yoke of the Mosaic law. One key element of that law code was the collection of commands that forced Israel to be separate from its neighboring Gentile peoples (see above on 2:13).

Yet in Christ there is a climactic development in redemptive revelation because there is climactic development in *redemption*. Christ, through his cross, has obliterated the dividing wall erected under the theocracy of Moses that kept Gentiles separated from free access to the promised inheritance of the saints (e.g., 1:18). The Mosaic law served as the constitution of Israel's theocracy and its citizenship, but the theocracy has expired, and the theocratic constitution has been supplanted by the new covenant.[86] This is implied by Paul's statement about the "covenants of promise" in v. 12. All the promises are fulfilled in Christ and in the giving of the promised Holy Spirit in the new covenant (2 Cor 1:20; 3:6–18; Gal 3:14).

This development informed Paul's choice of terms to describe the old and new situation through the language of citizenship.[87] Formerly, under the old covenant, Gentiles could ordinarily only be saved through circumcision and all that this entailed, including citizenship in the nation-state of Israel; i.e., they had to acquire new "passports." But as the promised messianic King, the crucified and risen Jesus annulled the old citizenship regulations of the law and its resulting enmity between Jew and Gentile and has created his truly international church.

The international nature of this church explains why Paul develops the notions of new creation and of a new human race (vv. 10, 15) alongside language of citizenship with the (other) saints (v. 19). If he had stuck to citizenship terminology only, it would seem that the church now forms a new earthly theocracy of its own. Certainly, this misconception would have been easy to make by the Ephesians, whose civil realm centered on a goddess and her city and temple.[88]

However, the term suggested above is the *organic* development of redemptive revelation. *Organic* here expresses the *unity* of this revelation from Genesis to Revelation. The covenants of promise were in their original intent looking forward to these great redemptive acts of Christ. One particularly clear expression of this idea is Gal 3:8, where we are told that the

86. This does not mean that the law's expression of God's holy requirements for his creatures as a perfect rule of righteousness has expired, but only those aspects of Torah that integrated the worship of God with the theocratic society.

87. As noted under vv. 12 and 19, this terminology includes "stranger" (ξένος) and "resident free alien" (πάροικος) as well as "citizen(ship)" (πολιτεία and συμπολίτης).

88. While Ephesus was not a "temple city" like Delphi or the like, its most famous characteristic was as the guardian (νεωκόρος) of Artemis Ephesia and of her temple (so Acts 19:35) as her "hometown" (πάτρις; *IvE* 24B). In later decades and centuries, Ephesus and other Asian cities touted their roles as νεωκόροι of the Roman imperial cult* (e.g., *IvE* 232–33, 237–38, 241–42). Cf. Trebilco, *Early Christians*, 30–37; S. R. F. Price, *Rituals and Power: The Roman Imperial Cult in Asia Minor* (Cambridge: Cambridge University Press, 1984); and the recent study of Beate Dignas, *Economy of the Sacred in Hellenistic and Roman Asia Minor* (New York: Oxford University Press, 2002).

promise of Gentiles joining Abraham in eschatological blessings through faith was the original motive for the Scripture's "preproclamation" (προευαγγελίζομαι) of the (Pauline) gospel to Abraham. From Genesis 3:15, 9:27; 22:18; 49:10; Deut 18:15; through the great messianic psalms, the unfolding mystery of Christ's coming was administered and grew like an acorn to a sapling until it burst out into a fully grown tree of life, overshadowing the whole world in Christ.[89]

Application and Devotional Implications

I often ponder what my (predominantly Welsh) ancestors were like at the time of Christ. Like all the other Gentile peoples, they were pagans, perhaps of the most brutal and ignorant sort whose Druidic practices would even be outlawed by pagan Rome (e.g., Tacitus, *Ann.* 14.30; Pliny, *Nat.* 16.95). This is not just a narcissistic exercise but a reminder of God's immeasurable grace and, equally important, a reminder that no one has any ethnic superiority in the church as if they come from some pure strain of godly people. The clear implication from Eph 2:11–22 is that every single believer, no matter what his or her ethnic background, sex, social identity, income, or any other thing, has equal standing with all the saints in light as a full citizen of the inaugurated new creation by the grace of Christ our Lord.[90]

Selected Bibliography

Barth, M. *The Broken Wall: A Study of the Epistle to the Ephesians.* Valley Forge, PA: Judson University Press, 1959.

Beale, G. *The Temple and the Church's Mission.* NSBT 17. Downers Grove, IL: InterVarsity Press, 2004.

Bickerman, E. "The Warning Inscriptions of Herod's Temple." *JQR* 37 (1947): 387–405.

Breytenbach, C. *Grace, Reconciliation, Concord: The Death of Christ in Graeco-Roman Metaphors.* NovTSup 135. Leiden: Brill, 2010.

---

89. The phrase "unfolding mystery" and the acorn-to-tree analogy are borrowed from Edmund P. Clowney, *The Unfolding Mystery: Discovering Christ in the Old Testament* (Phillipsburg, NJ: P&R, 1989) and from Geerhardus Vos, *Biblical Theology: Old and New Testaments* (Grand Rapids: Eerdmans, 1948).

90. Cf. Bruce W. Fong, "Addressing the Issue of Racial Reconciliation according to the Principles of Eph 2:11–22," *JETS* 38 (1995): 565–80.

Clowney, E. *The Unfolding Mystery: Discovering Christ in the Old Testament.* Phillipsburg, NJ: P&R, 1989.

Dignas, B. *Economy of the Sacred in Hellenistic and Roman Asia Minor.* New York: Oxford University Press, 2002.

Dunning, B. "Strangers and Aliens No Longer: Negotiating Identity and Difference in Ephesians 2." *HTR* 99 (2006): 1–16.

Fong, B. "Addressing the Issue of Racial Reconciliation according to the Principles of Eph 2:11–22." *JETS* 38 (1995): 565–80.

Kline, M. *The Structure of Biblical Authority.* 2nd ed. Grand Rapids: Eerdmans, 1975.

Knibbe, D. "Ephesos—Nicht nur die Stadt der Artemis: die 'anderen' ephesischen Götter." In *Studien zur Religion und Kultur Kleinasiens II. Festschrift für Friedrich Karl Dörner zum 65. Geburtstag am 28. Februar 1976*, edited by S. Şahin, E. Schwertheim, and J. Wagner, 489–503. Leiden: Brill, 1978.

Martin, R. *Reconciliation: A Study of Paul's Theology.* Atlanta: John Knox, 1981.

MacDonald, M. "The Politics of Identity in Ephesians." *JSNT* 26 (2004): 419–44.

McKelvey, R. "Christ the Cornerstone." *NTS* 8 (1962): 352–59.

———. *The New Temple: The Church in the New Testament.* New York: Oxford University Press, 1969.

Moritz, T. *A Profound Mystery: The Use of the Old Testament in Ephesians.* New York: Brill, 1996.

Morris, L. *The Apostolic Preaching of the Cross.* Grand Rapids: Eerdmans, 1965.

Price, S. *Rituals and Power: The Roman Imperial Cult in Asia Minor.* Cambridge: Cambridge University Press, 1984.

Rese, M. "Die Vorzüge Israels in Röm 9,4f und Eph 2,12: exegetische Anmerkungen zum Thema Kirche und Israel." *TheolZeit* 31 (1975): 211–22.

Schlier, H. *Christus und die Kirche im Epheserbrief.* BHT 6. Tübingen: Mohr Siebeck, 1930.

Smith, D. "Cultic Language in Ephesians 2:19–22: A Test Case." *ResQ* 34 (1989): 207–17.

Stuhlmacher, P. "'He Is Our Peace' (Eph 2:14)—On the Exegesis and Significance of Eph 2:14–18." In *Reconciliation, Law, & Righteousness: Essays in Biblical Theology*, 182–200. Philadelphia: Fortress, 1986.

Suh, R. "The Use of Ezekiel 37 in Ephesians 2." *JETS* 50 (2007): 715–33.

Vickers, B. *Jesus' Blood and Righteousness: Paul's Theology of Imputation.* Wheaton, IL: Crossway, 2006.

Vos, G. *Biblical Theology: Old and New Testaments.* Grand Rapids: Eerdmans, 1948.

Wallace, D. *Granville Sharp's Canon and Its Kin: Semantics and Significance.* SBG 14. New York: Peter Lang, 2009.

Warden, P., and R. Bagnall. "The Forty Thousand Citizens of Ephesus." *CPhil* 83 (1988): 220–23.

White, R. "Gaffin and Grudem on Eph 2:20: in Defense of Gaffin's Cessationist Exegesis." *WTJ* 54 (1992): 303–20.

The Mystery of Redemption and Its Revelation (3:1–13)

Introduction

In Ephesians 3:1–13 Paul pauses to assure his Gentile audience that his imprisonment does not mean that God has rejected him from his apostolic office so as to compromise their inheritance in Christ. Paul opens with an intention to express praise flowing from the truths of Eph 1–2 and his hope for his audience's further sanctification. Yet he is diverted from this purpose in v. 1 when he identifies himself as a prisoner, which calls for some clarifications in vv. 2–13 (cf. 6:19–20). Hence, one must skip to vv. 14–19 to see the direction of thought that was started in v. 1 (see on v. 14).

What is the point of the digression in vv. 2–13? One common view interprets this section as Paul—or, for many, a pseudonymous author—defending his apostolic office and authority.[1] Yet this does not seem to fit the matters Paul covers in Ephesians in general, and there is no evidence of a challenge to his apostolic position at Ephesus.[2]

Instead, Paul swerves from his intended track when he mentions his imprisonment in v. 1. He feels like this calls for explanation, as seen in his conclusion in v. 13: "I ask you not to lose heart at my tribulations on your

1. Cf. Timothy Gombis, "Ephesians 3:2–13: Pointless Digression, or Epitome of the Triumph of God in Christ?" *WTJ* 66 (2004): 313–23; and Aaron Sherwood, "Paul's Imprisonment as the Glory of the Ethnē: A Discourse Analysis of Ephesians 3:1–13," *BBR* 22 (2012): 97–112. It does not seem compelling for a pseudonymous author to defend Paul's apostolic authority. What would be the point? This problem is occasionally acknowledged by defenders of non-Pauline authorship; e.g., Martin Kitchen writes, "One is still left wondering why the writer devotes twelve verses to an exposition of Paul's status" (Kitchen, 30).

2. See Ignatius (*Eph.* 12.2), who compliments the Ephesians as Παύλου συμμύσται, "sharers in the rites along with Paul," and mentions no conflict or questions about his apostleship.

behalf, which is your glory." Paul anticipates that there is an apparent disconnect between the exultant victory and enthronement of Christ to all authority in this age in the church, which he had just taught on (i.e., Eph 1–2), and his imprisonment and therefore the apparent defeat and impotence of Christ's apostolic representative to the nations, Paul. How does the Messiah reign if his people suffer at the hands of a conquered world? The digression is an answer to this irony.[3] Paul may be in chains, but the gospel is not hindered, and Christ does indeed rule. The mystery of worldwide Christianity is now divinely revealed (below) and effectively set into action (v. 11b), as Tertullian famously grasped: "But nothing whatever is accomplished by your cruelties, each more exquisite than the last. It is the bait that wins men for our school. We multiply whenever we are mown down by you; the blood of Christians is seed" (*Apol.* 50.13; LCL trans.).

The digression (vv. 2–13), then, is Paul's attempt to encourage his audience despite his own afflictions "on behalf of you Gentiles" (v. 1). Specifically there seem to be three potential misconceptions that Paul is trying to quell as background for this assurance. Perhaps Paul's imprisonment means that he was never a true apostle and therefore his gospel is errant. Or perhaps this imprisonment means that God has dismissed Paul from his office. Or worse, as mentioned above, perhaps Christ's exaltation to cosmic rule, described so vividly in Eph 1–2, is a shattered failure, since he cannot even protect Paul from custody and various other unnamed afflictions. Hence Paul calms his audience by pointing to the indisputable nature of his apostolic call to office. He sees this as another example that God delights to use weak instruments in order to manifest his inscrutable wisdom in victory and power through the gospel (3:6–8, 10; esp. 1 Cor 1:17–25), which was planned from all eternity.[4]

One prominent thread in this passage centers on the disclosure of redemptive revelation in the person and work of Christ and especially in the extension of the benefits of Christ's accomplishment among the Gentiles

---

3. This view is convincingly argued by Timothy Gombis, "Ephesians 3:2–13." One can also see such irony of "conquered victors" or of a "triumphant dead Lamb" as a main theme in other NT works, such as Revelation; cf. Dennis E. Johnson, *Triumph of the Lamb* (Phillipsburg, NJ: P&R, 2001).

4. Cf. Michael Wolter, "Verborgene Weisheit und Heil für die Heiden. Zur Traditionsgeschichte und Intention des 'Revelationsschemas,'" *ZTK* 84 (1987): 297–319.

(vv. 6–8). For instance, note these repeated words and concepts: κατὰ ἀποκάλυψιν ἐγνωρίσθη μοι ("was made known to me by a revelation"; v. 3) … ὡς νῦν ἀπεκαλύφθη ("as it has now been revealed"; v. 5) … ἵνα γνωρισθῇ νῦν ("so that [God's wisdom] might now be made known"; v. 10). And in contrast, previously this revelation was a "mystery" (vv. 3, 9), ἑτέραις γενεαῖς οὐκ ἐγνωρίσθη ("was not made known to the sons of men in other generations"; v. 5) … ἡ οἰκονομία τοῦ μυστηρίου τοῦ ἀποκεκρυμμένου ἀπὸ τῶν αἰώνων ("the design of the mystery hidden from time immemorial"; v. 9), even though it was long planned (vv. 9, 11). Paul's calling as apostle to the Gentiles is itself a new stage in revelation through his distinctive calling (vv. 1–3, 7–9) alongside the other apostles and prophets (v. 5).

The basic structure of Eph 3:1–13 consists of the opening to Paul's intended discussion (v. 1), the digression (vv. 2–12), and the reason for the digression and expression of Paul's desire for the audience's encouragement (v. 13).[5] The outline of the passage below shows that the digression itself can be divided into two parts: vv. 2–7 ("Redemptive Revelation as a Mystery") and vv. 8–12 ("The Revelation of this Mystery").[6] An inclusio* between the first and last periods of vv. 2–7, with the repeated words "the grace of God given to me" (τῆς χάριτος τοῦ θεοῦ τῆς δοθείσης μοι; vv. 2b and 7b), and the

5. Codex Vaticanus (B) and the Euthalian Apparatus present 3:1–13 as one section. The repeated phrase ὑπὲρ ὑμῶν ("on your behalf") at the beginning and end (vv. 1b and 13b) may signal a demarcation for the whole section. Codex Alexandrinus (A) has breaks at vv. 12 and 13; see the introduction to the commentary for other MS divisions. NA[28] starts a new paragraph at v. 8 (also NKJV; both ESV and NIV break at v. 7), while UBS[4] and SBL editions have vv. 1–13 as one paragraph (also NASB). The different divisions of the text show once again that applying modern written and syntactical principles of text division for an ancient text meant for oral presentation and reception is not always the most accurate way to analyze the structure of that text.

6. It should also be noted that there are some striking similarities between Eph 3:1–7 and Col 1:23–29, which has led some to see Ephesians as dependent on Colossians by a pseudonymous writer (e.g., Lincoln, 168–69). This is not, of course, the only interpretation of the similarities. The same author writing to similar groups at the same time can be expected to say similar things, while his writings in earlier times may be different. Modern scholars look primarily at the use of vocabulary for decisions on authorship instead of key elements for a Greek author's style—which the ancients themselves would have concentrated on—like periodicity, length of cola*, meter, and more subtle things like "clashing of inconsonant letters" versus "those which are melodious, smooth, polished and free from any conflict of sound" (Dionysius, *Thuc.* 24).

fact that v. 8 opens with a grammatically independent statement allows a natural division of vv. 1–13 into two at vv. 1–7 and 8–13.

In the first half (3:1–7), Paul explains that his call to the apostleship was specifically "on behalf of you Gentiles" (v. 1b; cf. 2b and 13b). In this light, Paul interprets his office as a gift, not for his own glory and prestige but for theirs (v. 13); hence, he is a servant in chains. In the second half (3:8–13), Paul expands on his unique office as apostle to the Gentiles and the cosmic purpose of God to establish the glory of his grace before all creation.

The unifying themes of Paul's apostolic call and ministry can be seen in a number of repeated words and concepts throughout the pericope. The main ones concern "you Gentiles" or "you" or "Gentiles" (vv. 1–2, 6, 8, 9 ["all"], 13); the "mystery" of Gentile inclusion (vv. 3–4, 9); and verbs that concern the disclosure of this mystery (vv. 3–4, 8–10). Obviously, the Gentile ministry of Paul is paramount here.

My suggested division of the text into periods and cola* is as follows:

A

[1] τούτου χάριν ἐγὼ Παῦλος
ὁ δέσμιος τοῦ Χριστοῦ ὑπὲρ ὑμῶν τῶν ἐθνῶν—

B

[2] εἴ γε ἠκούσατε τὴν οἰκονομίαν
τῆς χάριτος τοῦ θεοῦ τῆς δοθείσης μοι εἰς ὑμᾶς
[3] κατὰ ἀποκάλυψιν ἐγνωρίσθη μοι τὸ μυστήριον

C

καθὼς προέγραψα ἐν ὀλίγῳ
[4] πρὸς ὃ δύνασθε ἀναγινώσκοντες
νοῆσαι τὴν σύνεσίν μου ἐν τῷ μυστηρίῳ τοῦ Χριστοῦ

D

[5] ὃ ἑτέραις γενεαῖς οὐκ ἐγνωρίσθη
τοῖς υἱοῖς τῶν ἀνθρώπων
ὡς νῦν ἀπεκαλύφθη
τοῖς ἁγίοις ἀποστόλοις αὐτοῦ καὶ προφήταις ἐν πνεύματι

E

[6] εἶναι τὰ ἔθνη συγκληρονόμα καὶ σύσσωμα
καὶ συμμέτοχα τῆς ἐπαγγελίας ἐν Χριστῷ Ἰησοῦ
διὰ τοῦ εὐαγγελίου

F

[7] οὗ ἐγενήθην διάκονος κατὰ τὴν δωρεὰν
τῆς χάριτος τοῦ θεοῦ τῆς δοθείσης μοι
κατὰ τὴν ἐνέργειαν τῆς δυνάμεως αὐτοῦ

G [8] ἐμοὶ τῷ ἐλαχιστοτέρῳ πάντων ἁγίων
ἐδόθη ἡ χάρις αὕτη
τοῖς ἔθνεσιν εὐαγγελίσασθαι
τὸ ἀνεξιχνίαστον πλοῦτος τοῦ Χριστοῦ

H [9] καὶ φωτίσαι πάντας
τίς ἡ οἰκονομία τοῦ μυστηρίου
τοῦ ἀποκεκρυμμένου ἀπὸ τῶν αἰώνων
ἐν τῷ θεῷ τῷ τὰ πάντα κτίσαντι

I [10] ἵνα γνωρισθῇ νῦν ταῖς ἀρχαῖς καὶ ταῖς ἐξουσίαις
ἐν τοῖς ἐπουρανίοις διὰ τῆς ἐκκλησίας
ἡ πολυποίκιλος σοφία τοῦ θεοῦ
[11] κατὰ πρόθεσιν τῶν αἰώνων
ἣν ἐποίησεν ἐν τῷ Χριστῷ Ἰησοῦ τῷ κυρίῳ ἡμῶν

J [12] ἐν ᾧ ἔχομεν τὴν παρρησίαν καὶ προσαγωγὴν ἐν πεποιθήσει
διὰ τῆς πίστεως αὐτοῦ

K [13] διὸ αἰτοῦμαι μὴ ἐγκακεῖν ἐν ταῖς θλίψεσίν μου ὑπὲρ ὑμῶν
ἥτις ἐστὶν δόξα ὑμῶν

Often the modern versification represents a fair division of the text into Greek periods. Hence, vv. 5–9, 12–13 are one period each. Yet there are clear exceptions as well as possible exceptions. As for the latter, I have combined vv. 10–11 into one period when each verse could be a period. Yet v. 11 only has two cola* and would result in an unusually short period if it stood on its own.[7] Verse 1 does consist of two cola*, but that is because Paul breaks off his thought in a digression (also vv. 12–13; see comment). Here is what Paul starts to say when we include his resumption in v. 14:

7. One could also attach v. 11 with v. 12 as so:
[11] κατὰ πρόθεσιν τῶν αἰώνων
ἣν ἐποίησεν ἐν τῷ Χριστῷ Ἰησοῦ τῷ κυρίῳ ἡμῶν
[12] ἐν ᾧ ἔχομεν τὴν παρρησίαν καὶ προσαγωγὴν ἐν πεποιθήσει
διὰ τῆς πίστεως αὐτοῦ
but this is not as attractive as proposed above. Relative clauses, like ἐν ᾧ at the beginning of v. 12, frequently signal the start of a new period in Ephesians (e.g., 1:11, 13; 2:3; 2:21; yet see 1:7 and 2:21).

> 1 τούτου χάριν ἐγὼ Παῦλος
> ὁ δέσμιος τοῦ Χριστοῦ ὑπὲρ ὑμῶν τῶν ἐθνῶν
> 14 [τούτου χάριν] κάμπτω τὰ γόνατά μου πρὸς τὸν πατέρα …

All of this shows the difficulty at times of dividing the text as the author composed and/or as the reader presented the original material. Greek prose is not poetry, with its demands for symmetrical forms and (complex) regular meters.

In one instance above, however, I am rather confident that my division is correct. That v. 3a does belong with v. 2 is seen by parallelism with v. 7 (a complete period) as follows:

> 2 … τὴν οἰκονομίαν
> τῆς χάριτος τοῦ θεοῦ τῆς δοθείσης μοι εἰς ὑμᾶς
> 3 κατὰ ἀποκάλυψιν ἐγνωρίσθη μοι τὸ μυστήριον

> 7 … κατὰ τὴν δωρεὰν
> τῆς χάριτος τοῦ θεοῦ τῆς δοθείσης μοι
> κατὰ τὴν ἐνέργειαν τῆς δυνάμεως αὐτοῦ

The first colon* of each ends with a feminine accusative noun (οἰκονομίαν … δωρεὰν), both second cola* have the same phrase (τῆς χάριτος τοῦ θεοῦ τῆς δοθείσης μοι), and the third cola* begin with clauses having the same preposition (κατά).

As we have seen up to this point in the epistle, it is instructive to see how each period ends. In 3:1–7 alone we have: "the mystery" (v. 3a), "in the mystery of Christ" (v. 4b), "in the Spirit" (v. 5e), "through the gospel" (v. 6c), and "in accordance with the effectiveness of his power" (v. 7c). One could almost compose a summary sentence for vv. 2–7 out of these phrases. The second section (vv. 8–13) likewise has concluding phrases that help us focus on Paul's main points here: "the untraceable riches of Christ" (v. 8:d), "in God who created all things" (v. 9d), "that he executed in Christ Jesus our Lord" (v. 11b), "through our faith in him" (v. 12c), and "which is your glory" (v. 13c).

Outline

VI. The Mystery of Redemption and Its Revelation (3:1–13)
- A. Opening to (delayed) prayer (3:1)
- B. Redemptive revelation as a mystery (3:2–7)
- C. The revelation of this mystery (3:8–12)
- D. Conclusion not to grow disheartened (3:13)

Original Text

1 Τούτου[a] χάριν ἐγὼ Παῦλος ὁ δέσμιος τοῦ Χριστοῦ Ἰησοῦ[b] ὑπὲρ ὑμῶν τῶν
ἐθνῶν[c] **2**—εἴ γε ἠκούσατε τὴν οἰκονομίαν τῆς χάριτος τοῦ θεοῦ τῆς δοθείσης μοι
εἰς ὑμᾶς, **3** κατὰ[d] ἀποκάλυψιν ἐγνωρίσθη μοι τὸ μυστήριον, καθὼς προέγραψα
ἐν ὀλίγῳ, **4** πρὸς ὃ δύνασθε ἀναγινώσκοντες νοῆσαι τὴν σύνεσίν μου ἐν τῷ μυστηρίῳ τοῦ Χριστοῦ, **5** ὃ ἑτέραις γενεαῖς οὐκ ἐγνωρίσθη τοῖς υἱοῖς τῶν ἀνθρώπων
ὡς νῦν ἀπεκαλύφθη τοῖς ἁγίοις ἀποστόλοις αὐτοῦ καὶ προφήταις ἐν πνεύματι,
6 εἶναι τὰ ἔθνη συγκληρονόμα καὶ σύσσωμα καὶ συμμέτοχα τῆς ἐπαγγελίας[e]
ἐν Χριστῷ Ἰησοῦ διὰ τοῦ εὐαγγελίου, **7** οὗ ἐγενήθην διάκονος κατὰ τὴν δωρεὰν
τῆς χάριτος τοῦ θεοῦ τῆς δοθείσης[f] μοι κατὰ τὴν ἐνέργειαν τῆς δυνάμεως αὐτοῦ.
8 Ἐμοὶ τῷ ἐλαχιστοτέρῳ πάντων ἁγίων[g] ἐδόθη ἡ χάρις αὕτη, τοῖς ἔθνεσιν εὐαγγελίσασθαι τὸ ἀνεξιχνίαστον πλοῦτος τοῦ Χριστοῦ **9** καὶ φωτίσαι πάντας[h] τίς
ἡ οἰκονομία τοῦ μυστηρίου τοῦ ἀποκεκρυμμένου ἀπὸ τῶν αἰώνων ἐν τῷ θεῷ τῷ
τὰ πάντα κτίσαντι, **10** ἵνα γνωρισθῇ νῦν ταῖς ἀρχαῖς καὶ ταῖς ἐξουσίαις ἐν τοῖς
ἐπουρανίοις διὰ τῆς ἐκκλησίας ἡ πολυποίκιλος σοφία τοῦ θεοῦ, **11** κατὰ πρόθεσιν
τῶν αἰώνων ἣν ἐποίησεν ἐν τῷ Χριστῷ Ἰησοῦ τῷ κυρίῳ ἡμῶν, **12** ἐν ᾧ ἔχομεν
τὴν παρρησίαν καὶ προσαγωγὴν ἐν πεποιθήσει διὰ τῆς πίστεως αὐτοῦ. **13** διὸ
αἰτοῦμαι μὴ ἐγκακεῖν ἐν ταῖς θλίψεσίν μου ὑπὲρ ὑμῶν[i], ἥτις ἐστὶν δόξα ὑμῶν[i].

Textual Notes

1.a. P^{46} has the accusative τούτο χάριν rather than the genitive τούτου χάριν, but this seems to be a simple copyist omission of the *upsilon*.

1.b. The second colon* of v. 1 reads ὁ δέσμιος τοῦ Χριστοῦ ὑπὲρ ὑμῶν τῶν ἐθνῶν, whereas the UBS^{4} has τοῦ Χριστοῦ [Ἰησοῦ], with "Jesus" in brackets and marked with a "C" to show the editors' uncertainty on whether it is original. P^{46}, ℵ (second hand), A, B, D2, and many other MSS have Ἰησοῦ ("of Jesus") here, while ℵ (original hand), D*, F, G, and others have the reading without "Jesus." Confusion over the original is indicated by the presence of the readings τοῦ Ἰησοῦ Χριστοῦ, τοῦ κυρίου Ἰησοῦ, ἐν Χριστῷ, and ἐν Χριστῷ Ἰησοῦ in various witnesses. The external testimony is quite good for reading "Jesus" as original here, but it is not easy to see why a scribe would accidentally or deliberately drop it (*lectio difficilior**), hence the uncertainty of our modern editors and why it was not included here.

1.c. The hanging nominative ἐγὼ Παῦλος here begs for a verb (which is not given until v. 3, when the syntax changes), so a few MSS add either πρεσβεύω ("I am an ambassador"; D, 104) (from 6:20) or κεκαύχημαι ("I take pride in"; 2464) at the end of v. 1. The first verb is picked up from 6:20, and the second is not at all likely original.

3.d. The UBS/NA editors supply ὅτι in brackets as the first word of v. 3, indicating doubts as to its originality, though it does help the sense somewhat, and it is found in some early and good MSS, including ℵ, A, C, D, Ψ, 33, 1739, 1881, et al. The fact that ὅτι is missing in P⁴⁶, B, F, G, and some other MSS and the difficulty of explaining its omission by a copyist (*lectio difficilior**) lead me to omit it here.

6.e. The presence of αὐτοῦ ("his"; D¹, F, G, Ψ, M) for the phrase τῆς ἐπαγγελίας αὐτοῦ, "of his promise," is one of the more common variant readings in the NT. The article τῆς here may already carry the idea of the possessive pronoun, and the scribe is simply adding a word that brings out the implicit meaning of the text.

7.f. Many mss. (D², Ψ, 1739, 1881, M) have accusative τὴν δοθεῖσαν ("given") instead of the genitive of the best MSS adopted in the UBS/NA. The difference is that the accusative would suggest that the gift (δωρεάν) was given by God rather than (gen.) grace (χάριτος). Both the gift and grace, of course, come from God to Paul.

8.g. P⁴⁶ omits ἁγίων ("saints"), but this appears to be an accidental omission.

9.h. The UBS/NA brackets πάντας ("all") in the first colon*: καὶ φωτίσαι [πάντας] ("to enlighten [all]"), because it is missing from ℵ*, A, 424c, 1739, 1881, etc., but πάντας is found in P⁴⁶, ℵ (second corrector), B, C, D, and the vast majority of other MSS. As Metzger observes, "The verb φωτίσαι seems to require an expressed accusative (which it usually has elsewhere in the New Testament)."[8] Metzger explains further that if πάντας were not original, we could expect other readings like αὐτούς ("them") and the like in the witnesses to fill the hole in the text, but only πάντας is found in the MSS. We could add that such a short colon* as καὶ φωτίσαι (four syllables) is unlikely, whereas πάντας bumps it up to six syllables, which is still short but more in the range of Paul's colon* length. This plus the fact that πάντας does carry good external attestation leads me to treat it as original.

13.i. Both occurrences of ὑμῶν ("of you") in this verse read as ἡμῶν ("of us") in various MSS.[9] This confusion between ὑμῶν and ἡμῶν probably occurred because *upsilon* and *eta* in these words came to be pronounced similarly and explains the substitution of one for the other by scribes.

Translation

1 For this reason even[10] I, Paul, the prisoner of Christ[11] on behalf of you Gentiles— **2** you have surely[12] heard about the management[13] of God's grace that was given to me for your sake, **3** this[14] mystery was made known to me

---

8. Bruce M. Metzger, *A Textual Commentary on the Greek New Testament*, 2nd ed. (New York: United Bible Societies, 1994), 534.
9. The NA[28] reports on only the first occurrence of ὑμῶν, while the UBS[4] and Metzger's *Textual Commentary* (535) report on the second.
10. This is an attempt to bring out the emphasis in the added pronoun, **ἐγὼ** Παῦλος.
11. ESV and NRSV have "a prisoner *for* Christ Jesus." The gen. connecting the two nouns (ὁ δέσμιος τοῦ Χριστοῦ) simply connects the two, and one must understand the most likely meaning from context (cf. NKJV, NASB, NIV).
12. The phrase εἴ γε "makes explicit an underlying assumption of the preceding assertion" (O'Brien, 226n5), as in 4:21; Col 1:23; cf. 2 Cor 5:3; Gal 3:4, which are the only other NT uses of the phrase; cf. NIV; BDAG, 278, "inasmuch as."
13. For οἰκονομία, which occurs also in v. 9 with a different meaning. See the translation note for v. 9.
14. The article here (**τὸ** μυστήριον, "*this* mystery") reverts to its earliest, demonstrative ("deictic") function, evidenced all the way back into the Homeric era. Cf. Herbert Wier Smyth, *Greek Grammar*, rev. Gordon M. Messing (Cambridge, MA: Harvard University Press, 1956; original ed., 1920), §1120; Daniel B. Wallace, *Greek Grammar beyond the Basics* (Grand Rapids: Zondervan, 1997), 221. The "mystery" is in apposition to the whole clause of v. 2.

by a revelation, just as I briefly[15] wrote about beforehand. **4** When you read about it,[16] you can perceive my insight[17] into the mystery of Christ, **5** which was not made known to the sons of men in other generations as it has now been revealed to his holy apostles and prophets in the Spirit. **6** This mystery is that the Gentiles are fellow heirs,[18] fellow body members, and fellow partakers[19] of the promise in Christ Jesus through the gospel. **7** Of which I was made a servant as[20] the gift of God's grace, which was given me in

15. The phrase ἐν ὀλίγῳ is only found here and in Acts 26:28–29 (twice) in the NT. The phrase implies a noun; either χώρῳ ("in a short *space*") or, more likely here, χρόνῳ ("in a brief *time*"); LSJ, 1215 (meaning 3). Either meaning shows Paul does not view his previous discussion of the issue to be as extensive as he may have liked.
16. The opening phrase πρὸς ὅ identifies the subject matter "in reference to which" the audience can review from earlier in the epistle (LSJ, 1498) and is the equivalent of a simple dative of respect. The neuter relative pronoun refers to the mystery in v. 3a.
17. "Insight" (σύνεσις) points to the "content of understanding or comprehension" (BDAG, 970; cf. Col 1:9; 2:2; and 2 Tim 2:7 [also with the verb νοέω, "perceive," as in Eph 3:4]).
18. Cf. *New Docs*, 2.75 (p. 97), for discussion of the word συγκληρονόμα ("fellow heirs" or "coheirs"). BDAG, 952, gives the reading of Hicks (*The Collection of Ancient Greek Inscriptions in the British Museum* [Oxford: Clarendon, 1890], 633) for an Ephesian inscription in which the right side of a tomb is said to belong to Cumfuleius Bassus and to his wife, Eutychis, as his "coheir": σ[υγ]κληρονό[μου αὐ]τοῦ. The more recent edition of the Ephesian inscriptions (*IvE* 1633), however, has the more expected mention of the tomb belonging to Bassus and to "his heirs," καὶ κληρονό[μων αὐ]τοῦ. It would be extraordinary for a husband and wife to be coheirs in the Graeco-Roman world (i.e., unless they were brother and sister), whereas tombs were regularly designated for family members (including children, freedmen, and slaves) and sometimes for their "descendants" (ἐκγόνοι; e.g., *IvE* 1635) and heirs (e.g., *IvE* 2200B).
19. The rendering with "fellow-" for the three adjs. συγκληρονόμος ("fellow heirs"), σύσσωμος ("fellow body members"), and συμμέτοχος ("fellow participants") is a bit clumsy in English but tries to bring out the use of the συν- prefix here, which make them notable and parallel. The modern spelling of this prefix just given on the adjs. (συγ-, συσ-, and συμ-, respectively) is not represented on, e.g., P[46], which has **συν**κληρονόμος, **σύν**σωμος, and **συν**μέτοχος (cf. original text of B, which has the same with correction to the spelling in our modern editions above each prefix), making the parallelism here even more obvious. Note also the συν- verbs in 2:5 and comments there.
20. Κατά is more often rendered "according to" here (KJV, NASB, ESV, NRSV), but it refers to the nature of Paul's office "as" or "by way of" a gift given to him; see BDAG, 513 (meaning 5bβ) (NIV "by the gift"). Cf. Rom 4:4, "it is not accounted *as a gracious favor* (κατὰ χάριν) but *as an obligation* (κατὰ ὀφείλημα)."

accordance with the effectiveness[21] of his power. **8** This grace was given to
me, the very least of all saints,[22] to proclaim to the Gentiles the untraceable
riches of Christ, **9** and to enlighten all as to what is the design[23] of the mystery hidden from time immemorial[24] in God who created all things, **10** so
that through the church the multifaceted[25] wisdom of God might now be
made known to the rulers and authorities in the high-heavenlies,[26] **11** ac-

21. As at 1:19 (but not at 4:16) ἐνέργεια is often translated as "working" (NASB, NIV, ESV), yet this noun does not point here to the process of bringing something about but to its actual accomplishment (BDAG, 335, where "manifestation" of power is suggested). Hence the reference is to the actual accomplishment of God's powerful acts; also 4:16; cf. Col 1:29; Phil 3:21.

22. The adj. ἐλαχιστότερος ("very least") is a vernacular comparative derived from the superlative ἐλάχιστος ("smallest, least"; from μικρός, "small," or earlier ἐλαχύς), but it has a superlative sense here; cf. Wallace, *Greek Grammar*, 302, who renders it "less than the least of all the saints"; BDF 60 (2); 61 (2). The word *saints* should be rendered without an English definite article ("the"), since the Greek article is missing here where it is expected (as σὺν πᾶσιν **τοῖς** ἁγίοις in below in v. 18). We expect τῷ ἐλαχιστοτέρῳ πάντων **τῶν** ἁγίων; because of τῷ in the word it is joined with in a gen. relation; Apollonius' canon; Wallace, *Greek Grammar*, 239–40; 250–52.

23. This rendering of οἰκονομία is a little clearer than "plan" (ESV; NRSV); cf. "administration" (NASB; NIV); or, unlikely, "fellowship" (KJV; NKJV). There are two meanings of the same word (οἰκονομία) in this passage. In v. 2 it points to the function or activity of a "manager" (οἰκονόμος) in fulfilling his office; here in v. 9 the idea is a design or blueprint that the manager follows to carry out his tasks, i.e., a "business *plan*" (cf. 1:10). The word rendered "plan" in v. 11 is πρόθεσις (cf. 1:11) and refers to a mental activity, an intent, purpose, or determination that one fixes in one's will in order to accomplish something (from the verb προτίθημι, used in 1:9). Cf. BDAG, 869; LSJ, 1480–81; John H. P. Reumann, "OIKONOMIA = 'COVENANT'; Terms for *Heilsgeschichte* in Early Christian Usage," *NovT* 3 (1959): 282–92; and Reumann, "Οἰκονομία-Terms in Paul in Comparison with Lucan *Heilsgeschichte*," *NTS* 13 (1967): 147–67.

24. Cf. Sasse, *TDNT*, 1.199; BDAG, 32–33, for the phrase ἀπὸ τῶν αἰώνων denoting the history of creation up to this point, though BDAG takes the reference in Eph 3:9 and Col 1:26 as personal, "the Aeons."

25. The compound πολυποίκιλος appears just here in the NT. Compounds with πολυ- ("much, a great many") are exceedingly common in Greek (a glance at LSJ, 1438–46, will show this), but the simple adj. ποικίλος already means "manifold" or "diversified" (1 Pet 4:10), so it is a bit of extravagance, i.e., "multi-manifold," "very diversified." Coining terms or using vocabulary beyond the ordinary was considered the province of poetry rather than of prose in antiquity, but this was a mark of a more flamboyant rhetoric that touches Paul's own style in a small way at times.

26. See on 1:3 for the rendering "in the high-heavenlies."

cording to the eternal plan[27] that he executed[28] in Christ Jesus our Lord,
12 in whom we have bold access[29] with confidence through our faith in him.
13 Wherefore, I ask you not to lose heart at my tribulations on your behalf,
which[30] is your glory.

Commentary

3:1 Τούτου χάριν, "For this reason." As is commonly pointed out (e.g., Lincoln, 167–72; O'Brien, 223–24), Paul breaks off his statement after v. 1 only to resume it in v. 14, where the unusual opening phrase (*τούτου χάριν* ... *τούτου χάριν*) is repeated in order to signal the resumption of thought (see also on 2:1, 5).[31] The following section of vv. 2–13 is therefore a digression. What Paul had started out to do was to respond with praise for the great truths

---

27. For *κατὰ πρόθεσιν τῶν αἰώνων*; see note on v. 6 above for references.

28. The Greek verb *ποιέω* is a flexible verb that pointed generally to either the process of "making" or "doing" to the actual accomplishment of a task and therefore allows a wide variety of English word substitutes. Here "carried out" (NASB), "accomplish" (NIV), or "realized" (ESV) would also bring out the idea well.

29. The two nouns *παρρησία* ("boldness, confidence") and *προσαγωγή* ("access") constitute one idea as hendiadys* ("one-through-two"; BDF, §442 [16]; A. T. Robertson, *A Grammar of the Greek New Testament in the Light of Historical Research*, 4th ed. [New York, 1923], 1179–83), which is then expanded with the phrase "with confidence," making a rather extravagant statement about our most "bold, confident access." Cf. "boldness and confident access" (NASB) or "we may approach God with freedom and confidence" (NIV). Wallace, *Greek Grammar*, 286, discusses the use of the two nouns "boldness" and "access" in relation to the Granville Sharp rule, where two nouns are modified by one article (i.e., **τὴν** *παρρησίαν καὶ προσαγωγὴν*), though he does not here discuss hendiadys*.

30. The fem. relative pronoun (*ἥτις*) is sg., but the closest fem. noun, "tribulations" (θλίψεις), is pl. It is possible to take the antecedent as fem. sg. "faith" (*πίστις*, v. 12c), but most commentators take the antecedent as "tribulations" (as Origen in Origen and Jerome, 152) and point to grammars that note the irregular lack of concord in number with relative pronouns in Greek (e.g., Hoehner, 469–70; Best, 331). One further point to make is that the meter would change if Paul had used more proper *αἵ* (–) or *αἵτινες* (– ˘ ˘) instead of *ἥτις* (– ˘), which may explain the unusual form of the pronoun. While Paul was not overly concerned for meter in his prose, he still does show some feel for nice cadences, especially at the end of his cola*.

31. Outside v. 1 and v. 14, *τούτου χάριν* only appears in Titus 1:5 in the NT. In contrast, synonymous *διὰ τοῦτο* ("for this reason, because of this") occurs over twenty times in Paul's writings (see 1:15; 5:17; 6:13). The improper prep. *χάριν* only appears nine times in the NT, with no occurrences in the LXX.

of the unity of Jews and Gentiles in one new creation he had recited in Eph 1–2 by stating that he "bows his knee to the Father" (v. 14).[32] But before engaging in this praise, he digresses with an explanation of the now-revealed mystery of Christ's redemption.[33] Proclamation of these truths to the nations outside Israel was Paul's particular task as an apostle (e.g., Acts 9:1–7; 2 Cor 12:1–2; Gal 1:12; 2:2).

Both Jerome and Origen regard v. 1 as containing a grammatical solecism and comment on Paul's lack of rhetorical polish and yet powerful preaching:

> He, therefore, who committed solecisms in speech, who could not render a hyperbaton and round off a period (*qui non potest hyperbaton reddere, sententiamque concludere*), boldly claims wisdom for himself and says, "That the mystery was made known to me in revelation, just as I wrote above in a few words" (Origen and Jerome, 143).[34]

While issues such as hyperbaton and the rounding of periods certainly were matters of fine compositional style, they also served a more prosaic function for readers in marking the contours of an author's cola* and periods.[35] These things would have been particularly important when writing practices utilized little to no punctuation or other features such as capitalization, spacing, and the like (not to mention versification and chapter divisions), which our modern Greek editions fully employ as if ancient Greek were a

32. See the introduction above for elaboration.

33. It is tempting for silent readers of this text to be distracted by such a long digression; in an oral setting the digression and resumption of thought only takes a few moments to transpire, and one can pick up the train of thought rather easily. Cf. the introduction to 3:14–21 for more on digressions in antiquity.

34. "Hyperbaton is the separation of two syntactically very closely linked words by the insertion of a (one-word or two-word) sentence part which does not directly belong at this point," Heinrich Lausberg, *Handbook of Literary Rhetoric: A Foundation for Literary Study*, ed. David E. Orton and R. Dean Anderson (Boston: Brill, 1998), §716. Cf. below on v. 10 and Acts 1:2 for hyperbaton and a rounded period. Hyperbaton may extend far beyond one or two words.

35. So the thesis of Markovic that hyperbaton was used for "signaling or reinforcing the end of syntactical and semantic units in the Greek (and, by analogy, Latin) literary sentence" (Daniel Markovic, "Hyperbaton in the Greek Literary Sentence," *GRBS* 46 [2006]: 127). In the NT this is easiest to see in Hebrews.

modern language. In this light, Origen and Jerome may be excused some exasperation that Paul was simply hard to understand at points. For the modern exegete, the study of ancient compositional theory gives us not only an appreciation for the niceties of language but also may help refine our abilities to see the contours and essential links of thought in the ancient texts.

The opening phrase, *τούτου χάριν* ("for this reason"), points back to 2:19–22 to the new phase in God's redemptive economy in which the Gentiles are being built together with believing Jews into a new, eschatological temple. It is for this reason that Paul—ironically, an apostle, even an ambassador, in chains (6:20)—is prepared to bow his knee to the exalted Creator and Lord of heaven and earth (v. 15). Paul sees this divine work executed in Christ Jesus (v. 11b) as the opening curtain of the age to come when the nations stream into it (Gen 9:27; Psa 86:9; Isa 2:2; 60:3; 66:18–23; Mic 4:1–2; etc.) and the Abrahamic promise finds its fulfillment (see on v. 6).

ἐγὼ Παῦλος, "even I, Paul."[36] The phrase "I Paul [personally]" (ἐγὼ Παῦλος), with the expressed pronoun, has a rather solemn sound and is used by him only a few times elsewhere (2 Cor 10:1; Gal 5:2; Col 1:23; 1 Thess 2:18; Phlm 1:19). Paul is pointing to himself *personally* and leads into his following statements about his personal apostolic office to bring the gospel to the Gentiles.

ὁ δέσμιος τοῦ Χριστοῦ Ἰησοῦ ὑπὲρ ὑμῶν τῶν ἐθνῶν, "the prisoner of Christ on behalf of you Gentiles." Paul suffered imprisonment or confinement several times in the service of Christ (4:1; 6:20; Acts 16:23; 24:23; Col 4:10; Phil 1:7; 2 Tim 1:8; Phlm 1, 9), and hence he refers to himself as "Christ's prisoner."[37] Paul's suffering and bonds for his gospel ministry go back to

36. This is not exactly the *nominativus pendens* (Wallace, *Greek Grammar*, 51–53) or a Semitic use of a nominative without regard to the construction (BDF §466 [2]), since the construction is broken off until v. 14. Hence bringing subject and verb together from vv. 1 and 14 we have: "[E]ven I, Paul, the prisoner of Christ ... bow my knees to the Father."

37. In 4:1 Paul modifies this designation to ὁ δέσμιος ἐν κυρίῳ ("the prisoner in the Lord"). Cf. Craig S. Wansink, *Chained in Christ: The Experience and Rhetoric of Paul's Imprisonments*, JSNTSup 130 (Sheffield: Sheffield Academic, 1996), 27–95; and in general: Harry W. Tajra, *The Trial of St. Paul: A Judicial Exegesis of the Second Half of the Acts of the Apostles*, WUNT 2.35 (Tübingen: Mohr Siebeck, 1989); Tajra,

his original call (Acts 9:15; cf. Acts 21:11; 2 Cor 6:5; 11:23). He experienced these trials "on behalf of you Gentiles," since he was their particular apostle, teacher, and preacher (v. 13; 2 Cor 1:6; Col 1:24; 1 Tim 2:7; 2 Tim 1:11). If Paul (Saul) had not been converted, one can only surmise at the heights he could have obtained in the Jerusalem power structure, though, of course, he most likely would not have survived the war of AD 68–70 anyway.

3:2 εἴ γε ἠκούσατε τὴν οἰκονομίαν τῆς χάριτος τοῦ θεοῦ τῆς δοθείσης μοι εἰς ὑμᾶς, "you have surely heard about the management of God's grace that was given to me for your sake." Paul states that he has been granted "management" (οἰκονομία) of God's grace for his (Gentile) audience's sake (cf. vv. 7, 9; Rom 1:5; Col 1:25).[38] The basis for this claim is that "the mystery of Christ" was revealed to him (v. 3a) as a special appointment as apostolic οἰκονόμος ("manager") of those divine mysteries of the gospel (6:9; 1 Cor 4:1). It sounds strange in English to say that God's grace is "managed," but the term *manager* in its original setting communicates that Paul is a servant who has charge of administration of someone else's property and dependents—in this instance, "you" (as illustrated so well in Matt 25:14–30; Luke 16:1–9).[39] Similar is 1 Peter 4:10, where Peter speaks of church officers who should be "good stewards (οἰκονόμοι) of God's variegated grace" (cf. 1 Tim 1:4; Ignatius, *Eph.* 6.1).

Paul frequently mentions that "grace was given" to him (ἡ χάρις ἡ δοθεῖσά μοι; Rom 12:3, 6; 15:15; 1 Cor 1:4; 3:10; Gal 2:9; cf. Eph 3:7–9; Hoehner, 423). He himself was shown grace as a persecutor of the church (Acts 9:1–2; 22:4; 26:11; 1 Cor 15:9; Gal 1:13), which made him all the more trustworthy as a steward of God's grace to be proclaimed to others: "This is how one should regard us, as servants of Christ and stewards (οἰκονόμοι) of the

---

The Martyrdom of St. Paul, WUNT 2.67 (Tübingen: Mohr Siebeck, 1994); T. J. Cadoux, "The Roman Carcer and Its Adjuncts," *Greece & Rome* 55 (2008): 202–21.

38. οἰκονομία ("[household] management") is possibly continuing a play on words built on οἶκος ("house") Paul had used in 2:19–22 (see introductory comment there). See the translation notes on οἰκονομία for vv. 2 and 9. In the latter verse the word has a different meaning and is rendered "design" (see on 1:10 also; cf. O'Brien, 228; Lincoln, 174).

39. The term for a manager (or "steward") is οἰκονόμος, which Paul uses in Gal 4:2 for servants who oversee the property of a minor heir (cf. Titus 1:7).

mysteries of God. Moreover, it is required of stewards that they be found trustworthy" (1 Cor 4:1–2).[40]

3:3 *κατὰ ἀποκάλυψιν ἐγνωρίσθη μοι τὸ μυστήριον*, "this mystery was made known to me by a revelation." The opening colon* of v. 3 belongs with the material of v. 2. Grammatically, *τὸ μυστήριον* ("this mystery") is in apposition to all of v. 2 and therefore explains the "management" of God's grace to the Gentiles; see v. 9 for *ἡ οἰκονομία τοῦ μυστηρίου* ("the design of the mystery"), where the terms *οἰκονομία* and *μυστήριον* are brought together. Taken together, vv. 2–3 show that Paul's appointment to his "management" of divine grace was granted through a revelation. It further shows that "this mystery" made known to him relates to God's grace, which he is charged to openly proclaim to all peoples. This is the "mystery of the gospel" that Paul makes known (6:19; cf. Col 4:3) in his proclamation, though he be in chains (6:20); his message of mystery is not secret knowledge that he was to protect like a new kind of mystery religion (see "Excursus: The Mystery of Christ").

As noted in the introduction, one should take v. 3a as the last colon* of the rather short v. 2. This is confirmed by the parallel construction of the whole period with that of v. 7:

[2] ... τὴν οἰκονομίαν
τῆς χάριτος τοῦ θεοῦ τῆς δοθείσης μοι ...
[3] κατὰ ἀποκάλυψιν ...

[7] ... τὴν δωρεὰν
τῆς χάριτος τοῦ θεοῦ τῆς δοθείσης μοι
κατὰ τὴν ἐνέργειαν ...

40. See John K. Goodrich, "Paul, the *Oikonomos* of God: Paul's Apostolic Metaphor in 1 Corinithians and Its Greco-Roman Context" (PhD diss., Durham University, 2010), who considers various contemporary backgrounds (including Ephesian epigraphical sources [!]) for Paul's *οἰκονόμος* metaphor and argues helpfully for the role of an estate manager in private affairs. While a slave or freedman *οἰκονόμος* was subserviant to a *κύριος*, he might hold considerable authority in the administration of the master's domains when acting on his behalf. Cf. Dale K. Martin, *Slavery as Salvation: The Metaphor of Slavery in Pauline Christianity* (New Haven, CT: Yale University Press, 1990).

The period is also unified by having the two words in apposition appear at the end of their respective cola*:

> 2 εἴ γε ἠκούσατε τὴν **οἰκονομίαν**
> τῆς χάριτος τοῦ θεοῦ τῆς δοθείσης μοι εἰς ὑμᾶς
> 3 κατὰ ἀποκάλυψιν ἐγνωρίσθη μοι τὸ **μυστήριον**

Repetition of this sort appears elsewhere in Paul's writings (e.g., 2:21–22; Rom 5:15–17) and reinforces the points he is making regarding the grace he has received as the apostle to the Gentiles.

Paul says that he received the knowledge of this mystery κατὰ ἀποκάλυψιν ("by revelation"). This is a point made about him and by him elsewhere (e.g., Act 22:17; 26:16–18; 2 Cor 12:1; Gal 1:12) in order to underline that he "was the recipient rather than the originator of the knowledge of the mystery" (Hoehner, 426). Perhaps equally important, such an experience of being taken into the "council chamber of God" was an essential authenticating experience for a true prophet (Amos 3:7; Isa 6 [cf. Rev 4]; 1 Kgs 22:19; Jer 23:16–18; Rev 1:9–20) and, in this case, an apostle (1 Cor 15:7–8).[41]

καθὼς προέγραψα ἐν ὀλίγῳ, "just as I briefly wrote about beforehand." When Paul says that he "wrote beforehand" (προέγραψα), it makes it appear at first glance that he may be referring to some earlier epistle he sent to his audience (Calvin, 158; Chrysostom, *Homily* 6) or to a different known epistle such as material in Colossians (Bruce, 312).[42] Most interpreters, including some early fathers, believe the reference is actually to material on the gospel mystery Paul has just briefly (cf. Heb 13:22; 1 Pet 5:12) written about in Ephesians (Hodge, 161; Hoehner, 428; Lincoln, 175; O'Brien, 229), especially the issue of Gentile inclusion as fellow heirs with the Jews in 2:11–22.[43] This view is strengthened by references given in the lexicons, in which other authors use this verb (προγράφω) to refer to material "before-mentioned" or "written above" in the same document (LSJ, 1473; BDAG, 867; cf. Wallace,

---

41. Cf. Peter R. Jones, "1 Corinthians 15:8: Paul the Last Apostle," *TynB* 36 (1985): 3–34.

42. Calvin (158) says that the reference is to a previous epistle was "the general opinion" in his day.

43. E.g., Theodoret: "The words, *I wrote a little before* do not mean, as some think, that he has written another letter. ... For he is referring to 'the mystery made know to me by revelation.' ... For this has been his subject from the outset right up to this passage," *ACCS*, 146.

Greek Grammar, 565). Hence, it seems best to take the reference as narrowly the statement of v. 3a ("the mystery [that] was made known to me by revelation") and more broadly the content of that mystery in Gentile inclusion into full citizenship with the saints that Paul had discussed in the previous chapters of Ephesians (O'Brien, 236).

3:4 *πρὸς ὃ δύνασθε ἀναγινώσκοντες νοῆσαι τὴν σύνεσίν μου ἐν τῷ μυστηρίῳ τοῦ Χριστοῦ*, "When you read about it, you can perceive my insight into the mystery of Christ." The neuter relative pronoun in the first phrase of v. 4 (*πρὸς ὅ*) can refer to this whole statement or only to a part, specifically to the neuter noun *μυστήριον* ("mystery") itself.

To modern readers of Ephesians, who may own multiple Bibles, it seems trivial for Paul to say in vv. 3–4 that one can reread what he had just written previously. But if one is hearing the letter for the first time, it assumes that a copy of the letter would be made available for future reference and for personal study of the previous points. Paul expected his epistles to be studied and reread (or more probably, reheard), as indeed they have been for close to two thousand years so far.

Paul points out his insight here not to magnify himself (cf. v. 8) but, in light of the thesis of vv. 1–13, to confirm that his calling and the revelation he received are genuine (cf. Barth, 330–31). "Even if I am unskilled in speaking, I am not so in knowledge; indeed, in every way we have made this plain to you in all things" (2 Cor 11:6).

3:5 *ὃ ἑτέραις γενεαῖς οὐκ ἐγνωρίσθη τοῖς υἱοῖς τῶν ἀνθρώπων*, "which was not made known to the sons of men in other generations." As discussed in "Excursus: The Mystery of Christ," v. 5 shows that the mysterious character of the Son of God is that his redemption for all peoples was not fully disclosed before his incarnation but that it has been "now" (*νῦν*, v. 5c).[44] This is an historical point, not a mystery such as found in Graeco-Roman paganism.

---

44. "Now" refers not to a momentary point in time but to the current era commenced with the incarnation and redemptive work of Christ (i.e., the "mystery of Christ"; v. 4). It is "this age" as opposed to "other [previous] generations" (*ἑτέραι γενεαί*; cf. 1:21) or the future "age to come" (1:21; 2:7). Gentile inclusion in the "promise of Christ" (v. 6), elaborated on in 2:11–22, is what particularly marks this "now" era for Paul.

Biblical revelation has an essential unity: It has divine origin (2 Tim 3:16; Heb 1:1–2), through the Spirit (Acts 1:16; Heb 10:15–16; 2 Pet 1:21), about Christ and his redemptive work (John 5:46; 1 Pet 1:10–12; Gal 3:8), and was sufficient to give the saints of old genuine faith into eschatological events Christ has inaugurated and guaranteed (Gal 3:9; Heb 11:13–16).[45] Yet this revelation is not static because it is tied to redemptive accomplishment in history. As the history of God's dealings with the human race unfolds, so does redemptive revelation. For this reason there is true *development* in revelation, and 3:5–6 is a demonstration of this.[46] Until the Son of God came to unite all his people from the ends of the earth into a new human race, this union was clearly hinted at in previous generations but effectively hidden from "the sons of men" (1 Cor 2:6–10; 1 Pet 1:10–12 again). Hence, redemptive revelation is most intimately bound up with God's work of redemption itself, which, specifically in this context, is the integration of believing Gentiles with Jewish saints into the church (v. 6). It is now no longer a secret, but it is to be broadcast to the ends of the earth.

ὡς νῦν ἀπεκαλύφθη τοῖς ἁγίοις ἀποστόλοις αὐτοῦ καὶ προφήταις ἐν πνεύματι, "as it has now been revealed to his holy apostles and prophets in the Spirit." A couple of questions that have occupied scholars on this verse can be summarily addressed. First, Christ is the closest possible referent to αὐτοῦ ("his") from v. 4, so we could read it as "*Christ's* holy apostles and prophets." But the decisive factor for understanding the referent of "his" is that God (the Father) is clearly the implied subject of the verb ἀπεκαλύφθη in this colon*, so αὐτοῦ most likely refers to God the Father (e.g., Lincoln, 178–79; Hoehner, 442–43).

Second, ἐν πνεύματι ("in the Spirit") is sometimes taken to be attached only to the prophets and not to the apostles (e.g., Schlier, 150–51) because of the syntax. It is best, however, to take ἐν πνεύματι as qualifying the verb ἀπεκαλύφθη and indicating that the Father's revelation to all his

45. Cf. S. M. Baugh, "The Cloud of Witnesses in Hebrews 11," *WTJ* 68 (2006): 113–32. For this redemptive-historical character of Scripture, see esp. Geerhardus Vos, ""The Idea of Biblical Theology as a Science and as a Theological Discipline," in *Redemptive History and Biblical Interpretation* (Phillipsburg, NJ: P&R, 1975), 3–24.

46. As one example, see the unveiling of "the faith" in Gal 3:22–23 in the NT era even though NT saints join *believing* Abraham in faith in Gal 3:9, 29.

servants (e.g., Rev 1:1–3) was given through the Holy Spirit's activity (cf. esp. 1 Cor 2:10–13; so most commentators).[47]

Finally, while it is possible (but not preferred above) to take "prophets" who were allied with the apostles as the foundation of the church in 2:20 as the prophets of the OT era, here in 3:5 it seems clear that Paul can only be referencing NT prophets, since the revelation occurs *now* (ὡς νῦν ἀπεκαλύφθη). This also fits with Paul's teaching in 4:11, where Christ gives "some as apostles, some as prophets" to his church along with others in this new covenant era (cf. 1 Cor 12:28). Hence, people like Agabus or the four daughters of Philip (Acts 2:17; 11:28; 21:8–10) are the prophets in view as recipients of new covenant-era divine revelation along with the apostles.

An issue that calls for a little more discussion is how to take the phrase τοῖς ἁγίοις ἀποστόλοις αὐτοῦ καὶ προφήταις ("to his holy apostles and prophets") and especially how the words interrelate. For example, O'Brien accepts a common view when he says, "The syntax suggests that both 'his' and 'holy' qualify only 'apostles,' but not both nouns" (O'Brien, 233; cf. Lincoln, 178–79; Schnackenburg, 133–34). I do not find this interpretation persuasive (as also Hoehner, 442) and would like to offer two reasons.

First, the main basis for separating apostles from prophets here is because αὐτοῦ ("his") is attached only to the first noun and does not come after both (O'Brien, 233n32). Hence we have:

> τοῖς ἁγίοις ἀποστόλοις **αὐτοῦ** καὶ προφήταις

rather than:

> τοῖς ἁγίοις ἀποστόλοις καὶ προφήταις **αὐτοῦ**

or

> τοῖς ἁγίοις ἀποστόλοις καὶ **τοῖς** προφήταις **αὐτοῦ**[48]

---

47. E.g., "Many years you … warned them by your Spirit through your prophets' (Neh 9:30) where there are three agents involved ("you," "your Spirit," and "your prophets"); cf. "Thus says the Lord God, 'Woe to the foolish prophets who follow *their own spirit*, and have seen nothing!' " (Ezek 13:3, emphasis added).

48. Usually a noun modified by a gen. pronoun has an article, as **τοῖς** ἁγίοις ἀποστόλοις **αὐτοῦ**. Further examples nearby are: τὴν σύνεσίν μου (v. 4), τῆς δυνάμεως αὐτοῦ (v. 7), διὰ τῆς πίστεως αὐτοῦ (v. 12), and ἐν ταῖς θλίψεσίν μου (v. 13). There are exceptions to this pattern caused by other mitigating factors.

But there are problems here. The first option above would appear to place "prophets" in apposition to "apostles" so that both nouns refer to the same individuals, reading: "to his holy apostles, even the prophets." This is what we have, for example, in τῷ δὲ θεῷ καὶ πατρὶ ἡμῶν, "to God, even our Father" (Phil 4:20), and τὸν μόνον δεσπότην καὶ κύριον ἡμῶν, "our only Master and Lord" (Jude 4). It might even be possible to see the two nouns as hendiadys* ("prophetic apostles"), as in this example: κατὰ τὴν ἀποκαραδοκίαν καὶ ἐλπίδα μου, "my expectation and hope" becomes "my hope-filled expectation" (Phil 1:20).[49]

The second possible option above separates the two groups too much. "to his (= τοῖς) holy apostles as well as to his prophets."[50] For example, τοῖς ὄχλοις καὶ τοῖς μαθηταῖς αὐτοῦ, "to the crowds as well as to his disciples" (Matt 23:1), refers to two separate groups (also Luke 1:58).[51] While one can read this second option as referring to two associated groups, it is not as clear or necessary as the way Paul actually states the matter.

In addition, that the genitive pronoun αὐτοῦ ("his") is directly attached to the first noun ("apostles") does not mean that its meaning is restricted to that noun. Context is the defining factor, but there are several examples where the pronoun would clearly be understood as referencing the second noun also.[52] There is a particularly instructive example for the whole matter in the LXX of Daniel: τοῖς βασιλεῦσιν ἡμῶν καὶ δυνάσταις καὶ τοῖς πατράσιν ἡμῶν, "to our kings and to (our) princes as well as to our fathers" (Dan 9:8). The meaning seems clear. The first two groups (kings and princes) are closely

---

49. For hendiadys* see BDF §442 (16) or A. T. Robertson, *A Grammar of the Greek New Testament in the Light of Historical Research*, 4th ed. (New York, 1923), 1179–83.

50. E.g., similar τὰς καρδίας ὑμῶν καὶ τὰ νοήματα ὑμῶν ἐν Χριστῷ Ἰησοῦ, "your hearts along with your minds in Christ Jesus" (Phil 4:7); οἱ υἱοὶ αὐτοῦ καὶ τὰ θρέμματα αὐτοῦ, "his sons as well as his livestock" (John 4:12). Cf. Acts 1:25; 2 Thess 1:4; 1 Pet 1:21.

51. Cf. Ἡρῴδης τοῖς γενεσίοις αὐτοῦ δεῖπνον ἐποίησεν τοῖς μεγιστᾶσιν αὐτοῦ καὶ τοῖς χιλιάρχοις καὶ τοῖς πρώτοις τῆς Γαλιλαίας, "Herod gave a banquet on his birthday for his kinsmen, for his nobles, and for his generals, as well as for the leading men of Galilee" (Mark 6:21). These are three separate groups, indicated in part by the repetition of the articles.

52. E.g., ἐν τοῖς ὠσὶν τῶν γυναικῶν ὑμῶν καὶ θυγατέρων, "in the ears of your wives and of (your) daughters" (Exod 32:2) and αἷμα υἱῶν αὐτῶν καὶ θυγατέρων, "the blood of their sons and of (their) daughters" (Psa 105[106]:38) in the LXX.

tied together as political groups even though distinguishable, so they get one article, and the first noun has the possessive pronoun. The third group ("fathers") is more distinguishable from the first two, so the noun has its own article and another pronoun added (καὶ **τοῖς** πατράσιν **ἡμῶν**).

The summary on syntax is that Paul's expression τοῖς ἁγίοις ἀποστόλοις αὐτοῦ καὶ προφῆται should be read as two groups that can be distinguishable, yet they are closely allied, much as Daniel's kings and princes in the example above.[53] In context, the point is that apostles and prophets are both special agents of divine disclosure of full Gentile inclusion in the new covenant blessings in Christ. And both groups are understood to be "his"; i.e., God's holy apostles and God's holy prophets as one united yet distinguishable group.

My second comment on the common scholarly view of the phrase τοῖς ἁγίοις ἀποστόλοις αὐτοῦ καὶ προφήταις is that this and other issues for interpretation seem to only be treated today on the level of syntax. However, there are also interpretive benefits of looking at the NT Greek text in light of how ancient texts were composed and read in antiquity. In particular, syntax was important for clarity or obscurity for the ancients, but scansion, the sounds of syllables and words and how they interact with nearby sounds, colon* length, and other such matters were also part of the bedrock of ancient literary composition, not syntax alone. Consider, for example, this statement by Dionysius of Halicarnassus regarding Greek and Latin at the grammar school level:

> When we are taught to read, first we learn by heart the names of the letters, then their shapes and their values, then, the same way, the syllables and their effects, and finally words and their properties, by which I mean the ways they are lengthened, shortened, and scanned; and similar functions. And when we have

53. This meaning is discussed and illustrated by Daniel B. Wallace, *Granville Sharp's Canon and Its Kin: Semantics and Significance*, SBG 14 (New York: Peter Lang, 2009), 137–38 (cf. 142–54; 214–28). For example the two groups who were quite disparate, οἱ Φαρισαῖοι καὶ Σαδδουκαῖοι ("the Pharisees and Sadducees"; Matt 16:1), are linked by one article because they were allied against Jesus in the context. Other classical examples are provided in Smyth, *Greek Grammar*, §1143 (e.g., οἱ στρατηγοὶ καὶ λοχαγοί, "the generals and commanders"; Xenophon, *Anab.* 2.2.8; but see §1144 for where Xenophon repeats the article in this same phrase to stress each word).

acquired knowledge of these things, we begin to write and read, syllable by syllable. (Dionysius of Halicarnassus, *Comp.* 25)

From this vantage point, the colon* of Eph 3:5d as Paul has expressed it is already the longest colon* in Eph 3:1–13, at eighteen syllables.[54] This passage is filled with short cola*, as seen in the first and last cola*: τούτου χάριν ἐγὼ Παῦλος ("For this reason even I, Paul"; v. 1a) and ἥτις ἐστὶν δόξα ὑμῶν ("which is your glory"; v. 13c), with eight syllables each. The point is, Paul, who demonstrates a rugged, native appreciation of Greek style in places, is composing fast phrases, and τοῖς ἁγίοις ἀποστόλοις αὐτοῦ καὶ προφήταις ἐν πνεύματι is already long enough and communicates quite well his meaning. To have added supplementary words like an extra article or possessive pronoun would have lengthened the colon* too much (twenty-one to twenty-four syllables total). And since this colon* ends the period (where the presenter takes a breath), Paul expresses ἐν πνεύματι at the very end even though it goes with the verb ἀπεκαλύφθη, expressed seven words (fourteen syllables) previously, because he wants the Holy Spirit's involvement in this divine disclosure "to his holy apostles and prophets" to be prominent in the audience's mind, hence "in the Spirit" is the last phrase of the period before the speaker takes a breath.

A final issue is the adjective "holy" here in v. 5. As stated, I take it to refer not only to the apostles but to the second noun as well: "to his holy apostles and to (his holy) prophets."[55] The term ἅγιος used as an adjective in this context means that the apostles and prophets are commissioned by and belong to God (cf. Rom 1:2), like the "holy angels" (e.g., Luke 9:26; Rev 14:10) over against false prophets (e.g., Matt 24:11, 24; 1 John 4:1; Rev 2:20) and false apostles (2 Cor 11:13; cf. Rev 2:2). The point in the flow of the context and particularly of Paul's overarching concern in the digression of vv. 2–13

54. Vv. 3a, 4b, and 11b each have seventeen syllables, but most are in the range of seven to fifteen. The four cola in v. 5 are twelve, seven, seven, and eighteen syllables long, respectively.

55. For "holy prophets" elsewhere see Luke 1:70; Acts 3:21; 2 Pet 3:2, where the holy prophets appear alongside "your apostles." Scholars use "holy apostles" as evidence of a pseudonymous author boasting about his understanding. In fact a pseudonymous author would be boasting in *Paul's* understanding, not his. As O'Brien notes, however (230), this whole theory of pseudonymity causes more problems with the text here than it solves.

is that the apostolic and prophetic revelation the Ephesians have relied on for their faith does indeed come from God and is authentically true.

3:6 εἶναι τὰ ἔθνη συγκληρονόμα καὶ σύσσωμα καὶ συμμέτοχα τῆς ἐπαγγελίας ἐν Χριστῷ Ἰησοῦ διὰ τοῦ εὐαγγελίου, "This mystery is that the Gentiles are fellow heirs, fellow body members, and fellow partakers of the promise in Christ Jesus through the gospel." As noted under 2:5–6, Paul has a fondness for words prefixed with συν- ("together with", "fellow," or "co-"), which he uses to express the corporate bond that believers have with Christ and with one another. Here the bond is first with one another as "coheirs" (συγκληρονόμα), "co-body members" (σύσσωμα), and "co-partakers" (συμμέτοχα), but then he adds "in Christ Jesus" to show that the incarnate Son ever mediates the church's relation not only to God but to one another.[56] These great truths of Jews and Gentiles together in a newly re-created human family are the substance of what God has revealed to his agents of revelation and proclamation through the Spirit (3:5) and published worldwide "through the gospel."

Although this new creation is inaugurated in Christ's completed work (see on 2:10), it remains as an inheritance for his people. This implies that believers have full title to and a sealed, guaranteed possession of the consummation of this new creation in a new heavens and new earth in resurrection (see on 1:13–14 and 5:5). But it is not yet consummated.[57] This is why believers are "coheirs" and "co-partakers of *the promise*." The inheritance is still promised (e.g., Heb 6:17) and shared with the OT saints (e.g., Heb 11:9, 39–40; Rom 4:11–16) as well as with all the Christian saints in the current age (Gal 3:29). And see particularly Rom 8:17 in this connection, where believers inherit all the vast domains that now belong to the risen Christ because they are "coheirs" (συγκληρονόμοι) with him as well as with the elect of all ages.

56. Paul is not concerned with the mixed legal and body metaphors here. He develops and works with these and related conceptions elsewhere: inheritance and promise (1:11, 13–14, 18; 2:12) and body (1:22–23; 4:4, 12–16).

57. The lengthy work by G. K. Beale (*A New Testament Biblical Theology: The Unfolding of the Old Testament in the New* [Grand Rapids: Baker Academic, 2011]) is centered on this dynamic; cf. Andrew T. Lincoln, *Paradise Now and Not Yet*, SNTSMS (Cambridge: Cambridge University Press, 1981).

Paul develops the idea that Gentiles are partakers in the promise along with all the saints from the fact that they were formerly "strangers from the covenants *of promise*" (2:12), but through Christ's work they are now full (new) covenant members as "coheirs," etc., along with believing Israelites (2:19). This great movement in redemptive history in v. 6 is stated as being "the mystery of Christ," which was not disclosed to prior generations (vv. 4–5).[58] However, it *was* disclosed that the Gentiles would stream into Zion to worship the true God of Israel, bringing their treasures (e.g., Gen 9:27; Psa 86:9; Isa 2:2; 60:3; 66:18–23; Mic 4:1–3). But the Gentiles appear in those places as captives or subject peoples bearing tribute to God, who comes in judgment and for the glory of a revived, conquering Israel (e.g., Gen 49:10; Psa 96; 98; Isa 18:3–7). Yet Paul says the Gentiles do not come in as enslaved captives or subjects but as "coheirs" and sharers in the OT covenant promises. Hence, the mystery that was not formerly disclosed is now revealed in the Gentile mission (vv. 5, 9).[59]

The fact that the church's inheritance comes through a proclaimed message ("through the gospel") would be stunning to an ancient audience. For someone outside the family to receive an inheritance means that he must be brought in, normally through adoption (see on 1:5). But for the *slaves* in the Ephesian congregation (6:5), adoption into any sort of inheritance—much less being adopted to be members of *God's* own household (2:19)—means the world has been turned upside down. The closest analogy to this for an ordinary Ephesian would be the various imperial freedmen like C. Julius Nicephorus (*IvE* 859 and 859A) or Earinus ('Εάρινος, "Springtime"; *IvE* 1564), and especially the two wealthy freedmen of M. Vipsanius Agrippa, the powerful friend of Augustus and of King Herod, named Mazaeus and Mithridates, who built the south gateway into the

58. The inf. εἶναι ("to be") leading off v. 6 acts as the content (epexegetical) of the mystery (v. 4) that was formerly not disclosed (οὐκ ἐγνωρίσθη) but now revealed (νῦν ἀπεκαλύφθη; v. 5) to God's messengers. We could paraphrase: "God has now revealed *the former mystery that the Gentiles are fellow heirs* ... to his holy apostles and prophets."

59. Origen and Jerome have a long section (Origen and Jerome, 144–48) discussing Eph 3:5–7 and how believing OT saints and prophets could not have known of the mystery of Christ when they certainly did to some extent. This is also discussed by Chrysostom and Theodoret (*ACCS*, 147). The idea of unfolding revelation ("organic development") is the answer to this apparent disparity. (See "Biblical Theological Comments" at the end of 2:11–22 above.)

Ephesian square marketplace (*IvE* 851 and 3006).[60] Such freedmen acquired vast resources and handed down privileges to their heirs—yet they earned it after years of loyal service. But the fact that the stunning privilege of adoption and inheritance into God's family comes via a *message* rather than by manumission payment or by the believer's own heroic and loyal deeds (2:9) is further proof that the riches of Christ are indeed "untraceable" (3:8) in their awesome depth.

3:7 οὗ ἐγενήθην διάκονος κατὰ τὴν δωρεὰν τῆς χάριτος τοῦ θεοῦ τῆς δοθείσης μοι, "Of which I was made a servant as the gift of God's grace, which was given me." Note the unusual alliteration with words beginning with "δ" in this period: διάκονος … δωρεάν … δοθείσης … δυνάμεως.[61] This unifies the period and gives it a certain dignity. Also see above on vv. 2–3a for the structure of this period, which mirrors that one.

Paul opens this period with "of which [gospel] I was made a servant," where the word "servant" is διάκονος, whence English gets "deacon" (cf. Acts 9:15; Rom 12:3; 1 Cor 3:5; 2 Cor 3:6; Col 1:23, 25). The word denotes a servant or official who is charged with an area of responsibility, especially people connected to service of a god. For example, we know the names of some διάκονοι in service of "Cretan" Zeus, Hera, and Ares, listed alongside priests and other cult* personnel at Ephesus. For example, Oikeios son of Dionysius was διάκονος of Cretan Zeus (*IvE* 3414.8–9); his name in Greek is Οἰκεῖος ("Domestic"), which probably refers to him as a "house-born" slave in contrast to a slave who was purchased, suggesting that a διάκονος was not an exalted position in the cult*. While διάκονος does not itself necessarily denote someone of servile status, Paul chooses a word in Eph 3:7 for himself that expresses neither "his importance or personal

---

60. The square marketplace is the tetragonos agora, and the gateway is called a *triodos* ("three-way") building; see Peter Scherrer, ed., *Ephesus: The New Guide* (Turkey: Zero, 2000), 138–39. Visitors to Ephesus today see the Mazaeus and Mithridates *triodos* immediately to the right of the famous Celsus Library (which was built several decades after Paul's day). The monuments and remains of all these freedmen benefactors would have been well known to the audience of Ephesians. For thorough discussion on various related subjects to slaves and freedmen see Henrik Mouritsen, *The Freedman in the Roman World* (Cambridge, Cambridge University Press, 2011).

61. In contrast, v. 6 has only one word beginning with δ (διὰ) and v. 8 has none; cf. Col 1:23.

renown" (Best, 314).[62] He *serves* both God and his Gentile audience as διάκονος even with its attendant persecutions:

> We put no obstacle in anyone's way, so that no fault may be found with our ministry, but as servants (διάκονοι) of God we commend ourselves in every way: by great endurance, in afflictions, hardships, calamities, beatings, imprisonments, riots, labors, sleepless nights, hunger; by purity, knowledge, patience, kindness, the Holy Spirit, genuine love; by truthful speech, and the power of God; with the weapons of righteousness for the right hand and for the left; through honor and dishonor, through slander and praise. (2 Cor 6:3–8)

Consequently, Paul was duty-bound to proclaim the gospel, yet as a gift of God's grace, because he served out of gratitude for the grace that he himself had received (κατὰ τὴν δωρεὰν τῆς χάριτος τοῦ θεοῦ τῆς δοθείσης μοι, "as the gift of God's grace, which was given me"). Note that Paul has not been given "authority" or "priesthood" in connection with his office but "grace."[63] Paul, "the very least of all the saints" (v. 8), loved much because he had been forgiven much (Luke 7:47), so that the mercies of God could be demonstrated through him to all the world (1 Tim 1:12–16).

κατὰ τὴν ἐνέργειαν τῆς δυνάμεως αὐτοῦ, "in accordance with the effectiveness of his power." Granting that Paul was called to service of God and of the church—rather than to kingly rule—he yet wants to stress alongside this that his office came to him and continues to be marked by divine empowerment. The early work of Seyoon Kim is still valuable to show that the blinding glory of the risen and exalted Christ that overcame Paul in great power on the road to Damascus had influenced him all his life (Acts 9:3; 22:6, 11; 26:13).[64] Paul was called on the Damascus road to be the "servant (ὑπηρέτης) and witness" of Christ (Acts 26:16) "before the Gentiles and

62. See O'Brien, 238–39, 33–37, for a penetrating analysis that the rather humble portrait of Paul here does not fit the work of a pseudonymous author.

63. See esp. Rom 12:3, where Paul declares instructions that must govern the lives of Christ's followers, yet he does so "through the grace given to me" (cf. Rom 15:15; 1 Cor 3:10; 15:10; Gal 2:9); cf. James R. Harrison, *Paul's Language of Grace in Its Graeco-Roman Context*, WUNT 2.172 (Tübingen: Mohr Siebeck, 2003).

64. Seyoon Kim, *The Origin of Paul's Gospel* (Eugene, OR: Wipf & Stock, 2007; original ed., 1982).

kings and the children of Israel" (Acts 9:15). The experience never left him; hence, he says in v. 7 that his office as διάκονος was "in accordance with the effectiveness of his power" (cf. 1 Cor 15:10; Col 1:29). Therefore, as the thesis of this passage above describes, Paul is showing his Gentile audience that they should not think that God's purpose for them has been thwarted by his imprisonment. It is perfected in weakness (2 Cor 12:9; 13:4).

3:8 Ἐμοὶ τῷ ἐλαχιστοτέρῳ πάντων ἁγίων ἐδόθη ἡ χάρις αὕτη, "This grace was given to me, the very least of all saints." God's wisdom (specifically his inclusion of Gentiles into his family) is revealed in Christ, which was a mystery before its full revelation in Christ. As stated in the introduction to 3:1–13, vv. 8–13 form the last subsection in the longer passage, but it should not be separated from it. Paul is still concerned to assure his Gentile audience that his imprisonment does not mean that God has rejected him from his apostolic office so as to compromise their redemption in Christ. Paul is turning now to expand on how this redemption of Gentiles and Jews in one new-creation people was formerly hidden yet now revealed.

It was no false humility on Paul's part to call himself "the very least of all saints," since he was acutely aware that he had once been a persecutor of Christ and of his church (Acts 9:4; Phil 3:6; 1 Tim 1:13).[65] Paul's particular calling as the apostle to the Gentiles (Acts 9:15; 18:6; Gal 2:8; 1 Tim 2:7) was to proclaim the good news of the gospel to them (cf. 1 Cor 15:9).

τοῖς ἔθνεσιν εὐαγγελίσασθαι τὸ ἀνεξιχνίαστον πλοῦτος τοῦ Χριστοῦ, "to proclaim to the Gentiles the untraceable riches of Christ." The infinitive εὐαγγελίσασθαι, along with φωτίσαι in the next verse, expresses purpose. We could paraphrase: "This grace was given to me *in order to proclaim the gospel ... and to enlighten*." The aorist form of εὐαγγελίσασθαι ("proclaim a favorable message") expresses the idea of the verb simply, without elaboration, whereas the present-tense form presents the event as an engagement in an activity of proclamation.[66]

---

65. See on 1:1 for the meaning of *saints* here as a reference to all covenant members rather than to a select group of believers. This verse, where Paul by implication assumes that he too is a saint like the Ephesians (though the very least), confirms this interpretation.

66. The inf. forms of εὐαγγελίζω in the NT occur as follows: pres. form: Rom 15:20 ("to engage in a proclamation ministry"); 1 Cor 1:17 (parallel with pres. βαπτίζειν and similar to Rom 15:20 in meaning); aor. form: Luke 1:19; 4:18, 43; Acts 16:10;

The English versions have come up with many different ways to render the adjective ἀνεξιχνίαστος ("untraceable"), which modifies "the riches of Christ": "unsearchable" (KJV; NIV; ESV), "inscrutable" (NAB), "boundless" (NRSV), and "unfathomable" (NASB).[67] In the LXX this adjective occurs four times (Job 5:9; 9:10; 34:24; *Odes. Sol.* 12:6) in parallel with ideas like "great," "glorious," "marvelous," "without number," and "without measure." The image, then, is that Christ represents an enormous expanse of riches that extends far beyond the horizon.[68] "Oh, the depth of the riches and wisdom and knowledge of God! How unsearchable are his judgments and how inscrutable (ἀνεξιχνίαστος) his ways!" (Rom 11:33).

3:9 καὶ φωτίσαι πάντας, "and to enlighten all." The period begins with "and to enlighten all [people]," which is a parallel purpose clause with "to proclaim to the Gentiles" in v. 8 (cf. 1:18; 2 Tim 1:10). This serves to expand on the nature of Paul's calling to proclaim the gospel, which was itself a disclosure of the new era in God's redemptive epochs to the whole world (1 Tim 2:6–7). Indeed, this era marks the inauguration of the consummation of all ages (Heb 9:26) now that the times of Gentile ignorance and groping in the darkness are past (Acts 17:24–31). Paul seems to have chosen φωτίζω ("enlighten") here in contrast with his audience's former life in "darkness" (5:8, cf. 5:9–13). The metaphorical use of "darkness" (or "night") and "light" (or "day") for moral states appears elsewhere in Paul's writings (e.g., 2 Cor 6:1; 1 Thess 5:5) and is quite common in other ancient sources, including the Dead Sea cave texts.[69]

Rom 1:15; 2 Cor 10:16; Eph 3:8; Rev 14:6. The simple idea predominates, as expected. The distinction here can be illustrated with a more common, analogous verb, ποιέω, as an inf. pres.: Παρακαλῶ οὖν πρῶτον πάντων ποιεῖσθαι δεήσεις, "As a first priority, I strongly urge that petitions *be made*" (i.e., "that you engage in making petitions"; 1 Tim 2:1); aor.: ταῦτα δὲ ἔδει ποιῆσαι, "You must *do* these things [justice and the love of God]" (Luke 11:42; cf. Matt 23:23).

67. The adj. ἀνεξιχνίαστος is built off a verb (ἐξιχνιάζω) that refers to tracking game in a hunt.

68. I am taking the gen. here as appositive (BDF §167): Christ is himself the riches (so Lincoln, 183–84 [though he mislabels it as an objective gen.]; and contra O'Brien, 241n79). The less likely option is simple possession: "the inexhaustible riches which belong to Christ."

69. E.g., 1QS 3.13–4.26 ("Treatise on the Two Spirits"), opening with the Teacher being told to instruct the "sons of light" (בני אור) concerning the twin spirits of truth and of deceit that God placed in man at creation. Cf. G. L. Borchert, "Light

τίς ἡ οἰκονομία τοῦ μυστηρίου τοῦ ἀποκεκρυμμένου ἀπὸ τῶν αἰώνων ἐν τῷ θεῷ τῷ τὰ πάντα κτίσαντι, "as to what is the design of the mystery hidden from time immemorial in God who created all things." That which Paul illuminates for all (*φωτίσαι πάντας*) is "the design of the mystery hidden from time immemorial," where the phrase "design of the mystery" is *ἡ οἰκονομία τοῦ μυστηρίου*.[70] Paul is referring to the *content* of the gospel mystery. He is showing people in his preaching what this former mystery was about: free grace and forgiveness in a new creation for all, Jew and Gentile, who entrust themselves to the one Mediator, Jesus Christ. That is the "plan" or "project" that God the Creator had previously "hidden from time immemorial" and now has powerfully brought into light.[71] It is interesting to contrast this with this statement from the *Testament of Moses:*

> He created the world on behalf of his people, but he did not make this purpose of creation openly known from the beginning of the world so that the nations might be found guilty. … But he did design and devise me [Moses], who (was) prepared from the beginning of the world, to be the mediator of his covenant. … Therefore, those who truly fulfill the commandments of God will flourish and will finish the good way, but those who sin by disregarding the commandments will deprive themselves of the good things which were declared before. (*T. Mos.* 1:12–14; 12:10–11; trans. J. Priest)[72]

---

and Darkness," *DPL*, 555–57. This theme is particularly prominent in John's Gospel; cf. Etienne Trocmé, "Light and Darkness in the Fourth Gospel," *Didaskalia* 6 (1995): 3–13.

70. Earlier, in v. 2, *οἰκονομία* had the meaning "administration," but here the meaning is "plan" or "design" (like πρόθεσις or βουλή in 1:11 and 3:11). The two meanings are conceptually related yet distinct. Cf. the translation note above.

71. See previous comments on vv. 5–7 above and esp. two other places in Paul: "Now to him who is able to strengthen you according to my gospel and the preaching of Jesus Christ, according to the revelation of the mystery that was kept secret for long ages" (Rom 16:25); "the mystery hidden for ages and generations but now revealed to his saints" (Col 1:26).

72. James H. Charlesworth, ed., *The Old Testament Pseudepigrapha* (New York: Doubleday, 1983, 1985), 1:927, 934.

The nations are "found guilty," and their only hope is to convert to Judaism and to adhere to the Mosaic covenant stipulations along with faithful Israel and to not sin. Compare especially Eph 2:11–22.

Why does Paul add the qualification regarding God as Creator here (ἐν τῷ θεῷ τῷ τὰ πάντα **κτίσαντι**, "in God who created all things")? There are three other references with κτίζω in Ephesians, yet all refer to *new* creation and to the new human race forged in Christ (2:10, 15; 4:24 [cf. Col 3:10–11]). There are other references to the original creation with this verb κτίζω in Paul's writings (Rom 1:25; 1 Cor 11:9; Col 1:16; 1 Tim 4:3), but why here? The best answer seems to be that when Paul reflected on the long ages when God had kept "the design of the mystery hidden," he wished to accent that God as the creator had never abandoned his compassion for the work of his hands, the multitude of nations who had wandered off into a pagan night, "who do not know their right hand from their left" (Jonah 4:11; Dan 4:34–35).

3:10 ἵνα γνωρισθῇ νῦν ταῖς ἀρχαῖς καὶ ταῖς ἐξουσίαις ἐν τοῖς ἐπουρανίοις διὰ τῆς ἐκκλησίας ἡ πολυποίκιλος σοφία τοῦ θεοῦ, "so that through the church the multifaceted wisdom of God might now be made known to the rulers and authorities in the high-heavenlies." The word order in 3:10 is a little unusual. Paul opens with a passive verb construction (ἵνα γνωρισθῇ, "in order to be made known") but suspends the subject (σοφία, "wisdom") until over a dozen words later, in v. 10c.[73] It is impossible to carry this off in English, but it might go something like: "so that the following might now be made known to the rulers and authorities in the high-heavenlies through the church,

73. Hyperbaton (suspension of words out of normal sequence) may function to create tension and finally resolution and "to make the sentence appear of equal value to a period," even though it can counteract the ideal in composition for simplicity and clarity (Lausberg, *Literary Rhetoric*, §716); see above on v. 1. Ancient Latin rhetoricians preferred verbs at the end of periods, yet in Greek prose style, an author may place his verb at other places, such as in the middle of a colon*: παρ᾽ ᾧ τὸ λοιπὸν **διέτριβε** τοῦ βίου μέρος (Polybius, *Hist.* 3.19.8–9; "at whose court he *spent* the rest of his life"; LCL trans.; emphasis added). Here the verb, διέτριβε, sits in the middle of an article and its noun (τὸ ... μέρος) and the noun's qualifiers (λοιπὸν ... τοῦ βίου); cf. Heb 2:9.

namely, *the multifaceted wisdom of God!*" The delay puts stress and focus on the subject phrase of v. 10c.[74]

What should not be missed is that God's wisdom here in v. 10 refers back to the "design of the mystery," which was formerly "hidden from time immemorial" in v. 9 and was not perceived by any of the world forces at the incarnate Son's appearance (1 Cor 2:6–9). God formerly did not fully disclose this eternal purpose but has now revealed it by its execution "in Christ Jesus our Lord" (3:11). Hence, it is a wisdom that defies the world's logic and values (1 Cor 1:18–25). God's handling of the history of the world and its redemption as creator and providential suzerain is wise beyond compare; but this is only seen *now* in light of the incarnation and redemptive work of God's Son.

"Now" (v. 10a) refers to this age, in contrast with the time before Christ's first coming and the consummation of this age, when the final and full disclosure of God's redemptive plan is unveiled to all of his creatures. "Now" is not a point in time but the current era of eschatological inauguration (cf. 2:2; 3:5; esp. Rom 3:26; 5:9; Titus 2:11–12). What comes as something of a surprise is that the unveiling of God's mystery and wisdom is not (only) made on earth (cf. 6:19) but "to the rulers and authorities in the high-heavenlies." It may be assumed that these are only evil powers (cf. 6:12), but there is no reason to think that this is exclusively so (cf. Rev 12:1–12). God's redemption of his people has ever been of interest to the holy angels (1 Pet 1:12) and to the whole host of heaven (including the elect who have gone before; e.g., Heb 12:22–23), who give even more praise to God when they behold it in wonder (Psa 148; Rev 7:9–12; 19:1–8).

Yet the focus now in v. 10 on revelation of these things in heaven is that the risen Christ Jesus is on display at God's right hand in triumph (see on 1:20–22; cf. Col 2:15) despite pockets of resistance (6:12). There, among those "high-heavenly" rulers, eschatology is far less "inaugurated" than "consummated." Yet, sadly, the triumphant ascent of Christ and the free

---

74. Markovic sees delayed elements as primarily signaling and reinforcing the end of a colon* or period but allows for it functioning for emphasis or focus ("Hyperbaton," 132–33). Cf. esp. the notable example of hyperbaton already seen in 2:1–6. The emphasis in the subject is also marked with the emphatic, "poetic" adj. πολυποίκιλος, "(very) multifaceted"; see translation note and O'Brien, 245.

offer of eternal life is still hidden to most people on earth (e.g., 1 Cor 1:18; 2 Cor 4:3; 2 Thess 2:9–12).

The passive "make known" assumes that God is the one making his mystery and wisdom known to the celestial powers, but he uses an intermediary expressed in the phrase "through the church."[75] One might expect the revelatory mediators to be "apostles and prophets" (and teachers; 3:5, 4:11), but it is in the church's existence as a multicultural and multiethnic body dwelling in unity that the church witnesses to the power of the new creation.[76] This activity implies the critical fact that the earthly gatherings of God's people have a vital link with Christ in his high-heavenly exaltation, to where believers too have been raised and seated (2:6). Hence, the church is in essence both earthly and heavenly and is linked as a body to Christ its head through the Holy Spirit (Matt 18:20; Heb 12:22–24; Rev 1:13, 20; 2:1).[77]

3:11 *κατὰ πρόθεσιν τῶν αἰώνων ἣν ἐποίησεν ἐν τῷ Χριστῷ Ἰησοῦ τῷ κυρίῳ ἡμῶν*, "according to the eternal plan that he executed in Christ Jesus our Lord." Insofar as some of the "powers and authorities" addressed in v. 10 are in league with the spirit who formerly kept the Gentiles enslaved in death (2:1–2; cf. Heb 2:14–15), God executed his long-held plan to vindicate his elect before them in Christ at the Savior's own vindication in resurrection (Rom 3:25–26; 1 Tim 3:16).[78] Jewish literature roughly contemporary with Paul expressed the hope for vindication of faithful martyrs in their resurrection (e.g., 2 Macc 7 and *T. Mos.* 10), but the focus was on vindication before their tormentors in the world rather than before heavenly beings (also Rev 6:9–11). Here in v. 11, though, saints like Joshua the high priest

---

75. Cf. Rom 9:22–24 with several parallels of concepts with Ephesians: "What if God, desiring to show his wrath and *to make known* his power, has endured with much patience vessels of wrath prepared for destruction, *in order to make known* the riches of his glory for vessels of mercy, which he has prepared beforehand for glory—even us whom he has called, not from the Jews only but also from the Gentiles?" (emphasis added).

76. Cf. O'Brien, 246, with references; Wallace, *Greek Grammar*, 434.

77. This is communicated in a novel way by representing and addressing seven local congregations through their "angels" in Rev 2–3 "to remind the churches that already a dimension of their existence is heavenly," G. K. Beale, *The Book of Revelation*, NIGTC (Grand Rapids: Eerdmans, 1999), 218.

78. Cf. Beale, *New Testament Biblical Theology*, 492–95. For similar ideas in Romans see J. R. Daniel Kirk, *Unlocking Romans: Resurrection and the Justification of God* (Grand Rapids: Eerdmans, 2008).

(Zech 3:1–5) are now vindicated before their satanic accusers, and the host of heaven wonders at the intervention of Christ and of his righteousness for his church (esp. 5:25–27; cf. Rev 12:7–12). Note that this was all according to God's "eternal plan that he executed in Christ Jesus our Lord" (3:11) in the fullness of time (1:10).

3:12 ἐν ᾧ ἔχομεν τὴν παρρησίαν καὶ προσαγωγὴν ἐν πεποιθήσει, "in whom we have bold access with confidence." This verse forms a very quick period, with only two cola* and twenty-eight syllables.[79] Obviously, Paul is moving fast in transition to the end of the long digression spanning vv. 1–13. This also accounts for the same colon* structure in v. 13 as well, as can be seen in the following (with syllable count in parentheses):

> [12] ἐν ᾧ ἔχομεν τὴν παρρησίαν καὶ προσαγωγὴν ἐν πεποιθήσει (20)
> διὰ τῆς πίστεως αὐτοῦ (8)
>
> [13] διὸ αἰτοῦμαι μὴ ἐγκακεῖν ἐν ταῖς θλίψεσίν μου ὑπὲρ ὑμῶν (19)
> ἥτις ἐστὶν δόξα ὑμῶν (8)

Besides its intrinsic interest for compositional analysis, there is a point to this analysis, which will be pointed out in the discussion of διὰ τῆς πίστεως αὐτοῦ below.

As v. 7 above was unified around words beginning with δ- (*delta*), this period of v. 12 arrests us with four words that begin with plosive *pi*: **π**αρρησίαν ... **π**ροσαγωγὴν ... **π**εποιθήσει ... **π**ίστεως (cf. 1:23). Boldness, access, and confidence (cf. 2 Cor 3:4; Phil 3:9) are all the supreme outcome of God's work for his elect in Christ and received by faith alone. In him believers confidently approach God in prayer, knowing that he attends to them from his "throne of grace" (cf. 2:18; Heb 4:16; 10:19; Rom 5:2).[80] The church has the ear of the sovereign King of creation, who listens with real interest

---

79. In contrast, for example, v. 5 contains forty-four syllables, and many of the other cola* in vv. 1–11 are longer than those in vv. 12–13. Though these cola* are equal or nearly equal in syllable length, they do not seem to form a case of *isocolon* because they are not coordinated grammatically; cf. Lausberg, *Literary Rhetoric*, §§719–24.

80. The opposite is a timorous faith that wavers in unbelief, as illustrated, for example, by the wavering father of a demon-possessed boy in Mark 9:22–24 and the kind of "faith" that James characterizes as being δίψυχος ("bi-souled" or "of two minds"; Jas 1:6–8).

and compassion to those who are now members of his own family (2:19; cf. Exod 3:7, 9; Psa 103:13; Rev 5:8; 8:3).

διὰ τῆς πίστεως αὐτοῦ, "through our faith in him." The referent of αὐτός ("him") in this phrase is undoubtedly "Christ Jesus our Lord" from v. 11b, which is also the antecedent of the relative pronoun ἐν ᾧ ("in whom") that begins v. 12. The relation of the genitive pronoun (αὐτοῦ) to its head noun (πίστις) in the phrase διὰ τῆς πίστεως αὐτοῦ, "through faith *in him*," has been discussed at great length over the past thirty years or so (cf. Hoehner, 466–67; Best, 226, 330; Barth, 347, O'Brien, 249n114; Wallace, *Greek Grammar*, 115–16). (For elaboration on the discussion, see "Additional Exegetical Comments" below.) The translation here takes "him" as the object of faith, "through our believing in him" (cf. 1:15; 2:8), and therefore takes the genitive as objective (as, e.g., Lincoln, 190), though many other interpretations have been proposed. Origen, the first commentator on Ephesians and an accomplished Greek speaker, also takes the genitive in this phrase as objective by paraphrasing it as ἡ πίστις ἡ εἰς τὸν Χριστόν, "faith which is in Christ."[81]

The entire final colon*, διὰ τῆς πίστεως αὐτοῦ, is a short eight syllables, in keeping with the colon* structure of both v. 12 and v. 3, noted above, as Paul moves quickly to wrap up his digression (vv. 1–13). The point is that analysis of the genitive relation between πίστις and αὐτοῦ should take these types of compositional factors into consideration when analyzing a phrase like this (but it typically is not). Our phrase, διὰ τῆς πίστεως αὐτοῦ, was intentionally a kind of shorthand for the sake of brevity. Paul could have written an unambiguous phrase like διὰ τῆς καθ' ὑμᾶς πίστεως ἐν τῷ κυρίῳ Ἰησοῦ ("through your faith in the Lord Jesus"), much like the phrase above in 1:15.[82] However, this would have taken too long for his purpose—i.e., doubling the

81. The larger statement in this regard is interesting: "It is a great thing not simply to have boldness, but boldness in confidence, and access because of our certainty, again, in confidence. And the foundation [ἀρχή; cf. Heb 3:14] of our confident boldness and access is our faith in Christ. We have often said that the one who does everything with reason has put his trust in Christ the Logos (πεπίστευκεν εἰς τὸν Χριστὸν Λόγον), and the one who has grasped wisdom has put his trust in Christ our Wisdom" (my trans.; Greek text from TLG).

82. Eph 1:15 reads: Διὰ τοῦτο κἀγὼ ἀκούσας / τὴν καθ' ὑμᾶς πίστιν ἐν τῷ κυρίῳ Ἰησοῦ / καὶ τὴν ἀγάπην τὴν εἰς πάντας τοὺς ἁγίους, "For this reason, when I received word of your faith in the Lord Jesus and of your love for all the saints." The objs. of πίστις and ἀγάπη are both clarified by prepositional phrases.

colon* syllable count from eight to sixteen—so he used a shorthand form nicely afforded by the objective genitive, which is as clear from context as ἐν φόβῳ Χριστοῦ in 5:21 signifies the believer's fear of Christ not Christ's own fear. (Again, see also "Additional Exegetical Comments" below.)

3:13 διὸ αἰτοῦμαι μὴ ἐγκακεῖν ἐν ταῖς θλίψεσίν μου ὑπὲρ ὑμῶν, "Wherefore, I ask you not to lose heart at my tribulations on your behalf." In grammar, the subject of the infinitive ἐγκακεῖν must be supplied from context, and all major English versions add "you" as the subject of "lose heart."[83] Jerome thinks this is possible but prefers to see Paul as the subject: " 'Wherefore I ask that *I* do not lose heart in my afflictions for you,' etc. This, therefore, is what the apostle asks for and earnestly seeks from the Lord, that he does not lose heart in his distresses" (Origen and Jerome, 152; emphasis added). This view, however, is not likely and out of accord with the overall thrust of vv. 1–13, in which Paul seeks to assure his audience at the possible problem of his imprisonment.[84] Paul seems more interested in the discouragement of his Gentile converts than of himself: "If we are afflicted, it is for your comfort and salvation; and if we are comforted, it is for your comfort. ... Therefore, having this ministry by the mercy of God, we do not lose heart" (2 Cor 1:6; 4:1).

ἥτις ἐστὶν δόξα ὑμῶν, "which is your glory."[85] In the genitive phrase δόξα ὑμῶν ("which is your glory"), δόξα is unexpectedly anarthrous with the genitive pronoun (ὑμῶν, "your").[86] It could be that the article was dropped for the sake of the rhythm, but the real effect is that there is a slight pause in midcolon (caused by the conj. of the liquid-plosive combination ν-δ in ἐστὶν

83. As though Paul had written αἰτοῦμαι **ὑμᾶς** μὴ ἐγκακεῖν; cf. Calvin, 165; Hodge, 176–77; Lincoln, 191; Best, 330–31 (but assumed pseudonymous authorship becomes a main determiner of the text's meaning for Best—a frequent problem in modern works).

84. Interestingly, Jerome's Vg. reads like the modern consensus: *Propter quod peto ne deficiatis* ["that *you* not faint"] *in tribulationibus meis pro uobis*.

85. Origen points out that the relative pronoun is sg. (ἥτις, "which") when it should be pl. in agreement with θλίψεις, "tribulations" (Origen and Jerome, 152), but this is a case where the subject pronoun agrees with the predicate noun (δόξα, "glory"); BDF, §132.

86. In the vast majority of cases such a noun is articular (**ἡ** δόξα ὑμῶν) as nearby διὰ **τῆς** πίστεως αὐτοῦ ("through [our] faith in him"; v. 12) or ἐν **ταῖς** θλίψεσίν μου ("in my tribulations"; v. 13).

δόξα, which could be avoided by using the article: ἐστὶν ἡ δόξα). This makes the last two words pronounced with stress on both: "which is … *glory* … *for you*." Why? Because Paul is showing how his imprisonment is not at all a sign of the failure of his gospel or of Christ's exaltation to all power—it is just the opposite.[87] It is their glory that Paul suffers tribulations in order that the power of God may be revealed in the apostle's weakness (2 Cor 12:9; 13:4; cf. 1 Cor 15:43). Paul did not suffer because he was a criminal, but "for your sakes" (cf. above v. 1 and 2 Cor 1:6). Christ had specially honored the Gentiles by appointing an apostle for them who would willingly lay down his life for their sakes in imitation of Christ (Col 1:24–29; Acts 9:15; Rom 11:13; 1 Tim 2:7).

As stated in the introduction, Paul is concerned in this long passage to assure his Gentile audience that their redemption is secure even though he is in prison. God has not abandoned Paul or them. He supports this by showing that this divine work had remained hidden from previous ages and is only now being disclosed in an inaugurated way.

Application and Devotional Implications

As Paul assures his audience from prison of Christ's supreme rule, he reminds us that we too live our lives and serve the Lord in the light of the cross. God has ever preferred to use weak instruments to conquer his enemies. One has only to think of Gideon and how the Lord was not willing to use the whole army to defeat Midian but sifted them down to Gideon and a mere one hundred men (Judg 7). God has not changed. He uses *us* to glorify his name, even though we are much more "the very least of all saints" (3:8) than was Paul. By realizing this, we too will not lose heart at the opposition to the gospel and to us as Christ's people that we will face. "If the world hates you, know that it has hated me before it hated you. If you were of the world, the world would love you as its own; but because you are not of the world, but I chose you out of the world, therefore the world hates you" (John 15:18–19).

---

87. Cf. Peter W. Gosnell, "Honor and Shame Rhetoric as a Unifying Motif in Ephesians," *BBR* 16 (2006): 105–28; for Eph 3:1–13 see pp. 118–19.

Additional Exegetical Comments: Faith in/of Christ

As mentioned in the comment on 3:12, there is a longstanding debate on the meaning of a genitive phrase in Paul's writings, διὰ πίστεως Χριστοῦ ("through faith [in/of] Christ")—with minor variations—in Rom 3:22, 26; Gal 2:16 (2x), 20, 22; Phil 3:9. The issue is often referenced as the "*pistis Christou* debate."[88] The phrase διὰ τῆς πίστεως αὐτοῦ in Eph 3:12 is not usually treated in the discussion because many scholars regard Ephesians as post-Pauline, but it is relevant nevertheless.[89] In a nutshell, the debate arose when scholars read the phrase πίστις Χριστοῦ as referring not to the believer's "faith in Christ" (objective gen.), but to some sort of "faith" or "faithfulness" of Christ himself (subjective gen.). The outcome of the analysis of the genitive relationship of these two words leads sometimes to breathtakingly overstated claims that it "lays the groundwork for an entirely different paradigm in the theology of the NT."[90] While the study of a couple of isolated Greek *commata* (phrases) hardly results in such sweeping changes to a Protestant theology forged sometimes at great cost by many centuries of ardent students of the Bible, it is worth spending a little time on the meaning of διὰ τῆς πίστεως αὐτοῦ (Χριστοῦ) ("through faith in him/Christ") in Eph 3:12.

88. See the collection of essays in Michael F. Bird and Preston M. Sprinkle, eds., *The Faith of Jesus Christ: Exegetical, Biblical, and Theological Studies* (Peabody, MA: Hendrickson, 2009), where the "The *Pistis Christou* Debate" appears on the cover near the title. This book provides a lengthy bibliography (309–30) on an issue that has generated much discussion since the first edition in 1983 of Richard B. Hays, *The Faith of Jesus Christ: The Narrative Substructure of Galatians 3:1–4:11*, 2nd ed., BRS (Grand Rapids: Eerdmans, 2002).

89. So also Paul Foster, "The First Contribution to the πίστις Χριστοῦ Debate: A Study of Ephesians 3.12," *JSNT* 85 (2002): 75-96; Foster, "Πίστις Χριστοῦ Terminology in Philippians and Ephesians," in *Faith of Jesus Christ*, 91–109; and Richard H. Bell, "Faith in Christ: Some Exegetical and Theological Reflections on Philippians 3:9 and Ephesians 3:12," in *Faith of Jesus Christ*, 111–46.

90. Sigve Tonstad, "Πιστις Χριστου: Reading Paul in a New Paradigm," *AUSS* 40 (2002): 37–59 (quote from 57). A similar call to reevaluate Paul's whole theology on the basis of two words in his epistles was made earlier by Douglas A. Campbell, "Romans 1:17—A Crux Interpretum for the ΠΙΣΤΙΣ ΧΡΙΣΤΟΥ Debate," *JBL* 113 (1994): 265–85; yet see Brian Dodd, "Romans 1:17—A Crux Interpretum for the ΠΙΣΤΙΣ ΧΡΙΣΤΟΥ Debate?" *JBL* 114 (1995): 470–73.

Let me begin by mentioning summarily my own orientation to the issue regarding the phrase διὰ τῆς πίστεως αὐτοῦ in 3:12 and more broadly to "the *pistis Christou* debate." For starters, there is often discussion of whether "grammar" or "exegesis" is the main determiner of the genitive's meaning (e.g., Winer, *Grammar*, 232). This could be refined to be more helpful. In general, a genitive substantive relates to its head substantive in any possible way the referents of these two terms may relate granting the phrase is not technical or idiomatic.[91] The genitive itself simply connects the two words. The genitive relationship itself in this situation must be determined from the meanings of the words and from various other contextual factors. Hence, in ἡ πίστις αὐτοῦ the personal pronoun (αὐτοῦ) relates to its head substantive (πίστις) in any way that a person can relate to the referent of πίστις. This means that the meaning of πίστις in Eph 3:12 is a limiting factor in the genitive relationship.[92]

As an aside, the presence of the article in the phrase διὰ **τῆς** πίστεως αὐτοῦ (3:12) or its lack in other related phrases (e.g., διὰ πίστεως Ἰησοῦ; Rom 3:22; Gal 2:16) has been understood by some to signal the nature of the genitive relationship.[93] Unfortunately, this has sometimes been treated

---

91. Cf. Smyth, *Greek Grammar*, §1295. This excludes words in a gen. that relate to verbs or that fall in other parts of speech, like the gen. abs.* construction. "Referents" assumes that the words in the construction are not self-referential (onomatopoeia) and therefore point to an obj., person, event, conception, quality, etc., in the world. Here "substantive" particularly includes nouns, substantive adjs., and pronouns. Substantive ptcs. would require more refinement. In technical or idiomatic phrases ("Son of Man," "man of sin," "children of wrath," etc.), the whole phrase carries a meaning often slightly detatched from or independent of the lexis of each term. This would be similar to English phrases like "piece of cake," "heat of the moment," "drop of the hat," "ball of fire," etc.

92. In other phrases, of course, the referent of the gen. word can also limit or signal the meaning of the gen. relation. For example, ἐν … πίστει ἀληθείας (2 Thess 2:13) can be rendered "in genuine faith" (adj. gen.), where the gen. word denotes a quality or characteristic (though most English versions take this particular gen. as adj., "belief in the truth"). It is also possible to take the head noun as modifying the gen. word: ἐν πίστει ἐλπίδος (Sir 49:10 "with confident hope"; RSV). I call this the "reversed adjectival gen."; S. M. Baugh, *A First John Reader: Intermediate Greek Reading Notes and Grammar* (Phillipsburg, NJ: P&R, 1999), 101–2; cf. Lausberg, *Literary Rhetoric*, §521 (ἀντίπτωσις).

93. See esp. Foster, who calls it a "grammatical rule" and "syntactical pattern" and says that the Greek article signals a subjective (versus objective) gen. (Foster, "First Contribution," 80). Hultgren thinks this factor is decisive in deciding the nature

too mechanically and without understanding the subtleties of Greek article usage that relate to prepositional phrases, personal names, and article usage with genitive personal pronouns.[94] There are well over two thousand examples in the NT of the Greek article used in a phrase where a genitive personal pronoun is attached to a substantive; hence, the article in διὰ **τῆς** πίστεως αὐτοῦ in 3:12 signals only that Paul is using Greek properly and has no unusual emphasis or semantic function signaling the meaning of the genitive relationship.[95] In the end, such "grammatical" solutions to the genitive relationship conundrum are unfruitful.[96]

So far, then, the phrase διὰ τῆς πίστεως αὐτοῦ is ordinary Greek in form.[97] The personal pronoun (αὐτοῦ) refers to "Christ Jesus our Lord" from v. 11b; hence, πίστις stands in relation to a person rather than to a quality or some

---

of the gen. relationship between πίστις and Χριστοῦ (A. J. Hultgren, "The *Pistis Christou* Formulation in Paul," *NovT* 22 [1980]: 248–63; esp. 253). I disagree.

94. For brief discussion of some of these article patterns, see "Excursus: Articular Χριστός as Messianic Title" below.

95. Article usage on substantives with gen. pronouns was also the norm in earlier periods of Greek (cf. Smyth, *Greek Grammar*, §1184). In Eph 3:11–13 alone there are two examples besides διὰ **τῆς** πίστεως αὐτοῦ of this use of the article: **τῷ** κυρίῳ ἡμῶν ("our Lord"; v. 11) and ἐν **ταῖς** θλίψεσίν μου ("in my tribulations"; v. 13). In fact, the few places where an article is *not* used call for comment as, for instance, (anarthrous) δόξα ὑμῶν in v. 13 (see comment). The word order in διὰ τῆς πίστεως αὐτοῦ (with the pronoun last) is also normal. Other word orders with different placement of the pronoun are occasionally found, ἐν τῷ **αὐτοῦ** αἵματι ("in his blood"; Rom 3:25; cf. Eph 5:28–29, 33) or **μου** τὴν χαρὰν ("my joy"; Phil 2:2; cf. Eph 6:9), but these are uncommon and signal emphasis or distinctive focus. (The word order in Eph 3:1 has a different meaning. In ὑπὲρ **ὑμῶν** τῶν ἐθνῶν, the substantive is appositive to the pronoun; woodenly: "on behalf of you, [namely] the Gentiles.") An interesting example of change of normal word order and lack of the article is σου ἀνήρ in John 4:18, where the meaning is "[the man you now have is not] *your* husband [but someone else's]"; cf. normal τὸν ἄνδρα σου in John 4:16. See also the comment on αὐτοῦ γάρ ἐσμεν ποίημα ("for we are *his* creation") in 2:10 above.

96. All of the key πίστις Χριστοῦ passages elsewhere in Paul occur with anarthrous πίστις yet within prepositional phrases (Rom 3:22, 26; Gal 2:16 [2x], 20, 22; Phil 3:9). One needs to recall that "The article is very often omitted in phrases containing a preposition" even with definite substantives (Smyth, *Greek Grammar*, §1128).

97. Cf. Roy A. Harrisville III, "Before ΠΙΣΤΙΣ ΧΡΙΣΤΟΥ: The Objective Genitive as Good Greek," *NovT* 48 (2006): 353–58, who shows places in classical authors where the objective gen. with πίστις is found and is therefore "good Greek," *contra* claims by Richard Hays in particular.

other kind of referent.[98] The meaning of πίστις that I preferred above renders it as "faith," where it points to belief or trust in someone.[99] I grant that other meanings are clearly possible for πίστις in other contexts, as brought out by the glosses: "faithfulness," "loyalty," "reliability," "commitment," "honesty," etc. (BADG, 818–20; LSJ, 1408). Yet, in all of these options, it is important to note that πίστις is connected to a verbal event of some sort, whether to a state or to a condition (e.g., "be reliable," "show loyalty") or to an act of trusting in someone, as I read it in Eph 3:12, and is communicated often in the NT for saving faith with the related verb πιστεύω and objects of this faith, marked by prepositions ἐν, εἰς, or ἐπί.[100]

Since πίστις has a verbal referent, the objective and subjective genitive relationship are possible notions for διὰ τῆς πίστεως αὐτοῦ, since the person denoted by αὐτοῦ can be conceived as either the subject of the event denoted by πίστις or to be its object. As the case stands, one can now only decide between these two genitive options by contextual factors, since the same phrase can be employed by the same author with either objective or subjective genitive meanings. As just one illustration among the dozens possible, take the following analogous phrase: γνῶσις θεοῦ, which means either knowledge that God has (subjective gen.; Rom 11:33) or knowledge

98. The well-known attempt to see Χριστοῦ as having an adj. quality in the *pistis Christou* phrase notably by Hultgren ("*Pistis Christou* Formulation"; "christic faith"; better would be "Messianic faith"?) is unpersuasive and does not relate to Eph 3:12, where αὐτοῦ cannot convey this idea. Likewise the less defined idea of an eschatological phenomenon or such ("Christ-faith"; cf. Preston M. Sprinkle, "Πιστίς Χριστοῦ as an Eschatological Event," in *Faith of Jesus Christ*, 165–84) also does not work here in Ephesians.

99. Cf. Wally V. Cirafesi, "ἔχειν πίστιν in Hellenistic Greek and Its Contribution to the πίστις Χριστοῦ Debate," *BAGL* 1 (2012): 5–37.

100. BDAG, 816–18 (esp. meaning 2). Other meanings of πίστις, such as commercial "credit," "safe-conduct," an "argument" in a speech, or a body of Christian beliefs or doctrine (Eph 4:5, 13; "the faith"), are not considered for Eph 3:12 as obviously ill-fitting to the context. It should be observed that often "obedience" is substituted for πίστις when it is taken as Christ's own "act of faithfulness" (cf. Barth, 273), which then becomes "Christ's obedience to the Father's will" (Foster, "First Contribution," 93). This seems to push this lexeme* into the realm of ὑπακοή ("obedience," in contrast with παρακοή), where it does not wish to go even though Paul certainly does speak of Christ's obedience (ὑπακοή) as the ground of justification of the believer (Rom 5:19 and context). Cf. εἰς τὴν ὑπακοὴν τοῦ Χριστοῦ (2 Cor 10:5; "to obey Christ"; ESV), where Christ is the person obeyed (objective gen.), not the one rendering obedience (subjective gen.).

where God is the person known (objective gen.; 2 Cor 10:5). Likewise, πίστις θεοῦ can refer to God's fidelity to his word and general trustworthiness (Rom 3:3; in contrast with ἡ ἀπιστία αὐτῶν, "their infidelity," a subjective gen., "they were untrusting") or to "trust in God" (Mark 11:22 and the πίστις Χριστοῦ passages?).[101]

Hence, I grant that the subjective genitive reading of πίστις Χριστοῦ and of ἡ πίστις αὐτοῦ here in Eph 3:12 is quite possible in other contexts. But Christ's "faith" or "trust" in his Father is not elaborated on by Paul anywhere and has no salvific value to "those who believe in Christ Jesus" (Eph 1:1). Hence, to read πίστις as referencing Christ's "faith" versus possibly his "fidelity" or "faithfulness" is not compelling or warranted by the context of Eph 3:12. On the other hand, Christ's obedience to his Father's will and to the "task" (ἔργον) mandated of him as the believer's substitutionary Mediator is both biblical (e.g., John 4:34; 5:30; 6:38–39; 17:4) and Pauline (e.g., Rom 5:12–21; 2 Thess 3:3), even though Paul could have easily said this more clearly by writing διὰ τῆς ὑπακοῆς αὐτοῦ ("through his obedience") rather than with πίστις if that were his meaning.[102]

Even though the idea of Christ's faithfulness is biblical, and the words of the target phrase in Eph 3:12 could mean "through his fidelity" or the like (e.g., Barth, 326), nevertheless, previous statements in Ephesians and factors in the immediate context still lead me to take πίστις in Eph 3:12 as referring to the believer's faith and, hence, αὐτοῦ (Christ) as the object of this

101. For the first meaning see the LXX for τὴν πίστιν τοῦ Σιμωνος, "Simon's faithfulness" (1 Macc 14:35 RSV), where Simon Maccabaeus' deeds are recounted in context, including τὴν πίστιν, "his loyalty" to his nation. There are many unobjectionable examples of objective gens. with πίστις, such as Acts 3:16; Phil 1:27; Col 2:12; Jas 2:1; Rev 14:12. In Ephesians, see the interesting if not exactly analogous ἡ ἐλπὶς τῆς κλήσεως αὐτοῦ ("the hope to which *he has called* you"; 1:18), where gen. αὐτοῦ is subjective and the verbal idea of "calling" is act., but ἡ ἐλπὶς τῆς κλήσεως ὑμῶν ("the hope to which *you have been called*"; Eph 4:4), where ὑμῶν is subjective with a pass. verbal idea (cf. Eph 4:1, which clarifies this interpretation of the gen.).

102. From very early days Protestant theology (including Luther and Calvin in seminal form) has articulated that the "active obedience" of Christ in perfect fulfillment of God's law is imputed to believers as their only righteousness before God in justification; see R. Scott Clark, "Do This and Live: Christ's Active Obedience as the Ground of Justification," in *Covenant, Justification and Pastoral Ministry: Essays by the Faculty of Westminster Seminary California*, ed. R. Scott Clark (Phillipsburg, NJ: P&R, 2007) 229–65; cf. John Murray, "The Obedience of Christ," in *Collected Writings* (Carlisle, PA: Banner of Truth, 1977) 2:156–57.

faith.[103] One of these reasons was mentioned above in the comment on v. 12: Paul is writing in short cola* as he speeds to the end of the section ending in the next verse (v. 13). The phrase constituting the last colon* of v. 12 (διὰ τῆς πίστεως αὐτοῦ) is a very brief eight syllables, in keeping with the brevity in the surrounding context in contrast with something less ambiguous along the lines of διὰ τῆς καθ' ὑμᾶς πίστεως ἐν τῷ κυρίῳ Ἰησοῦ (see 1:15), διὰ τῆς πίστεως τῆς ἐν αὐτῷ, or the like. Paul is writing succinctly here and expects the objective genitive to be clear enough from the context, much as he did with both θεοῦ in the phrase κατὰ τῆς γνώσεως τοῦ θεοῦ ("[arrayed] against knowing God") and Χριστοῦ in the phrase εἰς τὴν ὑπακοὴν τοῦ Χριστοῦ ("to obey Christ")—both objective gens.—in 2 Cor 10:5 (cf. 2 Thess 3:5).

Part of the context for our reading of Eph 3:12 comes from earlier in Ephesians. In support of a different reading of 3:12 as referring to Christ's faithfulness (or faith), some scholars (e.g., Barth and Foster) want "faith" in Eph 2:8 also to refer to Christ's faithfulness or obedience. While salvation by grace through faith (v. 8a) is a divine gift (θεοῦ τὸ δῶρον, v. 8c), the believer *believes* in trust and confident reliance (3:12) on the Savior for this complete salvation. The opposition in Eph 2:8–9 is a classic Pauline "faith" versus "works" dichotomy: διὰ πίστεως ... οὐκ ἐξ ἔργων ("through faith ... not from works"; 2:8–9; cf. Rom 3:28; 9:32; Gal 2:16; 3:5). The word ἔργα in 2:9 (οὐκ ἐξ ἔργων) must refer to the works *of the believer*, hence πίστις refers to the believer's faith as well because, for Christ, this salvation earned for his people *was* by works in obedience to his Father's will. To read these verses as saying: "[F]or by grace you are saved *through the faithfulness of Christ*" must go on to say "*not from (Christ's) works*, so that no one may boast," which is patent nonsense.

One helpful step in the exegetical process is to ask how an author would have expressed an alternative idea. In this case, how would Paul have expressed the notion of Christ's own πίστις in v. 12 rather than that of the believer? The answer is easy and would have fit the brevity of his statements in 3:12–13 very well: διὰ τῆς πίστεως. Here the article is not required

103. For other Pauline passages see R. Barry Matlock, "The Rhetoric of πίστις in Paul: Galatians 2.16, 3.22, Romans 3.22, and Philippians 3.9," *JSNT* 30 (2007): 173–203, which has some interesting structural observations on the texts in question.

in the construction, as it is when the genitive personal pronoun is added.[104] The meaning could easily be taken as "through *his* faithfulness," with the article understood as conveying the notion of a personal pronoun from context—though, admittedly, it could as well mean "through *our* faith." There is an interesting analogous example of this in Matthew: ἀπὸ δὲ τοῦ φόβου αὐτοῦ ἐσείσθησαν, "they shook violently in (their) fear of him" (Matt 28:4); and ἀπὸ τοῦ φόβου ἔκραξαν, "they cried out in *their* fear" (Matt 14:26).[105] The first example is identical with how I am taking the analogous phrase in Eph 3:12, and the second shows how Paul could have expressed the other idea easily.

To show the form of the text once again, the period of which διὰ τῆς πίστεως αὐτοῦ is a part reads as follows:

> (ἣν ἐποίησεν ἐν τῷ Χριστῷ Ἰησοῦ τῷ κυρίῳ ἡμῶν)
> 12 ἐν ᾧ ἔχομεν τὴν παρρησίαν καὶ προσαγωγὴν ἐν πεποιθήσει
> διὰ τῆς πίστεως αὐτοῦ

Here the "bold access with confidence" is the believer's because it is "in our Lord Jesus Christ," which is how the opening relative pronoun clause functions: ἐν τῷ Χριστῷ Ἰησοῦ τῷ κυρίῳ ἡμῶν **ἐν ᾧ** (vv. 11–12). After referencing Christ with ἐν ᾧ in v. 13, Paul then moves to the confidence and access into God's presence, which "faith in him" brings through the gospel. This then leads directly into v. 13, where this confident faith of the Ephesians leads them "not to lose heart at my tribulations on your behalf." Therefore, because Christ's role as mediator has already been indicated by ἐν ᾧ in v. 12, the πίστις later in the verse in the phrase διὰ τῆς πίστεως αὐτοῦ most likely refers to the faith the believer exercises as the means for appropriating confident, bold access to the Father "in Christ."

Finally, the structure of the text and ideas in 3:11–12 turn out to be very similar to what Paul says in 1:12–13: ἐν τῷ Χριστῷ ἐν ᾧ καὶ ὑμεῖς ἀκούσαντες … ἐν ᾧ καὶ πιστεύσαντες ("in the Messiah in whom you as well, when you heard … in whom also when you believed"). It is believers who believe (cf. Eph 1:13,

---

104. See above on articles regularly used when a substantive is qualified with a gen. personal pronoun. Perhaps saying the article is "required" is too strong, but it certainly is a pattern of usage in, I would guess, 95 percent of the instances of this construction.

105. For other examples of φόβος with an objective gen. see John 19:38; 20:19; Acts 9:31; Rom 3:18; 2 Cor 5:11; 7:1; 1 Pet 3:14; Rev 18:10, 15.

15, 19; 3:17; 4:13; 6:16, 23), not Christ. Yes, he was faithful and obedient, and he trusted his Father and entrusted himself to him (cf. John 2:24), but when Paul elaborates on how the Mediator's work relates to the redemption he accomplished, he states that it was effected through the cross, redemption, blood, death, exaltation to all rule, etc. (e.g., 1:7, 20–23; 2:5–6, 13–14, 16), not to Christ's own πίστις per se.

Selected Bibliography

Bird, M., and P. Sprinkle, eds. *The Faith of Jesus Christ: Exegetical, Biblical, and Theological Studies*. Peabody, MA: Hendrickson, 2009.

Brown, R. *The Semitic Background of the Term "Mystery" in the New Testament*. Philadelphia: Fortress, 1968.

Caragounis, C. *The Ephesian* Mysterion: *Meaning and Context*. CB 8. Lund: CWK Gleerup, 1977.

Cirafesi, W. "ἔχειν πίστιν in Hellenistic Greek and Its Contribution to the πίστις Χριστοῦ Debate." *BAGL* 1 (2012): 5–37.

Clark, R. S. "Do This and Live: Christ's Active Obedience as the Ground of Justification." In *Covenant, Justification and Pastoral Ministry: Essays by the Faculty of Westminster Seminary California*, edited by R. S. Clark, 229–65. Phillipsburg, NJ: P&R, 2007.

Foster, P. "The First Contribution to the πίστις Χριστοῦ Debate: A Study of Ephesians 3.12." *JSNT* 85 (2002): 75–96 .

Gombis, T. "Ephesians 3:2–13: Pointless Digression, or Epitome of the Triumph of God in Christ?" *WTJ* 66 (2004): 313–23.

Goodrich, J. "Paul, the *Oikonomos* of God: Paul's Apostolic Metaphor in 1 Corinthians and Its Greco-Roman Context." PhD diss., Durham University, 2010.

Gosnell, P. "Honor and Shame Rhetoric as a Unifying Motif in Ephesians." *BBR* 16 (2006): 105–28.

Harrisville, R. "Before ΠΙΣΤΙΣ ΧΡΙΣΤΟΥ: The Objective Genitive as Good Greek." *NovT* 48 (2006): 353–58.

Hays, R. *The Faith of Jesus Christ: The Narrative Substructure of Galatians 3:1–4:11*. 2nd ed. BRS. Grand Rapids: Eerdmans, 2002; first ed., 1983.

Hultgren, A. "The *Pistis Christou* Formulation in Paul." *NovT* 22 (1980): 248–63.

Kim, S. *The Origin of Paul's Gospel*. Eugene, OR: Wipf & Stock, 2007; first published 1982.

Kirk, J. R. D. *Unlocking Romans: Resurrection and the Justification of God*. Grand Rapids: Eerdmans, 2008.

Lincoln, A. *Paradise Now and Not Yet*. Grand Rapids: Baker, 1981.

Mare, W. "Paul's Mystery in Ephesians 3." *BETS* 8 (1965): 77–84.

Martin, D. *Slavery as Salvation: The Metaphor of Slavery in Pauline Christianity*. New Haven, CT: Yale University Press, 1990.

Mouritsen, H. *The Freedman in the Roman World*. New York: Cambridge University Press, 2011.

Reumann, J. "OIKONOMIA = 'COVENANT'; Terms for *Heilsgeschichte* in Early Christian Usage." *NovT* 3 (1959): 282–92.

———. "Οἰκονομία-Terms in Paul in Comparison with Lucan *Heilsgeschichte*." *NTS* 13 (1967): 147–67.

Rogers, G. *The Mysteries of Artemis of Ephesos: Cult, Polis, and Change in the Graeco-Roman World*. New Haven, CT: Yale University Press, 2012.

Sherwood, A. "Paul's Imprisonment as the Glory of the *Ethnē*: A Discourse Analysis of Ephesians 3:1–13." *BBR* 22 (2012): 97–112.

Tajra, H. *The Martyrdom of St. Paul*. WUNT 2.67. Tübingen: Mohr Siebeck, 1994.

———. *The Trial of St. Paul: A Judicial Exegesis of the Second Half of the Acts of the Apostles*. WUNT 2.35. Tübingen: Mohr Siebeck, 1989.

Tonstad, S. "Πιστις Χριστου: Reading Paul in a New Paradigm." *AUSS* 40 (2002): 37–59.

Vos, G. "The Idea of Biblical Theology as a Science and as a Theological Discipline." In *Redemptive History and Biblical Interpretation*, 3–24. Phillipsburg, NJ: P&R, 1975.

Wansink, C. *Chained in Christ: The Experience and Rhetoric of Paul's Imprisonments*. JSNTSS 130. Sheffield: Sheffield Academic, 1996.

Wolter, M. "Verborgene Weisheit und Heil für die Heiden. Zur Traditionsgeschichte und Intention des 'Revelationsschemas.'" *ZTK* 84 (1987): 297–319.

Paul's Resumed Prayer (3:14–21)

Introduction

In Ephesians 3:14–21 Paul resumes his praise to the Father from v. 1 and reports on his prayers that God would dwell with his audience and that they would grow in love and knowledge of the Lord. As shown in the discussion of the previous passage, vv. 14–21 expresses what Paul had begun to say earlier in v. 1; hence, this section is a resumption of thought that Paul had broken off with a digression in vv. 2–13.

The transition out of a digression (παρέκβασις) is called an ἄφοδος ("return"; also, "departure") by rhetoricians.[1] Some digressions can be quite long.[2] For example, the Greek historian Polybius has a long digression in which he justifies his huge work on the Punic Wars for its unity of narrative and edifying benefits (Polybius, *Hist.* 3.31–32), then he reorients the reader with a quick note: "I interrupted my narrative to enter on this digression (τὴν γὰρ παρέκβασιν ἐντεῦθεν ἐποιησάμεθα) at the point where the Roman ambassadors were at Carthage" (Polybius, *Hist.* 3.33.1).[3] In comparison with just this one from Polybius, Paul's digression in vv. 2–13 is quite brief, and he simply reorients to his point by repeating τούτου χάριν from v. 1 in the opening of v. 14.

---

1. Quintilian, *Inst.* 9.3.87; Heinrich Lausberg, *Handbook of Literary Rhetoric: A Foundation for Literary Study*, ed. David E. Orton and R. Dean Anderson (Boston: Brill, 1998), §340.
2. Romans 6–7 is a digression. Hence, Rom 8:1 continues from 5:21 in what would otherwise be a seamless text.
3. To give a better sense of how long this digression in Polybius is, it is about one-third the size of Paul's whole epistle to the Ephesians (roughly 700 words to nearly 2,500 words in Ephesians). See another of Polybius' long digressions on historical method, which he places (frustratingly!) just at the point where Hannibal and Publius Scipio are about to engage in a critical battle in Italy (Polybius, *Hist.* 3.57–59).

This section is itself a form of intercessory prayer (or "intercessory prayer-report").[4] It certainly opens with that in mind in vv. 14–15; yet, like 1:15–23 earlier, in vv. 16–19 Paul speaks to his audience ("that he may grant you"; v. 16) rather than to God and thereby allows them to listen in as he intercedes for them, and Paul seems to transition into a report of his prayer on their behalf and to the content of what he wants God to give them. Prayer, petition, praise, intercession, and thanksgiving (6:18; cf. Phil 4:6; 1 Tim 2:1–2) are behind what is said, and it is finished off with a blessing of God in vv. 20–21 (a form of prayer), which concludes the whole of the first half of the epistle. Hence, this section is both a prayer report and a form of prayer mixed together.

Like other previous passages, the division of this composition into periods and cola* comes with a certain amount of flexibility of interpretation, particularly with monocolon or bicolon verses like vv. 14–5, 18, or 19 that fit a more conversational than periodic Greek style.[5] The following is a suggested division, with the understanding that it may not perfectly capture the original presentation:

A
14 τούτου χάριν κάμπτω τὰ γόνατά μου πρὸς τὸν πατέρα
15 ἐξ οὗ πᾶσα πατριὰ ἐν οὐρανοῖς καὶ ἐπὶ γῆς ὀνομάζεται

B
16 ἵνα δῷ ὑμῖν κατὰ τὸ πλοῦτος τῆς δόξης αὐτοῦ
δυνάμει κραταιωθῆναι διὰ τοῦ πνεύματος αὐτοῦ
εἰς τὸν ἔσω ἄνθρωπον

C
17 κατοικῆσαι τὸν Χριστὸν διὰ τῆς πίστεως
ἐν ταῖς καρδίαις ὑμῶν
ἐν ἀγάπῃ ἐρριζωμένοι καὶ τεθεμελιωμένοι

---

4. Cf. Gordon P. Wiles, *Paul's Intercessory Prayers: The Significance of the Intercessory Prayer Passages in the Letters of Paul*, SNTSMS 24 (Cambridge: Cambridge University Press, 1974; repr., 2007) 156–258.

5. That the material in vv. 14–19 is "one long unwieldy sentence" (Best, 335) with "no logical structure, no clearly structuring elements" (Schnackenberg, 144) is too harsh (see the structure of Paul's requests in comments on v. 16). The flow of the sentence, though "rugged" in places, has many redeeming features in the ancient Greek aural experience. There are some nice observations along these lines for this passage in Witherington, 272–73.

D [18] ἵνα ἐξισχύσητε καταλαβέσθαι σὺν πᾶσιν τοῖς ἁγίοις
τί τὸ πλάτος καὶ μῆκος καὶ ὕψος καὶ βάθος
[19] γνῶναί τε τὴν ὑπερβάλλουσαν τῆς γνώσεως ἀγάπην τοῦ Χριστοῦ
ἵνα πληρωθῆτε εἰς πᾶν τὸ πλήρωμα τοῦ θεοῦ.

E [20] τῷ δὲ δυναμένῳ ὑπὲρ πάντα ποιῆσαι
ὑπερεκπερισσοῦ ὧν αἰτούμεθα ἢ νοοῦμεν
κατὰ τὴν δύναμιν τὴν ἐνεργουμένην ἐν ἡμῖν

F [21] αὐτῷ ἡ δόξα ἐν τῇ ἐκκλησίᾳ καὶ ἐν Χριστῷ Ἰησοῦ
εἰς πάσας τὰς γενεὰς τοῦ αἰῶνος τῶν αἰώνων
ἀμήν.

In general, vv. 14–21 contain two clear grammatical units: the long "sentence" in vv. 14–19 and the concluding blessing of God in vv. 20–21.[6] This passage differs from some of the previous sections and divisions by containing two rather long cola* at the beginning (vv. 14–15) that are unified in content as well as somewhat in sound: ... **π**ρὸς τὸν **π**ατέρα (v. 14) ἐξ οὗ **π**ᾶσα **π**ατριὰ (v. 15). Strictly speaking, Paul could have written κάμπτω τὰ γόνατά μου τῷ πατρί with the dative instead of πρὸς τὸν πατέρα as in Rom 11:4; 14:11, but πρὸς adds another word that opens with *pi*.

There seems to be some parallelism of expression in vv. 16 and 17 as follows:

[16b] ... κραταιωθῆναι
  διὰ τοῦ πνεύματος αὐτοῦ
    εἰς τὸν ἔσω ἄνθρωπον

[17] κατοικῆσαι ...
  διὰ τῆς πίστεως
    ἐν ταῖς καρδίαις ὑμῶν

This does seem somewhat attractive, especially with "in your inner man" (v. 16c) and "in your hearts" (v. 17b) explaining each other and with the concluding colon* (ἐν ἀγάπῃ ἐρριζωμένοι καὶ τεθεμελιωμένοι, "and that you may be rooted and founded in love") capping off the thoughts in both verses.

6. This corresponds to the division of the text in all four MSS surveyed in the Introduction (B, ℵ, A, and C).

Yet the parallelism is not exact in meaning everywhere (i.e., "through his Spirit" and "through faith"), and the infinitives are not parallel in function, so I will not press the resemblance of the two verses further.[7]

In the comments on vv. 20–21, I call these verses a "song," but it should be emphasized that this material does not match the regular metrical requirements for Greek hymnody. Nevertheless, it does have some interesting metrical features. For example, there is a definite rhythmical movement, as the first verse is longer than the second, yet it has many more short syllables.[8] This means that although verse 21 has fewer syllables (thirty-four to forty-three), it takes just a fraction longer to pronounce with its sixty-seven morae to the sixty-six morae of v. 20.[9] Finally, v. 20c has an interesting bit of rhythmical symmetry with two anapests and two cretics, and finishes with a bacchius: κατὰ τὴν δύναμιν τὴν ἐνεργουμένην ἐν ἡμῖν, ˘˘¯ | ˘˘¯ | ¯˘¯ | ¯˘¯ | ˘¯¯. I'm not sure how much of this was carefully crafted by Paul rather than the result of his native feel for the language, for the composition here seems rather more spontaneous than deliberate.

Outline

- VII. Paul's Resumed Prayer (3:14–21)
  - A. Posture of prayer before the Father (3:14–15)
  - B. Report of content of intercession for audience (3:16–19)
    - 1. For divine indwelling and love (3:16–17)
    - 2. For understanding (3:18–19)
  - C. Concluding blessing of God (3:20–21)

---

7. The first inf. (κραταιωθῆναι; v. 16b) is the obj. of ἵνα δῷ ("that he might grant"), while the second (κατοικῆσαι; v. 17a) is best taken as expressing result. See the translation note on v. 17.

8. Verse 20 has forty-three syllables, of which twenty are short, while v. 21 has thirty-four syllables, of which only five are short.

9. As a reminder, a mora is a measurement of a syllable's pronunciation time: a long syllable generally takes twice as long to pronounce as a short syllable, hence a long syllable is two mora and a short syllable is one.

Original Text

14 Τούτου χάριν κάμπτω τὰ γόνατά μου πρὸς τὸν πατέρα, **15** ἐξ οὗ πᾶσα πατριὰ ἐν οὐρανοῖς καὶ ἐπὶ γῆς ὀνομάζεται, **16** ἵνα δῷ ὑμῖν κατὰ τὸ πλοῦτος τῆς
δόξης αὐτοῦ δυνάμει κραταιωθῆναι διὰ τοῦ πνεύματος αὐτοῦ εἰς τὸν ἔσω ἄνθρωπον, **17** κατοικῆσαι τὸν Χριστὸν διὰ τῆς πίστεως ἐν ταῖς καρδίαις ὑμῶν, ἐν
ἀγάπῃ ἐρριζωμένοι καὶ τεθεμελιωμένοι, **18** ἵνα ἐξισχύσητε καταλαβέσθαι[a] σὺν
πᾶσιν τοῖς ἁγίοις τί τὸ πλάτος καὶ μῆκος καὶ ὕψος καὶ βάθος, **19** γνῶναί τε τὴν
ὑπερβάλλουσαν τῆς γνώσεως ἀγάπην τοῦ Χριστοῦ, ἵνα πληρωθῆτε[b] εἰς πᾶν τὸ
πλήρωμα τοῦ θεοῦ. **20** Τῷ δὲ δυναμένῳ ὑπὲρ[c] πάντα ποιῆσαι ὑπερεκπερισσοῦ
ὧν αἰτούμεθα ἢ νοοῦμεν κατὰ τὴν δύναμιν τὴν ἐνεργουμένην ἐν ἡμῖν, **21** αὐτῷ ἡ
δόξα ἐν τῇ ἐκκλησίᾳ καὶ ἐν Χριστῷ Ἰησοῦ εἰς πάσας τὰς γενεὰς τοῦ αἰῶνος τῶν
αἰώνων, ἀμήν.

Textual Notes

18.a. Instead of our text with the aorist infinitive καταλαβέσθαι ("to grasp") in the first colon*, P^{46} has the present infinitive καταλαμβάνεσθαι. The infinitive functions as the complement of ἐξισχύω ("be fully able to"), and though this is the only occurrence of compound ἐξισχύω in the NT, simple ἰσχύω ("able to") is followed by only an aorist infinitive complement in the NT, not the present, suggesting that the aorist, not the present, is the expected tense form here.

19.b. The final colon* reads ἵνα πληρωθῆτε εἰς πᾶν τὸ πλήρωμα τοῦ θεοῦ, "that you might be filled for all the fullness of God," but P^{46}, B, 33, 1175, and a few other witnesses have πληρωθῇ, "that all God's fullness might be filled up." Some other readings occur in this same phrase (e.g., πληροφορήθητε in 81), showing that scribes had difficulty with the sense of the original reading and created other options, unintentionally or otherwise. The accepted original reading (ἵνα πληρωθῆτε) has excellent external testimony in ℵ, A, C, D, F, G, K, L, P, Ψ, M, etc.

20.c. P^{46}, D, F, G, and a few other MSS omit ὑπὲρ ("far more") in the first colon* (3:20a), which replicates part of the compound preposition a few words later: ὑπερεκπερισσοῦ ("far more exceedingly). As Metzger notes, this was simple removal of redundancy and should be retained because it has excellent external attestation and marks the forceful speech of the original text of Ephesians.[10]

Translation

14 For this reason, I bow my knees before[11] the Father, **15** from whom the whole[12] family[13] in heaven and on earth receives its name,[14] **16** that[15] he may grant you to be strengthened[16] with power in accordance with the riches

10. Bruce M. Metzger, *A Textual Commentary on the Greek New Testament*, 2nd ed. (New York: United Bible Societies, 1994), 536.

11. For πρός, which has a relational ("friendly") or local ("in the presence of"; like πρὸς τὸν θεόν in John 1:1) sense here; cf. BDAG, 873–75 (esp. meaning 3d).

12. For this rendering and meaning of πᾶς here see comment.

13. Paul is engaging in a minor wordplay, since πατριά connects with πάτηρ in v. 14; i.e., a "paternal" group under one "Pater." Πατριά refers to a family, clan, or any group derived from a common father or ancestor; cf. BDAG, 788; Gottlob Schrenk, *TDNT*, 5:1015–19. Schrenk points out that πατριά and γενεά ("generation")—which can also sometimes be rendered "family"—occur near each other in Eph 3:15 and 3:21 as well as in the LXX of 1 Esd 5:37 and Esth 9:27. One does not want to make too much out of this, though. The interpretation that πατριά means "fatherhood" as an abstract concept is not a likely meaning of this noun; see Barth, 368 (esp. n. 2) and Best, 338.

14. Ὀνομάζω in general refers to calling or naming someone (i.e., "apostles" [Mark 3:14] or "Peter" [Luke 6:13]), but with ἐκ ("from") as here it refers to the derivation of a word (Xenophon, *Mem.* 4.5.12) or someone's patronymic: "calling each man by his lineage and his father's name" (*Il.* 10.68; πατρόθεν ἐκ γενεῆς ὀνομάζων ἄνδρα ἕκαστον); cf. BDAG, 714; LSJ, 1232–33. Hence Greek names like "Theodoros" ("Gift of God") or "Theophilos" ("Friend of God") would derive from "God." But naming things in Genesis is probably referenced here in Ephesians by Paul; see comment.

15. The ἵνα clause in vv. 16, 18 expresses the content of Paul's prayer as an alternative ὅτι or inf. clause; BDF, §388.

16. *Omicron*-contract verbs originated as causatives and often continued to convey that idea; hence, κραταιόω refers to *causing* someone or something to be strong (κραταιός). The gloss "become strong," as given in BDAG (564), is technically an inceptive idea bound up with the aor. form κραταιωθῆναι here in Eph 3:16. Such an inceptive meaning is also implied in the gloss "strengthen" so that any more overt inceptive rendering is overkill. This verb's other NT uses in Luke 1:80; 2:40 (both impf. indics.) and 1 Cor 16:13 (pres. impv.; cf. 2 Sam 10:12 LXX with aors.) show the stative meaning "be strong," though the mildly inceptive idea is common elsewhere (e.g., all four infs. of κραταιόω in the LXX are aor. and inceptive).

of his glory through his Spirit in your[17] inner man,[18] **17** so that Christ may take up his dwelling[19] in your hearts through faith and that you may be rooted and founded in love,[20] **18** that[21] you may be fully able to grasp[22] with all the saints what is the breadth and length and height and depth, **19** and likewise[23] to know the love of Christ that exceeds our understanding,[24] that

17. As commonly in Greek, and seen many times already in Ephesians, the article functions as a personal pronoun.

18. Ἄνθρωπος here refers to "man" (KJV, NASB) in its generic sense to include women as well. Hence some versions understandably prefer to render with "being" (ESV, NIV, NRSV). "Man" was chosen here in order to more clearly show its connection with the creation of the human race ("man") as explained in the comment.

19. The simple infinite κατοικῆσαι ("dwell") in v. 17 functions in one of two ways. It could express the result of the grant of divine strengthening in v. 16 ("so that"; as NASB, NIV, ESV), or it could be parallel with the inf. κραταιωθῆναι ("to be strengthened"; v. 16) without a conj. (asyndeton*; "and that"; NRSV). See the comment for reasons to prefer taking the inf. as expressing result. The aor. tense form of the inf. κατοικῆσαι conveys an inceptive idea here ("take up one's dwelling"; cf. Acts 7:2 and Col 1:19) in contrast with the pres.-tense inf. (κατοικεῖν, "dwell") found in Acts 17:26 (also pres. οἰκεῖν twice in 1 Cor 7:12–13). Generally one looks for an inceptive aor. in forms where the pres. tense is default, which is the case for κατοικέω, given that its LXX usage as an inf. predominates in the the pres.-tense form (38x compared with 6x as aor.); cf. Gen 13:6 and Psa 22(23):6 (pres.) with Gen 19:30 or 2 Sam 7:5 (aor.) and as well as the variant in Judg 18:1.

20. See the comment for taking the two ptcs. ἐρριζωμένοι and τεθεμελιωμένοι as parallel with the inf. κατοικῆσαι at the beginning of the verse.

21. The ἵνα clause expresses an obj. clause in v. 16 (see note there). We expect a conj. like καί or δέ to make this period parallel with v. 16, but this is a simple case of asyndeton* that is so prevalent in Ephesians.

22. For ἵνα ἐξισχύσητε καταλαβέσθαι, where I'm following BDAG for ἐξισχύω as an intensive idea for this compound verb form, which is unique to the NT: "to be fully capable of doing or experiencing someth[ing]" (BDAG, 350). Simple ἰσχύω or δύναμαι (e.g., v. 20 or **ἵνα** δυνηθῆτε in 6:13) are less intensive and more common ways to communicate "be able to." The verb καταλαμβάνω in the middle as here can refer to seizing a person or "grasping" an idea, among other things. For intellectual understanding as here in Eph 3:18 see Acts 4:13; 10:34; 25:25; John 1:5 (where a double meaning is intended); cf. BDAG, 519–20.

23. Τέ is a less common, more "literary" conj. than its cousin δέ (BDAG, 993; LSJ, 1763–65; BDF, §443).

24. The ptc. ὑπερβάλλουσαν ("immeasurable") is attributive, modifying ἀγάπην ("love"), and one might expect the statement τὴν ὑπερβάλλουσαν τῆς γνώσεως ἀγάπην τοῦ Χριστοῦ to mean "the immeasurable love of the knowledge of Christ," on analogy with the similar construction in 2:7 (cf. 1:19; 2 Cor 3:10; 9:14). But if that were the meaning, the word order would swap τῆς γνώσεως with ἀγάπην (τὴν

you may be filled to all the fullness of God. **20** Now to him who is able to accomplish[25] far more exceedingly than anything[26] we may request or imagine[27] in accordance with his power, which is at work[28] in us, **21** to him be the glory in the church and in Christ Jesus for all generations, forever and ever,[29] amen.

ὑπερβάλλουσαν ἀγάπην τῆς γνώσεως). As it stands, γνώσις is the gen. obj. of the ptc. ὑπερβάλλουσα; i.e., the love "goes beyond" or "exceeds" our comprehension or understanding (cf. BDAG, 1032; BDF, §177). Woodenly, we could paraphrase: "the 'exceeding-all-knowledge' love of Christ."

25. The rendering "accomplish" (as NRSV) takes the aor. of the inf. ποιῆσαι as resultative in meaning here. The idea is that God will actually bring all these marvelous things into fulfillment, not just be engaged in certain activities. As a complement of δύναμαι ("be able to"), the verb ποιέω appears as a pres. inf. seven times in the NT, with the meaning "bear" fruit (Matt 7:18), "perform" signs (John 3:2; 9:16) and generally to be "engaged" in various actions (John 5:19, 30; 9:33; 15:5). As an aor. inf. in this construction ποιέω appears five times with the meaning best rendered "accomplish," possible also in Matt 9:28 and Mark 6:5 (cf. Matt 5:36; Mark 14:7). For the "resultative" (or "consummative") aor. see E. Burton, *Syntax of the Moods and Tenses in New Testament Greek* (Edinburgh: T&T Clark, 1898), §§42 and 87; Daniel B. Wallace, *Greek Grammar beyond the Basics* (Grand Rapids: Zondervan, 1997), 559–61.

26. This renders ὑπὲρ πάντα ... ὑπερεκπερισσοῦ ὧν, where the gen. of the relative pronoun ὧν is comparative (BDF §185[1]) and ὑπερεκπερισσοῦ is emphatic, "*far more* exceedingly" (see BDAG, 1033).

27. "Image" for νοέω (as NIV, NRSV; BDAG, 675), in contrast with "perceive" or "think" (KJV, NASB, ESV). "Imagine" implies thinking that moves beyond the ordinary, and that is certainly what Paul expresses about what God has and will accomplish.

28. See notes above on 1:11 and 1:20 for ἐνεργέω as "bring into effect." Here the meaning is probably "to put one's capabilities into operation" (BDAG, 335), "be active," or "be at work."

29. The pleonastic phrase εἰς πάσας τὰς γενεὰς τοῦ αἰῶνος τῶν αἰώνων (woodenly, "unto all generations of the age of ages") is without parallel in the NT and LXX, whereas εἰς τοὺς αἰῶνας τῶν αἰώνων is relatively common; e.g., Gal 1:5; Phil 4:20; 1 Tim 1:17; 4:18 in Paul's writings, and thirteen times in Revelation (most concluded with ἀμήν, as in Eph 3:21). The LXX has more than four dozen examples of this latter phrase, usually with αἰῶν in the sg., as εἰς τὸν αἰῶνα τοῦ αἰῶνος, including three times in Psa 110 (111).

Commentary

3:14 Τούτου χάριν, "For this reason." This lead phrase is repeated from the same opening in 3:1, and by it Paul signals his return to the thought that he had interrupted for a long digression (vv. 2–13; see comments above and, e.g., Lincoln, 167–72; O'Brien, 223–24). What makes this certain is that τούτου χάριν is quite a rare conjunctive phrase (only 3:1, 14; Titus 1:5 in the NT), showing a clear intent on Paul's part to take the two in vv. 1 and 14 together. Διὰ τοῦτο ("for this reason") or διὰ ταῦτα ("for these reasons") or the like are far more common ways to express the idea of "for this reason" that Paul could have used otherwise.[30] Paul repeats terms to link passages or signal a return from digression (e.g., 2:1 with 2:5; cf. Rom 5:12 with 5:18). Hence, the reference of **τούτου** χάριν in v. 14 reaches all the way back to 2:19–22, where Paul had narrated the new phase in God's redemptive economy with Gentiles being built alongside believing Jews into a new, eschatological temple. It is "for this reason" that Paul bows his knees before the Father. The two passages (2:19–22 and 3:14–21) are quite removed from one another, but the separation of the two was caused by the digression of 3:2–13. This viewpoint becomes particularly important for interpreting v. 19 (see below).

κάμπτω τὰ γόνατά μου πρὸς τὸν πατέρα, "I bow my knees before the Father." Bowing of one's knee is a sign of fealty and respect. As fealty, one may bow the knee to a conqueror, to a king or other kind of ruler (Gen 41:43), to a god (Baal, Rom 11:4 from 1 Kgs 19:18), or to the true God at the end of the age (Rom 14:11 from Isa 45:23; Psa 95:6; of Christ, Phil 2:10).[31] It is also a posture of prayer in places (e.g., Dan 6:10), though standing (1 Sam 1:23; Matt 6:5; Mark 11:25; Luke 18:11) or bowing one's head (1 Chr 29:20) are also found among the Jews. Here Paul bows in intercessory prayer on behalf of his audience before the Father of "the whole family" of believers alive and in glory (v. 15).[32]

---

30. E.g., see for both expressions Eph 1:15; 5:6, 17; 6:13; and 2:11; 3:13; 4:8, 25; 5:14 for similar διό.

31. Milder signs of respect and greeting would be a polite kiss (Rom 16:16; 1 Cor 16:20; 2 Cor 13:12; 1 Thess 5:26; 1 Pet 5:14).

32. "Father of the Fatherland" (*pater patriae*) was a special Roman title for certain leaders and for many later emperors. The Roman senate voted the title for Nero in AD 56; he had earlier declined it, at his accession to power at the age of seventeen

The intercession in 3:14–21 is not a direct continuation of Paul's prayer report in 1:15–23 (cf. O'Brien, 254), though there are topical connections between the two passages, and this later one "has significant continuity" with the earlier one (Arnold, 204). In particular, Paul expresses his desire in both places for the strengthening and knowledge of his audience, particularly in light of the spiritual warfare in which all Christians are engaged, as he will explain later (6:10–20). Prayer and the equipment of the Holy Spirit (v. 16 and 6:18–20) are the effective weapons in this fight.

3:15 ἐξ οὗ πᾶσα πατριὰ ἐν οὐρανοῖς καὶ ἐπὶ γῆς ὀνομάζεται, "from whom the whole family in heaven and on earth receives its name." How one translates πᾶς in the phrase πᾶσα πατριὰ leads to quite different understandings of this phrase and this verse.[33] To render it as "every family" leads to understanding God as the Father or Creator who names all groupings of peoples and angelic beings in heaven and on earth.[34] In support of this, one does normally see the meaning "the whole" or "the entire" in a phrase with the adjective πᾶς when its noun is articular and πᾶς is placed in the attributive position (i.e., ἡ πᾶσα πατριὰ) as, for example, ὁ ... πᾶς νόμος, "the whole law"

(Suetonius, *Nero* 8); cf. David Shotter, *Nero*, 2nd ed. (New York: Routledge, 2005; 1st ed., 1997), 23. The term appears in imperial inscriptions at Ephesus. For example, *IvE* 259B is a Greek inscription (statue base?) for Claudius that includes his title as πατὴρ πατρίδος, and *IvE* 262 is a bilingual honorific for Titus in which the Latin version simply abbreviates *pater patriae* as "p · p ·," while the Greek spells it out (with dative): [π]ατρὶ [πα]τρίδ[ο]ς, "for the father of the fatherland." Interestingly, *IvE* 2065 is an honorific for another Ephesian noble as κτίστης πατρίδος, "*creator* of the fatherland," which seems to use *creator* as a near synonym for *father* (or *benefactor*; εὐεργέτης). See Eph 3:15 for God as Father and Creator of his whole family.

33. It can refer to each or every instance of multiple individual referents, "every family" (NASB, ESV, NRSV; cf. O'Brien, 252; Lincoln, 202–3; Hoehner, 474–75; Arnold, 208–9; Barth, 367; Best, 338–39; Gnilka, 181 ["each clan"]). Or it can reference an entire single group, "the whole family" (KVJ) or "his whole family" (NIV), as I am taking it here; so KJV, NIV; Hodge, 179–81; C. F. D. Moule, *An Idiom Book of New Testament Greek*, 2nd ed. (Cambridge: Cambridge University Press, 1959), 94–95; cf. BDAG, 783–84; LSJ, 1345.

34. Cf. Jas 1:17 for God as "the Father of lights," or Heb 12:9 "the Father of spirits," and Eccl 6:10 for God naming all, including the stars, in Psa 147:4 and Isa 40:26. In his exaltation, Christ is head of everything in heaven and on earth (Eph 1:10; cf. Col 1:15–17) that can be named (Eph 1:21).

(Gal 5:14).[35] And rendering πᾶς as "every" or "all" is seen for anarthrous nouns with πᾶς in other places in Ephesians, at 1:3, 21; 4:14, 16, 29.

Nevertheless, the idea of an entire single group for πᾶς, rendered "the whole," is possible even when the noun it is modifying is anarthrous, supporting my understanding and translation. A few examples include one from earlier in Ephesians: πᾶσα οἰκοδομὴ, "the whole building" (Eph 2:21)—not "every [different] building"; πᾶς οἶκος Ἰσραὴλ, "the whole house of Israel" (Acts 2:36); ἐπὶ πάσῃ γῇ Αἰγύπτῳ, "in the whole land of Egypt" (Jer 51:26 LXX [Jer 44:26]); and ἐγενήθην γέλως παντὶ λαῷ μου, "I have become a laughingstock to all my people" or "to my whole people" (Lam 3:14 LXX). This usage is particularly appropriate with πατριὰ in Eph 3:15 because it is a collective noun like οἶκος ("household," "nation") or λαός ("people") in the examples just cited.[36] The outcome of this view is that Paul is not referencing all of creation here with πᾶσα πατριὰ but the whole of the church family on earth and in heaven. The heavenly members of the family are the saints who have gone before into the presence of their Father.

The verb ὀνομάζω in general refers to calling or naming someone (i.e., calling "apostles" [Mark 3:14] or renaming Simon "Peter" [Luke 6:13]). But with ἐκ, as here in Eph 3:15 (ἐξ οὗ), it refers to the derivation of a word (Xenophon, *Mem.* 4.5.12) or to someone's patronymic: "calling each man by his lineage and his father's name" (Homer, *Il.* 10.68; πατρόθεν ἐκ γενεῆς ὀνομάζων ἄνδρα ἕκαστον; cf. BDAG, 714; LSJ, 1232–33). Directly, Greek names like "Theodoros" ("Gift of God") or "Theophilos" ("Friend of God") would derive from θεός, "God." But naming things in Genesis is probably in the background in Eph 3:15, where naming objects or persons is a royal act in the opening chapters of Genesis that God does initially and then

35. Best (338) writes, "What is named is *every* πατριά, not the *whole* πατριά; the latter would be πᾶσα ἡ πατριά"; he cites three grammars (emphasis original). However, this is not correct. Πᾶσα ἡ πατριά would be glossed "every family" or "all the family," whereas ἡ πᾶσα πατριά is "the whole family" (cf. Herbert Wier Smyth, *Greek Grammar*, rev. Gordon M. Messing [Cambridge, MA: Harvard University Press, 1956; original ed., 1920], §§1163, 1174), and one of the grammars Best cites goes against his view by taking the phrase as "the whole family" (Moule, *Idiom Book*, 94–95).

36. Cf. BDAG, 783–84; meaning 4, who say that this meaning normally occurs with geographic or proper names. Examples in LSJ, 1345, include πᾶσα ὕλη ("the whole forest"), which is a collective sg. noun like πατριά.

is joined by Adam as an expression of his creation in the divine image (Gen 1:5, 8, 10; 2:19–20, 23).

Paul's point in v. 15 is that the one new family (2:19; 3:6), constituted in Christ from every nation, both Jews and Gentiles, on earth and in heaven, all have their most meaningful patronymic and hence their family unity from the "one God and Father of all, who is over all and through all and in all" (4:6). There are no tribal, clan, or filial distinctions "according to the flesh" (Rom 4:1; 9:3, 5) for those who are in Christ Jesus (e.g., Rom 4:9–12; 2 Cor 5:16; Gal 3:29). "There is but one family which ought to be reckoned, both in heaven and on earth, both among angels and among men—if we belong to the Body of Christ. For outside of Him there is nothing but dispersion" (Calvin, 166).

3:16 *ἵνα δῷ ὑμῖν κατὰ τὸ πλοῦτος τῆς δόξης αὐτοῦ δυνάμει κραταιωθῆναι*, "that he may grant you to be strengthened with power in accordance with the riches of his glory." Paul had assumed the posture of deeply reverent prayer in vv. 14–15 and now informs his audience of his intercession for them as he in effect prays. The content of Paul's prayer consists of three parallel sections, each of which begins with *ἵνα* as the object of his prayer.[37] Here is an outline of the syntax and parallelism of the three object clauses and their major elements:

[14] *τούτου χάριν κάμπτω τὰ γόνατά μου* (prayer introduced)

1. [16] *ἵνα δῷ ὑμῖν* (first request)
   κραταιωθῆναι (obj. of *δῷ*)
   [17] *κατοικῆσαι τὸν Χριστὸν* (result)
   ἐρριζωμένοι καὶ τεθεμελιωμένοι (parallel result)
2. [18] *ἵνα ἐξισχύσητε* (second request)
   καταλαβέσθαι (complement of *ἐξισχύσητε*)
   [19] *γνῶναί τε* (parallel with *καταλαβέσθαι*)
3. *ἵνα πληρωθῆτε* (third request)

37. The *ἵνα* clause is an obj. clause and the equivalent of *ὅτι* here and in vv. 18–19 (cf. 1:17, where *ἵνα δῷ* also appears as the obj. of prayer). The meaning is: "I bow my knees before the Father [praying] *that* he may grant you ..."; see translation notes above on vv. 16 and 18 and Burton, *Moods*, §203.

The content of each of these requests gets shorter and faster, with the climactic last one in v. 19b a mere eight words.[38] And the content of v. 19b is fittingly climactic in meaning ("that you may be filled to all the fullness of God") to fit the climactic form (see below).

In v. 16 Paul employs the kind of extravagant language ("riches of his glory with power") that has characterized what he wants his audience to understand so far in the epistle; particularly, God's "wealth" (1:7, 18; 2:7; 3:8), "glory" (1:6, 12, 14, 17–18; 3:21), and "power" (1:19, 21; 3:7, 20)—terms that do not appear again in the coming chapters. Paul's petition flows out of his concern that the Ephesians not be disheartened (v. 13) and that they have a grasp of Christ's supremacy over the powers that they had sought to placate in their uneasy ignorance as pagans before their conversion (1:15–23; cf. Arnold, 209–10).

Paul uses the phrase "riches of [God's] glory" elsewhere (Rom 9:23; Col 1:27; cf. Phil 4:19) and has used it earlier in Ephesians to describe "his inheritance for the saints" (1:18). In 3:16 the riches of glory are associated with God's power that is to provide strength for believers (cf. Rom 6:4; Col 1:11).[39] More precisely, Paul asks that God powerfully strengthen the audience "in accordance with" (κατὰ) his wealth of glory, which represents the standard or measurement against which the action is requested.[40] "May you *be strengthened with all power, according to his glorious might*, for all endurance and patience with joy" (Col 1:11; emphasis added), "And my God will supply every need of yours *according to his riches in glory* in Christ Jesus" (Phil 4:19; emphasis added).

38. The first ἵνα request (vv. 16–17) consists of six cola* (thirty-four words), the second (vv. 18–19a) has three cola* (twenty-five words), and the last (v. 19b) is one colon* with eight words. The second and and third ἵνα requests open and close the final period, comprising vv. 18–19, as I have divided the text above (see also on v. 19 below).

39. The pass. inf. κραταιωθῆναι functions as the obj. of the grant (ἵνα δῷ) Paul is requesting. Here God is the assumed subject of the event. The verb κραταιόω itself is not common in the NT (only Luke 1:18; 2:40; 1 Cor 16:13)—but see related κράτος ("might") in 1:19 and 6:10. Cf. the exhortation in 6:10 that the Ephesians "grow strong in the Lord" (ἐνδυναμοῦσθε).

40. Cf. O'Brien, 257 and n. 143, for the OT background of this idiom (e.g., Pss 51:1; 109:26). For analogous expressions of qualifying the verb "strengthen" (κραταιόω) with a dative noun for power (δύναμις) in the Dead Sea Scrolls, see Lincoln, 205.

διὰ τοῦ πνεύματος αὐτοῦ εἰς τὸν ἔσω ἄνθρωπον, "through his Spirit in your inner man." In the NT it is common to connect "power" with the Holy Spirit (Luke 1:35; 4:14; Acts 1:8; 10:38; Rom 1:4; 15:13, 19; 1 Cor 2:4; Gal 3:5; 1 Thess 1:5; Heb 2:4). In Romans 1:4 in particular the Spirit is associated with the power of God when he raised Christ from the dead, which connects with what Paul says in Eph 1:19–20. Here Paul takes for granted the earlier flood of the Holy Spirit washing over the Gentiles (e.g., Acts 10:44–48), sealing them with "every blessing of the Spirit" (1:3, 13), and Paul requests that the Spirit will continue to work in the Ephesians with power and strength.

The strengthening Paul desires for his audience is unlike that exhibited by Samson, in his "outer man" (ὁ ἔξω ἄνθρωπος; cf. 1 Tim 4:7–8). Instead it is in the "inner man" (ὁ ἔσω ἄνθρωπος; cf. Rom 7:22), where "man" for ἄνθρωπος is retained from older translations (e.g., KJV, NASB) in order to connect with the creation of "man (אָדָם) ... both male and female" (Gen 1:27). The meaning is that strength comes to one's "inner human person" as originally created, which is already being transformed through the regenerating presence of the Holy Spirit in a renewed likeness of Christ (4:13; Rom 8:29; cf. 1 Cor 15:49) into a vital component of the "new man," that is, human persons united into a new human race (see above on 2:15). The Spirit has already begun this work in the Ephesians, as evidenced by their coming to faith in Christ through the gospel and displaying love (1:13, 15). Now Paul desires that this new, inner "man" be further renewed and strengthened even as the "old man" (ὁ παλαιὸν ἄνθρωπος; 4:22; Rom 6:6; Col 3:9) gives way to the new (4:24; Col 3:10) as the inaugurated new creation is effectively advanced (2:9–10; 2 Cor 4:16; Col 3:10 again).[41] Furthermore, this inner strengthening is connected with Christ's dwelling in the believers' hearts in the next verse.

3:17 κατοικῆσαι τὸν Χριστὸν διὰ τῆς πίστεως ἐν ταῖς καρδίαις ὑμῶν, "so that Christ may take up his dwelling in your hearts through faith."[42] As noted in the translation note above, I take the infinitive κατοικῆσαι ("take up his dwelling"), which opens v. 17, as expressing the result of the strengthening

41. Cf. Herman Ridderbos, *Paul: An Outline of His Theology*, trans. John De Witt (Grand Rapids: Eerdmans, 1975), 223–31.

42. Or "the Messiah" instead of "Christ" for articular τὸν Χριστὸν. Cf. Barth, 370, and "Excursus: Articular Χριστός as Messianic Title" below.

for which Paul asks in v. 16.[43] The outline is: ἵνα δῷ ὑμῖν ... κραταιωθῆναι ... κατοικῆσαι τὸν Χριστὸν, "that he may grant you to be strengthened ... so that Christ may take up his dwelling." O'Brien (258n151) reports that "most commentators," including himself, take κατοικῆσαι as parallel with κραταιωθῆναι and therefore also an event Paul requests be granted.[44] This interpretation is possible but unlikely because there is no conjunction linking the two infinitives (i.e., asyndeton*).[45] Asyndeton* does appear quite frequently in Ephesians with nouns, prepositional phrases, participles, and other parts of speech, but not with infinitives.[46] Where Paul does join two parallel infinitives together he uses a conjunction; this occurs three times in Ephesians, including in the next two verses (vv. 18–19): ἵνα ἐξισχύσητε καταλαβέσθαι ... γνῶναί **τε**, "that you may be fully able to grasp ... *and likewise* to know."[47]

We have seen the church as a new, spiritual temple being indwelt by God through the Spirit already in Eph 2:22. Now in v. 17 Paul intercedes further for the Ephesians that, as a result of the strength he asks God to grant them, Christ may "take up his dwelling" in their hearts. Their "hearts" are the center of their "inner man" (v. 16) and the source of a transformed existence characterized by love (v. 17b; cf. Matt 12:34–35; 15:18–19).[48] Such love arising out of faith in the gospel is the goal of Paul's ministry (1 Tim 1:5),

---

43. See also the translation note for v. 17 above for the aor. tense form of κατοικῆσαι expressing an inceptive idea, brought out in the rendering "*take up* [his] dwelling" rather than simply "that Christ may dwell," as the major English versions have it (e.g., KJV, NASB, NIV, ESV, NRSV).

44. Cf. Lincoln, 206; Gnilka, 184. Best (341) writes: "Since no particle links this verse to the preceding it is probably parallel to it, yet also clarifies it." To express this more precisely, he take the second inf. as epexegetical or appositional with the meaning: "that he may grant you to be strengthened ... (namely) that Christ may take up his dwelling," where the second inf. is an elaboration or definition of the first (also Barth, 369–70). But this use of the inf. is normally found in connection with nouns or pronouns (e.g., τοῦτο), not with other infs. (BDF §394; Burton, *Moods*, §385; Wallace, *Greek Grammar*, 606–7) and is not a good option in Eph 3:17.

45. See Hoehner, 480–82, who also takes the inf. as expressing result, as I am taking it here.

46. I.e., the three parallel ἵνα clauses in vv. 16–19 are not connected with conjs. Cf. 5:26–27 for another example of asyndeton* with parallel ἵνα clauses in Ephesians.

47. The other two places are in 3:8–9: ἐδόθη ... εὐαγγελίσασθαι ... **καὶ** φωτίσαι; and 4:22–24: ἀποθέσθαι ... ἀνανεοῦσθαι **δὲ** ... **καὶ** ἐνδύσασθαι.

48. Cf. Rom 5:5, where God's love is poured out in the believer's heart through the Holy Spirit.

and he labored among the Gentiles that they may be "rooted and built up (ἐρριζωμένοι καὶ ἐποικοδομούμενοι) in him [Christ] and established in the faith" (Col 2:7; cf. Col 1:23).

That Paul prays that *Christ* may dwell in the believer's heart is not to deny the incarnate Son's genuine, continued humanity. It is instead an affirmation of his essential identity with God and therefore his union with the Spirit even in his resurrected human existence, which is itself now πνευματικός ("spiritual"; cf. 1 Cor 15:45; 2 Cor 3:17).[49] Hence, Jesus can assure his disciples of the Holy Spirit's presence with them as well as of his own (e.g., John 14:18–28; cf. Matt 28:20; Heb 13:5, 8). Christ is "in" believers (2 Cor 13:5; Gal 2:20; Col 1:27). This is expressed in a remarkable passage where Paul says that the "Spirit of God," the "Spirit of Christ," "Christ," "the Spirit," and "the Spirit of him who raised Jesus from the dead" dwells in the believer (Rom 8:9–11). "The external works of the Trinity are undivided ... yet each [divine] person contributes distinctively to every work."[50]

Christ's dwelling with his people is further remarkable in that it shows that he is the Lord of the new covenant. As God promises to dwell with his people as the heart of the "covenant bond" (see above on 2:17), now we see Christ fulfilling that promise to dwell with his new covenant church. Among other elements in and of the Christian life, the sacrament of the Lord's Supper expresses this bond most intimately.[51] And all of this is acquired by the believer διὰ τῆς πίστεως ("through faith"), which is a "remarkable praise of faith, that through it the Son of God is made our own, and has His dwelling with us" (Calvin, 167–68).

ἐν ἀγάπῃ ἐρριζωμένοι καὶ τεθεμελιωμένοι, "and that you may be rooted and founded in love." Most English versions starting with KJV connect these two participles, ἐρριζωμένοι and τεθεμελιωμένοι, with the first colon* in the

49. This theological truth is graphically portrayed in John's visionary prophecy in Rev 3:1; 5:6.

50. Michael Horton, *The Christian Faith: A Systematic Theology for Pilgrims on the Way* (Grand Rapids: Zondervan, 2011), 551; cf. James D. G. Dunn, *Romans 1–8*, WBC 38A (Dallas: Word, 1988), 446: "Paul implies that the risen Christ is now experienced in and through the Spirit, indeed as the Spirit of God, the Spirit of creation and of prophecy. It is not that 'Christ' and 'Spirit' are synonymous, but 'Spirit *indwelling*,' 'Christ *in you*.' Christ's effective lordship over his own is coterminous with the Spirit's activity in their lives" (emphasis original).

51. Cf. Horton, *Christian Faith*, 777–85 (covenant, not metaphysics, is the "scriptural habitat" of the sacraments).

following verse (ἵνα ἐξισχύσητε ...): "that ye, being rooted and grounded in love, may be able to ..." (KJV; also NASB, NIV, ESV).[52] However, this understanding would require that ἵνα in v. 18 precede the participles in v. 17, not follow them, which would constitute an emendation of the text without warrant from the ancient MSS.[53] Instead, the participles express two truths that parallel the infinitive κατοικῆσαι ("to take up his dwelling") earlier in v. 17, not the following purpose clause in v. 18. This explains why the participle forms are in the nominative case (rather than gen., agreeing with ὑμῶν at the end of v. 17a).[54] The same use of nominative participles paralleling an infinitive is found in 4:1–3: Παρακαλῶ ... ὑμᾶς ... περιπατῆσαι ... ἀνεχόμενοι ... σπουδάζοντες ("I strongly urge you to walk ... and to bear with ... and to be eager to").

The prepositional phrase ἐν ἀγάπῃ ("in love") connects with the participles ἐρριζωμένοι καὶ τεθεμελιωμένοι ("rooted and founded"), but we expect it to be expressed after the participles, not before. It has been brought forward ("fronted"), just as we saw in 1:4–5, and the effect is to give "love" more prominence here, as it did in 1:4–5. It certainly is possible and makes good sense to see this love as God or Christ's love for his people, but it seems slightly better here to take it as the believer's love toward God and neighbor,

---

52. Contrast NRSV, "through faith, as you are being rooted and grounded in love. I pray that you may have the power ..."

53. So Origen, who recommends moving ἵνα forward from v. 18; Origen and Jerome, 160–61.

54. So BDF §468 (2); MHT, 2:248–49 ("the participle is used for the *verbum finitum,* and in the great majority it is in the nominative"); Winer, *A Treatise on the Grammar of New Testament Greek* (Edinburgh: T&T Clark, 1882), 716–17. Other, less likely views on how to take the ptcs. are surveyed in Hoehner, 483–84, who cites BDF §468 (2) as attaching the ptcs. with the ἵνα clause, but BDF actually just points to Eph 3:17 as having parallel ptcs.; cf. Best, 342; O'Brien, 259–60 (misreading BDF here); Lincoln, 197 (taking the ptcs. as further requests where "dwell," "rooted," and "grounded" are all parallel, "grant you be strengthened" in v. 16); and Wallace, *Greek Grammar*, 631n47 (causal, with a question mark on Eph 4:17). Barth (371) takes the ptcs. as exhortations. Origen says the ptcs. should be dative, agreeing with ὑμῖν ("to you") in v. 16; Origen and Jerome, 160–61. In the end my reading has the advantage of simplicity and conforms to a later function of ptcs. in 4:1–3 as well as throughout Hellenistic Greek.

which characterizes Christian sanctification.[55] The participles ἐρριζωμένοι and τεθεμελιωμένοι convey an agricultural and building metaphor. One pictures a plant that already has roots being transplanted into new, fertile soil, or a building's foundation being sunk down into bedrock (Matt 7:24–25).[56] "Here in Ephesians love is the soil in which believers are to be rooted and grow, the foundation on which they are to be built" (Lincoln, 207).

The whole of vv. 16–17 taken together, then, communicates that Paul prays for the Father to strengthen the Ephesians through his Spirit and in consequence that the Son may dwell in their hearts by faith. Redemption from sin and guilt and salvation from divine wrath is by faith alone, but genuine Christian faith is never alone; it necessarily issues in love toward God and one's neighbor. Paul has already expressed the twins of faith and love in 1:15, and the practical outworking of love in the good works for which believers have been re-created in Christ (2:10) is the subject of Paul's instruction and exhortations to follow in chaps. 4–6. It is for this reason that Paul adds the phrase with two participles at the end of v. 17: "and that you may be rooted and founded in love." This grounding of their lives in love is the result of God's predestination and salvation in his great and inexplicable love (1:4–5; 2:4) and of their faith in Christ because of his covenant bond with them, purchased through his sacrificial love (5:2, 25).

3:18 *ἵνα ἐξισχύσητε καταλαβέσθαι σὺν πᾶσιν τοῖς ἁγίοις*, "that you may be fully able to grasp with all the saints." This verse (along with v. 19a) comprises the second of the three requests Paul makes on his audience's behalf. It is shorter than the first (vv. 16–17); Paul's final request (v. 19b) is the shortest of all. The structure of the requests was outlined and discussed briefly above on v. 16.

The heart of Paul's second request is *ἵνα ἐξισχύσητε καταλαβέσθαι ... γνῶναί τε*, "that you may be fully able to grasp ... and likewise to know." The introductory verb ἐξισχύω is intensive, with the attached ἐξ- prepositional

55. There are similar ideas in Col 1:23 and 2:7 that refer to Christian faith and love that contain the same ptc. forms τεθεμελιωμένοι and ἐρριζωμένοι. Cf. Hodge, 186–87; Gnilka, 185; Lincoln, 207; O'Brien, 260; Best, 343; Arnold, 213.

56. There is an interesting possible connection between the first and last words in v. 17, which refer to buildings: **κατοικῆσαι** τὸν Χριστὸν ... **τεθεμελιωμένοι**, "so that Christ may take up his dwelling ... founded" (i.e., refering to a building's foundation).

prefix (see translation note). Hence, the idea is "fully able" or "entirely capable." And καταλαμβάνω (in its middle voice form) can mean to "seize" someone or, as here, to grasp a concept or intellectual reality (cf. LSJ, 897). Paul may have chosen the uncommon verb καταλαμβάνω here (versus the more common γινώσκω, οἶδα, or συνίημι) as a vivid, ironic metaphor for "getting one's mind around" the immeasurable "breadth and length and height and depth."[57] In any event, he is making a request to God to give understanding as only he can of such spiritual matters, which is the noetic aspect of the sanctification process God effects through the Holy Spirit in his people (e.g., Rom 12:2; 1 Cor 2:6–16). Paul expresses similar desires for their understanding in 1:15–23 (esp. vv. 17–19), which is connected with 3:14–21.

This last point explains why Paul adds "with all the saints" here in v. 18. Depth of understanding of divine matters is not disclosed to a chosen few in the church, as in later gnostic thought. And in Gnosticism, enlightenment comes from contemplation or intellectual discovery of some sort—usually of some contradictory truths—allowing the knower to penetrate the veil of personal identity, dualistic distinctions, bodily existence, etc., into the underlying monistic πᾶν ("the All"), where no distinctions exist (e.g., *Ap. John* 2.1, 2–3; *Gos. Thom.* 2.2, logia 3, 11, 19, 29, 49–51; 114).[58] Paul is *not* enabling this sort of gnostic search in v. 18, and neither does it stand in the background as some supposed source for our text. He is interceding for his audience in a prayer directed to the Christian's heavenly Father to grant insight into something that "*all* the saints," even children, can expect to perceive through divine grant (cf. 6:1; Matt 11:25; Jas 1:5).

τί τὸ πλάτος καὶ μῆκος καὶ ὕψος καὶ βάθος, "what is the breadth and length and height and depth." What exactly is Paul praying the Ephesians will join all the saints in fully understanding? "Scholars are in disarray" over the answer (Lincoln, 208). No stone has gone unturned as a possible backdrop to Paul's meaning: Stoicism, Gnosticism, magical papyri, apocrypha, other biblical passages (e.g., Rom 8:39; Job 11:8–9), or other things like the new Jerusalem (Rev 21:16), the mystery of Christ, his cross, or the church as the

57. He could have used the more common synonym συνίημι/συνίω instead (BDAG, 972).

58. For an expression of pantheism at Ephesus see Christoph Börker, "Eine pantheistische Weihung in Ephesos," *ZPE* 41 (1981): 181–88.

body of Christ.[59] "But," writes Nils Dahl, "no one set of parallels has provided the key to the interpretation of Eph 3:18 within the context of the letter."[60]

Of the myriad views, two fit the context of Eph 3:18 better than the others. Clinton Arnold has argued that the dimensional references here are to God's limitless *power*.[61] Paul has already reported on his prayer that the Ephesians would grasp the extent of God's immense power toward them in Christ in 1:16–20, a passage connected with 3:14–21 to some degree. Further, Arnold believes certain magical formulas that call on breadth, length, height, and depth as mystic powers in attempts to appropriate power over hostile forces or other ills would have been a formula with which the Ephesians would have been familiar or have themselves utilized before conversion.[62]

While I am in agreement with Arnold's understanding of the prevalence of "magic" in the Ephesian background, and I recognize the value of his treatment of Eph 1:15–23 in particular, I can't follow him here for Eph 3:18. If pagans attempted to call on cosmic powers of breadth, length, height, and depth, why would Paul pray that the Ephesians fully comprehend

---

59. The most helpful survey of options is provided by Lincoln, 208–13; for focus on patristic and other earlier views see Hoehner, 486–88. One field that still needs examination by more NT scholars is the bountiful epigraphical, numismatic, and archaeological sources from Ephesus itself and its neighbors.

60. Nils A. Dahl, "Cosmic Dimensions and Religious Knowledge (Eph 3:18)," in *Jesus und Paulus* (Göttingen: Vandenhoeck & Ruprecht, 1975), 57–75; repr. in *Studies in Ephesians*, WUNT 131 (Tübingen: Mohr Siebeck, 2000), 365–88 (quote on 366). As Best points out, the four words in v. 18b denote three dimensions, not four, as is sometimes stated, since breadth and length are on one plane, not two (Best, 344).

61. Arnold, 214–17; Clinton E. Arnold, *Ephesians: Power and Magic: The Concept of Power in Ephesians in Light of Its Historical Setting*, SNTSMS 63 (New York: Cambridge University Press, 1989), 89–96.

62. Arnold examines *PGM* 4:964–74, 979–85 in particular (Arnold, *Ephesians: Power and Magic*, 91–92). Scholars sometimes express doubts about Arnold's view because the *PGM* texts date to several centuries after Ephesians was written and require "the readers' intimate knowledge of the magical formulae" (e.g., Lincoln, 209). While this is a fair point, in general magical texts tended to preserve ancient techniques and formulas that predate the MSS we have found, and what we call *magic* (spells, charms, incantations, making signs, etc.) permeated ancient pagan life with little change over the course of many centuries. Furthermore, nearly everyone in antiquity had some degree of acquaintance with these things (see comments on 1:19–21 above).

them? Or would the audience understand that what is meant by these dimensions—which are presented as unified with one article (**τὸ** πλάτος καὶ μῆκος καὶ ὕψος καὶ βάθος)—belong particularly to God or have expressed his power?[63]

In the end, a significant number of interpreters are right to see the reference in v. 18b as a reference to the boundless, inscrutable character of Christ's love (v. 19; cf. 5:2).[64] The love of Christ has tremendous "breadth, length, height and depth," and it is this love that leads into v. 18 from v. 17 and then into "the love of Christ that exceeds our understanding" in v. 19, which is where we end up at the end of Paul's second request, spanning vv. 18–19a.[65] It is because God is rich in love (2:4) that he bestows on his people "the untraceable riches of Christ" (3:8) out of his immensity.

3:19 γνῶναί τε τὴν ὑπερβάλλουσαν τῆς γνώσεως ἀγάπην τοῦ Χριστοῦ, "and likewise to know the love of Christ that exceeds our understanding." At this place, the versification could have been improved to bring vv. 18 and 19 together, or at least to show the connection of v. 19a with v. 18, to which it belongs as the completion of Paul's second request on behalf of his audience. Verse 19b forms the very brief final request, which forms a mild inclusio* as the following schema of the three requests opening with **ἵνα** shows:

> **ἵνα δῷ** ὑμῖν ... (v. 16)
>
> **ἵνα ἐξισχύσητε** καταλαβέσθαι σὺν πᾶσιν τοῖς ἁγίοις (v. 18a)
> τί τὸ πλάτος καὶ μῆκος καὶ ὕψος καὶ βάθος
> γνῶναί τε τὴν ὑπερβάλλουσαν τῆς γνώσεως ἀγάπην τοῦ Χριστοῦ (v. 19a)
>
> **ἵνα πληρωθῆτε** εἰς πᾶν τὸ πλήρωμα τοῦ θεοῦ (v. 19b)[66]

---

63. Paul could easily have expressed this more clearly with one short word: τὸ πλάτος καὶ μῆκος καὶ ὕψος καὶ βάθος **θεοῦ** ("of God") or **αὐτοῦ** ("his"—referring to Christ in v. 17).

64. So Calvin, 168–69; Hodge, 188–90; Barth, 373; Best, 346; Lincoln, 212; Hoehner, 488; O'Brien, 263.

65. Again, the one colon* of v. 19b is Paul's third intercessory request of the Father for the Ephesians, not part of v. 19a.

66. It is not just that each request starts with ἵνα here, but that the subjunctive verb is the next word in each case. (Admittedly, there are eleven other examples of this word order in Ephesians, but there are nine other ἵνα clauses where the verb is *not*

That v. 19a belongs with v. 18 is further supported by the use of the particle τέ in the opening (*γνῶναί τε*), which is found only here in Ephesians. It could conceivably have been used instead of the far more common δὲ due to alliteration with the following article: *γνῶναί* **τε τὴν** *ὑπερβάλλουσαν* … (yet see δὲ **τῷ** in 4:23). But it is more likely that Paul chose τέ to connect *γνῶναι* more closely in parallel with *καταλαβέσθαι*, "to grasp … *and likewise* to know," which is a main function of this particle (BDAG, 993; BDF §443).

The reason I stress that v. 19a goes with v. 18 is that this colon* on Christ's inconceivable love is joined closely with the previous colon* ("what is the breadth and length and height and depth") and clues us in to the meaning of the enigmatic dimensions (as noted above on v. 18). In any case, the irony of what Paul says here should not be lost on us: He prays that his audience will *know* (γνῶναι) what surpasses *knowledge* (γνῶσις), Christ's love (cf. Phil 4:7).

ἵνα πληρωθῆτε εἰς πᾶν τὸ πλήρωμα τοῦ θεοῦ, "that you may be filled to all the fullness of God." As stated several times above (see on v. 16), this is the final request of the three that Paul makes to the Father on behalf of the Ephesians.[67] It is also the most striking, not least of which because of the arresting alliteration with π (ἵνα **π**ληρωθῆτε εἰς **π**ᾶν τὸ **π**λήρωμα τοῦ θεοῦ), with which Paul also dramatically concluded his paragraph in 1:23 in a passage connected to this one (τὸ **π**λήρωμα τοῦ τὰ **π**άντα ἐν **π**ᾶσιν **π**ληρουμένου, "the fullness of him who fills everything entirely"; see comment on 1:23; cf. 4:10 and Col 1:19, 29–2:10). When it comes to the meaning of this statement of Eph 3:19b, it is important to start by seeing that Paul is not asking that the audience be filled *with* the divine fullness, but *to* (εἰς) all his fullness as a goal.[68] In English we would say "filled to the brim" as a very rough

---

the next word.) Cf. especially a similar request in 1:17 (**ἵνα** ὁ θεὸς τοῦ κυρίου ἡμῶν Ἰησοῦ Χριστοῦ, ὁ πατὴρ τῆς δόξης, **δώῃ** ὑμῖν) with 3:16 (**ἵνα δῷ** ὑμῖν). Witherington (273) refers to this anaphora in vv. 16–19 and repeated ἵνα as "reduplication" and cites Quintilian as saying this gives "force or emphasis" to the discourse. I tend to see it more as a structuring device for parallel elements here rather than strictly an expression of emphasis.

67. See Lincoln, 197; O'Brien, 253; Best, 335; and others for seeing this request as the climax of the three.

68. See BDAG, 827–29, and BDF §195. The verb πληρόω ("fill") and synonym πίμπλημι ("fill") occur many times where that with which someone is filled is expressed in the gen. case (e.g., Rom 15:14) or the dative case (e.g., Rom 1:29; cf. Eph

equivalent. But very many things make up God's "fullness" or "sum total" (πλήρωμα, BDAG, 830). What exactly is Paul praying that the Ephesians will receive that equals God's measure of fullness?

The options given by scholars to this last question over the years have various nuances and represent much careful thought and reflection. The most prominent views of what Paul hopes the Ephesians will experience may be summarized briefly as follows. Best suggests that Paul hopes the Ephesians will grow in that love that also fills God (Best, 348). Similar to Best is Calvin (169): "everything necessary for perfection in God. … Men imagine that they are complete in themselves, but only because they swell with waste matter or wind." Hodge (190–92) sees Eph 3:19 as directly connected to Eph 4:13 in that Paul wants the Ephesians "to grow to the stature of Christ; to be perfect as our Father is perfect [Matt 5:48]; to be filled unto the measure of the fulness of God," i.e., to his moral perfection. Several commentators view the divine fullness as simple: "that excellence of which God himself is full" (Chrysostom, as cited by Hodge, 190); "the divine perfection in its wholeness" (Ambrosiaster, *ACCS*, 156). Others view it as having particular aspects: "his presence, life, and power" (O'Brien, 265); "God's moral excellence, perfection, and power … a combination of God's righteousness and God's love that must be experienced by believers" (Hoehner, 491); God's own life and power—that the Ephesians may be filled with God himself (Lincoln, 214–15; because our text is based on Col 1:29–2:10 in his judgment; cf. Gnilka, 190–91). Finally, Barth (373–74) sees Paul requesting filling to the measure of "God's presence, glory, and power," yet he adds the intriguing note: "Eph 3:19 may intend to say that the saints shall be the sanctuary of God filled by his glory; cf. 2:21–22" (Barth, 374).

Robert Foster develops the last idea of Markus Barth, which is how I also see the reference to God's fullness in v. 19.[69] As stated above, because

---

5:18 with ἐν). This is the only place in the NT or LXX where either verb occurs with εἰς expressing the goal of the filling. Cf. Ignatius (*Eph.* preface): τῇ εὐλογημένῃ ἐν μεγέθει θεοῦ πατρὸς πληρώματι … τῇ ἐκκλησίᾳ τῇ ἀξιομακαρίστῳ τῇ οὔσῃ ἐν Ἐφέσῳ τῆς Ἀσίας, "to that most blessed in the magnificent fullness of God the Father … the church most worthy of beatitude which is in Ephesus of Asia."

69. Robert L. Foster, " 'A Temple in the Lord Filled to the Fullness of God': Context and Intertextuality (Eph. 3:19)," *NovT* 49 (2007): 85–96. While I too saw a new temple reference in v. 19b earlier, the details of the following comments are

Paul has given us a long digression in vv. 1–13, it is important to see vv. 14–21 as directly flowing out of the end of chapter 2. In particular, when Paul says, "For this reason, I bow my knees before the Father" (3:14), the reason is that Gentile believers have been merged with believing Jews into a new "holy temple in the Lord" (ναὸς ἅγιος ἐν κυρίῳ; 2:21) as part of a new "dwelling of God in the Spirit" (κατοικητήριοντοῦ θεοῦ ἐν πνεύματι; 2:22).[70] Therefore Paul prays to God the Father that they will be strengthened by the Spirit (3:16) and that Christ would take up his dwelling with them (3:17), joining the Father and the Spirit in the new temple building, the church (see 1:23; 4:10).

Moving now to "God's fullness," we could paraphrase Paul's passive expression in v. 19b with an act.: "That God may fill you to the full measure of his own presence." Paul's request, then, is that God would fill his new creation temple, the new covenant church, with his glorious presence through the Spirit (2:22). God's glory had filled the Mosaic tabernacle after it was constructed (Exod 40:34–35), as well as Solomon's temple (the "house"; LXX οἶκος in 1 Kgs 8:10–11; 2 Chr 7:1–2). Early in Ezekiel's visions, he had seen the Lord's glory departing from the Solomonic temple, which had been profaned with idolatry before its desolation (Ezek 8:5–18; 10:3–4, 18–19), but then he saw and described a glorious, new-creation temple:

> Then he led me to the gate, the gate facing east. And behold, the glory of the God of Israel was coming from the east. And the sound of his coming was like the sound of many waters, and the earth shone with his glory. … And I fell on my face. As the glory of the LORD entered the temple by the gate facing east, the Spirit lifted me up and brought me into the inner court; and behold, the glory of the LORD filled the temple. (Ezek 43:1–5)[71]

This is the background to the divine filling and fullness in Eph 3:19b and leads directly to Paul's hymn in vv. 20–21, where he ascribes to God "glory in

---

dependent on Foster's work, which I gratefully acknowledge.

70. Foster, "Temple in the Lord," 88. Foster sees a linguistic connection between the nouns θεμέλιος ("foundation," 2:20) and κατοικητήριον ("dwelling," 2:22) with the verbs κατοικέω ("dwell," 3:17) and θεμελιόω ("founded," 3:17). The connection is tempting, but the statements about these things don't quite match up; in particular, the foundation of the apostles and prophets in 2:20 and founded in love in 3:17.

71. Cf. Foster, "Temple in the Lord," 89–91.

the church and in Christ Jesus for all generations, forever and ever" (v. 21).[72] In v. 19b, Paul is praying for the Lord to fill his inaugurated new creation temple, the church—of which these Gentile Ephesians were a part—with his glory in full measure (cf. Rev 21:23–24).

3:20 Τῷ δὲ δυναμένῳ ὑπὲρ πάντα ποιῆσαι ὑπερεκπερισσοῦ ὧν αἰτούμεθα ἢ νοοῦμεν κατὰ τὴν δύναμιν τὴν ἐνεργουμένην ἐν ἡμῖν, "Now to him who is able to accomplish far more exceedingly than anything we may request or imagine in accordance with his power, which is at work in us." Paul concludes his prayer (mixed as a prayer report) to the Father in vv. 14–19 with a brief doxological song in vv. 20–21, which also acts to cap off all of Eph 1–3, before he moves into material that is characterized by exhortations.[73] While it is not formulaic, the song of vv. 20–21 does fit patterns found elsewhere in both the OT and NT and helps us to understand what Paul has in mind with the "psalms, hymns, and spiritual songs" (5:19–20) with which he wants the Ephesians to occupy themselves.[74]

To give glory to God is a general description of worship, thanksgiving, acknowledgement, or confession in the Bible (Luke 17:18; John 9:24; Rom 4:20; Rev 4:9; 11:13; 14:7; 16:9; 19:7).[75] To "ascribe" or "give" glory is found as an exhortation a few times in the OT as a call to worship and confession of the true God (1 Chr 16:28–29; Pss 29:1–2; 96:7–8). This last Psalms text is particularly interesting for its connections with Paul's ministry, seen more clearly in the LXX version:

---

72. Cf. ibid., 93.

73. Cf. Jerome H. Neyrey, *Give God the Glory: Ancient Prayer and Worship in Cultural Perspective* (Grand Rapids: Eerdmans, 2007). For other literature on NT "hymns" and "songs" see the introduction to 1:3–14 above and below on 5:19–20; cf. discussions and literature in Lincoln, 200, 216; Gnilka, 191–93.

74. See the introduction to this section above for observations on how this "song" does not fit the metrical requirements of Greek poetry and hymns even though it has some interesting metrical features.

75. The Ephesian believers in their former lives before coming to faith engaged in private worship of various forms, including ones not found (legitimately) in biblical religion. For example, a marble altar was found in the main marketplace area of Ephesus with the following dedication: θεῷ ὑψίστῳ Ἀλέξανδρος Ἀττάλου εὐξ[άμενος ἀνέθηκεν], "Alexander son of Attalos dedicated (this) to Zeus Hypsistos ["God Most High"] in fulfillment of a vow" (*IvE* 1234). It is at least possible that worship of θεὸς ὑψίστος arose from Jewish influence; cf. A. Thomas Kraabel, "*Hypsistos* and the Synagogue at Sardis," *GRBS* 10 (1969): 81–93.

> ἀναγγείλατε ἐν τοῖς ἔθνεσιν τὴν δόξαν αὐτοῦ
> ἐν πᾶσι τοῖς λαοῖς τὰ θαυμάσια αὐτοῦ …
> ἐνέγκατε (Heb. יָהַב) τῷ κυρίῳ αἱ πατριαὶ τῶν ἐθνῶν
> ἐνέγκατε τῷ κυρίῳ δόξαν καὶ τιμήν
> ἐνέγκατε τῷ κυρίῳ δόξαν ὀνόματι αὐτοῦ
> ἄρατε θυσίας καὶ εἰσπορεύεσθε εἰς τὰς αὐλὰς αὐτοῦ
>
> Announce his glory among the nations
> his marvelous acts among all the peoples. …
> Ascribe to the Lord, families of the nations,
> ascribe to the Lord glory and honor,
> ascribe to the Lord glory to his name,
> bring sacrifices and enter into his courts (LXX Psa 95:3, 7–8 [96:3, 7–8]; my trans.).

Paul himself ascribes glory to God in Eph 3:20–21 on behalf of "the families of the nations," that is, the Gentiles who have now been brought near to the Lord's courts—as themselves made into components of a new temple—with their own bold and confident access into the divine presence (2:13, 18; 3:12).

That Ephesians 3:20–21 is a song appears in particular parallels in the book of Revelation, where the sung (or chanted) words are part of worship accompanied by the lyre and can be identified as an "ascription hymn," in which virtues—especially glory—are ascribed to God and to the Lamb (Rev 1:5–6; 5:13–14; 7:12; cf. Luke 2:13–14; Psa 66:2). Other examples of this format of ascription of glory, usually concluded with "forever and ever" and the "amen," are found elsewhere in Paul and other NT authors (Rom 11:36; 16:25 [textually uncertain]; Gal 1:5; Phil 4:20; 1 Tim 1:17; 2 Tim 2:18; Heb 13:20–21; 1 Pet 4:11; 2 Pet 3:18; Jude 24–25; and the Revelation texts just cited).

That God can do "far more exceedingly" than believers can ask or imagine may give them only faint comfort.[76] He can, but will he? Paul has already answered that question when he points to the "superabundant magnitude of his power toward us who believe in accordance with the effectiveness of

76. Lincoln (216) has a nice statement on the rhetorical buildup of Paul's extreme expression "far more exceedingly than anything," which he renders "infinitely more abundantly above all."

the strength of his might" (1:19). God has *already* demonstrated his mighty salvation to the Ephesians and to anyone who believes, and he is able and willing to do "far more exceedingly than anything we may request or imagine in accordance with his power, which is at work in us."

3:21 *αὐτῷ ἡ δόξα ἐν τῇ ἐκκλησίᾳ καὶ ἐν Χριστῷ Ἰησοῦ εἰς πάσας τὰς γενεὰς τοῦ αἰῶνος τῶν αἰώνων, ἀμήν.* "to him be the glory in the church and in Christ Jesus for all generations, forever and ever, amen."[77] The form of this ascription of glory has just been discussed under v. 20, but what calls for comment here is the unique reference to God's glory, which resides in the church and in Christ.

That God's glory resides in Christ is an expression of the latter's incarnate divinity (e.g., John 1:14; 17:1, 5; Col 1:19; Phil 2:6–11) and that he himself was the reality the OT tabernacle/temple pictured (e.g., Matt 12:6; John 2:19–22 [cf. Matt 27:40]; Rev 21:22). Just as God's glory filled the OT tabernacle and temple, so his glory fills Jesus (Col 1:19 again), who fills "all in all" with his own fullness as the covenantal mediator of God's new creation (cf. 1:23; 4:10). But Paul adds an expression in v. 21 that God's glory is "in the church." This is the only place where a doxological song (or prayer) of this sort expresses God's glory "in the church." The glory is God's, but his radiant presence (e.g., Exod 24:16) resides in the church alongside and through Christ Jesus. As stated above on v. 19, Paul is expressing the idea of God's dwelling with his people as his inaugurated new temple building (2:21–22).

In the OT period God expressed his covenant bond with his people by taking up his habitation with them in the tabernacle and later in the temple (e.g., Exod 29:45; 1 Kgs 6:13).[78] Yet after Israel's exile for breaking their covenant with the Lord, he graciously promised to dwell in their midst again:

77. The implied copulative verb here with αὐτῷ ἡ δόξα would be an optative expression of a wish or prayer (without ἄν): αὐτῷ ἡ δόξα **εἴη**, "to him *may there be* glory"; Smyth, *Greek Grammar*, §1814; BDF §128 (5); cf. Hoehner, 494. Some prefer to read an indic. here and the dative as poss.: "To him belongs glory" (so Lincoln, 216; cf. Gnilka, 192). This is less attractive here because Paul is expressing a wish in prayer. But it is a minor point.

78. In addition to literature already cited on this theme, add L. Michael Morales, *The Tabernacle Pre-Figured: Cosmic Mountain Ideology in Genesis and Exodus*, BTS 15 (Leuven: Peeters, 2012), for early imagery of "dwelling in the divine Presence," which is "the kernal of [Scripture's] principal theme" (1).

"Sing and rejoice, O daughter of Zion, for behold, I come and I will dwell in your midst, declares the LORD" (Zech 2:10). But this text goes further and promises that Israel would not be alone as a nation: "And many nations shall join themselves to the LORD in that day, *and shall be my people*. And I will dwell in your midst, and you shall know that the LORD of hosts has sent me to you" (Zech 2:11 [cf. v. 6 for the exile]; emphasis added).

Paul recognizes the fulfillment of this promise articulated by Zechariah in Christ Jesus. Thus he sees the fullness of God's glory residing with his new-covenant, united people, consisting of believing Jews and Gentiles as a new temple building.[79] Paul states that this new reality in the church will never end in his unprecedented extravagant expression of eternity: "for all generations, forever and ever, amen." God's glory will never depart from his church until the day when his resurrected people will enter the reality of the heavenly Jerusalem (Rev 21:1–22:5), which has already come into inaugurated fulfillment in the resurrected "Jesus, the Mediator of the new covenant" (Heb 12:22–24).

The implications of this are most significant. In the OT era, people had to travel long and hard to the distant land of Israel to inquire of the Lord or to discover his dwelling place (e.g., 1 Kgs 10:1–10; 2 Kgs 5:1–19). Now, in the new covenant era, the Lord dwells wherever his church is established together (Matt 18:20), even to the ends of the earth, as his church expands through the proclamation of the gospel (Matt 24:14; Acts 1:8; 13:46–8; Rom 10:18) in the power of the Spirit (1 Cor 2:4; Gal 3:5; Eph 3:16; 1 Thess 1:5)."To the Spirit particularly is attributed the dignity of transforming created space into covenantal place: a home for communion between Creator and creatures, extending to the ends of the earth in waves of kingdom labor."[80] As the church expands, it does so as the embodiment of Christ and as the temple home of the glory of God wherever it is on earth through the Holy Spirit (2:22). As one of my friends, Rev. Wayne Forkner, puts it, the church is an embassy of the new creation in this world.

---

79. The sg. reference to "church" in 3:21 instead of pl. "churches" shows that Paul conceives of the church as a unified whole, not as isolated and scattered communities (see 4:4–6).

80. Horton, *Christian Faith*, 552.

Application and Devotional Implications

It seems a bit presumptuous to discuss the application of this text, since Paul himself will be teasing out divinely inspired applications from what he has just taught in the chapters that follow. Yet if we need one practical reminder in our day from Eph 3:14–21, it is that Christians are both individuals and components of a united body. Individual believers matter to the Lord. He finds each one of his people inconceivably valuable, and he calls each of his sheep by name (John 10:3, 27). And the Lord has a strong desire that each one will be with him in glory (John 17:24), and he guards each one to that end (John 17:12). The individual believer appears in 3:14–21 in that Paul prays that the Holy Spirit would strengthen the "inner man" of each one (v. 16).

Yet believers are not only individuals but also corporately one in the church alongside others. This comes out in 3:14–21 and its connection to 2:19–22 in that the church is a single "house" of God, an inaugurated new-creation temple filled with his glory. Although Paul can talk about the bodies of individuals as holy sanctuaries of God (1 Cor 6:19; cf. John 2:21), here in Ephesians he presents the united house of God as composed of the whole of individuals brought together into one building, from nearby believing Jews to the far-flung believing Gentiles who have now been brought near. This corporate aspect comes out nicely in Peter's similar presentation of believers not as isolated and individual temples but as "living stones" of the one temple of God resting on a "chosen and precious" cornerstone, Jesus Christ (1 Pet 2:4–6). The exhortations that immediately follow in Eph 4:1–16 build on this unity and diversity in Christ's one body and house, made up of many, prized members, whom he loved even to the death (5:2, 25).

Selected Bibliography

Dahl, N. "Cosmic Dimensions and Religious Knowledge (Eph 3:18)." In *Jesus und Paulus*, 57–75. Göttingen: Vandenhoeck & Ruprecht, 1975. Repr. in *Studies in Ephesians*, 365–88. WUNT 131. Tübingen: Mohr Siebeck, 2000.

Foster, R. "'A Temple in the Lord Filled to the Fullness of God': Context and Intertextuality (Eph. 3:19)." *NovT* 49 (2007): 85–96.

Horton, M. *The Christian Faith: A Systematic Theology for Pilgrims on the Way*. Grand Rapids: Zondervan, 2011.

Morales, L. *The Tabernacle Pre-Figured: Cosmic Mountain Ideology in Genesis and Exodus*. BTS 15. Leuven: Peeters, 2012.

Neyrey, J. *Give God the Glory: Ancient Prayer and Worship in Cultural Perspective*. Grand Rapids: Eerdmans, 2007.

Wiles, G. *Paul's Intercessory Prayers: The Significance of the Intercessory Prayer Passages in the Letters of Paul*. SNTSMS 24. Cambridge: Cambridge University Press, 1974. Repr., 2007.

Paul's Exhortation to Unity in Love (4:1–6)

Introduction

In Ephesians 4:1–6 Paul strongly urges the church to unity in love based on the truths of the one God, his calling, and his one work of redemption. With v. 1, Paul transitions from the first part of his epistle, which has focused on doctrinal instruction related to believers' redemption, to unfolding exhortations specifying their obedience, which must flow from the divine grace of their deliverance and from the work of the Holy Spirit in them.[1] The ideal of ecclesiastical unity and love is central not only to 4:1–6 but to much of the material to follow in this chapter and beyond.

Ephesians 4:1–6 fits into a larger section consisting of 4:1–16 as its paraenetic introduction and statement of the main theme of unity. Codex Vaticanus (B) preserves 4:1–16 as one section, while other early MSS subdivide the text into smaller units by writing initial letters in the margin (*ekthesis*) or with punctuation marks and blank spaces.[2] I have divided discussion of 4:1–16 into two sections (vv. 1–6 and 7–16), but it should be understood that these are components of the larger text, which should remain in view while interpreting smaller elements of the whole.

1. As Sinclair Ferguson (*Holy Spirit,* 141) notes regarding the OT: "The pattern of holiness is always in the form of impvs. of obedience arising out of indics. of grace. God has redeemed his people from bondage, *therefore* they are to be conformed to his patterns (Ex. 20:1–2)" (emphasis original). For treatment of how the impvs. in Ephesians cohere with its doctrinal content see Ester Petrenko, *Created in Christ Jesus for Good Works: The Integration of Soteriology and Ethics in Ephesians*, PBM (Milton Keynes, UK: Paternoster, 2011).

2. Codex Sinaiticus (א) divides 4:1–16 into four divisions (vv. 1–6, 7–10, 11–13, 14–16); Alexandrinus (A) has six sections (vv. 1–3, 4, 5–6, 7–10, 11–14, 15–16); and Ephraemi Rescriptus (C) has seven (vv. 5–6, 7–8, 9–10, 11–12, 13–14, 15–16).

Contrary to the earlier periodic style of Eph 1–3, the style in what follows in chaps. 4–6 is composed of shorter cola* and less elaborate periods.[3] The character of the discourse is more conversational and fits with its series of imperatives and Paul's concern to give appeals for behavior and particular ethical practices. Sometimes there is simply a loose grouping of statements, some of which appear with machine gun-like rapidity, such as the two word predications in v. 5.[4] At other times the "periods" are longer and more involved (e.g., vv. 13 and 14). I will continue to speak of periods, but the term does not have a technical meaning of "rounding" in style here. It simply shows the grouping of cola* that have some sort of unity and may possibly represent the contours of the oral composition and presentation to the audience, since *period* to the ancients may refer to what could be delivered in one breath.

Here is my suggested arrangement of Eph 4:1–6:

A 1 Παρακαλῶ οὖν ὑμᾶς
ἐγὼ ὁ δέσμιος ἐν κυρίῳ
ἀξίως περιπατῆσαι τῆς κλήσεως ἧς ἐκλήθητε
2 μετὰ πάσης ταπεινοφροσύνης καὶ πραΰτητος

B μετὰ μακροθυμίας ἀνεχόμενοι ἀλλήλων ἐν ἀγάπῃ
3 σπουδάζοντες τηρεῖν τὴν ἑνότητα τοῦ πνεύματος
ἐν τῷ συνδέσμῳ τῆς εἰρήνης

C 4 ἓν σῶμα καὶ ἓν πνεῦμα
καθὼς καὶ ἐκλήθητε
ἐν μιᾷ ἐλπίδι τῆς κλήσεως ὑμῶν

3. Dionysius of Halicarnassus speaks clearly about the need for variation of style, with some parts expressed in periods (ἐν περιόδῳ) and some without (ἔξω περιόδου) to provide relief from monotony. In addition, he suggests that some cola* should also have variety, as we find in Eph 4:1–6, where "one is short, another long, one more crudely wrought, another with more refinement" (*Comp.* 19).

4. A series of short κόμματα (two- to four-word "phrases") lends some excitement and speed to the tone of the passage and is known to the rhetors as "rapidity" (γοργότης; Lat. *velocitas*); cf. Hermogenes, *Peri ideon* 2.1. I have separated these short predications (e.g., εἷς κύριος, μία πίστις, ἓν βάπτισμα [v. 5]) into their own line instead of putting them together on one line with commas. The effect is the same either way when read aloud, since a slight pause for oral presentation is indicated by the modern comma mark.

D 5 εἷς κύριος
μία πίστις
ἓν βάπτισμα
6 εἷς θεὸς καὶ πατὴρ πάντων
ὁ ἐπὶ πάντων καὶ διὰ πάντων καὶ ἐν πᾶσιν

As mentioned above, the style in this section of Ephesians is moving to a more informal, plain style of ordinary discourse than the Greek of Eph 1–3, even if it has a certain rhetorical power and appeal. This is clear particularly in v. 5, with its short bursts of phrases that have none of the flowing character that we saw in the previous chapters. There is also present here a coordination of prepositional phrases in v. 2, with *μετά* and without a conjunction like *καί* or *δέ*, that becomes particularly important for interpretation of the meaning of vv. 1 and 3 (see comments below) and will continue to interest us especially in 4:12.

The only other thing of note is an interesting inverted pairing (chiasm*) of words that have the same forms between vv. 1 and 4 as follows: 1 κλήσεως … ἐκλήθητε … 4 ἐκλήθητε … κλήσεως. However, this does not seem to function as a structuring device here and may have occurred simply because Paul wanted to reinforce the concept of calling in the passage.

Outline

VIII. Paul's Exhortation to Unity in Love (4:1–6)
- A. The exhortation proper (4:1–3)
  1. The worthy walk (4:1c–2a)
  2. Patient endurance in love (4:2b)
  3. Zeal for the church's unity in peace (4:3)
- B. The basis of the exhortation (4:4–6)

Original Text

1 Παρακαλῶ οὖν ὑμᾶς ἐγὼ ὁ δέσμιος ἐν κυρίῳ ἀξίως περιπατῆσαι τῆς κλήσεως
ἧς ἐκλήθητε, **2** μετὰ πάσης ταπεινοφροσύνης καὶ πραΰτητος, μετὰ μακροθυμίας, ἀνεχόμενοι ἀλλήλων ἐν ἀγάπῃ, **3** σπουδάζοντες τηρεῖν τὴν ἑνότητα τοῦ
πνεύματος ἐν τῷ συνδέσμῳ τῆς εἰρήνης· **4** ⸀Ἓν σῶμα καὶ[a] ἓν πνεῦμα, καθὼς καὶ

ἐκλήθητε ἐν μιᾷ ἐλπίδι τῆς κλήσεως ὑμῶν· **5** εἷς κύριος, μία πίστις, ἓν βάπτισμα,
6 εἷς θεὸς καὶ πατὴρ πάντων, ὁ ἐπὶ πάντων καὶ διὰ πάντων καὶ ἐν πᾶσιν.[b]

Textual Notes

4.a. B, 323, 326, and a few other MSS do not have καί in the expression "just as *also* you were called," but this can be viewed as a simple accidental omission of a word that is not absolutely necessary to the meaning of the statement (cf. Col 3:15).

6.b. The earliest and best MSS with a wide geographical distribution (including P[46], ℵ, A, B, 33, 88, 424, 460, cop, eth, and geo) read the last phrase as ἐν πᾶσιν, while the Textus Receptus and most Byzantine MSS read either ἐν πᾶσιν ὑμῖν, "among all *you*" ("in you all" [KJV]), or ἐν πᾶσιν ἡμῖν, "among all *of us*" (Vg.: *in omnibus nobis*). Metzger correctly labels these latter readings as "explanatory glosses."[5]

Translation

1 I therefore, the prisoner in the Lord[6], strongly urge[7] you to set out[8] in a manner worthy of the calling with which[9] you have been called, **2** accompanied

5. Bruce M. Metzger, *A Textual Commentary on the Greek New Testament*, 2nd ed. (New York: United Bible Societies, 1994), 536.
6. Some English versions have "the prisoner of the Lord" (KJV, NASB) for the phrase ὁ δέσμιος ἐν κυρίῳ, as though Paul had said ὁ δέσμιος τοῦ κυρίου as in 3:1. Other versions have "a prisoner for the Lord" (ESV, NIV) as well as"the prisoner in the Lord" (NRSV). The last rendering is preferred in order to show that Paul is a prisoner in union with Christ—the referent of κύριος here. Without this connection to Christ, Paul would not be a prisoner or suffer from the world's outrage (2 Tim 1:11–12; cf. Gal 1:10; 6:12).
7. See the comment for the strong sense of παρακαλέω as "strongly urge." English versions vary considerably in their renderings: ESV, NIV "urge"; KJV "beseech"; νasb "entreat"; and (least satisfactory) NRSV "beg."
8. BDF §337 (1) properly take the aor. inf. περιπατῆσαι as ingressive (inceptive), as also in 2:10. Contrast with pres. περιπατεῖν in 4:17. "Set out" is my attempt to convey the inceptive idea of "walk" lexically in English.
9. The relative pronoun ἧς is attracted to the gen. case of its antecedent κλήσεως; cf. BDF §294.

with[10] all humility and gentleness, and with patience[11] to bear[12] with one another in love, **3** and to take pains[13] to maintain the unity of the Spirit in the bond of peace. **4** There is one body and one Spirit—just as also you were called to the[14] one hope from[15] your calling— **5** one Lord, one faith, one baptism, **6** one God and Father of all, who is over all and through all and in all.

Commentary

4:1 Παρακαλῶ οὖν ὑμᾶς ἐγὼ ὁ δέσμιος ἐν κυρίῳ, "I therefore, the prisoner in the Lord, strongly urge you." The inferential conjunction οὖν shows that Paul sees the behavior he enjoins on his audience in the chapters to follow to be a clear implication of the doctrinal realities he has been teaching up to this point in the epistle (1:3–3:21). Yet the closer context also plays a

---

10. The phrase "accompanied with" renders μετά here, which ties the phrase μετὰ πάσης ταπεινοφροσύνης καὶ πραΰτητος ("accompanied with all humility and gentleness") with the previous statement to "set out in a manner worthy of the calling" in v. 1c; cf. BDAG, 637.

11. Μετά in the phrase μετὰ μακροθυμίας here is a marker of association, just as previously in v. 2a (see previous note). Despite the commas in the Greek editions and English versions, the phrase attaches to the following ptc. ἀνεχόμενοι (see comment). The dynamic transformation of the prepositional phrase into an English impv. by the NIV is unique: "and gentle; *be patient,* bearing with one another in love" (emphasis added).

12. As also seen with the "parallel" ptcs. (my term) in 3:17 (cf. 4:15; 5:15–21; 6:5–9), the two nominative ptcs. ἀνεχόμενοι and σπουδάζοντες are used to mirror an inf. (here περιπατῆσαι) without conjs. Hence the progression παρακαλῶ ... περιπατῆσαι ... ἀνεχόμενοι ... σπουδάζοντες is the equivalent of παρακαλῶ ... περιπατῆσαι ... καὶ ἀνέχεσθαι ... καὶ σπουδάζειν. See "Excursus: Parallel Participles" below.

13. See previous note for use of the ptc. σπουδάζοντες.

14. Often in Greek, an anarthrous noun acting as the obj. of a prep. may be definite, as here in v. 4 where anarthrous ἔλπις ("hope") is definite: ἐν μιᾷ **ἐλπίδι** τῆς κλήσεως ὑμῶν ("in *the* one hope from your calling"). The definite gen. phrase τῆς κλήσεως ὑμῶν attached to ἔλπις shows that is a specific hope that flows from their divine summons (cf. ESV and NRSV).

15. The gen. "call" or "calling" here (ἐν μιᾷ ἐλπίδι τῆς **κλήσεως** ὑμῶν) acts as the source of the believer's hope. Source (or origin) is one of the fundamental meanings of the gen. case, derived from an original Indo-European ablative (cf. Smyth, *Greek Grammar*, §§280, 1279, 1410; A. T. Robertson, *A Grammar of the Greek New Testament in the Light of Historical Research*, 4th ed. [New York, 1923], 514). Cf. "to one hope when you were called" (NIV); "to the one hope that belongs to your call."

role because holiness of life is especially required for those who are being constructed into an inaugurated new-creation temple filled with God's glorious presence (see on 3:19 and 21; cf. Exod 29:21): "You shall be holy, for I the LORD your God am holy" (Lev 19:2; cf. Lev 11:44–45; Deut 23:14; Joel 3:17; 1 Pet 1:15–16). Furthermore, Paul sees the power of God unleashed within believers at their conversion and regeneration (e.g., 1:13–14, 19–20) as necessarily leading to a holy, new-creation life, as was clearly articulated in Eph 2:8–10.[16]

Paul uses παρακαλέω over fifty times in his epistles, and the term often marks a transition into exhortations that concentrate on Christian living with παρακαλῶ οὖν ὑμᾶς ("I therefore strongly urge you") in Rom 12:1; 1 Cor 4:16; and 1 Tim 2:1 besides here in Eph 4:1.[17] The word παρακαλῶ is a term of a superior addressing inferiors (including royal exhortations); hence, it represents a strong appeal or exhortation to an action from someone who carried a certain authority over his audience (LSJ, 1311 ["demand, require"]; BDAG, 765).[18] This strong meaning of παρακαλῶ is combined with two other elements in v. 1. The first is Paul's expression of the pronoun ἐγώ, which is not needed by the verb, and the second is his reference to himself as "the prisoner in the Lord."[19] The word ἐγώ might add a certain

16. Cf. Herman Ridderbos, *Paul: An Outline of His Theology*, trans. John De Witt (Grand Rapids: Eerdmans, 1975), 205–326.

17. Paul uses synonymous διὸ παρακαλῶ ὑμᾶς in 2 Cor 2:8 and similar παρακαλῶ δὲ ὑμᾶς in Rom 15:30; 16:17; 1 Cor 1:10; 16:15; 1 Thess 4:10; 5:14 (the last two places with pl. παρακαλοῦμεν because of joint composition with Silvanus and Timothy).

18. See James D. G. Dunn, *The Theology of Paul the Apostle* (Grand Rapids: Eerdmans, 1998), 574, citing C. J. Bjerkelund. The pres. indic. tense form παρακαλῶ here is "performative" and therefore self-referential (sometimes called a "speech-act"). That is, it does not describe some other event, but the utterance of this statement is itself the event of the verb. The rendering that brings this out would be: "I *hereby* strongly urge"; see esp. Buist M. Fanning, *Verbal Aspect in New Testament Greek* (Oxford: Clarendon, 1990), 188–90. Grammars sometimes refer to this as "aoristic," but this is not the best label or treatment of the meaning; so E. Burton, *Syntax of the Moods and Tenses in New Testament Greek* (Edinburgh: T&T Clark, 1898), §13; BDF §320; Daniel B. Wallace, *Greek Grammar beyond the Basics* (Grand Rapids: Zondervan, 1997), 517–18.

19. The nominative personal pronoun (ἐγώ) is used alongside παρακαλῶ by Paul only in Eph 4:1 and 2 Cor 10:1: Αὐτὸς δὲ ἐγὼ Παῦλος παρακαλῶ ὑμᾶς, "I, Paul, do personally urge you most seriously"; cf. Gal 5:2, with λέγω with a different tone from Eph 5:32.

emphasis to an utterance especially stressing personal involvement ("I *personally* did this") or contrasting the speaker with another ("It was *I*, not *him*").[20] Here, though, Paul seems to use ἐγώ as a way to accent his imprisonment—"on your behalf" (3:1, 10)—which recalls the long digression explaining how it was an outcome of his apostolic call to preach the gospel among the nations (3:1–13). Thus he satisfies any concerns the audience may have for his authority to make demands for their lives as Christians.

ἀξίως περιπατῆσαι τῆς κλήσεως ἧς ἐκλήθητε, "to set out in a manner worthy of the calling with which you have been called." This is the first of the three, interconnected elements of Paul's exhortation: the worthy walk (vv. 1c–2a), patient endurance in love (v. 2b), and zeal for the church's unity in peace (v. 3). The "calling" (κλῆσις) here is the summons issued by God, which is "irrevocable" (Rom 11:29; cf. 8:28), "upward" (Phil 3:14), "holy" (2 Tim 1:9), and brings hope (Eph 1:18; 4:4; cf. 1:4–5). Hence, Paul urges his Ephesian audience to "walk worthily" (ἀξίως) of their calling inasmuch as "God's calling establishes the norm or criterion to which their conduct should conform" (O'Brien, 275–76).[21] Similarly, Paul prays in Col 1:10 that the Colossians may receive gifts "to walk worthily of the Lord" (περιπατῆσαι ἀξίως τοῦ κυρίου; cf. Col 2:6; Phil 1:27), while the Thessalonians were implored "so that you might walk worthily of the God who calls you into his own kingdom and glory" (εἰς τὸ περιπατεῖν ὑμᾶς ἀξίως τοῦ θεοῦ τοῦ καλοῦντος ὑμᾶς εἰς τὴν ἑαυτοῦ βασιλείαν καὶ δόξαν; 1 Thess 2:12; cf. 2 Thess 1:11).

Paul opens with mention of the believer's calling, because he or she is not called to be alone in a cell but to enter the church of Christ. "And let the peace of Christ rule in your hearts, to which indeed you were called in one body (εἰς ἣν καὶ ἐκλήθητε ἐν ἑνὶ σώματι)" (Col 3:15; cf. Eph 3:10). Paul develops similar ideas here in Eph 4:1–6 as in Col 3:12–15.

4:2 μετὰ πάσης ταπεινοφροσύνης καὶ πραΰτητος, "accompanied with all humility and gentleness." This colon* belongs with v. 1c. The modern

---

20. For the former see, for example, Rom 9:3, or the seven uses of ἐγώ in Rom 7:9–25; the contrastive use of ἐγώ is aptly illustrated in 1 Cor 1:12 (cf. 3:4): "*I* am in Paul's party, well, *I* am in Apollos', *I*, in contrast, belong to Cephas, *I* am Christ's!"

21. The inf. περιπατῆσαι is dependent on opening παρακαλῶ (similar to indirect discourse, yet with a verb of command or entreaty) and represents an original impv. idea; cf. Burton, *Moods*, §§204, 337, 391; BDF §392 (1c). The metaphor of "walking" (περιπατέω) refers to the conduct of life (2:1–2, 10; cf. ἀναστρέφω in 2:3).

versification and punctuation of our text follows a different line of interpretation, and English translations and commentaries often follow suit by attaching this prepositional phrase (along with μετὰ μακροθυμίας with the participle ἀνεχόμενοι that follows in v. 2b). Or they leave the meaning somewhat ambiguous.[22] The unwarranted ambiguity comes across in our versions and Greek editions when the prepositional phrase in v. 2a and the opening one in v. 2b are separated off from their surrounding context by commas: ἧς ἐκλήθητε, μετὰ πάσης ταπεινοφροσύνης καὶ πραΰτητος, μετὰ μακροθυμίας, ἀνεχόμενοι ἀλλήλων, "to which you have been called, with all humility and gentleness, with patience, bearing with one another ..."[23] In my judgment there should only be one comma after πραΰτητος.

All of this is to say that v. 2a gives an initial indication of how exactly the believer is to set out to live "in a manner worthy of the calling with which" he or she has been called (v. 1c). That life is worthy of the believer's call when it is "accompanied with all humility and gentleness."[24] This does not mean that v. 2a is hermetically sealed off from what follows—just the opposite, for it leads directly into v. 2b.

As is often pointed out (e.g., Lincoln, 235–36), ταπεινοφροσύνη ("humility") is not a positive attribute in the Graeco-Roman world at large but suggests degrading "humiliation" or "debasement" (cf. Col 2:18, 23; LSJ, 1756–57), which was abhorrent in a world where public honor, as

22. NIV removes this close connection of the prepositional phrase with what goes before entirely and turns it into an impv. starting out a new sentence: "Be completely humble and gentle." This interpretation is not followed here and may possibly have arisen because of too much dependence on the modern verse division between vv. 1 and 2. Cf. Barth (425–27), who also translates the first μετά phrase this way, but takes the second with the following ptc. as do I: "Be altogether humble and gentle. Patiently bear one another in love."

23. The ambiguity leads one to possibly take both prepositional phrases with what goes before (even with παρακαλῶ [i.e., "I strongly urge you ... with all humility"]) or with what comes after. The commas in the Greek text come from the NA[28] but can also be traced back a long way; for example, the same three commas in Eph 4:2 are found in Desiderius Erasmus's Greek edition of 1516. The issue here is yet another benefit of working with the NT text in terms of periodic and colon* divisions endemic to ancient Greek compositions.

24. Hence, grammatically the μετά phrase modifies περιπατῆσαι in v. 1c.

opposed to shame, was consummately valued.[25] In the biblical world, humility is a positive virtue in contrast with haughtiness, especially when it is combined with πραΰτης ("gentleness"), as marks Jesus' own character (e.g., Matt 11:29) and thus also marks those who are being remade into his image (e.g., Acts 20:19; Phil 2:3; Col 3:12; 1 Pet 3:8; 5:5).[26]

μετὰ μακροθυμίας, ἀνεχόμενοι ἀλλήλων ἐν ἀγάπῃ, "and with patience to bear with one another in love." The walk characterized by all humility and gentleness is easy to project in a vacuum or when surrounded by admirers and friends. But now Paul gives shape to what genuine humility and gentleness looks like when they enter the crucible of real life in the church: patient forbearance with one another in love. The word ἀνέχω only appears in the middle voice in the NT and means here to patiently tolerate someone who is difficult or foolish (cf. Col 3:11–15; 2 Cor 11:1–20; BDAG, 78, "endure, bear with, put up with"). This is why Paul brings in "patience" to qualify the bearing with one another he enjoins. One can easily tolerate a mildly irritating personality, but patience is especially needed for the foolish or difficult brother or sister in Christ.

As was defended above, I understand the prepositional phrase μετὰ μακροθυμίας ("with patience") to be used for emphasis to modify the following participle ἀνεχόμενοι, not the previous idea of "walking" (περιπατῆσαι) in v. 1 found in other interpretations.[27] The prepositional phrase μετὰ μακροθυμίας is brought forward in its colon* ("fronted") to the place of stress or focus, while the trailing ἐν ἀγάπῃ is at the end; thus the two phrases flank

25. The opposing pair of honor and shame in ancient Mediterranean society has happily received significant treatment in recent literature; e.g., David A. DeSilva, *Honor, Patronage, Kinship & Purity: Unlocking New Testament Culture* (Downers Grove, IL: InterVarsity, 2000), 23–93.

26. "He has told you, O man, what is good; and what does the LORD require of you but to do justice, and to love kindness, and to walk humbly with your God?" (Mic 6:8).

27. *Contra* Hoehner, 507–8, who has a long and helpful discussion of the options. Lincoln (236) says, " 'Bearing with one another in love' is an amplification of what is meant by patience," but this reverses the meaning of the Greek. Ptcs. don't amplify their qualifying adv. phrases but vice versa.

the participle ἀνεχόμενοι. The word order is unusual—hence, the focus or stress is perceivable to the audience—but not unprecedented.[28]

The participle ἀνεχόμενοι is almost universally interpreted as being imperatival here (cf. Hoehner, 510 and 510n6). While this is true, what gives it imperatival force is that it occurs in parallel with the infinitive περιπατῆσαι ("to walk") in v. 1, which itself functions as an imperative with a verb of command or admonition (παρακαλῶ ["strongly urge"]; see comment on v. 1). Hence, the participle acts like an imperative only because the word it parallels has imperatival force. The same is true of the next participle σπουδάζοντες at the beginning of v. 3.[29]

The phrase ἐν ἀγάπῃ gives the motive for patiently bearing with the difficult fellow church member. The most trenchant statement Paul says that bears on this admonition is in his magnificent encomium on love: "Love is patient. ... It does not take account of any wrong (received). ... Love bears all things ... endures all things" (1 Cor 13:4–7). Paul, the least of all saints (3:8), intimately knows that the only Christian motive for his own love for his neighbor is gratitude for Christ's self-sacrificial love received by grace through faith (e.g., 2:4–9; 5:2). Unity in the church may be secured by the bonds of peace (v. 3), but the links of that irenic chain are forged out of love.

4:3 σπουδάζοντες τηρεῖν τὴν ἑνότητα τοῦ πνεύματος ἐν τῷ συνδέσμῳ τῆς εἰρήνης, "and to take pains to maintain the unity of the Spirit in the bond of peace." This is the third of the three elements of Paul's exhortation: the worthy walk (vv. 1c–2a), patient endurance in love (v. 2b), and zeal for the church's unity in peace (v. 3). The grammar at the heart of this analysis takes the two adverbial participles in vv. 2–3 as parallel with the infinitive περιπατῆσαι in v. 1 (see "Excursus: Parallel Participles"). The three elements can be outlined as follows:

---

28. For example, in 1:4–5, where the prepositional phrase in v. 4 modifies the ptc. in v. 5, and this ptc. also has two flanking prepositional phrases: **ἐν ἀγάπῃ** προορίσας ἡμᾶς **εἰς υἱοθεσίαν** ("In love he predestined us for adoption"). There is fronting and therefore stress on ἐν ἀγάπῃ in this statement. Cf. 6:18.

29. One might expect the ptcs. to be expressed in their acc. case forms in agreement with ὑμᾶς (in v. 1 or as implied subject of the inf. περιπατῆσαι), but in this parallel function the adv. ptcs. are usually nominative, as are both ἀνεχόμενοι and σπουδάζοντες. See "Excursus: Parallel Participles" below for discussion.

1 Παρακαλῶ οὖν ὑμᾶς
ἀξίως περιπατῆσαι
2b ἀνεχόμενοι ἀλλήλων
3 σπουδάζοντες τηρεῖν[30]

The verb σπουδάζω means "to be especially conscientious in discharging an obligation" (BDAG, 939). Paul urges the church as a community to be eagerly intent on the goal of their unity and peace with one another. This is the concern that undergirds many of the details of Paul's exhortations in Eph 4–6. This unity (ἑνότης, or "oneness") Paul enjoins is reinforced by him in what follows through repetition of the word "one" (εἷς, μία, ἕν), which appears seven other times in vv. 4–5. The connection between ἑνότης and εἷς, μία, and ἕν later is clearly intentional; ἑνότης is a rare term, occurring only in 4:3 and 4:13 in the NT, in contrast with other terms for living in unity or harmony Paul could have chosen.[31]

Yet Paul does not just call for unity, but "the unity of the Spirit" (τὴν ἑνότητα τοῦ πνεύματος).[32] It is tempting to interpret the genitive "of the

30. The inf. τηρεῖν ("to maintain") is a complement of σπουδάζοντες ("to take pains"). The pres.-tense form predominates for atelic τηρέω (ten pres. inf. forms versus two aor. forms in the NT), though σπουδάζω more often takes an aor. inf. complement (three pres.-tense infs. versus eight aor. tense in the NT). The aor. form of τηρέω would be expected to convey an inceptive idea, as it does in Acts 25:21 (τηρηθῆναι, "put under guard"), where it is immediately followed by pres.-tense τηρεῖσθαι ("kept under guard").

31. E.g., τὸ αὐτὸ φρονεῖν ("live in harmony") in Rom 12:16; 15:5; 2 Cor 13:11; Phil 2:2; 4:2 (cf. ὁμόφρων in 1 Pet 3:1), συμφονία, or ὁμόνοια and ἕνωσις, which are found in Ignatius, whose interest in ecclesiastical unity has many echoes from Ephesians; e.g., "Do nothing apart from your bishop, preserve your flesh as a sanctuary for God (ναὸν θεοῦ), love your unity (ἕνωσιν), flee divisions, be imitators of Jesus Christ as he himself is of his Father" (*Phld.* 7.2); cf. *Eph.* 4.2, 14–15; *Smyrn.* 3.3; *Magn.* 7.1 (and more reported in BDAG, 338); cf. John Paul Lotz, *Ignatius and Concord: The Background and Use of the Language of Concord in the Letters of Ignatius of Antioch* (New York: Peter Lang, 2007). Ignatius' concern for unity becomes more poignant if his trip to Rome for execution was brought about by rivals in the Antiochian church, as hinted at in *Phld.* 10.1; *Smyrn.* 11.2; and *Pol.* 7.1; cf. William R. Schoedel, *Ignatius of Antioch*, Hermeneia (Philadelphia: Fortress, 1985), 10–11.

32. To take πνεῦμα as a unifying human spirit present in the church, as if he had said "spirit of gentleness" (1 Cor 4:21; Gal 6:1) or the like (cf. Rom 11:8), is linguistically possible but does not fit the context and flow of the passage; cf. Lincoln, 237; Barth, 428.

Spirit" as specifying the source or origin of the church's unity: "the church's unity, brought about by the Spirit." This would be true, but given what is said in v. 4, it is better to take the genitive as simple possession, "the Holy Spirit's own unity." This is why Paul calls on the Ephesians to "maintain" or "preserve" this unity rather than to make or create it (for more see comment on v. 4 below).

It is ironic that Paul, who is δέ σμιος (i.e., *bound* as a prisoner, in chains [6:20]), should refer here to a "bond" or "shackle" (σύνδεσμος; Acts 8:23) of peace in an exhortation to the church. It is further ironic that "bond" should be associated with "peace," since chains were often used to restrain violence (e.g., Mark 5:3–4). But this is not just wordplay. Paul knows that peace in the Christian community is necessary for their unity, whereas hostility, strife, jealousy, envy, harsh language, gossip, and other intemperate behavior, which he warns against elsewhere (e.g., 4:25–32; 2 Cor 12:20; Gal 5:20; 1 Tim 6:4–5), lead quickly and inexorably to ecclesiastical divisions (1 Cor 3:3–4). Such actions arise out of hatred (Titus 3:3), not the love that binds all to one another in perfect harmony (Col 3:14).

Ephesus at the time was not necessarily a harmonious, unified city. There had been long-standing rivalries between Ephesus, Smyrna, and Pergamum in particular, which were to continue into the second century as the cities vied for claims of special allegiance to Rome in the form of νεωκόρος ("superintendent"; cf. Acts 19:35) of the imperial cult*, which resulted in forms of special treatment from the ruling power.[33] Furthermore, given the rebuke later for the decline in love in the Ephesian church (Rev 2:4; despite their theological acumen; Rev 2:2, 6), Paul's call for unity and

33. This is well documented in various places, including: S. R. F. Price, *Rituals and Power: The Roman Imperial Cult in Asia Minor* (Cambridge: Cambridge University Press, 1985); Steven Friesen, "The Cult of the Roman Emperors in Ephesos: Temple Wardens, City Titles, and the Interpretation of the Revelation of John," in *Ephesos, Metropolis of Asia*, ed. Helmut Koester (Valley Forge, PA: Harvard Divinity School Press, 1995), 229–50; Dietmar Kienast, "Zu den Homonoia-Vereinbarungen in der römischen Kaiserzeit," *ZPE* 109 (1995): 267–82; and John Paul Lotz, "The *Homonoia* Coins of Asia Minor and Ephesians 1:21," *TynB* 50 (1999): 173–88. Imperial temples brought significant financial benefits to the cities during connected festivals and contests (Tacitus, *Ann.* 4.15.55–56); cf. Reinhold Merkelbach, "Der Rangstreit der Städte Asiens und die Rede des Aelius Aristides über die Eintracht," *ZPE* 32 (1978): 287–96.

harmony in love looks a little more pointed than a general appeal he would make to other churches.

4:4 Ἓν σῶμα καὶ ἓν πνεῦμα, "There is one body and one Spirit." This verse moves away from the exhortation proper into truths that support the call for unity that is just concluded.[34] Paul accomplishes two things at once with this line, which explains what is referred to by "unity of the Spirit" in the previous verse. First is a metaphor. The church is unified as the body of Christ (2:16; cf. 1:23; 4:12; 5:23, 30), and just as one human being has only one body, so he or she has only one spirit. From there the metaphor ends and the reality it points to begins. There is only one church, the one body of Christ; so also this church is filled by the one Holy Spirit, who unifies the church with his glorious presence and brings access to the Father to all (2:18). Hence the ἑνότης of the Spirit makes the church ἓν σῶμα, even though believers are each various "members" (5:20; cf. 4:16; Rom 12:4; 1 Cor 10:17; 12:12–20).[35] Christians do not lose their individual existence to be absorbed into the divine essence, but the one Holy Spirit, poured out in their hearts (Rom 5:5; Titus 3:5–6), ties them mysteriously together in union with Christ and with one another:

> Do we not have one God, and one Christ, and one gracious Spirit that has been poured out upon us, and one calling in Christ? Why do we mangle and mutilate the members of Christ and create factions in our own body? Why do we come to such a pitch of madness as to forget that we are members of one another? (*1 Clem.* 46.6–7; LCL trans.)

This is how v. 4a explains what is meant by "unity of the Spirit" in v. 3a.

καθὼς καὶ ἐκλήθητε ἐν μιᾷ ἐλπίδι τῆς κλήσεως ὑμῶν, "just as also you were called to the one hope from your calling." By returning to the words "call" (καλέω) and "calling" (κλῆσις) from v. 1, Paul is reminding the audience that to fulfill the mandate of maintaining ecclesiastical unity is their divine calling. This is not an offhand or insignificant part of their Christian life but

34. Though one certainly could expect γάρ here as a way of indicating the logical connection between v. 4a and what precedes. This leads many to see vv. 4–6 as having a textual background in a creed or baptismal confession (so Gnilka, 200 and n. 3). See below on v. 5 for discussion.

35. Many of these same themes are expressed in the larger passage of 1 Cor 12:4–31.

is at its very center, as he will develop further in 4:11–16 (esp. vv. 15–16). And by mentioning the "hope from your calling" here, he reminds the Ephesian Gentiles that they formerly had no hope (2:12), but that God had effectively called them into the hope of eternal life into a glorious new inheritance powerfully effected through Christ Jesus (1:18–20), which is the same for all, Jew and Gentile. "The Holy Ghost dwelling in them gives rise to the same aspirations, to the same anticipations of the same glorious inheritance, to a participation of which they have been called" (Hodge, 205).

4:5 εἷς κύριος, μία πίστις, ἓν βάπτισμα, "one Lord, one faith, one baptism." In this quick verse Paul continues the rationale for his appeal to the audience to preserve the Spirit's unity in the church. "For we all were baptized into one body in the one Spirit" (1 Cor 12:13; cf. Rom 12:5). So also there is only the one Lord, one faith, and one baptism at the heart of the church's unity.[36] Note that the church does not *create* this harmony, but *maintains* (τηρεῖν, v. 3) that unity that is founded on the oneness of the Spirit (v. 4), of the Lord Jesus, and of God the Father (v. 6). As already stated, the accent on "one," occurring seven times in vv. 4–6, binds together the "oneness" (ἑνότης; v. 3) Paul urges on his audience.

For roughly 150 years scholars have discussed passages like vv. 5–6 (many would include v. 4 here) as remnants of either an early Christian hymn, or more often as a creed or confession of faith used especially at baptism.[37] Early on scholars thought that the first such creeds only appeared in the second century (i.e., the Apostles' Creed), but in the last century scholars started proposing that confessions "of a looser sort, lacking the fixity and the official character of the later formularies but none the less foreshadowing them" may be traced to NT times.[38] As a result, commentators regularly say of Eph 4:5 that it "carries the forceful character of an acclamation" (Gnilka, 200–201) and is a "Pauline rephrasing of traditional confessions" (Barth, 471), a "baptismal catechism" (Schnackenburg, 165–66), or "a

36. Obviously, εἷς ... μία ... ἓν is an element of every ancient (and modern) student's creed when reciting the paradigms of Greek. It is also captured in the Vg. with "*unus* Dominus *una* fides *unum* baptisma."

37. For an overview see Barth, 462–72; J. N. D. Kelly, *Early Christian Creeds*, 3rd ed. (New York: Continuum, 1972; 1st ed., 1950), 1–29.

38. Kelly, *Creeds*, 7.

traditional confessional acclamation which had its origin in a baptismal setting" (Lincoln, 229).[39]

My own judgment is that in Eph 4:5–6 we are possibly dealing with an adaptation of concepts developed elsewhere, for there certainly are expressions of the faith that were semicodified in the apostolic age (see below on *κύριος Ἰησοῦς* and *μία πίστις*).[40] But who composed these concepts if not apostles like Paul? How exactly can we tell through precise historical inquiry devoid of speculative foundations that Paul did not express Eph 4:5–6 as a freely composed creedal statement for the Ephesian church?[41] Or, just as likely, he had expressed similar ideas elsewhere and rephrases them here for the purpose of his admonition, stated in vv. 1–3. Paul may even have had these, his own ideas, written down in a personal anthology for use when the occasion fit, for we know that ancient authors regularly kept notebooks for this purpose.[42] Without discovery of Christian creedal texts antedating the NT—or of Paul's personal notebooks (2 Tim 4:13)—these questions must remain unanswered and the idea of a prior, non-Pauline confessional origin of Eph 4:5–6 must remain only possible but unproven.

However, we can say one further thing here (and a couple more in a moment). When scholars analyze the material they think is confessional or hymnic in the NT, they often talk about it having "artistic structure,

39. For Lincoln, the whole of vv. 4–6 are "one or two pieces of creedal material that the writer has taken up in his own rhetorical stress on unity" (Lincoln, 228) in addition to his supposed dependence on Colossians, which Lincoln stresses throughout his treatment of Ephesians.

40. And Paul quite obviously and naturally derived inspiration from his focus on "one" from the Shema (Deut 6:4); see below on v. 6.

41. See Michael Peppard, " 'Poetry', 'Hymns' and 'Traditional Material' in New Testament Epistles or How to Do Things with Indentations," *JSNT* 30 (2008): 319–42, for critique of the undefined or inaccurate criteria used in the scholarly search for poetic or hymnic background to passages like this, as well as the corresponding indentation of these texts in our current Greek editions. It sometimes allows a fresh reading of the biblical text to remove or deemphasize chapter and verse divisions as well as the modern punctuation marks our editors and translators have inserted into the Greek text.

42. See E. Randolph Richards, *The Secretary in the Letters of Paul*, WUNT 2.42 (Tübingen: Mohr Siebeck, 1991), 158–68.

rhythmic style and stately bearing."[43] In line with this, Schnackenburg (166) calls the statement of εἷς-μία-ἕν in v. 5 a "sonorous trinity." I can easily grant that Eph 4:5–6 (indeed much of Ephesians) is "artistic" in a rough, powerful way. But scholars often speak of the "rhythmic" or "sonorous" character of texts that have no such rhythm or sonorous character in Greek. For example, **ἓν βάπτισμα** in v. 5c, with its conjunction of liquid *nu* next to plosive *beta*, is just the sort of thing audiences would find *not* sonorous, for it causes an awkward pause (hiatus) in pronunciation in the middle of its colon*.[44] Perhaps "sonorous" refers to the predominance of long syllables in the text (see above on 2:1–3) or that there are repetition of sounds. While there are five words in v. 6 that open with *pi* (a favorite in Ephesians at the end of a periodic development), that is about all that could be called sonorous in Eph 4:5–6.[45] And "rhythm" in Greek relates to accentual "beat," but in prose rhythm is more often related to quantitative metrical regularity of long and short vowels, but there are no repeated metrical feet in Eph 4:5–6.[46]

The most likely scenario regarding Eph 4:5–6 itself is that it is either a prior Pauline composition he employed or adapted here because the occasion called for it, or Paul composed it on the spot. There are certainly

43. Ralph P. Martin, "Aspects of Worship in the New Testament Church," *VE* 2 (1963): 6–32 (quote from 17–18); cf. Ralph P. Martin, *A Hymn of Christ: Philippians 2:5–11 in Recent Interpretation and in the Setting of Early Christian Worship*, 3rd ed. (Downers Grove, IL: InterVarsity Press, 1997), 18–19.

44. Paul shows little regard for such conjunction of sounds in his cola*, as I have pointed out earlier, and the effect in εἷς κύριος, μία πίστις, ἓν βάπτισμα is a focus on each single word, as if pronouncing them with a pause between each word.

45. Twelve to fifteen of the thirty-four syllables in Eph 4:5–6 are short. (Short syllables like **πίστις** and **βάπτισμα** may be considered long [or semilong] because they occur at the end of their cola*.)

46. The scansion of each line in v. 5 is: εἷς κύριος (¯ ˘ ˘ ˘), μία πίστις (˘ ˘ ¯ ˘), and ἓν βάπτισμα (¯ ¯ ¯ ˘). Each line has four syllables but no other resemblance of meter. The first colon* in v. 6 is interesting, with two cretics and a spondee: εἷς θεὸς καὶ πατὴρ πάντων (¯ ˘ ¯ | ¯ ˘ ¯ | ¯ ¯), while the first few words of 1 Cor 8:6 (another reputed rhythmic text) have an interesting inversion of a dactyl and anapest: εἷς θεὸς ὁ πατὴρ (¯ ˘ ˘ | ˘ ˘ ¯), but these are about the only points of metrical interest. Cf. Kelly's remarks on the "hymn-like scrap ... in rhythmic lines" of 1 Tim 3:16, which is obviously an interesting parallel composition that expressed the ὁμολογουμένως μέγα ("confessionally great") mystery of godliness; it too has no regular meter (˘ ˘ ˘ ¯ | ˘ ¯ ˘ ˘) and is therefore not rhythmic in Greek.

"trustworthy" sayings (1 Tim 1:15; 3:1; 4:9; etc.) apparently derived from others Paul quoted or commended, but we cannot tell for certain whether vv. 5–6 is such a text. There certainly were elementary confessions like κύριος Ἰησοῦς ("Jesus is Lord"; see next paragraph) in current use in the apostolic circles, but there is no direct evidence these were used in baptism. It is possible but not proven. It seems more profitable to deal with texts such as vv. 5–6 before us in their various, actually knowable contexts, even if they turn out to have been influenced somehow by other summary statements of the "one faith" current at the time.

In Ephesians 4:5, κύριος, in the assertion that there is but one Lord, refers to Christ Jesus, whose lordship as the Messiah is accented in Ephesians (1:2–3, 15, 17; 3:11; 4:1; etc.). Elsewhere κύριος Ἰησοῦς ("Jesus is Lord"; 1 Cor 12:3; cf. 1:2; Rom 10:9; Phil 2:11; Col 2:6) appears to be the summary of a basic Christian confession, even if they are "hardly more than catchwords."[47] Nevertheless, κύριος Ἰησοῦς and the host of other places where κύριος is associated with Jesus indicate how this word, which had earlier been used in the LXX to render the distinctive covenant name of God, is associated uniformly with Jesus in the NT.[48]

That there is "one Lord (Jesus)" is a bare assertion of Jesus' ascent to supreme rule over every competing power in creation (esp. 1:15–23 and 4:7–10). But it also has an implication that he is bringing the nations to himself through the gospel to unitedly confess that "Jesus is Lord." "On that day living waters shall flow out from Jerusalem, half of them to the eastern sea and half of them to the western sea. It shall continue in summer as in winter. And the LORD will be king over all the earth. On that day the LORD will be one and his name one" (Zech 14:8–9).

---

47. Kelly, *Creeds*, 16.

48. Note how εἷς κύριος ("one Lord") resembles the Shema of Deut 6:4 (κύριος εἷς ἐστιν, "the Lord is one"); see below on v. 6. Cf. Richard Bauckham, *Jesus and the God of Israel: God Crucified and Other Studies on the New Testament's Christology of Divine Identity* (Grand Rapids: Eerdmans, 2008); and Larry W. Hurtado, *One God, One Lord: Early Christian Devotion and Ancient Jewish Monotheism* (Philadelphia: Fortress, 1988). Cf. James F. McGrath, *The Only True God: Early Christian Monotheism in Its Jewish Context* (Urbana and Chicago: University of Illinois Press, 2009), who examines much the same material but with quite different (unpersuasive) results.

The assertion that there is "one faith" refers to the faith in its concrete form (1 Tim 1:19; Titus 1:13) as a "deposit" (παραθήκη; 1 Tim 6:20; 2 Tim 1:14; cf. 1 Cor 11:23; 15:3) and a "confession" (ὁμολογία; Heb 3:1; 4:14; 10:23; cf. 6:2; Jude 3). It would be ironic if Eph 4:4–6 did turn out to be a confessional statement, since these verses themselves would embody the "one faith," i.e., the heart of its doctrinal content that the apostle recognizes as essential to ecclesiastical unity.

Regardless of its origin though, vv. 5–6 *do* form elements of the "one faith," albeit not *all* of the faith. Paul is not here interested in fleshing out Christian doctrine for his audience—important elements of which comprise Ephesians itself—but in asserting the unity of the truth as part of the basis for the church's own unity. Later, in v. 13, Paul holds out the "unity of the faith" (ἡ ἑνότης τῆς πίστεως), which is distilled into "the knowledge of the Son of God" as the goal of Christian ministry in service of the church. Paul is himself engaged in this ministry in this epistle. And there is only one objective faith in Christianity, based on the one Lord, rather than one for Jews and one for Gentiles (Rom 3:29–30; cf. 1 Tim 2:4–6).

There is a natural development in the three affirmations in v. 5. The redemptive work and ascent to glory of the Lord Jesus (εἷς κύριος, "one Lord") leads to conversion and faith through Paul's gospel and its doctrinal truths (μία πίστις, "one faith"), which leads to baptism by those who are converted (ἓν βάπτισμα, "one baptism"). Hence, Paul is not counteracting false notions that more than baptism is required in true Christianity, and neither is there evidence of some sort of competing baptism in the background. He is simply saying that believers enter into union with Christ by faith, which is sacramentally signified and sealed through baptism (Gal 3:27–28; 1 Cor 12:13; cf. Rom 6:3–4; Col 2:12). There is only one baptism because there is only one Lord who has brought all together in one united body (2:13–18).

4:6 εἷς θεὸς καὶ πατὴρ πάντων ὁ ἐπὶ πάντων καὶ διὰ πάντων καὶ ἐν πᾶσιν, "one God and Father of all, who is over all and through all and in all." Paul caps off the foundation of his appeal for church unity with God the Father's own oneness. He had referenced the Spirit (v. 3) and the Son (v. 5) and finishes with the Father. Verse 6 constitutes the final two cola* of the last period of 4:1–6 in my arrangement above. Part of what indicates v. 6 as the end of a textual subsection (vv. 1–6) before the start of the second and last subsection of 4:1–16 in v. 7 is how Paul finishes it off with a series of words beginning with *pi*: εἷς θεὸς καὶ **πατὴρ πάντων** ὁ ἐπὶ **πάντων** καὶ διὰ **πάντων** καὶ ἐν **πᾶσιν**. He has already done this twice before in 1:23 and 3:19 (cf. 2 Cor 9:8) at the end of his periods.[49]

That there is only one, Triune God is a watchword of biblical religion, particularly over against the multiplicity of gods among contemporaries of God's people through the ages. Over against this, Jews in the OT era repeated their essential confession, the Shema, given in Deut 6:4: "Hear, O Israel, the LORD our God, the LORD is one" (LXX: ἄκουε Ισραηλ κύριος ὁ θεὸς ἡμῶν κύριος εἷς ἐστιν; cf. the first commandment, Exod 20:3).[50] In addition, there are other OT texts that connect with Eph 4:6. For example (using the LXX version): "Did not the one God create you? Is there not one Father for you all?" (Mal 2:10; οὐχὶ θεὸς εἷς ἔκτισεν ὑμᾶς; οὐχὶ πατὴρ εἷς πάντων ὑμῶν; the Hebrew has first-person pronouns).

Given OT teaching and Second Temple Judaism's concentrated notions that there is only one God, it is no surprise that Paul would also affirm this as well. Indeed, this must be seen as the major reason he founds his insistence on the church's diligent care to maintain its unity on the oneness of God.[51] God's oneness is what the Ephesians have now confessed at their

---

49. As a variation, there is an interesting piling up of ἐν- sounds in Col 1:29: εἰς ὃ καὶ κοπιῶ ἀγωνιζόμενος κατὰ τὴν **ἐν**έργειαν αὐτοῦ τὴν **ἐν**εργουμένην **ἐν** ἐμοὶ **ἐν** δυνάμει ("For which I labor and fight in accordance with his effectiveness which is effected in me in power").

50. Cf. Kim Huat Tan, "The Shema and Early Christianity," *TynB* 59 (2008): 181–206. The connection between Jesus affirmed as κύριος and his identification with the covenant God of OT Israel has already been noticed on v. 5 above. For the confession of God as one in second temple Judaism see Bauckham, *Jesus and the God of Israel*, 60–126; see also, for example, Ignatius, *Magn.* 8.2, εἷς θεὸς ἐστιν ("God is one"). Lincoln (238) provides some helpful references to Jewish sources on the Shema. However, his English version of Philo, *Virt.* 3.5 makes it appear to be a closer parallel with Eph 4:1–6 ("the highest and greatest source of this unanimity is their creed of a single God, through which, as from a fountain, they feel a love for each other, uniting them in an indissoluble bond") than it is in Greek. The text of Philo is a loose recounting of Num 25 and the entrapment of Israel into idolatry by the Midianites and their daughters. The statements are put in the mouths of the Midianites, who discuss Israel's "unanimity and agreement (ὁμονοία καὶ συμφονία)" because of their opinion (not "creed") that there is one God (ἡ τοῦ ἑνὸς θεοῦ δόξα), from which "they derive a unifying and indissoluble friendly regard [not "love"] toward one another" (ἑνωτικῇ καὶ ἀδιαλύτῳ φίλια κέχρηνται πρὸς ἀλλήλους).

51. See discussion above on v. 5 about possible but unproven confessional sources for Paul's notions here.

conversion to Christ in distinction from the myriads gods they formerly worshiped.[52] But Paul is Trinitarian. There is one Lord Jesus, who is also divine, so he qualifies v. 6 that he is speaking of the *Father* in this instance.

There is a central text in 1 Cor 8:6 that can inform our understanding of Eph 4:6. The context involves—much as it would be for any Jew who invokes God's oneness—the predominance of false pagan gods. The text reads:

> ἀλλ' ἡμῖν
> εἷς θεὸς ὁ πατὴρ ἐξ οὗ τὰ πάντα καὶ ἡμεῖς εἰς αὐτόν
> καὶ εἷς κύριος Ἰησοῦς Χριστὸς δι' οὗ τὰ πάντα καὶ ἡμεῖς δι' αὐτοῦ.
>
> [There are many false gods] "Yet for us, there is but one God, the Father, from whom are all things even as we exist for him, and but one Lord, Jesus Christ, through whom are all things even as we exist through him."[53]

Similarities to our text consist of the one God's fatherly relation to his people and as their *summum bonum*, and the existence of only one Lord Jesus, who has mediated both creation and the redemption of his people (e.g., Col 1:15–20; Heb 1:1–3).

Back to Ephesians 4:6, the question arises regarding the understanding of πάντων ("of all") in the phrase πατὴρ πάντων ("Father of all"). Is God the Father of all "things" (taking πάντων as neuter)? Or of all "people" (taking πάντων as masc. and universal in scope)? The first option seems possible as

---

52. As mentioned above, Ephesians venerated a whole panoply of gods besides their state goddess, Artemis Ephesia. For just one indication of this, the person who dedicated an altar (?) at Ephesus wanted to cover all bases, devoting it (in Latin) "to all the gods and goddesses"; in Dieter Knibbe and Bülent Iplikçioglu, "Neue Inschriften aus Ephesos, VIII," *JAÖI* 53 (1981/82): [Hauptblatt] 87–150, no. 131. Cf. Richard Oster, "Ephesus as a Religious Center under the Principate," *ANRW* 2.18.3 (1990): 1661–1728 (esp. 1667–98); Paul Trebilco, *The Early Christians in Ephesus from Paul to Ignatius* (Grand Rapids: Eerdmans, 2008; first published 2004), 19 (esp. n. 47 for mention of the names of the many gods worshiped at Ephesus).

53. First Cor 8:6 is also regarded as arising from an early creedal affirmation by many. Kelly (*Creeds*, 19) remarks: "The formulary character of this is unmistakable, and is emphasized by the careful parallelism and artificial construction." For extensive discussion of this text in its OT and contemporary contexts see Erik Waaler, *The Shema and the First Commandment in First Corinthians: An Intertextual Approach to Paul's Re-reading of Deuteronomy*, WUNT 253 (Tübingen: Mohr Siebeck, 2008).

a statement of God's creation of all things (3:9; Jas 1:17).[54] The second idea is a derivative of the first; it is abstractly possible to speak of God as Father of all human beings as their Creator, but this is at best a very rare idea in Scripture.[55]

For a number of reasons, it is far preferable to take the "all" in the statement εἷς θεὸς καὶ πατὴρ πάντων ("one God and Father of all") as a reference to all believers, in relation to whom God is their Father. This is a case where πάντες refers to "all indiscriminately," that is, both Jew and Gentile without distinction in the church, which Paul is generally interested in affirming (e.g., Rom 3:9, 22; 4:11, 16; 10:12; 1 Tim 2:4–5) and particularly in Ephesians, as he had written about briefly in chaps. 1–3. We see this meaning flowing out of what was said earlier in 1:13–14 and 2:19–22 that *all* who believe, both Jew and Gentile, are adopted and placed into the one united family (3:14–15) of the Father. Furthermore, the added qualifications that he is "over all and through all and in all" (cf. 1 Cor 8:6; Rom 9:5; 11:36) relate to the church as statements of the Father's glorious filling of his new-temple "house" that had just occupied Paul in 3:19–21 and earlier.[56] Paul opens most of his epistles with the name of God as "*our* Father," as he had in 1:3.

---

54. The text of 1 Cor 8:6 quoted above is not an exact parallel of this idea because it does not say that God is the Father of all things but that they came "from" him (ἐξ οὗ τὰ πάντα).

55. Possibly the meaning in Mal 2:10 cited above. This is how some wish to read Eph 4:14–15, as Father of all families in creation, and to connect it with our text (e.g., Barth, 471; O'Brien, 284–86), but I do not follow that interpretation of 3:14–15. Cf. the common title of Zeus/Jupiter by both Greeks and Romans as "the father of gods and men" (in many cases literally); e.g., Hesiod, *Theog.* 2.453; Homer, *Il.* 20.54; *Od.* 1.28 (and often as an formulaic epithet); Cicero, *Nat. d.* 2.25. One of the early discourses of the late first-century AD Stoic Epictetus has a discussion of this *(Diatr.* 1.3). Cf. Jerome (Origen and Jerome, 170), who points to similar ideas in Virgil.

56. Although he misses Paul's distinct use of πᾶς here and in the other passages in favor of a Stoic background, nevertheless Eduard Norden has provided a number of interesting texts to compare with Paul's in his classic *Agnostos Theos: Untersuchungen zur Formengeschichte religiöser Rede* (Leipzig and Berlin: Tuebner, 1913), 241–50. Interestingly, the "Ouroboros" ornament on the title page of Norden's book is an ancient gnostic monistic symbol (ἕν τὸ πᾶν, "the All is one").

Application and Devotional Implications

When Jesus was asked to summarize God's law (Mark 12:28–34; cf. Matt 22:34–40), he pointed to the commandment to love the Lord in Deuteronomy: "You shall love the LORD your God with all your heart and with all your soul and with all your might" (Deut 6:5; Mark 12:30). This verse was on every true Israelite's heart because it was immediately preceded by the famous confession of faith in the one true God that inspired Paul's statements in Eph 4:3–6: "Hear, O Israel: The LORD our God, the LORD is one" (Deut 6:4). Jesus also quotes this verse (Mark 12:29).

But Jesus surprises us in Mark 12:28–34. He was only asked to name the one greatest commandment, but he adds a second unasked: "The second is this: 'You shall love your neighbor as yourself.' There is no other commandment greater than these" (Mark 12:31; cf. Lev 19:18). Why the second commandment? Because he knew that it is easy to profess love for the one true God and at the same time to hate one's neighbor. And not just any neighbor, but even a neighbor who is a brother or sister in Christ. The Apostle John has some pointed words on this topic in his first epistle: "If anyone says, 'I love God,' and hates his brother, he is a liar; for he who does not love his brother whom he has seen cannot love God whom he has not seen. And this commandment we have from him: whoever loves God must also love his brother" (1 John 4:20–21).

In Ephesians 6:1–6 Paul founds the initial, main exhortation section of Ephesians on these same principles. There is only one faith in the one true God through the one Lord and Savior, Jesus (4:5–6). And a Christian life founded on these truths is characterized by humility, gentleness, and, particularly, love toward fellow Christians in the one body of Christ, evidenced by bearing with them (4:2). Love of God means love of neighbor.

Additional Exegetical Comments: Ephesians 4:1–6 and Colossians 3:12–15

It has been my considered purpose to avoid repeated interaction with the widespread opinion that Ephesians is an adaptation of Colossians by a post-Pauline author.[57] It simply seems more worthwhile to treat the text of Ephesians on its own terms rather than to engage in debate on supposed sources and authorship at every turn.[58]

This is not to say, of course, that there are no similarities between Ephesians and Colossians, which common involvement of Paul in both explains quite adequately. In order to facilitate the reader's own judgment on the interrelations of Eph 4:1–6 and Col 3:12–15, the latter text is given here with my suggested division into its cola* and periods. The careful reader will see obvious similarities and differences in the style and statements here:

A
12 Ἐνδύσασθε οὖν
ὡς ἐκλεκτοὶ τοῦ θεοῦ ἅγιοι καὶ ἠγαπημένοι
σπλάγχνα οἰκτιρμοῦ χρηστότητα
ταπεινοφροσύνην πραΰτητα μακροθυμίαν

B
13 ἀνεχόμενοι ἀλλήλων
καὶ χαριζόμενοι ἑαυτοῖς ἐάν τις πρός τινα ἔχῃ μομφήν
καθὼς καὶ ὁ κύριος ἐχαρίσατο ὑμῖν
οὕτως καὶ ὑμεῖς

C
14 ἐπὶ πᾶσιν δὲ τούτοις τὴν ἀγάπην
ὅ ἐστιν σύνδεσμος τῆς τελειότητος

D
15 καὶ ἡ εἰρήνη τοῦ Χριστοῦ βραβευέτω ἐν ταῖς καρδίαις ὑμῶν
εἰς ἣν καὶ ἐκλήθητε ἐν ἑνὶ σώματι
καὶ εὐχάριστοι γίνεσθε.

---

57. For example, it is ironic that Ephesians is viewed by many scholars as the product of a member of the "Pauline school" and that Pauline Colossians is the *Vorlage** that he adapted for his writing. The irony is that, at face value, *Ephesians* is more purely Paul's own composition and *Colossians* was written in conjunction with a member of his "school," Timothy (Col 1:1). If either of the two documents has non-Pauline compositional elements, it would be the Timothy strata in Colossians, not Ephesians. Cf. the introduction on authorship for discussion and literature.

58. This is the equivalent of the groundswell in Gospels scholarship to treat these books on their own terms without delving into possible oral or written sources, especially by narrative critics. The background of this groundswell is the signal failure of the various "scientific" (*wissenschaftlich*) criticisms to reach any sort of consensus on sources "behind" these Gospels despite several generations of concentrated work.

> "Put on then, as God's chosen ones, holy and beloved, compassion, kindness, humility, meekness, and patience, bearing with one another and, if one has a complaint against another, forgiving each other; as the Lord has forgiven you, so you also must forgive. And above all these put on love, which binds everything together in perfect harmony. And let the peace of Christ rule in your hearts, to which indeed you were called in one body. And be thankful." (Col 3:12–15)

Selected Bibliography

Bauckham, R. *Jesus and the God of Israel: God Crucified and Other Studies on the New Testament's Christology of Divine Identity*. Grand Rapids: Eerdmans, 2008.

Cooper, G., after Küger, K. *Attic Greek Prose Syntax.* 4 Vols. Ann Arbor: University of Michigan Press, 1998.

DeSilva, D. *Honor, Patronage, Kinship & Purity: Unlocking New Testament Culture*. Downers Grove, IL: InterVarsity Press, 2000.

Friesen, S. "The Cult of the Roman Emperors in Ephesos: Temple Wardens, City Titles, and the Interpretation of the Revelation of John." In *Ephesos, Metropolis of Asia*, ed. H. Koester, 229–50. Valley Forge, PA: Harvard Divinity School Press, 1995.

Hurtado, L. *One God, One Lord: Early Christian Devotion and Ancient Jewish Monotheism*. Philadelphia: Fortress, 1988.

Kelly, J. *Early Christian Creeds.* 3rd ed. New York: Continuum, 1972; 1st ed., 1950.

Kienast, D. "Zu den Homonoia-Vereinbarungen in der römischen Kaiserzeit." *ZPE* 109 (1995): 267–82.

Lotz, J. *Ignatius and Concord: The Background and Use of the Language of Concord in the Letters of Ignatius of Antioch.* New York: Peter Lang, 2007.

Martin, R. "Aspects of Worship in the New Testament Church." *VE* 2 (1963): 6–32.

McGrath, J. *The Only True God: Early Christian Monotheism in Its Jewish Context.* Urbana and Chicago: University of Illinois Press, 2009.

Norden, E. *Agnostos Theos: Untersuchungen zur Formengeschichte Religiöser Rede.* Leipzig and Berlin: Tuebner, 1913.

Peppard, M. " 'Poetry,' 'Hymns' and 'Traditional Material' in New Testament Epistles or How to Do Things with Indentations." *JSNT* 30 (2008): 319–42.

Petrenko, E. *Created in Christ Jesus for Good Works: The Integration of Soteriology and Ethics in Ephesians*. PBM. Milton Keynes, UK: Paternoster, 2011.

Tan, K. "The Shema and Early Christianity." *TynB* 59 (2008): 181–206.

Gifts from the Ascended Messiah to Unify His Church (4:7–16)

Introduction

In Ephesians 4:7–16 Paul sketches out the triumphant Lord's provision for his church's protection and growth in unity and love. As mentioned above, this is the second part of the larger passage, spanning vv. 1–16. This last section in vv. 7–16 does have its own intrinsic unity even though it is intimately wedded with the first section (vv. 1–6). The ties between vv. 1–6 and 7–16 are seen in the repetition of the adjective εἷς ("one"), used seven times in vv. 4–6 and used in an unusual expression (εἷς ἕκαστος, "each one") in vv. 7 and 16 (see comment).[1] Verses 7–16 are unified as a subdivision by a number of repeated terms throughout (e.g., "give" [δίδωμι] in vv. 7–8, 11, and "measure" [μέτρον] in vv. 7, 13, 16[2]).

Verses 7–16 comprise just a sketch of major theological ideas because Paul has already opened the paraenetic portion of his epistle in 4:1 with the classic line "I therefore strongly urge you" (cf. Rom 12:1; 1 Cor 4:16; 2 Cor 10:1; 1 Tim 2:1). In vv. 7–16, however, he breaks off the exhortation proper in order to establish the basis for this exhortation in the work of God in Christ more directly related to his exhortation than was already done in Eph 1–3. It is not until later in the chapter (vv. 25–26) that Paul returns to his exhortation regarding truthful speech in love, which expresses and concretizes the type of gentleness and patient forbearance in love he had called for earlier (vv. 1–3).

1. Also, the word "unity" or "oneness" (ἑνότης) in the phrases "unity of the Spirit" and "unity of the faith" only occurs in Ephesians in vv. 3, 13.

2. The terms εἷς ἕκαστος ("each one") and μέτρον ("measure") only occur in these verses in Ephesians.

Two portions of 4:7–16 are among the most discussed in Ephesians, if not in the whole NT. The first is Paul's use of Psa 68 in vv. 7–10 to prepare the way for understanding the word-based ministries in the church as Christ's own provision for his body (vv. 11–16). The second entails how exactly to read and interpret certain phrases in vv. 11–12: "pastors and [separate] teachers" or "pastor-teachers" (v. 11), and whether the saints in general engage in "the task of ministry" (v. 12). It is easy to get overwhelmed in the surge of scholarly work on these issues, but in the course of our examination of the text, I will attempt to keep the focus on how the particulars of each verse relate to the whole discourse. In its original setting, these verses take about two to three minutes to read; the audience was expected to retain from them the big idea that Christ's gifting of the church in his triumph was to bring about unifying, truth-telling lives of edification and love.

In the division of this long text into its component cola* and periods I have followed the contours of the versification, with the exception of vv. 7–8 and vv. 9–10, which could be separated but seem to be united. Verses 7–8 are joined by the giving of grace and of gifts in both the first and last cola* (vv. 7a and 8c), while vv. 9–10 are developing the identity of the "Ascender" as the same as the "Descender." Here is my proposed division of the text:

A
7 ἑνὶ δὲ ἑκάστῳ ἡμῶν ἐδόθη ἡ χάρις
κατὰ τὸ μέτρον τῆς δωρεᾶς τοῦ Χριστοῦ
8 διὸ λέγει
ἀναβὰς εἰς ὕψος ᾐχμαλώτευσεν αἰχμαλωσίαν
ἔδωκεν δόματα τοῖς ἀνθρώποις

B
9 τὸ δὲ ἀνέβη τί ἐστιν εἰ μὴ ὅτι καὶ κατέβη
εἰς τὰ κατώτερα μέρη τῆς γῆς;
10 ὁ καταβὰς αὐτός ἐστιν καὶ ὁ ἀναβὰς
ὑπεράνω πάντων τῶν οὐρανῶν
ἵνα πληρώσῃ τὰ πάντα

C
11 καὶ αὐτὸς ἔδωκεν
τοὺς μὲν ἀποστόλους τοὺς δὲ προφήτας
τοὺς δὲ εὐαγγελιστάς τοὺς δὲ ποιμένας
καὶ διδασκάλους

D [12] πρὸς τὸν καταρτισμὸν τῶν ἁγίων
εἰς ἔργον διακονίας
εἰς οἰκοδομὴν τοῦ σώματος τοῦ Χριστοῦ

E [13] μέχρι καταντήσωμεν οἱ πάντες
εἰς τὴν ἑνότητα τῆς πίστεως καὶ τῆς ἐπιγνώσεως τοῦ υἱοῦ
τοῦ θεοῦ
εἰς ἄνδρα τέλειον
εἰς μέτρον ἡλικίας τοῦ πληρώματος τοῦ Χριστοῦ

F [14] ἵνα μηκέτι ὦμεν νήπιοι
κλυδωνιζόμενοι καὶ περιφερόμενοι παντὶ ἀνέμῳ
τῆς διδασκαλίας
ἐν τῇ κυβείᾳ τῶν ἀνθρώπων
ἐν πανουργίᾳ
πρὸς τὴν μεθοδείαν τῆς πλάνης

G [15] ἀληθεύοντες δὲ ἐν ἀγάπῃ
αὐξήσωμεν εἰς αὐτὸν τὰ πάντα
ὅς ἐστιν ἡ κεφαλή Χριστός

H [16] ἐξ οὗ πᾶν τὸ σῶμα συναρμολογούμενον
καὶ συμβιβαζόμενον διὰ πάσης ἁφῆς τῆς ἐπιχορηγίας
κατ' ἐνέργειαν ἐν μέτρῳ ἑνὸς ἑκάστου μέρους
τὴν αὔξησιν τοῦ σώματος ποιεῖται
εἰς οἰκοδομὴν ἑαυτοῦ ἐν ἀγάπῃ

As mentioned above, my division into periods follows the traditional versification with only the exception of vv. 7–8 and 9–10. This is true even though some periods are quite a bit shorter than others. For example, vv. 11–12 and 15 range from twenty-nine to thirty-one syllables, while vv. 13–14 and 16 range from fifty-four to seventy-one syllables. Such variety was generally preferred in prose, though some studied rhetors often kept their cola* at least roughly equal in syllables, words, or syntactic groupings.[3]

3. Called "isocola"; cf. Heinrich Lausberg, *Handbook of Literary Rhetoric: A Foundation for Literary Study*, ed. David E. Orton and R. Dean Anderson (Boston: Brill, 1998), §§719–23.

As will be discussed below on the individual periods, there is some anaphora and inclusio* displayed in vv. 11–16 in particular. The most important ones for comment are the parallel prepositional phrases in v. 12, which are discussed below, and the use of anaphora with the phrase "in love" (ἐν ἀγάπῃ), which unifies v. 15a with v. 16e even though v. 15 is tied grammatically with the previous verse by the subjunctive verbs: ἵνα μηκέτι ὦμεν … δὲ … [ἵνα] αὐξήσωμεν.

Once more, we see the concern in Paul's periodic composition for the last word or phrase in the periods, which is the place for focus or emphasis. Verses 12 and 13 both end with the repeated phrase "of the body *of Christ*" and "of the fullness *of Christ*." This concern to end his cola* and periods with Christ as the focal point explains the otherwise somewhat awkward use of "Christ" in apposition to "the Head" in the last colon* of v. 15.

Outline

- IX. Gifts from the Ascended Messiah to Unify His Church (4:7–16)
    - A. Gifts from Christ's triumphant victory and ascent (4:7–10)
        - 1. Gifts of grace (4:7)
        - 2. Psalm 68:18 (4:8)
        - 3. Gifts given to loyal subjects after Christ's victory in death (4:9–10)
    - B. Word-based church officers as gifts for edification (4:11–13)
    - C. The outcome of the gifts in operation (4:14–16)
        - 1. Protection from error and deceit (4:14)
        - 2. Doctrinal maturity in love (4:15)
        - 3. Ecclesiastical unity in love (4:16)

Original Text

7 Ἑνὶ δὲ ἑκάστῳ ἡμῶν ἐδόθη ἡ χάρις κατὰ τὸ μέτρον τῆς δωρεᾶς τοῦ Χριστοῦ.
8 διὸ λέγει· ἀναβὰς εἰς ὕψος ᾐχμαλώτευσεν αἰχμαλωσίαν, [a]ἔδωκεν δόματα[b] τοῖς
ἀνθρώποις. **9** τὸ δὲ ἀνέβη τί ἐστιν, εἰ μὴ ὅτι[c] καὶ κατέβη[d] εἰς τὰ κατώτερα μέρη[e]
τῆς γῆς; **10** ὁ καταβὰς αὐτός ἐστιν καὶ ὁ ἀναβὰς ὑπεράνω πάντων τῶν οὐρανῶν,
ἵνα πληρώσῃ τὰ πάντα. **11** Καὶ αὐτὸς ἔδωκεν[f] τοὺς μὲν ἀποστόλους, τοὺς δὲ
προφήτας, τοὺς δὲ εὐαγγελιστάς, τοὺς δὲ ποιμένας καὶ διδασκάλους, **12** πρὸς
τὸν καταρτισμὸν τῶν ἁγίων εἰς ἔργον διακονίας, εἰς οἰκοδομὴν τοῦ σώματος

τοῦ Χριστοῦ, **13** μέχρι καταντήσωμεν οἱ πάντες εἰς τὴν ἑνότητα τῆς πίστεως
καὶ τῆς ἐπιγνώσεως τοῦ υἱοῦ τοῦ θεοῦ, εἰς ἄνδρα τέλειον, εἰς μέτρον ἡλικίας
τοῦ πληρώματος τοῦ Χριστοῦ, **14** ἵνα μηκέτι ὦμεν νήπιοι, κλυδωνιζόμενοι καὶ
περιφερόμενοι παντὶ ἀνέμῳ τῆς διδασκαλίας ἐν τῇ κυβείᾳ τῶν ἀνθρώπων, ἐν
πανουργίᾳ πρὸς τὴν μεθοδείαν τῆς πλάνης.[g] **15** ἀληθεύοντες[h] δὲ ἐν ἀγάπῃ αὐξήσωμεν εἰς αὐτὸν τὰ πάντα, ὅς ἐστιν ἡ κεφαλή, Χριστός,[i] **16** ἐξ οὗ πᾶν τὸ σῶμα
συναρμολογούμενον καὶ συμβιβαζόμενον διὰ πάσης ἁφῆς τῆς ἐπιχορηγίας κατ᾽
ἐνέργειαν ἐν μέτρῳ ἑνὸς ἑκάστου μέρους τὴν αὔξησιν τοῦ σώματος ποιεῖται εἰς
οἰκοδομὴν ἑαυτοῦ ἐν ἀγάπῃ.

Textual Notes

8.a. Many early corrections (second hand of א, C*, 3, D^{2}) and early and widespread MSS (B, Ψ, 81, 424, 459, 1739, 1881, syr, arm, geo) add the conjunction *καί* before "he gave" (καὶ ἔδωκεν), while quite a number of others lack the conjunction (P^{46}, א*, A, C^{2}, D*, 33, 1241, vg, cop, slav, Irenaeus, Jerome, etc.). This is a case of *lectio difficilior** where it is harder to conceive of a scribe omitting the conjunction rather than supplying one to conform to more normal Greek style, in which conjunctions between finite verbs are common.[4]

8.b. Instead of plural "gifts" (δόματα), the scribe of P^{46} wrote the singular "gift" (δόμα), probably because the article following this noun opens with a *tau* (writing ΔΟΜΑΤΟΙΣ instead of ΔΟΜΑΤΑΤΟΙΣ).

9.c. Instead of εἰ μὴ **ὅτι**, "except that," P^{46} has an unintelligible dative participle of the verb "to be" (εἰ μὴ **ὄντι**, "except *for the one who exists* he also descended"). This is just an uncorrected copyist mistake.

9.d. The adverb "beforehand" (πρῶτον) is found after "he descended" (κατέβη) in a number of corrections and MSS (e.g., the second corrector of א, B, C^{3}, Ψ, 104, 424*, 459, and M). The earliest and geographically widespread MSS lack this adverb (P^{46}, א*, A, C*, D, 424c, vg, cop, eth, etc.), making its inclusion appear to be a scribal, explanatory gloss.[5]

4. So also Bruce M. Metzger, *A Textual Commentary on the Greek New Testament*, 2nd ed. (New York: United Bible Societies, 1994), 536.
5. Cf. ibid.

9.e. The inclusion of μέρη ("regions") is the least certain variant in 4:1–16. It is missing in a number of important and early MSS (including P[46], D*, F, G, 921, it, cop, eth, Irenaeus, Jerome). There is, however, strong early manuscript witness for inclusion of μέρη (א, A, B, C, D[2], Ψ, 33, 1739, 1881, and M), which caused the UBS and NA editors to include the word in brackets (with a "C" rating in UBS[4]). Metzger says that μέρη is "virtually superfluous," and the meaning of the neuter plural would be simply "to the depths of the earth" (cf. Matt 21:9 and parallels for similar "in the most high [places]").[6] I treat the word as original because of the strong external witness to it and because it is more difficult to see a scribe deleting a word—superfluous or not—since the tendency in the scribal tradition was to expand the original text with explanatory words.

11.f. Instead of the aorist ἔδωκεν ("he gave"), P[46] has the perfect δέ δωκεν ("he has given"), but the aorist is more likely and would mirror the form of the verb in the quotation in v. 8c.

14.g. Alexandrinus (A) adds τοῦ διαβόλου ("of the Devil") at the very end (v. 14e; "for the scheme *of the Devil's* deceit"), but there is no reason to regard this editorial comment witnessed in one MS as original. It is better in any regard to see the deceitful scheming here as coming from humans, as specified in v. 14c.

15.h. The opening of this brief period has the participle ἀληθεύοντες, "speak the truth," in nearly all Greek MSS except the ninth-century codices F (Codex Augiensis) and G (Codex Boernerianus), which read ἀλήθειαν δὲ ποιοῦντες, a Hebrew idiom in the LXX for "act uprightly (or 'with fidelity')"; e.g., ἱκανοῦταί μοι … ἀπὸ πάσης **ἀληθείας** ἧς **ἐποίησας** τῷ παιδί σου, "I am not worthy … of all the fidelity which you have shown to your servant" (Gen 32:11; cf. 1 John 1:6). In the NT the verb ἀληθεύω occurs only here and in Gal 4:16 as the equivalent of λαλεῖτε ἀλήθειαν found in v. 25 (quoting Zech 8:16).[7]

15.i. The last colon* in v. 15 (2:15c) reads ὅς ἐστιν ἡ κεφαλή Χριστός, which is a little unusual in Greek (cf., however, Luke 2:11; 24:19; Col 2:2). One does

6. Ibid., 537.

7. Notwithstanding the support drawn for the other reading by Jean-Daniel Dubois, "Eph IV 15: ἀληθεύοντες δὲ or ἀλήθειαν δὲ ποιοῦντες," *NovT* 26 (1974): 30–34.

not expect the second nominative noun in apposition (Χριστός): "who is the Head, namely, Christ." An inattentive reader or copyist might expect this to be a different kind of phrase, which is what happened when the copyist of P[46] wrote ὅς ἐστιν ἡ κεφαλή τοῦ Χριστοῦ (i.e., XPY versus XPC when abbreviated), "who is the Head *of Christ*"! This mistake is easy to spot, but shows once again that our earliest, nearly complete copy of Ephesians does not necessarily contain only the original readings, and that some of its mistakes show a paid copyist who was not always at his best.

Translation

7 Yet[8] to each one of us grace was given according to the measure of the gift of Christ, **8** therefore it[9] says, "When he ascended on high, he took captivity[10] captive,[11] and he distributed gifts[12] to his people."[13] **9** Now,[14] this[15]

8. All the major English versions have "but" here for δέ, expressing a contrast between what begins in v. 7 and the foregoing statements about the unity of God, the church, the faith, etc., in vv. 1–6. It seems possible to understand δέ here as simply drawing out implications of this unity or furthering the discussion ("*Now*, to each one of us ..."), as below in v. 9. However, the contrast is slightly more likely as a contrast between the one Lord and the diverse gifts distributed to his church through its officers in v. 11.

9. Λέγει here could be rendered, "*He* says" (cf. KJV; NKJV footnote only), referring to God or even to the Son (as Heb 10:5), but it does not seem warranted here. Cf. Jas 4:5–6.

10. The noun αἰχμαλωσία appears only here and twice in Rev 13:10 in the NT and either refers to an abstract "captivity" (as in Revelation; so KJV, NRSV) or through transferred meaning to indicate a group of captured prisoners of war, "captives" (NASB, NIV, ESV); cf. Num 31:12; BDAG, 31. Either meaning is defensible, though the former has a slight advantage here. This is an example of a cognate acc. (with αἰχμαλωτεύω; BDF §153).

11. The verb αἰχμαλωτεύω—otherwise found as αἰχμαλωτίζω four times in the NT—appears some thirty-nine times in the LXX. Both forms refer to the capture of prisoners in war; BDAG, 31; LSJ, 45.

12. This is another cognate acc. (ἔδωκεν δόματα), as previously with ᾐχμαλώτευσεν αἰχμαλωσίαν.

13. As NRSV; see comment.

14. The conj. δέ here serves merely to advance the discussion, much like English "now" can (cf. NASB). "Now" is not intended here as a temporal marker ("at this time," νῦν or νυνί).

15. The neuter article in the expression τὸ δὲ ἀνέβη serves to identify a quoted word or phrase; cf. BDF §267; Smyth, *Greek Grammar*, §1153g. It is worth pointing out that the aor. ptc. ἀναβὰς is referenced by Paul with an aor. indic. ἀνέβη, showing

"he ascended," what does it mean except that he had also descended[16] to the nether regions of the earth?[17] **10** He who descended is himself also the one who ascended far beyond[18] all the heavens, that he might fill all things. **11** And he did himself give some as apostles,[19] some as prophets, some as evangelists, some as shepherds and teachers **12** for preparation[20] of the saints, for the task[21] of ministry, for building up of the body[22] of Christ **13** until all of us[23] attain[24] to the unity of the faith and of the knowledge[25] of

---

that he took the aor. of the ptc. as indicating a prior action.

16. While κατέβη is aor., the English pluperfect is sometimes the best way to render it as here; E. Burton, *Syntax of the Moods and Tenses in New Testament Greek* (Edinburgh: T&T Clark, 1898), §48 (cf. §46 for English perf. for aor.).

17. This phrase εἰς τὰ κατώτερα μέρη τῆς γῆς has received much attention and is discussed in the comment. The translation leaves the interpretation of the phrase open, as KJV, NKJV, NASB, NRSV, whereas NIV has "the lower, earthly regions," and ESV similarly has "the lower regions, the earth." Cf. BDF §167, who want "the regions under the earth" as Büchsel, *TDNT*, 3:640–42.

18. For emphatic ὑπεράνω ("far above" or here "far beyond") see the translation note on 1:21 and BDAG, 1031.

19. The construction ἔδωκεν τοὺς ... ἀποστόλους κτλ is a double acc. construction with an obj. and predicate (BDF §157), with the articles functioning as pronouns (BDF §§249–50). The rendering of the articles as "some" is due to the force of the μὲν ... δέ construction, enumerating the various offices in an alternating series (BDAG, 629–30, meaning 1c). We could also render the series with: "some as apostles, others as prophets, others as evangelists" etc. See comment.

20. See comment.

21. Ἔργον refers here to "that which one does as a regular activity" (BDAG, 391), hence, "task" or even "occupation."

22. Οἰκοδομή and σῶμα used here recall the building and body metaphors found throughout Ephesians (e.g., 1:23; 2:16, 19–22).

23. It is difficult to bring out the force of the article and the word order in the first colon* (i.e., καταντήσωμεν οἱ πάντες), which I have rendered above as "until all of us attain." We expect πάντες καταντήσωμεν where anarthrous πάντες precedes the verb (cf. 1 Cor 10:17; 2 Cor 5:10). Stronger emphasis would be to say ἡμεῖς πάντες (as 2:3; cf. John 1:16; Acts 10:33), which would also change the meter of the colon* with an extra syllable. As Paul expressed it, there is slight stress on the "all" who attain to unity: "each and every one," "all of us" (cf. BDAG, 784 [4.d]).

24. For use of the subjunctive in the temporal clause μέχρι καταντήσωμεν without ἄν where it might be expected see BDF §383 (2). Both ἄχρι(ς) and μέχρι(ς) are followed by aor. subjunctives in the NT; hence, the aor. tense form of καταντήσωμεν is default here and has minimal to no semantic value.

25. Ἐπίγνωσις with an impersonal obj. can refer to perception or recognition of something (e.g., Rom 3:20, of sin through the law), but with a personal obj. as here in Eph 4:13 it implies a maturing personal experience with that person (see also

the Son of God, to the mature man, to the measure of the full stature[26] of Christ, **14** so that we may no longer be toddlers,[27] tossed about and swept along by every wind of teaching in the trickery of men, in cunning, for their deceitful designs,[28] **15** but so that[29] by speaking the truth[30] in love we may grow[31] in every way in him who is our head, namely, Christ, **16** from whom the whole body, as it is joined together[32] and united through every connection he supplies, according to the functioning[33] capacity of each individual part,[34] produces the growth of the body for building itself up in love.

1:17; Col 1:10; 2 Pet 1:2–3, 8; 2:20; cf. Prov 2:5; BDAG, 369; LSJ, 627).

26. The rendering "to the measure of the full stature of Christ" (NRSV) for εἰς μέτρον ἡλικίας τοῦ πληρώματος τοῦ Χριστοῦ takes gen. πληρώματος here as adj., modifying ἡλικία. Other versions, like ESV's "to the measure of the stature of the fullness of Christ," amount to the same thing but are not as clear in English.

27. A νήπιος can refer to a child who may have been weaned (cp. βρέφος for "nursling, infant"; Luke 18:15) but for whom milk was still their main nourishment (e.g., Matt 21:16 parallel with θηλαζόντες, "nursing babes"; Heb 5:13; 1 Cor 3:1–2) and therefore refers to children who were younger than a more generic "child" (παιδίον, τέκνον, or τεκνίον). Νήπιος is used metaphorically for someone underage and immature (e.g., Matt 11:25; Gal 4:1; 1 Cor 13:11 [a "chatterbox"]).

28. See comment.

29. This expresses the implied repetition of ἵνα from v. 14 (see note on αὐξήσωμεν below).

30. The adv. ptc. ἀληθεύοντες expresses the means for achieving growth in the church: [ἵνα] αὐξήσωμεν, "[so that] we may grow through our truthful speech in love"; cf. Burton, *Moods*, §443. The subjunctive αὐξήσωμεν is parallel with ἵνα μηκέτι ὦμεν in v. 14 (see next note).

31. The subjunctive αὐξήσωμεν is grammatically dependent on the ἵνα in v. 14 and parallels it here: ἵνα μηκέτι ὦμεν νήπιοι … δὲ … [ἵνα] αὐξήσωμεν, "so that we may no longer be toddlers … but [in contrast] … we may grow [up out of infancy]." The aor. tense form of this telic verb in the subjunctive is default (also Matt 13:31 and 1 Pet 2:2). If not, the idea would be inceptive ("that we may *begin to* grow"), but that idea is not required by the context.

32. For the only other NT use of συναρμολογέω and discussion see translation note on 2:21; cf. BDF §119 (1).

33. In 1:19 and 3:7 ἐνέργεια referred to the production that resulted from effort or work ("effectiveness"), but here the idea is the process of working, "functioning" (cf. BDAG, 335, 644).

34. I have adopted the translation offered in BDAG wholesale for the colon* κατ' ἐνέργειαν ἐν μέτρῳ ἑνὸς ἑκάστου μέρους (644 [μέτρον]). The phrase ἐν μέτρῳ is sometimes rendered "proper" in the English versions (e.g., "the proper working" in NASB and NKJV, and "as each part is working properly" in NRSV and ESV ["while each part"]). The rendering "proper," though, does not bring out the idea

Commentary

4:7 Ἑνὶ δὲ ἑκάστῳ ἡμῶν, "Yet to each one of us." This phrase may initially seem to have emphasis or stress because Paul could easily have dropped ἑνί and said ἑκάστῳ ἡμῶν, "to each of us" (cf. 4:25; 5:33; 6:8; Rom 12:3; 1 Cor 7:7, 11; 15:23; Gal 6:4–5). The adjective εἷς is indeed found with ἕκαστος, where there seems to be some stress like "each one individually" or even "one-by-one" as a near equivalent of κατὰ ἑνά (e.g., Matt 26:22; Luke 4:40; Acts 2:3; Col 4:6; 1 Thess 2:11; 2 Thess 1:3). But the reason for εἷς here (see also v. 16) is that Paul is further developing his call for the church's devotion to "unity" (ἑνότης) of the Spirit (v. 3) because of the "oneness" (εἷς, μία, ἕν) of the Lord, the faith, God the Father, etc., from vv. 4–6. The focus in vv. 1–6 is unity and oneness, but in vv. 7–16 the focus shifts to *diversity* within the one body of Christ. Paul makes a connection between the "unity with diversity" or the "one and many" dynamic between the two passages by using εἷς with ἕκαστος to open this second part of 4:1–16, where he discusses the diversity of gifts (as also in 1 Cor 12:18; cf. Rom 12:3).

ἐδόθη ἡ χάρις κατὰ τὸ μέτρον τῆς δωρεᾶς τοῦ Χριστοῦ, "grace was given according to the measure of the gift of Christ." Paul frequently speaks of his apostleship as a "grace" given to him by God (see on 3:2, 7; cf. Rom 1:5; 12:3, 6; 15:15; 1 Cor 1:4; 3:10; Gal 2:9). Χάρις ("grace") blends the idea of divine favor, seen prominently in Ephesians already (e.g., 1:6–7; 2:5, 8), and a gracious benefaction (χάρισμα; see esp. Rom 12:6; 1 Cor 12:4; 1 Pet 4:10; cf. BDAG, 1080). In v. 7 Paul extends the idea of "grace" given to other special offices to be enumerated in v. 11 as also gifts portioned out by Christ's gifting.[35] Yet, it turns out, the gifts are also the special officers themselves, distributed to the church and for its benefit. Hence, the officers receive their offices by a gracious gifting from Christ so that they themselves might be his gifts to the church.

---

of proportionality conveyed with μέτρον ("measure, quantity"). "According to the proper working" would be κατ' ἴδιαν ἐνέργειαν.

35. This takes the second gen. in the phrase τῆς δωρεᾶς τοῦ Χριστοῦ as denoting source, "the gift that Christ gives," "from Christ" (Hoehner, 523). This is confirmed by what follows (esp. vv. 8–11), where Paul explains that the gifts are given by Christ, the head of the church (see v. 15; 1:22; 5:23), as a result of his triumph; cf. O'Brien, 286–88.

4:8 διὸ λέγει, "therefore it says." Because this is not Paul's common way of citing Scripture, some scholars see this phrase as a signal that he is instead referring to Christian tradition or to some other secondary material.[36] Yet the phrase is used in three other places for Scripture citation, and the quote that follows is intended to represent the meaning of Psa 68.[37] Even where this is recognized, διὸ λέγει is called a "formula" (e.g., O'Brien, 288; Hoehner, 523; cf. Lincoln, 242; Schnackenburg, 176; Gnilka, 206 [*die Einführungsformel*]; Barth, 430–31; Muddiman, 188).[38] However, this is mistaken. One can call γέγραπται ("it is written") and its participle forms a formula for introducing Scripture citations because they appear about one hundred times in the NT by various writers. But διὸ λέγει is too rare to be a formula.[39]

I call attention to διὸ λέγει because, if treated as a formula, it is easy to discount or to pass over the inferential conjunction διό or to reverse the logic of what is said.[40] This latter is the case with Hoehner, who says, "Paul had

36. E.g., Best, 378; Muddiman, 188–98 (a Christian "hymn"); cf. Thorsten Moritz, *A Profound Mystery: The Use of the Old Testament in Ephesians*, SNT 85 (New York: Brill, 1996), 56–86.

37. Διὸ λέγει introduces a composite quote in 5:14 (see comments there), a quote from Proverbs in Jas 4:6, where it is clear from Jas 4:5 that the subject is "Scripture" (ἡ γραφὴ λέγει ... διὸ [ἡ γραφὴ] λέγει), and Heb 10:5 discussed below as an important parallel for Eph 4:8.

38. Barth (430–31) references "he says" (λέγει) as a "quotation formula," citing 5:14; Gal 3:16; 1 Cor 6:16; 2 Cor 6:2; Rom 15:10; Jas 4:6; Heb 1:6; 2:12; etc. These are useful cross-references for λέγει, but he and others are discounting διό in the statement. Muddiman (188) renders διὸ λέγει with "As the saying goes," which is notably inaccurate.

39. See Moritz, *Profound Mystery*, 69–70, for discussion of the phrase and a search for its use elsewhere, which turns up only three parallels and leads him to focus on Ephesians alone for its meaning. He concludes: "In Ephesians δίο [*sic*] firmly links the phrase that it introduces with what precedes. In the present instance this means that the quoted text of v8 probably serves to sum up the christological and ecclesiological message of v7" (70). I am departing from this interpretation but appreciate that Moritz does not merely gloss over the phrase.

40. The individual elements of a formula may lose their semantic value. For example, ἀποκριθεὶς καὶ εἶπεν ("he answered and said"), found well over one hundred times in the Gospels, is used as a formula, since the speaker may not be "answering" anyone in the discourse that follows. For διό see 2:11; 3:13; 4:25; 5:14; cf. BDAG, 250. Διό marks a conclusion or inference from a stated or implied premise. E.g., "(Because) he humbled himself in obedience leading to his death, even that death on the cross, *therefore* (διό) God highly exalted him" (Phil 2:8–9). "For this reason"

just made a statement about the giving of gifts to each believer and this can be *inferred* from the OT passage of Scripture which he quotes" (Hoehner, 523, emphasis added; cf. O'Brien, 289). However, διό marks the inference, not the premise, as Hoehner's analysis would require. If Paul were inferring Christ's gifting from the Psa 68:18 passage, he would have said, "(Scripture) says 'He gave gifts to men' … *therefore* (διό) to each one of us grace was given." What Paul actually says, in effect, is: "(Because) to each one of us grace was given … *therefore* (διό, in consequence of this), Scripture says, 'When he ascended on high …' "[41] I will return to this point in a moment, but this is why Paul feels that he can tease out the *meaning* of Psa 68 in light of Christ's fulfillment rather than woodenly convey the wording of one of its verses.

ἀναβὰς εἰς ὕψος ᾐχμαλώτευσεν αἰχμαλωσίαν, ἔδωκεν δόματα τοῖς ἀνθρώποις, "When he ascended on high, he took captivity captive, and he distributed gifts to his people." This is the reference to Psa 68:18 introduced in v. 8a. The last colon* in particular obviously supports Paul's point about the gifting Christ has made for his church (vv. 7a, 11a), though, interestingly, the next two verses (vv. 9–10) are occupied not with "he distributed (ἔδωκεν) gifts to his people" but with "he ascended on high" and its implications. Yet to draw out the point of distribution of gifts in particular, Paul has not cited the text of this psalm exactly; he has made certain changes.

The main changes can easily be seen by comparing Eph 4:8 with the LXX version of Psa 68:18 (67:19 in the LXX; 68:19 in the MT), which follows the Hebrew text closely:

Psalm 68:18	**Ephesians 4:8**
ἀνέβης εἰς ὕψος	ἀναβὰς εἰς ὕψος
ᾐχμαλώτευσας αἰχμαλωσίαν	ᾐχμαλώτευσεν αἰχμαλωσίαν
ἔλαβες δόματα ἐν ἀνθρώπῳ	ἔδωκεν δόματα τοῖς ἀνθρώποις

or "in consequence" are also possible glosses for διό, but the logical relation to a premise is the same.

41. Most uses of the introductory formula γέγραπται ("it is written") in Paul are accompanied by καθώς ("just as") or γάρ ("for"), showing that Scripture is the standard for understanding something or foundational facts for the inferences or conclusions he is making. The phrase διότι γέγραπται in 1 Pet 1:16 does not mark the inference but is a "marker used to indicate why someth[ing] just stated can reasonably be considered valid" (BDAG, 251 [meaning 3]).

The changes in the first two lines are relatively minor.[42] In the third line, Paul changes ἔλαβες ("you received"; Heb. לָקַחְתָּ) to ἔδωκεν ("he distributed" or "gave"), which is the most important switch, whereas ἐν ἀνθρώπῳ ("by man"?) in the LXX version of the psalm woodenly mimics בָּאָדָם ("from the human race," or even "men as gifts").[43] Paul smoothes it out for the Ephesian Greeks with the dative plural τοῖς ἀνθρώποις ("to his people").[44]

The reason why Paul has felt free to change "you took ..." to "he gave ..." in particular has led to an extraordinary amount of scholarly discussion.[45]

---

42. Paul changes indic. ἀνέβης ("you ascended") to the ptc. ἀναβὰς ("when/after he ascended"), which he represents in v. 9 with 3 sg. indic. ἀνέβη, to put more focus on the main verb ᾐχμαλώτευσεν ("he led captive"), which is switched to the third person in Eph 4:8 from the second-person ᾐχμαλώτευσας ("you led captive") in Psa 68:18.

43. The LXX rendering ἔλαβες ... ἐν here is not the most lucid Greek, as is often the case with old Greek renderings of the Hebrew. It should be noted that Psa 68 itself "swarm[s] with obscure expressions and phrases" and "has hitherto defied every critical attempt at analysis, interpretation, and dating"; Samuel Iwry, "Notes on Psalm 68," *JBL* 71 (1952): 161; cf. Gary V. Smith, "Paul's Use of Psalm 68:18 in Ephesians 4:8," *JETS* 18 (1975): 184–85, who reports (187) that בָּאָדָם is read by Dahood in light of Ugaritic to mean "from their hands."

44. My translation treats the article in the phrase **τοῖς** ἀνθρώποις as having the force of a poss. pronoun, as very often in Greek. The "men" or "people" here are the faithful military and other supporters of the triumphant Lord in the psalm; see Psa 68:35.

45. In addition to works already cited and the commentaries, see especially: W. Hall Harris III, "The Ascent and Descent of Christ in Ephesians 4:9–10," *BSac* 151 (1994): 198–214; Harris, *The Descent of Christ: Ephesians 4:7–11 and Traditional Hebrew Imagery*, AGJU 32 (Grand Rapids: Baker, 1998); Timothy G. Gombis, "Cosmic Lordship and Divine Gift-Giving: Psalm 68 in Ephesians 4:8," *NovT* 47 (2005): 367–80; Gombis, *The Drama of Ephesians: Participating in the Triumph of God* (Downers Grove, IL: InterVarsity Press, 2010); Andrew T. Lincoln, "The Use of the OT in Ephesians," *JSNT* 14 (1982): 16–57; Jonathan M. Lunde and John Anthony Dunne, "Paul's Creative and Contextual Use of Psalm 68 in Ephesians 4:8," *WTJ* 74 (2012): 99–117; Martin Pickup, "New Testament Interpretation of the Old Testament: The Theological Rationale of Midrashic Exegesis," *JETS* 51 (2008): 353–81; Richard A. Taylor, "The Use of Psalm 68:18 in Ephesians 4:8 in Light of the Ancient Versions," *BSac* 148 (1991): 319–36; Frank S. Thielman in *Commentary on the New Testament Use of the Old Testament*, ed. G. K. Beale and D. A Carson (Grand Rapids: Baker Academic, 2007), 819–25; William N. Wilder, "The Use (or Abuse) of Power in High Places: Gifts Given and Received in Isaiah, Psalm 68, and Ephesians 4:8," *BBR* 20 (2010): 185–200.

Richard Taylor conveniently reviews eight proposals that would explain the variation between the psalm and Ephesians:

1. Paul simply misquotes the psalm.
2. He quotes an early Christian hymn and not Psa 68:18 itself.
3. Paul had a lapse of memory (facilitated by difficulty of finding passages when one has to unroll scrolls).
4. He quotes a collection of OT passages used in catechesis.
5. Paul is correcting a common Jewish understanding of Psa 68 that also had the wording "he [Moses] gave."
6. The meaning is virtually the same despite the difference in wording.
7. Paul is engaging in *midrash pesher* (explained below).
8. Paul is using a variant text form of Psa 68 that differed from the MT and the LXX.[46]

Of the various views on this, one of the more fully pursued is that Paul was quoting a translation of the psalm into Aramaic (the Targum) preserved in the OL and in other places that had this or a similar change of wording (view five above).[47] There are several problems with this view, not least of which is whether these texts were contemporary with and known by Paul, as well as whether he would cite them authoritatively. Furthermore, some of these other texts contain a common Jewish interpretation of Psa 68 as referring to the ascent of Moses into heaven to receive the Torah and his

46. See Taylor, "Use of Psalm 68:18," 324–29. Taylor holds to the last view.

47. See Richard Rubinkiewicz, "Ps LXVIII 19 (= Eph IV 8) Another Textual Tradition or Targum?" *NovT* 17 (1975): 219–24; Harris, *Descent*, 64–142; Moritz, *Profound Mystery*, 60–63; Taylor, "Use of Psalm 68:18," 330–35; Barth, 473–76; Lincoln, 242–44; Gnilka, 206–9. Rubinkiewicz sees Paul utilizing a textual tradition similar to the Targum as found in the *Testament of the Twelve Patriarchs* (*T. Dan* 5.10–11), which speaks of taking "captivity" from Beliar and says, "he will give to all those who call on him eternal peace" (from the Greek as cited by Rubinkiewicz, "Ps LXVIII 19," 221; my trans.). He also cites the OL of Psa 68:18 as: *Dominus in illis in Sinai, in sancto ascendens in altum, captivam duxit captivitatem, dedit dona hominibus*, "The Lord is among them on Sinai, ascending on high in holiness, he led captivity captive, he gave gifts to men" (as given in Rubinkiewicz, "Ps LXVIII 19," 222; my trans.). The Vg. reads more like the Hebrew and LXX (*accepisti dona in hominibus,* "you received gives among men").

descent to distribute its words to Israel. There is no trace of this reference to Moses in Ephesians, and Paul evidences no interest in appropriating secondary sources for his Scripture citation.[48]

The second view that is much discussed is that Paul's citation of Psa 68 was "a restrained use of *midrash pesher*," which, as far as I can discern, means an interpretive commentary that adapts wording of the biblical text for its application to the current situation.[49] Other scholars simply prefer to call Paul's method of citing Psa 68:18 here *midrash*, even though at least one scholar insists that Eph 4:8 "is not midrashic."[50] The problem stems from the slippery term *midrash*. As Addison Wright remarks: "The word midrash at present is an equivocal term and is being used to describe a mass of disparate material. Indeed, if some of the definitions are correct, large amounts, if not the whole of the Bible, would have to be called midrash."[51]

Arising out of the discussion above, a number of scholars see Eph 4:8 not just as a wooden quote of one verse in the psalm but as a reference to the teaching of the whole psalm in context and to other OT teachings on the Lord as a triumphant warrior.[52] Psalm 68 is a triumphant song of

48. See Harris, *Descent*, 77–122; cf. O'Brien, 290–91; Hoehner, 524–30. While Paul probably knew Aramaic, as one of the leading Torah students of his day (e.g., Acts 26:24; Gal 1:14), he would have had the Psalms if not the OT memorized in Hebrew, while Greek was his first language. He regularly cites the OT in either of those two languages directly.

49. Taylor, "Use of Psalm 68:18," 329; cf. Pickup, "New Testament Interpretation," 355n10 for literature and attempted definition of terms, on which there is admittedly little precise unanimity.

50. E.g., pro-*midrash* is Martin Pickup, "New Testament Interpretation"; the anti-*midrash* quote is from Smith, "Paul's Use," 188. Wilder ("Use [or Abuse] of Power," 199) prefers the term "adaptive paraphrase" and says—helpfully—that Paul interprets Christ's exaltation "in canonical context" in light of a pattern of biblical teaching from a number of OT passages (Isaiah and the whole of Psa 68) that refer to an Adamic and Davidic messianic king.

51. Addison G. Wright, "The Literary Genre Midrash," *CBQ* 28 (1966): 105–38, 417–57 (quote from 108); cf. Jacob Neusner, *What Is Midrash?* (Philadelphia: Fortress, 1987); Gary G. Porton, "Rabbinic Midrash," in *A History of Biblical Interpretation*, ed. Alan J. Hauser and Duane F. Watson (Grand Rapids: Eerdmans, 2003), 1:198–224. For example, Lincoln calls Paul's drawing out the implications of the psalm quote in vv. 9–10 "midrash" and "midrashic" (Lincoln, 225).

52. Most notably Gombis, "Cosmic Lordship"; Lunde and Dunne, "Paul's Creative and Contextual Use"; and Wilder, "Use (or Abuse) of Power." See Lunde and Dunne, "Paul's Creative and Contextual Use," 107n35, for reference to a few other

Yahweh's deliverance of his people from his and their enemies in salvation from death (Psa 68:20), and then the song lauds his victorious ascent to dwell among his people in peace. The women divide up the spoils of battle (Psa 68:12), and the conquered kings of the earth bear gifts of tribute to the divine Victor (Psa 68:29) as the whole world is called on to worship the Lord (Psa 68:31–32). Then Yahweh, enthroned in his holy place (Psa 68:24), with his loyal subjects attending him, distributes "power and strength to his people" (Psa 68:35). The themes of triumph and the Gentiles streaming in to worship the Lord, as well as the Lord's largesse from the riches of his grace, are prominent concerns throughout Ephesians (e.g., 1:15–23; 2:11–22; 3:5–13) that had been both revealed and hidden from earlier generations as a mystery (see above on 3:1–13 and "Excursus: The Mystery of Christ").

Although Psalm 68 presents difficulties for understanding its significance in its own time (see 1 Pet 1:10–12), as redemptive history unfolded this "preliminary announcement of the gospel" (προευαγγελίζομαι; Gal 3:8) came into focus as pointing ahead to the incarnation, death, and triumphant ascension of Christ, and to the distribution of the spoils of his victory to his compatriots. "Paul's use of the OT is both *christological*—or '*christotelic*'—as well as contextual."[53] This view will be addressed more fully below after consideration of vv. 9–10.

4:9 *τὸ δὲ ἀνέβη τί ἐστιν, εἰ μὴ ὅτι καὶ κατέβη εἰς τὰ κατώτερα μέρη τῆς γῆς; ὁ καταβὰς αὐτός ἐστιν καὶ ὁ ἀναβὰς ὑπεράνω πάντων τῶν οὐρανῶν, ἵνα πληρώσῃ τὰ πάντα*, "Now, this 'he ascended,' what does it mean except that he had also descended to the nether regions of the earth? He who descended is himself also the one who ascended far beyond all the heavens, that he might fill all things." In the suggested periodic division in the introduction, vv. 9–10 are

---

works along the same lines, and see especially 116 for references for the well-known practice of NT writers to quote a phrase or a verse in the OT as a pointer to the whole of the passage in context.

53. Lunde and Dunne, "Paul's Creative and Contextual Use," 116; cf. Timothy Gombis: "The author [of Ephesians] has no intention of quoting Ps. 68:19 verbatim, but rather has in mind the full narrative movement of the entire psalm. He thereby appropriates the imagery of Yahweh ascending his throne after a victory and refocuses it christologically. Consequently Christ is depicted as the triumphant divine warrior who defeats his enemies in his death, ascends his throne as the exalted and victorious Lord, and blesses his people with gifts" (Gombis, "Cosmic Lordship," 379–80).

treated as one period. Some commentators properly address the two verses together in one place (e.g., O'Brien, 293–97; Lincoln, 244–48). The signal that the cola* of v. 10 belong with v. 9 is the lack of a conjunction like δέ, which could have been used easily; i.e., ὁ **δὲ** καταβὰς αὐτός ἐστιν would have set v. 10 apart from what went before (as does τὸ **δὲ** ἀνέβη τί ἐστιν opening v. 9).

Scholars have focused on particular phrases in vv. 9–10, but as to the meaning of the verses themselves, scholars have found "little agreement about their purpose" beyond treating them as a digression (Lincoln, 225).[54] Yet this is no digression. In fact, it is vital to answer the question of why Paul says what he does here. We may have questions on what he means by "nether regions" (τὰ κατώτερα) or "filling all things" (ἵνα πληρώσῃ τὰ πάντα), but Paul is only concerned with one point here: that the one who ascended is the same person who descended. We must concentrate on his central concern in a moment and on the overall interpretation of vv. 8–10 after reporting on the best understanding of some of the individual phrases.

The meaning of τὰ κατώτερα μέρη τῆς γῆς ("the nether regions of the earth"; cf. esp. Psa 63:9; Isa 44:23; John 3:13; 6:41, 51, 58) has drawn significant discussion over the centuries, with three prominent understandings of its meaning. It refers to: (1) Christ's descent into hell; (2) the earth itself; or (3) Christ's death.[55] The first view was popular in the early church in conjunction with their view of 1 Pet 3:19 ("he went and proclaimed to the spirits in prison"), but it is hard to defend this interpretation today (see Barth, 433; Hoehner, 533–35).[56] The second view of εἰς τὰ κατώτερα μέρη τῆς γῆς takes the genitive τῆς γῆς ("of the earth") as expressing apposition: "to the nether regions, namely, to the earth" (e.g., Barth, 433–34; O'Brien, 294; cf. Harris, *Descent*, 46–54). "Therefore, the descent of Christ mentioned in 4:9 denotes his incarnation and, most likely his crucifixion" (Barth, 434). This is an attractive option, but it makes τὰ κατώτερα unnecessary. Why didn't Paul simply say κατέβη εἰς τὴν γῆν ("he descended to the earth")? The advantage of the third view is that "the nether regions of the

54. English versions (KJV, NASB, NIV, ESV, NRSV, etc.) treat vv. 9–10 as a digression by setting them off in parentheses.

55. Harris, *Descent*, 1–63, provides a thorough review of the different views.

56. Though a descent to "the realm of the dead" is defended by William Bales, "The Descent of Christ in Ephesians 4:9," *CBQ* 72 (2010): 84–100.

earth," namely the grave (Sheol), expresses the purpose of the Son of God's descent and includes the idea of the cross and the death of Christ that has concerned Paul as paving the way for his exaltation to the highest place over all creation by freeing his people from sin (e.g., 1:7, 20–22; 2:1–7, 16; 5:2).[57] So, "by 'the lower parts of the earth' he means 'death' " (Chrysostom, 195).

The phrase referring to Christ's "filling all things" (ἵνα πληρώσῃ τὰ πάντα) is less controversial, but it needs to be pointed out that it minimally refers to Christ's glory, power, and sovereign prerogative to dispense gifts to his people. To arrive at this position, Christ has "passed through the heavens" (Heb 4:14) and even been "exalted above the heavens" (Heb 7:26; cf. Eph 1:20–23; Phil 2:9). "Be exalted, O God, above the heavens! Let your glory be over all the earth!" (Psa 108:5). As Marius Victorinus says, the phrase means that "nothing in the cosmos is left untouched by Christ" (*ACCS*, 165).

But we need also remember that "filling" and "fullness" earlier in Ephesians refer to God's glory filling his inaugurated new-creation temple, the church (see above on 2:21–22; 3:17, 19, 21). In 3:17 Paul had included in his prayer that "Christ may take up his dwelling in your hearts" as the Lord of the covenant, fulfilling his oath-sealed pledge to dwell with his people (see above on 3:17). In the reference to "filling all things," Paul expresses Christ's presence in the church through his Spirit (Rom 8:9–11).[58]

---

57. For a careful and interesting interpretation somewhat along these lines but incorporating Johannine irony where Christ's being "exalted" is both to heaven and on the cross (esp. John 3:13) see Muddiman, 195–98. Friedrich Büchsel (*TDNT*, 3:640–42) says that the phrase refers to Christ's "entry into the sphere of the dead by death." Then his exaltation to "fill all things" spans the deepest netherworld of the dead to the very heights of heaven—spanning all creation. He continues: "[Christ taking captivity captive] does not mean that He victoriously invaded Hades and liberated the dead there. Eph[esians] does not speak in these terms. The point is that He who is raised from the dead (1:20) and exalted to the right hand of God has subdued all the spirits (1:21) which previously ruled over men and kept them captive in sins, as expressly stated in 2:1–7. ... To Christ alone belongs cosmic greatness" (3:642).

58. This expresses a similar concern (but in a quite different way) to the position of Hall Harris ("Ascent and Descent" and *Descent*) and a few others (e.g., Lincoln, 246–47) who interpret the "descent" of Christ to be subsequent to his ascent as the giving of the Holy Spirit in Pentecost. "This Jesus God raised up, and of that we all are witnesses. Being therefore exalted at the right hand of God, and having received from the Father the promise of the Holy Spirit, he has poured out this that

The final thing to say about Eph 4:9–10 is the most important. Why does Paul add these statements? I have already mentioned that vv. 9–10 are not merely parenthetical remarks, as if unimportant, and that scholars are not united on what they mean. By focusing on individual phrases in these verses, sometimes their main point gets lost from view. Furthermore, in v. 8, we tend to focus on the colon* "he distributed gifts to his people," *but Paul does not elaborate on this at all* in vv. 9–10. His attention is elsewhere.

That being said, Paul's real concern is summarized in v. 10a: ὁ καταβὰς αὐτός ἐστιν καὶ ὁ ἀναβὰς, which can be paraphrased, "That one who descended is the very same person (αὐτός) who also ascended." In v. 9 Paul teases out the implication that the psalm, speaking of Yahweh's ascent, implies that he has also descended.[59] Yahweh dwells above the heavens and will rend the heavens and come down to redeem his people (e.g., 1 Kgs 8:27; Isa 33:5; 64:1; 66:1; Matt 23:22). What Paul is interested in here is that the acts of Yahweh dimly foreshadowed in Psa 68 were accomplished in Jesus Christ. *He* is the one who came down and went back up to be exalted "far beyond all the heavens" (ὑπεράνω πάντων τῶν οὐρανῶν; v. 10b) and is in a position to distribute gifts to the church, which is his fullness (1:23). "And no one has ascended into heaven except he who descended from heaven, namely, the Son of Man" (John 3:13).

We may finally pull together all the threads from vv. 7–10 to form a coherent picture of what Paul is doing in Eph 4:7–10. It begins with διὸ λέγει ("therefore he says"; v. 8) which, as pointed out, is not a formula but a meaningful indicator of how Paul views Psa 68:18. To understand how Paul interprets this psalm depends on an understanding that Scripture is an organic development of redemptive revelation, as outlined in "Biblical Theological Comments" after 2:11–22. Even more pointedly, all Scripture has Christ—his earthly mission and redemption on the cross, and his resurrection and exaltation to cosmic supremacy—as its central orientation from beginning to end. Christ was the rock that followed Israel in the wilderness (1 Cor 10:4), the recipient of the Abrahamic promise (Gal 3:16),

---

you yourselves are seeing and hearing. For David did not ascend into the heavens …" (Acts 2:32–34). Most commentators dissent from this view; cf. Gombis, "Cosmic Lordship," 368–72, for critique.

59. In the view of Harris and others mentioned in the previous note, the descent of Christ is *after* his ascent, not prior. Given that "nether parts of the earth" means Christ's death, it does seem best to see the descent as prior to his ascent.

which remained valid until he should arrive (Gal 3:19) in fulfillment of the intratrinitarian covenant of redemption (Gal 3:20–22; cf. Eph 1:3–14).[60] Abraham saw his day (John 8:56; cf. Heb 11:8–16) because the Scripture spoke the promise of the gospel to him in a preliminary proclamation (προευαγγελίζομαι) because God would fulfill it in Christ (Gal 3:8). And Moses—who preferred "the reproach of Christ" to the treasures of Egypt (Heb 11:26)—and Isaiah—who saw Christ's glory—both wrote of him (John 5:46; 12:41) through the prophetic "Spirit of Christ" (1 Pet 1:10–12). Indeed, Christ and his mission are the subject of all the divisions of the OT Scriptures (Luke 24:26–27). And, as we will see, Christ's relationship to the church forms the archetype of the creation ordinance of marriage itself (Eph 5:31–32).

Hence, Paul interprets Psa 68:18 as originally given to reveal—in a mysterious, preliminary way—the gifting of gifts from the victorious Christ to his church, stated in v. 7. Paul develops this image by saying the gifts were given "to his people" (τοῖς ἀνθρώποις; Eph 4:8c), which is the distribution of gifts of captured spoils of war (cf. Psa 68:12) to the victorious king's army and supporters (cf. 6:10–20; Col 2:15): "he gives power and strength to his people" (Psa 68:35). It turns out in Eph 4:11 that the gifts the exalted Messiah has given to strengthen his people are gifted men who are called to spend themselves in service of Christ's church.[61]

For Paul, this is why (διό) Psa 68:18 was originally written and speaks of Christ's gifts. In order to confirm this, Paul is at pains in vv. 9–10 to show that Christ is the one who ascended in the psalm at his resurrection/exaltation, because it is he who had descended "to the nether regions of the earth" in death to lead a host of captives captive into glory.[62] Jesus Christ is the

60. See S. M. Baugh, "Galatians 3:20 and the Covenant of Redemption," *WTJ* 66 (2004): 49–70.

61. And women prophets in the apostolic era (Acts 2:17; 21:8–9). My focus on "men" here and in the subsequent discussion is not intended to diminish the important contribution of female prophets in the initial generation, or of the "general office" (see below) contributions of women today. It arises out of a conviction that Christ gives men to fill the "special office" ministry throughout this age (evangelists, shepherds, teachers).

62. Cf. the view of Smith that the spoils were the church officers of v. 11 on analogy with the OT Levites (Smith, "Paul's Use," 187–89); and Muddiman, 190–92, where 2 Cor 2:14 and 1 Cor 4:9 are noted (cf. Rom 16:7; Phlm 23; Col 4:10) for the apostles as prisoners (cf. Eph 3:1; 4:1) and Christ's captives given to the church.

incarnate, divine Son whose existence and revelation was concurrent with the psalm. This same outlook of a psalm is found in another place where διὸ is used in connection with λέγει:

> For it is impossible for the blood of bulls and goats to take away sins. Therefore (διό), when Christ came into the world, he said (λέγει), "Sacrifices and offering you did not desire, but a body you prepared for me. ... Then I said, 'Here I am—it is written about me in the scroll—I have come to do your will, O God.' [Psa 40:6–8] ... And by that will, we have been made holy through the sacrifice of the body of Jesus Christ once for all" (Heb 10:4–5, 10 NIV).

William Lane remarks here, "The writer [of Hebrews] understands the cited passage as a word addressed by the Son to the Father on the occasion of the incarnation, which the psalmist, as it were, overheard."[63] In Ephesians 4:8 Paul similarly gives a free paraphrase of Psa 68:18 by incorporating elements of the whole psalm in light of its fulfillment in Christ's ascent and gifting because he views the psalm as part of the organic development in the stream of supernatural revelation of this great event.[64] "The Scripture saw" Christ's ascent to glory "ahead of time" (προϊδοῦσα ἡ γραφή; Gal 3:8).

4:11 Καὶ αὐτὸς ἔδωκεν τοὺς μὲν ἀποστόλους, τοὺς δὲ προφήτας, τοὺς δὲ εὐαγγελιστάς, τοὺς δὲ ποιμένας καὶ διδασκάλους, "And he did himself give some as apostles, some as prophets, some as evangelists, some as shepherds as well as

---

63. William L. Lane, *Hebrews 9–13*, WBC 47B (Dallas: Word, 1991), 263; see also 255 (note m) and 262–63 for the LXX of Psa 40:6–8 as an "interpretive paraphrase" of the MT. Cf. Geerhardus Vos, *The Teaching of the Epistle to the Hebrews* (Grand Rapids: Eerdmans, 1956; repr., Phillipsburg, NJ: P&R, n.d.), 49–87.

64. The phrase "organic development" expresses the organic connection of the revelation of Christ in Psa 68 with Eph 4:8–11, yet acknowledges that there is true development of redemptive revelation from those two points in history, which progresses as redemptive accomplishment itself progresses. Hence, there was true mystery in the OT era, which is now disclosed in the coming of Christ. This contrasts with seeing Paul somehow violating proper biblical interpretive principles and imposing a distinctive "Christotelic" interpretation on the OT as, for example, Peter Enns, "Apostolic Hermeneutics and an Evangelical Doctrine of Scripture: Moving Beyond a Modernist Impasse," *WTJ* 65 (2003): 263–87; Enns, *Inspiration and Incarnation* (Grand Rapids: Baker, 2005).

teachers." Paul opens vv. 11–16 with a backward look to Christ's triumphant ascent to comprehensive rule over "all things" (v. 10c) and resulting largesse to his loyal subjects with the opening colon* of v. 11: "And he did himself give" (καὶ αὐτὸς ἔδωκεν).[65] It is difficult to render the exact force of αὐτὸς here. It is clearly emphatic, but more importantly we must evaluate the force of the emphasis, which in this place serves to link the Lord here with what was previously said about him. A free paraphrase conveys the idea: "*This same ascended and triumphant Lord* is the one who gave some as ..."[66]

We actually should be surprised with the statement of v. 11. The Lord, ascending to his throne in triumphant glory, could be expected to dole out property or wealth to his people as reward for their loyal service in the wars (6:10–20), but instead he gives *men.* And these men are given to help equip the church to ward off attacks of deceitful, scheming teachers (v. 14; cf. esp. 2 Pet 2:1).

One of the more prevalent features of Greek style in ancient literature is the use of contrasting elements, represented here with the familiar μέν ... δέ, "on the one hand ... on the other" sequence.[67] One nice thing about this sequence that would not be lost on the audience is the rhyming of the final syllables of the titles of office, with the first and last forming an inclusio*: ἀποστόλ**ους** ... προφήτ**ας** ... εὐαγγελιστ**άς** ... ποιμέν**ας** ... διδασκάλ**ους**. This is not accidental but part of nice, if not extravagant, compositional care, marking Ephesians and many parts of Paul's writings.

---

65. "Christ now sets out to accomplish the goal of filling all things by supplying his people with everything necessary to foster the growth and perfection of the body (v. 13)" (O'Brien, 297).
66. The repetition of δίδωμι ("give") and cognate δωρεά and δόμα ("gift") also bind vv. 7–11 together.
67. The μέν ... δέ sequence is an exceedingly common feature of extrabiblical Greek and is found in the NT, if not quite as frequently. See also the variation on it such as: οἱ μέν ... ἄλλοι δέ ... ἕτεροι δέ ... ("some ... others ... and still others"; Matt 16:14). We also find καί ... καί ... καί as common connectors in NT lists; e.g., Luke 14:21; Acts 2:9; Eph 1:21; 3:8; 2 Tim 1:11. The occurrence of the particle μέν in 4:11 is its only use in Ephesians. It is fairly common in Romans and the Corinthians epistles, but it is rare in most other Pauline books; e.g., Galatians (3x), Colossians (1x), 1 Thessalonians (1x), and 2 Thessalonians (0x). In the LXX μέν is found most often in nontranslation Greek of the Maccabean literature and less often in translations from Hebrew, such as the Psalms, with only one occurrence where it could have been expected in its many strophes* that express alternation and contrast.

The construction ἔδωκεν τοὺς … ἀποστόλους κτλ is a double accusative with an object and predicate (BDF §157), with articles functioning as pronouns (BDF §§249–50). The rendering of the articles as "some" is due to the force of the μὲν … δέ construction enumerating the various offices in a contrasting series (BDAG, 629–30; meaning 1c). We could also render the series with: "he gave some *to be* apostles," "some *to be* prophets," etc., or we could accent the contrast in the series with "some as apostles, *others* as prophets, *others* as evangelists," etc.

Some scholars read τοὺς μὲν ἀποστόλους, τοὺς δὲ προφήτας, etc., not as a double accusative but as a simple direct object of ἔδωκεν: "He gave the apostles, the prophets …" (e.g., O'Brien, 297–98n101; Lincoln, 249; Schnackenburg, 180–81).[68] The effect of this reading allows taking τοὺς δὲ ποιμένας καὶ διδασκάλους ("shepherds as well as teachers") as essentially one office ("he gave … the pastor-teachers"). However, the double accusative is to be preferred because it is dictated by ἔδωκεν with two connected accusative substantives, not merely by the article with the μέν … δέ sequence (as Lincoln, 249).[69] There is a parallel example of the grammar of Eph 4:11 in (Pseudo-)Plutarch when he writes:

> τῶν γὰρ δούλων τῶν σπουδαίων τοὺς μὲν γεωργοὺς ἀποδεικνύουσι, τοὺς δὲ ναυκλήρους τοὺς δ' ἐμπόρους τοὺς δ' οἰκονόμους τοὺς δὲ δανειστάς
>
> For from their virtuous slaves they designate some as (i.e., *to be*) caretakers of their farms, some as their ship-masters, some as merchants, some as stewards, and some as their money-lenders. (*Lib. ed.* 4A–B; my trans.)[70]

68. Cf. Ernest Best, "Ministry in Ephesians," *IBS* 15 (1993): 146–66.
69. For δίδωμι taking a double acc. see: αὐτὸν ἔδωκεν κεφαλὴν, "he gave him (to be) Head" (Eph 1:22); δοῦναι τὴν ψυχὴν αὐτοῦ λύτρον ἀντὶ πολλῶν, "to give his life (to be) a ransom for many" (Matt 20:28; Mark 10:45); and ἔδωκεν αὐτοῖς ἐξουσίαν τέκνα θεοῦ γενέσθαι, "he gave to them the right to become children of God" (John 1:12), where the predication implied in the double acc. construction is made explicit with copulative γενέσθαι ("to become"); cf. Matt 16:26; John 12:49; 2 Thess 3:9; 1 Tim 2:6.
70. The passage continues (LCL trans.): "But these people heedlessly make any convenient slave, even drunkards or gluttons, the παιδαγωγός ["guardian"; Gal 3:24–25] of their son." The verb ἀποδείκνυμι ("designate [someone to be], appoint

There are two questions that typically come up in discussion of v. 11: (1) which and whether all the special offices listed here continue today and (2) whether we should take "shepherds" and "teachers" as one group or two. The first question was addressed in our comment on 2:20, that the "apostles and prophets" were foundational offices for the apostolic period (cf. Acts 13:1; 1 Cor 12:28) and were not continued after the Lord had laid the groundwork for his church in the first generation of the new covenant era (cf. Hoehner, 540–47; O'Brien, 298–99). The second question requires a bit more attention here.

As noted already, the five offices listed in v. 11 are given in a μέν ... δέ clause construction, with the last syllable of the first and last office forming an inclusio*. What is more, the first two cola* in the list are balanced against each other with two offices in each cola*. But the last mentioned office, teachers, has no corresponding partner, as so:

> τοὺς μὲν ἀποστόλους τοὺς δὲ προφήτας
> τοὺς δὲ εὐαγγελιστάς τοὺς δὲ ποιμένας
> καὶ διδασκάλους.

What this means is that if Paul had kept up the same format and had said τοὺς δὲ διδασκάλους, we would expect one more office to be listed as its partner. But there is no other office to mention because this is a complete list of offices in the church whose primary responsibility revolves around *proclaiming and teaching the word of God* for the church's maturity and protection from false teaching (vv. 13–14).[71]

This lack of balance in the structure is part of why attempts to read the one article governing "shepherds" as also governing "teachers" (τοὺς δὲ ποιμένας καὶ διδασκάλους) and forming one office with two components (i.e., "teaching shepherds") are unpersuasive.[72] Paul joins "teachers" to the

---

[someone as]") here takes the same double acc./predication construction as δίδωμι in Eph 4:11.

71. Hence, "deacons" and "elders" are not listed here as elsewhere (e.g., 1 Tim 3:1-13); cf. H. Merklein, *Die kirchliche Amt nach den Epheserbrief*, SANT 33 (Munich: Kösel, 1973). For NT lists of church officers see Rom 12:6–8; 1 Cor 12:8–10, 28:30; cf. 1 Pet 4:10–11.

72. E.g., Barth, 438–39. "Granville Sharp's Canon" applies strictly to sg. noun pairs with certain kinds of nouns; cf. Daniel B. Wallace, *Granville Sharp's Canon and Its Kin: Semantics and Significance*, SBG 14 (New York: Peter Lang, 2009), 228–30,

previous list with a simple καί, giving the list a termination. This is the adjunctive meaning of καί (BDAG, 495–96), communicating "along with" or "as well as," and it has this function in other, similar lists.[73] Teachers, then, should be viewed as an office that can be distinguished from "shepherds" as a special branch of overseers charged particularly with instruction in God's word (e.g., 1 Tim 5:17). If there is any connection between shepherds and teachers intended, it is most likely that these are the two offices in this list more directly connected to local congregations than the other three.[74]

The term "evangelist" (εὐαγγελιστής) designates someone like a modern missionary. The term itself occurs only here and in Acts 21:8 of Philip (cf. Acts 8:4–5) and 2 Tim 4:5 of Timothy (cf. 1 Thess 3:2; Phil 2:22; Gerhard Friedrich, *TDNT*, 2:736–37).[75] Their "task of ministry" (v. 12) centers on proclamation of the gospel (εὐαγγέλιον) as foundation for planting

---

who says "this text is the most abused pl. personal construction in the NT" (228). As just one example, Plutarch writes about: τοὺς μὲν οὖν εὐπόρους καὶ πρεσβυτέρους καὶ τῶν γεωργῶν τὸ πλῆθος, "the men who were well-to-do, and the elderly men, and most of the farmers" (*Nicias* 9.5; LCL trans.) where τοὺς … εὐπόρους καὶ πρεσβυτέρους ("the rich and the elderly") are listed with only one article but are two separate groups (cf. Plutarch, *Pomp.* 9.1, τοὺς μὲν ἄλλους ἡγεμόνας καὶ στρατηγούς, "the rest of his officers and generals" [LCL trans.]—two groups with one article; there is no corresponding τοὺς δέ member in the context, just the καί).

73. Here are a few clear examples of the adjunct "along with" meaning for καί and some where δέ is the main connector: Matt 1:2, 11; 2:3; Acts 26:30; Jude 1:25; and outside the NT: Gen 3:8; 4:5; 45:16; *3 Macc* 4:8–19; Dan 1:7; 12:2; Diogenes Laertius, 8:2, 77; Onasander, 1:1. Cf. Eph 4:31, where σύν rounds out the list as variation from καί.

74. This is the view of Chrysostom, who gives Timothy and Titus as examples. Although he references pastors and teachers together (Ποιμένας καὶ διδασκάλους, τοὺς ὁλόκληρον ἐμπεπιστευμένους ἔθνος, "Pastors and teachers, who were entrusted with an entire nation") he distinguishes them separately with separate articles in what follows: Τί οὖν; **οἱ** ποιμένες καὶ **οἱ** διδάσκαλοι ἐλάττους; "What then? Are pastors and teachers inferior?" (*Hom. Eph.* 82.45–50; emphasis added; accessed via TLG). Cf. Origen and Jerome, 174–75, where Origen clearly takes them as separate groups and Jerome does not.

75. In 2 Tim 4:5 in particular, Timothy is to fulfill the "task" (ἔργον) of an evangelist, which is called his "ministry" (διακονία) and therefore connects to εἰς ἔργον διακονίας ("for the task of ministry") in Eph 4:12. The LXX of Psa 68 quoted in Eph 4:8 has an interesting statement that may relate to evangelists: κύριος δώσει ῥῆμα τοῖς εὐαγγελιζομένοις δυνάμει πολλῇ, "The Lord will give the word to his evangelists with great power" (Psa 68:11; LXX 67:12; cf. MT 68:12).

new congregations.[76] In the OT, judges and kings were the shepherds (ποιμένες) of the people (e.g., 2 Sam 5:2; 7:7); in the NT era, elders "shepherd" by watching over, counseling, and nurturing the church: "And I will give you shepherds after my own heart, who will feed you with knowledge and understanding" (Jer 3:15; cf. Acts 20:28; 1 Cor 12:5–6; 12:28; 1 Pet 5:1–2).

4:12 πρὸς τὸν καταρτισμὸν τῶν ἁγίων εἰς ἔργον διακονίας, εἰς οἰκοδομὴν τοῦ σώματος τοῦ Χριστοῦ, "for preparation of the saints, for the task of ministry, for building-up of the body of Christ." There are two interpretations of the interrelation of the prepositional phrases in this period, which are understood as having significant impact on one's understanding of ministry in the church.[77] They line up as follows:

4:12 πρὸς τὸν καταρτισμὸν τῶν ἁγίων
εἰς ἔργον διακονίας
εἰς οἰκοδομὴν τοῦ σώματος τοῦ Χριστοῦ

A common view today is represented in translations like the ESV, which reads: "to equip the saints for the work of ministry ..." and thereby communicates that it is believers ("general officers") who execute the church's ministry (διακονία).[78] This idea is communicated in translation by having no comma after "saints" and makes the second phrase subordinate to the first.[79] The other view is brought out in my translation ("for preparation of

76. This is how the early church understood this ministry as witnessed in Eusebius, *Hist. eccl.* 5.10.1–4. Notice in particular there how evangelists functioned "for the growth and edification of the divine word" (ἐπ' αὐξήσει καὶ οἰκοδομῇ τοῦ θεοῦ), with possible echoes to the same terms in Eph 4:12, 16.

77. Talbert (113) calls this issue a "battleground."

78. See Barth, 439, 78–84, for a strong defense of this interpretation; cf. Gnilka, 213; O'Brien, 301–5; Hoehner, 547–50; Talbert, 113–14. For an equally strong defense of the opposite view see T. David Gordon, " 'Equipping' Ministry in Ephesians 4?" *JETS* 37 (1994): 69–78; Juan Manuel Granados Rojas, "Ephesians 4,12. A Revised Reading," *Bib* 92 (2011): 81–96; Sydney H. T. Page, "Whose Ministry? A Re-Appraisal of Ephesians 4:12," *NovT* 47 (2005): 26–46; Henry P. Hamann, "The Translation of Ephesians 4:12—A Necessary Revision," *Concordia Journal* 14 (1988): 42–49; cf. Calvin, 180–81; Hodge, 227–30; Lincoln, 253–54; Schnackenburg, 182–84.

79. Hence the period would have to be presented as:
πρὸς τὸν καταρτισμὸν τῶν ἁγίων εἰς ἔργον διακονίας
εἰς οἰκοδομὴν τοῦ σώματος τοῦ Χριστοῦ.

the saints, for the task of ministry"—note the comma; cf. KJV). This interpretation takes the three cola* here as parallel (or coordinate) despite the lack of conjunctions in front of the two εἰς clauses (asyndeton*); all three phrases thus describe the ministry of the special officers of v. 11.

The primary reason for taking the three cola* as parallel is stylistic, as well as that it is what is required as the passage moves forward (below on vv. 14–16). It is sometimes noted that we can expect the two εἰς clauses to be preceded by conjunctions if they refer to actions of the officers in v. 11 and are therefore what I am calling *parallel.* Technically what we are dealing with is a figure of speech called "accumulation," which involves expansion of an idea in subsequent parallel phrases or cola* (Lausberg, *Literary Rhetoric*, §671).

Furthermore, asyndeton* with two or more parallel prepositions and other parts of speech occurs quite frequently in Ephesians and can be found elsewhere in Paul's writings, as these examples—which include the next two verses—illustrate:[80]

4:13 μέχρι καταντήσωμεν οἱ πάντες
εἰς τὴν ἑνότητα τῆς πίστεως καὶ τῆς ἐπιγνώσεως
τοῦ υἱοῦ τοῦ θεοῦ
εἰς ἄνδρα τέλειον
εἰς μέτρον ἡλικίας τοῦ πληρώματος τοῦ Χριστοῦ

4:14 ἵνα μηκέτι ὦμεν νήπιοι
κλυδωνιζόμενοι καὶ περιφερόμενοι
παντὶ ἀνέμῳ τῆς διδασκαλίας
ἐν τῇ κυβείᾳ τῶν ἀνθρώπων
ἐν πανουργίᾳ
πρὸς τὴν μεθοδείαν τῆς πλάνης

80. Other examples of the same phenomenon are found in 1:14, 18; 2:2; 4:2, 18; 5:26–27 (with ἵνα clauses); cf. 2 Cor 10:15–16; Rom 15:2; 2 Cor 10:15–16; 2 Tim 3:16.

6:12 ὅτι οὐκ ἔστιν ἡμῖν ἡ πάλη
πρὸς αἷμα καὶ σάρκα **ἀλλὰ πρὸς** τὰς ἀρχάς
πρὸς τὰς ἐξουσίας
πρὸς τοὺς κοσμοκράτορας τοῦ σκότους τούτου
πρὸς τὰ πνευματικὰ τῆς πονηρίας ἐν
τοῖς ἐπουρανίοις

Rom 15:2 ἕκαστος ἡμῶν τῷ πλησίον ἀρεσκέτω
εἰς τὸ ἀγαθὸν
πρὸς οἰκοδομήν
("Let each of us please his neighbor for his good, to build him up")

2 Tim 3:16 πᾶσα γραφὴ θεόπνευστος καὶ ὠφέλιμος
πρὸς διδασκαλίαν
πρὸς ἐλεγμόν
πρὸς ἐπανόρθωσιν
πρὸς παιδείαν τὴν ἐν δικαιοσύνῃ
("All Scripture is breathed out by God and profitable for teaching, for reproof, for correction, and for training in righteousness")

Although the text form above shows the parallel phrases visually, there would be a slight pause before the start of each colon* in the original oral presentation of these texts, which marked out the prepositions as parallel with asyndeton*. Our interpretation of the phrases in v. 12, therefore, fits the demonstrable style of Ephesians and highlights the three statements of the church officers in v. 11 as parallel or coordinate.

Finally, for many scholars, the interpretation of these phrases hinges on the shift from πρός to εἰς, "which means at least the first two prepositional phrases are not coordinate" (Talbert, 114). I find this argument problematic. The three prepositional phrases can be coordinate but say different things—as indeed they do.[81] The first colon* (πρὸς τὸν καταρτισμὸν, "for

81. Note how the ESV takes εἰς τὸ ἀγαθὸν and πρὸς οἰκοδομήν in Rom 15:2 above as coordinate by inserting a comma in translation: "for his good, to build him up." In fact, the second prepositional phrase is in apposition, expanding on the meaning of the first: "for his good, [which means] to build him up." See the mention above

preparation of the saints") is the equivalent of a result clause (= "so that the saints may be prepared"), while the second (εἰς ἔργον διακονίας, "for the task of ministry") and third (εἰς οἰκοδομὴν, "for building up of the body of Christ") are the equivalent of purpose clauses (= "in order that they may fulfill their task of ministry [to the church], in order to build up the body of Christ") (cf. 5:26–27a; Rev 13:6).[82]

The noun καταρτισμός ("preparation"; v. 12a) occurs only here in the NT and LXX and would be expected to mean "maturation" (like κατάρτισις in 2 Cor 13:9) or "restoration," which do not fit this context. It is normally rendered "equip" or "equipping" (NKJV, NASB, ESV, NRSV; as suggested in BDAG, 526; KJV has "perfecting"), yet other renderings and meanings are possible. LSJ (910) suggests "training" or "discipline" and "furnishings," as found in nonliterary sources.[83] We are guided here by etymology (with all due caution) for a rare word, especially since the -ισμός class of nouns are derived from verbs. Hence, καταρτισμός is derived from καταρτίζω, and so the meaning of the noun (derived from the verb; cf. BDAG, 526) seems to be "preparation," as one arranges and prepares an army for battle. Here the saints are prepared for withstanding human cunning in false teaching (v. 14).

In conclusion, then, v. 12 outlines three responsibilities of the special officers of v. 11, with their central obligation being the most general. We can paraphrase the whole as: "to fulfill the task of ministry (to the church), to provide for the saints, (and) to build up the body of Christ." By saying that this is the "task of ministry" (διακονία), Paul shows that these officers are not lords over but servants (διάκονοι) of the church, as was the Lord Jesus

---

on this use of asyndeton* as the "accumulation" rhetorical figure, which fits Rom 15:2 also.

82. For πρός as the equivalent of a result clause see BDAG, 874 (meaning 2cγ); εἰς as purpose, BDAG, 290 (meaning 4f). Note that these uses of the preps. require their nominal objs. to carry a verbal idea, which all three in v. 12 do. Rojas ("Ephesians 4,12") proposes that πρός expresses "agreement" (?), that the first εἰς clause is purpose and the second is result. This last idea is certainly possible: "that (as a result of the church officers' task of ministry) the body of Christ be built up." Page ("Whose Ministry?," 28–30) argues that the preps. are synonyms for purpose ("telic force"). The difference between purpose and result is merely one of intent (purpose), whether accomplished or not, and actual accomplishment (result).

83. See G. H. R. Horsley, *New Docs*, 3:70 nr. 42; cf. Page, "Whose Ministry?," 32–35.

(e.g., Mark 10:42–45) and Paul himself (e.g., 3:7).[84] While it is true that the church in general has responsibilities for what is termed "service" or "ministry" with the same term, διακονία, found in v. 12b (e.g., 1 Cor 12:5; 2 Cor 9:12–13; Rev 2:19), in our passage Paul is focusing on the ministry of the word for tasks and benefits articulated in vv. 13–14, whereas the general office service is referenced particularly in vv. 15–16.[85]

4:13 μέχρι καταντήσωμεν οἱ πάντες εἰς τὴν ἑνότητα τῆς πίστεως καὶ τῆς ἐπιγνώσεως τοῦ υἱοῦ τοῦ θεοῦ, "until all of us attain to the unity of the faith and of the knowledge of the Son of God." While only some are given to the church as special officers, the outcome of their service, when properly executed, leads to *all* attaining to the unity of the faith and to the knowledge of Christ. There are no special tutors to the wealthy and exclusive people in the church, as characterized education at large in antiquity.[86] Christ's people embody a wonderful irony: A diverse gifting brings about their unity (so 1 Cor 12:4–13, with many parallels to Eph 4).

The object of knowledge here is of "the Son of God," a title for Christ found in Ephesians only here and not frequently in Paul's writings elsewhere (Rom 1:4; Gal 2:20). This title brings out either Christ's kingly identity, reaching back to the promise to David that his royal seed would be to God as a son (2 Sam 7:14; Col 1:13; cf. Rev 21:7), or more likely here it displays the perfect, divine stature of the incarnate Son, whose "full stature" serves as the standard for measuring Christian maturity.

εἰς ἄνδρα τέλειον, εἰς μέτρον ἡλικίας τοῦ πληρώματος τοῦ Χριστοῦ, "to the mature man, to the measure of the full stature of Christ." In the incarnate

84. However, see John N. Collins, *Diakonia: Re-interpreting the Ancient Sources* (Oxford: Oxford University Press, 1990) for a study that concludes that *diakonia* does not imply servile status but has ties with delivering a message for another as a spokesman or courier. This certainly fits the "task of ministry" of the word-based church officers in Eph 4:11–12 very well; cf. Page, "Whose Ministry?," 35–40.

85. The classic terms "special office" and "general office" I am using are that pastors, teachers, elders, and deacons hold a special office, while all other members of the church hold "the general office of believer," which gives them their own duties and callings in the overall ministry of the church; cf. Edmund P. Clowney, *The Church* (Downers Grove, IL: InterVarsity Press, 1995), 199–214.

86. There were some publicly or privately funded schools in antiquity; e.g., Pliny, *Ep.* 4.13 (before Pliny's intervention mentioned in this letter, students had to travel from Comum to Milan for school).

Son is the full expression of both divine and human perfection in one person (see 1:23; 3:19; Col 1:19, 28; 2:9), in whose image believers are being renewed (Rom 8:29; 1 Cor 15:49; 2 Cor 3:18). He is the maturity by which all Christian maturity must be measured as the fountain and standard of the new human race in the new creation inaugurated in the Firstborn. Paul is here extending the body metaphor used earlier and in the following verses for the church and contrasts this with the stature of doctrinal "toddlers" in the next verse (cf. Heb 5:11–14). The work of the gifted ministers in v. 11 is to proclaim and to teach the word centering on Christ rather than on speculative or eccentric teachings of their own (1 Cor 2:2). The necessary outcome of their "task of ministry" is the maturity of others, not their own aggrandizement (cf. 1 Tim 6:3–6; Jas 3:1, 14; Jude 16–20).

4:14 ἵνα μηκέτι ὦμεν νήπιοι, "so that we may no longer be toddlers." This is the first of two outcomes of the maturity brought about by the proper operation of the word-based ministry.[87] The second outcome is a contrasting parallel statement with ἵνα elided: [ἵνα] δέ ... αὐξήσωμεν εἰς αὐτὸν τὰ πάντα ("but ... [so that] we may grow in every way in him"; v. 15b). The contrast is between the "toddler" stage and "growing up."

Hebrews 5:13 provides an illuminating parallel for v. 14a with its statement about νήπιοι ("children," "toddlers") addicted to milk rather than to the solid food of Christian teaching that is for "mature" (τέλειοι) adults (cf. ἄνδρα τέλειον in v. 13 above and also in 1 Cor 3:1–2; cf. 1 Cor 14:20; 2 Cor 4:2; 11:3). Paul is teaching in v. 14 and context that Christians must become doctrinally "mature" in order not to become ensnared by the crafty schemes of deceiving false teachers. The special-office ministers of v. 11 labor to bring this about, ideally, in self-sacrificial service for the benefit of the church (see esp. Col 1:28–29).

87. English versions sometimes add an unwarranted element of exhortation here: "We must no longer be children" (NRSV), leaving out the force of ἵνα entirely, as if ὦμεν were a hortatory subjunctive (it is not); similar is: "As a result, we are no longer to be children" (NASB); cf. "Then we will no longer be infants" (NIV); "so that we may no longer be children" (ESV). For ἵνα used to introduce result see BDAG, 477 (meaning 3); BDF §391 ("The classical boundaries of ἵνα are here overstepped"); C. F. D. Moule, *An Idiom Book of New Testament Greek*, 2nd ed. (Cambridge: Cambridge University Press, 1959), 142–46.

κλυδωνιζόμενοι καὶ περιφερόμενοι παντὶ ἀνέμῳ τῆς διδασκαλίας ἐν τῇ κυβείᾳ τῶν ἀνθρώπων, ἐν πανουργίᾳ πρὸς τὴν μεθοδείαν τῆς πλάνης, "tossed about and swept along by every wind of teaching in the trickery of men, in cunning, for their deceitful designs." The figure of blasts of storm winds and of a ship being tossed about and swept along is especially poignant for Paul. It recalls the several storms and shipwrecks he had experienced on the Mediterranean Sea, which could terrify even the most experienced sailors (Acts 27:13–44; cf. Jonah 1:4–14). Paul could certainly understand being "swept along" by tempestuous rollers, especially considering the small size of the ships of his day.[88]

While one may be tempted to think of false teaching in the church as innocent error—and there certainly is such—there is malice to certain forms of doctrinal heresy intended to shipwreck the faith of the naive and credulous, i.e., of "toddlers" (cf. 1 Cor 14:20). Paul refers to "the trickery of men, in cunning, for their deceitful designs" in most vivid terms. Κυβεία ("trickery")—whence we derive "cube"—refers to "dice" and is taken to refer to something akin to English "playing against loaded dice." Πανουργία and μεθοδεία are similar terms for "wiles," "cunning," "schemes," "[deceptive] designs," and piling up these terms shows that false teachers "worm their way into" (Gal 2:4) congregations in order to captivate them for their own gain (cf. 1 Tim 6:3–5; Jude 4; 1 Pet 2:1; 1 John 2:18–19; 4:1–3) and are serving the purposes of evil spirits (6:12; 2:2; 1 Tim 4:1) and their own evil schemes.

For πρὸς τὴν μεθοδείαν τῆς πλάνης ("for their deceitful designs"; v. 14e), most modern versions follow BDAG (625 [μεθοδεία]) with "in deceitful scheming" (NRSV, NKJV), "in deceitful schemes" (ESV), or "in their deceitful scheming" (NIV), as if πρὸς τὴν μεθοδείαν were expressed as ἐν τῇ

88. I once had an analogously memorable experience aboard a ship during a hurricane in the North Atlantic. That was on a large ship, of some 530 feet in length, whereas most ancient Mediterranean ships were more in the range of 30–70 feet in length; cf. Hubert Cancik and Helmuth Schneider, ed., *Brill's New Pauly: Encyclopaedia of the Ancient World* (Boston: Brill, 2008), 13:387–403; cf. Lucian, *Nav.* 35.5–6 for a huge ancient ship, about 180 feet long. All it would take for one of those small sailing vessels to "turn turtle" and sink is a rogue wave that would snap a mast or tiller oar, leaving the vessel susceptible to taking a killer surge on its beam. On a stormy night in utter blackness rarely experienced on land, lurking death is fearfully unseen. Needless to say, Paul's sea storm imagery is vivid!

μεθωδείᾳ like the two previous clauses, which have ἐν. It is possible for πρός to be part of a general adverbial expression (BDAG, 875; Jas 4:5 as the only NT example), but it is more likely that πρὸς τὴν μεθοδείαν τῆς πλάνης expresses the goal of false teachers: They toss Christ's people about with their false doctrine in order to accomplish their "deceitful designs" or "schemes" (where τῆς πλάνης is an adjectival genitive, as universally accepted). The KJV conveys a similar notion with "whereby they lie in wait to deceive." See 6:11–12 for μεθοδεία and πλάνη used together again (cf. LSJ, 1091 and supplement, 204).

The Ephesians were commended for putting false apostles to the test (Rev 2:2), but the story of the impostor Peregrinus is a most vivid example of the reason for Paul's warning here. As Lucian relates, Peregrinus banished himself from his homeland because of a pending charge of patricide and other offenses. Afterward, the fellow attached himself to the church in Palestine and "quickly had them looking like children" (παῖδες), becoming their "prophet, brotherhood-leader, and synagogue head." In time Peregrinus left Christianity only to end up as a ludicrous Cynic publicity-seeker who flamboyantly immolated himself before a horrified Olympic game crowd in AD 165, just a century after Ephesians was written. His life finally became the subject of mockery from the satirist Lucian.[89]

4:15 *ἀληθεύοντες δὲ ἐν ἀγάπῃ αὐξήσωμεν εἰς αὐτὸν τὰ πάντα, ὅς ἐστιν ἡ κεφαλή, Χριστός*, "but so that by speaking the truth in love we may grow in every way in him who is our head, namely, Christ." It is possible to take αὐξήσωμεν ("we may grow") as a hortatory subjunctive here, "Let us grow" or "we must grow up," as do many English versions.[90] This is especially communicated when they begin a new English sentence at v. 15; e.g., "... in deceitful schemes. Rather, speaking the truth in love, we are to grow up" (ESV). However, most commentators treat v. 15 as a positive statement (growth into maturity), which stands in contrast with v. 14 (immaturity as children susceptible to false teachers). So, for example, Ernest Best:

---

89. The story is related in Lucian's *Death of Peregrinus*, taking into account Lucian's embellishment of the truth for the sake of his biting sarcasm.

90. So NASB, ESV, NRSV (NIV has a curious future idea, "Instead ... we will in all things grow up"). For the view that αὐξήσωμεν is transitive ("we may cause the cosmos to grown up to him") and the problems with this view see Lincoln, 260–61; Schnackenburg, 188.

"This verse contrasts with (δέ) and is parallel to v. 14; its main verb is subjunctive being controlled by the ἵνα of v. 14; that verse was negative in tone; this is positive."[91]

Accordingly, we can outline the two verses as ἵνα μηκέτι ὦμεν νήπιοι ... δὲ ... [ἵνα] αὐξήσωμεν εἰς αὐτὸν, "so that we may no longer be toddlers ... but [so that] we may grow in him." The term δέ expresses the contrast between being toddlers and growing in Christ, though the intervention of the adverbial participle clause (ἀληθεύοντες ἐν ἀγάπῃ, "by speaking the truth in love") makes this a little difficult to perceive at first glance. Furthermore, vv. 14–15 are grammatically and conceptually tied together through chiasmus. The schema is:

v. 14 A That we may not be toddlers subject to
B lies of deceivers

v. 15 B′ but by speaking the truth
A′ that we may grow into maturity.[92]

The participle ἀληθεύοντες ("by speaking the truth") communicates a means for producing the church's growth (also Barth, 443). The verb ἀληθεύω itself can mean a variety of things related to the truth, such as "to live uprightly."[93] But here the contrast with deceit and lies in v. 14 makes "speaking" or "telling" the truth the best meaning.[94]

Such truthful speech is seasoned by love. In the previous verses Paul has been talking about the objectives of the special word-based ministry

---

91. Best, 406; cf. Calvin, 184–85; Lincoln, 223–24, 261; Hoehner, 566; Barth, 443–45; O'Brien, 310; cf. Hodge, 239–40, who seems ambiguous on the issue. Note that Codex Sinaiticus (א) divides 4:7–16 into three units at vv. 7–10, 11–13, 14–16. This ties vv. 14 and 15 together, as the analysis above.

92. Even though v. 15 is thus tied grammatically and thematically to v. 14, it also ties in with v. 16. Verse 15 is very short, at only twenty-nine syllables, allowing a quick transition to the much longer period of v. 16, which has seventy-one syllables. And the two periods are formally joined by an inclusio* with ἐν ἀγάπῃ in the first and last cola (vv. 15a and 16e), as well as by the repetition of the etymologically related terms αὐξήσωμεν (v. 15b) and αὔξησιν (v. 16d).

93. E.g., the LXX of Prov 21:3 has ποιεῖν δίκαια καὶ ἀληθεύειν, where the first phrase means to practice righteous actions and ἀληθεύειν means to be upright and just ("To do righteousness and justice is more acceptable to the LORD than sacrifice").

94. Cf. 4:25; Gal 4:16; BDAG, 43. Add as witness to this meaning for ἀληθεύω a Samos inscription from the fourth century BC; see Horsley, *New Docs*, 4:145.

in the church, but here truth telling and love are to characterize all in the church. This results in the unity and growth in maturity developed in v. 16 that finishes off vv. 11–16.

The truth leads Christians in growth toward maturity, which is defined here as growing up εἰς αὐτὸν τὰ πάντα, "in him in every way." The accusative τὰ πάντα is used adverbially for specification to define the extent of the growth, while "in him" refers to Christ again as the measure of Christian growth, as in v. 13d–e.[95] This, in turn, displays what Paul has in mind by calling Christ the church's "head" here. It is the part of the body that controls, directs, and guides the body in all of its activities (see 5:23; 1 Cor 11:3).

4:16 ἐξ οὗ πᾶν τὸ σῶμα συναρμολογούμενον καὶ συμβιβαζόμενον διὰ πάσης ἁφῆς τῆς ἐπιχορηγίας κατ' ἐνέργειαν ἐν μέτρῳ ἑνὸς ἑκάστου μέρους τὴν αὔξησιν τοῦ σώματος ποιεῖται εἰς οἰκοδομὴν ἑαυτοῦ ἐν ἀγάπῃ, "from whom the whole body, as it is joined together and united through every connection he supplies, according to the functioning capacity of each individual part, produces the growth of the body for building itself up in love." The last, rather long period is actually straightforward in meaning, though it may seem unwieldy in translation.[96] The general meaning is the same as more briefly stated in Col 2:19: "the Head, from whom the whole body, nourished and knit together through its joints and ligaments, grows with a growth that is from God" (see also Rom 12:4–21). In Ephesians 4:16, Christ, the head of the church, provides all of its nourishment as the individual members grow in love and the unity of faith and of the Spirit (vv. 3, 13). This unity and growth in love is illustrated below in vv. 25–32 (cf. esp. Matt 25:31–43; 26:6–13).

The focus of the passage as a whole has been on the special offices of pastoral ministry. But Paul has not ignored the general officers of the church—believers. And they are not merely passive recipients of ministry, but here we see their vital contribution to the life of the body "according

95. Cf. BDF §160, who calls this use an acc. of respect or adv.; see the many examples in Smyth, *Grammar*, §§1600–1611. The meaning of τὰ πάντα, then, is "that we may *fully* grow up" or "in every way," as I have rendered it.

96. "The general sense is clear though many details are not" (Best, 409); "Paul has not explained himself clearly due to his desire to say everything at once" (Chrysostom, *ACCS*, 168). The details involve ancient medical terminology that implies a different understanding from modern medicine. Best (409–13) has a lengthy and helpful discussion of the details, yet the clear, general sense should not be lost in these details.

to the functioning capacity of each individual part," since the whole body of believers "produces the growth of the body for building itself up in love."

Application and Devotional Implications

The analysis of an ethical action requires us to consider three elements: its goal, motive, and standard. This is at the heart of a Christian life of gratitude for a free salvation from sin and guilt by grace through faith alone. Let us look at each of these three elements.

The ultimate goal of the Christian life is to glorify God. We may have shorter steps and goals to accomplish God's glory, such as providing for one's family, loving our spouse, hard study in school, etc., but all these serve the greater goal: to glorify God. This element is not a prominent, overt part of Eph 4:7–16, but it is implied. The gifting that allows each member to contribute to the edification of the body of Christ is a gift of grace that all receive from the exalted, triumphant Messiah "for the praise of the glory of his grace" (1:6, 12, 14).

The motive for Christian living is prominent in Eph 4:7–16 and just about everywhere else in the Scriptures: love (4:15–16). It is the love of God in Christ and love of one's neighbor. "Faith, hope, and love abide, these three, but the greatest of these is love" (1 Cor 13:13). And without this love, supreme displays of self-sacrifice and flamboyant altruism are as meaningful as the clash of cymbals and castanets easily carried off by the wind and remembered no more (1 Cor 13:1–3).

Finally, the standard for true Christian living is always ultimately a proper interpretation of the Word of God. Some texts are easy to interpret, and some require wisdom and serious reflection to understand. But the main guidelines for our lives before the Lord are clear. In Ephesians 4:7–16 Paul is making clear that the foundation of maturity in true Christian faith entails knowledge of Christ (4:13), rejecting the deceitful errors of false teachers (4:14), and receiving the benefits of the gifted ministers of the word and their pastoral oversight (4:7–13), which have been provided by Christ. This obviously entails living in a community of believers in Christ and exercising the gifts of grace he has given to us for the good of our fellow Christians (4:13, 15–16). As John Calvin concludes:

> That man is mistaken who desires his own separate growth. For what would it profit a leg or an arm if it grew to an enormous size, or for the mouth to be stretched wider? It would merely be afflicted with a harmful tumour. So if we wish to be considered in Christ, let no man be anything for himself, but let us all be whatever we are for others. This is accomplished by love; and where love does not reign, there is no edification of the Church, but a mere scattering. (Calvin, 185)

Selected Bibliography

Collins, J. *Diakonia: Re-interpreting the Ancient Sources*. Oxford: Oxford University Press, 1990.

Gombis, T. "Cosmic Lordship and Divine Gift-Giving: Psalm 68 in Ephesians 4:8." *NovT* 47 (2005): 367–80.

———. *The Drama of Ephesians: Participating in the Triumph of God*. Downers Grove, IL: InterVarsity Press, 2010.

Gordon, D. " 'Equipping' Ministry in Ephesians 4?" *JETS* 37 (1994): 69–78.

Hamann, H. "The Translation of Ephesians 4:12—A Necessary Revision." *Concordia Journal* 14 (1988): 42–49.

Harris, H., III. "The Ascent and Descent of Christ in Ephesians 4:9–10." *BSac* 151 (1994): 198–214.

———. *The Descent of Christ: Ephesians 4:7–11 and Traditional Hebrew Imagery*. AGJU 32. Grand Rapids: Baker, 1998.

Iwry, S. "Notes on Psalm 68." *JBL* 71 (1952): 161–65.

Lincoln, A. "The Use of the OT in Ephesians." *JSNT* 14 (1982): 16–57.

Lunde, J., and J. Dunne. "Paul's Creative and Contextual Use of Psalm 68 in Ephesians 4:8." *WTJ* 74 (2012): 99–117.

Merklein, H. *Die kirchliche Amt nach den Epheserbrief*. Munich: Kösel, 1973.

Moritz, T. *A Profound Mystery: The Use of the Old Testament in Ephesians*. SNT 85. New York: Brill, 1996.

Page, S. "Whose Ministry? A Re-Appraisal of Ephesians 4:12." *NovT* 47 (2005): 26–46.

Pickup, M. "New Testament Interpretation of the Old Testament: The Theological Rationale of Midrashic Exegesis." *JETS* 51 (2008): 353–81.

Rojas, J. "Ephesians 4,12. A Revised Reading." *Bib* 92 (2011): 81–96.

Rubinkiewicz, R. "Ps LXVIII 19 (= Eph IV 8) Another Textual Tradition or Targum?" *NovT* 17 (1975): 219–24.

Smith, G. "Paul's Use of Psalm 68:18 in Ephesians 4:8." *JETS* 18 (1975): 181–89.

Taylor, R. "The Use of Psalm 68:18 in Ephesians 4:8 in Light of the Ancient Versions." *BSac* 148 (1991): 319–36.

Wilder, W. "The Use (or Abuse) of Power in High Places: Gifts Given and Received in Isaiah, Psalm 68, and Ephesians 4:8." *BBR* 20 (2010): 185–200.

The New Way of Life versus the Old (4:17–24)

Introduction

In Ephesians 4:17–24 Paul solemnly continues his exhortation that his audience live new lives of the inaugurated new creation in contrast with their old, corrupted mind-set and practices that still characterize the nations. The solemnity of Paul's speech is signaled by the unusual combination of λέγω ("I declare") and μαρτύρομαι ("I testify"; see comment). But the note of solemnity needs to be explained, and that arises because Paul has just taught in 4:7–16 about the risen, exalted Messiah's provision for his church to grow in holiness and because of what he will now say about their own participation in the new creation (vv. 22–24). This lends a note of urgency for believers to abandon their former lives and to join in communal, new-creation existence, characterized by genuine righteousness and devotion to the Lord.

The exhortation in 4:17–24, however, does not get very far. It is essentially just v. 17a–b, as Paul gets caught up again with elaborating on both what causes and what is wrong with the old life of sin and on the radical transformation of life God has brought about in Christ for his people. It is not until v. 25 that Paul begins his more sustained teaching on Christian ethical practices, which is then more or less kept up until the end of the epistle.

Andrew Lincoln (273; cf. 276–77) lines up the Greek in vv. 17–19 with Rom 1:21, 24, which has impressive parallels:

Romans	Ephesians
1:21 ἐματαιώθησαν ἐν τοῖς διαλογισμοῖς αὐτῶν	4:17 ἐν ματαιότητι τοῦ νοὸς αὐτῶν
1:21 καὶ ἐσκοτίσθη ἡ ἀσύνετος αὐτῶν καρδία	4:18 ἐσκοτωμένοι τῇ διανοίᾳ ὄντες
1:24 παρέδωκεν αὐτοὺς ὁ θεὸς … εἰς ἀκαθαρσίαν	4:19 ἑαυτοὺς παρέδωκαν … εἰς ἐργασίαν ἀκαθαρσίας πάσης.

We should not be surprised that a teacher has passages that resemble each other, even if they have differences of focus, as do Rom 1:21–24 and Eph 4:17–19.[1] Teachers repeat themselves not only to different audiences but also to the same audience in order to drive their points deep into their minds.[2] More importantly, these parallels to Romans show a habit of mind and interpretation that is both thoroughly Jewish in its evaluation of Gentile lifestyles (Lincoln, 277) and heavily influenced by the OT Scriptures (e.g., Jer 10:1–5; Isa 44:9–20).

As throughout this work, I offer a suggested grouping of cola* and periods that graphically shows the possible pauses, both long and short, in the oral presentation of the original and its compositional contours. Here are the suggested divisions:

A ⠀⠀[17] τοῦτο οὖν λέγω καὶ μαρτύρομαι ἐν κυρίῳ
μηκέτι ὑμᾶς περιπατεῖν
καθὼς καὶ τὰ ἔθνη περιπατεῖ
ἐν ματαιότητι τοῦ νοὸς αὐτῶν

B ⠀⠀[18] ἐσκοτωμένοι τῇ διανοίᾳ ὄντες
ἀπηλλοτριωμένοι τῆς ζωῆς τοῦ θεοῦ
διὰ τὴν ἄγνοιαν τὴν οὖσαν ἐν αὐτοῖς
διὰ τὴν πώρωσιν τῆς καρδίας αὐτῶν

C ⠀⠀[19] οἵτινες ἀπηλγηκότες
ἑαυτοὺς παρέδωκαν τῇ ἀσελγείᾳ
εἰς ἐργασίαν ἀκαθαρσίας πάσης ἐν πλεονεξίᾳ

1. See also similar wording and ideas between Eph 4:19–24 and Col 3:5–10, also given in Lincoln, 273.
2. The old axiom for the student also guides the teacher: *repetitio mater studiorum* ("repetition is the mother of learning").

D [20] ὑμεῖς δὲ οὐχ οὕτως ἐμάθετε τὸν Χριστόν
[21] εἴ γε αὐτὸν ἠκούσατε καὶ ἐν αὐτῷ ἐδιδάχθητε
καθώς ἐστιν ἀλήθεια ἐν τῷ Ἰησοῦ

E [22] ἀποθέσθαι ὑμᾶς κατὰ τὴν προτέραν ἀναστροφὴν
τὸν παλαιὸν ἄνθρωπον τὸν φθειρόμενον
κατὰ τὰς ἐπιθυμίας τῆς ἀπάτης

F [23] ἀνανεοῦσθαι δὲ τῷ πνεύματι τοῦ νοὸς ὑμῶν
[24] καὶ ἐνδύσασθαι τὸν καινὸν ἄνθρωπον
τὸν κατὰ θεὸν κτισθέντα
ἐν δικαιοσύνῃ καὶ ὁσιότητι τῆς ἀληθείας.

The division of the text follows the versification except for the exceedingly short cola* of v. 20 (thirteen syllables) and v. 23 (fifteen syllables). Each of these short verses goes well conceptually with the verses that follow, though v. 23 in particular connects with v. 22.[3]

There is very little evidence of the careful crafting of flowing prose we encountered earlier in Ephesians. For example, we do not see much concern for ending the cola* and periods with repeating elements. (However, v. 20 ends with "Christ," and its period at 21c ends with "Jesus," which is significant.) In fact, in some ways the style of Eph 4:17–24 resembles more conventional Pauline prose. Consider the following passage from Rom 1:21–24, referenced above but lined out here:

A [21] διότι γνόντες τὸν θεὸν
οὐχ ὡς θεὸν ἐδόξασαν ἢ ηὐχαρίστησαν
ἀλλ' ἐματαιώθησαν ἐν τοῖς διαλογισμοῖς αὐτῶν
καὶ ἐσκοτίσθη ἡ ἀσύνετος αὐτῶν καρδία

B [22] φάσκοντες εἶναι σοφοὶ ἐμωράνθησαν
[23] καὶ ἤλλαξαν τὴν δόξαν τοῦ ἀφθάρτου θεοῦ
ἐν ὁμοιώματι εἰκόνος φθαρτοῦ ἀνθρώπου
καὶ πετεινῶν καὶ τετραπόδων καὶ ἑρπετῶν

3. It is tempting to take vv. 22–24 as one very long period (with vv. 24a and 24b expressed as one colon*), but v. 22 does set up a contrast with vv. 23–24.

C [24] διὸ παρέδωκεν αὐτοὺς ὁ θεὸς
ἐν ταῖς ἐπιθυμίαις τῶν καρδιῶν αὐτῶν
εἰς ἀκαθαρσίαν
τοῦ ἀτιμάζεσθαι τὰ σώματα αὐτῶν ἐν αὐτοῖς.

Grammatically, these passages are dissimilar because Eph 4:17–24 has so much indirect discourse, while Rom 1:21–24 is a string of mostly indicatives for factual statements. But there are similarities nonetheless. Each has groupings of three or four cola* of modest length with relatively straightforward interrelations.[4] And there is little concern for symmetry. For example, in Rom 1:21c–d, Paul could have made a nice parallel with the verbs and nouns by moving things around and changing some of the forms. Instead of:

ἀλλ' ἐματαιώθησαν ἐν τοῖς διαλογισμοῖς αὐτῶν
καὶ ἐσκοτίσθη ἡ ἀσύνετος αὐτῶν καρδία[5]

But they became futile in their thoughts,
and darkened became their futile heart.

He could have said:

ἐματαιώθησαν δ' οἱ διαλογισμοὶ αὐτῶν
καὶ αἱ ἀσύνετοι καρδίαι αὐτῶν ἐσκοτίσθησαν

4. Cf. 1 Pet 1:17–19, which has some surface similarities with Eph 4:17–24 (e.g., the "empty conduct of your former lives inherited from your fathers" in v. 18c). But this is quite different Greek style :
A [17] καὶ εἰ πατέρα ἐπικαλεῖσθε τὸν ἀπροσωπολήμπτως κρίνοντα κατὰ τὸ ἑκάστου ἔργον
ἐν φόβῳ τὸν τῆς παροικίας ὑμῶν χρόνον ἀναστράφητε
B [18] εἰδότες ὅτι οὐ φθαρτοῖς ἀργυρίῳ ἢ χρυσίῳ ἐλυτρώθητε
ἐκ τῆς ματαίας ὑμῶν ἀναστροφῆς πατροπαραδότου
[19] ἀλλὰ τιμίῳ αἵματι ὡς ἀμνοῦ ἀμώμου καὶ ἀσπίλου Χριστοῦ.
Not least of the differences is the "sandwiching" of gen. and pronominal forms in v. 17b (τὸν τῆς παροικίας ὑμῶν χρόνον) and in v. 18b (ἐκ τῆς ματαίας ὑμῶν ἀναστροφῆς). Ephesians texts rarely do this except for some reason (cf. Eph 3:19).

5. The word order of ἡ ἀσύνετος αὐτῶν καρδία has the gen. personal pronoun sandwiched between the article (ἡ) and its noun (καρδία). This may seem stylistically nice, but it creates a pause midcolon with the *nu* and *kappa*, αὐτῶν καρδία, which could easily have been avoided with ἡ ἀσύνετος καρδία αὐτῶν. We see this sort of thing in Ephesians often also.

But futile became their thoughts,
and their senseless hearts became darkened.

Prose balance is not a major concern of Paul's. He can certainly turn very nice phrases and state interesting, powerful prose statements, but he does not "polish his periods" to perfection like a professional rhetor.[6]

Outline

X. The New Way of Life versus the Old (4:17–24)
   A. Solemn exhortation to turn away from the old life (4:17)
   B. The old life is futility, ignorance, and impurity (4:17–19)
   C. Converts to Christ have made a definitive break with the past (4:20–24)

Original Text

17 Τοῦτο οὖν λέγω καὶ μαρτύρομαι ἐν κυρίῳ, μηκέτι ὑμᾶς περιπατεῖν, καθὼς
καὶ τὰ ἔθνη περιπατεῖ ἐν ματαιότητι τοῦ νοὸς αὐτῶν, **18** ἐσκοτωμένοι τῇ διανοίᾳ
ὄντες, ἀπηλλοτριωμένοι τῆς ζωῆς τοῦ θεοῦ διὰ τὴν ἄγνοιαν τὴν οὖσαν ἐν αὐτοῖς,
διὰ τὴν πώρωσιν[a] τῆς καρδίας αὐτῶν, **19** οἵτινες ἀπηλγηκότες[b] ἑαυτοὺς παρέδωκαν τῇ ἀσελγείᾳ εἰς ἐργασίαν ἀκαθαρσίας πάσης ἐν πλεονεξίᾳ. **20** ὑμεῖς δὲ οὐχ
οὕτως ἐμάθετε τὸν Χριστόν, **21** εἴ γε αὐτὸν ἠκούσατε καὶ ἐν αὐτῷ ἐδιδάχθητε,
καθώς ἐστιν ἀλήθεια ἐν τῷ Ἰησοῦ, **22** ἀποθέσθαι ὑμᾶς κατὰ τὴν προτέραν ἀναστροφὴν τὸν παλαιὸν ἄνθρωπον τὸν φθειρόμενον κατὰ τὰς ἐπιθυμίας τῆς ἀπάτης,
23 ἀνανεοῦσθαι[c] δὲ τῷ πνεύματι τοῦ νοὸς ὑμῶν **24** καὶ ἐνδύσασθαι[d] τὸν καινὸν
ἄνθρωπον τὸν κατὰ θεὸν κτισθέντα ἐν δικαιοσύνῃ καὶ ὁσιότητι τῆς ἀληθείας.

---

6. Cf. the nice balance in the second and third cola* in Rom 6:3:
   ἢ ἀγνοεῖτε ὅτι
   ὅσοι ἐβαπτίσθημεν εἰς Χριστὸν Ἰησοῦν
   εἰς τὸν θάνατον αὐτοῦ ἐβαπτίσθημεν;

This and many other features of Paul's style are discussed in John D. Harvey, *Listening to the Text: Oral Patterning in Paul's Letters* (Grand Rapids: Baker, 1998) (cf. 128), which regrettably does not treat Ephesians.

Textual Notes

18.a. Scribal spelling variations are commonly present in the ancient MSS and are standardized in our modern editions. One such lapse is πόρρωσιν (not found as a word in LSJ) in P[46] for πώρωσιν ("hardness").

19.b. The rare verb ἀπαλγέω ("become insensible, callous"), which only occurs here in the NT (as ἀπηλγηκότες), has led some scribes to substitute forms of ἀπελπίζω, "despair" ("expect in return," in Luke 6:35). The support for this reading is found in P[99] and several Western witnesses (D, F, G, P, 1241[s]) but is not strong enough to overturn ἀπαλγέω as original.[7]

4:23–24c–d. Instead of the two infinitives ἀνανεοῦσθαι ("to be renewed") and ἐνδύσασθαι ("to don," "put on"), some MSS have second-person imperative forms: [α]νανεουσθε in P[46], D1, K, 33, 323, etc., and [ε]νδυσασθε in P[46], ℵ, B, D1, K, 104, 323, 1241, 1881, etc. This variation is not followed in the other major MSS (e.g., P[49] has infinitives here: [ανα]νεουσθαι and [ἐνδύσασ]θαι [apparently]), and so the imperatives should be regarded as a copyist error that is perpetuated in various MSS.

Translation

17 So I declare and testify[8] in the Lord[9] as follows,[10] that you must no longer walk[11] as the Gentiles do, in the futility of their minds, **18** for they are

7. Cf. Bruce M. Metzger, *A Textual Commentary on the Greek New Testament*, 2nd ed. (New York: United Bible Societies, 1994), 537.
8. The declaration (λέγω) and testimony (μαρτύρομαι) here are solemn affirmations of the truth, the content of which is conveyed by the inf. in indirect statement (see note under τοῦτο and comment).
9. The phrase ἐν κυρίῳ is not an invocation of the Lord (i.e., "I call the Lord to witness"), but Paul is speaking in union with Christ as his apostle. See comment.
10. Τοῦτο points ahead to the following indirect statement, expressed with the inf. περιπατεῖν (v. 17); cf. BDF §§290 (3), 394; 1 Cor 7:29; 15:50.
11. The pres. inf. περιπατεῖν in indirect discourse represents a pres. impv. in direct statement; here impv. περιπατεῖτε ("walk") would present the atelic event as the sort of activity that would characterize someone's life (as in 5:2 and 8). Περιπατέω appears as a pres. impv. fourteen times in the NT, with no aor. forms.

darkened in their mind-set,[12] alienated[13] from the life of God because of the ignorance that is in them, due to their hardness[14] of heart, **19** who[15] in their callousness[16] have given themselves over to licentiousness,[17] greedy to practice every kind of impurity,[18] **20** whereas, in contrast,[19] you did not learn the Messiah[20] in that way. **21** For surely[21] you have heard about him[22] and

12. The noun διάνοια refers to the "mind" as a faculty or mode of thinking rather than to thoughts themselves (BDAG, 234). Hence "mind-set" is preferred here (cf. "thinking" in NIV) rather than "understanding," found in most other versions.
13. The perf. ptc. ἀπηλλοτριωμένοι is parallel with ἐσκοτωμένοι and has the same function; see note in the comment below.
14. Πώρωσις ("hardness"), particularly of the heart as here, refers to obstinacy or insensibility in resisting the light of nature and of divine revelation; BDAG, 900; cf. O'Brien, 322.
15. Οἵτινες (ὅστις, ἥτις, ὅτι) in earlier stages of Greek meant "whoever" (Herbert Wier Smyth, *Greek Grammar*, rev. Gordon M. Messing [Cambridge, MA: Harvard University Press, 1956; original ed., 1920], §2496), but in NT times it (and other forms, such as ἥτις) was regularly used for the simple relative pronoun οἵ, perhaps to avoid confusion with the unaccented article (οἱ). Cf. S. M. Baugh, *A New Testament Greek Primer,* 3rd ed. (Phillipsburg, NJ: P&R, 2012), 111–12.
16. For causal use of the ptc. see E. Burton, *Syntax of the Moods and Tenses in New Testament Greek* (Edinburgh: T&T Clark, 1898), §439.
17. See esp. 2 Cor 12:21 and Gal 5:19 for ἀσέλγεια ("licentiousness") with other similar vices (BDAG, 141).
18. This is the (very nicely put) ESV and NRSV rendering for εἰς ἐργασίαν ἀκαθαρσίας πάσης ἐν πλεονεξίᾳ, whereas the NASB and NKJV represent the Greek idiom more closely: "for the practice of every kind of impurity with greediness."
19. The nominative personal pronoun with a finite verb (ὑμεῖς ... ἐμάθετε) normally communicates emphasis, which here conveys stress on the contrast between the audience and the Gentiles of vv. 17b–19. The rendering is an attempt to bring this out, albeit not in the smoothest English.
20. Or "Christ"; see excurses below.
21. See comment for εἴ γε communicating a firm assertion of truth.
22. The acc. of a personal referent with ἀκούω (as here: **αὐτὸν** ἠκούσατε, "about him") usually refers to the subject matter of the hearing (= acc. of respect or specification; BDF §160), while a gen. obj. normally means that one hears the person (e.g., **οὗ** οὐκ ἤκουσαν, "whom they have not heard"; Rom 10:14; cf. 2 Cor 13:3); cf. BDF §173; Smyth, *Greek Grammar*, §1361. Cf. Barth, 530.

were taught[23] in him, since[24] truth is in Jesus, **22** that you have shed[25] your old man, in regard to[26] your former manner of life, which is perishing due to[27] its deceitful desires,[28] **23** and[29] that you are undergoing renewal in the spirit of your minds,[30] **24** and that you have donned[31] the new man, who was created after the likeness of God[32] in true righteousness and devotion.[33]

---

23. The firm assertion conveyed by εἴ γε at the beginning of the colon* (see note above and comment) governs both statements: "For surely you have heard about him and were *surely* taught in him."

24. See BDAG, 494, for καθώς referencing cause; otherwise it conveys a close comparison ("just as" or "as," found in most English versions).

25. As with many versions (e.g., ESV, NIV, NRSV), ἀποθέσθαι, as well as ἀνανεοῦσθαι and ἐνδύσασθαι, is the subject matter of what the Ephesians were taught in v. 21. See comment.

26. For κατὰ τὴν προτέραν ἀναστροφὴν, where the phrase introduced by κατά specifies what particular aspect of the "old man" is discarded; BDAG, 511–13 (meaning 6).

27. Here κατά moves from being the norm for an action to its reason or basis; BDAG, 511–13 (meaning 5aδ).

28. The prep. κατὰ in the phrase κατὰ τὰς ἐπιθυμίας τῆς ἀπάτης communicates the norm that guides actions (as BDAG, 513). The gen. ἀπάτης acts as an adj., qualifying the nature of the "desires" (BDF §165).

29. The conj. δέ conveys slight contrast with "your former manner of life," but not enough to render *but* rather than *and* here. The pres. tense of the inf. ἀνανεοῦσθαι ("you are undergoing renewal") communicates a progressive aspectual idea in this place (cf. Col 3:14); comparable is 2 Cor 4:16, where a synonym is used and the progressive idea is made explicit with an adv. clause: ἀλλ' ὁ ἔσω ἡμῶν ἀνακαινοῦται **ἡμέρᾳ καὶ ἡμέρᾳ**, "yet our inner (man) is being renewed *day by day*." (Cf. the aor. inf. ἀνανεώσασθαι, used five times in 1 Maccabees.)

30. Sg. νοῦς with the pl. poss. ὑμῶν is a distributive sg. (BDF §140); cf. ἡ ὀσφῦς ὑμῶν, "your waist(s)," in 6:14.

31. The inf. ἐνδύσασθαι ("don," "put on") with καί is parallel in meaning with ἀποθέσθαι ("shed," "take off") in v. 22. The aor. tense form of ἐνδύσασθαι here is default for a verb denoting a telic event, as also found with aor. ἀποθέσθαι in v. 22; cf. aor. infs. of ἐνδύω in 1 Cor 15:53 and LXX Lev 21:10, with no pres.-tense-form infs. used in biblical literature (see also other moods at 6:11, 14).

32. The idea of God's *likeness*, going back to Genesis, is implied in the succinct phrase κατὰ θεὸν; cf. NASB, NKJV, NIV, ESV, NRSV. See also 1 Pet 4:6; 5:2 (and LXX *4 Macc* 15:3), where κατὰ θεὸν is used with comparable pregnant meanings.

33. This takes gen. ἀληθείας in the phrase ἐν δικαιοσύνῃ καὶ ὁσιότητι τῆς ἀληθείας as adj. or "gen. of quality" (BDF §165), modifying both preceding nouns as done in NIV, ESV, NRSV (cf. KJV, "in righteousness and true holiness").

Commentary

4:17 Τοῦτο οὖν λέγω καὶ μαρτύρομαι ἐν κυρίῳ, "So I declare and testify in the Lord as follows." Paul links this new section with what went before with οὖν (here "so"; elsewhere "therefore"), which ties what he now says with his opening exhortation in 4:1–3 as its continuation (BDAG, 736–37; Hoehner, 582).

Furthermore, this is a unique opening to an exhortation. True, Paul does say **Λέγω** γὰρ διὰ τῆς χάριτος τῆς δοθείσης μοι παντὶ τῷ ὄντι ἐν ὑμῖν μὴ ὑπερφρονεῖν, "For I declare, through the grace given to me, to everyone of you not to think more highly of yourselves ..." in Rom 12:3.[34] But normally when he uses this kind of language he is bearing testimony, followed by indicative predications, not exhortations.[35] The main example of this is Gal 5:2–3, which reads: Ἴδε ἐγὼ Παῦλος **λέγω** ὑμῖν ὅτι ἐὰν περιτέμνησθε, Χριστὸς ὑμᾶς οὐδὲν ὠφελήσει. **μαρτύρομαι** δὲ πάλιν παντὶ ἀνθρώπῳ περιτεμνομένῳ ὅτι ὀφειλέτης ἐστὶν ὅλον τὸν νόμον ποιῆσαι, "Behold, *I*, Paul, *declare* to you that if you take on circumcision, Christ profits you nothing! And again, I *testify* to every many man who wants to become circumcised that he is debtor to personally complete the whole law!"[36] The word λέγω ("declare") itself can have a special force of solemnity. Indeed, λέγω is how Roman

---

34. Romans 12:3 also has an inf. standing for an impv. in indirect discourse (μὴ ὑπερφρονεῖν = μὴ ὑπερφρονεῖτε), as does Eph 4:17. See comment below.

35. BDAG, 619, gives two meanings for μαρτύρομαι: "to affirm someth[ing] with solemnity" (the meaning here in Eph 4:17) and "to urge someth[ing] as a matter of great importance." Unfortunately, this second meaning is inaccurate and has led to the rendering "insist" (e.g., NIV, NRSV; Best, 414; Barth, 488–89) instead of "testify" (KVJ, ESV). BDAG give texts from Polybius, Judith, and Josephus for the second meaning that, instead, on examination means either "protest" or "call to witness"; cf. LSJ, 1082 and supplement, 203. The supposed other example of BDAG's second meaning is 1 Thess 2:12, which also carries the idea of solemn affirmation as testimony rather than "insist."

36. For defense of the nuances of this rendering see S. M. Baugh, "Galatians 5:1–6 and Personal Obligation: Reflections on Paul and the Law," in *The Law Is Not of Faith: Essays on Works and Grace in the Mosaic Covenant,* ed. B. Estelle, J. V. Fesko, and D. VanDrunen (Phillipsburg, NJ: P&R, 2009), 265–70.

emperors or governors opened their communications in the Greek world to impose their will on their subjects, "I *decree*."[37]

And still further, Paul normally introduces an exhortation with *παρακαλέω* ("I strongly urge," as in Eph 4:1 and a dozen other times in his epistles).[38] Here, rather than repeat *παρακαλέω*, Paul uniquely uses λέγω and μαρτύρομαι for the opening of his exhortation in v. 17a, giving it a startlingly solemn tone. Why? At the least, it shows how seriously he regards the necessity that converts break away from their former, sinful life. It is not optional. More directly, Paul is grounding this exhortation to live new lives of new creatures renewed in God's image, on which he teaches in vv. 22–24 (see comment there).

The phrase ἐν κυρίῳ modifies both Paul's declaration (λέγω) and testimony (μαρτύρομαι); "he does so because he and his readers are members of the church" (Best, 154; cf. 4:14–17). Hence, the statements are "in the Lord" (KJV, NIV, ESV, NRSV), rather than "with the Lord" (NKJV and NASB), or "I call the Lord as witness," which would require an accusative: μαρτύρομαι τὸν κύριον.[39] Paul is the Lord's gifted apostle to the Gentiles (vv. 7, 11) and speaks in union with him (cf. 2:21; 4:1; 5:8; 6:1, 10, 21). See Hoehner, 173–74, who

37. E.g., [ἀγαθῇ] τύχῃ· Λ. Ἀντώνιος Ἄλβος ἀνθύπατος λέγει·, "To good fortune. L[ucius] Antonius Albus the Proconsul decrees [as follows]" (*IvE* 23; AD 146/7; cf. *IvE* 24, 25, or 1521 [AD 6–14]). See edicts of Augustus in *SEG* IX.8, where λέγει is written in larger letters than the rest ("Augustus ... DECREES!") or has more spaces between the letters ("d e c r e e s"), making it emphatic; cf. Victor Ehrenberg and A. H. M. Jones, eds., *Documents Illustrating the Reigns of Augustus and Tiberius*, 2nd ed. (Oxford: Clarendon, 1976), no. 311. The opening of each of the seven edicts in Rev 2–3 has the similar LXX prophetic formula of divine speech: Τάδε λέγει ("Thus declares [the Lord]"). This formal use of λέγω appears more than 160 times in dominical statements of Jesus in the four Gospels (with and without ἀμήν or ναί). For example, λέγω occurs with this sense nine times alone in Matt 5:22–44, including Matt 5:34, 39, with infs. of indirect discourse that have imperatival sense, as found in Eph 4:17; cf. Pauline texts: Rom 9:1; 11:13; 12:3; Gal 1:9; 1 Tim 2:7.

38. Cf. synonyms for παρακαλέω found in Luke-Acts: παραβιάζομαι (Luke 24:29; Acts 16:17) and παραινέω (Acts 27:9, 22).

39. So LSJ, 1082; cf. Jdt 7:28, μαρτυρόμεθα ὑμῖν τὸν οὐρανὸν καὶ τὴν γῆν καὶ τὸν θεὸν ἡμῶν καὶ κύριον τῶν πατέρων ἡμῶν, "We call to witness against you heaven and earth and our God and the Lord of our fathers" (with ὑμῖν as dative of disadvantage). As noted, BDAG, 619, cites this text but assigns μαρτύρομαι an inaccurate meaning here.

lists "in the Lord" and a dozen related expressions (e.g., ἐν Χριστῷ, "in Christ") occurring in thirty-nine places in Ephesians (cf. Gnilka, 66–69).

μηκέτι ὑμᾶς περιπατεῖν, καθὼς καὶ τὰ ἔθνη περιπατεῖ ἐν ματαιότητι τοῦ νοὸς αὐτῶν, "that you must no longer walk as the Gentiles do, in the futility of their minds." What is most remarkable here is that believers who were formerly "Gentiles in the flesh" (2:11) are now no longer "Gentiles," as it were, whom Jews like Paul would have shunned (e.g., Matt 18:17; 5:46–47; Acts 10:28). Being in Christ makes these Gentiles a part of a new human race in the new creation, as Paul has stated (2:15) and will further explore in vv. 22–24.

> Do not lie to one another, seeing that you have put off the old self (ὁ παλαιὸς ἄνθρωπος) with its practices and have put on the new self (ὁ νέος [ἄνθρωπος]), which is being renewed in knowledge after the image of its creator. Here there is not Greek and Jew, circumcised and uncircumcised, barbarian, Scythian, slave, free; but Christ is all, and in all. (Col 3:9–11)

The believers' participation in the death and resurrection of Christ has removed them not only from the guilt of their former lives in sin but its power as well (see esp. on 2:1–10; Rom 6:1–23; cf. 1 Thess 2:12).

As one consequence of this new reality, the audience must no longer live "in the futility of their minds," since "the spirit of their minds" has and is undergoing renewal in Christ (v. 23). "Futility" or "emptiness" (ματαιότης) marks the frustration and "dead-ended-ness" of life in this creation after the fall (Rom 8:20). Paul echoes here the eloquent theme of Ecclesiastes, ματαιότης ματαιοτήτων τὰ πάντα ματαιότης, "Futility of futilities, all is futility" (Eccl 1:2 LXX), found also in Peter's words regarding Gentile believers' former "futile way of life," from which they have now been redeemed (ἡ ματαία ἀναστροφή; 1 Pet 1:18). Even the most lofty aspirations of those outside Christ fall under this judgment: "The Lord knows the machinations of the wise, that they are futile (μάταιοι)" (1 Cor 3:20; cf. Rom 1:21; Col 2:18).[40] "The light of human reason differs little from darkness; for, be-

40. The word for "machinations" or "rationalizations" (διαλογισμοί) in 1 Cor 3:20 may simply be "thoughts" or "conclusion[s] reached through use of reason" (BDAG, 232). Yet it is more likely "machinations" (e.g., Matt 15:19), since they are "futile" or "empty" in their content and actually lead away from the truth. Cf. κύριος

fore it has shown the way it is extinguished" (Calvin, 186; cf. 1 Pet 4:3–4; 2 Pet 2:17–19).

4:18 ἐσκοτωμένοι τῇ διανοίᾳ ὄντες, ἀπηλλοτριωμένοι τῆς ζωῆς τοῦ θεοῦ, "for they are darkened in their thinking, alienated from the life of God."[41] It is easy to forget that, while Paul is speaking of the Gentiles, he is probably speaking autobiographically here as well. He was once an unbelieving, brilliant student of Scripture and Jewish tradition beyond his contemporaries, well known for great learning (Gal 1:14; Acts 26:24). He had probably thought of himself as "enlightened" (cf. Heb 10:32), yet only after Christ blinded him with light on the road to Damascus (Acts 9:3) did he come to see that he had been walking in utter darkness (see John 9:38–41) with "his mind-set darkened." This is especially true of those who "claiming to be wise, have become fools," who are "futile in their understanding" (Rom 1:21–32).

Acts 17:16 reads: "Now while Paul was waiting for them at Athens, his spirit was provoked within him as he saw that the city was full of idols" (cf. Acts 17:22–23). This verse gives us a telling insight into Paul. Why should specifically Athenian idols provoke Paul's spirit? There can be no doubt that he encountered an endless host of temples, altars, shrines, statues, heroes, Herms, and all manners of wayside sacred trees, caves, grottoes, springs, etc., in every single place he visited throughout Asia Minor and Greece.[42] Yet Acts 17:16 is the only time we are told Paul's spirit was provoked. Why? My take is that, like other idealistic Hellenists who were impressed by the high ideals of classical Athenian literature, he had imagined that glittering Athens would rise above the squalor of pagan superstition and idolatry. The reality revealed that the true symbol of even the highest pagan divine knowledge and piety was embodied in an altar Ἀγνώστῳ θεῷ, "to the

---

γινώσκει τοὺς **διαλογισμοὺς** τῶν ἀνθρώπων ὅτι εἰσὶν **μάταιοι**, "the Lord knows the machinations of men, that they are futile" (Psa 94:11 [LXX 93:11]; my trans.).

41. Both the perf. ptc. ἐσκοτωμένοι ("darkened") and ἀπηλλοτριωμένοι ("alienated") act as predicates with the copulative ptc. ὄντες, denoting the existing state of darkness and of alienation; cf. Burton, *Moods*, §155 (also Col 1:21); BDF §352. The masc. gender form (ἐσκοτωμένοι) agrees with the implied human reference of the neuter τὰ ἔθνη in v. 17 as *construction ad sensum* (BDF §134 [2]). The ptc. ὄντες is adv., relating to περιπατεῖ in v. 17c as the reason why they "walk" in futility; cf. Burton, *Moods*, §439 (causal).

42. See comment on 2:12 above for a note on the host of deities worshiped at Ephesus.

Unknown God" (Acts 17:22–23). Despite their claims of wisdom, Gentile philosophers devoted to seeking wisdom (Acts 17:18, 21) were ἄθεοι ("without God") in the world (Eph 2:12) and therefore "alienated" from his life.

There are several possible meanings of διάνοια (BDAG, 234), but the most likely one here refers to the human reasoning and thinking faculty rather than to human thoughts themselves. This is "their 'mind-set,' the total person viewed under the aspect of thinking" (Best, 417). If the capacity to think is "darkened" by being directed by "the will of the flesh" and its "rationalizations" (2:3), all the resulting thoughts are bent and distorted as a result (see comment on 2:3; cf. Rom 11:10). "Gentile thinking suffers from the consequences of having lost touch with reality and is left fumbling with inane trivialities and worthless side issues" (O'Brien, 320).

διὰ τὴν ἄγνοιαν τὴν οὖσαν ἐν αὐτοῖς, διὰ τὴν πώρωσιν τῆς καρδίας αὐτῶν, "because of the ignorance that is in them, due to their hardness of heart."[43] Obviously, Paul knows that Gentiles are not ignorant in general terms by lacking native intelligence or even education in all cases. As mentioned above, Gentiles were born ἄθεοι ("without God"; 2:12). But in this case the ignorance is one that is *culpable* because it represents a willful ignorance (cf. Acts 3:17; Heb 5:2; 9:7; 1 Pet 1:14) of those who have rejected the knowledge and acknowledgment of the true God out of "the hardness of their hearts" (cf. Mark 3:5; Rom 11:7, 25; 2 Cor 3:14). Romans 1:19–32 is pertinent here to show the dynamic of deliberate rejection of the knowledge of God, which God has actively revealed to them. Yet, by calling Paul to be apostle to the Gentiles, God shows that although he is willing to overlook the season of Gentile ignorance, he now commands all people everywhere in his creation to repent (Acts 17:30).

At its heart, then, the ignorance and hard-heartedness of Gentiles manifests itself in their idolatry (again, being ἄθεοι, "without God"). It's hard to shake the possibility that there is a link here to the Gentile "futility" (ματαιότης) of the previous verse and this idolatry. In Hebrew, idols are

43. The prepositional phrases starting each colon* are parallel, as we have seen often in Ephesians (esp. 4:12–14), as Best, 420; yet some see the second clause as the reason for the first: Pagan Gentiles are ignorant due to their hardness of heart (O'Brien, 322; Lincoln, 278). This makes good sense and is possible, but one could also say that willful ignorance leads to hardness of heart due to a mind-set that rejects the knowledge of God because it is driven by evil desires (v. 19). For Paul, all of this is summarized by "the flesh" (e.g., Rom 8:5–13; Gal 5:16–24).

sometimes referred to as הֶבֶל ("nothings"), which appears sometimes as τὰ μάταια ("futilities") in the LXX (e.g., 1 Kgs 16:2, 13, 26; Isa 2:20). For example, we read this of the fall of the northern kingdom through the influence of Gentile idolatry:

> But they would not listen, but were stubborn as their fathers had been, who did not believe in the LORD their God. They despised his statutes and his covenant that he made with their fathers and the warnings that he gave them. They went after false idols (אַחֲרֵי הַהֶבֶל, ὀπίσω τῶν ματαίων) and became false (וַיֶּהְבָּלוּ, ἐματαιώθησαν), and they followed the nations that were around them, concerning whom the LORD had commanded them that they should not do like them. (2 Kgs 17:14–15; cf. Jer 2:5)

Could it be that Paul has this in mind? Certainly idolatry, which surrounded the Ephesians and dominated their former lives, is nearby. They had become hardened children of wrath (2:3) before their conversion.

4:19 οἵτινες ἀπηλγηκότες ἑαυτοὺς παρέδωκαν τῇ ἀσελγείᾳ εἰς ἐργασίαν ἀκαθαρσίας πάσης ἐν πλεονεξίᾳ, "who in their callousness have given themselves over to licentiousness, greedy to practice every kind of impurity."

The word ἀπαλγέω ("callousness") only appears here in the NT.[44] BDAG, 96, suggests two meanings: either "to be so inured that one is not bothered by the implications of what one is doing" or "to be filled with a heavy sense of loss or deprivation, *be despondent.*" The former meaning fits the context better, though LSJ, 176, gives only the latter meaning. BDAG cites Polybius (*Hist.* 16.12.7) for the first meaning (ἀπηλγηκυία ψυχή, "blunted intelligence" [LCL], but in context it indicates hardness of heart] and Polybius (*Hist.* 1.35.5; αἱ ἀπηλγηκυίαι ψυχαὶ τῶν δυνάμεων, "the *deadened* spirit of its soldiers" [LCL]) for the second. The meanings are similar, and in Eph 4:18 the word refers to people with "seared" consciences (1 Tim 4:2)

44. "Callous" as ESV and NASB; cf. "being past feeling," KJV, or "lost all sensitivity," NIV and NRSV.

who have no human sympathy or regard for anything but their own greed and passions.[45]

These are home invaders, cartel minions, human traffickers, terror bombers, and the like, who would as soon shoot someone as look at him.[46] The worst part of it all for them is that they have been handed over (also παραδίδωμι) by God to evil practices (Rom 1:24–28), to which "they have handed themselves over." It is at once self-judgment and divine judgment (Schnackenburg, 198). Hence, the urgency of Christians to separate themselves from this mind-set and wanton lifestyle.

The vice list in v. 19b–c is a very quick description, meant to summarize rather than to describe at length (also 5:3): "licentiousness, greedy to practice every kind of impurity." There are three main traits of depravity mentioned in the portrait here. "Licentiousness" (ἀσελγεία) refers to abandonment of oneself to unrestrained practices, especially in sexual excesses (e.g., Mark 7:22; Rom 13:13; 2 Cor 12:21) alongside other "deeds of the flesh" (Gal 5:19) and idolatry (1 Pet 4:3). "Impurity" (or "filth"; ἀκαθαρσία) has a religious connection, since all sin is oriented as an offense to God (e.g., Matt 23:27 [the content of graves]; Rom 1:24; Col 3:5; 1 Thess 4:7; and other verses cited for ἀσελγεία).[47] Here the impurity erupts from the callous heart and leads to actions that embody "every sort of filth" (εἰς ἐργασίαν ἀκαθαρσίας πάσης; BDAG, 34). The word πᾶς here does not refer to every single act of uncleanness possible but to representative acts that cover a broad spectrum, of "every kind" (BDAG, 784, meaning 5). All of this is

45. The adv. ptc. ἀπηλγηκότες here explains the cause of their turning themselves over to sensuality and could also be rendered "because of their callousness of heart." The perf. tense form communicates their state of mind after they have morally desensitized themselves.

46. The Bible has many accounts of such people, for example: 1 Sam 2:12–25; Mark 6:21–28.

47. John Chrysostom writes: " 'Impurity' is every sort of adultery, sexual immorality, lust after boys, envy, every kind of wantonness and licentiousness" (Ἀκαθαρσία πᾶσα μοιχεία, πορνεία, παιδεραστία, φθόνος, πᾶσα ἀκολασία καὶ ἀσέλγεια; *Hom. Eph.* 13; my trans.).

fueled by a self-centered "greed" or "covetousness" and an insatiable lust for more (πλεονεξία, cf. BDAG, 824), like "brute beasts" (1 Pet 2:12–19).[48]

This is a portrait of total depravity, which refers to the infection of sin that has permeated the whole person of those who are "by nature children of wrath" (2:3). But total depravity is not *absolute* depravity. Indeed, many if not most people outside Christ have a veneer of decency and decorum held in place by God's common grace and restraining influence. But Paul's words express the viewpoint of the last judgment that pierces all such veneers, no matter how thick and attractive on the outside. "Woe to you, scribes and Pharisees, hypocrites! For you are like whitewashed tombs, which outwardly appear beautiful, but within are full of dead people's bones and all uncleanness" (Matt 23:27).

4:20–21 *ὑμεῖς δὲ οὐχ οὕτως ἐμάθετε τὸν Χριστόν, εἴ γε αὐτὸν ἠκούσατε καὶ ἐν αὐτῷ ἐδιδάχθητε, καθώς ἐστιν ἀλήθεια ἐν τῷ Ἰησοῦ*, "whereas, in contrast, you did not learn the Messiah in that way. For surely you have heard about him and were taught in him, since truth is in Jesus." Paul now contrasts in earnest the audience's current lives as Christians to those they have abandoned. Verses 20–24 pave the way for specifics of the Christian lifestyle, which he will elaborate on from 4:25 to the end of the epistle. In some ways vv. 20–24 are a reprise of things he has already taught to this point, which accounts for the compressed nature of the language here (see below).

The structure of the statements in vv. 20–24 is particularly dependent on the interpretation of the meaning of each colon* and clause. This interpretation varies widely in the versions and commentators and is not always transparent without a few added ideas. My understanding, to be defended below, can be outlined as follows:

(The audience is separated from their past mindset and lives of sin, because:)

v. 20 They learned the Messiah
(which involves two things:)

48. "To the pure, all things are pure, but to the defiled and unbelieving, nothing is pure; but both their minds and their consciences are defiled. They profess to know God, but they deny him by their works. They are detestable, disobedient, unfit for any good work" (Titus 1:15–16).

v. 21 Hearing about him in the gospel
and
Being taught in him
Since truth is in him (Jesus) (over against the futility of their past)
(the teaching in him entails:)
v. 22 Shedding their old-creation man
v. 23 Renewal of their spirits and minds
v. 24 Putting on the new-creation man

The phrase "you did not learn the Messiah" is unusual in that the verb "learn" (μανθάνω) does not take a personal object elsewhere, as most commentators discuss (e.g., Hodge, 256; Barth, 529; Hoehner, 593–94).[49] It would be unusual, for example, to say, "You learned *the Emperor*." However, there is a near equivalent in Gal 4:9, where the aorist of γινώσκω ("know") carries an inceptive idea and means "come to know," "discover," "learn." Hence, we read νῦν δὲ γνόντες θεόν, "Now that you have *come to know* God"—a reading that is confirmed by what immediately follows: μᾶλλον δὲ γνωσθέντες ὑπὸ θεοῦ, "Or rather, now that *you have come to be known* by God." This is a distinctly LXX use of γινώσκω, which is personal and covenantal (e.g., Hos 6:3; Isa 11:9; Jer 38:34). This is what Paul means: To learn the Messiah means to know him (as 2 Cor 5:16; Phil 3:10; cf. John 17:3).[50] "'To learn Christ' does not mean merely, to learn his doctrines, but to attain the knowledge of Christ as the Son of God, God in our nature, the Holy one of God, the Saviour from sin, whom to know is holiness and life" (Hodge, 256).

49. To take the acc. as specification or respect (learn *about* the Messiah) is warranted here. Gnilka (226–27) and others take the learning and knowledge of Christ here as "mystical," but Barth responds that this "is too far-fetched to be convincing. Why should the mists of mysticism substitute for the sober thoughts and solid learning that befit a school?" (Barth, 530–31).

50. Chrysostom, again, is interesting on this point: Ἄρα καὶ τοῦτο μαθεῖν ἐστι τὸν Χριστὸν, τὸ ὀρθῶς βιοῦν. Ὁ γὰρ πονηρῶς βιῶν, ἀγνοεῖ τὸν Θεὸν, καὶ ἀγνοεῖται παρ' αὐτοῦ, "So then this is what it means to learn the Messiah, to live uprightly. For, the one who lives wickedly, does not know God, and is not known by him" (he cites Titus 1:16; *Hom. Eph.* 13; my trans.).

As noted above on 3:2, where εἴ γε ἠκούσατε also appears, Paul is not expressing doubts about whether his Ephesian audience has heard of Christ—he affirms their faith and love (1:13, 15) and that they were taught Christ (v. 20). The phrase εἴ γε does not mean "if indeed" (as NASB and NKJV), but "you most surely have heard" or "if, as I take for granted" (Hodge, 257); as Chrysostom notes: "This, 'Surely you have heard about him,' is not from one who is in doubt, but from one who is most certain."[51] The same note of confidence should also govern the next phrase in v. 21a also: εἴ γε … ἐν αὐτῷ ἐδιδάχθητε, "For surely you … were taught in him."

Paul expands on what he means by learning the Messiah in v. 21a: "For surely you have heard about him and were taught in him." There are two stages here, with a logical progression. The first stage is to hear about Christ in the proclamation of the gospel of peace (see 2:17), the gospel of their salvation (1:13). But the second stage of being taught "in him" implies that the hearers have responded to the gospel in faith and have been baptized "into him" (e.g., 1:13, 15; Matt 24:19–20; Rom 10:14–17; Col 1:5–7, 23).[52] For instruction "in him" means that the teaching is in communion with Christ through the ministry of evangelists and teachers whom Christ has gifted for this (see on 4:11–16). Marcus Barth (529–33) sees an extended school imagery in vv. 20–21 and states nicely, "When Jesus Christ is the headmaster, the teaching matter, the method, the curriculum, and the academy, then the gift of new life takes the place of a diploma" (Barth, 530; cf. 529–33).

The concluding colon* of this period ("since truth is in Jesus") has led to extended discussion in the literature, centering on three questions. First, how is καθώς to be understood? It may introduce a close comparison ("just as," NASB, or "as," KJV, ESV, NRSV), but the better option here is to see it as causal ("since"; see translation note above). Secondly, some read anarthrous

---

51. Τὸ, Εἴ γε αὐτὸν ἠκούσατε, οὐκ ἀμφιβάλλοντός ἐστιν, ἀλλὰ καὶ σφόδρα διαβεβαιουμένου (*Hom. Eph.* 13; my trans.); he continues by citing 2 Thess 1:6 with εἴπερ for the same meaning. Cf. BDAG, 278.

52. Matthew 24:19–20 is especially interesting, for the lead noun in the impv. μαθητεύω is etymologically related to μανθάνω ("learn") and μαθητής ("student," "disciple"). The aor. impv. μαθητεύσατε in Matt 24:19 is inceptive and means something like "enroll [all the nations] as my disciples." As the Twelve were the Messiah's distinct μαθηταί ("students," "disciples"), so now the circle of disciples extends even to the Gentiles. Ephesus was home to several important schools and teachers, particularly in rhetoric, philosophy, and medicine.

ἀλήθεια ("truth") as definite "*the* truth" (e.g., KJV, ESV, NIV; O'Brien, 325–26). To be sure, Greek article usage is a very complex issue, and there are many situations where anarthrous nouns are definite.[53] But there does not seem to be a compelling reason to see a definite meaning here (cf. 1:13; 4:24–25; 5:9; 6:14).[54] Third, Paul does not usually simply call the Lord "Jesus," as here, instead of "Christ Jesus" or "Jesus Christ" (e.g., 1:1–3, 5, 17; 2:6–7, 10). He does refer to the Ephesians' faith "in the Lord Jesus" (ἐν τῷ κυρίῳ Ἰησοῦ) in 1:15, but simple "Jesus" is unusual and should be explained.[55]

Fortunately, the difficulties outlined above can be cleared up by seeing the period of vv. 20–21 as having cohesive unity.[56] To this point we have seen periods that have linguistic markers for their thematic unity, such as: ἧς ἐχαρίτωσεν ... τῆς χάριτος αὐτοῦ (1:6b–7c), ἐν ᾧ ... ἐν τῷ Χριστῷ (1:11–12), τὰ ἔθνη ἐν σαρκί ... ἐν σαρκὶ χειροποιήτου (2:11), and ἐν Χριστῷ Ἰησοῦ ... ἐν τῷ αἵματι τοῦ Χριστοῦ (2:13). There is nothing mechanical about this; it is simply a compositional option that Paul sometimes employs. Such may be the case again in vv. 20–21, which I have suggested be organized as:

20 ὑμεῖς δὲ οὐχ οὕτως ἐμάθετε τὸν **Χριστόν**
21 εἴ γε αὐτὸν ἠκούσατε καὶ ἐν αὐτῷ ἐδιδάχθητε
καθώς ἐστιν ἀλήθεια ἐν τῷ **Ἰησοῦ**

whereas, in contrast, you did not learn the Messiah in that way.
For surely you have heard about him and were taught in him,
since truth is in Jesus.

---

53. For instance, as the obj. of a prep.: "belt up your waist with *the* truth (ἐν ἀληθείᾳ)" in 6:14; cf. Rom 2:2; 15:8. One even finds anarthrous nouns in Greek that must be rendered with a poss. pronoun; e.g., καὶ ἐπέστρεψαν πρός με **νῶτον** καὶ οὐ **πρόσωπον**, "they have turned *their* back to me and not *their* face" (Jer 32:33 [LXX 39:33]).

54. For example, Peter O'Brien notes, "It is not unusual for abstract nouns to appear without the article (e.g., sin, death, and grace)" (O'Brien, 325–26). This is true, but one has to look at each case. And the fact is, abstract nouns in Greek often have an article where they are rendered indefinitely in English; BDF §258 ["in some instances the problem is rather to account for the presence of the article than its absence"]; cf. Smyth, *Greek Grammar*, §§1131–35. As just one example see **τῆς** ἀληθείας ("of truth") below in v. 24.

55. There is full discussion of these issues in O'Brien, 324–26; Lincoln, 279–83.

56. Of course, one has to see v. 20 as part of the same period as v. 21, but the unity of thought here is obvious. Modern versification, again, must not dictate our understanding of the contours of the ancient Greek text. It is often helpful but frequently not.

"Jesus" at the end of the period corresponds with his title, "the Messiah," at the end of the first colon* and possibly was arranged to give his whole name, Christ Jesus.

More importantly, the line "since truth is in Jesus" in v. 21b must be connected to vv. 20–21a because it explains its meaning. Paul had focused on the deceit and ignorance of the Ephesians' former lives (4:18, 22). It was life shot through with ματαιότης, "futility" (v. 17). But believers like Paul's audience have "learned Christ" and have been instructed in the truth through the servants the exalted Christ has provided for their maturity and growth in him (4:14–16). "You were taught *in him,* since truth is *in Jesus.*" Apart from communion with Christ, there is only the ματαιότης of unbelief and paganism. In Jesus there is genuine ἀλήθεια, "truth" (e.g., John 14:6; 1 Cor 1:24). Οὐ ματαιότης τὰ παρ' ἡμῖν, ἀλλ' ἀλήθεια, "Our lives are not futility, but truth" (John Chrysostom, *Hom. Eph.* 13).

4:22 ἀποθέσθαι ὑμᾶς κατὰ τὴν προτέραν ἀναστροφὴν τὸν παλαιὸν ἄνθρωπον τὸν φθειρόμενον κατὰ τὰς ἐπιθυμίας τῆς ἀπάτης, "that you have shed your old man, in regard to your former manner of life, which is perishing due to its deceitful desires." The infinitive ἀποθέσθαι ("shed") and the two other infinitives in vv. 23–24 are grammatically all dependent on ἐδιδάχθητε ("you were taught") in v. 21, as object clauses in indirect discourse: ἐδιδάχθητε … ἀποθέσθαι ὑμᾶς … ἀνανεοῦσθαι δὲ … καὶ ἐνδύσασθαι, "you were taught … that you have shed … and that you are undergoing renewal … and that you have donned."[57] Therefore, vv. 22–24 should be viewed together as a unity and are outlined in the introduction to v. 20 above as:

The teaching in Christ entails:

v. 22	Shedding their old-creation man
v. 23	Renewal of their spirits and minds
v. 24	Putting on the new-creation man

I have translated these verses and their infinitives as indicative statements of fact about what the Ephesians were taught subsequent to their conversion and baptism (see on v. 21 above). This is in contrast with most modern English versions and many interpreters, who read these statements in

57. As also in 3:5–6 with: νῦν ἀπεκαλύφθη … εἶναι τὰ ἔθνη, "now revealed … that the Gentiles would be"; cf. 3:13; 4:1, 17.

vv. 22–24 as imperative duties that the Ephesians were taught to fulfill; for instance, "You were taught to put away ... and to be renewed ... and to clothe yourselves" (NRSV) and, "Since this whole section consists of moral exhortation, versus 22–24 must have imperatival force" (Muddiman, 217).[58] Grammatically, this is possible (e.g., v. 17), since the infinitive in indirect discourse can represent either an indicative or an imperative. But only the context decides what is meant by the author or speaker, and there are many reasons for reading vv. 22–24 as statements of fact rather than as imperatives The two most prominent of these are simple contextual observations and, just as importantly, theological truths that require us to read these as statements about Christians rather than as things they should do.

In context, Paul must be speaking about points of fact in vv. 22–24, because he uses those facts as the basis for his exhortation in v. 25: "For this reason (διό), each of you must put aside (ἀποθέμενοι) falsehood and speak truth." It makes no sense to say that they were told "to put aside (ἀποθέσθαι) their old man" then to conclude from this that they must "put aside" falsehood. Exhortations flow as conclusions from facts, not from other exhortations (e.g., 4:1; 5:7; Rom 6:12; 15:7; 1 Cor 14:13; Gal 5:1; Col 2:16; 1 Thess 5:11). Furthermore, Paul says the Ephesians learned Christ, heard of him, and were taught in him as truth over against the futility of their former lives. In the background of this distinction between truth and futility is the new creation, and Paul expresses their own participation in that new creation as "the new man who was created after the likeness of God in true righteousness and devotion" (v. 24). These are truths about Christians in other parts of Ephesians (e.g., 2:10, 15; 5:8) and elsewhere, not things they can perform.[59]

---

58. It should be noted that this is not an accurate or compelling exegetical argument. Verses 17c–21 are statements of fact and *cannot* be interpreted with imperatival force simply because there are impvs. in the vicinity. Optionally taking the infs. as connected with truth in Jesus (Gnilka, 229) is not a likely possibility (cf. Lincoln, 283–84). See "Additional Exegetical Comments" for further discussion of the infs.

59. Hoehner, 598–602, has a long defense of the view taken here, which can be consulted with profit. Although John Murray takes the infs. as result clauses (possible as resulting from all of vv. 20–21), he otherwise has a nearly identical view as adopted here in *Principles of Conduct* (Grand Rapids: Eerdmans, 1957), 214–19; cf. Witherington, 298–99, who cites O'Brien (326–27) in support of the indic. view, but O'Brien actually agrees with Schnackenburg (199–200), Lincoln (285–86), and others that the infs. "have an implied imperatival force ... in terms of their

"The old way of life was cast off like an old garment. The old person is not who these Christians are anymore. The old lifestyle was self-destructive, full of wicked desires and deceits" (Witherington, 298). "Every trait of the Old Man's behavior is putrid, crumbling, or inflated like rotting waste or cadavers, stinking, ripe for being disposed of and forgotten" (Barth, 507). In Christ, believers have "shed," stripped off, and discarded their old man.[60] He is dead—and good riddance. "According to 4:22–24 there is no way whatsoever to improve, repair, reform, or in any other sense to preserve and continue sinful man" (Barth, 539). "Our first man is buried: buried not in earth, but in water; not death-destroyed, but buried by death's destroyer" (Chrysostom, *Hom. Col.* 7).[61]

This is the foundation of all Christian ethics: The old has passed away and the new has dawned in bright array (Eph 5:8, 14; 2 Cor 5:17). Believers have died with Christ on the cross, along with the slavery to sin that marked the old life in Adam (Rom 6:8; Gal 2:20; 5:24; 6:14; Col 2:20; 3:3; cf. Eph 2:5). This is stated as a truth of Christians in Col 3:9–10 as well as threading through Rom 6:1–23. Paul assumes it to be a key part of all Christian catechism (v. 21), and the believer's death with Christ states the negative side of regeneration, while vv. 23–24 are the positive. Paul specifies that believers no longer live in relation to τὴν προτέραν ἀναστροφὴν ("your former manner of life"). This phrase in v. 22a zeroes in on that precise part of their "old man" that believers are rid of in Christ, even if they continue to fight against the residue of that old existence in this life until the

---

continuing to live out the implications of their mighty break with the past." This sounds plausible in isolation, but the actual implications of the believer's break with the past are drawn out by Paul in 4:25–6:18, not in 4:22–24.

60. For ἀποτίθημι, which is used for "taking off" clothing but also ridding oneself of something worn out or unwanted (BDAG, 123–24). Barth, 540–43 ("Stripping, Clothing and Renewal"), discusses the clothing symbolism for "shed" and "don" in v. 24 in some detail: "The OT and NT show traces of almost all known features of garment and clothing symbolism" (Barth, 541); cf. Eph 6:11–17 for donning armor and weapons. The aor. inf. ἀποθέσθαι is unusual in indirect discourse when it represents an aor. indic. statement; so Burton, *Moods*, §114; see discussion including helpful input from Daniel Wallace in Hoehner, 600–601 (esp. n. 5); cf. Daniel B. Wallace, *Greek Grammar beyond the Basics* (Grand Rapids: Zondervan, 1997), 605. Examples from classical literature in Smyth, *Greek Grammar*, §1867d, can be added to these two aor. infs. in v. 22 and 24 (ἀποθέσθαι and ἐνδύσασθαι).

61. Translation is *NPNF*[1], 13:290.

resurrection.[62] In one phrase Paul looks back at that old, Gentile manner of life that they are now to shun (vv. 17–19) and points ahead to its "poetic parallel" (Barth, 506), namely their new creation existence created κατὰ θεόν, "after the likeness of God" (v. 24).

All humans have been created in the likeness of God (Gen 1:26–7; 9:6), but that likeness was irreparably infected with decay through sin as Adam sired descendants in his fallen corruption (Gen 5:3; Rom 5:12–21; 1 Cor 15:21–22). Hence, the "old man" is "perishing due to its deceitful desires."[63] "Perishing" (φθείρω as a pass.) in Eph 4:22 is a pregnant term for falling into ruin and the corruption of death (e.g., 4:29; Gen 6:11–12; Psa 14:3; 1 Cor 15:35–55; 2 Cor 4:16 [διαφθείρω]; Gal 6:8; cf. LSJ, 1928; BDAG, 1054).

One concluding point needs to be made. To have v. 22 be an exhortation, "you must put off the old person" (Talbert, 123), is not compelling because it is impossible.[64] Even suicide is out of the question because one must then, correspondingly, "don the new man" (v. 24), i.e., in self-resurrection, which, apart from the sinless, incarnate Son (John 10:18), the dead cannot do.[65] One can certainly "shed" lies (see 4:25), the old practices and mind-set of darkness and sin—which elsewhere believers are told to do (Rom 13:12; Col 3:8; cf. Heb 12:1; Jas 1:21; 1 Pet 2:1). But the death of the old man and his world, condemned to futility (ματαιότης; Rom 8:20; Eph 4:17d) and to "slavery to decay" (φθορά; Rom 8:21), requires a new creation, and for humans, a resurrection.[66] "For this corrupted body (τὸ φθαρτὸν τοῦτο) must

62. What follows deserves far more discussion and qualification than can be given here. In dogmatic terms, the material throughout 4:20–22 and much of the surrounding context relates to the interaction of regeneration and sanctification; cf. Herman Bavinck, *Reformed Dogmatics: Holy Spirit, Church, and New Creation*, trans. John Vriend (Grand Rapids: Baker Academic, 2008), 4:46–95, 230–70.

63. "The heart is deceitful above all things, and desperately sick; who can understand it?" (Jer 17:9); cf. Rom 3:10–18; 2 Cor 11:3; Heb 3:13.

64. The quote in Diogenes Laertius, attributed to the philosopher Pyrrho, is often brought up here (e.g., Lincoln, 285; Talbert, 123–24): χαλεπόν ἐστιν τὸν ἄνθρωπον ἐκδῦναι, "It is difficult to shed our human nature." Most difficult indeed.

65. Note also Barth's insightful comment: "This understanding implies that Eph 4:22–24 is an equivalent to, though a new way of phrasing, the Pauline doctrine of sin and justification" (Barth, 539). As justification is not the believer's work (see 2:8–9)—"God is the one who justifies" (Rom 8:33; cf. Luke 10:29)—neither is putting off the old man.

66. See below on v. 24 for preserving "man" in translation for ἄνθρωπος in v. 22; cf. 2:15.

don incorruptibility, and this mortal body must don immortality, then shall the recorded word come to pass, 'Death has been swallowed up in victory!' " (1 Cor 15:53–54). "Our old man has been co-crucified [with Christ] (ὁ παλαιὸς ἡμῶν ἄνθρωπος συνεσταυρώθη), in order to destroy the body of sin" (Rom 6:6). Paul will put this another way soon: "You were formerly darkness, but now you *are* light in the Lord" (5:8, emphasis added).

4:23 ἀνανεοῦσθαι δὲ τῷ πνεύματι τοῦ νοὸς ὑμῶν, "and that you are undergoing renewal in the spirit of your minds." This short verse belongs with v. 24 and is a necessary transition to it as well as connecting with what has gone before. The surrounding statements in both v. 22 ("shed the old man") and v. 24 ("don the new man") focus on their characteristic elements: deceitful desires over against genuine righteousness and devotion. Renewal of the "spirit of your minds" gets to the core of the transformational effect of regeneration and justification in the life of the genuine believer.[67] Sanctification begins immediately in the inner καινὸς ἄνθρωπος ("new man" or "human person") after the "old man" (v. 22) is renewed in regeneration (John 3:3–6; cf. Eph 1:13–14), and it then undergoes a process of constant renewal: "But even if our outer man is rotting away (διαφθείρεται), our inner man is undergoing renewal (ἀνακαινοῦται) day after day" (2 Cor 4:16).[68]

The inner transformation is accomplished by the Holy Spirit, but that is not what is said here in Eph 4:23 with τῷ πνεύματι, "in the spirit," not

---

67. Sometimes the two verbs Paul uses for "renew" (ἀνανεόω, found only here in Eph 4:23 in the NT, and ἀνακαινέω, used only in 2 Cor 4:16 and Col 3:10) are differentiated (cf. ἀνακαινώσις in Rom 12:2). For example, Schnackenburg, 200, thinks that the use of ἀνανεόω "includes human effort." But the two terms are simple synonyms; cf. R. A. Harrisville, "The Concept of Newness in the New Testament," *JBL* 74 (1955): 69–79; expanded in Harrisville, *The Concept of Newness in the New Testament* (Minneapolis: Augsburg, 1960); O'Brien, 329; Hoehner, 607–8; BDAG, 64, 68.

68. Paul shifts tenses from the two aor. infs. in vv. 22 and 24 (ἀποθέσθαι and ἐνδύσασθαι) to the pres.-tense ἀνανεοῦσθαι, expressing "undergo renewal" as a pass. The inf. in indirect discourse represents a pres. indic. (ἀνανεοῦσθε, "you are undergoing renewal"), which expresses the idea of the event as in progress. In contrast, Paul could conceivably have used the aor. form here (ἀνανεωθῆναι) to convey a simple idea of renewal that has transpired, like the aors. in vv. 22 and 24: "you have been renewed." But he presents the renewal as a process with the pres.-tense form; cf. analogous ποιεῖν in John 3:2 ("to be performing" signs) or ἰᾶσθαι in Luke 5:17 ("to perform acts of healing"); cf. Burton, *Moods*, §9; Wallace, *Greek Grammar*, 518–19.

"by the Spirit."[69] This would have Paul say, "your minds are undergoing renewal by the Spirit," which would require "your mind(s)" to be expressed in the accusative rather than genitive τοῦ νοὸς ὑμῶν ("of your minds"). This differentiates between the human mind as the seat of intellectual life and the believer's spirit as the link with the Holy Spirit that guides the inner life (Rom 8:16; 1 Cor 2:10–16; cf. 1 Cor 14:14) and connects with the new creation (below).[70] But the reason for this focus on both the spirit and the mind is to contrast the believer's renewed mind and spirit with the former corrupted mind-set they are to abandon (vv. 17–19), particularly that mind (νοῦς) mired in futility in v. 17d (cf. Rom 12:2). Paul will expand on the implications of these things with concrete examples of evil thoughts, words, and deeds to reject and others to adopt (4:25–6:9).

4:24 καὶ ἐνδύσασθαι τὸν καινὸν ἄνθρωπον τὸν κατὰ θεὸν κτισθέντα ἐν δικαιοσύνῃ καὶ ὁσιότητι τῆς ἀληθείας, "and that you have donned the new man, who was created after the likeness of God in true righteousness and devotion." Paul concludes here his summary sketch of what the Ephesians—and presumably all in the apostolic-era church—had been taught regarding their regeneration and the foundation of their sanctification. This verse obviously corresponds to what was said in v. 22. As they had shed the old, they had donned the new "man" in Christ.

In other places, ἐνδύω ("don," "put on") is used as an exhortation, "But put on (ἐνδύσασθε) the Lord Jesus Christ, and make no provision for the flesh, to gratify its desires" (Rom 13:14), and as an accomplished act, "For as many of you as were baptized into Christ have put on (ἐνεδύσασθε) Christ" (Gal 3:27; cf. Eph 6:11, 14; Rom 13:12). Here the latter idea is communicated,

---

69. The dative for πνεύματι is locative, as Wallace, *Greek Grammar*, 153–55 ("sphere"); cf. BDF §199.

70. The "spirit of the mind" does not appear elsewhere in biblical literature. Another possible option is to regard the two terms "spirit" and "mind" as synonymous and pleonastic for the inner person (see Lincoln, 287; Barth, 508). Hodge, 263–64, has a helpful discussion and concludes, "The spirit of the mind therefore is its interior life; that of which the νοῦς, καρδία, ψυχή are the modes of manifestation. That, therefore, which needs to be renewed, is not merely outward habits or modes of life; not merely transient tempers or dispositions, but the interior principle of life which lies back of all that is outward, phenomenal, or transient" (Hodge, 264).

but the identification of both the "old man" (v. 22) and "the new man" (v. 24) needs exploration.[71]

Some persist in seeing a gnostic myth of a redeemer in the background, but, besides being anachronistic, this is hardly likely. Paul has little resemblance to the monistic dualism of gnostic speculations. Others see a connection between Paul here and Jewish sources that discuss the first man, Adam, but these texts simply discuss the creation of Adam (e.g., *4 Ezra* 3:21; 4:30–32) rather than anything like what Paul is doing with "the old man." More promising is the idea of Philo that there were two men at creation, one created in the image of God, who was spiritual, and a second who was of the earth and subject to corruption (e.g., *Alleg. Interp.* 1.31–42, 53–55; 2.4; cf. Barth, 538n200). But this connection is only persuasive if one finds pure Platonic allegory a likely source for Paul's imagery.[72]

More likely is to understand the "old man" in v. 22 as Adam and the "new man" in v. 24 as Christ. Hence, the meaning is that believers have (or need to) "shed Adam" and "don[ned] Christ"—the latter of which Paul teaches in Rom 13:14 and Gal 3:27, quoted above. Further, both Adam and the Last Adam are corporate individuals (Rom 5:12–21; 1 Cor 15:20–28). As such, Paul's language in Eph 4:22–24 is not mythological but poetic (Barth, 538–40). This is very attractive, with only one niggly problem: The new man is "created" (κτίζω). The Son exists in the image of God (Col 1:15) and is the radiance of his Father's glory and the corresponding stamp of his being (Heb 1:3), but he is not created. Begotten, not made.

---

71. For reasons that will become clear as the discussion progresses, the popular glosses "self" or "person" for ἄνθρωπος were not used in either v. 22 or v. 24, especially since these abstract nouns divert the reader from the allusion to Genesis, which Paul intends; cf. Barth, 537; G. K. Beale, *A New Testament Biblical Theology: The Unfolding of the Old Testament in the New* (Grand Rapids: Baker Academic, 2011), 278 (esp. n. 57). "Human race" was used for ἄνθρωπος in 2:15, which also has Genesis connections, but that would not suit in either v. 22 or v. 24.

72. In fact the resemblance is only on a very thin surface layer, for the two "men" of Philo represent a Platonic dualism: The one represents philosophers like Philo who have learned to control their urges, and the second lesser mortals who are controlled by their senses and passions and vices. Both Philo's men were described in Eph 4:17–19. Cf. George van Kooten, *Paul's Anthropology in Context: The Image of God, Assimilation to God, and Tripartite Man in Ancient Judaism, Ancient Philosophy and Early Christianity*, WUNT 1.232 (Tübingen: Mohr Siebeck, 2008).

Along with this poetic view is one that interprets the old man as the mass of humanity under Adam and the new man as the *church* under Christ.[73] This is the meaning of the "one new human race" (εἷς καινὸς ἄνθρωπος) in 2:15, but one does not "don" the church.[74]

Where, then, does that leave us? The answer is certainly informed by the latter two views mentioned above, but Paul gives us a hint when he references the *spirit* of the mind in v. 23. The new, resurrection body is πνευματικός ("of the Spirit"; cf. 1:3, 13–14; 1 Cor 15:44–46). The renewed new man is therefore spiritual, and the inauguration of the new creation is experienced in the spirit of the believer through the operation of the Holy Spirit. The idea that elucidates Paul's meaning the best is to see the old man as the old *existence* in Adam and in the fallen old creation. Therefore the new man is the new *existence* in the inaugurated new creation, which was pioneered by the resurrected Mediator as firstfruits (e.g., 2:5–6, 10, 15; 1 Cor 15:20–23).[75] Paul references this new existence, for example, in Gal 2:20, ὃ δὲ νῦν ζῶ ἐν σαρκί, ἐν πίστει ζῶ τῇ τοῦ υἱοῦ τοῦ θεοῦ, which we can paraphrase: "That new life that I now live in my continuing existence in this age, I live by faith in the Son of God" (cf. Rom 6:10).

We will come back to this when looking at 5:8, but there is a link between 4:22–24 and the new- creation imagery of believers as light. They *are* light because when they fled the world by belief in Christ they donned the inaugurated resurrection existence, which can only be equated in its scope

73. Or, similarly, the Old and New Testaments respectively, as maintained by "bad philosophers" (Calvin, 190).

74. If this is the equivalent of "become a Christian" (Martin Dibelius, as cited in Barth, 537n196), then we certainly cannot have an exhortation in 4:22–24. How many times does a Christian have to become a Christian? Cf. Nils Dahl, "Kleidungsmetaphern der alte und der neue Mensch," in *Studies in Ephesians*, WUNT 131 (Tübingen: Mohr Siebeck, 2000), 389–411.

75. "The new man created after God (Ephesians 4:24) is surely the new creation (Ephesians 2:10)," Murray, *Principles*, 217. Murray also argues against taking the infs. as impvs. in Eph 4:22–24: "Paul is not exhorting believers to put off the old man and to put on the new. He is urging them to desist from certain sins, sins which are indeed characteristic of the old man, and the reason he adduces for such abstinence is that they have put off the old man and have put on the new man. Since this is the case, Paul is saying in effect, do not practice those sins which are after the pattern of the old man but behave as new men, as indeed you are" (214).

and importance with the original creation of light in Genesis.[76] And the church is the inaugurated, physical manifestation of this new-man existence in this creation (e.g., 2 Cor 5:17; Gal 6:15; Col 3:10). The Messiah (4:20) is the king of this existence, for it is his kingdom, the cosmic kingdom of God, over which he is enthroned (1:20; 5:5). The incarnate and resurrected Son of God is its head, cornerstone, firstfruits, the standard for full maturity of the new man (4:13)—in a word, "all in all" (1:23; 4:10).

This existence in the new man constitutes a new creation inaugurated when newly minted citizens of this heavenly kingdom are "created after the likeness of God" (τὸν κατὰ θεὸν κτισθέντα; cf. Gen 1:26–27; 1 Cor 15:49). "Created" (κτισθείς) is aorist because the creation is a simple act that was already done, just as believers have already been coenlivened, coraised, and coseated with the Messiah in the high-heavenlies, so they have donned the new existence through the act of a God who is rich in love (2:4–10). And that existence is now characterized by "true righteousness and devotion" in contrast to the callous greed and impurity (v. 19) from before.

The term ὁσιότης, "devotion," appears only here in the NT but occurs in the canonical parts of the LXX at Deut 9:5 (with δικαιοσύνη); 1 Sam 14:41; 1 Kgs 9:4; Prov 14:3.[77] Most English versions render the term "holiness" (Vg. *sanctitas*), whereas LSJ says that this word is more equivalent to Latin *pietas* ("devotion") and that this word group appears with the δικαι- word group often (LSJ, 1260–61). The meaning in Eph 4:24 seems to be "disposition to observe divine law, piety" (LSJ, 1261; BDAG, 728; cf. Hoehner, 612; Barth, 510–11) and corresponds to εὐσέβεια ("godliness" or "piety"). "The meaning is personal piety. ... Whereas Plato, in true G[ree]k fashion, defines ὁσιότης as an ἐπιστήμη of right conduct toward the gods, the NT regards it as a

76. Note again. Believers are not exhorted to *become* light in 5:8; they *are* light because they are believers united to Christ in new creation. What they are exhorted to do is to *act* as children of the light, that is, they must act like what they actually are. Faith in Christ for justification is continued as believers grow in sanctification *by faith* in the truth about themselves in Christ. Hence Eph 4:22–24 is also what believers *are*, whereas the exhortation about how they should act begins in v. 25 with "therefore" (διό).

77. And five times in the Apocrypha, where two meanings, "holiness" and "devotion," are found: λατρεύειν αὐτῷ ἐν ὁσιότητι καὶ δικαιοσύνῃ ἐνώπιον αὐτοῦ πάσας τὰς ἡμέρας ἡμῶν, "to serve him with devotion and righteousness before him all our days" (*Odes Sol.* 9:75) and λήμψεται ἀσπίδα ἀκαταμάχητον ὁσιότητα, "he will take holiness as an invincible shield" (Wis 5:19 RSV).

consequence of the new birth" (Friedrich Hauck, *TDNT*, 5:493). It is possible for ὁσιότης to act as a synonym of ἁγιοσύνη ("holiness" or "sanctity") in some few cases, but it is not the best view here.[78] "Of truth" (τῆς ἀληθείας) qualifies both "righteousness" and "devotion" as an adjectival genitive (so also Calvin, 191).

Application and Devotional Implications

Church leaders have often been nervous about supposed antinomianism where the gospel of free and complete justification by grace through faith alone is proclaimed and taught. As my good friend and colleague R. Scott Clark says, "They don't think people will behave." But to preach any other gospel is not the genuine gospel (Gal 1:6–9). And it is not as if Paul himself has not considered and addressed this issue head-on (Rom 6:1, 15). Protestants have responded time and again to a charge of teaching antinomianism by saying that genuine, justifying faith in the finished work of Christ *always does* produce fruit of sanctification and good works out of gratitude.[79] It must do so because it flows from the sanctifying power of God unleashed in us through his Spirit. Believers are (re)created for these

---

78. Different terms for "holiness," "purity," and "piety" are used in connection with the cult* of Artemis Ephesia (e.g., *IvE* 1578B, cited under comment on 1:4 above, uses ἁγνῶς "with purity" and εὐσεβῶς, "piously"). *IvE* 3217 is an edict of the provincial governor under Trajan around AD 113/4, who refers to the emperor with the superlative adj. ὁσιωτάτος, which probably means "most sacred" or possibly even "most revered." But this is of little help for deciding the meaning of ὁσιότης in Eph 4:24.

79. For instance: "We believe that this true faith, being wrought in man by the hearing of the Word of God and the operation of the Holy Spirit, sanctifies him and makes him a new man, causing him to live a new life, and freeing him from the bondage to sin. Therefore it is so far from being true that this justifying faith makes men remiss in a pious and holy life, that on the contrary, without it they would never do anything out of love to God, but only out of self-love or fear of damnation. Therefore it is impossible that this holy faith can be unfruitful in man; for we do not speak of vain faith, but of such a faith which is called in Scripture a 'faith working through love,' " *Belgic Confession of Faith*, article 24 ("Man's Sanctification and Good Works"), written in 1561. Cf. *Westminster Confession of Faith*, chap. 16 "Of Good Works"; and Murray, *Principles*, 218–19: "This definitive transformation, summed up in the putting off of the old man and the putting on of the new, does not remove the necessity or the fact of progressive renewal," which is expressed in renewal of the mind in Eph 4:23.

good works (2:10). We walk in light because we *are* now light (5:8). Put in terms of dogmatics, personal sanctification is the necessary fruit of justification. They are distinguishable but inseparable.

In the text we have just seen (4:22–24), believers have shed the old man and donned the new because *it is a work of God*. This death of the old man was done in Christ on the cross, and we were raised anew with Christ (2:5–6). Yet for some believers this is precisely the place where problems arise. We do not *see* this change itself in us (except by its resulting good works). And some people with sensitive consciences see nothing but what appears to be the old man battling every halting step forward in the Christian life and none of the evidence that we are in fact new creatures in Christ. What do you do now? Spiritual disciplines? Tried and true "steps" to a happy and victorious life? Positive thinking? Hypnotism?

The place to start for the biblical answer is in our passage. The fact is, just as justification is by faith alone, this same faith in Christ's finished work is also the essential means for our growth in sanctification and in the new life of holiness. We believe that we have donned the new man not because we see it, but because the Bible teaches it and we believe God and his Word to be true. We "consider" ourselves to be dead to sin and alive to God (Rom 6:11)—an act of faith—because it is the foundational truth for a believer in Christ. We have been set free! Now we *walk* in that freedom by faith (Eph 4:1, 17, 25; 5:2, etc.). Sanctification is by faith. We will never see enough good fruit to satisfy our conscience if we look to that fruit as the source of our hope (1 John 3:19–20). If you have truly entrusted yourself to Christ Jesus, you *are* a new creation. You *are* light, now walk as children of the light by faith!

Additional Exegetical Comments: Infinitives in 4:22–24

Some interpreters may wish to see the infinitives in vv. 22–24 (ἀποθέσθαι ὑμᾶς ... ἀνανεοῦσθαι δὲ ... καὶ ἐνδύσασθαι, "that you have shed ... that you are undergoing renewal ... and that you have donned") as functioning as independent imperatives. But this is a specialized legal and poetic use of the infinitive (the latter of which goes back to Homer) with only one clear NT use (Phil 3:16). The few other possible NT examples sometimes cited, such as Rom 12:15, may function in indirect discourse dependent on a remote or implied λέγω (cf. E. Burton, *Syntax of the Moods and Tenses in New Testament Greek* [Edinburgh: T&T Clark, 1898], §§364–65; Smyth, *Greek Grammar*, §§2013–14; BDF §389). For true imperatival infinitives in legal use see, for example, three given in Polybius with thirteen such infinitives.[80]

Unfortunately, C. F. D. Moule and others following him label the infinitives of indirect discourse in Eph 4:22–24 as "epexegetic," which is the wrong label and confusing.[81] (Moule himself says the idea is subtle.) An epexegetic infinitive either stands in apposition to or explains the purpose, destination, or meaning of a pronoun (i.e., τοῦτο; as in 3:8), noun, adjective, or adverb; e.g., αἰσχρόν ... καὶ λέγειν, "shameful even to talk about" (5:12); cf. Burton, *Moods*, §§376–79, 386 (cf. §§390–91 for indirect discourse); Smyth, *Greek Grammar*, §§1987, 2001–7; BDF §§392–94. The infinitives in Eph 4:22–24 are content (or obj.) clauses in indirect discourse, which are to be expected when one specifies through paraphrase what is said, thought, supposed, or, in this case, taught; for other examples of content infinitives with διδάσκω see Luke 11:1; Rev 2:14, 20; and content clauses with ὅτι in Mark 8:31; 1 Cor 11:14.

Selected Bibliography

Ehrenberg, V., and A. Jones, eds. *Documents Illustrating the Reigns of Augustus and Tiberius.* 2nd ed. Oxford: Clarendon, 1976.

Harrisville, R. "The Concept of Newness in the New Testament." *JBL* 74 (1955): 69–79.

———. *The Concept of Newness in the New Testament.* Minneapolis: Augsburg, 1960.

Harvey, J. *Listening to the Text: Oral Patterning in Paul's Letters.* Grand Rapids: Baker, 1998.

Murray J. *Principles of Conduct.* Grand Rapids: Eerdmans, 1957.

van Kooten, G. *Paul's Anthropology in Context: The Image of God, Assimilation to God, and Tripartite Man in Ancient Judaism, Ancient Philosophy and Early Christianity.* WUNT 1.232. Tübingen: Mohr Siebeck, 2008.

80. Polybius, *Hist.* 1.62; 3.22; 21.42–43. Alongside the imperatival infs. are impvs. and a parallel ptc. acting as an impv. (ἀναζητηθὲν ἀποδοθήτω, "let it be sought after and restored"). There are several other passages given in Polybius that could be adduced as well.

81. C. F. D. Moule, *An Idiom-Book of New Testament Greek*, 2nd ed. (Cambridge: Cambridge University Press, 1959), 127, 139

The New Creation Walk in Love (4:25–5:2)

Introduction

In Ephesians 4:25–5:2 Paul continues his instruction on how citizens of the new creation are to walk together in love, thought, word, and deed. This is a place where the chapter division has to be overridden to keep related material together, since 5:1–2 belongs with 4:25–32 (and connects also with 5:3–14 to follow).[1] Furthermore, the unity of the whole passage revolves around the theme provided in 5:2, "walk in love," which illustrates the new-creation life in true righteousness and devotion (v. 24). This simple theme of walking in love connects further with earlier verses, so that we see in 4:25–5:2 a sketch of what it means to walk in a manner worthy of one's calling (4:1) and not in the way of the unbelieving Gentiles (4:17; cf. 5:8, 15).

Paul had opened the previous two sections (4:1–16, 17–24) with exhortations, but he was then slightly diverted with theological truths or divine redemptive provisions that bear on the rationale and power for Christian behavior. In 4:25–5:2 Paul finally seems ready to elaborate on the kind of practices that must characterize true believers. He does deal further with rationale for specific instruction, but at most he reminds the audience of the Holy Spirit's sealing work in v. 30 (from 1:13–14) and by holding up God's loving forgiveness and self-sacrificial redemption in his Son as providing the believer's model for a life of love (4:32c–5:2).

As with other sections in Ephesians and throughout the NT, scholars have searched at length for models Paul utilized for the paraenesis in this and later sections of the epistle, especially in contemporary virtue and vice

1. Also many commentators; for example, Schnackenburg, 203–6, O'Brien, 334; Lincoln, 292; Best, 442. Note that Sinaiticus (א) has vv. 4:32–5:2 as one subunit without division.

lists.[2] Some trace the ideas here back to Stoicism, but this runs into several problems.[3] While ethics is certainly a concern of nearly all Graeco-Roman writers, Paul does not seem to be overly impressed by Gentile ethics, wisdom, or knowledge (4:17–19; 1 Cor 1:17–22; 3:19; Col 2:23).[4] Furthermore, the difference between Paul and the Stoics is clear in a number of ways, including the simple issue of degree. Paul writes a few words on anger (vv. 26, 31) only after a thorough foundation has been laid on the gospel of God's gracious works in Christ. Around a decade earlier, the Stoic Seneca, for example, wrote three very long books "On Anger" (*De ira*). Seneca thinks that lengthy portrayal of anger's evils (book I), discussion of whether it springs from choice or natural impulses (book II), and finally advice on how to tame it (book III) will remedy someone's heart of rage.[5] But Paul grounds his few words in a completely non-Stoic gospel of divine power in death and resurrection.

More fruitful as background to Paul's ethical injunctions are Jewish sources and particularly the OT, specifics of which will come up in the comments. But some observations for general orientation can be noted. First, the influence of the teaching of Jesus and of the OT should be stressed. This seems *prima facie* plausible given Paul's estimation of Jesus as the "all

2. Cf. René A. López, "Vice Lists in Non-Pauline Sources," *BSac* 168 (2011): 178–95; cf. Lincoln, 294–97; Barth, 550–53. In our passage only vv. 31–32 is a "list" per se (cf. 5:3–5). The formal resemblance of such "lists" between Paul and other writers may merely be a matter of style learned in the Graeco-Roman schools rather than indicating borrowing or pagan influence on the apostle. Cf. Paul's use of asyndeton* in quick, anaphoric* cola* noted above on 4:12 with Seneca's similar passages in *De ira* ("On Anger"; e.g., 1.2.1–3 [*Aspice* ("Behold") three times and *alium* ("one man") ... *alium* ("another") three more times]). (This sort of thing is common in Seneca's essays.) The "list" may simply be a similar way of enumerating a number of evils and virtues in quick, summary fashion that typifies the style of Paul's paraenesis and that of other ancient authors.

3. E.g., Burton S. Easton, "New Testament Ethical Lists," *JBL* 51 (1932): 1–12.

4. Similarities between biblical and nonbiblical ethics are more likely traced to the common creation law written "by nature" (φύσει) in the human heart (e.g., Rom 2:12–16); cf. David VanDrunen, *Divine Covenants and Moral Order: A Biblical Theology of Natural Law* (Grand Rapids: Eerdmans, 2014).

5. The discrepancy between Seneca's teachings and his life includes charges of ἀσελγεία ("licentiousness"; see v. 19b above) in antiquity (e.g., Cassius Dio, 61.10; Tacitus, *Ann.* 13.4; 14.52–56); cf. Denis Henry and B. Walker, "Tacitus and Seneca," *Greece & Rome* 10 (1963): 98–110.

in all" of this creation and of the next. The influence of works that fully exposit the divine commandments, such as Leviticus, Deuteronomy, and the various prophets (cf. 2:20), seem like obvious influences on Paul and other NT writers.[6] The only texts Paul quotes or clearly alludes to in Ephesians are from the OT. Second, Ephesians 4:25–5:2 has clear connections to what has gone before in this epistle.[7] He could certainly have adapted material he used and read elsewhere, but the ethical exhortations in Ephesians are not simply a stock list he copies. More importantly, Paul sees the lifestyle he urges here as based on the church being the embassy of the new creation in this age and being the new-temple house. These truths give his ethical imperatives distinctive coloring, which should not be lost from view.

The compositional style of this section consists of short bursts of thematically related material. The loose collection of suggested cola* and periods can be divided as:

A

25 διὸ ἀποθέμενοι τὸ ψεῦδος
λαλεῖτε ἀλήθειαν ἕκαστος μετὰ τοῦ πλησίον αὐτοῦ
ὅτι ἐσμὲν ἀλλήλων μέλη

B

26 ὀργίζεσθε καὶ μὴ ἁμαρτάνετε
ὁ ἥλιος μὴ ἐπιδυέτω ἐπὶ παροργισμῷ ὑμῶν
27 μηδὲ δίδοτε τόπον τῷ διαβόλῳ

C

28 ὁ κλέπτων μηκέτι κλεπτέτω
μᾶλλον δὲ κοπιάτω
ἐργαζόμενος ταῖς ἰδίαις χερσὶν τὸ ἀγαθόν
ἵνα ἔχῃ μεταδιδόναι τῷ χρείαν ἔχοντι

D

29 πᾶς λόγος σαπρὸς ἐκ τοῦ στόματος ὑμῶν μὴ ἐκπορευέσθω
ἀλλὰ εἴ τις ἀγαθὸς πρὸς οἰκοδομὴν τῆς χρείας
ἵνα δῷ χάριν τοῖς ἀκούουσιν

6. For example of the prophets see Ira Jolivet, "The Ethical Instructions in Ephesians as the Unwritten Statutes and Ordinances of God's New Temple in Ezekiel," *ResQ* 48 (2006): 193–210.

7. So Ester Petrenko, *Created in Christ Jesus for Good Works: The Integration of Soteriology and Ethics in Ephesians*, PBM (Milton Keynes, UK: Paternoster, 2011).

E 30 καὶ μὴ λυπεῖτε τὸ πνεῦμα τὸ ἅγιον τοῦ θεοῦ
ἐν ᾧ ἐσφραγίσθητε
εἰς ἡμέραν ἀπολυτρώσεως

F 31 πᾶσα πικρία καὶ θυμὸς καὶ ὀργὴ καὶ κραυγὴ
καὶ βλασφημία
ἀρθήτω ἀφ' ὑμῶν
σὺν πάσῃ κακίᾳ

G 32 γίνεσθε δὲ εἰς ἀλλήλους
χρηστοί εὔσπλαγχνοι χαριζόμενοι ἑαυτοῖς
καθὼς καὶ ὁ θεὸς ἐν Χριστῷ ἐχαρίσατο ὑμῖν

H 5:1 γίνεσθε οὖν μιμηταὶ τοῦ θεοῦ ὡς τέκνα ἀγαπητὰ
2 καὶ περιπατεῖτε ἐν ἀγάπῃ
καθὼς καὶ ὁ Χριστὸς ἠγάπησεν ἡμᾶς
καὶ παρέδωκεν ἑαυτὸν ὑπὲρ ἡμῶν
προσφορὰν καὶ θυσίαν τῷ θεῷ εἰς ὀσμὴν εὐωδίας

With the exception of the very short, one-colon verses 4:27 and 5:1, the versification in our text otherwise corresponds to the Greek periods. The unity of 5:1–2 is reinforced by three forms of "love": ἀγαπητός (adjective, "beloved"; v. 1), ἀγάπη (noun, "love"; v. 2a), and ἀγαπάω (verb, "I love"; v. 2b).[8] Otherwise the structure is thematic, where three of the periods (vv. 25, 28, 29) open with prohibitions of negative behavior and end with exhortation to the positive side of that matter. A reminder of the motivation for these works is supplied in vv. 27, 30, and 5:1–2.

Outline

XI. The New Creation Walk in Love (4:25–5:2)
- A. In word (4:25)
- B. In thought (4:26–27)
  - (Reason #1: do not give the devil an opportunity [4:27])
- C. In deed (4:28)
- D. In word again (4:29)
  - (Reason #2: Do not grieve the Holy Spirit [4:30])

8. We also have a possible inclusio* with **πᾶσα** πικρία ... σὺν **πάσῃ** κακίᾳ in v. 31.

E. In thought and word (4:31–5:2)
(Reason #3: Imitate God in love [5:1–2])

Original Text

25 Διὸ ἀποθέμενοι τὸ ψεῦδος λαλεῖτε ἀλήθειαν ἕκαστος μετὰ τοῦ πλησίον αὐτοῦ,
ὅτι ἐσμὲν ἀλλήλων μέλη. **26** ὀργίζεσθε καὶ μὴ ἁμαρτάνετε· ὁ ἥλιος μὴ ἐπιδυέτω
ἐπὶ παροργισμῷ[a] ὑμῶν, **27** μηδὲ δίδοτε τόπον τῷ διαβόλῳ. **28** ὁ κλέπτων μηκέτι
κλεπτέτω, μᾶλλον δὲ κοπιάτω ἐργαζόμενος [b]ταῖς ἰδίαις χερσὶν τὸ ἀγαθόν, ἵνα[c]
ἔχῃ μεταδιδόναι τῷ χρείαν ἔχοντι. **29** πᾶς λόγος σαπρὸς ἐκ τοῦ στόματος ὑμῶν
μὴ ἐκπορευέσθω, ἀλλὰ εἴ τις ἀγαθὸς πρὸς οἰκοδομὴν τῆς χρείας,[d] ἵνα δῷ χάριν
τοῖς ἀκούουσιν. **30** καὶ μὴ[e] λυπεῖτε τὸ πνεῦμα τὸ ἅγιον τοῦ θεοῦ, ἐν ᾧ ἐσφραγίσθητε εἰς ἡμέραν ἀπολυτρώσεως. **31** πᾶσα πικρία καὶ θυμὸς καὶ ὀργὴ καὶ κραυγὴ
καὶ βλασφημία ἀρθήτω ἀφ᾽ ὑμῶν σὺν πάσῃ κακίᾳ. **32** γίνεσθε δὲ[f] εἰς ἀλλήλους
χρηστοί, εὔσπλαγχνοι, χαριζόμενοι ἑαυτοῖς, καθὼς καὶ ὁ θεὸς ἐν Χριστῷ ἐχαρίσατο ὑμῖν[g] **5:1** Γίνεσθε οὖν μιμηταὶ τοῦ θεοῦ ὡς τέκνα ἀγαπητὰ **2** καὶ περιπατεῖτε ἐν ἀγάπῃ, καθὼς καὶ ὁ Χριστὸς ἠγάπησεν ἡμᾶς[h] καὶ παρέδωκεν ἑαυτὸν
ὑπὲρ ἡμῶν[i] προσφορὰν καὶ θυσίαν[j] τῷ θεῷ εἰς ὀσμὴν εὐωδίας.

Textual Notes

26.a. The article τῷ is missing in the phrase ἐπὶ **τῷ** παροργισμῷ ὑμῶν ("on your vexation") in early, key MSS P^{49}, *א, A, B, and 1739* but found in almost all other MSS. (The phrase appears at the bottom of a page in P^{46}, which is fragmentary and therefore missing. The text picks up again with ὑμῶν at the top of the next page.) The UBS and NA editions put the article in brackets, ἐπὶ [τῷ] παροργισμῷ ὑμῶν, indicating questions about its originality. Any noun qualified by a genitive personal pronoun (as ὑμῶν ["your"] here) is definite and would normally have an article, but definite nouns that are the object of prepositions (as ἐπί here) are also sometimes anarthrous. Therefore, the article was probably added by later scribes as required by the sense. The meaning is unchanged either way.

28.b. The five words (ταῖς ἰδίαις χερσὶν τὸ ἀγαθόν) are included in many key, early MSS (א*, A, D, F, G, 81, 104, 365, 1175, it, vg) with good geographical distribution. But there are several other readings here: ταῖς χερσὶν ἀγαθόν in P^{46}, P^{49}, (apparently) second hand of א, and B; τὸ ἀγαθόν in P, 6, 33, 1739, and 1881; τὸ ἀγαθόν ταῖς χερσὶν in K and 1505; and ἐν ταῖς αὐτοῦ χερσὶν τὸ ἀγαθόν in 629. The meanings of these variants are all similar to ταῖς ἰδίαις χερσὶν τὸ ἀγαθόν, and they seem to be smoothing out what was perceived to be a rough phrase.

28.c. It is sometimes easy to lose sight of the fact that ancient MSS were the products of people who were doing something supremely tedious and wearisome, writing seated on the ground, fingers and legs cramped, welcoming any small distraction. One small but obvious mark of this humanity is found in P[46] at 4:28b, where instead of writing INA (i.e., ἵνα, "in order that"), the scribe only wrote IN. This creates an elision with the next word, ἵν' ἔχῃ, though this was probably not intended.[9] It is easy to see in the letters leading up to INA that the scribe's (reed) pen was becoming dull. The lines get thick and heavy, so much so that the iota of INA is very heavy and the typical "serifs" this scribe makes on his iotas on both top and bottom to the left of the letter are nearly merged into the vertical line. Because of this, the scribe either swapped out his pen for one already sharpened or paused to sharpen his pen in the middle of ἵνα and began again without writing the alpha. The characters after this IN are notably thinner—so much so that the scribe moves his pen up and down two or three times on his verticals for certain letters. This seems to indicate that he was writing syllable by syllable rather than word by word, which accounts for other mistakes in the MS, such as the one below in v. 30.

29.d. Instead of the phrase πρὸς οἰκοδομὴν τῆς χρείας (loosely, "for building up where there is need"), several predominantly Western texts (D*, OL Vg., Victorinus, etc.) read τῆς πίστεως ("for building up in faith"). This latter reading makes the phrase easier, and so χρείας is preferred simply due to being more difficult to imagine as a scribal invention or mistake (*lectio difficilior**). Adding that χρείας has early and widespread external attestation makes it certain to be the original reading.

30.e. One of the more unique and shocking variants in our manuscript evidence is found in P[46], where instead of the textually certain μὴ λυπεῖτε, "do

9. I.e., ἵνα is not elided in this manuscript, as places like 2:7 (ἵνα ἐνδείξηται) or 3:18 (ἵνα ἐξισχύσητε), where it could be. It seems likely that the scribe simply picked up his dull pen and failed to write the alpha when he resumed.

not grieve [the Holy Spirit of God]," the copyist left out the negative μὴ and would have Paul enjoin us to grieve the Spirit! There is no obvious reason for this blunder. The scribe had paused to sharpen his pen three lines up, and it was still writing well.[10] The other occurrence of μή occurs far enough away that it should not have interfered with writing it here. For all we know, it might have been the end of a long day for our hardworking scribe and he simply made an obvious mistake. What is, frankly, more shocking is that no one corrected the mistake, though there are relatively few corrections of the Ephesians text in P46. Whatever the case, we are in no doubt about the reading of the original.

32.f. The editors of the UBS and NA editions provide δὲ ("but, however") in the main text in brackets, suggesting that it is doubtful.[11] This conjunction is found in P49 (but the *delta* is not fully visible), ℵ, A, D2, Υ, 33, 1739mg, and M, while there is no conjunction in P46, B, 104*, 1739*, and 1881. (The conj. οὖν, "therefore," is found in a few later MSS such as D*, F, G, and some Latin sources and seems to have been influenced by the phrase γίνεσθε οὖν found in 5:1; accordingly, it should not be considered original.) Greek style expects the use of a conjunction like δέ here, which leads one to posit that a scribe inserted it here. On the other hand, the ending of the verb before the conjunction (γίνεσθε δὲ) shares sound features (i.e., an aspirated dental and a dental), which may have caused a reader to skip over the conjunction accidentally.[12] Because of this latter possibility and the early and widespread attestation to δέ, I treat it as original.

32.g. The ὑμῖν ("you") in the phrase "God forgave you" at the end of v. 32 is supported by P46, ℵ, A, F, G, P, 81, and other MSS and seems to be required in the context by the second-person verb leading off the period (γίνεσθε ... χρηστοί, "[you] be kind"). P49, B, 33, 1739, 1881, and M have ἡμῖν ("God forgave *us*") here, which does not materially change Paul's point. The common confusion of these pronoun forms in our manuscript deposit

10. See the textual note on 4:28.
11. Discussion of this variant is missing in the UBS4 and therefore Bruce M. Metzger, *A Textual Commentary on the Greek New Testament*, 2nd ed. (New York: United Bible Societies, 1994).
12. A similar variety of variants occurs in Acts 6:3, where a similar sound situation occurs (ἐπισκέψασθε δέ with variants of οὖν and the omission of δέ in some MSS, as in Eph 4:32).

is usually explained as being caused by *upsilon* (ὑμῖν) and *eta* (ἡμῖν) being pronounced the same way at the time when even our earlier manuscripts were copied. See on 5:2 for the same phenomenon.

2.h.–i. There are two variants in this verse where the 1 plural pronouns are 2 plural in some MSS. The first is for ἡμᾶς ("us"), which is supported by P[46], the second hand of א, D, F, G, K, L, 33, 1739, 1881, and M, and which is early and geographically dispersed, while the reading ὑμᾶς ("you") has some other good MSS support (e.g., א*, A, B, P, 81, 326, and 1175). The second variant is for ὑπὲρ ἡμῶν ("on our behalf"), which is challenged with the second-person pronoun (ὑπὲρ ὑμῶν, "on your behalf") only by B, 1175, and some Latin MSS and fathers. This is a common type of variant explained on 4:32 above, but Paul's meaning is not materially changed either way since it is clear that the whole of the church is meant in either case.

2.j. The early papyrus witness P[46] reads **ὀσμὴν** τῷ θεῷ εἰς ὀσμὴν εὐωδίας, "fragrance to God as an attractive fragrance," in place of the original **θυσίαν** τῷ θεῷ, "sacrifice to God." Obviously the occurrence of ὀσμὴν in the next clause influenced this incidental copyist error, which went uncorrected.

Translation

25 For this reason, each of you must put off falsehood[13] and "speak truth[14] with his neighbor," for we are members alongside[15] one another. **26** "Be angry, yet[16] do not sin." Do not let the sun set on your vexation,[17] **27** nor give

13. This follows the NIV, which handles the ptc. ἀποθέμενοι acting in parallel with impv. λαλεῖτε very nicely; see "Excursus: Parallel Participles" below for this use of the ptc. The exhortations are negative and positive sides of the issue of speech. See BDAG, 1097, for ψεῦδος as abstract (or collective) "falsehood" rather than a specific lie, and references to other places where ψεῦδος is contrasted with ἀλήθεια ("truth").
14. This is a quotation of Zech 14:8, where ἀλήθεια ("truth") is also anarthrous in the LXX. See commentary. I have moved ἕκαστος, "each (of you)," into the first part of the exhortation simply for smoother English.
15. "Alongside one another" is more accurate for Paul's meaning that "we are members of one another" (e.g., NASB); see comment.
16. Καί is used under Semitic or colloquial influence in this proverbial type of statement (cf. Pss 4:4; 37:8), where Greek would normally show the contrast with ἀλλά or δέ (cf. BDAG, 494 [meaning 1bβ]).
17. Cf. "wrath" (KJV), "anger" (NASB, ESV, NRSV; cf. NIV). See comment.

the Devil any opportunity. **28** Let the thief[18] engage in thievery no more, but rather let him engage in productive labor[19] with his own hands, that he may have something to share with someone in need.[20] **29** Do not let any foul language come out of your mouth but only whatever is wholesome to edify as needed,[21] that it may give grace to those who hear. **30** And do not grieve the Holy Spirit of God, in whom you were sealed for the day of redemption. **31** All bitterness and fury and anger and shouting and slander must be removed from you, along with any other kind of malice. **32** Instead, be[22] kind to one another, compassionate, forgiving each other, just as also God has forgiven[23] you in Christ. **5:1** So be[24] imitators of God as beloved

18. BDF §275 (6) suggest "he who used to steal" for ὁ κλέπτων and have "[he] who stole up to now" in §339 (3). The latter section explains that a pres. ptc. may substitute for an impf. that refers to previous or customary events and therefore stands for something like ὃς ἔκλεπτεν.

19. The phrase κοπιάτω ἐργαζόμενος ... τὸ ἀγαθόν is a little unwieldy in English. Our versions have: "but rather he must labor, performing ... what is good" (NASB, NKJV); "rather let him labor, doing honest work" (ESV; cf. NRSV); "but must work, doing something useful" (NIV). In my "let him engage in productive labor," I am trying to preserve the toilsome character of work communicated by κοπιάω with "labor" (BDAG, 558) and the idea that the labor is beneficial or productive (in contrast with stealing), to which τὸ ἀγαθόν refers (BDAG, 3–4).

20. For ἵνα ἔχῃ μεταδιδόναι τῷ χρείαν ἔχοντι, which needs a few words added in English; cf. "so as to have something to share with the needy," NRSV.

21. Some degree of paraphrase of the Greek idiom needs to be applied here (ἀλλὰ εἴ τις ἀγαθὸς πρὸς οἰκοδομὴν τῆς χρείας, woodenly: "but whatever wholesome [word] for edification of need"). For example, note the words supplied by the NASB in italics: "but only such *a word* as is good for edification according to the need *of the moment.*" The phrase οἰκοδομὴν τῆς χρείας in particular shows how the gen. relation is a kind of shorthand in Greek, requiring fleshing out of the interrelation of the two words in English. Other versions have: "to the use of edifying" (KJV); "for building others up according to their needs" (NIV); "for building up, as fits the occasion" (ESV); "for building up, as there is need" (NRSV).

22. The verb γίνομαι most often refers to coming into existence, "become." But with certain adjs., as here, it means to "possess certain characteristics" (BDAG, 196–99, meaning 7) and is rendered like εἰμί, "be"; cf. Matt 10:16; Luke 6:36; 1 Cor 10:32.

23. See E. Burton, *Syntax of the Moods and Tenses in New Testament Greek* (Edinburgh: T&T Clark, 1898), §§46, 52, for using an English perf. to render a Greek aor. (ἐχαρίσατο, "has forgiven").

24. See note on γίνομαι for 4:32 above.

children, **2** and walk in love, just as also Christ loved us and gave himself up for us as[25] an offering and sacrifice to God, as a fragrant aroma.[26]

Commentary

4:25 Διὸ ἀποθέμενοι τὸ ψεῦδος λαλεῖτε ἀλήθειαν ἕκαστος μετὰ τοῦ πλησίον αὐτοῦ, "For this reason, each of you must put off falsehood and 'speak truth with his neighbor.' " The word διὸ ("for this reason") indicates that the exhortations that follow in v. 25 and beyond flow from the truths in which the audience had just been instructed (see 4:21–24), just as διό in 2:11 introduces an inferential imperative from the truths of 2:1–10 (cf. Rom 15:7; 1 Cor 14:13; 2 Cor 6:17; 1 Thess 5:11). This same message is communicated in only a slightly different way in Colossians:

> μὴ ψεύδεσθε εἰς ἀλλήλους, ἀπεκδυσάμενοι τὸν παλαιὸν ἄνθρωπον σὺν ταῖς πράξεσιν αὐτοῦ καὶ ἐνδυσάμενοι τὸν νέον τὸν ἀνακαινούμενον εἰς ἐπίγνωσιν κατ' εἰκόνα τοῦ κτίσαντος αὐτόν
>
> Do not lie to one another, since you have shed the old man with its practices, and you have donned the new man which is being renewed in knowledge in the image of his Creator. (Col 3:9–10)

The reuse of the verb ἀποτίθημι in Eph 4:25 ("put off") is a clear link back to shedding the old man and his manner of life in 4:22, where the same verb was used.[27] As noted there, the believer *has* shed this old man, who was embedded in the futility of the old creation, but his "former manner of life"

25. This renders the second of a double acc. construction with an obj. and predicate (παρέδωκεν ἑαυτὸν ... προσφορὰν καὶ θυσίαν); cf. BDF §§155, 157. And see BDF §157 (5) for use of εἰς for the predicate in this construction, which accounts for **εἰς** ὀσμὴν at the end of the verse.

26. See previous note for εἰς in an obj. and predicate (double acc.) construction. The gen. (ὀσμὴ **εὐωδίας**, woodenly, "aroma of fragrance") functions adjectivally for a quality (BDF §165); this phrase is also found in Phil 4:18 and almost fifty times in the LXX (e.g., Gen 8:21; Exod 29:18; Lev 6:14; Ezek 20:41; cf. BDAG, 729).

27. As observed in the translation note, the ptc. ἀποθέμενοι is parallel with the following impv. λαλεῖτε ("speak") and therefore acts as an impv. for that reason (also Heb 12:1; Jas 1:21; 1 Pet 2:1). That the ptc. is aor. represents the implied impv. form as aor. (ἀπόθεσθε), as found in Col 3:8; cf. aor. hortatory subjunctive ἀποθώμεθα ("let us put off") in Rom 13:12. This meaning is simply telic, so the verb tended to the aor. in imperatival uses. See also v. 31 and "Additional Exegetical Comments" below.

(ἡ πρότερα ἀναστροφή; 4:22a) still clings to the believer and must also be "shed" or "laid aside." This first focus of that old life is "falsehood" (τὸ ψεῦδος; see translation note) and contrasts with speaking the truth and with the true righteousness and devotion (v. 24) of the new creation that conditions the life of true faith in Jesus, in whom is truth (v. 21; cf. 5:9; 6:14).[28]

Paul opens with rejection of the old, do not lie, but immediately urges the audience to the positive: "speak truth each one of you with his neighbor" (also vv. 28–29, 31–32; cf. 4:15). This second part of the exhortation is a quotation from part of Zech 8:16: "Speak the truth each one to his neighbor."[29] Some scholars (e.g., Gnilka, 234; Lincoln, 300) believe that Paul is not quoting Zechariah directly but a secondary Jewish source (esp. *T. Dan* 5:2). While this is possible in abstract (assuming Paul had read the *Testament of Dan*), it is better to take the link with Zechariah as intentional here.[30]

The Zechariah quote (Zech 8:16) talks about speaking truth with one's *neighbor* who, in context, is a fellow Israelite brought back as a remnant to the new Jerusalem (Zech 8:1–15). Paul applies this prophecy to the new covenant community because the church is this eschatological people consisting of the remnant Jews (Rom 11:1–5) and Gentiles, like Paul's audience, brought into one new house as a new human race (2:13–21; and see comment on 3:21).[31]

> Thus says the LORD of hosts: Peoples shall yet come, even the inhabitants of many cities. The inhabitants of one city shall go to another, saying, "Let us go at once to entreat the favor of the LORD and to seek the LORD of hosts; I myself am going." Many peoples and strong nations shall come to seek the LORD of hosts

---

28. There is continuity with creation ethics in that speaking the truth and avoiding falsehood is a reflection on the ninth commandment (Exod 20:16) and its implications.

29. The LXX of Zech 8:16 is λαλεῖτε ἀλήθειαν ἕκαστος πρὸς τὸν πλησίον αὐτοῦ, where the only difference with Eph 4:25 is the change of the prep. from πρός ("to") to μετά ("with"). Paul's μετά is closer to the Hebrew (אֵת), from which he may be giving his own translation. The MT of the Zech 8:16 quote is: אֶת־רֵעֵהוּ .

30. The construction with a 2 pl. impv. and sg. "each" (λαλεῖτε ... ἕκαστος) is only found in Eph 4:25 in the NT, with about twenty LXX occurrences rendering a Hebrew idiom (with אִישׁ). Paul apparently knows the Hebrew text.

31. See esp. O'Brien, 337–38.

> in Jerusalem and to entreat the favor of the LORD. Thus says the LORD of hosts: In those days ten men from the nations of every tongue shall take hold of the robe of a Jew, saying, "Let us go with you, for we have heard that God is with you." (Zech 8:20–23)

The exhortations of 4:25–5:2 and beyond are predicated on and flow from church members' experience of eschatological, "new man" existence in Christ (see 4:24; cf. 2:15).

ὅτι ἐσμὲν ἀλλήλων μέλη, "for we are members alongside one another." This phrase is often rendered strictly as "we are members of one another" (e.g., NASB, ESV, NRSV), yet ἀλλήλων μέλη is a compressed phrase standing for the idea of being fellow members of the body of Christ *alongside* one another (see 5:30; cf. Rom 12:5). That is, believers are not members of each other's body but of Christ's body (cf. 1:23; 2:16; 4:4, 12, 16; 5:23, 30). So also NIV, "we are all members of one body." The genitive simply connects ἀλλήλων to μέλη with whatever relation warranted by context.

More importantly, with this last colon* (v. 25c) we can see that Paul's concern in this place and throughout 4:25–5:2 is with life *within* the covenant community and building that unity he insists on elsewhere (e.g., 4:1–6; 15–16). This does not imply that Christians are free to lie to their nonbelieving neighbors but only that life within the church is Paul's focus here.[32]

4:26 ὀργίζεσθε καὶ μὴ ἁμαρτάνετε· ὁ ἥλιος μὴ ἐπιδυέτω ἐπὶ παροργισμῷ ὑμῶν, "'Be angry, yet do not sin.' Do not let the sun set on your vexation." The imperative ὀργίζεσθε ("be angry") gives one pause since it seems counter to Paul's admonitions that "anger (ὀργή) ... must be removed from you" (4:31; cf. Gal 5:20; Col 3:8; etc.). Some scholars have suggested the first imperative is conditional and offer a paraphrase: "You may be angry as far as I am concerned (if you can't help it), but do not sin thereby."[33] However, this has been rejected by Daniel Wallace and others who say that the construction here does not accord with taking "be angry" as conditional, and they take it

32. Cf. Vern S. Poythress, "Why Lying Is Always Wrong: The Uniqueness of Verbal Deceit," *WTJ* 75 (2013): 83–95, for some recent debates.
33. BDF §387 (1); cf. Lincoln, 301.

as a command for judicial anger, even as a "shorthand expression for church discipline."[34]

Yet, as the single quotes indicate, Paul is quoting a line from the OT here (Psa 4:4).[35] This is not a *command* to anger per se. It is a recognition that there are certain kinds of anger and vexation that are warranted and permissible for the godly in this life, especially from unjust accusations (Psa 4:2–3). The psalmist asks: ἵνα τί ἀγαπᾶτε ματαιότητα καὶ ζητεῖτε ψεῦδος, "Why do you love futility [see 4:17] and search out falsehood [see 4:25]?" (Psa 4:3 LXX).

But unrestrained anger is tantamount to murder (Matt 5:21–22; cf. *Did.* 3.2) and therefore is a violation of the sixth commandment (Exod 20:13). While "God is angry with the wicked every day" (Psa 7:11b KJV), this is the judicial wrath of God against sin and evil, which humans cannot normally exercise without sin: "For the wrath of man does not accomplish the justice of God" (Jas 1:20).[36] Hence we must make a distinction between divine judicial wrath and human, selfish fury.[37] This is why Paul adds to the psalm, "Do not let the sun set on your vexation." A righteous indignation may flare up, leading to vexation over evils believers may encounter, but it must be swiftly dealt with before it leads to sin.[38]

---

34. Daniel B. Wallace, *Greek Grammar beyond the Basics* (Grand Rapids: Zondervan, 1997), 492; cf. Wallace, "Ὀργίζεσθε in Ephesians 4:26: Command or Condition?" *CTR* 3 (1989): 353–72; Joseph D. Fantin, *The Greek Imperative Mood in the New Testament: A Cognitive and Communicative Approach*, SBG 12 (New York: Peter Lang, 2010), 304–6; Hoehner, 619–21; O'Brien, 339–40.

35. Psalm 4:5 in the LXX, which reads: ὀργίζεσθε καὶ μὴ ἁμαρτάνετε λέγετε ἐν ταῖς καρδίαις ὑμῶν καὶ ἐπὶ ταῖς κοίταις ὑμῶν κατανύγητε διάψαλμα, "Be angry and do not sin, speak in your hearts and on your beds be vexed. Selah" (or "be silenced" for κατανύσσω as pass.; LSJ, 903; LSJ 9th ed. supplement, 170); cf. Psa 37:8.

36. See the interesting discussion of Seneca against anger when administering capital punishment as a magistrate (*Ira* 1.16.5–7).

37. Even more we must contrast the judicial anger of an impassible, infinitely just, and good God with the selfish fits of jealousy and spite exhibited by the pagan gods of antiquity. For example, the theme of Virgil's *Aeneid* is the long, wearisome pilgrimage of the Trojan War refugees caused by the spiteful rage (*ira*) of cruel Juno (*saevae … Iunonis*; *Aen.* 1.4).

38. See O'Brien, 340, for parallels in both Plutarch and the Dead Sea texts for the idea of settling disputes before sunset. Yet see 1QS X, 20 "However, my anger I shall not remove from wicked men, nor shall I be appeased, until he [God] carries out his judgment. I shall not sustain angry resentment for those who convert from iniquity, but I shall have no mercy for all those who deviate from the path" (trans. F.

The term for "vexation" (παροργισμός) in v. 26 is unique to the NT in place of the more common terms ὀργή ("wrath," "anger") and θυμός ("fury"; see both in 4:31; Rom 2:8; Col 3:8; Rev 16:19; 19:15). In the LXX παροργισμός refers to provocation or cause of anger, except in the LXX of Jer 21:5, where ὀργή, θυμός, and παροργισμός are all used together as synonyms. In this context and in light of Jer 21:5, "vexation" seems to be the best rendering.[39] Verse 27 is connected with v. 26.

4:27 μηδὲ δίδοτε τόπον τῷ διαβόλῳ, "nor give the Devil any opportunity." This colon* belongs with v. 26 as part of the motivation to turn aside from anger and its consequent thoughts and acts. It is also parallel with the admonition not to grieve the Spirit in v. 30. In its other NT uses, the phrase δίδωμι τόπον refers to (1) giving up one's place at a banquet (Luke 14:9) or (2) leaving room for someone or something (metaphorically, divine wrath in Rom 12:19; cf. Jas 4:7).[40] The second meaning fits best here, where τόπος refers to an opportunity for accomplishing something. BDAG provides a helpful paraphrase: "*[D]o not give the devil a chance* to exert his influence"(BDAG, 243 and 1012; emphasis original).

The focus in 4:25–5:2 is clearly on the peace and unity of the covenant community. Believers are informed here in v. 27 that this peace is not a trivial earthly matter but part of a wider affair with cosmic involvement (see 3:10; 6:12). The church is a portal to the realm of heaven and of eschatological realities that must be kept in mind by its members, for the enemy of peace and of the work of God wants nothing more than that the church be torn apart with fury, tumult, hostilities, divisions, and all other malevolent effects of unresolved anger (v. 31). "Any kingdom divided against itself will be desolated, and any city or house divided against itself will not stand" (Matt 12:25). The church is an incursion of the kingdom of God and of Christ (5:5), which will ultimately prevail (Matt 16:18), but not without its losses (e.g., Rev 2:18–29).

García Martínez and E. J. C. Tigchelaar, *The Dead Sea Scrolls Study Edition* [New York: Brill, 1997–1998]).

39. See BDAG, 780; LSJ, 1343. The terms ὀργή and θυμός occur some four hundred times in the canonical OT alone, usually of God's wrath (cf. 5:6).

40. Cf. "give ground" in a military sense in Judg 20:36 LXX. For the pres.-tense form of δίδοτε in 4:27 see "Additional Exegetical Comments" below.

4:28 ὁ κλέπτων μηκέτι κλεπτέτω, μᾶλλον δὲ κοπιάτω ἐργαζόμενος ταῖς ἰδίαις χερσὶν τὸ ἀγαθόν, ἵνα ἔχῃ μεταδιδόναι τῷ χρείαν ἔχοντι, "Let the thief engage in thievery no more, but rather let him engage in productive labor with his own hands, that he may have something to share with someone in need" (see also 1 Thess 4:11–12; 2 Thess 3:11–12; cf. 1 Pet 4:15). There is nothing particularly difficult to understand about this verse.[41] But it is worth pointing out that Paul develops the eighth commandment against stealing (Exod 20:15; cf. Rom 13:9) by exhorting the audience not only to refrain from this sin but to replace it with fruitful labor to share with those in need.[42] It is easy to extend the pattern Paul uses here to other lifestyle sins the saints are to stop practicing and the corresponding virtues they are to positively develop for holy lives (see also vv. 31–32).

At the heart of stealing is "covetousness" (πλεονεξία; 4:19; 5:3, 5; Exod 20:17 [the tenth commandment]) and laziness (see esp. Prov 1:11–19; 21:25–26). But the thief is to displace his past mind-set with a positive life of diligent labor and generosity.[43] Generosity is the key here because it directly counteracts covetousness (greed). However, it should be noted that Paul says κοπιάτω, "let him *labor*." This Greek verb is particularly used of toilsome, manual labor (BDAG, 558; cf. ποιέω or ἐργάζομαι), which Paul knew both from his own labor in the gospel (e.g., Gal 4:11; Col 1:29; 1 Tim 4:10) and his "tentmaking" (Acts 18:3).[44] One of the more vivid portraits of labor in the ancient world comes from Egypt, even if much earlier:

---

41. For the pres.-tense form of κλεπτέτω in 4:27 see "Additional Exegetical Comments" below. The ptc. ἐργαζόμενος can be viewed as parallel with κοπιάτω, "let him labor (and) let him work," but the ptc. seems to be more closely connected with κοπιάω here, so it is probably better to read the ptc. as means: "let him labor *by working* ..." (cf. Burton, *Moods*, §443). My translation seeks merely to show the close interplay of these two synonyms: "let him engage in productive labor." Cf. καὶ κοπιῶμεν ἐργαζόμενοι ταῖς ἰδίαις χερσίν, "and we are hard at work with our own hands" (1 Cor 4:12).

42. For helping those in need see also Luke 3:11; Gal 6:10; Titus 3:8, 14.

43. For the point about covetousness and stealing see esp. 1 Cor 6:10, οὔτε κλέπται οὔτε πλεονέκται ... βασιλείαν θεοῦ κληρονομήσουσιν, "Neither thieves nor covetous people ... will inherit the kingdom of God."

44. The exact nature of Paul's "tentmaking" is not important for understanding Eph 4:28, but Peter Lampe makes a strong case for Paul dealing primarily in awnings used in commercial and residential applications; Peter Lampe, "Paulus—Zeltmacher," *BZ* 31 (1987): 256–60. The main alternative is Ronald Hock's idea that Paul was a leather-worker (primarily a cobbler) in Ronald F. Hock, *The Social*

> I have seen the smith at work at the opening of his furnace; with fingers like claws of a crocodile he stinks more than fish roe. The carpenter who wields an adze, he is wearier than a field-laborer; his field is the timber, his hoe the adze. There is no end to his labor, he does more than his arms can do. ... The potter is under the soil, though as yet among the living; he grubs in the mud more than a pig, in order to fire his pots. His clothes are stiff with clay, his girdle is in shreds; if air enters his nose, it comes straight from the fire. ... The gardener carries a yoke, his shoulders are bent as with age; there's a swelling on his neck and it festers. In the morning he waters vegetables, the evening he spends with the herbs, while at noon he has toiled in the orchard. He works himself to death more than all other professions.[45]

For Paul's own life of labor, see Acts 20:35; 1 Cor 4:11–12; 2 Thess 3:8; cf. 1 Thess 4:11–12. Ronald Hock thinks that Paul was an elitist who despised labor, but this idea has recently been challenged by Todd Still.[46] Anyone who has engaged in manual labor from sunrise to sundown, day after day, can sympathize with a preference for softer work! But I think Still makes a good case, even though Paul's point is not to revel in labor but to use it to develop generosity and to benefit the church.

The infinitive μεταδιδόναι ("to share") is a little tricky. It is possible to see this as simple result: ἵνα ἔχῃ μεταδιδόναι, "that he might have (something) *so that he can share*." But it is more likely (in good Greek fashion) to be functioning as means, "that he might have (something) *with which to share*," as is found in Matt 18:25: μὴ ἔχοντος δὲ αὐτοῦ ἀποδοῦναι, "But he did not have anything *with which to repay* (his debt)." This precise use does

---

Context of Paul's Ministry: Tentmaking and Apostleship (Philadelphia: Fortress, 1980); cf. Hock, "Paul's Tentmaking and the Problem of His Social Class," *JBL* 97 (1978): 555–64.

45. From "The Satire of the Trades" in Miriam Lichtheim, *Ancient Egyptian Literature: A Book of Readings* (Berkeley and Los Angeles: University of California Press, 1973), 186–87. Not all scholars view this ancient work as a satire (see 184), but even if it derides labor with some exaggeration (in contrast with the glories of the Egyptian scribal profession), subsistence labor is ever under the cloud of the common curse (Gen 3:17–19); cf. Eccl 12:12; Acts 26:24.

46. Todd D. Still, "Did Paul Loathe Manual Labor? Revisiting the Work of Ronald F. Hock on the Apostle's Tentmaking and Social Class," *JBL* 125 (2006): 781–95.

not get much treatment in the grammars, though note Burton (*Syntax of the Moods and Tenses in New Testament Greek* [Edinburgh: T&T Clark, 1898], §368), who talks about an infinitive of indirect object that can have a "similar dative relation" to a verb.

4:29 *πᾶς λόγος σαπρὸς ἐκ τοῦ στόματος ὑμῶν μὴ ἐκπορευέσθω, ἀλλὰ εἴ τις ἀγαθὸς πρὸς οἰκοδομὴν τῆς χρείας, ἵνα δῷ χάριν τοῖς ἀκούουσιν*, "Do not let any foul language come out of your mouth but only whatever is wholesome to edify as needed, that it may give grace to those who hear." The disciple of Christ must love the Lord with heart, mind, soul, and strength—and word. Paul now shows just how extensive the claims of Christ are on the lives of his hearers: It extends to the way they are to talk (cf. Matt 5:22; Rom 3:14; Col 4:6). From the diseased (*σαπρός*) tree comes rotten (*σαπρός*) fruit (Matt 12:33); so then, "every careless word that men shall speak, they shall render account for it in the day of judgment" (Matt 12:36 NASB). "The mouth of the righteous is a fountain of life, but the mouth of the wicked conceals violence" (Prov 10:11; cf. Prov 10:31–32; 13:3; 14:3; 15:2; Eccl 10:12; etc.).

The adjective *σαπρός* found in "foul language" in v. 29 refers to fish, fruit, or other products that are "spoiled," "rotten," or "putrid" (occurring only in Matt 7:17–18; 12:33; 13:47–48; Luke 6:43; Eph 4:29). Here the meaning is metaphorically transferred from the realm of foodstuffs to "unwholesome" or "foul" speech (BDAG, 913). Paul is speaking very broadly about harmful speech in contrast with that which builds up others (esp. O'Brien, 344–45). See also "obscene and foolish talk or base jesting" in 5:4 (*αἰσχρολογία*, "obscene talk"; cf. Col 3:8).

We should keep in mind that Paul is dealing with very few educated and political elites in the congregations he founded (e.g., 1 Cor 1:26).[47] The Ephesian audience no doubt contained at least partly a pretty rough crowd, and the Gentile contingent may have been unversed in OT wisdom literature and its plethora of statements on the mouth, the tongue, or the words of the wise and the fool. They may have been surprised to learn

47. In contrast to the people for whom the vast majority of Graeco-Roman literature is written.

that even the way they talk had to be reformed on conversion to Christ.[48] But here we see the unity of the congregation and its mutual growth and edification is paramount in Paul's mind (4:15–16; cf. v. 32; Rom 14:19). Furthermore, it does not take a call to the special offices of the church (4:11) to be able to "give grace to those who hear" with one's words; this is an obligatory privilege of all Christians as well.[49]

4:30 καὶ μὴ λυπεῖτε τὸ πνεῦμα τὸ ἅγιον τοῦ θεοῦ, ἐν ᾧ ἐσφραγίσθητε εἰς ἡμέραν ἀπολυτρώσεως, "And do not grieve the Holy Spirit of God, in whom you were sealed for the day of redemption." This is one of the more mysterious—and important—verses in the Bible. It is mysterious because God's ways and thoughts are not human (Isa 55:8–9), yet his church can grieve his Spirit (cf. 1 Thess 5:19). It is important because it is a reminder that the Triune God is personal and that his Spirit, who dwells among his people, is not an impersonal wind or power but a person.[50]

Paul is alluding in v. 30 to a passage in Isa 63 that has its own mysterious features. While looking forward to God's future deliverance—especially since the sanctuary of God was to be trampled down (Isa 63:18)—the prophet reflects back on God's redemption of his people from Egypt. Then we read of the Servant of the Lord's affliction and the vexation of the Holy Spirit at Meribah (Exod 17:1–7; Num 20:13, 24; 17:14; Deut 32:51; 33:8; Pss 81:7; 95:8; 106:32; Ezek 47:19; 48:28; cf. Heb 3:7–4:6)—which turned out to be a foreshadowing of Christ (1 Cor 10:1–6).[51] Then Isaiah prophesies:

> In all their affliction he was afflicted, and the angel of his presence saved them; in his love and in his pity he redeemed them; he lifted them up and carried them all the days of old. But they rebelled and *grieved his Holy Spirit*; therefore he turned to be

---

48. Confiscation of property and enslavement was a common punishment for criminals in antiquity; hence, criminal activity may be in the background of some of the Ephesian converts who were slaves (see on 6:5–7).

49. To "give grace" (δίδωμι χάριν) can refer to the extension of a benefaction or to benefit people with words (so "that it may benefit," NIV). Or perhaps it can even be a means of extending the grace of God to others (see BDAG, 1080).

50. So also Edward J. Young, *The Book of Isaiah* (Grand Rapids: Eerdmans, 1972), 3:482–83, who sees the link between Isa 63:10 and Eph 4:30 developed below, as do many others (but cf. Best, 457).

51. See esp. O'Brien, 346–49, for similar points made here and below.

their enemy, and himself fought against them. (Isa 63:9–10; emphasis added)[52]

Isaiah's prophecy became relevant for a new exodus, which had a near referent of a return of Israel from exile but is now interpreted by Paul in v. 30 for the "day of redemption" that lies ahead.[53] God had redeemed Israel from Egypt (e.g., Exod 15:13; Deut 7:8). Earlier in Ephesians Paul had identified redemption (ἀπολύτρωσις) as the forgiveness of sin in Christ's blood (1:7), by which God had redeemed his prized possession (1:13–14)—this redemption is finished (1:7, 13–14; cf. Col 1:14). The verdict of the final judgment for God's people has already been pronounced, and they are justified by Christ's righteousness, imputed to them as a gift (e.g., Rom 3:24; 5:12–21, esp. v. 17). But there is a new exodus ahead for those who possess the "firstfruits of the Spirit," and it will lead to "the redemption of our bodies" (Rom 8:23) in resurrection glory. As Israel had been led as pilgrims in the wilderness by the angel of God's presence (Exod 23:20–21), so also the new-covenant church is filled with the divine presence as pilgrims leading to the heavenly promise that the patriarchs saw from a distance and hailed (Heb 11:13–16).

Paul specifies the goal of the church's pilgrimage as "the day of redemption" (cf. Luke 21:28) on the "day of the Lord" (1 Cor 5:5; 1 Thess 5:2; 2 Thess 2:2; cf. 1 Cor 1:8; 2 Cor 1:14; Phil 1:6, 10; 2:16; Lincoln, 307).[54] This future redemption consists of resurrection and new creation, which is founded on a fully purchased redemption in the death of Christ; this dynamic of inauguration-consummation is the essence of biblical eschatology. For the genuine believer, this future redemption is "sealed" through regeneration (4:22–24) by the Holy Spirit, which acts as its guarantee (see

52. The LXX of the key phrase is καὶ παρώξυναν τὸ πνεῦμα τὸ ἅγιον αὐτοῦ, with a different verb (παροξύνω, "provoke" or "irritate") from Paul's λυπέω ("grieve" or "vex").

53. The idea of a new exodus from sin and death as the hallmark of Christianity is a main theme in the work of N. T. Wright, who also sees it in Ephesians (even as a mark of Pauline authorship); e.g., N. T. Wright, *The Resurrection of the Son of God* (Minneapolis: Fortress, 2003), 236–40. Cf. Rikki E. Watts, *Isaiah's New Exodus and Mark*, WUNT 2.88 (Tubingen: Mohr Siebeck, 1997).

54. The phrase εἰς ἡμέραν ἀπολυτρώσεως specifies the temporal goal of the Spirit's sealing ministry (BDAG, 288–91, on εἰς). The phrase has also been described as the purpose, which is essentially indistinguishable from a temporal goal; cf. Hoehner, 632–33.

comment on 1:13–14). In the meantime, because of the Spirit's dwelling in their midst both individually and corporately, the church must take care not to offend him with their lips (vv. 29, 31) or with other offensive actions that may disrupt "the unity of the Spirit in the bond of peace" (vv. 3, 26–27).

4:31–32 *πᾶσα πικρία καὶ θυμὸς καὶ ὀργὴ καὶ κραυγὴ καὶ βλασφημία ἀρθήτω ἀφ' ὑμῶν σὺν πάσῃ κακίᾳ. γίνεσθε δὲ εἰς ἀλλήλους χρηστοί, εὔσπλαγχνοι, χαριζόμενοι ἑαυτοῖς*, "All bitterness and fury and anger and shouting and slander must be removed from you, along with any other kind of malice. Instead, be kind to one another, compassionate, forgiving each other." As mentioned above on the previous verse, what lies behind Paul's command not to grieve the Spirit is Isa 63 and a reference to Israel's rebellion after the exodus (see esp. 1 Cor 10:1–6). Hence, it is not surprising that the next passage after v. 30 opens with *πικρία* ("bitterness"), since Israel grumbled against Moses at Marah; "the name of that place was 'bitterness' (*πικρία* LXX)" (Exod 15:23–24).[55] Ephesians 4:31 continues the theme of preserving "the unity of the Spirit in the bond of peace" (v. 3) among the covenant community in particular by rejecting attitudes and actions of the old man (v. 22) that would disrupt that unity, and then in v. 32 by adopting actions and attitudes that preserve and advance the church's inner harmony and growth in the image of Christ (cf. vv. 13, 26–27).

The evils that believers are to "remove" in v. 31 can be summarized as issues flowing from the anger forbidden in v. 26: "bitterness, and fury and anger," as well as "shouting and slander" as types of "foul language" in v. 29.[56] The imperative form for "remove" is passive *ἀρθήτω* (from *αἴρω*), which does not imply divine agency (as Barth, 522; cf. O'Brien, 349) but is an

55. Cf. Rom 3:14, "the mouth full of curses and of bitter words"; Heb 12:15; BDAG, 813.

56. Κραυγή can refer to various kinds of shouts, but here it is obviously a quarrelsome kind (as Acts 23:9; BDAG, 565–66). The English derivative from βλασφημία, "blasphemy," refers only to speech that denigrates or slanders God; while the Greek word is also used for this (e.g., Matt 12:31; Rev 13:6), it can also refer to "any kind of speech that is defamatory or abusive" (BDAG, 178), as here in Eph 4:30; cf. Matt 15:19; Col 3:8; 1 Tim 6:4.

impersonal construction equivalent to "let it be removed" (cf. Matt 21:21; Mark 11:23; Luke 9:17; 1 Cor 5:2).[57]

The phrase σὺν πάσῃ κακίᾳ ("with any other kind of malice") is appended to the end of the colon* to give it focus as a summary of any sort of evil to be avoided (cf. Rom 1:29; Col 3:8; Titus 3:3; 1 Pet 2:1).[58] Hence, v. 30 ties in with previous verses in 4:25–5:2 in a number of ways and serves as a quick summary of sins in thought, word, and deed that cannot characterize citizens of the inaugurated new-creation community. In addition, "The arrangement of these terms is climactic. The catalogue moves from a hidden state of the heart to public disgrace caused by words" (Barth, 521).

The positive mind-set that corresponds to the negative evils of v. 31 is given in v. 32 and centers on being kind, compassionate, and forgiving. This, in essence, lies at the heart of the theme of 4:25–5:2, "walk in love" (5:2). It also connects with v. 2 and patiently bearing with other members of the church.

The adjective χρηστός ("kind") can refer to something that is "easy" as a synonym of "light" or not burdensome (e.g., Matt 11:30), but here the meaning conveyed by the English terms "kind" or "benevolent" is clearly intended because of its neighbor εὔσπλαγχνοι, "compassionate," which is a related quality (cf. Luke 6:35; Rom 2:4; 1 Pet 2:3; 3:8; BDAG, 1090). The word εὔσπλαγχνοι itself only appears here and in 1 Pet 3:8 (and *Odes. Sol.* 12:7 in the LXX), but its meaning is clear and derived from its root, σπλάγχνον ("compassion"; Luke 1:78; Col 3:12; Phil 1:8; 1 John 3:17; cf. BDAG, 413, 938). Both χρηστός and εὔσπλαγχνοι ("kind and compassionate") prepare the way as the wellspring for the forgiveness of others that caps off the positive traits believers are to exhibit in v. 32.

> Put on then, as God's chosen ones, holy and beloved, compassion, kindness, humility, meekness, and patience, bearing with

---

57. The aor. tense form of the impv. ἀρθήτω ("must be removed") in v. 30 is default for αἴρω (twenty-two times in the aor. impv., four pres. impv. forms in the NT) and therefore has no aspectual significance here. See, for example, Matt 9:6; 16:24; Mark 2:9, where aor. impvs. of αἴρω are used in parallel with pres.-tense impvs. of other verbs, which is also true in Eph 4:30–31 (γίνεσθε). (See also "Additional Exegetical Comments" below.)

58. See BDAG, 784, for πᾶς in the sg. as denoting "everything belonging, in kind, to the class designated by the noun" (and referencing also Eph 1:3, 8, 21; 4:19; 5:3). For κακία as "malice," "ill-will," or "malignity," see BDAG, 500.

> one another and, if one has a complaint against another, forgiving each other; as the Lord has forgiven you, so you also must forgive. And above all these put on love, which binds everything together in perfect harmony. (Col 3:12–14)

καθὼς καὶ ὁ θεὸς ἐν Χριστῷ ἐχαρίσατο ὑμῖν, "just as also God has forgiven you in Christ." Grammatically, this colon* belongs with the earlier part of v. 32, but conceptually it leads into 5:1–2. It states the vital foundation of all Christian living: The walk of love flows from the love already shown the child of God: "Not that we have loved God but that he loved us. ... We love because he first loved us" (1 John 4:10, 19). Here in Ephesians 4:32 the opening conjunction καθὼς communicates a close comparative idea, "just as," i.e., "in close conformity to." Yet, conceptually, a comparison like this merges into the reason for an action and may be rendered as "since" or "in so far as."[59] This forms the strongest motivation for fulfilling Paul's ethical demands in the passage.

This colon* of v. 32 is seen as part of the NT "conformity" pattern in exhortations (see O'Brien, 351), though this is not strictly a NT idea but is found in central OT places as well: "For I am the LORD who brought you up out of the land of Egypt to be your God. You shall therefore be holy, for I am holy" (Lev 11:45; cf. 1 Pet 1:15–16). Even more importantly, Paul is building on the idea of believers experiencing the initial stage of the new creation, through which they are being renewed in the image of God in Christ (2:10; 4:13, 23; cf. Rom 8:29; 1 Cor 15:49; 2 Cor 3:18; Col 3:10). This conformity to God's image is the continuing sanctifying effect of God's working in them "to will and to work for his good pleasure" (Phil 2:13; cf. Heb 13:21). Sanctification is by faith as an ongoing work of God in which believers "walk" in this life.

The heart of sanctification by faith is rooted in justification and free redemption by faith alone. Paul's statement "God has forgiven you in Christ" (cf. 1:7) is a statement of fact forming the basis for conformity to the image of the God. Believers do not *acquire* forgiveness by forgiving others but forgive *because* they are forgiven. And hence they are being renewed in the image of the God, whose revealed self-identity, his name, includes

59. So BDAG, 493–94 (meaning 3), especially with καί here meaning "also"; cf. Gnilka, 241 (Καθὼς καί *ist sowohl vergleichend als auch begründend*).

his mercy and forgiveness: "And he said, 'I will make all my goodness pass before you and will proclaim before you my name "The LORD." And I will be gracious to whom I will be gracious, and will show mercy on whom I will show mercy' " (Exod 33:19; cf. Luke 6:36; Rom 9:15). This principle is so important that Jesus embedded it as the fifth petition of the prayer he taught his disciples: "forgive us our debts, as we also have forgiven our debtors" (Matt 6:12; Luke 11:4).

5:1–2 Γίνεσθε οὖν μιμηταὶ τοῦ θεοῦ ὡς τέκνα ἀγαπητὰ καὶ περιπατεῖτε ἐν ἀγάπῃ, "So be imitators of God as beloved children, and walk in love." The conjunction οὖν is often inferential (e.g., 4:1, 17), but it is also used frequently for continuation of a narrative or a discussion, as it is used here (BDAG, 736–37). This contributes to taking 5:1–2 as wedded to the previous 4:25–32 as its capstone and essentially expanding particularly on v. 32 (cf. O'Brien, 352; Lincoln, 310–11; cf. Hoehner, 643; Barth, 555). Believers are to forgive because they are forgiven, and so—more generally—they are to imitate God's character and actions.

As in 4:32, it is vital to see that believers do not *become* children or acquire God's love by imitating him, but they *are* children and so in consequence imitate him.[60] The fact that Christians are members of God's household with free access to their Father has already been stated (2:18–19; 3:12; cf. Rom 5:2), but now, in God's "beloved" Son (1:6), Paul affirms that believers—formerly "by nature children of wrath" (2:3)—are now adopted (1:5), beloved children (2:4).[61] This is the basis for walking in God's

---

60. Paul speaks elsewhere about Christians imitating him and the Lord Jesus (1 Cor 11:1; 1 Thess 1:6; cf. 1 Cor 4:16), but not imitating God specifically; cf. A. D. Clarke, " 'Be Imitators of Me': Paul's Model of Leadership," *TynB* 49 (1998): 329–60. R. A. Wild, " 'Be Imitators of God': Discipleship in the Letter to the Ephesians," in *Discipleship in the New Testament*, ed. F. F. Segovia (Philadelphia: Fortress, 1985), 127–43, sees Philo in the background of this statement of imitating God in 5:1 (cf. Lincoln, 310–11), a connection that is only persuasive when v. 1 is read in isolation from its new-creation context. To imitate God for Paul means to imitate his incarnate Son, who gave his life for his friends when they were yet enemies (John 15:13; Rom 5:10). Incarnation and resurrection are antithetical to any kind of Platonism that Philo represents as well as to other Hellenic philosophies (e.g., Acts 17:32).

61. Cf. Rom 1:7, where the Romans are addressed with the adj. ἀγαπητός as "beloved of God" and also Col 3:12; 1 Thess 1:4; 2 Thess 2:13, with the perf. ptc. of ἀγαπάω ("beloved"); or 1 Cor 4:14, where Paul addresses the Corinthians as his beloved children (cf. 1 Cor 4:17; Eph 6:21; Col 4:7; Phil 2:12).

love (v. 2) as those who are not just being renewed in the divine image as *creatures* (above on 4:32), but as *children* of God, and beloved ones at that.[62] God is the Father of his one, whole family (3:14–15), and Christians are his beloved children, who must walk in his way of love (2 Cor 13:11; 1 John 4:8, 16). "The beginning [of life] is faith, its end is love" (Ignatius, *Eph.* 14.1).

"Walk in love" (5:2a) is the summary theme of the exhortations in Ephesians (and in the Bible) and may serve as the distillation of the two great summary statements of God's royal law (Jas 2:8): to love God with heart, mind, soul, and strength, and to love one's neighbor as oneself (e.g., Lev 19:18; Deut 6:5; 11:1, 13; Josh 22:5; Psa 31:23; Matt 22:36–40; Mark 12:30; Luke 10:27; Rom 13:9; Gal 5:14). All the positive injunctions Christians must heed that Paul specifies in this epistle may be summarized as actions motivated by love: speaking the truth and practicing generosity, kindness, compassion, and mercy. But love also motivates rejecting the evils Paul mentions: putting away lies, foul language, bitterness, anger, etc.

καθὼς καὶ ὁ Χριστὸς ἠγάπησεν ἡμᾶς καὶ παρέδωκεν ἑαυτὸν ὑπὲρ ἡμῶν, "just as also Christ loved us and gave himself up for us." As above in v. 4:32c, καθὼς may have a causal meaning: "*since* Christ also loved us." But the close comparison seems to be more prominent here as illustrating the self-sacrificial character of the "walk in love" that Paul enjoins for the Christian life. Certainly there is no Christian life at all without Christ's love and sacrifice as its vivifying root.

Furthermore, bringing Christ into v. 2 gives Paul's earlier exhortation to imitate God concrete form. God "did not spare his own Son but delivered him over (παρέδωκεν) for us all" (Rom 8:32; cf. Rom 4:25), even while they, his enemies (Rom 5:10), were "delivering themselves over (παρέδωκαν) to licentiousness" (4:19). "You spare your friends. He spared his enemies" (Chrysostom, *ACCS*, 183). As the Father (2:4), so too the incarnate Son "loved us and gave himself up (παρέδωκεν) for us" (5:2b–c, as also 5:25). This is a classic Pauline statement of Christ's love for his people (see Gal 2:20 and 2 Thess 2:16; cf. Rom 8:37). The aorist verb ἠγάπησεν ("he loved") is explained by παρέδωκεν ("he gave himself up") as the way in which Christ's supreme love for his friends (John 15:13) is displayed. His people are to walk in the same way, that is, to live in self-sacrificial love: "By this we know love,

62. This is a major theme of 1 John, with the language of believers being "sired" (γεννάω) from God (1 John 2:29; 3:9; 4:7; 5:1, 4, 18; cf. John 1:13).

that he laid down his life for us, and we ought to lay down our lives for the brothers" (1 John 3:16).

προσφορὰν καὶ θυσίαν τῷ θεῷ εἰς ὀσμὴν εὐωδίας, "as an offering and sacrifice to God, as a fragrant aroma."[63] Animal and various plant offerings and sacrifices were an everyday feature of ancient life. Certainly the first-century Ephesians, who possessed the largest temple and altar complex in their day, knew intimately what this image of Christ's self-sacrifice conveyed (cf. above on 2:13). Bulls, birds, and barley, as well as rams, ewes, lambs, sheaves of wheat, wine, and more were all offered.[64] The same such sacrifices and offerings formed the foundation of contemporary Second Temple Judaism.[65] This universal familiarity with sacrifices may well explain why Paul never elaborates on the details of Christ's sacrifice beyond general terms such as those found in 5:2 and 5:25 (e.g., Rom 3:24–25; 5:9–10; 8:3; 1 Cor 5:7).

In this context, Paul presents Christ's sacrifice in substitutionary mediation in terms of an OT animal and grain sacrifice, which gave off a "pleasing aroma" to God. This aromatic character of sacrifices is a repeated description of the sacrificial experience. The phrase "pleasing aroma" (ὀσμὴ εὐωδίας in the LXX also) is found some forty-two times in the Pentateuch

---

63. The two acc. nouns προσφορὰν and θυσίαν are part of a double acc. construction (see translation note).

64. For surveys of Graeco-Roman sacrifical practices see: Walter Burkert, *Greek Religion*, trans. John Raffan (Cambridge, MA: Harvard University Press, 1985), 55–95; John Scheid, *An Introduction to Roman Religion*, trans. Janet Lloyd (Bloomington: Indiana University Press, 2003); cf. Jan Brenner and C. Rober Phillips III, "Sacrifice," in *Brill's New Pauly: Encyclopaedia of the Ancient World* (Boston: Brill, 2008), 12:846–54 (in the larger entry spanning 12:831–56); and Mareile Haase, "Libation," in *Brill's New Pauly*, 7:482–3 (including offerings to/for the dead). A votive offering would often have been some object of value or a token given to the god. Dining halls were often attached to ancient temples for eating parts of sacrifices that were not burnt whole. There were many altars and shrines for sacrifice at Ephesus besides the great Artemisium (which had an adjacent, very large altar structure on its west side; cf. Peter Scherrer, ed., *Ephesus: The New Guide* [Turkey: Zero, 2000], 53).

65. Leviticus and Numbers alone provide myriad OT sacrificial regulations, which reached their pinnacle in the Day of Atonement offering (Lev 16:1–34; cf. Heb 9:11–14; 10:1–4). For recent helpful essays on the topic see Roger T. Beckwith and Martin J. Selman, *Sacrifice in the Bible* (Grand Rapids: Baker, 1995).

in connection with the sacrifice of both animals and grains.[66] The point is that this sacrifice pleases God in fulfillment of his commands and satisfies his justice. In Christ alone, divine justice and unfathomable love kissed to fulfill at once all the OT sacrificial types and as a result provide the supreme model for the believer's own grateful, self-sacrificial acts of love: "I am well supplied, having received from Epaphroditus the gifts you sent, a fragrant offering, a sacrifice acceptable and pleasing to God" (Phil 4:18; cf. Rom 12:1; Heb 13:15–16; 1 Pet 2:5).

Application and Devotional Implications

Paul's admonitions in 4:25–5:2 and generally in Ephesians and in Paul's other epistles show, understandably, a heavy influence of the Torah and especially of the Ten Commandments. The question of the continuing relevance of these old-covenant commandments for members of the new covenant is an issue with a long history. Both Lutherans and Reformed in particular have agreed to a large extent on the moral law's relevance as a guide for grateful Christian living, calling it the "third use" or "third office" of the law.[67]

This does not mean that Christians are still "under the law" in Paul's terminology (e.g., Rom 6:14; Gal 5:18), but that the moral law reveals God's will for the lives of his people and guides them to "walk in love" (5:2). This becomes especially clear when Paul says, "For the whole law is fulfilled in one word: You shall love our neighbor as yourself" (Gal 5:14), and again, even more explicitly, "The commandments, 'You shall not commit adultery, You shall not murder, You shall not steal, You shall not covet,' and any other

---

66. For the pleasing odor, one should think of a modern barbeque. For just one example of the variety of items in sacrifice see Exod 29:22–25 for the consecration service of the Aaronic high priest, where parts of a sacrificial ram, leavened bread, a barley cake, and unleavened bread were all to be burned on an altar "as a pleasing aroma before the Lord" (v. 25).

67. For the Lutheran view, including antecedents of Luther's view in the ancient and medieval periods, see Edward A. Engelbrecht, *Friends of the Law: Luther's Use of the Law for the Christian Life* (St. Louis: Concordia, 2011). John Calvin summarizes his view in his *Institutes of the Christian Religion*, trans. Ford Lewis Battles (Philadelphia: Westminster, 1960), 2.7.6–12, where he says that "the third and principal use ... pertains more closely to the proper purpose of the law" (2.7.12); cf. John Hasselink, *Calvin's Concept of the Law* (Allison Park, PA: Pickwick, 1992).

commandment, are summed up in this word: 'You shall love your neighbor as yourself' " (Rom 13:9).

The main benefit of the "third use of the law" is that it puts flesh on the admonition to love. This is how Paul himself develops both the positive and negative side of these commandments in Eph 4:25–5:2. How do you love your neighbor? Do not steal from him (4:28), do not slander her (4:29), be compassionate and forgiving to all (4:32), etc. It is well worth our time to study the law of God and to see it as the "light for the path" of the believer (e.g., Psa 119) without fear as beloved children of God:[68]

> By this we know that we abide in him and he in us, because he has given us of his Spirit. And we have seen and testify that the Father has sent his Son to be the Savior of the world. Whoever confesses that Jesus is the Son of God, God abides in him, and he in God. So we have come to know and to believe the love that God has for us. God is love, and whoever abides in love abides in God, and God abides in him. By this is love perfected with us, so that we may have confidence for the day of judgment. ... We love because he first loved us." (1 John 4:13–19)

Additional Exegetical Comments: Imperatives in 4:25–5:2

There are thirteen imperative verbs in Eph 4:25–5:2 and more to follow, so this is a good time to lay out briefly the way I understand the use of the tense forms in this mood.[69] This is particularly acute because there are

68. Cf. Hywel Jones, *Psalm 119 for Life: Living Today in the Light of the Word* (Carlisle, PA: Evangelical, 2009).

69. I will not treat here parallel ptcs. functioning as impvs. (e.g., ἀποθέμενοι), infs. in indirect statements with impv. force, fut. indics. with impv. force, or hortatory and prohibitory subjunctives (neither of which are found in Ephesians). This is simply to conserve space in what could easily turn a commentary into a Greek grammar. There are thirty-four pres. impv. forms and six aors. in Ephesians. For a general study of impvs. in light of modern linguistics see Fantin, *Greek Imperative*, which includes a helpful survey of the history of interpretation of this mood. For other relevant works see the introduction to the commentary; cf. K. L. McKay, "Aspect in Imperatival Constructions in New Testament Greek," *NovT* 27 (1985):

prevailing misunderstandings or oversimplifications on Greek imperatives even among some grammarians.[70]

One key way to study the reasons for an ancient Greek author's selection of tense forms in the dependent moods is to look for passages where forms vary between the present and aorist forms in the same context by the same speaker.[71] For example:

> **ἐνέγκατε** [aor.] τῷ κυρίῳ δόξαν ὀνόματι αὐτοῦ **ἄρατε** [aor.] θυσίας καὶ **εἰσπορεύεσθε** [pres.] εἰς τὰς αὐλὰς αὐτοῦ, "*Bring* to the Lord glory to his name, *take along* a sacrifice, and *enter* into his courtyards." (Psa 95:8 [96:8]; LXX)

> [When Florus inquired of Agrippinus whether he should enter a festival put on by Nero, Agrippinus answers:] **ἄπελθε** [aor.] τοίνυν καὶ **τραγῴδει** [pres.], ἐγὼ δ' οὐ τραγῳδήσω, "*Go on* then and *play a part*, but *I'm* not going to play any part." (Epictetus, *Diatr.* 1.2.16–17)

> **ἐντρέπεσθε** [pres.] ἀλλήλους … ἐν Ἰησοῦ Χριστῷ ἀλλήλους διὰ παντὸς **ἀγαπᾶτε** [pres.] … **ἑνώθητε** [aor.] τῷ ἐπισκόπῳ, "Show deference to one another … in Jesus Christ love one another in every way … be united with your overseer." (Ignatius, *Magn.* 6.2, my trans.)

> εἴ τις θέλει ὀπίσω μου ἐλθεῖν, **ἀπαρνησάσθω** [aor.] ἑαυτὸν καὶ **ἀράτω** [aor.] τὸν σταυρὸν αὐτοῦ καὶ **ἀκολουθείτω** [pres.] μοι,"If anyone wants to follow me, *let him deny* himself and *let him take up* his cross *and follow* me!" (Matt 16:24)

201–26; James L. Boyer, "A Classification of Imperatives: A Statistical Study," *GTJ* 8 (1987): 35–54.

70. E.g., Nigel Turner, *Grammatical Insights into the New Testament* (Edinburgh: T&T Clark, 1965), 29–30. ("[A] present imperative was an order to do something constantly or to continue. … The aorist … expresses no more than one specific instance of the action of the verb, involving usually a single moment of time.") This highly inaccurate statement has no doubt influenced many unwary students.

71. There are only two perf. impvs. in the NT: πεφίμωσο (from φιμόω), "Be quiet!" (Mark 4:39); and idiomatic ἔρρωσθε (from ῥώννυμαι), "Farewell" (Acts 15:29), so only the pres. and aor. forms factor into tense-form choice considerations.

σοὶ λέγω, **ἔγειρε** [pres.] **ἆρον** [aor.] τὸν κράβαττόν σου καὶ **ὕπαγε** [pres.] εἰς τὸν οἶκόν σου, "I say to you, '*Get up, pick up* your mat and *go* to your home.' " (Mark 2:11)

μενέτω ἄγαμος ἢ τῷ ἀνδρὶ **καταλλαγήτω**, "*Let her remain* unmarried or l*et her be reconciled* to her husband." (1 Cor 7:11)

ἀλλὰ **ἐνδύσασθε** [aor.] τὸν κύριον Ἰησοῦν Χριστὸν καὶ τῆς σαρκὸς πρόνοιαν μὴ **ποιεῖσθε** [pres.] εἰς ἐπιθυμίας, "But *put on* the Lord Jesus Christ and *do not perform* the plans of the flesh leading to lusts." (Rom 13:14)

φέρε τὴν χεῖρά σου καὶ **βάλε** εἰς τὴν πλευράν μου, "*Bring* your hand (here) and *put* it into my side." (John 20:27)

παράλαβε [aor.] τὸ παιδίον ... καὶ **φεῦγε** [pres.] εἰς Αἴγυπτον, "*Take* the child ... and *flee* into Egypt." (Matt 2:13)[72]

While this list could be greatly expanded, it suffices to illustrate some key ideas for our purpose in Ephesians. At the very least, these examples simply show that we must take care not to oversimplify imperative tense form values. In Matthew 2:13 the author is not saying "flee [constantly] into Egypt," and neither is Mark 2:11 saying "Get up [constantly or repeatedly], pick up your mat [once for all], and go [progressively] to your home."

In fact, there are at least three factors at work in these examples, which I will simply state very briefly. First, it is idiomatic in Greek that certain verbs that refer to travel, movement from one place to another, or conveyance tend to their present-tense imperative forms. This accounts for present εἰσπορεύεσθε, ἀκολουθείτω, ἔγειρε, ὕπαγε, φέρε, and φεῦγε in the examples above, even when other verbs in the same context and utterances are expressed in their aorist forms.[73] In the context of Ephesians, this accounts

72. For the pres. impv. form of φεῦγε see also this example from Plutarch: [A friend of Julius Caesar counsels him to abandon his associations with Mark Anthony]: ὦ ἄνθρωπε, τί σοι πρᾶγμα πρὸς τοῦτον ἔστι τὸν νεανίσκον; **φεῦγ'** αὐτόν· ἐνδοξότερος εἶ, πρεσβύτερος εἶ ... "Sir, what business have you with this youth? *Avoid* him! Your repute is greater, you are older ..." (*Fort. Rom.* 320A; LCL trans.).

73. Other verbs fitting this category include ἄγω, ἔρχομαι, πορεύομαι, φέρω, and περιπατέω (along with their compounds, such as ὑπάγω). Of these verbs (and their compounds), there are about sixty occurrences of the pres. impv. forms and

for present-tense imperatives, ἐκπορευέσθω (4:29) and περιπατεῖτε (5:2) in particular.

Second, there is a tendency in the imperative for verbs that refer to an atelic verbal idea to be expressed in their present forms and telic verbs in their aorist forms.[74] In the examples above, this accounts for present-tense forms τραγῳδει, ἐντρέπεσθε, ἀγαπᾶτε, μενέτω, and ποιεῖσθε (atelic meanings) and for all the aorist imperative forms (telic). In Ephesians the six aorist imperative forms all express telic meanings: ἀρθήτω ("be removed"; 4:31); ἀνάστα ("arise"; Eph 5:14 [see pres. verb of movement ἔγειρε earlier]); ἐνδύσασθε ("put on"; 6:11); ἀναλάβετε ("take up"; 6:13); στῆτε ("stand [fast]"; 6:14); and δέξασθε ("receive"; 6:17).[75]

Third, granting the two qualifications and factors discussed above (and more not discussed), when an author wished to enjoin or forbid verbal events as a pattern of behavior in which to engage in the course of life, he used the present-tense form. This can be confused with a progressive idea (i.e., "do this repeatedly" or "do this all the time" or "constantly") but is more a matter of lifestyle than of constant occurrence. In effect, he says, "Make this your practice" or "Do this when appropriate." This is a "general precept" idea.[76]

The correspondingly opposite idea to that of the general precept is when an aorist-tense-form imperative is chosen (granting again the qualifying factors discussed above) when one wants to enjoin or forbid a simple occurrence near at hand.[77] This is not necessarily a one-time occurrence,

---

thirty-three as aor. forms (most of these aors. are telic compounds: ἐξέρχομαι or εἰσέρχομαι and the like).

74. For the atelic/telic idea see the commentary introduction.

75. This means that an aspectual description like continuation, iteration, attempt, or inception would possibly be found when an atelic verb is found in the aor. (**σχῶμεν** τὴν κληρονομίαν αὐτοῦ, "Let's kill him and *acquire* [inceptive] his inheritance" [Matt 21:38; a hortatory subjunctive that operates as an impv.]) or a telic verb in the pres.-tense form: **ἑτοίμαζέ** μοι ξενίαν, "*Keep* a guest-room *ready* for me" (Phlm 22; only aor. in the NT otherwise).

76. By far, most impvs. in the NT fit this category and account for why the pres. impv. outnumbers the aor. in the Pauline Epistles by about three to one. Cf. Fantin, *Greek Imperative*, 97–98, and Buist M. Fanning, *Verbal Aspect in New Testament Greek* (Oxford: Clarendon, 1990), 327–28.

77. Such impvs. are "narrow in focus and dependent upon the immediate circumstances" (Fantin, *Greek Imperative*, 98).

but it might be; only the context would communicate the idea of single occurrence. Let me illustrate with two uses of the same verb:

> μὴ **κρίνετε** [pres.], καὶ οὐ μὴ κριθῆτε, "Do not *judge* (others), then you will not be judged." (Luke 6:37 // Matt 7:1)

> κατὰ τὸν νόμον ὑμῶν **κρίνατε** [aor.] αὐτόν, [Pilate to the Jews:] "You *judge* him according to your law." (John 18:31)

The first example is a general precept, "Do not make judging others your practice," while the second verse enjoins the hearers to conduct a specific trial rather than to engage in a lifestyle of judging events.

In the final analysis, nearly all of the imperative forms in Ephesians fit into one or another of the categories discussed above. This is to be expected. Most utterances of Greek follow customary lines of usage; marked aspectual nuances in the imperative and in the other moods are the exception rather than the norm. Thus we find atelic verbs like μνημονεύετε ("remember"; 2:11), ὀργίζεσθε ("be angry"; 4:26), περιπατεῖτε ("walk"; 5:2, 8); or ἀγαπᾶτε ("love"; 5:25; cf. 5:33) in their normal present-tense forms, while telic ἀρθήτω ("be removed"; 4:31) and ἐνδύσασθε ("put on"; 6:11) are in their aorist forms, as expected. Furthermore, the predominance of present-tense imperatives over aorists in Ephesians (thirty-four to six) is also caused by Paul expressing events that should mark the mind-set and lives of his audience. It should be noted that there are also aorist-tense imperatives in these "general precept" contexts, but these are usually explicable not as one-time events but as general patterns of behavior for events whose telic nature led them to be expressed as aorists.[78]

Yet there are two imperatives that are not expressed in the tense form we might expect. The first is in the statement μηδὲ **δίδοτε** τόπον τῷ διαβόλῳ ("nor give the Devil any opportunity"; 4:27). The verb δίδωμι normally refers to a telic event, and we would expect the aorist rather than the present-tense form, as here, especially since the same idiom occurs elsewhere in Paul in the aorist: **δότε** τόπον τῇ ὀργῇ, "leave room for God's

78. The six aor. impvs. in Ephesians are at 4:31; 5:14; 6:11, 13–14, 17, and will be discussed in their place.

wrath" (Rom 12:19).[79] Both Romans 12:19 and Ephesians 4:27 are "general precept" contexts, but it could be that Paul felt that only the Ephesians context warranted the present-tense form alongside all the others in 4:25–5:2 (cf. Luke 6:30, 38; 1 Cor 7:3). The only other likely interpretation is that Paul assumes the event is already in progress and calls for it to stop: "And quit giving the Devil any opportunity" (see next example). Yet this does not seem warranted by the context.

The last example is the statement ὁ κλέπτων μηκέτι **κλεπτέτω** ("Let the thief engage in thievery no more"; 4:28). There are not that many examples of κλέπτω as imperatives or related forms to form a hard and fast opinion on this verb, yet the meaning "steal" seems more telic than atelic.[80] One simply "steals" something, and it is stolen. The particle μηκέτι ("no longer") in 4:28 provides the answer: The present tense of the imperative—particularly with a telic verb—may imply that the speaker assumes that the event is currently in progress and forbids its continuance.[81] Hence, μὴ κλεπτέτω should be understood to mean "Let him quit stealing," and with μηκέτι it clearly communicates this with "Let him quit stealing any more (as he has been)."

Selected Bibliography

Boyer, J. "A Classification of Imperatives: A Statistical Study." *GTJ* 8 (1987): 35–54.

Clarke, A. " 'Be Imitators of Me': Paul's Model of Leadership." *TynB* 49 (1998): 329–60.

Easton, B. "New Testament Ethical Lists." *JBL* 51 (1932): 1–12.

Fantin, J. *The Greek Imperative Mood in the New Testament: A Cognitive and Communicative Approach*. SBG 12. New York: Peter Lang, 2010.

Hock, R. *The Social Context of Paul's Ministry: Tentmaking and Apostleship*. Philadelphia: Fortress, 1980.

Jolivet, I. "The Ethical Instructions in Ephesians as the Unwritten Statutes and Ordinances of God's New Temple in Ezekiel." *ResQ* 48 (2006): 193–210.

López, R. "Vice Lists in Non-Pauline Sources." *BSac* 168 (2011): 178–95.

---

79. Δίδωμι and its compounds appear 219 times in their aor. impv. forms in the NT and LXX, but only eight times in their pres.-tense forms.

80. For example, see the aor. prohibitory subjunctives in Mark 10:19 and Luke 18:20, expressing the eighth commandment, which is otherwise expressed as a (categorical) fut. indic. (Exod 20:14; Matt 19:18), and see Rom 2:21.

81. Wallace, *Greek Grammar*, 336–38, discusses this nuance and helpfully cautions not to overdo it; cf. BDF §336 (3). See also comment on 5:18.

Poythress, V. "Why Lying Is Always Wrong: The Uniqueness of Verbal Deceit." *WTJ* 75 (2013): 83–95.

Still, T. "Did Paul Loathe Manual Labor? Revisiting the Work of Ronald F. Hock on the Apostle's Tentmaking and Social Class." *JBL* 125 (2006): 781–95.

Turner, N. *Grammatical Insights Into the New Testament*. Edinburgh: T&T Clark, 1965.

VanDrunen, D. *Divine Covenants and Moral Order: A Biblical Theology of Natural Law*. Grand Rapids: Eerdmans, 2014.

Wallace, D. "Ὀργίζεσθε in Ephesians 4:26: Command or Condition?" *CTR* 3 (1989): 353–72.

Wild, R. " 'Be Imitators of God': Discipleship in the Letter to the Ephesians." In *Discipleship in the New Testament*, edited by F. Segovia, 127–43. Philadelphia: Fortress, 1985.

Wright, N. T. *The Resurrection of the Son of God*. Minneapolis: Fortress, 2003.

The Saints and the Sinful World (5:3–14)

Introduction

In Ephesians 5:3–14 Paul continues his exhortation to the saints as citizens of the new creation and warns them to avoid the evil practices of those in the world. There is a transition here from the previous passage (4:25–5:2). In the earlier exhortations, the focus was on interactions within the covenant community, whereas here in 5:3–14 the focus is on the church's interaction with the world. The first part of vv. 3–14 concentrates on avoiding any sort of sexual immorality, impurity, or avarice (covetousness), along with the "sons of disobedience" (v. 6), with the center being the admonition in v. 7. There is a transition in v. 8 to a focus more on the reason why those who profess faith in Christ must no longer engage in these evils: They are light and are to walk as children of the light and to bear its fruit (vv. 8–9). Paul concludes this section with an interesting combination OT quote in v. 14 that ties together the theme of light and darkness.

Just as there were similarities between Eph 4:17–19 and Rom 1:21–24 reported above (see introduction to Eph 4:17–24), so also there are similarities between Eph 5:3–14 and a passage in Colossians:

> Put to death therefore what is earthly in you: sexual immorality, impurity, passion, evil desire, and covetousness, which is idolatry. On account of these the wrath of God is coming. In these you too once walked, when you were living in them. But now

> you must put them all away: anger, wrath, malice, slander, and obscene talk from your mouth. (Col 3:5–8)[1]

The connection between various passages with a common author (Paul alone for Romans and Ephesians and Paul with Timothy as cosender for Colossians) should not be very surprising, given that authors kept copies of their works and often reused or consulted portions of one for another.[2]

Here is a suggested division of Eph 5:3–14 into cola* and periods:

A ³ πορνεία δὲ καὶ ἀκαθαρσία πᾶσα ἢ πλεονεξία
μηδὲ ὀνομαζέσθω ἐν ὑμῖν
καθὼς πρέπει ἁγίοις

B ⁴ καὶ αἰσχρότης καὶ μωρολογία ἢ εὐτραπελία
ἃ οὐκ ἀνῆκεν
ἀλλὰ μᾶλλον εὐχαριστία

C ⁵ τοῦτο γὰρ ἴστε γινώσκοντες
ὅτι πᾶς πόρνος ἢ ἀκάθαρτος ἢ πλεονέκτης
ὅ ἐστιν εἰδωλολάτρης
οὐκ ἔχει κληρονομίαν ἐν τῇ βασιλείᾳ τοῦ Χριστοῦ καὶ θεοῦ

D ⁶ μηδεὶς ὑμᾶς ἀπατάτω κενοῖς λόγοις
διὰ ταῦτα γὰρ ἔρχεται ἡ ὀργὴ τοῦ θεοῦ
ἐπὶ τοὺς υἱοὺς τῆς ἀπειθείας

E ⁷ μὴ οὖν γίνεσθε συμμέτοχοι αὐτῶν

F ⁸ ἦτε γάρ ποτε σκότος νῦν δὲ φῶς ἐν κυρίῳ
ὡς τέκνα φωτὸς περιπατεῖτε
⁹ ὁ γὰρ καρπὸς τοῦ φωτὸς
ἐν πάσῃ ἀγαθωσύνῃ καὶ δικαιοσύνῃ καὶ ἀληθείᾳ

---

1. Andrew Lincoln (319) rearranges the Greek to make the parallelism between 5:3–14 and Col 3:5–8 seem closer than it is. Nils Dahl sees close similarity between Eph 5:3–14 and 1 Cor 5–6, suggesting a link with a lost letter to the Corinthians in Dahl, "Der Epheserbrief und der verlorene, erste Brief des Paulus an die Korinther," in *Studies in Ephesians*, WUNT 131 (Tübingen: Mohr Siebeck, 2000), 335–48. It would be interesting to find this lost letter.
2. See E. Randolph Richards, *The Secretary in the Letters of Paul*, WUNT 2.42 (Tübingen: Mohr Siebeck, 1991), 158–68.

G ¹⁰ δοκιμάζοντες τί ἐστιν εὐάρεστον τῷ κυρίῳ
¹¹ καὶ μὴ συγκοινωνεῖτε τοῖς ἔργοις τοῖς ἀκάρποις
τοῦ σκότους
μᾶλλον δὲ καὶ ἐλέγχετε

H ¹² τὰ γὰρ κρυφῇ γινόμενα ὑπ᾽ αὐτῶν
αἰσχρόν ἐστιν καὶ λέγειν
¹³ τὰ δὲ πάντα ἐλεγχόμενα
ὑπὸ τοῦ φωτὸς φανεροῦται

I ¹⁴ πᾶν γὰρ τὸ φανερούμενον φῶς ἐστιν
διὸ λέγει
ἔγειρε ὁ καθεύδων
καὶ ἀνάστα ἐκ τῶν νεκρῶν
καὶ ἐπιφαύσει σοι ὁ Χριστός

To start with the obvious, there is a parallel between vv. 3–4 in the use of the same conjunctions: *πορνεία* … **καὶ** *ἀκαθαρσία* … **ἢ** *πλεονεξία* (v. 3a) and *αἰσχρότης* **καὶ** *μωρολογία* **ἢ** *εὐτραπελία* (v. 4a). The parallel between v. 3 and v. 5 is equally obvious by repetition of related terms in the same sequence: *πορνεία* … *ἀκαθαρσία* … *πλεονεξία* (v. 3a) and *πόρνος* … *ἀκάθαρτος* … *πλεονέκτης* (v. 5b). From that point the unity of this text arises from the exhortation themes, cemented by a loose repetition of words such as "darkness" (vv. 8, 11), "light" (vv. 8–9, 13), and "become clear" (*φανερόω*; vv. 13–14).

The larger contours of this text present certain difficulties and have been divided differently. For example, both Codex Vaticanus (B) and Codex Alexandrinus (A) divide the text into two parts at 5:3–5 and 5:6–14 (also NRSV and Lincoln, 316). The NIV keeps vv. 5–6 together with paragraphs of 5:3–7 and 5:8–14 (also Gnilka, 241–42), while the ESV keeps 5:3–14 together as one paragraph (also O'Brien, 357; Schnackenburg, 215).[3]

There is merit to all these divisions of the text. The warning of v. 6 clearly seems to transition out of the presentation of the evils of the world (hence, vv. 3–5/6–14).[4] But *ταῦτα* in the phrase *διὰ ταῦτα* ("because of these things"; v. 6b) refers back to the evils of vv. 3–5 and ties v. 6 in with

3. Codex Sinaiticus (א) divides each statement of vv. 3–6 separately, then takes vv. 7–10 as one unit.

4. Verses 3–5 are each marked with three nouns expressing worldly evils.

those earlier verses. Next, it is very tempting to read v. 7 as finishing off v. 6 ("Do not let anyone deceive you. … Therefore do not join them") and the last colon* of that previous period, but v. 7 is set apart from what precedes by οὖν and is essentially restated in v. 11 ("Therefore do not join them. … And do not join with them in their fruitless works"), thereby connecting it with vv. 8–14.

The best solution seems to be to treat the one colon* v. 7 as a central hinge for the whole passage of vv. 3–14. The passage ties into v. 7 and revolves around it at the same time. It states the central exhortation not to share in the sinful practices of the evildoers of this world. Believers live in the world but cannot be of it.

Outline

- XII. The Saints and the Sinful World (5:3–14)
  - A. The sinful world's practices (5:3–5)
  - B. Exhortation to resist enticements of the world (5:6)
  - C. Central exhortation (5:7)
  - D. Walk wisely in the light and bear its fruit (5:8–14)

Original Text

3 Πορνεία δὲ καὶ ἀκαθαρσία πᾶσα ἢ πλεονεξία μηδὲ ὀνομαζέσθω ἐν ὑμῖν, καθὼς
πρέπει ἁγίοις, **4** καὶ αἰσχρότης καὶ μωρολογία ἢ εὐτραπελία, ἃ οὐκ ἀνῆκεν, ἀλλὰ
μᾶλλον εὐχαριστία. **5** τοῦτο γὰρ ἴστε γινώσκοντες, ὅτι πᾶς πόρνος ἢ ἀκάθαρτος
ἢ πλεονέκτης, ὅ[a] ἐστιν εἰδωλολάτρης, οὐκ ἔχει κληρονομίαν ἐν τῇ βασιλείᾳ [b]τοῦ
Χριστοῦ καὶ θεοῦ. **6** Μηδεὶς ὑμᾶς ἀπατάτω κενοῖς λόγοις· διὰ ταῦτα γὰρ ἔρχεται ἡ ὀργὴ τοῦ θεοῦ ἐπὶ τοὺς υἱοὺς τῆς ἀπειθείας. **7** μὴ οὖν γίνεσθε συμμέτοχοι
αὐτῶν· **8** ἦτε γάρ ποτε σκότος, νῦν δὲ φῶς ἐν κυρίῳ· ὡς τέκνα φωτὸς περιπατεῖτε **9**—ὁ γὰρ καρπὸς τοῦ φωτὸς[c] ἐν πάσῃ ἀγαθωσύνῃ καὶ δικαιοσύνῃ καὶ ἀληθείᾳ— **10** δοκιμάζοντες τί ἐστιν εὐάρεστον τῷ κυρίῳ, **11** καὶ μὴ συγκοινωνεῖτε
τοῖς ἔργοις τοῖς ἀκάρποις τοῦ σκότους, μᾶλλον δὲ καὶ ἐλέγχετε.[d] **12** τὰ γὰρ κρυφῇ[e] γινόμενα[f] ὑπ' αὐτῶν αἰσχρόν ἐστιν καὶ λέγειν, **13** τὰ δὲ πάντα ἐλεγχόμενα
ὑπὸ τοῦ φωτὸς φανεροῦται, **14** πᾶν γὰρ τὸ φανερούμενον φῶς ἐστιν. διὸ λέγει·
ἔγειρε, ὁ καθεύδων, καὶ ἀνάστα ἐκ τῶν νεκρῶν, καὶ ἐπιφαύσει[g] σοι ὁ Χριστός.

Textual Notes

5.a. The neuter relative pronoun in the phrase ὅ ἐστιν ("that is" or "that is to say") is strongly supported by a host of early witnesses (e.g., P46, ℵ, B, F, G, Ψ, 33, 81, 256, 424c, 1175, 1319, and 1739; see 6:17 for the same idiom). As Metzger notes, "overly punctilious scribes" in A, D, K, L, P, and M changed the text to the masculine pronoun ὅς to agree with the preceding masculine noun.[5]

5.b. P46, 1245, and 2147 do not have τοῦ Χριστοῦ ("of Christ") in the phrase "in the kingdom of Christ and of God" in v. 5d (which would have been abbreviated as: ΤΟΥ ΧΡΥ ΚΑΙ ΘΥ; cf. 3:19). The phrase "kingdom of God" is, of course, far more familiar from the Gospels, and the scribe probably unwittingly left off "of Christ" for that reason. A few other singular readings such as "of (the) Son of God" (υἱοῦ τοῦ θεοῦ) in 1836 or "of the Christ of God" (Χριστοῦ τοῦ θεοῦ) in 1739* attempt to make the phrase more familiar also.

5:9.c. The reading ὁ γὰρ καρπὸς τοῦ φωτὸς ("for the fruit of the light") is strongly attested by early and diverse witnesses such as P49, ℵ, A, B, D*, 33, 81, 1739*, and Latin, Syriac and other early translations. The phrase was changed to "fruit of the Spirit" (ΚΑΡΠΟΣ ΤΟΥ ΠΝΣ [abbreviating πνεύματος]) in P46, Dc, K, Ψ, 88, 614, and 1739mg, as found in Gal 5:22. The variant is not likely original.

11–12.d–f. P46 has some spelling variations here that show regional pronunciation variations and the flexibility of life before Webster; e.g., ελλεγχετε for ἐλέγχετε (v. 11c), κρυβη for κρυφῇ, and γεινομενα for γινόμενα (a very common spelling in many places, including the Ephesian inscriptions; v. 12a).

14.g. Some Western witnesses (D*, b, and some fathers) have ἐπιψαύσεις ("you will lightly touch") for ἐπιφαύσει ("the Messiah will *shine upon* you"). Metzger explains, "Apparently the readings arose from the legend that the cross on which Jesus was crucified was erected over the burial place of Adam, who was raised from the dead by the touch of the Savior's blood."[6]

---

5. Bruce M. Metzger, *A Textual Commentary on the Greek New Testament*, 2nd ed. (New York: United Bible Societies, 1994), 539.
6. Ibid., 540.

Translation

3 There must not even be a hint[7] of sexual immorality and any sort of impurity or avarice among you, as is fitting for saints, **4** as well as obscene and foolish talk or base jesting, which practices are not proper,[8] but instead expressions of thanks.[9] **5** For you know this full well,[10] that any sexually immoral or impure or avaricious person—that is to say,[11] an idolater—does not have an inheritance in the kingdom of Christ and of God.[12] **6** Do not let anyone deceive you with empty words; for it is because of these things that the wrath of God is coming upon the sons of disobedience. **7** So then do not join them in these things,[13] **8** for you were formerly darkness, but now you are light in the Lord. Walk as children of the light **9**—for the fruit of light is found in[14] all goodness and righteousness and truth— **10** and discern[15] what is pleasing to the Lord. **11** And do not join with them in

---

7. Cf. NIV. Or "let it not even be mentioned" for μηδὲ ὀνομαζέσθω (cf. BDAG, 714; NRSV).

8. The impf. ἀνῆκεν ("are not proper," from ἀνήκω) expresses present obligation; cf. E. Burton, *Syntax of the Moods and Tenses in New Testament Greek* (Edinburgh: T&T Clark, 1898), §32; BDF §358 (2); BDAG, 78–79. The sg. verb is used with a neuter pl. subject (ἅ) in accordance with the common rule of Greek known by an example: τὰ ζῷα τρέχει ("the animals run"; BDF §133).

9. Rendering sg. εὐχαριστία, since context warrants seeing this as a positive practice believers are to substitute for inappropriate use of language; cf. BDAG, 416.

10. See comment for taking the phrase ἴστε γινώσκοντες ("you know this full well") as representing a Semitic-inspired emphatic construction.

11. For the formulaic phrase ὅ ἐστιν ("that is to say," also in 6:17) see BDF §132 (2); cf. Schnackenburg, 219. The other way to take the relative pronoun is as a reference to the action of the "avaricious person" on analogy with ὃ γὰρ ἀπέθανεν ... ὃ δὲ ζῇ, "For *that death* which he died ... and *that life* which he lives" (Rom 6:10). But the overall meaning that it is the avaricious person who is the idolater is unchanged.

12. Some versions omit the second prep. here ("of Christ and God"; NASB, ESV, NIV in footnote; cf. KJV, NIV, NRSV). This revolves around an attempt to convey in English the idea that the two nouns refer to one person (Granville Sharp's canon), which is discussed in the commentary.

13. For μὴ ... γίνεσθε συμμέτοχοι αὐτῶν with "in these things" supplied from context; see comment.

14. As ESV and NRSV. The verb is elided in Greek and must be supplied; cf. "consists in" (NASB; NIV).

15. The ptc. δοκιμάζοντες may convey the result of the idea from v. 8: "but now you are light in the Lord. Walk as children of the light ... *so that [in consequence]* you may discern." My rendering, however, takes the ptc. as parallel here with an

their fruitless deeds of darkness, but rather expose them.[16] **12** For the things performed[17] by them in secret are shameful even to mention,[18] **13** whereas everything that is exposed[19] by the light comes into plain view, **14** for everything brought into view[20] is light. Therefore it says, "Arise,[21] O sleeper,[22] and rise up from the dead, and the Messiah will shine on you."

Commentary

5:3 *Πορνεία δὲ καὶ ἀκαθαρσία πᾶσα ἢ πλεονεξία μηδὲ ὀνομαζέσθω ἐν ὑμῖν, καθὼς πρέπει ἁγίοις*, "There must not even be a hint of sexual immorality and any sort of impurity or avarice among you, as is fitting for saints." As discussed above, places where Paul or other NT authors list vices for Christians to avoid or virtues for them to embody are seen by various scholars as carried over from contemporary lists especially popular with Stoic authors.[23] What is remarkable about v. 3, though, is how general it is. Paul does not engage in a very long list here, and his terms carry broad meanings.

---

impv. and so functions as another impv.; see "Excursus: Parallel Participles" below. The NIV rendering ("and find out what pleases") agrees.

16. Cf. BDAG, 315, "the darkness-light theme suggests exposure, with implication of censure"; cf. 5:13; John 3:20.

17. For substantive *τὰ γινόμενα*. See BDAG, 197 (meaning 2a), for *γίνομαι* as "perform" something (e.g., Luke 13:17). The idea is that they are *producing* fruitless deeds of darkness (v. 10) in contrast with "the fruit of light" (v. 11; cf. LSJ, 349, meaning 2).

18. For *καὶ λέγειν* as NIV, NRSV, while NASB and ESV have "speak of." The inf. *λέγειν* is epexegetic with *αἰσχρόν* and therefore explains what is shameful; cf. Burton, *Moods*, §§376–79, 386; Herbert Wier Smyth, *Greek Grammar*, rev. Gordon M. Messing (Cambridge, MA: Harvard University Press, 1956; original ed., 1920), §§1987, 2001–7; BDF §§392–94.

19. See note and comment on *ἐλέγχετε* in v. 11.

20. For *πᾶν τὸ φανερούμενον*, which connects to *φανεροῦται* in v. 13, rendered "comes into plain view"; cf. BDAG, 1048, "become visible" or "known."

21. *Ἔγειρω* can refer to awakening from sleep, hence the English versions have "wake up" or "awake" here. Cf. BDAG, 272 (meaning 13), and the idea of getting up from sleep or reclining. The connection with Christ's resurrection from the dead (e.g., 1:20) is obvious.

22. The nominative, articular ptc. (*ὁ καθεύδων*) is used with a voc. meaning; BDF §147.

23. See the introduction to 4:25–5:2 in particular for brief discussion and bibliography; cf. Lincoln, 318.

"Sexual immorality" (πορνεία) is a flexible term embodying a whole host of acts: adultery (Exod 20:14), prostitution, fornication, etc. (BDAG, 854). "Impurity" or "filth" (ἀκαθαρσία) is made even broader with the qualifier "any sort of" (πᾶσα) and refers to any kind of "vileness" or "filth," though sexual sins are also in its range of meaning (cf. Gal 5:19; BDAG, 34).[24] And these are topped by a sin that grips one's mind and heart: "avarice" or "covetousness" (πλεονεξία; see Exod 20:17; BDAG, 824; and v. 5).[25]

Paul is not being exhaustive with his list of sins in v. 3 but illustrative of deep-rooted sins that characterize any group of people in this fallen world. Yet the "saints" (see on 1:1) are not to be just any group of people, for they were chosen out of the world "to be holy and blameless" (1:4; 5:27). "Flee from sexual immorality. Every other sin a person commits is outside the body, but the sexually immoral person sins against his own body. Or do you not know that your body is a temple of the Holy Spirit within you, whom you have from God?" (1 Cor 6:18–19; cf. Gal 5:19; Col 3:5). Hence, what is "fitting" for the saints is that such sins as Paul mentions must not even be "hinted at" with them.[26]

5:4 *καὶ αἰσχρότης καὶ μωρολογία ἢ εὐτραπελία, ἃ οὐκ ἀνῆκεν, ἀλλὰ μᾶλλον εὐχαριστία*, "as well as obscene and foolish talk or base jesting, which practices are not proper, but instead expressions of thanks." The three terms αἰσχρότης ("obscene talk" or "obscenity"), μωρολογία ("foolish talk"), and εὐτραπελία ("base jesting") are found only here in the NT.[27] Combined with v. 3, Paul lists examples of "deeds," "thoughts," and now "words" to

---

24. See discussion on 4:19 above, where we find πᾶσα modifying ἀκαθαρσία along with πλεονεξία ("avarice") in the phrase εἰς ἐργασίαν ἀκαθαρσίας πάσης ἐν πλεονεξίᾳ, "greedy to practice every kind of impurity"; cf. BDAG, 782–84 (meaning 5).

25. Cf. Dio Chrysostom, "On Covetousness" [περὶ πλεονεξίας] (*Or.* 17).

26. See translation note for ὀνομάζω for the rendering "mention" here. This verb appears with other meanings in 1:21 and 3:15. A line from Psa 16 similarly speaks of avoiding even mention of idolaters in the covenant community: "As for the saints in the land, they are the excellent ones, in whom is all my delight. The sorrows of those who run after another god shall multiply; their drink offerings of blood I will not pour out *or take their names on my lips*" (Psa 16:3–4; emphasis added).

27. The abstract term αἰσχρότης, "obscenity," stands for concrete αἰσχρολογία, "obscene speech" (Col 3:8), according to BDAG, 29. Cf. *Did.* 3.3, which says that using "base words" (αἰσχρολόγος; along with lust and haughtiness) leads to sexual immorality (πορνεία).

cover the ethical illustrations the saints are to avoid.[28] Words come from and reveal the heart (Matt 12:34; 15:18), and a foolish heart is the wellspring of "evil madness" (Eccl 10:13), while the tongue, when unbridled, may lead to a firestorm of evils (Jas 3:1–12).

Furthermore, the types of speech Paul mentions here, he says, are "not proper" or "fitting."[29] New Testament scholars are rightly becoming sensitive to ancient ideas of societal honor and shame standing behind many NT texts. So also here we see that Paul is invoking the shamefulness of these various kinds of "foul language" (cf. 4:29 and Col 3:8) as a main reason for them to be avoided. This comes out particularly in v. 12, where such actions are to be "exposed."[30]

The two terms εὐτραπελία ... εὐχαριστία ("base jesting ... thanksgiving") are roughly homophones and may have been intentionally set up to be contrasted as the last word of the first and of the third cola* of v. 4.[31] Instead of "base jesting" or "coarse wittiness," believers are to use their speech for edification (cf. 4:29).[32] Some scholars see this contrast as leading to an austere, joyless form of Christianity. It should instead point to the kind of honor and privilege granted to the church as the place where God is pleased to dwell on earth as the new, holy temple (above on 2:21–22):

> The author of Ephesians ... and his readers probably knew, along with Sirach 23:12–15 and a host of pagan and Greek moralists, that such talk might lower them in the eyes of others. But

---

28. See "Application and Devotional Implications" below for Christian ethics covering "thought, word, and deed."
29. For ἀνῆκω, which can refer either to what is socially proper or to what is morally one's duty; BDAG, 78–79 (meaning 2); cf. Col 3:18; Phlm 8.
30. See Peter W. Gosnell, "Honor and Shame Rhetoric in Ephesians," *BBR* 16 (2006): 105–28; esp. 123–24. Cf. the conspicuous example of this feature at Ephesus in the inscription of a letter from Antoninus Pius castigating the city for not honoring one of their local grandees adequately (*IvE* 1491) already mentioned under 2:9 above.
31. The meter of the two words is similar but not identical: εὐτραπελία is ¯ ˘ ˘ ˘ ˘ and εὐχαριστία is ¯ ˘ ¯ ˘ ˘. Metrical exactness would matter to a professional rhetor.
32. The term εὐτραπελία can have a positive meaning of "wittiness," but a negative meaning is obvious here and has a few antecedents in antiquity, particularly related to ribald speech; BDAG, 414; LSJ, 735. For a full study see Jeremy F. Hultin, *The Ethics of Obscene Speech in Early Christianity and Its Environment*, SNT 128 (Leiden: Brill, 2008), who renders εὐτραπελία as "facetiousness." Cf. 1QS 10.21–23.

> Ephesians does not give these reasons any more than Leviticus explains why a priest with a physical defect cannot enter the sanctuary. ... Foul language (αἰσχρότης, μωρολογία) and even light language (εὐτραπελία) were inconsistent with the believers' holiness, and were inappropriate in God's holy presence.[33]

Believers are to dedicate themselves to thanksgiving, as a new, royal order of priesthood (cf. 5:20; Rom 12:1–2; Heb 13:15; 1 Pet 2:9).

5:5 τοῦτο γὰρ ἴστε γινώσκοντες, ὅτι πᾶς πόρνος ἢ ἀκάθαρτος ἢ πλεονέκτης, ὅ ἐστιν εἰδωλολάτρης, "For you know this full well, that any sexually immoral or impure or avaricious person—that is to say, an idolater." The connection between this verse and v. 3 has already been pointed out in the introduction above. The construction ἴστε γινώσκοντες would have represented an unusual turn of phrase to an Ephesian Greek who had no exposure to the Septuagint. The background is the Hebrew infinitive absolute construction, which is often conveyed by a cognate participle, as here in v. 5 (BDF §422). Normally the verbs used are the same, although a few instances of οἶδα and γινώσκω can be found together like this in the LXX.[34] The lead verb ἴστε (from οἶδα) can be either imperative (cf. Jas 1:19) or indicative, as I prefer (cf. Heb 12:17).[35] In the end, it does not make a significant difference because an indicative statement may have the effect of informing someone of what they *should* know. Obviously, it is imperative that everyone who professes Christ must know the subject matter of v. 5, yet regenerate saints who are not callous (4:19) do know: "By appealing to their own conscience, he intimates that there was nothing doubtful in this" (Calvin, 198).

---

33. Hultin, *Ethics*, 205. The Sirach reference says in part: "There is an utterance which is comparable to death; may it never be found in the inheritance of Jacob! For all these errors will be far from the godly, and they will not wallow in sins. Do not accustom your mouth to lewd vulgarity, for it involves sinful speech. ... A man accustomed to use insulting words will never become disciplined all his days" (RSV).

34. I found eight instances with only γινώσκω and four with a mixture of γινώσκω and οἶδα. For example, in one passage of 1 Samuel (1 Sam 20:3, 9), David says to Jonathan, "Your father knows full well" (γινώσκων οἶδεν), while Jonathan responds a little later, "If I had truly known ..." (ἐὰν γινώσκων γνῶ).

35. As an impv. only NRSV, while most modern English versions take the form as indic. (e.g., "For you may be sure of this"; ESV); cf. BDF §§99 (2), 353 (6); Hoehner, 659; Lincoln, 316.

The singular relative pronoun ὅ refers back only to the avaricious person in particular (πλεονέκτης; cf. 4:19; 5:3) rather than to all three preceding nouns. This is expressed explicitly in Col 3:5.[36] Compare the plural ἅ earlier in v. 4, which refers to the three nouns preceding it. "Avarice" refers to a lust for possessions in general, while "covetousness," forbidden in the tenth commandment (Exod 20:17), is lust for the possessions of others. Either manifestation of this mind-set involves a person placing ultimate allegiance in the acquisition of goods to such an extent that it becomes idolatry, which then often leads to other grave sins (e.g., 1 Kgs 21:1–19; cf. Matt 6:24; Luke 16:13; 1 Tim 6:10; Philo, *Spec. Laws* 1.23–27).

[πᾶς πόρνος ἢ ἀκάθαρτος ἢ πλεονέκτης ...] οὐκ ἔχει κληρονομίαν ἐν τῇ βασιλείᾳ τοῦ Χριστοῦ καὶ θεοῦ, "[any sexually immoral or impure or avaricious person ...] does not have an inheritance in the kingdom of Christ and of God."[37] This colon* brings out two main questions. Does this statement relate to true believers? Can a genuine believer in Christ thus lose his or her salvation and be disinherited from the kingdom? Second, what kingdom is this, and when and where is it constituted?[38]

To answer the second question first, Paul speaks clearly of Christ ruling now from the right hand of God (see on vv. 1:20–22; Rom 8:34; 1 Cor 15:24–27; Col 3:1; etc.), into whose redemptive kingdom believers have already been placed as citizens (2:6, 19; Col 1:13–14; Phil 3:20; cf. Matt 5:3, 7; Luke 12:32), although the messianic kingdom will only be consummated at Christ's second coming, when death is destroyed forever (1 Cor 15:20–24; 2 Tim 4:1). The kingdom of God proper for Paul is an

---

36. ... τὴν πλεονεξίαν, ἥτις ἐστὶν εἰδωλολατρία, "avarice, which is idolatry."

37. See esp. parallels in 1 Cor 6:10 and Gal 5:21. The construction πᾶς ... οὐκ ἔχει is a Semitic-inspired form of universal negation and is the equivalent of saying, "None of these people has ..."; BDF §302.

38. A third issue is how do the two gens. τοῦ Χριστοῦ καὶ θεοῦ ("of Christ [or, 'of the Messiah'] and of God") interrelate? Is this one person with two titles (Granville Sharp's canon), and hence is Christ called God here? (so Hodge, 286–87). While the incarnate Son's divine identity is a biblical notion, and Sharp's principle of article usage is helpful in several places, it does not seem to be as clearly intended here as elsewhere, since "kingdom of God" is itself a common phrase and Paul seems more interested in establishing that the kingdom belongs to both the Messiah and to God the Father; see esp. Daniel B. Wallace, *Granville Sharp's Canon and Its Kin: Semantics and Significance*, SBG 14 (New York: Peter Lang, 2009), 236–37; Hoehner, 661–62.

eternal realm that—although the elect hold its citizenship rights now—can only be entered through resurrection incorruptibility (1 Cor 15:50; 1 Thess 2:12), even though believers live now in light of its righteousness (Matt 6:33; Rom 14:17; 1 Cor 6:9–10; Gal 5:21; 2 Tim 4:18).[39] In summary, the current, inaugurated kingdom reality that believers experience in this age (over which Christ now rules) centers on a covenantally administered citizenship entitlement to the eternal kingdom that is to be consummated in the age to come (see esp. on 1:13–14, 20–22; 2:12; 3:6; and on 5:6 below).[40] Believers now have an "inheritance" of that eternal kingdom.

This latter is the key to answering the first question. The inheritance of the kingdom is covenantally administered to those who profess faith in Christ. The elect profess this faith because they have been sealed by the Holy Spirit as heirs for redemption and eternal life (see on 1:3–4, 13–14; 2:1–10; 3:6; 4:30). And these elect are not left in doubt about their place in this inheritance as beloved children through the internal testimony of the Holy Spirit, who has sealed them for this inheritance (1:13–14 again; Rom 8:16–17; 1 Pet 1:3–9).

Yet this side of the consummated new creation, the new covenant is administered more broadly than only to the elect because it is administered today to those who *profess* faith in Christ. Ministers who baptize a person can never know whether that person is elect, only that he or she makes a credible profession of faith in Christ.[41] Paul makes this distinction

---

39. Some interpreters believe that the kingdom of God refers to a future, theocratic reign of Christ on earth before the introduction of the eternal state in the new heavens and new earth. This is the "premillennial" view; cf. Stanley N. Gundry, ed., *Three Views of the Millennium and Beyond* (Grand Rapids: Zondervan, 1999); cf. Herman N. Ridderbos, *The Coming of the Kingdom* (Philipsburg, NJ: P&R, 1962); Kim Riddlebarger, *A Case for Amillennialism: Understanding the End Times* (Grand Rapids: Baker, 2003), 100–113.

40. Biblical covenants are legal, constitutional instruments for administering the kingdom of God. Hence kingdom and covenant are twin, foundational pillars of all of Scripture; cf. Meredith G. Kline, *Kingdom Prologue* (Overland Park, KS: Two Age, 2000), 4.

41. In the language of Reformed theology, baptism of a convert is on the basis of a "credible profession of faith." As a result, from very early days, a distinction has been made between the *administration* of the new covenant and its *substance*. The former is conveyed to all who are baptized, while the substance (*duplex beneficium,* the "twin benefit" of justification and sanctification) is granted only to the elect; see R. Scott Clark, *Caspar Olevian and the Substance of the Covenant: The*

in many places but never more clearly than in 1 Cor 5:1–13, where he is surprised that his audience did not make a distinction between those "outside" and the "one who bears the name of 'brother'" who openly practices sin (1 Cor 5:10–11, including sexual immorality, avarice, and idolatry, as also in Eph 5:5). Such a one is "from us" but not "of us" (cf. 1 John 2:19). Such a one is like Esau, who had a covenantal entitlement but sold it for pottage (Gen 25:29–34; see esp. Heb 12:15–17). Such a one is a "goat" to be sifted out of the messianic kingdom at the end of this age, for Christ never knew them (Matt 7:21–23; 25:31–46), whereas Christ says to his true people that they "inherit the kingdom prepared for you from the foundation of the world" (Matt 25:34). A person's deeds reveal the genuineness of this profession of faith: whether it be true or false (e.g., 2:10; Matt 12:33; Rom 2:6; Jas 2:18; 1 John 3:4–10), even if sanctification in this life is but "a small beginning" and discernment in these matters is painfully difficult.[42]

That being said, however, the work of the Holy Spirit in the lives of believers and in the life of the church of the new-covenant era is powerful, extending to all God's people (e.g., Jer 31:33–34; Heb 8:8–12; 2 Cor 3:1–6). Believers must presume the best of brothers and sisters in the church and work for their growth in grace (as enjoined frequently in Eph 4–5), expecting that this dire situation of apostasy will only occur in extreme cases after all attempts to reclaim wandering members is expended (e.g., Jas 5:20), and should this fail in the short term there should be good hope and prayers for restoration (e.g., 1 John 5:16; cf. 1 Tim 1:20). This was Paul's own attitude even for a church as confused and problem filled as that in Corinth:

> Do you not know that the unrighteous will not inherit the kingdom of God? Do not be deceived: neither the sexually immoral, nor idolaters, nor adulterers, nor men who practice homosexuality, nor thieves, nor the greedy, nor drunkards, nor revilers,

---

Double Benefit of Christ, Reformed Historical-Theological Studies (Edinburgh: Rutherford House, 2005; repr., Reformed Heritage, 2008). Olevianus was a student of Calvin and an important pioneer of modern Reformed theology.

42. This is obviously a very complex issue that deserves a fuller discussion than can be given here. The quoted words are from the Heidelberg Catechism (114), which reads: "Q. *But can those converted to God obey these commandments perfectly?* A. No. In this life even the holiest have only a small beginning of this obedience. Nevertheless, with all seriousness of purpose, they do begin to live according to all, not only some, of God's commandments."

> nor swindlers will inherit the kingdom of God. And such were some of you. *But you were washed, you were sanctified, you were justified in the name of the Lord Jesus Christ and by the Spirit of our God.* (1 Cor 6:9–11; emphasis added)

5:6 Μηδεὶς ὑμᾶς ἀπατάτω κενοῖς λόγοις· διὰ ταῦτα γὰρ ἔρχεται ἡ ὀργὴ τοῦ θεοῦ ἐπὶ τοὺς υἱοὺς τῆς ἀπειθείας, "Do not let anyone deceive you with empty words; for it is because of these things that the wrath of God is coming upon the sons of disobedience." Because the eschatological kingdom is inaugurated but not consummated, God's people must alertly live in a time when false teaching attempts to undermine the truth, even biblical teachings that are well known and clear (i.e., "you know this full well," v. 5a; cf. 4:14). Christians are at war over truths such as these (6:10–13) and need to keep watch lest they be led astray (e.g., Matt 24:4–5, 11, 24) or taken captive (Col 2:8; cf. 1 Cor 3:18; Gal 6:7; 1 John 3:7). This battle becomes particularly acute over the "empty words" that those who profess Christ are free to lead evil, licentious lives without consequences (e.g., 1 Cor 5:1–2, 6; 2 Tim 3:1–9; 2 Pet 2:1–3; Rev 2:14, 20).[43] Such deceit (ἀπατάτω) is not theoretical for the saints awaiting the day of redemption (4:30), who must still battle until then the "deceitful desires" (4:22; αἱ ἐπιθυμίαι τῆς **ἀπάτης**) deeply embedded in their old existence and surrounding them in the world (2:3; cf. Rom 7:23; Gal 5:17; 1 Pet 1:14).

The expression διὰ τοῦτο with the singular pronoun is a fairly common phrase that brings out an inference or makes a conclusion: "because of this, therefore" (so 1:15; 5:17; 6:13). But διὰ ταῦτα with the plural pronoun is unique to this verse in the NT; the plural ταῦτα summarizes the preceding practices from vv. 3–6a (impurity, avarice, obscene talk, false teaching, etc.) as the sorts of things that invoke God's wrath, as is also analogously stated in Col 3:6.[44]

---

43. "*Empty words* are words that are for a moment attractive but in no way are proved by deeds. They become a flimsy deceit" (Chrysostom, *ACCS*, 186).

44. Δι' ἃ ἔρχεται ἡ ὀργὴ τοῦ θεοῦ, "on account of *which things* the wrath of God is coming." Cf. BDAG, 741, meaning 1bα. See Luke 8:8; 11:27; 24:26; John 5:34; 15:11; 21:24 for ταῦτα referencing a number of preceding statements and events in the preceding context, as in Eph 5:6.

The present indicative ἔρχεται ("the wrath of God *is coming*") is used "vividly" for the future (E. Burton, *Syntax of the Moods and Tenses in New Testament Greek* [Edinburgh: T&T Clark, 1898], §§15–16). I prefer to call this use an "impending" present, since in this case and in several other passages where this form is used it conveys an ominous note. See, for example, ὅτι **ἔρχεται** ὅτι **ἔρχεται** κρῖναι τὴν γῆν, "For he is coming, he is surely coming to judge the earth" (LXX Psa 95:13 [96:13]); cf. Matt 24:42, 44; Luke 12:40; 1 John 2:18; Rev 1:7; 2:5, 16; 3:11; 16:15; 22:7, 12.

By mentioning the wrath of God here in v. 6 as future (cf. Rom 1:18; 1 Thess 2:16), Paul corroborates the interpretation of v. 5 above (cf. Col 3:6). The kingdom of Christ and of God in its consummated form follows the final judgment. The elect will be delivered from divine, eschatological wrath (e.g., Rom 5:10; 1 Thess 1:10; 5:9) because there is no condemnation for those who are in Christ by grace through faith alone (e.g., Eph 2:8–9; Rom 8:1). In fact, when the final judgment occurs, true believers will already be resurrected in a consummation of the transformation already begun in them (e.g., 1:13–14; 4:30). The objects of wrath at that judgment are the "sons of disobedience" (cf. 2:2), which is a Hebrew-inspired phrase referring to unrepentant apostates (cf. Rev 2:21–23). They profess Christ but live in disobedient sin and prove themselves to be subjects of the "the ruler of the realm of the air, the spirit who is now at work in the sons of disobedience" (2:2; cf. John 8:44; 1 John 3:10) like Judas, "the son of destruction" (John 17:12). This warning comes to the whole "mixed" covenant community (see above on v. 5), although one should expect these cases to be rare in Christ's body, which is to work tirelessly (Heb 3:13) for edification of all (e.g., 4:12, 16, 29; cf. Col 1:28).

5:7 μὴ οὖν γίνεσθε συμμέτοχοι αὐτῶν, "So then do not join them in these things" (cf. v. 11). This brief colon* belongs both with vv. 3–6 and with vv. 8–14; it acts as a transition between them and forms the thematic center of the passage. It is introduced with οὖν ("so then," "therefore") as an inference or practical conclusion one should draw from the preceding warnings of divine wrath (BDAG, 736–37, meaning 1). Paul had exposed the heinous character of sin and idolatry and its consequences and now admonishes the saints to turn aside from "fruitless deeds of darkness" (v. 11) and to bring forth fruit as "children of the light" (v. 8).

To be συμμέτοχοι with other people means to have intimate communion and/or share in some possession (Eph 3:6, the promise), practices, or relations with them.[45] The idea here is sharing in their sinful practices, anticipating συγκοινωνεῖτε in v. 11; for a vivid example of which see Prov 1:10–14. Compare "be partners with them" (NIV) or "associate with them" (ESV; NRSV is similar), which has the possibility of misunderstanding, since it may be taken to mean that one cannot have, for example, business relations with a nonbeliever. For that to be true, one would, as Paul says elsewhere, have to leave the world (1 Cor 5:9–10).

5:8 ἦτε γάρ ποτε σκότος, νῦν δὲ φῶς ἐν κυρίῳ· ὡς τέκνα φωτὸς περιπατεῖτε, "for you were formerly darkness, but now you are light in the Lord. Walk as children of the light." Paul has already asked the Gentile Ephesians to think back to what they were "formerly" (2:2–3, 11, 13; cf. Rom 11:30; Col 1:21; 3:7; Titus 3:3). Now he does so again as he develops why it is that they must not join with their nonbelieving, Gentile neighbors in the "fruitless deeds of darkness" (v. 11). (Ephesians 4:17 has taught his audience that they are no longer "Gentiles," as it were, but saints.)

The phrase "now you are light in the Lord" is key. The image of light and darkness as metaphors for the holiness of God and for his allied people over against the denizens and the evils of this world is common in the Bible and in various ancient Jewish documents (e.g., Isa 2:6; 5:20; 58:8; Matt 6:23; Luke 16:8; John 3:19; 12:35–36; Acts 26:18; 1 John 1:5; 2:8).[46] Paul also uses this image elsewhere when telling the church to avoid being "unequally yoked together with unbelievers" in 2 Cor 6:14 because "what fellowship has light with darkness?"

Yet in Ephesians 5:8 Paul does not just say that the saints dwell in the light (Col 1:12) as "sons of light" (1 Thess 5:5) who are to pick up

45. The word συμμέτοχος is used only in 3:6 and 5:7 in the NT; BDAG, 958; BDF §182. Origen does not recall seeing the compound with the σύν prefix before (Origen and Jerome, 217; [Origen's notes on 3:6 are not extant]). As mentioned above on 2:5, LSJ lists forty pages of συν- prefixed words alone (LSJ, 1690–1730), which does not include the words with the phonetic shift of συγ-, συλ-, or συμ-. One could add συν- to virtually any word in Greek. Cf. Carl B. Hoch Jr., "The Significance of the *Syn-* Compounds for Jew-Gentile Relationships in the Body of Christ," *JETS* 25 (1982): 175–83; and Brendan McGrath, " 'SYN' Words in Saint Paul," *CBQ* 14 (1952): 219–26.

46. For extrabiblical Jewish references see above on 3:9 and esp. Lincoln, 326–27.

"light's implements" (Rom 13:12); in v. 8a he says that the saints *are* light (cf. Phil 2:14–16; Matt 5:14–16). The background is the opening verses of Genesis. Those whom God has called out of darkness are now themselves "luminaries" (φωστῆρες; Gen 1:14) because, in the church, the new creation where the light and the darkness are divided from each other (Gen 1:4) has been definitively inaugurated by the Light of the World (John 8:12; 9:5; cf. above on 4:24). The saints do not *become* light by taking up deeds of light. They *are* light in union with Christ ("in the Lord"), experiencing the power of the inaugurated new creation through the Holy Spirit, and are being re created in the image of God for good works (2:10; 4:24) as they await the day of redemption in resurrection (4:30).[47]

As "luminaries," the saints are now to "walk as children of the light."[48] The imperative "walk" signifies the conduct of life (5:2; cf. 2:2, 3 [ἀναστρέφω], 10). Paul is reinforcing the exhortations given so far (esp. 4:25–5:2), but the near context for the "children of light" contrasts with the actions of the "sons of disobedience" (v. 6) and their "fruitless" works (see next verse).

5:9 —*ὁ γὰρ καρπὸς τοῦ φωτὸς ἐν πάσῃ ἀγαθωσύνῃ καὶ δικαιοσύνῃ καὶ ἀληθείᾳ*, "—for the fruit of light is found in all goodness and righteousness and truth." This short verse is normally set apart in the versions either by parentheses or dashes to signify its explanatory meaning.[49] Paul does not go on in the next several verses to elaborate on how exactly the saints are to "walk as children of the light" (v. 8), so this brief addition in v. 9 gives a short declaration of the nature of that "walk."

Paul combines here the metaphors of "light" and "fruit" (καρπός; cf. Rom 7:4; Gal 5:22) before going on in contrast to speak of the "fruitless

47. For ἐν κυρίῳ ("in the Lord") and union with Christ see above on 1:1 and 1:20; cf. Constantine R. Campbell, *Paul and Union with Christ: An Exegetical and Theological Study* (Grand Rapids: Zondervan, 2012); Michael S. Horton, *Covenant and Salvation: Union with Christ* (Louisville: Westminster John Knox, 2007).

48. The pres.-tense impv. περιπατεῖτε ("walk") is default for this verb with its atelic meaning (cf. v. 2) and in this "general" exhortation, meaning for acts that should characterize the audience's lives (περιπατέω occurs 14x in the NT as a pres. impv. with no aors.). There are seven pres. impvs. in Eph 5:3–14 and one aor. (ἀνάστα, "arise" in v. 14). Cf. "Additional Exegetical Comments" above after 4:25–5:2.

49. This meaning as an explanation is communicated by γάρ in Greek; cf. BDAG, 189–90 (meaning 2, "marker of clarification" for "[b]rief, explanatory parenthetical clauses").

(ἀκάρπος) deeds of darkness" in v. 10. Since the majority of people in antiquity worked in agriculture (e.g., Heb 6:7; Jas 5:7), the metaphor of bearing fruit is a common one (e.g., Matt 3:8; Mark 4:7–8; Luke 13:6–9; John 15:2–8; Rom 1:13; Col 1:10).[50]

The "fruit of the light" is given in a general triad, "all goodness and righteousness and truth," which corresponds in contrast to the three sets of three nouns in each of vv. 3–5. The terms in v. 9 are not pure antonyms of the evils in the previous verses, though both "goodness" (ἀγαθωσύνη) and "righteousness" (δικαιοσύνη) may be seen as the rough opposite of "impurity" (ἀκαθαρσία), while the three nouns in v. 4 ("obscene and foolish talk or base jesting") might be seen as counteracted by "truth" (ἀλήθεια).[51] His point is to provide a quick portrait with very broad strokes on what sort of characteristics define the saints' lives. Other parts of his paraenesis in the epistle fill in the details.

5:10 *δοκιμάζοντες τί ἐστιν εὐάρεστον τῷ κυρίῳ*, "and discern what is pleasing to the Lord." This colon* is closely tied in with both v. 9 and v. 11. The tie-in with v. 11 is grammatical in that *καὶ* ("and") creates a parallel of opposites, even though the verb forms in the two verses are not antonyms:

---

50. The rule of thumb is that 80 to 85 percent of the people in antiquity worked directly in food production: farming, fishing, hunting, animal husbandry, and similar activities such as beekeeping (a bee is commonly found as a symbol of the city on Ephesian coins). As mentioned earlier, the Ephesian Artemisium controlled some 77,000 acres of farmlands in the Cayster River valley (up to thirty miles from the city) to support its population (see above on 1:4). This area's main "fruit" (beside cereal grains) would have been grapes for wine production, while soft fruit trees were cultivated in the inland areas of Asia; see below on 5:18. Cf. Helmuth Schneider and Robin Osborne, "Agriculture," in *Brill's New Pauly: Encyclopaedia of the Ancient World* (Boston: Brill, 2008), 1.374–86. For examples from antiquity, the treatises of both Cato the Elder and Varro on agriculture are handily brought together in one Loeb volume (LCL 283), where Varro (1.1.8–9) reports that he knows of more than fifty Greek authors on agriculture, including the poet Menecrates of Ephesus (born ca. 340 BC; cf. *OCD*, 931).

51. Only Paul uses ἀγαθωσύνη ("goodness" or "generosity"; BDAG, 4) in the NT (only in Rom 15:14; Gal 5:22; 2 Thess 1:11), while the other two terms ("righteousness" and "truth") are very common. See the phrase "fruit of righteousness" in Phil 1:11; Jas 3:18. Paula Qualls and John D. W. Watts ("Isaiah in Ephesians," *RevExp* 93 [1996]: 249–59) show connection between these three terms and several passages in Isaiah.

δοκιμάζοντες … καὶ μὴ συγκοινωνεῖτε, "discern … and do not join."[52] In connection with v. 9, this colon* elaborates very briefly on how believers are to know goodness, righteousness, and truth (v. 9). Since the audience had formerly been "darkened in their mind-set" (4:18; cf. 2:1–3) and are now "light" (v. 8), they have discernment into what pleases the Lord, who is infinitely good, righteous, and true. What pleases him are concrete expressions of these three qualities.

Interestingly, NASB ("trying to learn"), ESV ("try to discern"), and NRSV ("try to find out") take δοκιμάζοντες as conveying a conative* meaning, where the event is attempted but not necessarily carried out (BDF §319; Burton, *Moods*, §11; cf. also BDAG, 255–56, meaning 1). This is possible, but it would be more likely if the context warranted that the event was not expected to be accomplished or was impossible to bring about, neither of which seems to be the case here. With "discern," the meaning is to scrutinize something in order to perceive its genuineness or character and has a companion in Romans in a passage with other links to Ephesians:

> So then I strongly urge you, brothers, through the mercies of God to present your bodies as a living sacrifice, holy, pleasing to God (εὐάρεστον τῷ θεῷ), which is your reasonable service (to him). And do not be conformed to this age, but be transformed by the renewal of your mind so that you may discern (εἰς τὸ δοκιμάζειν) what is God's will which is good and pleasing (εὐάρεστον) and perfect. (Rom 12:1–2; my trans.)

Discernment of this type is at the very heart of biblical wisdom as the renewed believer perceives how to please the Lord in the concrete situations of life (cf. Rom 14:18; Phil 4:18; Col 3:20; 1 Thess 2:4) and thereby to follow the dictates of righteousness and love.

5:11 καὶ μὴ συγκοινωνεῖτε τοῖς ἔργοις τοῖς ἀκάρποις τοῦ σκότους, μᾶλλον δὲ καὶ ἐλέγχετε, "And do not join with them in their fruitless deeds of darkness, but rather expose them." As mentioned for the previous verse, the opening καί here links v. 11 with v. 10 as its opposite pair, even though they are not true antonyms: δοκιμάζοντες … καὶ μὴ συγκοινωνεῖτε, "discern … and do not

52. See the translation note for taking δοκιμάζοντες ("discern") as a parallel ptc. and therefore functioning as an impv. alongside συγκοινωνεῖτε ("join").

join." Paul did not spend much time elaborating on what exactly the "fruit of the light" is, as he is more interested here in v. 11 and throughout most of 5:3–14 with "exposing" the "fruitless deeds of darkness" himself. (As also mentioned under v. 8, "fruitless" [ἄκαρπος] contrasts with the "fruit" [καρπός] of the light the saints are to yield.)

The verb συγκοινωνέω refers to any sort of connection one may have with someone (as Rev 18:4; BDAG, 952) or, in this case, with the "deeds" (ἔργα) of darkness, which are ephemeral shadows and waterless mists driven by the winds (Jude 12—another use of ἄκαρπος), which believers are to "cast off" (Rom 13:12). Such fruitless works are the kind Paul has been outlining above in thought, word, and deed. In v. 11 he restates the central concern of the passage (5:3–14) expressed in v. 7, that the saints are to put off their former unlawful behavior and to keep from joining their nonbelieving neighbors in sin.

The term μᾶλλον ("rather" or "instead") here introduces an alternative (BDAG, 613–14) and is combined with the twin conjunctions δὲ καί, which substitute for simple δέ. Earlier Paul had used μᾶλλον with simple δέ: μᾶλλον δὲ κοπιάτω, "but rather let him … labor" (4:28), as well as synonymous: ἀλλὰ μᾶλλον εὐχαριστία, "but instead expressions of thanks" (5:3; the only other uses of μᾶλλον in Ephesians). Why use both δὲ καί here in v. 11? The answer is a simple matter of style to avoid elision, since the next word opens with a vowel (i.e., μᾶλλον δ' ἐλέγχετε), where the force of δέ reinforcing the alternative idea tends to get lost in oral presentation (as also in v. 3; cf. 1 Cor 3:8; 5:8; 1 Tim 5:9; Titus 3:14).[53]

"Reprove not (μὴ ἔλεγχε) evil men lest they hate you; reprove (ἔλεγχε) a wise man and he will love you" (Prov 9:8 LXX; cf. Prov 9:7; 15:12; 19:25). "For everyone who practices evil things hates the light and does not come to the light, so that his deeds may not be exposed (ἵνα μὴ ἐλεγχθῇ τὰ ἔργα αὐτοῦ)" (John 3:20). Paul's exhortation to "expose" (ἐλέγχετε) the deeds

53. Otherwise, one would take καί as heightening the contrast: "but instead *even* expose them." The only other use of δὲ καί together in Ephesians is δὲ καὶ ἀκαθαρσία in v. 3. It should be noted that καί tended to get elided and combined with the word that followed it if that word opened with a vowel ("crasis") in spoken Greek, in which case the phrase would have been pronounced as μᾶλλον δὲ κἐλέγχετε.

of darkness comes with risks, which Christians are obliged to take.[54] This does not mean only avoiding them (the first part of the verse) or becoming a public nuisance, but revealing the "secrets of the heart" (1 Cor 14:24) through gospel proclamation "to exhibit [those deeds of darkness] in their true nature as vile and destructive," otherwise sinners would be left in their ignorance (4:18–19) and their sin would increase (Hodge, 291) and ultimately produce their death (Rom 6:21).[55] This was Paul's own charge from the risen Jesus, who sent him to the Gentiles "to open their eyes, so that they may turn from darkness to light and from the power of Satan to God, that they may receive forgiveness of sins and a place among those who are sanctified by faith in me," namely, "the saints in light" (Acts 26:18 and Col 1:12; cf. esp. Eph 3:6–9 and Phil 2:14–16).

5:12 *τὰ γὰρ κρυφῇ γινόμενα ὑπ' αὐτῶν αἰσχρόν ἐστιν καὶ λέγειν*, "For the things performed by them in secret are shameful even to mention." Since the ascension of Nero as emperor, not all shameful things were done in secret anymore, but some first-century practices were too vile for public notice even in Nero's day (e.g., several episodes in Petronius, *Satyr.*; cf. Tacitus, *Ann.* 13–16). The secretive nature of these actions suggests that they belong to the darkness. Even the pagan Romans were morally suspicious of certain practices of the Dionysian/Bacchic cults because they were "secret rites performed by night" (Livy, 39.8.4 [see further 39.8–18]).[56] Normally "a fool flaunts his folly" (Prov 13:16) in the open, but not these heinous things. Paul does not want to catalog these practices further, or his audience to

54. The verb ἐλέγχω has a number of meanings conveyed by "convict," "correct," "punish," etc., but BDAG notes "the darkness-light theme suggests exposure, with implication of censure" (BDAG, 315). The direct obj. for the verb, "them" (i.e., the deeds of darkness), must be supplied from context, as often in Greek when the meaning is obvious.

55. Cf. Gosnell, "Honor and Shame," 123–24, again for the role of public shame as a deterrent in the ancient Mediterranean world. See Rom 15:14 and 1 Thess 5:12 for similar "admonition" (νουθετέω) in the church; cf. 1 Tim 5:20 and "You shall not hate your brother in your heart, but you shall reason frankly with your neighbor, lest you incur sin because of him" (Lev 19:17).

56. Cf. Reinhold Merkelbach, "Die ephesischen Dionysosmysten vor der Stadt," *ZPE* 36 (1979): 151–56.

delve into them, for they are "shameful even to mention," much less to do (v. 7).[57]

Larry Kreitzer believes that Paul's references to shameful practices here demonstrates a Hierapolitan rather than an Ephesian destination for the epistle.[58] Not many have been persuaded by his evidence, but it is helpful as background color to Ephesians in contemporary ancient religious practices for the goddess Demeter (Cybele). Her cult* was also prominent at Ephesus (see above on 2:12), as evidenced by an inscription summarizing ancestral law (*κεφάλαιον νόμου πατρίου*) for offerings and adornment of the statue of Demeter the Fruit-Bearer (Καρπόφορος), which was lodged in the Ephesian Pryaneion, the equivalent of its city hall (*IvE* 10; cf. *IvE* 213 ["mysteries and sacrifices" to her], 1210, 1228, 1305, 3252).

5:13 *τὰ δὲ πάντα ἐλεγχόμενα ὑπὸ τοῦ φωτὸς φανεροῦται*, "whereas everything that is exposed by the light comes into plain view." This verse develops both vv. 11–12 in how "exposure" of "deeds of darkness" (v. 11) by the "children of the light" (v. 8) brings their true nature into view.[59] This is a general statement of truth that develops the light-darkness metaphor and explains how the church is equipped by being the embassy of the new creation to enlighten the world through the gospel (cf. Matt 5:14–16).

5:14 *πᾶν γὰρ τὸ φανερούμενον φῶς ἐστιν*, "for everything brought into view is light." If the prior emphasis has been on exposure of sinful deeds, the goal is not self-righteous glory of the saints over against the world but to challenge others also (v. 8a) to come into the light through faith in Christ (also John 3:19–21; and see on v. 11 above; cf. O'Brien, 372–74).[60] The mission of the saints is not merely moral improvement of the world's behavior but

---

57. See the translation note for λέγειν as an epexegetic inf.; cf. the same use here: σοὶ δὲ περὶ τῆς ἐκείνου ὀργῆς οὐδὲν ἔχω **λέγειν**, "I have nothing *to say* to you about the anger of that fellow" (Epictetus, *Diatr.* 1.15.5; λέγειν explains οὐδὲν).-

58. Larry J. Kreitzer, " 'Crude Language' and 'Shameful Things Done in Secret' (Ephesians 5.4, 12): Allusions to the Cult of Demeter/Cybele in Hierapolis?" *JSNT* 71 (1998): 51–77.

59. See BDAG, 1048, for φανερόω as "to cause to become visible, *reveal, expose publicly*"; in its pass. forms as φανεροῦται in 5:11 the meaning is intransitive, "become visible," so that it can be viewed or known.

60. Some believe the focus here is on the church (e.g., Schnackenburg, 227) or on lapsed believers, not on the world (e.g., Hoehner, 684–85).

its wholesale transformation through the gospel as the power of the age to come unleashed in new-creation light (6:14–20; cf. 2 Cor 6:6).[61] However, as Paul explains next, it turns out that though believers are themselves φῶς ("light"), it is *reflected* light, as of an unwinking, visible planet. The light comes from "the Messiah" (v. 14e).

διὸ λέγει· ἔγειρε, ὁ καθεύδων, καὶ ἀνάστα ἐκ τῶν νεκρῶν, καὶ ἐπιφαύσει σοι ὁ Χριστός, "Therefore it says, 'Arise, O sleeper, and rise up from the dead, and the Messiah will shine on you.' " The question of where this text comes from dominates the discussion of Eph 5:14. Before commenting on that, though, let us ignore its origin for a moment and see how it works in this context. Paul invokes these few lines to cap off vv. 3–14a, and especially the theme of light in vv. 8–14a. Earlier the saints are the light (v. 8) and illumine the dark works of their nonbelieving neighbors in hopes of raising them too from their ignorance and darkened hearts into the light of Christ (vv. 10–14a).

With this quotation in v. 14, we see that the saints are *reflective* lights as inaugurated lampposts, whose brightness will come to full radiance at the consummation of the Messiah's eternal kingdom (v. 5) when he wakes them from sleep into the glory of the bodily resurrection (cf. 2 Cor 3:4–18; Phil 3:20–21). As Paul moves forward from these truths in consequence (οὖν, "So then," v. 15), the audience is counseled to conduct their lives during these evil times (v. 16) in wisdom and thankful circumspection. Christians walk at once in the shadows of this age and in the light of the consummation (e.g., Jas 5:3).

> Besides this you know the time, that the hour has come for you to wake from sleep. For salvation is nearer to us now than when we first believed. The night is far gone; the day is at hand. So then let us cast off the works of darkness and put on the armor of light. Let us walk properly as in the daytime, not in

61. "The disclosure of people's sins effected through believers' lives enables men and women to see the nature of their deeds. Some abandon the darkness of sin and respond to the light so that they become light themselves" (O'Brien, 372); "As the children of light expose the deeds of darkness by their living, so what is exposed itself becomes illuminated by the sphere of light. In fact, as the further explanation asserts, whatever becomes illuminated in this way is then itself part of the sphere of light" (Lincoln, 331); cf. also Hodge, 295–96.

> orgies and drunkenness, not in sexual immorality and sensuality, not in quarreling and jealousy. But put on the Lord Jesus Christ, and make no provision for the flesh, to gratify its desires. (Rom 13:11–14)

Now we can ask where the quotation comes from. The most common scholarly opinion at present is that Paul is citing an early Christian hymn, particularly one used at baptism (e.g., Barth, 574–75; Lincoln, 318–19, 331; O'Brien, 374–77; Gnilka, 260–62).[62] We are told that the text has a certain "lilt" to it (Best, 497) and "rhythmic beat" as the first criterion for its hymnic background. But what is meant by terms such as "lilt" or "rhythmic beat" are either not clear or are not used properly for ancient Greek rhythm.[63] It has been pointed out several times already that the rhythms of ancient Greek music were "quantitative, based on patterns of long and short syllables which must correspond to patterns of long and short notes."[64] If the Ephesians knew the text Paul cites and sang it at their baptismal rites as a Greek song, we would naturally expect the passage that Paul cites to have one of the regular, repeated meters of Greek music (dactylic, anapaestic, iambic, ionic, etc.), but it does not.[65] The text cited is not a Greek hymn.

---

62. Cf. Michel Gourgues, "«Réveille-toi... » (Ep 5,14): de l'évocation de la Pâque baptismale à la motivation parénétique," *Science et esprit* 63 (2011): 367–83.

63. E.g., Thorsten Moritz, *A Profound Mystery: The Use of the Old Testament in Ephesians*, SNT 85 (New York: Brill, 1996), 101, speaks of a "rhythmic pattern" in a repeated word order (e.g., a lead verb followed by its subject), but this is not how analysis of Greek rhythm works.

64. M. L. West, *Ancient Greek Music* (Oxford: Clarendon, 1992), 130; cf. the introduction to Eph 1:3–14 and the discussion on 3:20–21; 4:8–10; 5:19–20.

65. The scansion of each line in v. 14c–e is as follows:

ἔγειρε ὁ καθεύδων ˘ - ˘ ˘ ˘ - -
καὶ ἀνάστα ἐκ τῶν νεκρῶν - ˘ - - - - - ˘ -
καὶ ἐπιφαύσει σοι ὁ Χριστός - ˘ - - - - ˘ ¯ x (anceps, either ˘ or ¯).

Even granting that poetic scansion allows for many variations and differences from prose (e.g., diphthongs -*αι* and -*οι* can be short), there is no regular meter here; cf. M. L. West, *Greek Metre* (Oxford: Clarendon, 1982); and esp. West, *Ancient Greek Music*, 129–59, for musical rhythms (cf. 324–26 for *P.Oxy.* 1786). See excursus below for a metrical hexameter line quoted in Titus 1:12.

This leaves us with the better alternative of seeing an OT background to the text.[66] Before looking at this, we must note especially that Paul introduces the quotation with διὸ λέγει ("therefore it says"), which he also used earlier, in 4:8.[67] Also, as noted earlier, Paul brings in these quoted words as an *inference* from his previous statements in the passage (indicated by διό). Therefore (also as in 4:8), Paul is not giving the words of the quotation as the underlying premise of his previous statements about the saints and the light, but he teases out the fuller *meaning* of the previous revelation he is quoting in light of its fulfillment in Christ.[68] As a result of this dynamic, Paul is not bound by the exact wording of the prophetic material he cites but is interpreting it through free paraphrase. He gives the gist of its meaning, which is clearer now that the "mystery" that had earlier been concealed (see above on 3:3–9) has now been revealed in Christ's advent.[69]

Scholars who see 5:14 arising from the OT settle on two main tributaries from Isaiah (cf. also Isa 9:2; 51:17; 52:1; Mal 4:2; John 5:25–29):

Isaiah 26:19	**Ephesians 5:14**
ἀναστήσονται οἱ νεκροί	ἔγειρε ὁ καθεύδων
καὶ ἐγερθήσονται οἱ ἐν τοῖς μνημείοις …	καὶ ἀνάστα ἐκ τῶν νεκρῶν
ἡ δόξα κυρίου ἐπὶ σὲ ἀνατέταλκεν	

66. Cf. esp. Jonathan M. Lunde and John Anthony Dunne, "Paul's Creative and Contextual Use of Isaiah in Ephesians 5:14," *JETS* 55 (2012): 87–110; Qualls and Watts, "Isaiah in Ephesians," 254–55; Moritz, *Profound Mystery*, 97–116.

67. See the rather long discussion under 4:8 on *not* taking διὸ λέγει ("it says") as a quotation *formula*. Calvin, 201–2, and Barth, 574–75, take the phrase as "*he* says." It was thus also noted above on 4:8 that the conj. διό ("therefore," "for this reason," "in consequence") marks an inference or conclusion drawn from previous statements (cf. 2:11; 3:13; 4:25), not the reverse.

68. The full discussion of this dynamic will not be repeated here; see on 4:8 and the discussion on the "organic development" of redemptive revelation in "Biblical Theological Comments" after 2:11–22.

69. "Paul's redactional adjustments [to Isaiah] closely cohere with his reflection on the nature of Christ's fulfillments of those texts," Lunde and Dunne, "Paul's Creative and Contextual Use," 109; cf. Qualls and Watts, "Isaiah in Ephesians," 256.

Isaiah 60:1

φωτίζου φωτίζου Ιερουσαλημ
ἥκει γάρ σου τὸ φῶς
καὶ ἡ δόξα κυρίου ἐπὶ σὲ ἀνατέταλκεν   καὶ ἐπιφαύσει σοι ὁ Χριστός

Obviously there are differences in the LXX text of Isaiah (and with the MT as well), which have been discussed at great length by others.[70] But, as stated above and noted also by others, Paul is not citing the prophet word for word but teasing out what is nascent in the earlier revelation in light of its fulfillment in Christ. This is even clearer as Isa 60:1 continues into a prophecy of the Gentile mission and the theme Paul has developed in Eph 5:7–14a (and Rom 13:11–14, cited above):

> For behold, darkness shall cover the earth, and thick darkness the peoples; but the LORD will arise upon you, and his glory will be seen upon you. And nations shall come to your light, and kings to the brightness of your rising. Lift up your eyes all around, and see; they all gather together, they come to you; your sons shall come from afar, and your daughters shall be carried on the hip. Then you shall see and be radiant; your heart shall thrill and exult. (Isa 60:2–5)

This resurrection light has been inaugurated through regeneration (see on 1:13–14) and must burn bright in the saints until "the Messiah shines on you" in the glory of his consummated kingdom.

---

70. Esp. Moritz, *Profound Mystery*, 100–105, and Lunde and Dunne, "Paul's Creative and Contextual Use." Translation of Isa 26:19; 60:1 in the ESV is: "Your dead shall live; their bodies shall rise. You who dwell in the dust, awake and sing for joy! For your dew is a dew of light, and the earth will give birth to the dead. … Arise, shine, for your light has come, and the glory of the LORD has risen upon you." Among the more interesting patristic references to this text is that of Clement of Alexandria (*Protr.* 9.70), who quotes Eph 5:14 (adding κύριος at the end, "the Lord Messiah") and expanding with: ὁ τῆς ἀναστάσεως ἥλιος, ὁ πρὸ ἑωσφόρου γεννώμενος, ὁ ζωὴν χαρισάμενος ἀκτῖσιν ἰδίαις, "the sun of the resurrection, He that is begotten 'before the morning star' [Psa 110:3], He that dispenses life by His own rays" (LCL trans.).

Biblical Theology Comments

The warning of Eph 5:5 about evildoers not having an inheritance in the kingdom of Christ and of God has caused considerable consternation in the church. In particular, the question is asked whether this warning is addressed to Christians or to nonbelievers.[71] Depending on how this question is answered, it bears on the vital question of whether believers can lose their inheritance in the future new creation.

In the discussion above on v. 5, I presented a view that has been hammered out through careful Scripture study over the course of many, many centuries. To be clear on the second question first, true believers can certainly *not* lose their inheritance in the new creation. To be regenerated by the Holy Spirit is to possess an initial experience of the resurrection, and this is an irreversible gift. All of God's chosen people will be saved.

What about the first question, then? Is Paul warning Christians or non-Christians in v. 5? This is the wrong way to pose the question, for it does not recognize that there are both sheep and goats (e.g., Matt 7:21–23; 25:31–46) or wheat and weeds (e.g., Mark 4:18–19) in the kingdom of Christ in *this* age (but not in the next; see on 1:21). Paul's warnings in Eph 5:5 and other places (such as in Hebrews) are addressed to the *whole* new-covenant community, but in the historic language again, this is a "mixed" community composed of both elect true believers and of those who make profession of faith in Christ but who have no root and sell their birthright like Esau.[72] This last reference is to Heb 12:12–17, where the warning is parallel with Eph 5:5 that there should be no fruitless person like Esau *in their midst* who had legal, covenantal claim on the inheritance, but he sold it and was rejected (cf. Rom 9:6–13). Not all who are in the church are of the church (cf. Rom 9:6). So the warning comes to *the church* as a mixed-covenant community.

71. For example, René A. López, "Paul's Vice List in Ephesians 5:3–5," *BSac* 169 (2012): 203–18, esp. 203–4, labeled, "Does the passage address Christians?" answers, "Hence Paul penned the contents of this letter to address Christian matters, and he considered his audience believers" (204).

72. Another way to think of this is that Jesus started out with twelve apostles. But this was a "mixed" group of eleven true apostles and one "son of destruction" (John 17:12), as time and Judas' deeds revealed.

One further point is vital to emphasize, however. The stern warning of v. 5 and the mixed character of the church should be a minor note in the church's life of praise and devotion (e.g., 4:24; 5:19). Every member should take the warning seriously and be vigilant (e.g., Rev 3:17–18; 16:15), but it cannot lead to fear and doubts, especially in light of all the focus on grace and God's powerful free gift of eternal life in his Son, dispensed through the power of the Holy Spirit, which dominates Ephesians. The Christian life individually and corporately is one of faith, hope, and love, not fear (1 John 4:17–19).

Application and Devotional Implications

In Christian ethics, "thought," "word," and "deed" cover comprehensively the three areas of human acts that fall under the sovereign legislation of God. If you think about it, there really is nothing else that we do: We think, we speak, we act. This means that God's claim on our lives is comprehensive: We are to love him with all of our heart, our mind, our soul, and our strength, that is, in thought, word, and deed.

As a sign of his incarnate identity as Son of God, Christ Jesus clearly calls his followers to this same total allegiance to himself and makes comprehensive demands on them in thought, word, and deed fitting only for God. For example, in the Sermon on the Mount (Matt 5–7), Jesus' call to personal allegiance comes out in the beginning when he conveys his kingdom citizenship and its blessings on his followers (Matt 5:3–10). Yet the last of these beatitudes shows clearly that his kingdom is going to be inaugurated but not consummated, so that as a result his followers can expect to be persecuted because of (ἕνεκεν) righteousness (5:10), which is explained as persecution "because of (ἕνεκεν) me" (5:11). Once Jesus has his followers' attention directed squarely on himself and his royal, divine authority (see Matt 7:28–29), he proceeds to stake his claim on their lives. As just one example, see Matt 5:21–22, where Jesus extends the sixth commandment (Exod 20:13) prohibiting murder (a sin of "deed") to his own prohibition of anger (cf. Eph 4:26, 31), a sin of "thought," and he further prohibits insults, a sin of "word." In our passage and throughout Ephesians and elsewhere, Paul likewise shows the comprehensive nature of Christian ethics as it applies to thought, word, and deed.

Selected Bibliography

Dahl, N. "Der Epheserbrief und der verlorene, erste Brief des Paulus an die Korinther." In *Studies in Ephesians*, 335–48. WUNT 131. Tübingen: Mohr Siebeck, 2000.

Gosnell, P. "Honor and Shame Rhetoric in Ephesians." *BBR* 16 (2006): 105–28.

Gundry, S., ed. *Three Views of the Millennium and Beyond*. Grand Rapids: Zondervan, 1999.

Hultin, J. *The Ethics of Obscene Speech in Early Christianity and Its Environment*. SNT 128. Leiden: Brill, 2008.

Kreitzer, L. " 'Crude Language' and 'Shameful Things Done in Secret' (Ephesians 5.4, 12): Allusions to the Cult of Demeter/Cybele in Hierapolis?" *JSNT* 71 (1998): 51–77.

López, R. "Paul's Vice List in Ephesians 5:3–5." *BSac* 169 (2012): 203–18.

Lunde, J., and J. Dunne. "Paul's Creative and Contextual Use of Isaiah in Ephesians 5:14." *JETS* 55 (2012): 87–110.

Qualls, P., and J. Watts. "Isaiah in Ephesians." *RevExp* 93 (1996): 249–59.

Ridderbos, H. *The Coming of the Kingdom*. Phillipsburg, NJ: P&R, 1962.

Riddlebarger, K. *A Case for Amillennialism: Understanding the End Times*. Grand Rapids: Baker, 2003.

West, M. *Greek Metre*. Oxford: Clarendon, 1982.

Summarizing Exhortation to the Whole Church (5:15–21)

Introduction

In Ephesians 5:15–21 Paul concludes his general exhortations to all the members of the church up to this point before transitioning to material related to specific groups in the household. Verse 21 acts as a transitional concluding exhortation for submission, which is then illustrated in how this works out for various groups within the family in 5:22–6:9. As such, v. 21—indeed all of 5:15–21—belongs to the larger grouping of material running through 6:9, but it is treated separately here for convenience.[1]

This section opens with an exhortation to "walk" (περιπατέω), a common Semitic metaphor (e.g., Psa 1:1) that marks major sections in Paul's paraenetic portion of the epistle as follows:

4:1	set out [start *walking*] in a manner worthy of [your] calling
4:17	you must no longer *walk* as the Gentiles do
5:2	*walk* in love
5:8	*walk* as children of the light
5:15	so then be very careful how you *walk*

As we saw in 2:1–10, this verb "walk" marked an inclusio* that opens with an elaboration on the audience's former lives, dominated by sin and lostness (2:2a), and ends with their new walk in good works as the result of God's loving initiation of the new creation in their lives through Christ (2:10). This new-creation walk or conduct of life is therefore elaborated on in the paraenesis of the latter half of the epistle. *How* does one walk in this

1. Codices Vaticanus, Sinaiticus, and Alexandrinus (B, א, and A) all have a division between v. 21 and v. 22, as adopted here (see the introduction to the commentary).

"newness of life" (Rom 6:4)? That can be seen as the question that guides the exhortations in Eph 4–6 and the Christian "walk."

In "Excursus: Parallel Participles," I elaborate on adverbial participles used in parallel with imperatives to act as supplementary imperatives. The use of participles in this way provides relief from a string of imperatives joined by "and" (καί), which would be regarded as unduly repetitive and stylistically inelegant.[2] It can be done in refined Greek, but one would not want too much of it, so the participles serve to break up monotony and a series of short coordinate cola* (parataxis).[3] We do see the use of four imperatives in a row in vv. 17–18, but these are part of a construction in which the imperative actions are presented as things to be avoided with alternatives to cultivate, where the mood of the verbs makes the parallelism explicit: "do not X ... but rather Y" (μή ... ἀλλά). Here is a listing of the five imperatives and six parallel participles in the passage:

> 15 Βλέπετε ...
> 16 ἐξαγοραζόμενοι ...
> 17 μὴ γίνεσθε ... ἀλλὰ συνίετε ...
> 18 καὶ μὴ μεθύσκεσθε ... ἀλλὰ πληροῦσθε ...
> 19 λαλοῦντες ... ᾄδοντες καὶ ψάλλοντες ...
> 20 εὐχαριστοῦντες ...
> 21 ὑποτασσόμενοι.

As would be the case with imperative mood verbs in parallel, some of these participles may be joined in close, explanatory relations with the verb forms around them, as will be discussed in some of the comments.

---

2. This would be an example of a "monocolon" (μονόκωλος) style, mentioned in the commentary introduction above, where each period (or sentence) consists of one colon*. "While I am still dwelling upon my own opinion in regard to education, I desire to say that in the first place a discourse composed of a series of short sentences (τὸν μονόκωλον λόγον) I regard as no small proof of lack of culture; in the second place I think that in practice such discourse soon palls, and in every case it causes impatience; for monotony is in everything tiresome and repellent, but variety is agreeable, as it is in everything else, as, for example, in entertainments that appeal to the eye or the ear" (*Lib. ed.* 7B–D; LCL trans.).

3. As noted by Cooper that parallel ptcs. avoid "boringly repetitive parataxis of finite forms" (Guy L. Cooper III, *Attic Greek Prose Syntax* [Ann Arbor: University of Michigan Press, 1998], 1:859).

All the imperative mood verbs and parallel participles are expressed in their present-tense forms. These should be regarded as events that are enjoined in a general exhortation to things one should do whenever appropriate and should mark the "careful walk" of the Christian life (see above after 4:25–5:2 for discussion). Only the tense-form choice of μεθύσκεσθε ("be drunk") in v. 17 will draw further specific comment.

The periodic divisions of this passage, like the earlier paraenetic material beginning at Eph 4, are less elaborate and flowing than we found particularly in Eph 1–3. Here is my suggested division:

A
15 βλέπετε οὖν ἀκριβῶς πῶς περιπατεῖτε
μὴ ὡς ἄσοφοι ἀλλ᾽ ὡς σοφοί
16 ἐξαγοραζόμενοι τὸν καιρόν
ὅτι αἱ ἡμέραι πονηραί εἰσιν

B
17 διὰ τοῦτο μὴ γίνεσθε ἄφρονες
ἀλλὰ συνίετε τί τὸ θέλημα τοῦ κυρίου

C
18 καὶ μὴ μεθύσκεσθε οἴνῳ ἐν ᾧ ἐστιν ἀσωτία
ἀλλὰ πληροῦσθε ἐν πνεύματι

D
19 λαλοῦντες ἑαυτοῖς ἐν ψαλμοῖς καὶ ὕμνοις καὶ
ᾠδαῖς πνευματικαῖς
ᾄδοντες καὶ ψάλλοντες τῇ καρδίᾳ ὑμῶν τῷ κυρίῳ

E
20 εὐχαριστοῦντες πάντοτε ὑπὲρ πάντων
ἐν ὀνόματι τοῦ κυρίου ἡμῶν Ἰησοῦ Χριστοῦ τῷ θεῷ
καὶ πατρί

F
21 ὑποτασσόμενοι ἀλλήλοις ἐν φόβῳ Χριστοῦ.

The exhortations in 5:15–21 are very brief, although thematically as well as grammatically one can easily group vv. 15–17 and 18–21 together into just two long subunits. It is better to keep them separate, and the end of each verse in vv. 17–21 may confirm this with focus on Christ and on God: the will of the Lord (v. 17) ... in the Spirit (v. 18) ... to the Lord (v. 19) ... to God the Father (v. 20) ... in the fear of Christ (v. 21). This focus is very similar to the long development seen in 1:3–14 and elsewhere.

Outline

XIII. Summarizing Exhortation to the Whole Church (5:15–21)
- A. Walk in wisdom, not folly (5:15–17)
- B. Not in drunken excess and license (5:18a)
- C. The church in God's presence in the Spirit as the new temple and priesthood (5:18b)
- D. Service in song (5:19)
- E. Service in thanksgiving (5:20)
- F. Service in submission (5:21)

Original Text

15 Βλέπετε οὖν ἀκριβῶς πῶς[a] περιπατεῖτε μὴ ὡς ἄσοφοι ἀλλ᾽ ὡς σοφοί, **16** ἐξαγοραζόμενοι τὸν καιρόν, ὅτι αἱ ἡμέραι πονηραί εἰσιν. **17** διὰ τοῦτο μὴ γίνεσθε
ἄφρονες, ἀλλὰ συνίετε τί τὸ θέλημα τοῦ κυρίου. **18** καὶ μὴ μεθύσκεσθε οἴνῳ, ἐν ᾧ
ἐστιν ἀσωτία, ἀλλὰ πληροῦσθε ἐν πνεύματι, **19** λαλοῦντες ἑαυτοῖς ἐν[b] ψαλμοῖς
καὶ ὕμνοις καὶ ᾠδαῖς πνευματικαῖς,[c] ᾄδοντες καὶ ψάλλοντες τῇ καρδίᾳ ὑμῶν τῷ
κυρίῳ, **20** εὐχαριστοῦντες πάντοτε ὑπὲρ πάντων ἐν ὀνόματι τοῦ κυρίου ἡμῶν
Ἰησοῦ Χριστοῦ τῷ θεῷ καὶ πατρί. **21** Ὑποτασσόμενοι ἀλλήλοις ἐν φόβῳ Χριστοῦ.

Textual Notes

15.a. Some predominantly Western and Byzantine MSS (D, F, G, Ψ, 1881, and M) invert the adverbs in the opening phrase (πῶς ἀκριβῶς, "how accurately" or "carefully"), which makes ἀκριβῶς ("accurately, carefully") go with περιπατεῖτε ("walk") rather than with βλέπετε ("see," "be watchful"), making the phrase mean: "Be watchful just how carefully you walk." The word order in the text is supported by better and earlier MSS such as P^{46}, א, B, 81, 1175, 1241, and 1739.

19.b. The critical editions give ἐν ("with") in brackets as being uncertain but helpful in the context. The plain vanilla dative of means is just as clear in Greek here, yet the fact that ἐν is found in P^{46}, B, 33, 1739, and other good witnesses argues for its originality. The similar statement in Col 3:16 does not have ἐν, which may explain why it was not given in most other ancient MSS here.

19.c. P[46], B, b, d, and Ambrosiaster omit the adjective πνευματικαῖς in the phrase ᾠδαῖς πνευματικαῖς ("with spiritual songs"). Metzger says this was an accident caused by skipping over the adjective because it has the same ending as its noun (homoeoteleuton: ᾠδ**αῖς** πνευματικ**αῖς**); cf. Col 4:16.[4]

Translation

15 So then be very careful how you walk, not like unwise people, but like those who are wise, **16** redeem[5] the time, for the days are evil. **17** Therefore, do not be foolish,[6] but understand what the will of the Lord is. **18** And do not be drunk with wine, which leads to debauchery,[7] but rather,[8] be filled in[9] the Spirit. **19** Address[10] each other[11] in psalms and hymns and songs of

---

4. Bruce M. Metzger, *A Textual Commentary on the Greek New Testament*, 2nd ed. (New York: United Bible Societies, 1994), 540–41.
5. Our passage is marked by a long series of impvs. and ptcs. where the ptcs. have imperatival force simply because they are used in parallel with impv. mood verbs, as discussed in "Excursus: Parallel Participles" below. The ptcs. in vv. 15–21 are rendered as impvs. without further explanation.
6. As noted in the translation note on 4:32 above, γίνομαι when used with a quality or characteristic does not point to entrance into that condition ("become") but is a synonym of εἰμί ("be); BDAG, 196–99 (meaning 7). Hence μὴ γίνεσθε ἄφρονες is "do not be foolish" rather than "do not become foolish," as if the audience has been wise and is in danger of a prudential change for the worse.
7. As NIV for ἐν ᾧ ἐστιν ἀσωτία ("in which is debauchery"; cf. "for that is debauchery," ESV, NRSV).
8. Related to its function to show contrast with what precedes, ἀλλά can provide an alternative idea, as here ("but rather," "instead"; cf. BDAG, 44–45; BDF §448).
9. The idea is fullness of God's presence in the sphere or realm of the Spirit as the "atmosphere" of the new-creation temple. The rendering "with" or "by" the Spirit (as all major English versions) suggests the content of being filled and is not the best interpretation of ἐν here. See comment.
10. The verb λάλεω can focus on the activity of speech ("converse," "chat") or the conveyance of other kinds of sounds (hissing, thunder, musical notes, etc.; BDAG, 582; LSJ, 1025–26). Here the first idea is conveyed: "address one another" or "express yourselves to each other."
11. "To one another" is normally the reciprocal pronoun ἀλλήλοις (as v. 21), but this meaning is also possible with the reflexive pronoun ἑαυτοῦ in the pl., as here (ἑαυτοῖς; cf. 4:32; BDAG, 268–69, meaning 2).

the Spirit,[12] sing and make melody[13] with your hearts[14] to the Lord. **20** Give thanks at all times on behalf of all[15] in the name of our Lord Jesus Christ to God the Father. **21** Be subject to one another in the fear of Christ.

Commentary

5:15 *Βλέπετε οὖν ἀκριβῶς πῶς περιπατεῖτε μὴ ὡς ἄσοφοι ἀλλ᾽ ὡς σοφοί*, "So then be very careful how you walk, not like unwise people, but like those who are wise." This verse should not be taken alone but connects more broadly with other places in Ephesians (see below). But it connects as a concluding statement (*οὖν*, "so then") about discerning the Lord's will as children of light and reproving works of darkness (vv. 10–11; Hodge, 298), and it also connects more directly with vv. 16–17 and acts as a minor swing verse or hinge. It introduces the idea of the Christian life as one of wisdom as a transformation out of the audience's previous futility, ignorance, folly, and vice (esp. 2:1–3; 4:17–19). Verses 16–17 add the ideas of the urgency of their care in the conduct of life and the insight needed to proceed in a thoughtful, wise manner.

As mentioned in the introduction, the directive to walk with great care culminates the four earlier sections that also enjoin the audience to engage in a Christian "walk" (4:1, 17; 5:2, 8; cf. O'Brien, 378). More importantly still, all these exhortations in Eph 4–5 are giving specifics on the kind of new "walk" in good works that God has laid out for them as the effect of their inaugurated new creation in Christ Jesus (2:10). Hence, the Christian never walks alone but alongside others in the Christian community and with the risen Christ through the Spirit (2:22; 3:16; 4:3; etc.).

The adverb *ἀκριβῶς* means to act with strict focus and attention to details: "thoroughly" in Matt 2:8 and "accurately" in Luke 1:3. The opposite

---

12. See note on 1:3 for *πνευματικός* as a reference to the Holy Spirit (cf. BDAG, 837).
13. The meaning of *ψάλλω* is much discussed; it can refer to playing a musical instrument (derived from "plucking" a bow, then a lyre) or to forms of singing. See BDAG, 1096; LSJ, 2018. See comments for more.
14. The simple dative *τῇ καρδίᾳ ὑμῶν* can be the location of the singing ("in your heart[s]"; KJV, NIV, NRSV) or instrumental, as I take it here (as NASB; ESV has "with all your heart").
15. The phrase *ὑπὲρ πάντων* refers to "on behalf of all" people (generic masc.) rather than to circumstances, events, or other "things" (neuter). See comment.

here would be to conduct the Christian life in a haphazard or thoughtless manner like those who are "unwise"[16] (see esp. v. 17). The attention to this careful, wise conduct of life in Christ is strengthened by the imperative βλέπετε ("see"), which here means to pay close attention to something (BDAG, 178–79). At the end of the day, this fits into the whole notion of biblical wisdom, which can be described as "the skill of godly living."[17] It is a skill developed through reflection on scriptural truths and applying them to the experiences of life. And true wisdom is not merely contemplative or abstract because its foundation consists in the fear of the Lord (e.g., Job 28:28; Psa 111:10; Prov 1:7; 9:10; Isa 11:2), hence it is marked by godliness (cf. 4:24).

As has marked Paul's exhortations many times previously, there is a behavior to put off from the old, Adamic existence (cf. 4:22) and one to put on in the Last Adam (cf. 4:24), which is marked by truth and righteousness (e.g., 4:25). Here in 5:15 the language is compressed and in effect summarizes what has gone before as rejecting a walk in folly and the need to substitute wisdom instead. The construction in v. 15b implies an imperative of "walk" in both clauses: μὴ [περιπατεῖτε] ὡς ἄσοφοι ἀλλ' [περιπατεῖτε] ὡς σοφοί, "Do not *walk* like unwise people, but instead *walk* like those who are wise." This structure of μή ... ἀλλά ("do not ... but instead") is also repeated in two other verses in the passage:

> 15 **μὴ** ὡς ἄσοφοι **ἀλλ'** ὡς σοφοί
> 17 **μὴ** γίνεσθε ἄφρονες **ἀλλὰ** συνίετε
> 18 καὶ **μὴ** μεθύσκεσθε οἴνῳ ... **ἀλλὰ** πληροῦσθε.

In v. 17 in particular, the idea of foolish and wise is virtually repeated but with enough change in vocabulary to build on v. 15 (see comment below).

5:16 ἐξαγοραζόμενοι τὸν καιρόν, ὅτι αἱ ἡμέραι πονηραί εἰσιν, "redeem the time, for the days are evil." This verse belongs with vv. 15 and 17 to intensify the need for Christians to walk wisely. It lends a note of urgency to the directive to reject the folly of moral laxity (v. 15) and to conduct lives with penetrating insight into God's will (v. 17).

---

16. The adj. ἄσοφος, "unwise" or "one who lacks discernment," occurs only here in the NT (BDAG, 144). Cf. ἄφρων, "foolish," in v. 17.

17. This can be derived specifically from a careful study of what amounts to a catechism for young people growing up in the OT covenant community, Prov 1–9.

To "redeem the time" is a vivid metaphor for making the best use of one's time and efforts.[18] This is true for everyone, since life seems to speed up as youth passes away like an early morning mist (Jas 4:14): "Remember also your Creator in the days of your youth, before the evil days come and the years draw near of which you will say, 'I have no pleasure in them' " (Eccl 12:1). Hence, one should make the most of any opportunity that presents itself: "The years of our life are seventy, or even by reason of strength eighty; yet their span is but toil and trouble; they are soon gone, and we fly away. … So teach us to number our days that we may get a heart of wisdom" (Psa 90:10, 12).

The "time" in v. 16, though, is not the latter part of an individual's life but the period of time from Christ's first coming to the Parousia; it is "this age" (1:21), which is evil (Gal 1:4; cf. Matt 12:39) and filled with supreme challenges for Christians as "the evil day" (Eph 6:13): "Therefore he who is prudent will keep silent in such a time, for it is an evil time" (Amos 5:13).[19] The main thing to note here is that this lends urgency to the seriousness in which believers must take care to conduct their lives. It also qualifies that although they are citizens of a new creation and enjoy inaugurated blessings of that reality now, these things are experienced in the midst of an evil age because they are inaugurated and not yet consummated.

5:17 διὰ τοῦτο μὴ γίνεσθε ἄφρονες, ἀλλὰ συνίετε τί τὸ θέλημα τοῦ κυρίου, "Therefore, do not be foolish, but understand what the will of the Lord is." By opening with διὰ τοῦτο ("therefore"), Paul makes a direct connection between this verse and the statement in v. 16 about redeeming the time in this evil age. This verse also serves as a restatement and conclusion of the exhortation in v. 15 to walk not as unwise but wise disciples of Christ.

18. The verb ἐξαγοράζω can refer to eternal redemption from the law's curse (Gal 3:13; 4:5), but with καιρός ("time" or "opportunity") in Eph 5:16 and Col 4:5 it refers to making the best use of opportunities that present themselves; cf. Dan 2:8 in LXX; BDAG, 343, 497–98. So Col 4:5: "Walk in wisdom toward those who are outside, and redeem the time (τὸν καιρὸν ἐξαγοραζόμενοι)."

19. Cf. Herman Ridderbos, *Paul: An Outline of His Theology*, trans. John De Witt (Grand Rapids: Eerdmans, 1975), 91.

The adjective ἄφρων ("foolish") means to lack sense or prudence, as opposed to someone who is φρόνιμος ("sensible" or "prudent").[20]

In v. 10 above, Christians were exhorted to "discern" (δοκιμάζω) what pleases the Lord. This calls for insight into the Lord's will and how it applies in different circumstances. Here, with the imperative συνίετε ("understand" or "comprehend"; BDAG, 972), Paul wants Christians to have a thorough and intelligent grasp of God's will in Christ. By saying "the Lord's will" (τὸ θέλημα τοῦ κυρίου; see Acts 21:14), where "Lord" refers to the incarnate Son rather than more generally to "God's will" (τὸ θέλημα τοῦ θεοῦ; cf. 1:1, 5, 9, 11; 6:6), Paul brings out both the Son's divine identity and the unity of the Son's and his Father's purposes and directives for Christian living (e.g., Matt 7:21; 12:50; 18:14; John 5:30; 6:38–40).

That is, seeing things as he sees them, and making his will or judgment the standard of yours, and the rule of your conduct. The will of the Lord is the will of Christ. That *Lord* here means *Christ* is plain not only from the general usage of the NT, so often referred to, but also from the constant use of the word in this chapter as a designation of the Redeemer. Here again, therefore, the divinity of Christ is seen to be a practical doctrine entering into the daily religious life of the believer. His will is the rule of truth and duty (Hodge, 301–2).

This "will" (θέλημα) of the Lord is not his secret counsel (βουλή) or good pleasure (εὐδοκία), which directs his actions from before time as emphasized in 1:3–14. This cannot be discerned until revealed by special revelation. Until then, it is a "mystery" (1:9; and see "Excursus: The Mystery of Christ"). Rather, "will" here is God's *revealed* will in Christ, which is accessed by wise application of biblical revelation at the concrete crossroads of life that believers encounter in this age (cf. Rom 12:2; Col 1:9; 1 Thess 4:3; 5:18).

5:18 καὶ μὴ μεθύσκεσθε οἴνῳ, ἐν ᾧ ἐστιν ἀσωτία, ἀλλὰ πληροῦσθε ἐν πνεύματι, "And do not be drunk on wine, which leads to debauchery, but rather,

20. See, for example: δουλεύσει δὲ ἄφρων φρονίμῳ, "the fool will serve the sensible man" (Prov 11:29; cf. Prov 17:10; BDAG, 159). Synonyms of ἄφρων include: ἄσοφος, "one who lacks discernment" (v. 15); μωρός, "foolish" or "stupid"; ἀνόητος, "dull-witted"; or ἀσύνετος, "one who lacks insight or understanding."

be filled in the Spirit."[21] In English, based on the Hebrew, Prov 23:31 reads: "Do not look at wine when it is red, when it sparkles in the cup and goes down smoothly." And there are many other places both in the Wisdom literature and elsewhere that counsel against overuse of wine and other forms of drink.[22] As a result, Paul's counsel here about not being drunk on wine has broad precedent in the Scriptures.[23]

More particularly, Paul's prohibition on drunkenness is a direct quote of the LXX version of Prov 23:31 quoted above, which is quite different from the Hebrew and English version:

> μὴ μεθύσκεσθε οἴνῳ ἀλλὰ ὁμιλεῖτε ἀνθρώποις δικαίοις καὶ ὁμιλεῖτε ἐν περιπάτοις ἐὰν γὰρ εἰς τὰς φιάλας καὶ τὰ ποτήρια δῷς τοὺς ὀφθαλμούς σου ὕστερον περιπατήσεις γυμνότερος ὑπέρου
>
> Do not be drunk on wine, but keep company with righteous men and keep their company in your travels, for if you let your eyes settle in your bowls and in your cups you will thereafter walk around more naked than a staff. (Prov 23:31 LXX; my trans.)[24]

---

21. For survey and treatment of this verse see Timothy G. Gombis, "Being the Fullness of God in Christ by the Spirit: Ephesians 5:18 in Its Epistolary Setting," *TynB* 53 (2002): 259–71.

22. E.g., "Wine is a mocker, strong drink a brawler, and whoever is led astray by it is not wise" (Prov 20:1; cf. Prov 23:20, 31–35; 31:4–7; 1 Cor 5:11; 1 Thess 5:7).

23. Note that this is not a command for total abstinence but care in the consumption of wine and, by implication, other alcoholic beverages. The dative οἴνῳ ("on wine") can be taken as a rare dative of content (as Daniel B. Wallace, *Greek Grammar beyond the Basics* [Grand Rapids: Zondervan, 1997], 170–71) in place of the more common gen. of content (cf. Psa 35:9 with ἀπό or Rev 17:2 with ἐκ). However, it works just as well to take the dative as its common instrumental use (means), explaining how drunkenness is brought on. The same dative is also found elsewhere in the LXX of Proverbs: οἵδε γὰρ σιτοῦνται σῖτα ἀσεβείας **οἴνῳ** δὲ παρανόμῳ μεθύσκονται, "For they eat the bread of wickedness, and they are drunk on lawless wine" (Prov 4:17; cf. Jdt 6:4 with ἐν).

24. There is some uncertainty in the last word, rendered "staff." τὸ ὕστερον is a "pestle" or similarly shaped implement like a "club" and occurs only here as a noun in the LXX or NT. I am taking it here as a "walking staff" as one "walks around," ἐν περιπάτοις … περιπατήσεις. It is not unusual for the LXX translators to guess at the meaning of Hebrew words if they do not understand them precisely (e.g., the earth was ἀόρατος, "invisible" in Gen 1:2), though both the Hebrew and LXX in Prov 23:31 agree as warnings against drunkenness.

We have seen Paul in Ephesians quoting portions of the OT before without notice (e.g., Psa 4:4 in Eph 4:26).[25] Drunkenness is pointed out to be a form of debauchery and sin in many of the OT texts referenced above, but the point in v. 18b is that intoxication itself is a cause of even more forms of "debauchery" or "reckless abandon" (ἀσωτία; cf. BDAG, 148). The word ἀσωτία only occurs here and in Titus 1:6 and 1 Pet 4:4 in the NT, but see Luke 15:13 for the "profligate" living (ζῶν ἀσώτως) of the prodigal son.

Scholars have wondered why Paul inserts a somewhat specific prohibition for drunkenness in the context of general exhortations on wisdom (vv. 15–17; e.g., Best, 506–8, coming to no clear conclusion). One good answer is that Paul's concentration on wisdom in vv. 15–17 brought up this common theme in the wisdom literature (even quoting Prov 23:31).[26] However, the more likely reason is the parallel positive substitute of being filled in the Spirit (versus mere abstinence from wine or such; cf. O'Brien, 388–91).

Some scholars see a link between drunkenness and being filled "by" the Spirit as somehow linked with a pagan background of "cultic inebriation" in drunken Dionysian (Bacchic) rites as a way "to cause Dionysius to enter and fill the worshiper's body."[27] I find myself skeptical of such theological romanticism that attempts to dignify these Dionysian rites. The ancient

---

25. The view that Paul is not quoting the OT but something else through "the medium of a Jewish paraenetic tradition" (Gnilka, 269; cf. Lincoln, 340) such as *T. Jud.* 14:1 is possible but seems to overlook that the only certain quotes in Ephesians are from the OT rather than from secondary material (cf. Thorsten Moritz, *A Profound Mystery: The Use of the Old Testament in Ephesians*, SNT 85 [New York: Brill, 1996], 94; O'Brien, 390, esp. n. 118).

26. There is no reason to suppose that the Ephesians were particularly addicted to wine and therefore to read the prohibition μὴ μεθύσκεσθε as forbidding an event that was going on (cf. Wallace, *Greek Grammar*, 724–25; BDF §336; E. Burton, *Syntax of the Moods and Tenses in New Testament Greek* [Edinburgh: T&T Clark, 1898], §165); cf. Peter W. Gosnell, "Ephesians 5:18–20 and Mealtime Propriety," *TynB* 44 (1993): 363–71, who sees a common gathering around meals by the Ephesian Christians similar to Greek symposia. μεθύσκω is a stative verb expressing a state or condition of the subject and is expected in its pres.-tense form in the impv. without aspectual nuance and fits in with all the other pres. indic. ideas in this context.

27. Moritz, *Profound Mystery*, 95; cf. Cleon L. Rogers Jr., "The Dionysian Background of Ephesians 5:18," *BSac* 136 (1979): 249–57; Barth, 580, with further literature cited there.

pagans may have papered these practices over with a thin veneer of religious language, but they all knew it was merely an excuse for unfettered partying (e.g., Clement of Alexandria, *Protr.* 2.11). That the believers of Ephesus themselves had a background in these practices is anyone's guess. Certainly the Dionysius cult* was present in first-century Ephesus, but so also was a more restrained and abstemious worship of Artemis Ephesia, the prudish virgin huntress.[28]

The Ephesian Christians have already been told that they have been "filled to all the fullness of God" (3:19) as his holy temple on earth "in the Spirit" (see 1:13–14; 2:18, 21–22; 3:5, 16; 4:30). So now they are to live according to that constant presence of God by being filled *in* (not "with") the Spirit, just as their new-creation existence is *in* Christ. While the preposition ἐν ("in") in the expression πληροῦσθε ἐν πνεύματι could possibly convey the content of filling, it is better to give ἐν ("in") its meaning as denoting "sphere" (as in 2:18, 22; 6:18).[29] The Spirit's presence in the church's midst—or better its members' existence *in him* as the "aether" of the eschatological, new-creation realm projected into the present (see above on 1:3)—is to be their source of life, thanksgiving, and service (vv. 19–21) in the Lord. Note especially in this connection how the church's prayers are to be made "in the Spirit" in 6:18. If wine controls the mind and ruins one's sense of

28. Archaeologists have recently viewed evidence in one of the "terrace houses" in Ephesus as indicating Dionysian cult* practices taking place there: Hilke Thür, "The House of C. Flavius Furius Aptus in Ephesos: Club House of a Dionysic Community?," a conference paper on Ephesus given in Memphis, Tennessee, May 18, 2012. For "purity" and sexual abstinence in worship of Artemis see references on 1:4 above and S. M. Baugh, "A Foreign World: Ephesus in the First Century," in *Women in the Church*, 2nd ed., ed. A. J. Köstenberger and T. R. Schreiner (Grand Rapids: Baker, 2005).

29. The idea of content for ἐν here with πληρόω is said to be unprecedented by Wallace, *Greek Grammar*, 171, 374–75 (cf. Hoehner, 702–5), who, along with others, argues for the idea of means: "by the Spirit." *Contra* means here are: C. John Collins, "Ephesians 5:18: What Does πληροῦσθε ἐν πνεύματι Mean?," *Presb* (2007): 12–30; and Kendell H. Easley, "The Pauline Usage of *Pneumati* as a Reference to the Spirit of God," *JETS* 27 (1984): 299–313, more clearly with the simple dative τῷ πνεύματι in 1:13 (cf. 3:16). Collins does find analogous uses of ἐν signifying the content of filling in the LXX and church fathers (Collins, "Ephesians 5:18," 19–20), though this makes the idea possible, not certain, in Eph 5:18. For the idea of sphere or "dynamic realm" see John Paul Heil, "Ephesians 5:18b: 'But Be Filled in the Spirit,'" *CBQ* 69 (2007): 506–16.

propriety, leading to debauchery, so in stark contrast being filled with the Triune God's presence (O'Brien, 392–93) in the Spirit leads to *self-control*, along with the other spiritual fruits: "love, joy, peace, patience, kindness, goodness, faithfulness, [and] gentleness" (Gal 5:22–23; cf. also Luke 1:15; Lincoln, 344–45).

How does the believer fulfill this admonition to be filled in the Spirit? Paul answers that question by giving some examples in the next three verses.[30]

5:19 λαλοῦντες ἑαυτοῖς ἐν ψαλμοῖς καὶ ὕμνοις καὶ ᾠδαῖς πνευματικαῖς, ᾄδοντες καὶ ψάλλοντες τῇ καρδίᾳ ὑμῶν τῷ κυρίῳ, "Address each other in psalms and hymns and songs of the Spirit, sing and make melody with your hearts to the Lord." The three participles λαλοῦντες ("address"), ᾄδοντες ("sing"), and ψάλλοντες ("make melody"), as well as εὐχαριστοῦντες ("give thanks") and ὑποτασσόμενοι ("be subject to") in vv. 21–22, are all connected to the admonition to "be filled in the Spirit" (πληροῦσθε ἐν πνεύματι) in v. 18. The precise nature of this connection is subject to discussion, but that these statements are interconnected should be emphasized from the start.

Daniel Wallace argues that the participles communicate the *result* of believers being filled "by the Spirit."[31] He rules out "attendant circumstance, and even imperatival!" which he says is rarely found in this construction, and he thinks that taking the participles as means leads to a "mechanical" idea of being filled "by" the Spirit. However, the "construction" is merely a lead imperative (πληροῦσθε, "be filled" in v. 18) followed by participles that pick up their function from the imperative (*parallel participles*). The participles break up the monotony of a string of imperatives joined by καί ("and") and yet still carry the exhortation forward. However, this is not to say that these imperative ideas are statically parallel and unconnected. Two or more imperatives can be interrelated temporally and logically as indicated by context.[32]

---

30. One should also see the preservation of unity in the Spirit (4:3) and not grieving the Spirit (4:30) as connected with living in the presence of God's fullness.

31. Wallace, *Greek Grammar*, 639; cf. O'Brien, 387–88.

32. For example: ἀναστὰς βάπτισαι καὶ ἀπόλουσαι τὰς ἁμαρτίας σου ἐπικαλεσάμενος τὸ ὄνομα αὐτοῦ, "Arise, be baptized and wash away your sins and call on his name" (Acts 22:16; two impvs. and two parallel ptcs. in a nice symmetrical arrangement). The baptism is effective for washing away sins because Paul called on the Lord's name in faith (e.g., Rom 10:9–13). Outside the NT there is a nice parallel in Polybius in a treaty that says: καὶ εἴ τι ἀπελήφθη ἀπ' αὐτῶν, **ἀναζητηθὲν** ἀποδοθήτω,

Therefore, in Ephesians 5:18–21, the participles conveying imperative notions could still communicate result as Wallace and others see it: "be filled … and *in consequence* address, sing, make melody," etc. This makes good sense; however, because of the interconnection between vv. 19–21 and v. 18, it is best to take the ideas here as the *means* of expressing the congregation's existence in the presence of God's fullness in the Spirit. Furthermore, "filling" provides the general admonition, while the participles in vv. 19–21 provide the specifics.[33] There is nothing mechanical about this. In fact, it is a very profound situation.

As v. 18 was interpreted above, the Ephesians were admonished to express their identity as "a holy temple in the Lord … a dwelling of God in the Spirit" (2:21–22), a "spiritual house" (1 Pet 2:5), expressing the divine fullness in Christ (1:23; 4:10; see above on 5:18).[34] Christians are a new temple of God. In the OT temple, Levitical singers were charged to provide music and song on behalf of Israel (e.g., 1 Chr 6:31–48; 25:1–31). For example:

> Then [King David] appointed some of the Levites as ministers before the ark of the LORD, to invoke, to thank, and to praise the LORD, the God of Israel. … Then on that day David first appointed that thanksgiving be sung to the LORD by Asaph and his brothers. (1 Chr 16:4, 7)

Likewise, special hymn composers and singers accompanied sacrifices and worship pageants in Ephesian public worship to Artemis, to the Roman emperors, and to others (see "Excursus: Hymns"). In the Christian

---

"And if anything else has been taken from them (the Rhodians by [defeated] King Antiochus), *it shall be sought out* and restored" (Polybius, *Hist.* 21.42.17; my trans.; LCL is similar). The restoration—the word in the impv. mood—of these items is the result of them being sought out (parallel ptc.) and identified as confiscated by the king and his allies.

33. Collins, "Ephesians 5:18," 22, has something similar: "The simplest relationship seems to be that of carrying out the command—that is, they indicate the content of it. Thus we have 'be filled with the Spirit, that is, *in addressing* one another in psalms and hymns and spiritual songs, *in singing and making melody …*' " (emphasis original). Cf. Gombis, "Fullness of God," 269–71.

34. For similar treatments see esp. Gombis, "Fullness of God"; and Andreas J. Köstenberger, "What Does It Mean to Be Filled with the Spirit? A Biblical Investigation," *JETS* 40 (1997): 229–40 (esp. 231–35).

congregation, however, *all without distinction* are a new, holy priesthood whose privilege it is to offer "spiritual sacrifices" (1 Pet 2:5) in song (v. 19) and thanksgiving (v. 20) to God as his prized, priestly possession (e.g., 1 Pet 2:9; above on 1:14). There is no more professional choir to act on behalf of God's people in worship; all believers are to devote themselves to this priestly service in the Spirit "that you may be filled to all the fullness of God" (3:19). It is important to note here the priesthood of all believers who all have equal access to God's presence "in one Spirit" (2:18) in light of the following arrangement of the Christian household, where submission is enjoined in some relationships (5:22–6:9).

There are two details of v. 19 worth further mention. The first relates to the exhortation that Christians are to "address" (λαλέω) one another in song. There are examples of λαλέω ("address" or "speak") used to introduce song in the LXX, e.g., when Moses "spoke" a song to Israel (Deut 31:30; the song is Deut 32:1–43; cf. Judg 5:12; Psa 17:1 [18:1]; Rev 5:9–14 for songs with λέγω). It is possible to see this "address" as a reference to antiphonal singing (Ezra 3:11; Best, 511), as is mentioned in Pliny the Younger's report on Christian worship from the first decade of the second century: *carmenque Christo quasi deo dicere secum invicem*, "and they would address each other antiphonally in song to Christ as to a god" (Pliny, *Ep.* 10.96.7).[35] Likewise, this "address" in song is often taken as explained in Col 3:16 (see below on v. 20) as instruction and admonition. Paul himself provides examples of this in his teaching in Ephesians (and elsewhere, of course) when he quotes the Psalms and includes material that is poetic forms of praise and song (e.g., 3:20–21). This does not have to be in public worship only but can be fulfilled in a number of contexts in the life of the Christian community together. There is no reason to choose between these two different understandings of λαλέω in v. 19, since the exhortation is broad and Paul could have expected it to be fulfilled in a variety of ways and situations.

The second detail is the identity of the "psalms, hymns, and spiritual songs." Some Christian communions understand what is meant here as either the OT Psalms alone or the Psalms plus other biblical, poetic texts

35. LCL has: "when they sang in alternate verses a hymn to Christ, as to a god"; note that Pliny has *dico secum* ("*address* one another") as the Latin equivalent of λέγω or λαλέω rather than *cano* ("sing"). The adv. *invicem* is "alternately" or here "antiphonally."

that alone are allowed to be sung in Christian worship.[36] In this connection, πνευματικός ("spiritual") in particular is interpreted to mean "inspired" by the Holy Spirit, and therefore Christians are instructed to sing *canonical* psalms, hymns, and songs.[37]

In this discussion, the adjective πνευματικός ("spiritual") is taken to mean narrowly musical compositions that are "inspired" by the Holy Spirit and therefore biblical texts alone, but because of the connection with 5:18, the various kinds of singing are "of the Spirit" because believers are singing "in the Spirit," just as they are "in Christ" in their acts of praise (cf. 1:3; 6:18). Paul himself is capable of expressing exalted, poetic compositions of praise and has already given a song of praise in 3:20–21.[38] It is true that prophetic utterance is "in the Spirit" (3:5) and therefore "inspired" so that the prophet's words are God's word (cf. 6:17). But Christians can and do engage in other actions in the Spirit that are *illuminated* by the Spirit (1:17; Col 1:9) but not inspired by him: "Pray with all prayer and supplication in every season *in the Spirit*" (6:18; emphasis added). The words of these prayers are those of believers offered through the Spirit in priestly service in the dwelling place of God (above on v. 18). The words of Scripture, especially the Psalms, are certainly to be used directly and to guide modern song, but not exclusively so any more than in other forms of prayer and praise.

Finally, the qualifying phrase τῇ καρδίᾳ ὑμῶν is not "*in* your heart" (as Col 3:16 with ἐν) but "*with* your heart" (cf. Rom 10:10) or "heartfelt," just as charitable giving should be heartfelt and not be from compulsion

---

36. For history of the broader discussion and defense of the latter view see R. Scott Clark, *Recovering the Reformed Confession: Our Theology, Piety, and Practice* (Phillipsburg, NJ: P&R, 2008), 227–91; cf. documents collected at: http://exclusivepsalmody.com/articles-exclusive-psalmody/ (accessed Jan. 27, 2014).

37. See O'Brien, 395; Best, 511; Schnackenburg, 238; for taking "spiritual" with all three nouns: psalms, hymns, and songs (BDF §135.3), not with "songs" (ᾠδαί) only (as Hoehner, 709); cf. Col 3:16, discussed under v. 20. The three terms for songs refer in the OT not only to canonical psalms but to other "religious songs" as well (e.g., O'Brien, 395–96; Lincoln, 345–46). The three terms ὕμνοι, ψαλμός, and ᾠδή appear together in Pss 66:1 (67:1); 75:1 (76:1) (in that word order with only "hymns" in the pl.); ψαλμός appears more than seventy times in the LXX of the Psalms, ὕμνος 13x, and ᾠδή (Exod 15:1; Deut 31:30; 32:1–43) over 40x in Psalms. Cf. esp. 1 Cor 14:26.

38. Cf. Rom 8:31–39; Col 1:15–20; Phil 2:6–10; see also Luke 1:46–55; 67–79; Rev 5:9–10; 15:3–4. For singing see also Matt 26:30; Mark 14:26; Acts 16:25; 1 Cor 14:15, 26; Jas 5:13.

or mere outward duty (2 Cor 9:7). Otherwise it would be possible to take "in your heart" in 5:19 as Christians singing "silently" (cf. 1 Sam 1:13). In English, we would say that such singing to the Lord should be "from the heart" (cf. Luke 10:27) and not with the lips alone (Isa 29:13 = Matt 15:8; Mark 7:6; cf. Ezek 33:31).[39]

5:20 εὐχαριστοῦντες πάντοτε ὑπὲρ πάντων ἐν ὀνόματι τοῦ κυρίου ἡμῶν Ἰησοῦ Χριστοῦ τῷ θεῷ καὶ πατρί, "Give thanks at all times on behalf of all in the name of our Lord Jesus Christ to God the Father." The Jewish people made offerings in the temple for the Roman emperor and people (Josephus, *J.W.* 2.10.4) and additional thanksgiving sacrifices on select occasions for the emperor (e.g., Philo, *Embassy* [45] 356). Here Paul continues his theme developed in vv. 18–19 that the NT church is the inaugurated new-creation temple and its members all occupy priestly roles and now take over this offering of thanks to God "on behalf of all":

> And when the builders laid the foundation of the temple of the LORD, the priests in their vestments came forward with trumpets, and the Levites, the sons of Asaph, with cymbals, to praise the LORD, according to the directions of David king of Israel. And they sang responsively, praising and *giving thanks to the LORD*. (Ezra 3:10–11; emphasis added)

The phrase ὑπὲρ πάντων ("on behalf of all") is ambiguous, since πάντων could be either masculine (referring generically to people) or neuter ("for everything," NIV, ESV, NRSV). The issue is decided on how one takes ὑπέρ, which would be expected on analogy of the statement in 1:16 ("giving thanks for you") and other places (3:1, 13; 5:2, 25; 6:19) to refer to thanks "on behalf" of all people (cf. 2 Cor 1:11) rather than for the benefit of or in place of things.[40] Paul wants the Ephesian church to pray with thanks not only for one another but to broaden their perspective in thanksgiving for "all the saints" (6:18; and esp. Rom 16:4) and even to zealously intercede as

39. See a similar point in the comments of Chrysostom and Ambrosiaster in *ACCS*, 192.

40. Cf. BDAG, 1030–31 (meaning A2). The synonym here is περί and the dative (e.g., Rom 1:8; Col 1:3; 1 Thess 1:2). For offering of thanks see esp. 5:4; 1 Thess 1:2; 2 Thess 1:3; Heb 13:15.

the priests of God on behalf of all as an expression of the church's mission to the world (6:19; cf. 1 Tim 2:1–2).[41]

To pray "in the name of" Jesus means to pray in faith, trusting in him as the church's mediator with God the Father on "the throne of grace" (John 14:6; Heb 4:16; 10:20; Jas 1:6–8). See also above on 1:21.

The interpretation of vv. 18–20 offered above was directed by what is said on its own terms. Often, however, the meanings of these verses are guided by the similar passage in Colossians:

A ¹⁵ καὶ ἡ εἰρήνη τοῦ Χριστοῦ βραβευέτω ἐν ταῖς καρδίαις ὑμῶν
εἰς ἣν καὶ ἐκλήθητε ἐν ἑνὶ σώματι
καὶ εὐχάριστοι γίνεσθε

B ¹⁶ ὁ λόγος τοῦ Χριστοῦ ἐνοικείτω ἐν ὑμῖν πλουσίως
ἐν πάσῃ σοφίᾳ διδάσκοντες καὶ νουθετοῦντες ἑαυτούς
ψαλμοῖς ὕμνοις ᾠδαῖς πνευματικαῖς
ἐν [τῇ] χάριτι ᾄδοντες ἐν ταῖς καρδίαις ὑμῶν τῷ θεῷ

C ¹⁷ καὶ πᾶν ὅ τι ἐὰν ποιῆτε ἐν λόγῳ ἢ ἐν ἔργῳ
πάντα ἐν ὀνόματι κυρίου Ἰησοῦ
εὐχαριστοῦντες τῷ θεῷ πατρὶ δι' αὐτοῦ.[42]

The similarity between these passages is obvious, but there are enough differences in style and content that I am more cautious about letting the wording in one passage settle interpretive issues in the other.[43] In particular,

41. O'Brien, 398n151, prefers to take it as neuter, "for everything," but lets "the parallel passage in Col 3:17" control the meaning in Ephesians. (See also Jerome in *ACCS* 192–93.) "For everything" or "in all circumstances" would be communicated by ἐν παντί or ἐν πᾶσιν (5:24 and 6:16; cf. Rom 8:37; 1 Cor 1:5; 2 Cor 4:8; 11:6; Phil 4:12).

42. "And let the peace of Christ rule in your hearts, to which indeed you were called in one body. And be thankful. Let the word of Christ dwell in you richly, teaching and admonishing one another in all wisdom, singing psalms and hymns and spiritual songs, with thankfulness in your hearts to God. And whatever you do, in word or deed, do everything in the name of the Lord Jesus, giving thanks to God the Father through him" (Col 3:15–17).

43. One interesting parallel is the opening prepositional phrase ἐν πάσῃ σοφίᾳ ("in all wisdom"), which is brought forward ("fronted") for stress in its colon*, perhaps informing Eph 1:8–9. Most scholars view Colossians as original and Ephesians as an adaptation of it (e.g., Lincoln, anywhere the two books are similar), yet O'Brien

the new-temple theology permeating the Ephesians passage is not as clear here in Colossians. The two passages complement rather than supplant each other.

5:21 Ὑποτασσόμενοι ἀλλήλοις ἐν φόβῳ Χριστοῦ, "Be subject to one another in the fear of Christ." This short colon* (fourteen syllables) belongs as the last exposition of how the church is to express its fullness of God's presence in the Spirit (v. 18) and serves to introduce Paul's admonition for order in the Christian family that follows: wives-husbands (5:22–33), children-parents (6:1–4), and slaves-masters (6:5–9; cf. Col 3:18–25).

Absolute mutual submission is popular today, particularly where egalitarian or democratic social and political philosophies rule. Paul's general idea of proper submission, however, is explained and illustrated through the particular examples of family relations he develops in 5:22–6:9 (cf. Hoehner, 717; Barth, 610). Submission is not absolute for any party, but an individual submits in some ways to some people and not in other ways to others.[44] The only absolute rule for Christian behavior that is to guide everyone at all times is love. As a general guideline, believers are to submit to one another by considering others and their concerns more highly than themselves (Phil 2:3–4) in mutual love and service (Gal 5:13), and they are to submit to governing authorities in the church and in the world (e.g., Rom 13:1, 5; Titus 3:1; Heb 13:17; 1 Pet 2:13; 5:5).[45]

---

says that Col 3:16 "may be based on Ephesians 5:19" (O'Brien, 395). One needs to also factor Timothy into the composition of Colossians (Col 1:1) but not of Ephesians (cf. introduction).

44. See, for example, the interaction of Wayne Walden, "Ephesians 5:21—A Translation Note," *ResQ* 45 (2003): 254; Walden, "Translating Ephesians 5:21," *ResQ* 47 (2005): 197–82 (locating various kinds of mutuality primarily in ἀλλήλοις); and Stanley N. Helton, "Ephesians 5:21: A Longer Translation Note," *ResQ* 48 (2006): 33–41, who, as I do here, locates the nature of the various kinds of mutuality as indicated by the larger discourse in 5:22–6:9: "The meaning of words themselves depends on semantic relationship to other elements in a phrase, a sentence, a paragraph, etc. ... Yes, Paul teaches wives, children, and slaves to be submissive to those 'over' them. However, Paul also demands a level of 'submission' from husbands, fathers, and masters premised on the self-giving nature of the incarnation" (41). See below on 5:25–33 for the radical nature of Paul's admonition to husbands.

45. The substantive ptc. οἱ ὑποτασσόμενοι (or Attic spelling ὑποταττόμενοι) is the normal way of referencing "subjects" of a king (e.g., Polybius, *Hist.* 21.42; LSJ, 1897); so the subjection of all things as subjects to the messianic King Jesus in 1:22;

The motive that guides believers in their interrelations is not to draw attention to themselves through false humility but out of " the fear of Christ." The Greek word φόβος ("fear," "reverence," or "respect"; BDAG, 1062) is a strong word that connotes not the terror of judgment (1 John 4:18) but the holy awe due to a divine person (for example, Rev 4:17). This term is used elsewhere for fear "of the Lord" (Acts 9:31; 2 Cor 5:4) or "of God" (Rom 3:18; 2 Cor 7:1) and motivates the willing submission to proper authority by the Christian (cf. 5:33; 6:5; 2 Cor 5:11; 1 Pet 2:18; 3:2).

Verse 5:21 was treated here with 5:15–21 because of its grammatical and logical connection to 5:18 especially; however, it is a transitional verse that belongs just as much to 5:22–6:9. See the introduction to 5:22–33 that follows for more on this point.

Application and Devotional Implications

The apostle has exhorted all members of the church to sing, praise, and rejoice in the Lord. As noted, all members have this privileged role in the church's worship as the new-creation priesthood. But this is a new creation *inaugurated.* In the great hope and future consummation of this kingdom in a new heavens and a new earth, there will be no more need for an exhortation to sing like this. Oh, yes, there will be one thundering great angelic summons to sing at the start:

> Hallelujah! For the Lord our God, the Almighty One has entered into his [consummation] reign! *Let us rejoice and be exultant and give him glory!* For the wedding feast of the Lamb has come, and his bride has prepared herself, and it was granted her to robe herself in radiant, fine linen. (Rev 19:6–8; my trans.; emphasis added)

But after that last invitation, we will never need any more prompting to sing and give heartfelt glory to our great God: Father, Son, and Holy Spirit. For the joy of his presence will erupt from us in song forever. Think of that the next time you experience just a little foretaste of that great day in worship alongside your brothers and sisters in the Lord on the Lord's day.

---

1 Cor 15:27–28; Phil 3:21; Heb 2:8; 1 Pet 3:22.

Additional Exegetical Comments: Wine in Ephesus

Paul's admonition against drunkenness on wine (v. 18) relates to the staple drink of most of the Mediterranean world, Ephesus included. At Ephesus, wine production was connected with the vast agricultural lands controlled by Artemis Ephesia (see above on 1:4 and 5:9). In fact, the agriculture of Asia Minor was so dominated by vineyards at the expense of land used for other staple foodstuffs that Domitian ordered half of its vineyards to be dug up in the late first century (Philostratus, *Vit. soph.* 520; Suetonius, *Dom.* 7.2).

The importance of the wine industry at Ephesus is further indicated by a public guild of the "Sacred Taste," the "Sacred Tasters," and more fully, "The College of the Sacred Wine Tasters" in the city (*IvE* 728; 2076; *SEG* 35 [1985] 1109). However, it should be noted that Ephesian wine did not have a particularly good reputation since it was laced with sea water (cf. Pliny, *Nat.* 14.10). The wine that was stored was usually rather concentrated and was mixed with water before drinking it, thereby decreasing its alcohol level. "We call a mixture 'wine,' although the larger of the component parts is water" (Plutarch, *Conj. praec.*, 140F; LCL trans.). So it was always possible to drink wine in moderation without drunkenness, and wine was thought to be mildly medicinal, especially where the water supply might be contaminated (see 1 Tim 5:23).

For a number of reasons, water was not an exclusive staple drink in the cities, and other potable liquids such as milk would be specialty items and undoubtedly relatively expensive. As for the drinking water in the city of Ephesus, an inscription from around AD 113/4 is instructive (*IvE* 3217). This is an edict from the Roman governor, A. Vicirius Martialis, regarding the water supply into the city. In the countryside, this supply apparently came via an open stream (in contrast with later aqueducts), which the farmers in the area were charged by Martialis to keep dredged where it crossed their properties. But when the water supply entered the city, it was conveyed through a lead pipe system. However, the edict addresses a problem caused by some city dwellers who were breaking holes into the pipes on their property and pouring all manners of disgusting material (πολλὰ ἄτοπα) into it.[46] It does not take much imagination to understand that water in the public fountains would not be very attractive for drinking; hence, people drank wine mixed with water.

Selected Bibliography

Cabaniss, A. "The Background of Metrical Psalmody." *CTJ* 20 (1985): 191–206.

Clark, S. *Recovering the Reformed Confession: Our Theology, Piety, and Practice.* Phillipsburg, NJ: P&R, 2008.

Collins, J. "Ephesians 5:18: What Does πληροῦσθε ἐν πνεύματι Mean?" *Presb* (2007): 12–30.

Easley, K. "The Pauline Usage of *Pneumati* as a Reference to the Spirit of God." *JETS* 27 (1984): 299–313.

Gombis, T. "Being the Fullness of God in Christ by the Spirit: Ephesians 5:18 in Its Epistolary Setting." *TynB* 53 (2002): 259–71.

Gosnell, P. "Ephesians 5:18–20 and Mealtime Propriety." *TynB* 44 (1993): 363–71.

Heil, J. "Ephesians 5:18b: 'But Be Filled in the Spirit.' " *CBQ* 69 (2007): 506–16.

Kostenberger, A. "What Does It Mean to Be Filled with the Spirit? A Biblical Investigation." *JETS* 40 (1997): 229–40.

Rogers, C. "The Dionysian Background of Ephesians 5:18." *BSac* 136 (1979): 249–57.

46. The fine assigned for this crime (ἁμαρτία) in the Martialis edict was quite large, at 12,500 denarii. To put this in perspective, in the late first to early second century one could buy four-and-a-half twelve-ounce "loaves" of Ephesian bread (more like pita) made from the best flour for one Roman denarius; cf. Naum Jasny, "The Breads of Ephesus and Their Prices," *Agricultural History* 21 (1947): 190–92.

Exhortations to Christian Households: Wives and Husbands (5:22–33)

Introduction

In Ephesians 5:22–33 Paul begins to illustrate his exhortation for mutual submission in the church family with marriage relations of submission and love as founded on God's eternal counsel and in Christ's redemption of the church. There are three areas in the ancient Christian household where Paul illustrates his general exhortation in v. 21, "Be subject to one another in the fear of Christ." These three areas are between married couples (5:22–33), parents and children (6:1–4), and the relations between slaves and owners (6:5–9).

Many ancient sources deal with advice for relations within and the management (οἰκονομία) of the ancient household. This has given rise to discussion of possible backgrounds for the apostle's teaching in 5:22–6:9 and elsewhere (e.g., Col 3:18–4:1) in ancient "household codes" (German *Haustafeln*). Some scholars propose a Graeco-Roman, particularly a Stoic, unwritten code as the influence on such analogous material in the NT.[1] Others see the influence as derived more from Graeco-Roman *Oikonomos* literature (e.g., Xenophon, *Oeconomicus*), while others propose Jewish—either OT or secondary—literature or oral sources in the background.

1. See esp. the inscribed regulations governing a house cult* from Philadelphia given in Stephen C. Barton and Greg H. R. Horsley, "A Hellenistic Cult Group and the New Testament Churches," *JAC* 24 (1981): 7–41; cf. Stanley K. Stowers, "A Cult from Philadelphia: *Oikos* Religion or Cult Association?" in *The Early Church in Its Context*, ed. Abraham Malherbe, Frederick Norris, and James Thompson (Leiden: Brill, 1998), 287–301. The inscription was reproduced in translation in S. M. Baugh, "Marriage and Family in Ancient Greek Society," in *Marriage and Family in the Biblical World*, ed. K. M. Campbell (Downers Grove, IL: InterVarsity Press, 2003), 125–26.

Finally, others believe that "codes" like this were the inventions of Paul and other NT writers to meet the special needs of the NT church communities.[2]

Regardless of the origin of the idea of directions for the various members of the church's households, the instructions in Eph 5:22–6:9 are very brief, with Col 3:18–4:1 even more brief and schematic. Paul distills each relationship down to two or three basic principles, which is quite unlike the much longer essays, dialogues, or instructional wisdom material one encounters in more thorough literary discussions found in Xenophon, Plutarch, Philo, Pseudo-Phocylides, et al. And the focus of Paul in the Ephesians material fits well with the epistle's overall, constant concern for unity in the inaugurated new-creation community. As Harold Hoehner concludes:

> The Ephesian household code was for the purpose of fostering unity of believers in that community in Asia Minor. Specific groups of believers are addressed regarding their responsibilities to other groups who may or may not have been believers. The believers are to carry out their responsibilities as to the Lord in the power of the Holy Spirit. (Hoehner, 729)

As regards Ephesians 5:22–24 in particular, the passage composed of these three verses (only six cola*), as much as any short passage in Ephesians or elsewhere in the Bible, is a modern skirmish field. It is rejected as a hopeless patriarchal relic of the past.[3] It is reinterpreted through various methodologies or hermeneutical commitments to be more compatible with modern egalitarian sensibilities on marriage.[4] And it is interpreted more dispassionately with a focus especially on the passage's literary, historical,

---

2. For survey of the literature and the issues, see the excursus in Hoehner, 720–29, and supplement with Timothy G. Gombis, "A Radically New Humanity: The Function of the *Haustafel* in Ephesians," *JETS* 48 (2005): 317–30; Benjamin G. Wold, "Family Ethics in *4QInstruction* and the New Testament," *NovT* 50 (2008): 286–300.

3. E.g., Elisabeth Schüssler Fiorenza, *In Memory of Her: A Feminist Theological Reconstruction of Christian Origins* (New York: Crossroad, 1989). For review of various feminist approaches ("rejectionist, loyalist, revisionist, sublimationist, liberationist") see Eileen R. Campbell-Reed, "Should Wives 'Submit Graciously'? A Feminist Approach to Interpreting Ephesians 5:21–33," *RevExp* 98 (2001): 263–76.

4. I.e., Campbell-Reed's "revisionist" and "liberationist" positions. E.g., Gregory W. Dawes, *The Body in Question: Metaphor and Meaning in the Interpretation of Ephesian 5:21–33* (Boston: Brill, 1998), who uses a metaphor theory and ends

and theological contexts.[5] There is much to be learned by an examination of all of these various approaches; however, it seems to me that a thorough review of all of them is easily obtained by reading the major works just cited and seeing comments and discussion in the various other commentaries (e.g., Barth, 651–62; Lincoln, 355–65). What I hope to provide is a general treatment of the particulars of the passage itself in light of certain historical issues that are not usually discussed and some theological considerations that are in the literature but are worth restatement or refinement.

As for the historical issues, the changing legal status of women in the first century and its societal effects has received some helpful attention recently.[6] One area of particular interest is recognition of the rising, relative freedom of women to divorce their husbands in the early imperial period.[7] All of this is illuminating for Eph 5:22–33 and helps explain Paul's particular concern to admonish wives and husbands to their various duties toward one another in order to "preserve the unity of the Spirit in the bond of peace" (4:3) and to act with wisdom (5:15–17) in the marriage relationship.[8]

---

by providing an opening for his own interpretation by charging the author of Ephesians with inconsistency in the use of words and expressions.

5. In addition to the commentaries, see esp. Stephen Francis Miletic, *"One Flesh": Eph. 5.22–24, 5.31, Marriage and the New Creation*, AnBib 115 (Rome: Pontifical Biblical Institute, 1988); Jack J. Gibson, "Ephesians 5:21–33 and the Lack of Marital Unity in the Roman Empire," *BSac* 168 (2011): 162–77; Cynthia Long Westfall, " 'This Is a Great Metaphor!' Reciprocity in the Ephesians Household Code," in *Christian Origins and Greco-Roman Culture: Social and Literary Contexts for the New Testament*, ed. Stanley E. Porter and Andrew W. Pitts (Boston: Brill, 2013), 561–98; Michelle Lee-Barnewall, "Turning Κεφαλή on Its Head: The Rhetoric of Reversal in Ephesians 5:21–33," in *Christian Origins and Greco-Roman Culture*, 599–614; cf. J. Paul Sampley, *"And the Two Shall Become One Flesh": A Study of Traditions in Ephesians 5:21–33* (Cambridge: Cambridge University Press, 1971); Andreas J. Köstenberger, "The Mystery of Christ and the Church: Head and Body, One Flesh," *TrinJ* 12 (1991): 79–94; G. W. Peterman, "Marriage and Sexual Fidelity in the Papyri, Plutarch and Paul," *TynB* 50 (1999): 163–72.

6. E.g., Bruce W. Winter, *Roman Wives, Roman Widows: The Appearance of New Women and the Pauline Communities* (Grand Rapids: Eerdmans, 2003); cf. Paul Trebilco, *The Early Christians in Ephesus from Paul to Ignatius* (Grand Rapids: Eerdmans, 2008; first published 2004), 507–52.

7. See esp. Winter, *Roman Wives*; Gibson, "Ephesians 5:21–33."

8. Ephesus in the mid-first century was demonstrably undergoing the beginnings of Roman imperial societal influences on its own historic Hellenic social structures. Hints as to this are given in the commentary's introduction.

But there are other areas of historical concern that should also be discussed beyond the legal and social position of women in the first century, which often goes unnoticed. If Paul were addressing modern wives in the United States, only 1 percent of them would be from fifteen to seventeen years of age at first marriage.[9] The median age at first marriage for women in the United States is about twenty-six years, and twenty-eight years for men (with less than 50 percent of these marriages lasting twenty years). Even fewer U.S. men (about 0.3 percent) marry between the ages of fifteen and seventeen years, with most of them marrying for the first time in the age range of twenty-four to forty-four years (with a median age of twenty-eight years). The average life expectancy from birth in 2011 in the United States for both men and women is 78.7 years.[10]

Now consider the married couples Paul was addressing in the first century. Not 1 percent but closer to *all* the wives to whom Paul wrote were married for the first time when they were twelve to seventeen years old; most were about fourteen years old at first marriage. Their husbands married later, depending primarily on family situation, but men at first marriage were in the range of eighteen to thirty years old.[11] Based on significant census records from Egypt, D. C. Barker says that close to 33

9. The following statistics are taken from Casey E. Copen, Kimberly Daniels, Jonathan Vespa, and William D. Mosher, "First Marriages in the United States: Data from the 2006–2010 National Survey of Family Growth," *National Health Statistics Reports* 49 (2012), a publication of the United States National Center for Health Statistics (NCHS).

10. From Donna L. Hoyert and Jiaquan Xu, "Deaths: Preliminary Data for 2011," *National Vital Statistics Report* 61 (2012), also published by the NCHS.

11. Obviously these figures are estimates from antiquity, but they are the result of various forms of research over the course of many decades among ancient historians into funerary and other archaeological and literary remains, as well as on analogy with more recent subsistence agrarian societies where such population records have been kept. The latter marked the groundbreaking essay by A. R. Burn, "*Hic Breve Vivitur*: A Study of the Expectation of Life in the Roman Empire," *Past and Present* 4 (1953): 2–31. For further discussion and resources see Baugh, "Marriage and Family in Ancient Greek Society," and also the essays on the Roman family by Susan Treggiari and the Second Temple Jewish family by David W. Chapman in the same volume. For the Roman situation see esp. Arnold A. Lelis, William A. Percy, and Beert C. Verstraete, *The Age of Marriage in Ancient Rome*, Studies in Classics 26 (Lewiston, NY: Edwin Mellen, 2003). The age of men at first marriage in classical Greece tended to be later (around thirty) and was younger (around eighteen to twenty-two years) for Roman men.

percent of Egyptian men were from eleven to more than thirty years older than their wives.[12]

Furthermore, the life expectancy in antiquity was substantially shorter than today:

> Rome exhibits the fundamental demographic condition of the so-called pre-modern world, under which of course the entire ancient world can be subsumed, that is mortality rates so high, and affecting especially the very young (up to 50% of children by the age of six) that average life-spans were in the 20–30 years range.[13]

Granted that the wife Paul was addressing in Eph 5:22–24 had survived her first six years, she could expect to live, on average, into her mid-thirties.[14] Very often, ancient women died young amid serious health issues, particularly due to iron deficiency in their diet (anemia).[15] This condition was exacerbated during menstruation and pregnancy and made ancient women susceptible to spontaneous abortion and to diseases such as pneumonia, bronchitis, and emphysema, and to death during or shortly after childbirth.[16]

One poignant example of death in childbirth is probably witnessed in this Ephesian grave inscription:

---

12. D. C. Barker, in *New Docs*, 10:114–18.

13. Lelis, Percy, and Verstraete, *Age of Marriage*, 3.

14. There are many epigraphical witnesses to infant mortality on Ephesian funerary memorials. For example: Eppia infant daughter (νηπία—see Eph 4:14) of Marcus (*IvE* 1639); Herakleides who lived eighteen months, twenty-four days, and five hours (*IvE* 2268); Hero who lived four years (*IvE* 2269); and Statonike six years (*IvE* 2104).

15. E.g., an unknown young woman (the stone is broken) who lived nineteen years and nineteen days κοσμίως ("with decorum"; *IvE* 2560).

16. For ancient problems from anemia see Vern L. Bullough in the preface to Lelis, Percy, and Verstraete, *Age of Marriage*, iii–viii. For a personal view into the reality of the danger in childbirth (cf. 1 Tim 2:15), see the second-century letter of a mother relaying her relief at the "escape" (ἐκφεύγω) of her daughter from a successful birth in S. R. Llewelyn, *New Docs*, 9:57–58.

Εὐτύχη-
ς τῇ ἰδίᾳ
γυναικί
Γερμάνᾳ κ-
αὶ τέκνῳ, ζῶσ-
ιν, ἐποίησεν
[the bottom of the stone is broken off][17]

Eutyches made [this memorial] for his wife, Germana, and child, they live.[18]

The child undoubtedly died with the mother in childbirth before he or she could receive a name, whereas in *IvE* 1653 Flavia Tation and her son (τέκνον), Tatianus, probably died together soon after childbirth, as the infant boy received his name (cf. Eph 3:15). Men, who lived into their early forties on average, normally outlived their wives in antiquity—and therefore often had more than one wife in succession.[19]

In other words, of the wives to whom Paul speaks in Ephesians, some were fifteen years old and nursing their first or second child with husbands ten to thirty years older than themselves.[20] Others were twenty-six years old—the age when a woman in the United States first gets married—and were in ill health with emphysema and chronic lethargy after delivering

17. Dieter Knibbe, Helmut Engelmann, and Bülent Iplikçioglu, "Neue Inschriften aus Ephesos XII," *JAÖI* 62 (1993): Hauptblatt 113–50; no. 42 (137).

18. Note the use of ἴδιος in the phrase τῇ ἰδίᾳ γυναικί ("for his [own] wife"), which is parallel with τοῖς ἰδίοις ἀνδράσιν ("to their own husbands") in v. 22.

19. Much older people are known from antiquity, of course, (e.g., P. Cordius Pharnaces, who died at 86; *IvE* 2240A in Latin). But these are the exception and are often from the elite, better-fed circles than the 80 to 85 percent of ancient people whose main occupation during most of their waking hours was in the production of food for themselves, for their families, and to create a small excess beyond what they needed to use for exchange of goods or cash. It should also be mentioned that "wife" and "husband" does not relate to ancient slaves who may, at best, have consorts by permission of their masters, usually for raising "houseborn" slaves to add to the workforce of the household.

20. See Sarah B. Pomeroy, *Xenophon Oeconomicus: A Social and Historical Commentary* (Oxford: Clarendon, 1994), esp. 269: "The average age of menarche was 14. Thus the young bride might well be a mother within a year or two of marriage." Menarche (age at first menstruation) was generally considered the marriageable age in Graeco-Roman antiquity.

their fourth, fifth, or sixth child. Some of the older wives were in their late thirties and enjoying being grandmothers but living in the household of their brothers or sons or nephews as widows.[21] Hence, Paul exhorts husbands to love in a self-sacrificial manner their child-brides (vv. 25–33), who were often laid up in bed one week or longer every month from anemia and other common health problems in antiquity (i.e., "weaker vessels"; 1 Pet 3:7) or with pregnancy complications (e.g., *diastasis symphysis pubis*).[22]

There are two other considerations to mention. First, ancient marriage was the union of families. It was normal for the husband and wife to have little, if any, contact before their marriage. They married as strangers. Furthermore, most young girls before marriage were sequestered, like the literary wife of Ischomachus in Xenophon's *Oeconomicus*, who was fourteen when she married but previously knew nothing of household management, "seeing, hearing and saying as little as possible" before Ischomachus had "received her from her father and mother" (*Oec.* 7.5). Within a year or

---

21. E.g., *IvE* 1636 (mid-1 AD) for the grave memorial of Claudia Magna, wife of Tib. Claudius Diognetos, identified as a grandmother (μάμμη) who lived thirty-eight years, two months, and four hours. See also the number of Egyptian legal papyri where women list their sons as κύριος ("legal representative"); e.g., *P. Ryl.* 174 (AD 112); *P. Amh.* 104 (AD 125); *P.Tebt.* 389 (AD 141); B. P. Grenfell and A. S. Hunt, eds., *The Oxyrhynchus Papyri* (London: Egypt Exploration Society, 1922), nos. 1.74, 73, and 70 respectively. These women were either divorced or widowed, and their sons were the legal heads of the household. In many cases, when the husband died, he left the house to his children with a proviso in his will that his wife should be allowed to live in the home. Census returns from Roman imperial Egypt show that most households held more than the nuclear family, with up to twenty-seven people living in one house; see D. C. Barker in *New Docs*, 4:87–93.

22. Not to mention health problems from hunger in lean times. The surrounding region of Ephesus was planted with an excess of vineyards, making the city susceptible to grain shortages. This is evident in a telling inscription from AD 129: "For the Emperor Caesar Trajanus Hadrian Augustus and Olympian (god), son of the deified Trajan Parthicus, grandson of the deified Nerva, (holding) tribunican authority for the thirteenth time, consul three times, father of his fatherland. The Council and People of the Ephesians, to their own founder and savior on account of his superabundant gifts to Artemis: he granted to the goddess rights over inheritances and deposits and her own laws, *he provided grain importation from Egypt* ..." (*IvE* 274; AD 129; emphasis added). The emperor directly controlled the grain supply from Egypt for Rome's needs but allowed some for Ephesus because of severe shortage. Note that Hadrian is declared to be the "founder" and "savior" (σωτήρ) of the city for his benefactions, which relates to σωτήρ in Eph 5:23.

so, this girl had a daughter, if she corresponds to the historical Chrysilla, wife of a known Ischomachus of the day, so her older and more experienced husband had to train her for her managerial role in the household.[23] "Guard a virgin in firmly locked rooms, and do not let her be seen before the house until her wedding day" (Pseudo-Phocylides 215–16).

Finally, it is reasonable to assume from 1 Cor 7:12–16 that some members of the Ephesian audience had an unbelieving spouse.[24] Paul is addressing these believing husbands and wives with unbelieving spouses in Eph 5:22–33 as well. These are some of the historical realities we must keep in mind as we deal with the following verses.

The following is my suggested division of the text into cola* and periods, granting again that it is provisional and not as deliberately composed everywhere as earlier in Ephesians:

[21 ὑποτασσόμενοι ἀλλήλοις ἐν φόβῳ Χριστοῦ]

A
22 αἱ γυναῖκες τοῖς ἰδίοις ἀνδράσιν ὡς τῷ κυρίῳ
23 ὅτι ἀνήρ ἐστιν κεφαλὴ τῆς γυναικὸς
ὡς καὶ ὁ Χριστὸς κεφαλὴ τῆς ἐκκλησίας
αὐτὸς σωτὴρ τοῦ σώματος

B
24 ἀλλὰ ὡς ἡ ἐκκλησία ὑποτάσσεται τῷ Χριστῷ
οὕτως καὶ αἱ γυναῖκες τοῖς ἀνδράσιν ἐν παντί

C
25 οἱ ἄνδρες ἀγαπᾶτε τὰς γυναῖκας
καθὼς καὶ ὁ Χριστὸς ἠγάπησεν τὴν ἐκκλησίαν
καὶ ἑαυτὸν παρέδωκεν ὑπὲρ αὐτῆς

D
26 ἵνα αὐτὴν ἁγιάσῃ
καθαρίσας τῷ λουτρῷ τοῦ ὕδατος ἐν ῥήματι
27 ἵνα παραστήσῃ αὐτὸς ἑαυτῷ ἔνδοξον τὴν ἐκκλησίαν
μὴ ἔχουσαν σπίλον ἢ ῥυτίδα ἤ τι τῶν τοιούτων
ἀλλ᾽ ἵνα ᾖ ἁγία καὶ ἄμωμος

23. Cf. Pomeroy, *Xenophon Oeconomicus*, 259–64.

24. See Plutarch's advice to the bride to worship her husband's gods and not to bring "queer rituals and outlandish superstitions" into the household (Plutarch, *Conj. praec.* 140D). This does not mean that Plutarch's advice was heeded by anyone, of course, but it is an interesting ancient opinion that may represent the ideas of others as well.

E [28] οὕτως ὀφείλουσιν οἱ ἄνδρες
ἀγαπᾶν τὰς ἑαυτῶν γυναῖκας
ὡς τὰ ἑαυτῶν σώματα
ὁ ἀγαπῶν τὴν ἑαυτοῦ γυναῖκα ἑαυτὸν ἀγαπᾷ

F [29] οὐδεὶς γάρ ποτε τὴν ἑαυτοῦ σάρκα ἐμίσησεν
ἀλλὰ ἐκτρέφει καὶ θάλπει αὐτήν
καθὼς καὶ ὁ Χριστὸς τὴν ἐκκλησίαν
[30] ὅτι μέλη ἐσμὲν τοῦ σώματος αὐτοῦ

G [31] ἀντὶ τούτου καταλείψει ἄνθρωπος
τὸν πατέρα καὶ τὴν μητέρα
καὶ προσκολληθήσεται πρὸς τὴν γυναῖκα αὐτοῦ
καὶ ἔσονται οἱ δύο εἰς σάρκα μίαν

H [32] τὸ μυστήριον τοῦτο μέγα ἐστίν
ἐγὼ δὲ λέγω εἰς Χριστὸν
καὶ εἰς τὴν ἐκκλησίαν

I [33] πλὴν καὶ ὑμεῖς οἱ καθ' ἕνα ἕκαστος τὴν ἑαυτοῦ γυναῖκα
οὕτως ἀγαπάτω ὡς ἑαυτόν
ἡ δὲ γυνὴ ἵνα φοβῆται τὸν ἄνδρα

It is tempting to regard vv. 22–24 as one period united around an inclusio* of repeated words in v. 22 and 24b (αἱ γυναῖκες τοῖς ἰδίοις ἀνδράσιν ... αἱ γυναῖκες τοῖς ἀνδράσιν). However, the adversative ἀλλά that starts v. 24 sets its two cola* off from vv. 22–23 and gives it a slight focus as the conclusion of Paul's address to women here, so I have set it off from the previous two verses.[25]

There are two places were versification may unhappily separate related material. Verses 26–27 belong together and carry a clearly united structure (see comment on v. 26), and vv. 29–30 are united with movement from σάρξ ("flesh"; v. 29a) to a related term, σῶμα ("body"; v. 30). Finally, we note the high density of ἐκκλησία ("church") in this passage (5:25, 27, 29, 32; cf. 1:22; 3:10, 21; 5:23–24), which in v. 32 overshadows the marriage relationship as its archetype.

---

25. See also the two parallel clauses in vv. 23a and 23b: κεφαλὴ τῆς γυναικὸς ... κεφαλὴ τῆς ἐκκλησίας.

Outline

XIV. Exhortations to Christian Households: Wives and Husbands (5:22–33)
- A. Exhortation to wives (5:22–24)
  1. First manner and motive (5:22)
  2. Rationale (5:23)
  3. Second manner and motive (5:24)
- B. Exhortation to husbands (5:25–32)
  1. Manner and rationale (5:25–27)
  2. Exhortation repeated with stress on union (5:28)
  3. Rationale in archetype of Christ and the church (5:29–32)
- C. Final exhortation to both husband and wife (5:33)

Original Text

22 αἱ γυναῖκες τοῖς ἰδίοις ἀνδράσιν ὡς τῷ κυρίῳ,[a] **23** ὅτι ἀνήρ ἐστιν κεφαλὴ τῆς
γυναικὸς ὡς καὶ ὁ Χριστὸς κεφαλὴ τῆς ἐκκλησίας, αὐτὸς σωτὴρ τοῦ σώματος·
24 ἀλλὰ ὡς ἡ ἐκκλησία ὑποτάσσεται τῷ Χριστῷ, οὕτως καὶ αἱ γυναῖκες τοῖς
ἀνδράσιν ἐν παντί. **25** Οἱ ἄνδρες, ἀγαπᾶτε τὰς γυναῖκας,[b] καθὼς καὶ ὁ Χριστὸς
ἠγάπησεν τὴν ἐκκλησίαν καὶ ἑαυτὸν παρέδωκεν ὑπὲρ αὐτῆς, **26** ἵνα αὐτὴν ἁγιάσῃ καθαρίσας τῷ λουτρῷ τοῦ ὕδατος ἐν ῥήματι, **27** ἵνα παραστήσῃ αὐτὸς ἑαυτῷ
ἔνδοξον τὴν ἐκκλησίαν, μὴ ἔχουσαν σπίλον ἢ ῥυτίδα ἤ τι τῶν τοιούτων, ἀλλ᾽ ἵνα
ᾖ ἁγία καὶ ἄμωμος. **28** οὕτως ὀφείλουσιν οἱ ἄνδρες[c] ἀγαπᾶν τὰς ἑαυτῶν γυναῖκας
ὡς τὰ ἑαυτῶν σώματα. ὁ ἀγαπῶν τὴν ἑαυτοῦ γυναῖκα ἑαυτὸν ἀγαπᾷ. **29** Οὐδεὶς
γάρ ποτε τὴν ἑαυτοῦ σάρκα ἐμίσησεν ἀλλὰ ἐκτρέφει καὶ θάλπει αὐτήν, καθὼς
καὶ ὁ Χριστὸς τὴν ἐκκλησίαν, **30** ὅτι μέλη ἐσμὲν τοῦ σώματος αὐτοῦ.[d] **31** ἀντὶ
τούτου καταλείψει ἄνθρωπος τὸν[e] πατέρα καὶ τὴν[e] μητέρα καὶ προσκολληθήσεται πρὸς[f] τὴν γυναῖκα αὐτοῦ, καὶ ἔσονται οἱ δύο εἰς σάρκα μίαν. **32** τὸ μυστήριον
τοῦτο μέγα ἐστίν· ἐγὼ δὲ λέγω εἰς Χριστὸν καὶ εἰς τὴν ἐκκλησίαν. **33** πλὴν καὶ
ὑμεῖς οἱ καθ᾽ ἕνα, ἕκαστος τὴν ἑαυτοῦ γυναῖκα οὕτως ἀγαπάτω ὡς ἑαυτόν, ἡ δὲ
γυνὴ ἵνα φοβῆται τὸν ἄνδρα.

Textual Notes

22.a. The text in the critical editions lacks a verb and is supported only by P46, B, and a few fathers.[26] Clearly, the verb implied is to be taken from the participle ὑποτασσόμενοι ("be subject to") in v. 21. Most MSS make this implied verb explicit by supplying either ὑποτάσσεσθε ("[you] be subject to"; e.g., D, F, G, and M) or ὑποτασσέσθωσαν ("let them be subject to"; e.g., ℵ, A, 33, 1175, and 1739). This verse started off a new reading section in the early church, and it could be that scribes supplied an implied verb here during this period of liturgical use of the text.[27]

25.b. Some Western and late witnesses add to τὰς γυναῖκας ("your wives") either ὑμῶν ("your"; F, G, OL, and Syriac) or ἑαυτῶν ("your own"; D, Ψ, and M). The article (τάς) already implies the pronoun "your," which is one of its common functions in Greek, so we have here another case of scribes making explicit what is already implicit in the text.

28.c. There are three main variants in this stretch of the text centering an inclusion of καί ("also") here: (1) ὀφείλουσιν οἱ ἄνδρες in ℵ, K, L, Ψ, 81, 104, 365, 630, and 1241s; (2) καὶ οἱ ἄνδρες ὀφείλουσιν ("[so] also husbands ought") in A, D, F, G, P, and a few others; and (3) ὀφείλουσιν καὶ οἱ ἄνδρες ("[so] ought also husbands") in P46, B, 33, 1175, and a few others. Because of its early attestation, the καί is included in brackets in the NA28, but I have omitted it here. It is not strictly necessary for the sense, and it seems more likely that a scribe would insert it here to bring out the meaning of husbands acting *also* as does Christ.

30.d. This short verse reads ὅτι μέλη ἐσμὲν τοῦ σώματος αὐτοῦ, "for we are members of his body," but Western and Byzantine MSS (including the second corrector of ℵ) add at the end: "from his flesh and from his bones," clearly influenced by Gen 2:23. The shorter text is supported by the earliest and better MSS (e.g., P46, ℵ*, A, B, 33, 81, 1739*, and 1881).

---

26. Both Origen and Jerome take the verb "be subject to" as implied; Jerome adds it in Latin but says, "The verb is understood so that it expresses ἀπὸ κοινοῦ ('in common') the idea"; Origen and Jerome, 233.

27. Cf. Bruce M. Metzger, *A Textual Commentary on the Greek New Testament*, 2nd ed. (New York: United Bible Societies, 1994), 541; B, ℵ, and A all have punctuation marking out Eph 5:22–24 as a new reading unit.

31.e. Both articles τὸν and τὴν are lacking in B, D*, F, and G but are found in the vast majority of other ancient MSS and versions (as well as in the LXX for Gen 2:24). The NA[28] puts brackets around both articles, but they are included here because of the overwhelming external witnesses.

31.f. The end of the quotation of Gen 2:24 reads προσκολληθήσεται πρὸς τὴν γυναῖκα αὐτοῦ, "and will adhere to his wife," in the LXX, where the prepositional prefix on the verb (προσ-) is repeated after the verb (cf. Mark 10:7). P[46], ℵ, A, 33, 81, 1739*, and a number of other MSS remove the redundant preposition and use a simple dative: προσκολληθήσεται τῇ γυναῖκι αὐτοῦ (cf. Matt 19:5). The meaning is not changed either way.

Translation

22 Wives,[28] be subject[29] to your own husbands as to the Lord.[30] **23** For a husband is the head of his wife as also Christ is the head of his church, he is the Savior of his body.[31] **24** Accordingly,[32] as the church is subject to Christ, so also wives should be subject[33] in everything to their husbands. **25** Husbands,[34] love[35] your wives, just as Christ loved his church and gave

28. This is the articular nominative (αἱ γυναῖκες) used in place of a voc.; BDF §147. Also οἱ ἄνδρες in v. 25.
29. The verb ὑποτάσσω must be brought in from the previous verse, as clear also from v. 24. "Submit" or "be in subjection to" are the best English options here. See also the textual note above on this verse for Origen and Jerome.
30. I.e., the Lord Jesus, not to her husband as "lord" (so also O'Brien, 412).
31. The versions prefer to connect "Savior" with "church" through interpretive license: "Christ is the head of the church, his body, and is himself its Savior" (ESV; cf. NIV, NRSV). It does read more smoothly in English this way but does not convey the original meaning very accurately.
32. We could expect ἀλλά here to be adversative, but see BDAG, 45 (meaning 5): "prob[ably] to be understood as an ellipsis, and can be expanded thus: *then just as the church is subject to Christ, wives should also be subject to their husbands.* Yet ἀλλά is also used to introduce an inference from what precedes: *so, therefore, accordingly*."
33. The verb ὑποτάσσω is again elided and assumed from the first part of the verse.
34. See translation note on αἱ γυναῖκες in v. 22 for the articular nominative (οἱ ἄνδρες) used as a voc.
35. This section continues general exhortations, hence the pres.-tense forms of the impv. (ἀγαπᾶτε in v. 25 and ἀγαπάτω in v. 33) are appropriate; cf. translation note on 4:27 and introduction, "Tense Form Choice."

himself up on her behalf, **26** that he might sanctify[36] her by cleansing[37] her with the washing of water with the word,[38] **27** so that he may himself present the church to himself resplendent,[39] so that she may not have spot or wrinkle or any such defect but instead be holy and blameless. **28** Thus husbands ought to love[40] their own wives, as their own bodies. The one who loves his own wife loves himself. **29** For no one has ever despised his own flesh, but he nourishes[41] and cherishes[42] it, just as Christ does the church, **30** because we are members of his body. **31** "For this reason, a man will leave his father and his mother and will adhere to his wife, and the two will be one flesh."[43] **32** This mystery is profound, for I[44] am speaking with regard

36. The aor. subjunctive of ἁγιάζω here (ἵνα ἁγιάσῃ) communicates an act of consecration rather than to the process of growth in personal holiness, as the pres.-tense form might suggest. See the same idea in Heb 13:12, ἵνα ἁγιάσῃ διὰ τοῦ ἰδίου αἵματος τὸν λαόν, "that he might consecrate his people with his own blood." Cf. the aor. subjunctive in the LXX at Exod 28:38; Lev 27:14, 16–18, 22; Deut 22:9; Ezek 44:19 versus one pres.-tense form at Lev 22:3.

37. The adv. ptc. καθαρίσας is instrumental here. E. Burton, *Syntax of the Moods and Tenses in New Testament Greek* [Edinburgh: T&T Clark, 1898), §443.

38. The phrase ἐν ῥήματι with ἐν may communicate accompaniment (like μετά or σύν), but it is instrumental here.

39. For ἔνδοξος see Luke 7:25 for splendid clothing (parallel with τρυφή, "luxury"); cf. BDAG, 332–33.

40. The pres. form of the inf. ἀγαπᾶν is default for this atelic verb, and so the tense form carries no significant aspectual nuance here. The pres. inf. of ἀγαπάω occurs 26x in the LXX and NT, while aor. ἀγαπῆσαι appears 5x in the LXX alone with no NT occurrences.

41. The compound form of this verb (ἐκτρέφω) appears only here and in 6:4, where it means "to bring up from childhood" (BDAG, 311).

42. Only here and 1 Thess 2:7, where the image is a mother cherishing a child; cf. BDAG, 442.

43. The use of εἰς marking the predicate is "under Semitic influence" but was also part of Greek "tendencies in the same direction" (BDAG, 289–91; meaning 8). This is a LXX quote, so the Hebrew obviously lies behind this construction, which is not part of Paul's own style (also 1 Cor 6:16; cf. 1 John 5:8).

44. It is difficult to bring out the force of emphatic ἐγώ here. It acts to show a contrast between Paul and Genesis—both the speakers and subject matter; cf. BDF §277 (1).

to Christ[45] and the church. **33** In any case,[46] let each and every one of you[47] love his wife as himself, let each of you love his own wife as himself, and see that[48] the wife respects[49] her husband.

Commentary

5:22 *αἱ γυναῖκες τοῖς ἰδίοις ἀνδράσιν ὡς τῷ κυρίῳ*, "Wives, be subject to your own husbands as to the Lord." The elision of the verb *ὑποτάσσω* links this verse closely with the general principle to "be subject to one another" in v. 21 and is made clear in the second half of the inclusio* in v. 24. Such elision of a noncopulative verb is unusual in Ephesians but serves here to make the connection between vv. 21 and 22 close. The imperative idea is stated directly in Colossians: *αἱ γυναῖκες, ὑποτάσσεσθε τοῖς ἀνδράσιν ὡς ἀνῆκεν ἐν κυρίῳ*, "Wives, be subject to your husbands as is fitting in the Lord" (Col 3:18; cf. 1 Cor 14:34; Titus 2:5; 1 Pet 3:1–7). The imperative idea in Eph 5:22 is picked up from context (see above on the parallel ptcs.

45. Both uses of *εἰς* ("with regard to") with *λέγω* ("I am speaking") communicate the connection or subject matter under discussion and mirror a simple acc. of specification, used a few times elsewhere (e.g., Rom 10:5); see BDAG, 288–91 (meaning 5).

46. See BDAG, 826 (meaning 1c), for this meaning of *πλήν*: "breaking off a discussion and emphasizing what is important" (cf. LSJ, 1419).

47. This is the meaning in English of the rather cumbersome Greek expression *καὶ ὑμεῖς οἱ καθ' ἕνα ἕκαστος* (woodenly: "and as for you, one by one, let each one ..."). For the expression *καθ' ἕνα* (or similar [*εἷς*] *κατὰ εἷς*), meaning either "individually," "in particular," or "one by one," see Mark 14:19; Rom 12:5; 1 Cor 14:31; Rev 4:8. Versions like NIV ("However, each one of you also must"), ESV ("However, let each one of you"), or NRSV ("Each of you, however") downplay the emphasis in the original expression.

48. The construction *ἵνα φοβῆται* here acts in parallel with impv. *ἀγαπάτω* and has the same imperatival force as also in 1 Cor 7:29 and 2 Cor 8:7; see BDF §387 (3). The idiom is explained in BDF §389 as a replacement for the rare imperatival inf. (found primarily in poetry or legal documents).

49. BDAG, 1060–62 (meaning 2b), gives only this verse as an instance of this meaning for *φοβέω/-ομαι* in the NT, but see ancient passages including LXX Lev 19:3 cited there. Cf. LSJ, 1946, where this meaning is not clearly reported; Horst Balz, *TDNT*, 9:189–219 (esp. 217, where it is equated with "a pure and patient and gentle heart").

in vv. 19–21), including the following imperative: "Husbands, *love* (ἀγαπᾶτε) your wives" (v. 25; cf. O'Brien, 411).

Note that Paul does not urge wives to *obey* their husbands, as if they were children or slaves (see 6:1, 5) to their husbands—even if some of the wives may be young girls in their mid-teens with husbands quite a bit older than themselves.[50] In all of life, people are in submission to other people and have authority over others. Both women and men are to be in submission to the Lord and to show honor to those who are appointed to serve their needs in word and sacrament ministry (4:11–14; Phil 2:29; 1 Tim 5:17).

Neither does Paul tell *women* to be in submission to *men*—but *wives* to their own *husbands* only. Believers of both sexes are equally created in God's image (Gen 1:26–28) and are heirs of eternal life together by faith in Christ (Gal 3:28–29) as "fellow heirs, fellow body members, and fellow partakers of the promise in Christ Jesus through the gospel" (3:6).[51] This comes out clearly from 5:18–19, where women are included in the new-covenant priesthood who also make up the NT choir for song and praise to God.

The submission Paul enjoins is a deference to the ultimate leadership of the woman's own husband for the health and harmonious working of the marriage relationship. The incarnate Son himself was in submission (ἦν ὑποτασσόμενος) to his human parents (Luke 2:51); all believers are to be in submission to various proper authorities (e.g., Rom 13:5; 1 Cor 16:16; Titus 3:1; 1 Pet 5:5). The focus of Ephesians is unity in the inaugurated new-creation community, which this submission is designed to facilitate. But even more pointedly, this is an expression of the wife's service to the Lord, who has subjected all things to himself (1:22) and to whom the church is in submission (v. 24a). So she voluntarily submits to her own husband as she does to the Lord Jesus (ὡς τῷ κυρίῳ; cf. 6:7; Col 3:23), especially given that her

50. See the introduction above for the historical background of marriage in the early Roman imperial era. For ὑποτάσσω see BDAG, 1042, which gives "obey" as a possible gloss but is not the best option for 5:22–24; cf. Hoehner, 734; Barth, 714.

51. Paul makes clear that wives are to submit to *their own* husbands with the adj. ἰδίοις here (BDAG, 466–67; as also in Titus 2:5 and 1 Pet 3:1, 5), where the Greek article alone would be sufficient to convey this idea, as found in v. 24 and **τὰς** γυναῖκας, "*your* wives" in v. 25. But see ἴδιος with the same function in the Eutyches inscription cited above in the introduction.

husband is charged to love her self-sacrificially, as Christ loves the church (vv. 25–33; cf. 5:2).[52]

The final clause, "as to the Lord," introduces both the manner and motive of the main exhortation of vv. 22–24. The passage is then structured by three uses of ὡς ("as"), with the lead (or main) exhortation as follows:

> *Lead exhortation #1:* [22] Wives, be subject to your own husbands
> > *Manner and motive #1*: as (ὡς) to the Lord
> > *Rationale:* [23] For a husband is the head of his wife
> > *Analogy:* as (ὡς) also Christ is the head of his church, he is the Savior of his body
> > *Manner and motive #2*: [23] Accordingly, as (ὡς) the church is subject to Christ,
>
> *Lead exhortation #2*: so also wives (should be subject) in everything to their husbands

In this structure there is repetition both of the main exhortation with the inclusio*, αἱ γυναῖκες τοῖς ἰδίοις ἀνδράσιν ... αἱ γυναῖκες τοῖς ἀνδράσιν (vv. 22, 24), and the repetition of ὡς ("as").[53]

5:23 ὅτι ἀνήρ ἐστιν κεφαλὴ τῆς γυναικὸς ὡς καὶ ὁ Χριστὸς κεφαλὴ τῆς ἐκκλησίας, αὐτὸς σωτὴρ τοῦ σώματος, "For a husband is the head of his wife as also Christ is the head of his church, he is the Savior of his body." The first part of this verse states the headship of the husband over his wife as the rationale for the wife's voluntary submission to him. Paul presents this as the reason (ὅτι, "for, because") for the submission stated as a fact without elaboration here.[54] Elsewhere he grounds this in creation as a creation ordinance (1 Cor 11:8–9; 1 Tim 2:11–13).[55] "But I want you to understand that

52. This latter point is rightly emphasized in Gibson, "Ephesians 5:21–33," 176–77.

53. For rather involved discussion of the simple comparative ὡς ("as") see Hoehner, 737–38. Cf. ὡς ... οὕτως καὶ ("as ... so also"), which sets up an analogy and explains how and why one fulfills the duty; cf. 5:1, 8; 6:7.

54. It should be stressed again that this is not male headship over females but characterizes the husband-wife relation in marriage.

55. As a "creation ordinance," marriage endures as long as does this creation (cf. Matt 22:30); cf. John Murray, *Principles of Conduct* (Grand Rapids: Eerdmans, 1957), 27–81. The problems of 1 Cor 7 are due to an "overrealized eschatology" in which some assumed that the inauguration of the new creation dissolved the marriage bond in this age.

the head of every man is Christ, the head of a wife is her husband, and the head of Christ is God" (1 Cor 11:3).

The second colon* (v. 23b) gives an analogy with which to understand the metaphor of the husband being head of his wife: "as (ὡς) also Christ is the head of his church." Christ's headship has already been expressed in 1:22 (cf. 4:15) as a result of all things in this age and in the next being *subjected* to him (ὑποτάσσω again). This relation of Christ to the church is the original archetype of marriage and establishes the role of husband as head of his wife (see below on v. 32).

The last colon* in this verse (v. 23c), "he is the Savior of his body," sets up the kind of headship the husband is to exercise on analogy with Christ's. As Christ is "Savior"—with the loaded term σωτήρ (cf. 2:5, 8)—so also the husband is to express his role as head with his wife's welfare as his constant aim. "Savior" is a familiar title on many of the Ephesian public monuments for their state goddess Artemis "Soteira," kings, emperors, and others who acted as benefactors (εὐεργέτης) for those under their authority, and it would have conveyed that sense here.[56]

Paul mixes his metaphors in an interesting way in v. 23. We expect him to say that Christ is "head of the body" (e.g., 1:22–23; Col 1:18, 24; 2:19) and "Savior of the church," but he switches them around:

ὁ Χριστὸς	κεφαλὴ	τῆς ἐκκλησίας
αὐτὸς	σωτὴρ	τοῦ σώματος

It does catch our ear and perhaps shows how "body" (σῶμα) is becoming a near synonym of "church" (ἐκκλησία) for him: "he [Christ] is head of the body, the church" (Col 1:18; cf. O'Brien, 414–15).

Headship of a husband would be easier to see in Greek antiquity where, as already stated, girls twelve to seventeen years old were given to husbands often ten to thirty years older than themselves in marriages arranged by their fathers. But just as Christ's position as "head" and "Savior" of the

56. This is a very common ancient notion and has widespread Ephesian attestation, discussed briefly in S. M. Baugh, " 'Savior of All People': 1 Tim 4:10 in Context," *WTJ* 54 (1992): 331–40; cf. F. W. Danker, *Benefactor: Epigraphic Study of a Graeco-Roman and New Testament Semantic Field* (St. Louis: Clayton, 1982); J. R. Harrison, *New Docs*, 9:4–5. Some of the Ephesian epigraphical records of interest are *IvE* 251, 274, 713, 1265, 1312, 1501, 3271, 3435. *IvE* 274 (Hadrian) was given in translation above. For Artemis Soteira (i.e., "the Saving") see *IvE* 1265.

church does not vary from one culture to another, neither also does the headship of a husband to his wife and her duty to submit to her husband "in everything" (v. 24).

Scholars sometimes read "source" as a lexical meaning of κεφαλή based on a few possible ancient uses of the term.[57] One interesting example of the use of this word near the time and place of Paul is found in the choliambic fable of Babrius, where the tail of a snake takes the lead over its head, but since the tail lacks eyes or other senses, the snake falls among sharp rocks and is injured. The tail repents, saying, "Mistress head (δέ σποινα κεφαλή), save us, if you will. … If you'll put me where I was at first I'll be more obe dient and you'll not worry about getting into trouble again under my leadership (ἀρχούσης ἐμοῦ)" (Babrius, 134; LCL trans.). This is the use of the κεφαλή metaphor in Eph 5:23 and elsewhere (e.g., 1:22) and shows some idea of leadership or authority.

Furthermore, it seems unlikely that a wife should "submit" to her own husband because he is her "source," even if Gen 2:21–23 were in the background and the lexical evidence for this meaning of κεφαλή were compelling. Submission is demonstrably performed to "one who is in authority" (Rom 13:3, 5). In the case of a husband, rather than a king, however, the wife's submission is as a fellow heir of life to someone who is charged to act like Christ with self-sacrificial love for her.[58]

5:24 ἀλλὰ ὡς ἡ ἐκκλησία ὑποτάσσεται τῷ Χριστῷ, οὕτως καὶ αἱ γυναῖκες τοῖς ἀνδράσιν ἐν παντί, "Accordingly, as the church is subject to Christ, so also

---

57. E.g., Catherine Kroeger, "Head," in *DPL*, 375–77; Peter Cotterell and Max Turner (*Linguistics & Biblical Interpretation* [Downers Grove, IL: InterVarsity Press, 1989] 141–45) use this interpretation of κεφαλή as "source" as an example of confusing the "lexical sense" of a lexeme* with its (metaphorical) use in one or two authors. They conclude that the word cannot be demonstrated to have this meaning in Paul. "Source" would more likely be conveyed by ἀρχή or metaphorically by πηγή ("spring," "source") in Greek.

58. For κεφαλή see also 1:22; BDAG, 541–42; cf. Wayne Grudem, "Does ΚΕΦΑΛΗ ('Head') Mean 'Source' or 'Authority Over' in Greek Literature?" *TrinJ* 6 (1985): 38–59; Richard S. Cervin, "Does Κεφαλή Mean 'Source' or 'Authority Over' in Greek Literature? A Rebuttal," *TrinJ* 10 (1989): 85–112; Grudem, "The Meaning of Κεφαλή ('Head'): A Response to Recent Studies," *TrinJ* 11 (1990): 3–72; Joseph A. Fitzmyer, "*Kephalê* in I Corinthians 11:3," *Int* 47 (1993): 52–59; Grudem, "The Meaning of Κεφαλή ('Head'): An Evaluation of New Evidence, Real and Alleged," *JETS* 44 (2001): 25–65.

wives should be subject in everything to their husbands."[59] This verse restates and summarizes the "manner and motivation" of the wife's voluntary submission to her own husband from vv. 22–23. In v. 22 she was to be subject "as to the Lord," which focuses on her own personal relationship with him. Now in v. 24 she is to act in subjection to her husband just as the whole church—husbands, wives, single men, single women, children, slaves, free persons, Jews, Gentiles, Scythians, Ephesians, etc.—are in subjection to Christ, that is, to the messianic King (τῷ Χριστῷ; see "Excursus: Articular Χριστός as Messianic Title"). Paul adds at the end the phrase "in everything" (ἐν παντί), which can signify "completely" (as 2 Cor 7:14; 11:6), but it is better taken to refer to submission in all the circumstances and conditions of life one may encounter (as 2 Cor 4:8; 6:4; Phil 4:6, 11; 1 Thess 5:18). Cf. v. 33 for the parting admonition to wives.

5:25 Οἱ ἄνδρες, ἀγαπᾶτε τὰς γυναῖκας, "Husbands, love your wives." Paul opens the second half of the passage (5:22–33) with a direct exhortation to husbands to love their wives, which is repeated in vv. 28, 33. Notably, Paul devotes over three times more space to the husband's duty (nine verses; twenty-four cola) than to the wife's (three verses; seven cola [includes v. 33c]). The apostle's exhortation to husbands is not elaborate in itself. They are to love their wives as themselves (v. 28), similar to the second great summary of God's law to love one's neighbor as oneself (e.g., Lev 19:18; Matt 19:19; 22:39; Rom 13:9; Gal 5:14). The difference here, though, is that—unlike neighbors—the husband and wife are joined together into one body, which requires some elaboration in vv. 28–32. Indeed, the bulk of vv. 25–33 are occupied with theological explanation of the rationale for husbands loving their wives and its archetypal foundation in Christ's love for and bond with his church.[60]

Granted that Paul's admonition to wives to be subject to their husbands is not a radical notion given its historical and creational background, this imperative for husbands to love their wives is indeed countercultural in its

---

59. "Accordingly" brings out the elipsis of a comparison with the church's subjection to Christ and of wives to their husbands; cf. BDAG, 44–45 (meaning 5).

60. See the outline above for the structure of the passage. Note that the similar exhortation in Colossians is rather spartan in comparison with Ephesians: "Wives, submit to your husbands, as is fitting in the Lord. Husbands, love your wives, and do not be harsh with them" (Col 3:18–19); cf. 1 Pet 3:7.

day.[61] As noted repeatedly above, husbands in the ancient world were very often marrying teenage girls one to three decades younger than themselves whom they may not have met personally before the wedding day. Marriage was for the purpose of raising legitimate children and heirs. Having a good, working relationship with one's wife as a companion is usually enjoined by Graeco-Roman authors in order to make the journey more pleasant and less troublesome.[62] But the advice is given because even this minimal companionship is not always the norm in antiquity:

> Socrates. "Is there anyone to whom you commit more affairs of importance than you commit to your wife?"
> Critobulus. "There is not."
> Socrates. "Is there anyone with whom you talk less?"
> Critobulus. "There are few or none, I confess." (Xenophon, *Oec.* 3.12; LCL trans.).[63]

---

61. Cf. Lee-Barnewall, "Turning ΚΕΦΑΛΗ on Its Head," 608–14.

62. Even in one of the few places where love toward one's wife was encouraged it was based on the pleasant outcomes: "Love your own wife, for what is sweeter and better than whenever a wife is kindly disposed toward (her) husband and a husband toward (his) wife till old age, without strife divisively interfering?" (Pseudo-Phocylides 195–97).

63. See also, for example, the letter from Serapion to his brothers inviting them to his marriage, contracted to the daughter of Hesperus—does he even know her name? (*P.Par.* 43; B. P. Grenfell and A. S. Hunt, eds., *The Oxyrhynchus Papyri* [London: Egypt Exploration Society, 1922], 1.99); or the object of Sostratos' desire in Menander's only complete extant play, *Dyskolos* ("Old Cantankerous," "The Grouch"). The young man only saw the girl in passing as she was adorning a shrine to the nymphs, yet the prospective bride has no speaking role or name in the play ("Girl"). (Granted that the eponymous character in Menander's *Girl from Samos* is named Chrysis.) Finally, an important inscription from Ephesus in mid-1 AD (*IvE* 20) lists contributors from the fish sellers and fishermen and their specific contributions for a fishing customs house. All but one of those named are men, with four of them simply specifying "with wife" (σὺν γυναικί); the exception is Pub. Cornelius Felix (a full Roman name), who lists his wife, Cornelia Ision; cf. G. H. R. Horsley, *New Docs*, 5:95–114.

So the idea of *loving* one's wife to the point of death was not a common thought at all in the Ephesians' world, yet that is precisely Paul's injunction for husbands in the church.[64]

καθὼς καὶ ὁ Χριστὸς ἠγάπησεν τὴν ἐκκλησίαν καὶ ἑαυτὸν παρέδωκεν ὑπὲρ αὐτῆς, "just as Christ loved his church and gave himself up on her behalf." The first colon* of v. 26a stands by itself as an exhortation to husbands that is repeated with variation and development in vv. 28 and 33a–b. In the other verses of vv. 25b–32 Paul expands on the grounds for husbands heeding his admonition to love their wives. Hence, the second and third cola* of v. 25, beginning with καθώς, serve to bring the focus of this grounds and model for the husband's love in Christ's love and self-sacrifice for his church (cf. O'Brien, 419). The same idea has already been conveyed earlier, when believers were exhorted to forgive *just as* God has forgiven them (4:32) and to love *just as* Christ loved them self-sacrificially (5:2). The latter passage forms a parallel with 5:25 (see comment on 5:2).

The husband's love—not dominion or rule—is the best guard against a wife's submission to her husband ending up as joyless slavery to spousal tyrannical despotism, which has no resemblance whatsoever to the Bible's teaching. The husband is bound by love to ensure that his wife finds their marriage a source of rich fulfillment and joyful service to the Lord. Husbands and wives have different roles in marriage, but they are equally indispensable and worthy of honor in the body of Christ (as 1 Cor 12:21–26).

5:26–27 ἵνα αὐτὴν ἁγιάσῃ καθαρίσας τῷ λουτρῷ τοῦ ὕδατος ἐν ῥήματι, ἵνα παραστήσῃ αὐτὸς ἑαυτῷ ἔνδοξον τὴν ἐκκλησίαν, μὴ ἔχουσαν σπίλον ἢ ῥυτίδα ἤ τι τῶν τοιούτων, ἀλλ' ἵνα ᾖ ἁγία καὶ ἄμωμος, "that he might sanctify her by cleansing her with the washing of water with the word, so that he may himself present the church to himself resplendent, so that she may not have spot or wrinkle or any such defect but instead be holy and blameless." Instead of moving directly back to the husband's duty toward his wife, Paul elaborates in both v. 26 and v. 27 on the effects of Christ's self-sacrifice for the church. The text is structured around three ἵνα clauses, which are not parallel but

64. Cf. Lincoln, 374. It is not as though husbands never loved their wives in antiquity! There may possibly be background here in the Lord's love for Israel modeled on the tender love and care of a husband for his wife in places like Isa 54:5–8; Ezek 16, 23; Hos 1–3; cf. O'Brien, 420.

develop in a chiastic pattern, with v. 27a as the central purpose of the whole of vv. 25–27 as follows:

25b	ὁ Χριστὸς ἠγάπησεν τὴν ἐκκλησίαν
25c	καὶ ἑαυτὸν παρέδωκεν ὑπὲρ αὐτῆς
26a	ἵνα … ἁγιάσῃ [purpose of v. 25c]
26b	καθαρίσας … [ptc. means for v. 26a]
27a	ἵνα παραστήσῃ … [central purpose of vv. 25c–27]
27b	μὴ ἔχουσαν … [ptc. purpose for v. 26b]
27c	ἀλλ᾽ ἵνα ᾖ … [alternative of v. 27b]

We can state the relationships as follows with some paraphrase and moving the central purpose (v. 27a) to the end, where English composition would prefer it:

25b	Christ loved his church	
25c	and gave himself up on her behalf	
	26a–A	in order that his self-sacrifice may sanctify her
	26b–B	by means of cleansing her with water
	27b–B′	so that she may not have any blemishes [relates to 26b]
	27c–A′	but instead be holy and blameless [relates to v. 26a]
27a	so that in consequence of all this, he may present the church to himself	

This kind of pattern, with the main point in the middle, is found especially in Semitic chiastic structures. It is important to keep this structure in mind so that we may read the last two cola* in v. 27 (v. 27b–c) not as dependent on v. 27a (the central purpose) but bypassing it to connect directly with v. 26 in an inverse, chiastic pattern (marked A-B, B′-A′). For this reason, I will discuss v. 27a last rather than in sequence as it occurs in the text.

These actions in vv. 26–27 are not those of the husband for his wife but of Christ for the church. As such, they illustrate the beneficial outcome of love in action for the husband, which moves beyond romantic love, as wonderful as that is. Even more importantly, Christ's model demonstrates a love toward someone who is not perfect or purely lovable—in the case of the church, she is full of warts, wrinkles, and impurities outside Christ's loving consecration and cleansing.

Paul combines two metaphors to explain the work of Christ in vv. 25b–27: sacrificial purification and the wedding day. While these two may seem totally separate to us, what unites them is stated in the central purpose of Christ's redemptive work in v. 27a: "so that he may himself present the church to himself resplendent." The church is Christ's bride, who must be sanctified from her impurity before she enters the divine presence of her husband. Before expanding on these two themes, note in particular that Paul's focus is on the one, universal ἐκκλησία ("church") of Christ, of which the Ephesians are a part, which is referenced four times in the passage.[65]

The idea of sacrificial purity comes across through the priestly actions of Christ's sacrifice (v. 25), who, as himself the sinless Son without blemish, had no need for the purifying offerings and sacrifices or the bath required of the Aaronic priests (e.g., Exod 29:1–21; Lev 21:17–24; 22:6; Num 19:1–9; Matt 3:13–15; Heb 7:26–28). Through his sacrifice, he "sanctifies" his people for his own possession (1:14; Titus 2:14; cf. Exod 29:21; Josh 7:13; Ezek 46:20; BDAG, 9–10). This act denotes a purification event rooted in Christ's death ("blood"; cf. 1:7; 2:13) to rid the church of impurity and guilt (e.g., 1 Cor 6:10–11; Heb 9:14–15; 13:12; Phil 2:15) rather than to a process of moral renovation to which the doctrine of sanctification refers.[66]

This act of purification is then elaborated on in v. 26b with a participle expressing the means used for the purification (καθαρίσας, "by cleansing

65. In vv. 25, 27, 29, 32, with only five other uses of ἐκκλησία in Ephesians, at 1:22 (Christ's body and fullness over which he is Head), 3:10, 21; 5:23–24. Cf. esp. 4:4.

66. The verb ἁγιάζω ("sanctify") is aor. in the expression ἵνα αὐτὴν ἁγιάσῃ as its default form in the subjunctive. Its close parallel in the NT is also aor. (Heb 13:12; cf. John 17:19 [perf. periphrastic]) with eight aor. and one pres.-tense form uses in the LXX (Exod 28:38; Lev 22:3; 27:14, 16–18, 22; Deut 22:9; Ezek 44:19). There is no temporal significance to the aor. subjunctive (cf. O'Brien, 421–22; it is conceptually *future* relative to "he gave himself" [v. 25] as a specification of a [future] purpose of that event with ἵνα), but as the default or unmarked form, the aor. tense form is semantically neutral and simply refers to the event as a whole without elaboration or description ("aspect").

her"; cf. Acts 15:9; Heb 10:2; Ignatius, *Eph.* 18.2; BDAG, 488–89).[67] Paul then elaborates on this cleansing as accomplished through a water bath "with the word." Bathing or washing with water was a common form of OT purification for priests and people (e.g., Exod 19:19–21; Lev 5:5–11; Heb 9:10) that was practiced and expanded on by the Pharisees in their daily lives (e.g., Matt 15:1–20; Luke 11:37–41).[68] The connection with baptism seems obvious (Acts 22:16; 1 Cor 6:11; Heb 10:22), but the key thing to observe is that the baptism of individuals connects them with an underlying, purifying reality of the cross (e.g., Rom 6:2–6; Gal 3:27) through the Spirit (1 Cor 12:13; cf. 1 Cor 10:1–4; and esp. Barth, 687–99). This is probably the best explanation for why Paul adds that this water purification for the church was "with the word" (ἐν ῥήματι), which refers to the powerful, divine creative force to bring the inauguration of the new creation (and its attendant sanctification) to pass (John 15:3; 17:17; Heb 6:4–5; Jas 1:18) through the Spirit (see Eph 6:17; cf. 1 Tim 4:5).[69]

As noted above, v. 27b–c relate directly to the water cleansing in v. 26 as its purpose. The first colon* (v. 27b) puts the matter negatively: "so that she may not have spot or wrinkle or any such defect." The adverbial participle here (ἔχουσαν) expresses purpose (intended result), which is confirmed by the parallel phrase in v. 27c ,where ἀλλ' ἵνα ("but instead [in order that she may] be") states the purpose explicitly, with ἵνα ("in order that," "so

---

67. The discussion of the temporal relation of the aor. ptc. καθαρίσας ("cleanse") with "sanctify" (ἁγιάσῃ) is not necessary (e.g., Barth, 626; Lincoln, 375; O'Brien, 421–22) since an adv. ptc. of means is logically prior to but temporally coincident with its outcome (cf. Gal 3:13; Heb 2:18; Burton, *Moods*, §§443, 447).

68. Cf. A. Oepke, *TDNT*, 4:295–307. While Greeks did bathe with water, it was more typical of the Romans. Elaborate gymnasium-bath complexes arose in Asia Minor under Claudius (Miletus), but the earliest known at Ephesus was under Domitian as part of a growing influence of Rome in the city's culture and building program; cf. L. Michael White, "Urban Development and Social Change in Imperial Ephesos," in *Ephesos Metropolis of Asia*, ed. Helmut Koester (Valley Forge, PA: Harvard Divinity School Press, 1995), 27–79; Martin Steskal and Martino la Torre, *Das Vedius Gymnasium in Ephesos: Archäologie und Baubefund* (Vienna: Österreichischen Akadamie der Wissenschaften, 2008), 1–3.

69. Analogous to the first creation word: "By the word of the Lord the heavens were made, and by the breath of his mouth all their host" (Psa 33:6; cf. 2 Pet 3:5). The other best option is that this "word" represents the gospel proclamation that the church believes for salvation (e.g., Rom 10:8–18; 1 Pet 1:22–25); so O'Brien, 423; cf. Hoehner, 754–57; cf. Calvin, 207.

that").[70] The second phrase acts as the positive alternative to the church having any defects: "but instead be holy and blameless."[71]

The two statements of v. 27 clarify what the sanctification (v. 26a–A) and the cleansing (v. 26b–B) consist of: removing all her defects (v. 27b–B′) and constituting the church as "holy and blameless" (v. 27c–A′). The defects here are expressed with the uncommon terms "spot" (σπίλος), "wrinkle" (ῥυτίδα), or "such like things" (τι τῶν τοιούτων).[72] Nevertheless, the reference is to the defects that prevent an Aaronite from serving as a priest in the temple (e.g., Lev 21:16–24), or an Israelite with skin disease from approaching God (Lev 13–14), as well as defects that disqualify an animal from being sacrificed (Lev 22:17–25). Once these are removed, the church is "holy and blameless," which also appears as a pair in 1:4 (see comment above) and Col 1:22.[73] This latter is the effect of the sanctification Christ's sacrificial death provides with a purity that goes to the very heart of guilt and sin rather than being merely external (Heb 9:11–15; cf. Eph 1:7).

Now we come to the purpose of all that is said in vv. 25b–27: "so that he may himself present the church to himself resplendent." The "presentation," expressed with the verb "present" (παρίστημι), may sometimes be used in a sacrificial context (e.g., Rom 12:1), but Christ is not presenting the church as a sacrificial offering to his Father.[74] The church does not constitute the

---

70. For the adv. ptc. of purpose see Burton, *Moods*, §442. The pres.-tense form of the ptc. in μὴ ἔχουσαν ("so that she may not have") is default for the atelic meaning "have" or "be in possession of," with well over two hundred uses in its pres.-tense form and no aor. ptcs. in the NT (cf. Eph 2:12; 4:28). The aor.-tense form here would give the ptc. an inceptive meaning: "so that she may not *acquire* any spot or wrinkle."

71. While the conj. ἀλλά can introduce a simple contrasting idea (BDAG, 44–45), in this case it marks an alternative event as a substitute: "I did not come to destroy the law, *but instead* (ἀλλά) to fulfill it" (Matt 5:17); cf. Eph 2:19; 5:4 (ἀλλὰ μᾶλλον, "but rather"); 5:15; 6:4; etc.

72. The term σπίλος ("spot"; BDAG, 938) occurs only at 2 Pet 2:13 (moral "blots" and "blemishes" [μῶμος; cf. ἄμωμος in 5:27]; cf. ἄσπιλος ["spotless"] in 1 Tim 6:14; 1 Pet 1:19; 2 Pet 3:14; Jas 1:27), while ῥυτίς ("wrinkle"; BDAG, 908; or "pucker," LSJ, 1578) occurs once; neither term appears in the LXX.

73. The term ἄμωμος ("blameless") can refer either to cultic* purity ("unblemished") or absence of moral fault or culpability (BDAG, 56).

74. The aor. subjunctive in the phrase ἵνα παραστήσῃ ("so that he may present") is default for a telic meaning (cf. note on ἁγιάζω above). Παρίστημι only appears three times as an aor. subjunctive in the NT and LXX (with no pres.-tense forms), but

sacrifice. Christ's loving self-sacrifice (v. 25) sanctifies her for access (2:18; 3:12) into the very presence of God to dwell with him forever:

> Therefore, brothers, since we have confidence to enter the holy places [better, "holy of holies"] by the blood of Jesus, by the new and living way that he opened for us through the curtain, that is, through his flesh, and since we have a great priest over the house of God, let us draw near with a true heart in full assurance of faith, with our hearts sprinkled clean from an evil conscience and our bodies washed with pure water. (Heb 10:19–21; cf. 2 Cor 4:14; Col 1:22)

But Paul's statement in v. 27 is that Christ—through his sanctifying sacrifice—presents the church to himself as his "resplendent" bride at the end of this creation in new-creation glory (cf. O'Brien, 424–25). "I feel a divine jealousy for you, for I betrothed you to one husband, to present (παραστῆσαι) you as a pure virgin to Christ" (2 Cor 11:2; cf. Isa 62:5).

The background for the bridal cleansing in vv. 26–27 is commonly taken to be Ezek 16:1–14 and the story the Lord tells of his washing the blood from a foundling infant girl, Israel, and raising and betrothing her to himself (e.g., O'Brien, 420; Mortiz, *Profound Mystery*, 150–52; Lincoln, 375–76). It is certainly an attractive connection, but Paul's story has a significant difference. In Ezekiel, the bride prostitutes herself with any passerby and pays for the service herself. This is the sad story of Israel's idolatry and the Lord's exacting covenant vengeance on her (Ezek 16:15–63). In Ephesians 5:26–27 the church is "resplendent" (ἔνδοξος) in utter purity—not of her own making—in preparation for the wedding feast at her entrance into eternal glory (Rev 7:14; 19:7–9; 21:2, 9–11). The new covenant was inaugurated by an intratrinitarian divine oath, which cannot be broken, and was sealed historically by the blood of the everlasting covenant (e.g., Heb 7:20–25; 13:20). All of this serves to model for husbands the kind of love and devoted care they are obliged to show their own brides.

5:28 οὕτως ὀφείλουσιν οἱ ἄνδρες ἀγαπᾶν τὰς ἑαυτῶν γυναῖκας ὡς τὰ ἑαυτῶν σώματα. ὁ ἀγαπῶν τὴν ἑαυτοῦ γυναῖκα ἑαυτὸν ἀγαπᾷ, "Thus husbands ought

---

uncompounded ἵστημι also appears predominantly as an aor. forty-one times in the NT and LXX against one pres.-tense use.

to love their own wives, as their own bodies. The one who loves his own wife loves himself." This verse is the first restatement of the main exhortation to husbands to love their wives from v. 25. The second is in v. 33. In 1 Peter 3:7 husbands are instructed to "live with your wives in an understanding way," since they are fellow heirs of eternal life. Furthermore, as noted above on v. 25, all followers of the Lord are to love their neighbors as themselves. But Paul's point in v. 28 is different. Neighbors do not love neighbors as their own bodies and by so doing love themselves. This implies an intimacy and connection between husband and wife that goes beyond any other human experience. This needs explanation, which Paul proceeds to give in vv. 29–32.

5:29 *Οὐδεὶς γάρ ποτε τὴν ἑαυτοῦ σάρκα ἐμίσησεν ἀλλὰ ἐκτρέφει καὶ θάλπει αὐτήν*, "For no one has ever despised his own flesh, but he nourishes and cherishes it." As preparation for his point to be made, Paul states a proposition that calls for universal agreement among the audience about care for one's own body. A similar use of this metaphor is found in a speech at the end of the Greek Social War in 217 BC before King Philip V of Macedon (238–179 BC), when Agelaus of Naupactus urged the king to "take thought for [the Greeks] as for your own body" (*ὡς ὑπὲρ ἰδίου σώματος*; Polybius, *Hist.* 5.104.5).

There have been people who have hated their bodies and done harm to their flesh, of course, but this sort of universal premise implies an understanding that it can be agreed to by all *reasonable* people.[75] Even more germane, there was a practice in rabbinic literature to present presumptions arising from "the nature of man," of which Eph 5:29 is a clear instance.[76] This kind of assumed, agreed-on truth (חֲזָקָה, *ḥazakah*) is found, for instance, in a discussion in the Talmud (*Ketubim* 75b) of how a man can divorce his wife for physical defects (e.g., "excessive perspiration, a mole, or offensive breath"). Two conflicting claims are taken for granted but impact

75. Witherington, 331n235, calls this statement hyperbolic and characteristic of Asiatic rhetoric. It might possibly be compelling if he gave support for this idea or examples in ancient authors. Ephesians 5:29 does not seem particularly hyperbolic.

76. See Isaac Levitats and Menachem Elon, "Ḥazakahm," in *Encyclopaedia Judaica*, 2nd ed. (New York: Thomson Gale, 2007), 8:486–91. Presumptions on the "psychological nature of man" constitute a legal principle that is still used in modern Israeli courts, according to Levitats and Elon.

deliberation on the issue: "The presumption is that no man drinks out of a cup unless he has first examined it" and "the presumption is that no man is reconciled to bodily defects."[77] The point is that Paul asks the reader to accept a similar kind of presumption from human nature in Eph 5:29 (see other examples at Rom 5:7; Gal 3:15; 2 Tim 2:4; cf. Eph 5:13).

The reasonable person cares for his body: "he nourishes (ἐκτρέφει) and cherishes (θάλπει) it." While this care is stated for one's own body, it does apply to express the tenderness of the husband's care for his wife by implication.[78] Even more importantly, "nourish" and "cherish" describe Christ's nurturing of his church in the next colon*.

5:29–30 *καθὼς καὶ ὁ Χριστὸς τὴν ἐκκλησίαν, ὅτι μέλη ἐσμὲν τοῦ σώματος αὐτοῦ*, "just as Christ does the church, because we are members of his body." The verbs "nourishes" (ἐκτρέφει) and "cherishes" (θάλπει) carry over in v. 29c from the previous colon*: "just as also Christ nourishes and cherishes the church." There's no reason to turn these into past-tense ideas, as we had in v. 25, when the focus of Christ's love was on its supreme expression on the cross, so that one can assume that Christ still loves and cherishes his people, as was expressed, for example, in 4:9–16.

Paul had reiterated a husband's self-sacrificial love for his wife from v. 25 in vv. 28–29b, but he had advanced the idea in the second passage by comparing this love to one's regard for his own body, himself, and his own flesh (cf. v. 33). Then he grounded that love in vv. 25b–27 in Christ's love for his body, the church. The remarkable twist made explicit in vv. 29–30 is that Christ's body for which he sacrificed himself was not his own person, but the church as his "body" (see on 1:23 and 4:12; cf. 1 Cor 6:15; 12:27).[79]

---

77. The first presumption is taken as a euphemism by an editor of the *Ketuboth* tractate.

78. The same language is found in an ancient papyrus marriage contract of a husband's duties toward his wife; see Gnilka, 285, or Lincoln, 379–80. The verb ἐκτρέφω ("provide food" or "bring up from childhood"; BDAG, 311) is only found in Eph 5:29 and 6:4, while θάλπω ("cherish," "comfort"; BDAG, 442) is found in Eph 5:29 and 1 Thess 2:7, which reads: "But we were gentle among you, like a nursing mother *taking care* of her own children" (emphasis added); cf. Hoehner, 766–67.

79. See esp. Hodge, 337–47, for a lengthy discussion of the nature of union with Christ here and various other views.

5:31 ἀντὶ τούτου καταλείψει ἄνθρωπος τὸν πατέρα καὶ τὴν μητέρα καὶ προσκολληθήσεται πρὸς τὴν γυναῖκα αὐτοῦ, καὶ ἔσονται οἱ δύο εἰς σάρκα μίαν, "'For this reason, a man will leave his father and his mother and will adhere to his wife, and the two will be one flesh.' " This is a quotation of Gen 2:24 with only a few minor differences from the LXX that do not affect the meaning.[80] Paul has cited other OT texts earlier without a citation introduction (e.g., 4:25–26; 5:18; cf. 6:2), and doing so here in particular serves to integrate the quotation of Gen 2:24 seamlessly into Paul's discussion (cf. O'Brien, 429–30). This becomes important when we consider how the citation is integrated into its context.

At first glance, it is puzzling why Paul quotes the whole of Gen 2:24 when all he really needs for his discussion is the last colon*, "the two will be one flesh," since this alone relates directly to his point about husband and wife being one bodily and, more importantly, the church being united to Christ as his body.[81] This last line is all Paul cites in his other use of Gen 2:24, which is worth citing:

> οὐκ οἴδατε ὅτι ὁ κολλώμενος τῇ πόρνῃ ἓν σῶμά ἐστιν; ἔσονται γάρ, φησίν, οἱ δύο εἰς σάρκα μίαν
>
> Don't you know that the man who unites himself with a prostitute is one in body with her? For, it says, "The two will be one flesh." (1 Cor 6:16)

Notice that Paul introduces the quote of Genesis with γάρ ("for"), marking the quotation as the evidence that establishes the previous conclusion. I paraphrase: "The man and the prostitute are one body, since Scripture clearly states this at creation by describing the union of a man and a woman as the two becoming one flesh." This is how one would expect the OT text to function. But Paul quotes the whole of Gen 2:24 because it opens with

80. The LXX has: ἕνεκεν τούτου καταλείψει ἄνθρωπος τὸν πατέρα αὐτοῦ καὶ τὴν μητέρα αὐτοῦ καὶ προσκολληθήσεται πρὸς τὴν γυναῖκα αὐτοῦ καὶ ἔσονται οἱ δύο εἰς σάρκα μίαν (Gen 2:24). See also the variant reading for Eph 5:31, reported in the textual notes for this verse above. Genesis 2:24 is also cited in 1 Cor 6:16; Matt 19:5; Mark 10:7–8.

81. E.g., Gnilka, 286–87; Best, 553. Note that Paul only quotes a phrase from OT passages in 4:25–26 and 5:18, not whole passages or verses.

"for this reason" or "because of this."[82] Once again (cf. 4:8; 5:14), Paul sees the OT text as derivative from the reality of Christ, not vice versa, as he explains next, and so will I.

5:32 τὸ μυστήριον τοῦτο μέγα ἐστίν· ἐγὼ δὲ λέγω εἰς Χριστὸν καὶ εἰς τὴν ἐκκλησίαν, "This mystery is profound, for I am speaking with regard to Christ and the church." Before moving to the interpretation of this verse, there are two grammatical issues to discuss. Some versions have τοῦτο ("this") as the subject of the first colon* and the adjective μέγας (here "profound"; BDAG, 623–25, meaning 4; LSJ, 1088–89, "weighty") as attributive: "This is a profound mystery" (NIV, ESV; cf. NRSV). But the word order does not favor this sentence structure, and the article with "mystery" shows that the *pronoun* is attributive—τὸ μυστήριον τοῦτο, "this mystery" (as also in Rom 11:25; cf. Eph 1:21; 2:2; 3:8; 6:12)—and therefore the adjective μέγας is predicate (as Titus 1:13). In the end, the difference is not drastic, but "the better alternative stresses the magnitude, importance, or profundity of the mystery" (Hoehner, 775).

The use of the nominative pronoun "I" in the phrase ἐγὼ δὲ λέγω ("for I am speaking") adds some stress on the subject and is used elsewhere for a solemn declaration (Gal 5:2) or an authoritative declaration in contrast with others (e.g., Matt 5:22, 28, 32, 34, 39, 44).[83] Sampley notes the work of Morton Smith regarding a possible rabbinic background to the phrase in legal opinions that cut against the grain of prevailing positions.[84] Hence, Paul is contrasting his interpretation with the surface view of Gen 2:24 that relates it only to human marriage. This would explain the use of ἐγώ ("I") here (cf. 3:1 and 4:1).

---

82. As already reported, the LXX of Gen 2:24 (also Mark 10:7) opens with ἕνεκεν τούτου, while Paul's quotation has ἀντὶ τούτου (Matt 19:5 has ἕνεκα τούτου). The two phrases are synonymous, and neither ἕνεκεν nor ἀντί is common in Paul's writings. For ἕνεκα/-εν see BDAG, 334; for ἀντί see BDAG, 87–88; BDF §208 (1); 2 Thess 2:10. It could be that Paul is citing from memory with a synonym or that he had a different Old Greek version than our LXX.

83. It should be noted that λέγω in the other places cited has a different force from in Eph 5:32. In the former, the verb is a "speech-act," which is self-referential of the utterance: "I (hereby) declare" (cf. 4:17 and comment there; "Aoristic," in Burton, *Moods*, §13). The force in Eph 5:32 refers to the subject matter of Paul's discussion in vv. 29–31 (i.e., "what I am talking about is …").

84. Sampley, "*One Flesh*," 88–89.

Along with the interpretation of 4:8 and 5:14, Paul has found an OT text that speaks to the christocentric truths of inaugurated eschatological realities. What is notable about those texts is that Paul sees the OT texts as shadowy pointers to NT fulfillments, texts that were originally given for that prophetic purpose. They were a *sufficient* though not a full disclosure of divine mysteries of redemptive history, revealed fully only in conjunction with the incarnate Son's completed redemptive work (see on 1:9; 3:3–4, 9; 6:19). Redemptive revelation follows redemptive accomplishment.

In the instance of Gen 2:24 cited in 5:31, Paul has cited it in such a way that it follows this same pattern but in a more "profound" (μέγας) way. Paul declares in v. 32 that the original created institution of union of husband and wife was itself modeled on Christ's union with the church as his "body" (v. 23) as its archetype. On the historical plane, marital union then becomes a type of the historical antitype of fulfillment in Christ.[85] Prior to this disclosure in Christ, the reality on which marriage was predicated and to which it would later refer was a "mystery."[86]

This does not mean that Gen 2:24 *only* speaks of this eschatological reality—it also establishes the creation ordinance of marital union. But it reveals more than this, which is now clear since Christ Jesus has united the whole church to himself and thereby to God "in one body" (2:16), which is composed of a great variety of peoples along with the saints of old (2:19; cf. Col 1:12) and which has been purified through the high-priestly intervention of himself (so vv. 25–27). Christ's bride has been sanctified to become "holy and blameless" (v. 27) before him, for which she was chosen before the foundation of the world (1:4).[87] This view alone explains how Paul cites Gen 2:24 in the previous verse: "we are members of his body '*for this reason* a man will leave his father ... and the two will be one flesh.' "[88] "Even all that

85. Many interpreters see only a typological (or allegorical or prophetic) relation of marriage and later soteriology in Christ in this reference; cf. Barth, 637–39; Hoehner, 775–78; Lincoln, 380–83.

86. See above on 3:1–12 and excursus below.

87. The two passages are intentionally linked by ἅγιος καὶ ἄμωμος.

88. See also O'Brien, 428–35; Lincoln, 381; cf. George W. Knight III, "Husbands and Wives as Analogues of Christ and the Church," in *Recovering Biblical Manhood and Womanhood: A Response to Evangelical Feminism*, ed. John Piper and Wayne Grudem (Wheaton, IL: Crossway, 1991), 165–78 (esp. 175–76).

is said of Adam and Eve is to be interpreted with reference to Christ and the church."[89]

5:33 πλὴν καὶ ὑμεῖς οἱ καθ' ἕνα, ἕκαστος τὴν ἑαυτοῦ γυναῖκα οὕτως ἀγαπάτω ὡς ἑαυτόν, ἡ δὲ γυνὴ ἵνα φοβῆται τὸν ἄνδρα, "In any case, let each and every one of you love his wife as himself, and see that the wife respects her husband." The conjunction πλὴν (here, "in any case") signals a return to the point of the discussion and its conclusion, i.e., concluding all of vv. 22–33 and vv. 25–33 in particular.[90] Paul had spent considerable space in both subsections of vv. 22–33 elaborating on the rationale for preserving and enhancing marital union with submission (vv. 22–24) and love (vv. 25–33) on the model of Christ's own love and union with his people in the church. Now he brings vv. 25–33 to a close by stating for a third time (vv. 25 and 28) that husbands are obliged to love their own wives.

Here in v. 33 Paul personalizes his instruction explicitly by stressing that this admonition comes not to an abstract class of men ("husbands") but to "each and every one of you." The upshot of Paul's point throughout vv. 25–33 is to show the dignity, privilege, and vital importance of husbands loving their own wives. The husband's interests and purposes and his wife's submission are not for his own honor and status but to turn his headship on its head by loving his wife self-sacrificially in imitation of Christ.[91]

Likewise, wives also mirror this relationship by modeling the church's "respectful (ἐν φόβῳ) and pure conduct" (1 Pet 3 2) toward her loving Savior (vv. 23, 25–27) by submitting to their husbands (vv. 22–24). So in v. 33c, Paul reiterates and concludes his admonition to wives by referencing the wife (sg.) specifically with her duty to "fear" her own husband. This is not slavish terror but "a profound measure of respect" (BDAG, 1060–62, meaning 2) for her husband. Jack Gibson helpfully concludes:

> Rather than focusing on the rights of the husbands and wives, rather than providing financial incentives for the promotion of marriage, Paul drove right to the heart of marital unity by

---

89. Jerome reporting the words of Gregory of Nazianzus in *ACCS*, 199; cf. Origen and Jerome, 240–41.
90. BDAG, 826; BDF §449.
91. The reversal image is taken from Lee-Barnewall's insightful "Turning ΚΕΦΑΛΗ on Its Head."

> presenting the sacrifice of Christ on the cross as the model for the relationship of the husband to the wife. … In the new οἰκονομία of God, the husband is called on to be willing to sacrifice everything for his wife, up to and including his life. For the husband, this is what it means for him to love his wife. The wife, in return is to respect her husband and show respect to him for his sacrifices on her behalf (v. 33). A marriage characterized by such love and respect will indeed be a unified marriage.[92]

In following Paul's admonition in vv. 22–33, both husbands and wives mirror the most fundamental purpose in creational existence: to glorify God and to dwell in his very presence in the full enjoyment of his self-sacrificial love in Christ forever.

Application and Devotional Implications

It seems superfluous to suggest an application from Eph 5:22–33 since the text is itself an application of the principle expressed in v. 21: "Be subject to one another in the fear of Christ. Wives, submit to your husbands. Husbands, love your wives." But perhaps there is something worth adding.

As repeatedly mentioned above, marriage in the ancient world contemporary with the NT was normally quite different from today. Marriages were usually arranged by families between what we would regard as underage girls and older boys or usually young or not-so-young men. Today things are quite different. It takes no interpretive skill to understand that husbands are to love their wives self-sacrificially today just as in the first century. It was not normally expected of husbands back then, but there are no real cross-cultural difficulties in understanding what marital love and self-sacrifice mean today from the ancient biblical text.

What is difficult, particularly in light of a generation of feminist and egalitarian efforts in Western societies, is whether a wife today is still bound to submit to her husband, and if so, how? Modern American women are marrying at age twenty-six on average, not fourteen. They can expect to live to around the age of eighty-one, not thirty-five. They have real access to professional careers and significant societal contributions their ancient

92. Gibson, "Ephesians 5:21–33," 177.

sisters could not even dream about. Submit? Isn't that just a bygone relic of long-discarded patriarchy?

Consider this, however: Are Paul's insights here about marriage based on his patriarchal social order in the first century, or are they based on creation? If the latter, then we are dealing with enduring fundamentals about marriage that do not change from one society to the next. But *submit*? Frankly, I think the whole issue of submission is poorly discussed in abstract. In practice, it does not look the same from one marriage to the next. How does a modern wife submit while retaining her God-given integrity as a fellow heir of life and fellow citizen with the saints? I think Paul answers that in 5:15: She submits with wisdom and careful reflection on biblical truths that bear on the issue. Ideally, this whole issue never becomes a problem or an issue between a man and wife when a godly husband lovingly cherishes his wife as Christ cherishes the church. But both wives and husbands must pray for and exercise wisdom in their submission and love.

It is notable that Paul says so much and so little in Eph 5:22–33. We may want more specifics about how exactly each married couple is to relate to each other. But that is the point above: Paul lays down a few, essential principles and leaves the rest for us to work out wisely through the study of Scripture and the principles it teaches. For Paul to have said more would make it appear that each marriage looks exactly the same, and to have said less would have left us without a solid foundation on which to build. Furthermore, we have a vital resource in the seasoned saints of our churches, to whom we can also look for models of godly lives, not only in marriage but in singleness and in our other walks of life.

Selected Bibliography

Barton, S., and G. Horsley. "A Hellenistic Cult Group and the New Testament Churches." *JAC* 24 (1981): 7–41.

Baugh, S. M. " 'Savior of All People': 1 Tim 4:10 in Context." *WTJ* 54 (1992): 331–40.

Burn, A. "*Hic Breve Vivitur:* A Study of the Expectation of Life in the Roman Empire." *Past and Present* 4 (1953): 2–31.

Campbell-Reed, E. "Should Wives 'Submit Graciously'? A Feminist Approach to Interpreting Ephesians 5:21–33." *RevExp* 98 (2001): 263–76.

Cervin, R. "Does Κεφαλή Mean 'Source' or 'Authority Over' in Greek Literature? A Rebuttal." *TrinJ* 10 (1989): 85–112.

Danker, F. *Benefactor: Epigraphic Study of a Graeco-Roman and New Testament Semantic Field*. St. Louis: Clayton, 1982.

Dawes, G. *The Body in Question: Metaphor and Meaning in the Interpretation of Ephesians 5:21–33*. Boston: Brill, 1998.

Fitzmyer, J. "*Kephalê* in I Corinthians 11:3." *Int* 47 (1993): 52–59.

Gibson, J. "Ephesians 5:21–33 and the Lack of Marital Unity in the Roman Empire." *BSac* 168 (2011): 162–77.

Gombis, T. "A Radically New Humanity: The Function of the *Haustafel* in Ephesians." *JETS* 48 (2005): 317–30.

Grudem, W. "Does ΚΕΦΑΛΗ ('Head') Mean 'Source' or 'Authority Over' in Greek Literature?" *TrinJ* 6 (1985): 38–59.

———. "The Meaning of κεφαλή ('Head'): An Evaluation of New Evidence, Real and Alleged." *JETS* 44 (2001): 25–65.

———. "The Meaning of Κεφαλή ('Head'): A Response to Recent Studies." *TrinJ* 11 (1990): 3–72.

Knibbe, D., H. Engelmann, and B. Iplikçioglu. "Neue Inschriften aus Ephesos XII." *JAÖI* 62 (1993): Hauptblatt 113–50.

Knight, G. "Husbands and Wives as Analogues of Christ and the Church." In *Recovering Biblical Manhood and Womanhood: A Response to Evangelical Feminism*, edited by J. Piper and W. Grudem, 165–78. Wheaton, IL: Crossway, 1991.

Kostenberger, A. "The Mystery of Christ and the Church: Head and Body, 'One Flesh.' " *TrinJ* 12 (1991): 79–94.

Lee-Barnewall, M. "Turning Κεφαλή on Its Head: The Rhetoric of Reversal in Ephesians 5:21–33." In *Christian Origins and Greco-Roman Culture: Social and Literary Contexts for the New Testament*, edited by S. Porter and A. Pitts, 599–614. Boston: Brill, 2013.

Lelis, A., W. Percy, and B. Verstraete. *The Age of Marriage in Ancient Rome*. Studies in Classics 26. Lewiston, NY: Edwin Mellen, 2003.

Miletic, S. "*One Flesh*": *Eph. 5.22–24, 5.31, Marriage and the New Creation*. AnBib 115. Rome: Pontifical Biblical Institute, 1988.

Peterman, G. "Marriage and Sexual Fidelity in the Papyri, Plutarch and Paul." *TynB* 50 (1999): 163–72.

Pomeroy, S. *Xenophon Oeconomicus: A Social and Historical Commentary*. Oxford: Clarendon, 1994.

Sampley, J. P. *"And the Two Shall Become One Flesh": A Study of Traditions in Ephesians 5:21–33*. Cambridge: Cambridge University Press, 1971.

Schüssler Fiorenza, E. *In Memory of Her: A Feminist Theological Reconstruction of Christian Origins*. New York: Crossroad, 1989.

Stowers, S. "A Cult From Philadelphia: *Oikos* Religion or Cult Association?" In *The Early Church in Its Context*, edited by A. Malherbe, F. Norris, and J. Thompson, 287–301. Leiden: Brill, 1998.

Westfall, C. " 'This Is a Great Metaphor!' Reciprocity in the Ephesians Household Code." In *Christian Origins and Greco-Roman Culture: Social and Literary Contexts for the New Testament*, edited by S. Porter and A. Pitts, 561–98. Boston: Brill, 2013.

Winter, B. *Roman Wives, Roman Widows: The Appearance of New Women and the Pauline Communities*. Grand Rapids: Eerdmans, 2003.

Wold, B. "Family Ethics in *4QInstruction* and the New Testament." *NovT* 50 (2008): 286–300.

Exhortations to Christian Households: Children and Parents in the Lord (6:1–4)

Introduction

In Ephesians 6:1–4 Paul urges proper, fundamental relations between children and parents in the Lord. This is the second of three specific examples of how the members of the congregation are to submit to one another in their households, developing out of the general exhortation of 5:21. The first was the interrelations of wives and husbands (5:22–33), and the third and last is slaves with masters (6:5–9). These are the three main relations in the ancient οἶκος ("household," "estate"), though one could extend these basics further to other common members of the house, such as widowed sisters and her children or freedmen (below). Yet Paul is not interested in a lengthy treatise on these relations but merely gives a few basic ideas as groundwork for Christians to apply to the great variety of circumstances and relational variations one encounters in life both in the world and in the church.

The cola* in this passage tend to be relatively short and more conversational than the more "literary" first few chapters of the epistle, which fits giving advice to one's friends and associates, represented in the exhortations of these later chapters. The cola* and periods become longer in 6:10–20 as Paul moves into an exalted exposition on Christian warfare.

Here is my suggested organization of 6:1–4:

A   [1] τὰ τέκνα ὑπακούετε τοῖς γονεῦσιν ὑμῶν ἐν κυρίῳ
      τοῦτο γάρ ἐστιν δίκαιον

B   [2] τίμα τὸν πατέρα σου καὶ τὴν μητέρα
      ἥτις ἐστὶν ἐντολὴ πρώτη ἐν ἐπαγγελίᾳ
      [3] ἵνα εὖ σοι γένηται
      καὶ ἔσῃ μακροχρόνιος ἐπὶ τῆς γῆς

C + καὶ οἱ πατέρες μὴ παροργίζετε τὰ τέκνα ὑμῶν
ἀλλὰ ἐκτρέφετε αὐτὰ
ἐν παιδείᾳ καὶ νουθεσίᾳ κυρίου

The second colon* in v. 1 is quite short and leads quickly into the OT quote of vv. 2–3. Speaking of versification, it seems odd to divide the OT quote into two verses in vv. 2–3, so I have put these cola* back together where they belong. The only other point of note is that reference to the Lord (κύριος) frames this passage by appearing in the first and last cola* (vv. 1a [ἐν κυρίῳ] and 4c [κυρίου]).

Outline

XV. Exhortations to Christian Households: Children and Parents in the Lord (6:1–4)
- A. Children to be obedient, as is right (6:1)
- B. OT justification (6:2–3)
- C. Parents' nurture of children in the Lord (6:4)

Original Text

1 Τὰ τέκνα, ὑπακούετε τοῖς γονεῦσιν ὑμῶν ἐν κυρίῳ[a]· τοῦτο γάρ ἐστιν δίκαιον.
2 τίμα τὸν πατέρα σου καὶ τὴν μητέρα, ἥτις ἐστὶν ἐντολὴ πρώτη ἐν ἐπαγγελίᾳ,
3 ἵνα εὖ σοι γένηται καὶ ἔσῃ μακροχρόνιος ἐπὶ τῆς γῆς. **4** Καὶ οἱ πατέρες, μὴ παροργίζετε τὰ τέκνα ὑμῶν ἀλλὰ ἐκτρέφετε αὐτὰ ἐν παιδείᾳ καὶ νουθεσίᾳ κυρίου.

Textual Notes

1.a. The words ἐν κυρίῳ ("in the Lord") are present in the vast majority of ancient Greek MSS, translations, and church fathers, but are missing in Vaticanus (B), some Western uncials (D*, F, G), and a few other witnesses. Vaticanus especially is weighty and is part of why the editors of the critical text include the words in brackets.[1] We are told that if the phrase is not original, then it may have been inserted by scribes recollecting 5:22 (ὡς τῷ κυρίῳ ["as to the Lord"]) or Col 3:20 (Τὰ τέκνα, ὑπακούετε τοῖς γονεῦσιν

1. Cf. Bruce M. Metzger, *A Textual Commentary on the Greek New Testament*, 2nd ed. (New York: United Bible Societies, 1994), 541–42.

κατὰ πάντα, τοῦτο γὰρ εὐάρεστόν ἐστιν ἐν κυρίῳ ["Children, obey your parents in everything, for this is well pleasing in the Lord"]). The arguments against the insertion, though, are that neither of the statements in Eph 5:22 and in Col 3:20 is the same. For instance, a copyist who wanted to parallel Eph 6:1 with the Colossians statement would not have inserted ἐν κυρίῳ at the end of the *first* colon* but after the *second* as so: τοῦτο γάρ ἐστιν δίκαιον **ἐν κυρίῳ** ("for this is right *in the Lord*"). Furthermore, Metzger notes regarding a variant in 6:19 that "in the Pauline corpus codex Vaticanus not infrequently displays a strand of Western contamination, and therefore the weight of its testimony, when united with Western witnesses, should not be over evaluated."[2] Remarkably, the committee did not heed this warning for this variant in v. 1. We should also note the early and strong witnesses for including the phrase in the first colon*, including P[46], א, A, D[1], Ψ, 33, 81, 1175, 1241, 1739, and 1881. For these reasons, I regard the phrase as original and as an important part of Paul's meaning.

Translation

1 Children,[3] obey[4] your parents in the Lord, for this is right. **2** "Honor your father and your mother" (which is the first[5] commandment with a promise) **3** "that it may go well with you and you may enjoy[6] long life[7] in the land."

---

2. Ibid., 542.

3. The articular nominative τὰ τέκνα ("children") functions as voc., as seen earlier; see translation notes on 5:22 and 25. The same occurs below as well and will draw no further notice: οἱ πατέρες ("fathers"; v. 4), οἱ δοῦλοι ("slaves"; v. 5), and οἱ κύριοι ("masters"; v. 9).

4. As noted earlier (esp. at 4:25–30), the pres.-tense form of the impv. found throughout this passage is appropriate for general exhortations that set one's behavior or lifestyle. So in vv. 1–4 we find: ὑπακούετε ... τίμα ... μὴ παροργίζετε ... ἐκτρέφετε ("obey ... honor ... do not provoke ... rear"; and see ὑπακούετε ["obey"] again in v. 5). There are no aor. impvs. in 6:1–4. For discussion see "Additional Exegetical Comments" after 4:25–5:2.

5. Cf. Best, 562, who renders this colon* as "for this is a pre-eminent commandment carrying with it a promise."

6. The word *enjoy* is added to conform to the English idiom for long life.

7. The only use of the adj. μακροχρόνιος ("long-lived"; BDAG, 613) in biblical literature is here in Eph 6:3 and in the LXX versions of the fifth commandment in Exod 20:12 and Deut 5:16; cf. synonymous πολυήμερος ("length of days") in Deut 22:7.

4 And fathers, do not provoke your children to anger, but rear[8] them in the training and reproof[9] of the Lord.

Commentary

6:1 Τὰ τέκνα, ὑπακούετε τοῖς γονεῦσιν ὑμῶν ἐν κυρίῳ, "Children, obey your parents in the Lord." As noted in the introduction, this is the second of three specific examples of how submission in the church is to be carried out in the Christian household from 5:21. Like the other two examples (5:22–33 and 6:5–9), Paul does not speak only about one party in the relationship but to both. Here in vv. 1–4 he speaks to both children (vv. 1–3) and to parents (v. 4).

The address to children to "obey" (rather than to "love") their parents is notable. Obedience requires a submission of will and cannot easily be feigned. Calvin takes obedience here as synecdoche* for the honor required toward parents in the fifth commandment, cited in vv. 2–3, because obedience is the more difficult form of honor and the other parts of honor will follow (Calvin, 212). It should also be noted that the incarnate Son of God was "in submission" (ἦν ὑποτασσόμενος) to both Mary and Joseph during his childhood (Luke 2:51; cf. Matt 19:19; Luke 18:20).

It is easy to overlook the radical character of Eph 6:1–3 in its own day. First, Paul is addressing children directly. The great moralists in antiquity certainly address issues of child-rearing at some length.[10] But this and other such essays are addressed to fathers. In Ephesians 6:1–3 Paul speaks directly to Christian children with the assumption that they are present with their parents when this epistle is read and that they are hearing the whole of its instruction as well (Lincoln, 403).

---

8. The compound form of the verb ἐκτρέφω appears only here and in 5:29 ("nourish") in the NT; cf. BDAG, 311.

9. The term νουθεσία used here reinforces the connection between this passage and OT wisdom, especially in Proverbs. See the comment.

10. For example, Pseudo-Plutarch on "The Upbringing of Children" (*Lib. ed.*; in Greek, Περὶ Παίδων Ἀγωγῆς) starts at the beginning with parentage—one should not sire a son with one's slave girls or with courtesans—then the type of nurse to whom to turn the boy over, noting particularly that the nurse should be able to speak Greek properly so that the boy learns to speak well without barbarisms; then he turns to the appointment of *paidagogoi* (Gal 3:24–25), etc. All of this is addressed to the father.

The second radical point to Eph 6:1–4 is that Paul addresses *children* (τέκνα)—that is, both boys and *girls*, and not boys alone. As mentioned above under 5:22–24, girls in the ancient Greek world were generally sequestered from public view except under very rigidly supervised circumstances until marriage, which occurred around age fourteen or so.[11] Yet Paul expects whole families, including their girls, to be present for the reading of the epistle, perhaps on the model of the synagogue.[12]

In contrast to reading τέκνα ("children") as including girls, Best, 563, says that τέκνα "would have been automatically understood by readers as meaning male children." He gives no evidence for such restriction, but it is a reasonable position given the general predominance of males in Hellenic public life and even more pointedly that girls were not in the parental home as long as boys.[13] However, the meaning of the text is not ultimately determined by the readers but by the author. And in this case, the author, Paul, believes that there is no male or female in Christ when it comes to matters of place in the new covenant and its inheritance (Gal 2:28). Furthermore, did Paul desire only sons to obey their parents and not daughters? Regardless, girls at Ephesus sometimes did have prominent public roles in a (munificent) office called the *prytany*.[14] In light of this and of other pertinent evi-

---

11. I.e., with attendants; however, note that Ephesian girls participated in certain public festivals for Artemis, discussed in S. M. Baugh, "A Foreign World: Ephesus in the First Century," in *Women in the Church*, 2nd ed., ed. A. J. Köstenberger and T. R. Schreiner (Grand Rapids: Baker, 2005), 26–35.

12. Cf. James Tunstead Burtchaell, *From Synagogue to Church: Public Services and Offices in the Earliest Christian Communities* (Cambridge: Cambridge University Press, 1992) for defense of continuity between synagogue and church. For children in the Christian community see Andreas Lindemann, "… ἐκτρέφετε αὐτὰ ἐν παιδείᾳ καὶ νουθεσίᾳ κυρίου (Eph 6:4): Kinder in der Welt des frühen Christentums," *NTS* 56 (2010): 169–90. Later Christians showed obvious concern for their children and their whole household; e.g., "Lord, have mercy on your servant (τῷ δούλῳ σου) Ago […] and on his child and on all his house. Amen" (*IvE* 1361).

13. For example, a girl entered her husband's home at marriage between fourteen and sixteen years of age, while a boy married at around twenty to thirty years old and often still lived afterward at his parents' home with his young bride (see above on 5:22–24).

14. See discussion in Baugh, "Foreign World," 31–32; and the poem of Claudia Trophime the Prytanis (*IvE* 1062), cited above in the introduction to 1:3–14 (cf. *IvE* 1066). There is also evidence that girls played a role in public festivals for Artemis Ephesia (Baugh, "Foreign World," 26–35).

dence, I do think that τέκνα would not automatically refer only to males to Paul's Ephesian audience. I will discuss this briefly in "Excursus: Boys and Girls at Ephesus."

The phrase ἐν κυρίῳ ("in the Lord") attaches to the verb "obey," not to "your parents," and implies that children are considered as members of the covenant community alongside their parents.[15] Hence, "in the Lord" qualifies the child's obedience as a religious service in deference to Christ (Hodge, 357). The obedience is due to both parents; the mother's submission to her husband (5:22–24, 33) does not remove her parental dignity but rather increases it. That Christ is the referent of κύριος ("Lord") here is clear from the fact that 6:1–4 is following up from the general notion of submission in 5:21 "in the fear of Christ." There is a parallel statement in Colossians that further illumines the idea:

> Τὰ τέκνα ὑπακούετε τοῖς γονεῦσιν κατὰ πάντα
> τοῦτο γὰρ εὐάρεστόν ἐστιν ἐν κυρίῳ
>
> Children, obey your parents in everything,
> for this is well pleasing in the Lord. (Col 3:20)

Andrew Lincoln states without support that v. 1 and its reference to children being "in the Lord" are "irrelevant for discussion of the issue of whether infants were baptized as part of households in the early church" (Lincoln, 403; cf. Gnilka, 295). Yet this text and others like it form the basis for infant baptism in the NT church.[16] Children of only one believing parent

---

15. To say "parents who are in the Lord" would require a second article: τοῖς γονεῦσιν ὑμῶν **τοῖς** ἐν κυρίῳ; cf. 1:5; Rom 3:24; 4:11; 7:10; 9:30; etc. Paul uses the phrase "in the Lord" to qualify mutual relationships with himself like "brother" (Phil 1:14; cf. Eph 6:21) or "child" (1 Cor 4:17); cf. Rom 16:11–13; 1 Cor 7:22, 39; Ezek 16:20–21. This mutual relationship in the Lord by parent and child in the covenant community together strengthens the commitment of both parties involved as an expression of mutual submission and love. Cf. Best, 563, for discussion of the possibility of children of pagan parents in the Christian community and citation of Mark 3:31–35; 10:29–30.

16. Pierre Ch. Marcel, *The Biblical Doctrine of Infant Baptism: Sacrament of the Covenant of Grace*, trans. Philip Edgcumbe Hughes (Cambridge: James Clarke, 1953), 187–245; John Murray, *Christian Baptism* (Philadelphia: P&R, 1974); cf. David F. Wright, *Infant Baptism in Historical Perspective: Collected Studies*, SCHT (Eugene, OR: Wipf & Stock, 2007); Wright, ed., *Baptism: Three Views* (Downers

are not "unclean, but the fact is they are holy" (1 Cor 7:14), and as Eph 6:1 affirms, they are fellow members of the covenant community "in the Lord." Children of believers are baptized precisely because they belong to the Lord (cf. Ezek 16:20–21) with the sacrament that signifies and seals God's covenant promises to them (as Eph 2:12). Not every theological doctrine or practice is based on explicit proof texts; some are drawn out from multiple texts by good and necessary inference. It should be noted, of course, that a significant portion of the church rejects this view on infant baptism in favor of believer- or adult-baptist theology and practice.[17]

τοῦτο γάρ ἐστιν δίκαιον, "for this is right." As discussed at 2:8 and very often in Greek (e.g., Col 3:20), neuter τοῦτο refers to the whole preceding statement as its antecedent. Hence, what is right is that children obey their parents in the Lord. The "rightness" of this act is derived because it is "obligatory in view of certain requirements of justice" (BDAG, 247), particularly in light of God's requirements (Acts 4:19), or there is a certain equity to it (Phil 1:7; 2 Thess 1:6). Here in Ephesians 6:1, the justice of this requirement for children to obey their parents is derived from the fifth commandment, which Paul cites in the next verse. "He proves it to be right, because the Lord has commanded it; for it is not lawful to dispute or call in question the appointment of Him whose will is the most sure rule of goodness and righteousness" (Calvin, 212). It should be noted that this requirement is evident to all people through general revelation in creation, as is implied when Paul invokes the effect of the law written on the hearts (Rom 2:14–15) of people created in God's image for a charge against them, which includes that they are γονεῦσιν ἀπειθεῖς, "disobedient to parents" (Rom 1:30; also 2 Tim 3:2).[18]

Grove, IL: InterVarsity Press, 2009); John V. Fesko, *Word, Water, and Spirit: A Reformed Perspective on Baptism* (Grand Rapids: Reformed Heritage, 2010).

17. An historic Reformed baptist position is embodied in the Second London Baptist Confession of 1689. Recent defenses of the believer or adult baptist position are: G. R. Beasley-Murray, *Baptism in the New Testament*, 2nd ed. (Carlisle, UK: Paternoster, 1997); Bruce A. Ware, "Believers' Baptism View," in Wright, ed., *Baptism: Three Views*, 19–50; and Thomas R. Schreiner and Shawn D. Wright, eds., *Believer's Baptism: Sign of the New Covenant in Christ* (Nashville: Broadman and Holman, 2006).

18. The Mosaic theocratic law specified the death penalty for the child who struck or cursed a parent (Exod 21:15–17; Lev. 20:9), which is cited along with the fifth commandment by Jesus in Matt 15:4//Mark 7:10. For discussion of parents and children in Graeco-Roman literature see Lincoln, 398–402.

6:2–3 τίμα τὸν πατέρα σου καὶ τὴν μητέρα, ἥτις ἐστὶν ἐντολὴ πρώτη ἐν ἐπαγγελίᾳ, ἵνα εὖ σοι γένηται καὶ ἔσῃ μακροχρόνιος ἐπὶ τῆς γῆς, " 'Honor your father and your mother' (which is the first commandment with a promise) 'that it may go well with you and you may enjoy long life in the land.' " Just as earlier in Ephesians and particularly at 5:31, Paul quotes an OT text to support his position without an introduction, such as "as it is written" (γέγραπται).[19] What is unusual is that Paul adds a parenthetical remark in the middle of the citation about this commandment being the first with a promise. This is not unprecedented, however, since a similar thing occurs in the second recitation of the fifth commandment itself in Deut 5:16.[20]

As mentioned above, the commandment to honor one's parents is narrowed by Paul for children to *obey* their parents as the more exacting and difficult to disguise part of honor. This is the point of Jesus' rebuke of Pharisees and scribes for teaching the violation of the fifth commandment for the sake of their tithing traditions, fulfilling the prophetic word that the people of God honor him with their lips but not with their hearts (Matt 15:1–9; quoting Isa 29:13; cf. Ezek 33:31; see also Mark 7:1–13). The commandment specifies that children show honor or deference to their parents, which takes various forms in different cultures; for example, children rising to their feet in the presence of a wise and godly mother in Prov 31:28.[21]

Paul's mention that the fifth commandment is the first one with an appended promise has drawn some discussion from early days.[22] There were

---

19. That Paul is quoting the LXX of Exod 20:12 and Deut 5:16 seems clear since he uses μακροχρόνιος ("long life"), used only in those two OT passages and Eph 6:3 in biblical literature, even though there are a few trivial differences. The most notable difference is that Paul uses [ἵνα] **ἔσῃ** μακροχρόνιος (the fut. indic.; see E. Burton, *Syntax of the Moods and Tenses in New Testament Greek* [Edinburgh: T&T Clark, 1898], §198) while the LXX uses the synonymous subjunctive of γίνομαι (γένῃ) here. Otherwise, Paul cuts off the specifications about the land, as discussed in the comment.

20. Deut 5:16 is a restatement of the fifth commandment but adds: ὃν τρόπον ἐνετείλατό σοι κύριος ὁ θεός σου, "in the manner in which [= just as] the Lord your God commanded you" (Deut 5:16 LXX).

21. See above on 4:2 for honor and shame as fundamental contrasting values in ancient Mediterranean cultures.

22. See Origen and Jerome, 244–46; Best, 566–67; Lincoln, 404; Gnilka, 297. The specification of blessing and curse appended to the second commandment (Exod 20:4–6) is not a promise to keep the commandment per se. The Lord sanctions the

earlier commands of God with promises (for example, Gen 17:1–2), but this is the first and only one of the Ten Commandments to specifically contain a promise (see also Exod 20:24; Deut 22:6–7).[23] Most commandments contain a curse for violation (Gen 2:17; Exod 20:7), but for children who honor their parents, the Lord promises a special blessing under the OT theocracy, which Paul observes by way of description. The theocratic character of the promise is clear in the OT forms of the promise because it specifies that it is "the land which the LORD your God is giving you" (Exod 20:12; Deut 5:16). Paul cuts off this last phrase to broaden the promise to "the earth" for his audience in a post-theocratic covenant world.

God does not promise all obedient children long life today, as though believers prolong their lives on earth through the merit of good works. As Jerome notes: "There have been many believers who were obedient to their parents but, nevertheless, died young, and there have been many who were impious toward their parents who have reached an extreme old age" (Origen and Jerome, 246). This would be especially true in the first-century world, where it is estimated that, on average, *one-half* of all children died before their sixth birthday.[24] Furthermore, Christians in Paul's day and throughout this age have and continue to face early deaths through persecution. The consistent promise believers hear is that they will suffer for Christ's sake (e.g., Matt 5:10–12; Phil 1:29; 1 Thess 2:14; Heb 10:32; 1 Pet 5:10; Rev 2:10), yet this is accompanied by the certain promise of *eternal life* in the world to come (Matt 19:29; Mark 10:30), not in this world. Nevertheless, wisdom notes that children who honor their parents will avoid the ills that naturally befall the foolish (e.g., Prov 10:10; 11:29; 21:20). Paul's remark is based on this wisdom observation, and thus it should be treated as one understands various biblical proverbs. They must

---

commandment with a curse on those who break the commandment out of hate for him but in Exod 20:6 brings up his steadfast love for those who keep the covenant stipulations (i.e., by faith) from one generation to the next (cf. Deut 5:29). This has been misunderstood as a promise, like that attached to the fifth commandment (also Lincoln, 404).

23. The Deut 22:6–7 command is to not take a mother bird with her chicks if found in the wild: ἀποστολῇ ἀποστελεῖς τὴν μητέρα τὰ δὲ παιδία λήμψῃ σεαυτῷ ἵνα εὖ σοι γένηται καὶ πολυήμερος ἔσῃ, "You shall surely release the mother [bird] but you may take her young for yourself, in order that it may be well with you and you will enjoy length of days" (Deut 22:7 LXX).

24. See the introduction to 5:22–33 above for discussion and literature.

be understood wisely and with appropriate qualifications from other biblical teachings.

6:4 Καὶ οἱ πατέρες, μὴ παροργίζετε τὰ τέκνα ὑμῶν ἀλλὰ ἐκτρέφετε αὐτὰ ἐν παιδείᾳ καὶ νουθεσίᾳ κυρίου, "And fathers, do not provoke your children to anger, but rear them in the training and reproof of the Lord." The focus on fathers in the reciprocal command in the parent-child relationship recognizes that the father has "headship" responsibility in the home. Yet there is no reason to believe that just as mothers are due honor from their children ("parents ... you father and your mother," vv. 1–2), so also mothers are included in the admonition to avoid angering their children and to contribute to their nurture in the Lord.[25] Proverbs 1–9 constitutes the equivalent of an OT catechism in godly wisdom, and both fathers and mothers are active in the instruction of their youths (e.g., Prov 1:8; 6:20; cf. 23:22; 31:1–9, 26–28).

The compound verb παροργίζετε is causative, indicating an act of provoking to anger. The NIV has "do not exacerbate" here, which nicely draws out the reference to children becoming frustrated and discouraged by overbearing or unfair treatment (cf. 4:26, 31), especially if they themselves are trying to be obedient to and honor their parents (vv. 1–3). The parallel statement in Col 3:21 has ἐρεθίζω, "provoke" or "embitter" (BDAG, 391). "So many parents do this. They do this by depriving them of their portion of the inheritance and their promises, by oppressing them with burdens, by treating them not as though they were free but as slaves" (Chrysostom, *ACCS*, 203).

The exhortation for parents to train and "reprove" their children has a long history in the biblical and Graeco-Roman world.[26] The term παιδεία ("training") has rich cultural associations in the Greek world for the

25. Cf. O'Brien, 445). He points to the Roman father's *patria potestas* ("fatherly authority"), which gave them at least theoretical power of life and death over their children. O'Brien thinks that this Roman institution had an impact on Hellenic societies such as at Ephesus, but this is not certain, since Roman influence at Ephesus was still only incipient in the mid-first century—though slowly growing as the first century gave way to the second.

26. Cf. Lindemann, "... ἐκτρέφετε αὐτά."

training and education of youths in a wide range of subjects and disciplines.[27] For example, Dio Chrysostom remarks that parents teach their children "to play the lyre and to wrestle, to read and write" (*Or.* 13.17) as the heart of their *paideia*.

Paideia also has a rich history in the biblical world. Parents are told plainly in Deut 6:1–9 to instruct their children in all of the Lord's instructions and commandments in every occasion of life, "when you sit in your house, and when you walk by the way, and when you lie down, and when you rise" (Deut 6:7).[28] This becomes the way that children encounter *the Lord's* training and reproof: "My son, do not despise the Lord's discipline [παιδεία] or be weary when you are reproved by him [ὑπ' αὐτοῦ ἐλεγχόμενος], for the Lord disciplines him whom he loves, and chastises every son whom he loves" (Prov 3:11–12; my trans. from the LXX; cf. Heb 12:6). Reproof is needed for children that they may abandon the negative and sinful practices they naturally develop (see 2:3) and that they adopt and wisely discern how to live holy lives that please their heavenly Father (5:10). "Whoever spares the rod hates his son, but he who loves him is diligent to discipline him" (Prov 13:24; cf. Heb 12:7–11). Hence, what makes parental "training" and "reproof" tolerable is that it is "in the Lord," where the passage begins (v. 1), and "of the Lord," where it ends (v. 4).

Application and Devotional Implications

Jesus cites the fifth commandment several times (Matt 15:4; 19:19; Mark 7:10; 10:19; Luke 18:20). And, as noted above, Luke 2:51 specifies that Jesus was in submission to Mary and Joseph in his youth. However, there are some interesting connections between the fifth commandment and what Jesus says in John's Gospel. When accused by Jewish leaders of being a

---

27. The classic work on this is Werner Jaeger's *Paideia: die Formung des classischen Menschen* (1933–47), translated as *Paideia: The Ideals of Greek Culture*, trans. Gilbert Highet, 3 vols. (New York: Oxford University Press, 1939–44); cf. Jaeger, *Early Christianity and Greek Paideia* (Cambridge, MA: Harvard University Press, 1965); BDAG, 748–49; LSJ, 1286; Georg Bertram, *TDNT*, 5:596–625.

28. Cf. Gen 18:19; Deut 4:9; 11:19; Pss 34:11; 78:4; Prov 19:18; 22:6; 29:17; and Timothy in 2 Tim 3:15. The Deut 6:4–9 passage (Shema) was central for Jewish piety and belief through its daily recitation, and it was written down (along with Deut 11:13–21) and placed in a container on the doorpost (*mezuzah*) of one's home.

Samaritan and having a demon, Jesus responds, "I do not have a demon, but I honor my Father, whereas *you* are dishonoring me" (John 8:49). His opponents think that the point of contention is their descent from Abraham and whether they are thereby children of God (John 8:39–42). What they do not grasp is that the only way to have God as one's Father and to do him honor is through the mediation of the incarnate Son in their midst to whom the Father has granted all judgment "in order that all might honor the Son just as they honor the Father. The one who does not honor the Son does not honor the Father who sent him" (John 5:23). But then comes the shocking clincher: "If anyone would serve me, he must follow me, and where I am, there also will my servant be. If anyone serves me, *my Father will honor him*" (John 12:26, emphasis added). The fifth commandment is turned on its head for us in glory through Jesus Christ; this is certainly "far more exceeding than anything we may request or imagine" (3:20).

Selected Bibliography

Beasley-Murray, G. *Baptism in the New Testament.* 2nd ed. Carlisle: Paternoster, 1997.

Burtchaell, J. *From Synagogue to Church: Public Services and Offices in the Earliest Christian Communities.* Cambridge: Cambridge University Press, 1992.

Jaeger, W. *Early Christianity and Greek Paideia.* Cambridge, MA: Harvard University Press, 1965.

Lindemann, A. "... ἐκτρέφετε αὐτὰ ἐν παιδείᾳ καὶ νουθεσίᾳ κυρίου (Eph 6:4): Kinder in der Welt des frühen Christentums." *NTS* 56 (2010): 169–90.

Marcel, P. *The Biblical Doctrine of Infant Baptism: Sacrament of the Covenant of Grace.* Translated by P. E. Hughes. Cambridge: James Clarke, 1953.

Murray, J. *Christian Baptism.* Philadelphia: P&R, 1974.

Schreiner, T., and S. Wright, eds. *Believer's Baptism: Sign of the New Covenant in Christ.* Nashville: Broadman and Holman, 2006.

Wright, D., ed. *Baptism: Three Views.* Downers Grove, IL: InterVarsity Press, 2009.

———. *Infant Baptism in Historical Perspective: Collected Studies.* SCHT. Eugene, OR: Wipf & Stock, 2007.

Exhortations to Christian Households: Slaves and Masters in the Lord (6:5–9)

Introduction

In Ephesians 6:5–9 Paul urges sincere, considerate relations between slaves and masters in the Lord. This is the third and last specification of submission to one another in the fear of Christ from 5:21 as it relates to the Christian household. The first was related to wives and husbands (5:22–33), while the second was to children and parents (6:1–4). The epistle will soon end after a long section to follow on the "warfare" of the Christian life (6:10–20). Until then, Paul establishes how slaves are to serve their masters "in the flesh" with sincerity "as to Christ" (v. 5) by specifying that they are to offer obedience, much as also children obey their parents.

In the prior two interrelations Paul has addressed (wives with husbands and parents with children), the relationships are rooted in creation. Slavery is not. Ancient slavery could make for the most debased kind of life—and it could lead to enormous wealth and political power. For most slaves, it certainly placed them at their master's mercy (cf. Matt 8:9; Luke 17:7–10), and mercy and restraint was not always exercised by masters.[1]

1. One point discussed by Jennifer Glancy is the sexual exploitation of slaves, which has elicited important attention in recent discussions. See Jennifer A. Glancy, "Obstacles to Slaves' Participation in the Corinthian Church," *JBL* 117 (1998): 481–501; and Glancy, *Slavery in Early Christianity* (Minneapolis: Fortress, 2006; repr. of 2002 ed.). Glancy does not think that Paul's instructions curtailed sexual use of slaves as "fornication" (πορνεία), though cf. Margaret Y. MacDonald, "Slavery, Sexuality and House Churches: A Reassessment of Colossians 3:18–4:1 in Light of New Research on the Roman Family," *NTS* 53 (2007): 94–113. Cf. J. Albert Harrill, *Slaves in the New Testament: Literary, Social, and Moral Dimensions* (Minneapolis: Fortress, 2006). Indication of the widespread character of this practice is witnessed by the offhand way ancient authors sometimes speak of it. For example, "Do not many Athenian men have intercourse with their maidservants,

Why then does not Paul here in Eph 6:5–9 and in other places (e.g., Col 3:22–4:1; Philemon) condemn slavery outright? This question is often asked as if Paul could simply condemn slavery and not expect there to be such serious repercussions that the continued existence of the church would be seriously threatened: "Let all who are under a yoke as slaves regard their own masters as worthy of all honor, *so that the name of God and the teaching may not be reviled*" (1 Tim 6:1, emphasis added; cf. Titus 2:5). Slavery was not an incidental feature of the ancient agrarian economies of the first century but part of its essential fabric. Even if a Roman emperor were to outlaw slavery by decree, there would be unimaginable inflation when newly freed farm workers—especially from the Roman *latifundia* ("plantations"), which often employed "chained slaves" (Pliny, *Ep*. 3.19; Dio Chrysostom, *Or.* 14.19)—would enter the urban workforce without skills or training for the relatively few craft jobs available.[2] Farms would stand vacant, and starvation and food riots would be the norm.[3] This is not by any means meant to justify ancient slavery, but Paul would have been most irresponsible and imprudent if he had simply spoken out against it and inspired Christians to social revolution.[4]

It is worthwhile to read the balanced and careful treatment of Charles Hodge at this point (Hodge, 361–63). Hodge observes that slavery was a lawful institution in Paul's world, just as much as the political system (Roman imperialism) to which he taught lawful obedience (e.g., Rom 13:1–7), even if it had despotic tendencies. Nevertheless, Hodge does not say that slavery, though tolerated by biblical writers as "lawful under given circumstances," does not mean that it "may be cherished and rendered perpetual" (Hodge,

---

some of them secretly, but others quite openly?" (Dio Chrysostom, *Or.* 15.5). This is an issue worth far more attention that I am giving it here.

2. Again, as noted above on 5:9: Up to 85 percent of ancient people worked directly in food production occupations.

3. This is a dire picture, I know, but some of these things did occur in antiquity already. For example there were strikes by the bakers at Ephesus in the early to mid-third century, requiring the unusual direct intervention of the Roman proconsul (*IvE* 215). Bread prices had doubled from the previous century (*IvE* 910, 923–24, 934, 938, 3010), and life in Ephesus was soon to go even further downhill as a marauding band of Goths sacked the Artemisium (the main deposit bank in Asia Minor) in AD 262/3. Ephesus never fully recovered from this.

4. This stands in contrast to modern forms of illegal slavery such as the "sex slave" trade, which Christians should and do vigorously oppose.

363). That is, Paul's teaching does *not* regard or establish slavery as a creation institution that God has sanctioned on the same order as the family. Hodge, one of the most widely read and respected theologians in America at the time, wrote his Ephesians commentary in 1857, just four years before civil war broke out between the industrialized North and agrarian South, with slavery as one of its main issues. Hodge no doubt lost students and friends in this vicious war, and Princeton Seminary, where he taught, housed southern students alongside northern students during the war.[5]

Paul did not condemn slavery outright, yet what he did do was tactful, wise, and led to the ultimate demise of slavery in the ancient world: He accented the full inheritance and citizenship of slaves in Christ's eschatological kingdom in places like 1 Cor 12:13, Gal 3:28, and Col 3:11—and by implication in Eph 6:5–9. In the meantime, he asks slaves to offer sincere obedience to their masters, and, more importantly, he reminds their masters that both their Lord and the Lord of the slaves is in heaven and has a particular concern for the fatherless and the dispossessed in the world (e.g., Deut 10:17–18; Psa 10:14–18; 82:3–4; Mal 3:5).

The text of Col 3:22–4:1 is similar enough to Eph 6:5–9 that it is worthwhile to cite it in full for comparison:

> [22] Οἱ δοῦλοι ὑπακούετε κατὰ πάντα τοῖς κατὰ σάρκα κυρίοις
> μὴ ἐν ὀφθαλμοδουλίᾳ ὡς ἀνθρωπάρεσκοι
> ἀλλ' ἐν ἁπλότητι καρδίας
> φοβούμενοι τὸν κύριον
>
> [23] ὃ ἐὰν ποιῆτε ἐκ ψυχῆς ἐργάζεσθε
> ὡς τῷ κυρίῳ
> καὶ οὐκ ἀνθρώποις
>
> [24] εἰδότες ὅτι ἀπὸ κυρίου ἀπολήμψεσθε τὴν ἀνταπόδοσιν τῆς κληρονομίας
> τῷ κυρίῳ Χριστῷ δουλεύετε

---

5. Cf. Paul C. Gutjahr, *Charles Hodge: Guardian of American Orthodoxy* (New York: Oxford University Press, 2011). Hodge himself had owned domestic slaves earlier but supported Lincoln's emancipation proclamation of Jan. 1, 1863. Nevertheless, slavery in America was a brutal exploitation of Africans that still has serious repercussions today. Slavery in antiquity was not restricted to any particular ethnic group but was sometimes just as brutal and exploitative.

[25] ὁ γὰρ ἀδικῶν κομίσεται ὃ ἠδίκησεν
καὶ οὐκ ἔστιν προσωπολημψία

[4:1] οἱ κύριοι τὸ δίκαιον καὶ τὴν ἰσότητα τοῖς δούλοις παρέχεσθε
εἰδότες ὅτι καὶ ὑμεῖς ἔχετε κύριον ἐν οὐρανῷ.[6]

In translation or lined up in Greek with similar words placed alongside those in Ephesians (so Lincoln, 412), the Colossians and Ephesians passages look more similar than they do when one notes the length and grouping into cola* that represent their probable original presentation. The two passages are quite different in structure (e.g., the unusual asyndeton* between Col 3:24a and 24b; and the three bicolon periods in Col 3:24–4:1 that are not found in Eph 6:5–9). Nevertheless, the text of Paul (Ephesians) and the text of Paul with his cosender, Timothy (Colossians) clearly speak to the same issues in a similar way.

My suggested division of Eph 6:5–9 into cola* and periods is as follows:

A [5] οἱ δοῦλοι ὑπακούετε τοῖς κατὰ σάρκα κυρίοις
μετὰ φόβου καὶ τρόμου ἐν ἁπλότητι τῆς καρδίας ὑμῶν
ὡς τῷ Χριστῷ

B [6] μὴ κατ᾽ ὀφθαλμοδουλίαν ὡς ἀνθρωπάρεσκοι
ἀλλ᾽ ὡς δοῦλοι Χριστοῦ
ποιοῦντες τὸ θέλημα τοῦ θεοῦ ἐκ ψυχῆς [7]μετ᾽ εὐνοίας
δουλεύοντες ὡς τῷ κυρίῳ καὶ οὐκ ἀνθρώποις

C [8] εἰδότες ὅτι ἕκαστος ἐάν τι ποιήσῃ ἀγαθόν
τοῦτο κομίσεται παρὰ κυρίου
εἴτε δοῦλος εἴτε ἐλεύθερος

D [9] καὶ οἱ κύριοι τὰ αὐτὰ ποιεῖτε πρὸς αὐτούς
ἀνιέντες τὴν ἀπειλήν
εἰδότες ὅτι καὶ αὐτῶν καὶ ὑμῶν ὁ κύριός ἐστιν ἐν οὐρανοῖς
καὶ προσωπολημψία οὐκ ἔστιν παρ᾽ αὐτῷ

---

6. "Slaves, obey in everything those who are your earthly masters, not by way of eye-service, as people-pleasers, but with sincerity of heart, fearing the Lord. Whatever you do, work heartily, as for the Lord and not for men, knowing that from the Lord you will receive the inheritance as your reward. You are serving the Lord Christ. For the wrongdoer will be paid back for the wrong he has done, and there is no partiality. Masters, treat your slaves justly and fairly, knowing that you also have a Master in heaven."

I have kept the two prepositional phrases together as the second colon* in v. 5, which could possibly be divided μετὰ φόβου καὶ τρόμου / ἐν ἁπλότητι τῆς καρδίας ὑμῶν, "with fear and trembling / in sincerity of heart." However, I think it best to see "sincerity of heart" as explaining "fear and trembling," which is why I kept the phrases (Greek, κόμματα) together in one colon*.

Given that all the modern punctuation and the versification are much later interpretive accessories to the biblical text, the exact delineation of vv. 6–7 is subject to debate. The UBS/NA critical texts agree with the early Stephanus edition of 1550 by punctuating the transition from v. 6 to v. 7 as follows: ποιοῦντες τὸ θέλημα τοῦ θεοῦ ἐκ ψυχῆς, [7] μετ᾽ εὐνοίας δουλεύοντες ... ("you must perform the will of God willingly, [7] serve with good intent ...").[7] Hence, v. 7 starts with a prepositional phrase that modifies a trailing participle; this is seen from time to time as a place of special focus ("fronting").[8] The SBL edition, following Westcott-Hort, places a comma after τοῦ θεοῦ ("of God"), making *both* prepositional phrases modify the trailing participle δουλεύοντες in v. 7: "willingly [7] serve with good intent." This agrees with the fifth century MS Alexandrinus (A), which has a "high dot" (*stigme teleia*) punctuation after θεοῦ.[9]

Finally, the Erasmus edition of 1516 interestingly adds an extra comma after μετ᾽ εὐνοίας ("with good intent"), which sets it off as appositional to the previous prepositional phrase: "you must perform the will of God willingly, [7] that is, with good intent, and serve ..." In this instance, with the way I have lined out the cola* of vv. 6–7 above, I am agreeing with Erasmus in taking both prepositional phrases (ἐκ ψυχῆς and μετ᾽ εὐνοίας) as modifying not the trailing δουλεύοντες ("serve") in v. 7 but the statement leading off with ποιοῦντες ("perform") in v. 6. The meaning of the text is not

7. Both the Stephanus and Erasmus editions were consulted via the Center for the Study of New Testament Manuscripts digital images at www.csntm.org (accessed March 1, 2014). Stephanus has ὡς in v. 7 in the margin.

8. As argued for 1:4–5 ἐν ἀγάπῃ [5] προορίσας ("predestined in love").

9. The vellum Alexandrinus is creased and has ink runs at this place in Ephesians that exaggerate the dot, but close examination of the digital photograph shows that this is indeed a dot (looking like a small "c" because of the way a dot was formed with the pen's nib), much like another such dot in Eph 6:1 on the same page (ΕΝ ΚΩ · ΤΟΥΤΟ). Other MSS I looked at (Vaticanus, Sinaiticus, and Boernerianus [012]) have no punctuation or spacing in either of these places. I am assuming the punctuation in these MSS is contemporary with their initial production, but that may be questionable.

significantly impacted by this, but it more clearly shows the intended parallel relationship between the participles ποιοῦντες and δουλεύοντες, which start off their cola*. Furthermore, it shows that the material in v. 7 is part of one period comprising vv. 6–7, which would have been read together in one breath originally.

Outline

XVI. Exhortations to Christian Households: Slaves and Masters in the Lord (6:5–9)
- A. Slaves obey their masters (6:5–8)
  1. With sincerity of heart (6:5)
  2. As to the Lord (6:6–7)
  3. Mindful of their eternal inheritance (6:8)
- B. Masters' mild treatment of their slaves (6:9)

Original Text

5 Οἱ δοῦλοι, ὑπακούετε τοῖς κατὰ σάρκα κυρίοις[a] μετὰ φόβου καὶ τρόμου ἐν
ἁπλότητι τῆς καρδίας ὑμῶν ὡς τῷ Χριστῷ, **6** μὴ κατ᾽ ὀφθαλμοδουλίαν ὡς ἀνθρωπάρεσκοι ἀλλ᾽ ὡς δοῦλοι Χριστοῦ ποιοῦντες τὸ θέλημα τοῦ θεοῦ ἐκ ψυχῆς, **7**
μετ᾽ εὐνοίας δουλεύοντες ὡς τῷ κυρίῳ καὶ οὐκ ἀνθρώποις,[b] **8** εἰδότες ὅτι ἕκαστος
ἐάν τι[c] ποιήσῃ[d] ἀγαθόν, τοῦτο κομίσεται παρὰ κυρίου εἴτε δοῦλος εἴτε ἐλεύθερος.
9 Καὶ οἱ κύριοι, τὰ αὐτὰ ποιεῖτε πρὸς αὐτούς, ἀνιέντες τὴν ἀπειλήν, εἰδότες ὅτι
καὶ αὐτῶν καὶ ὑμῶν ὁ κύριός ἐστιν ἐν οὐρανοῖς καὶ προσωπολημψία οὐκ ἔστιν
παρ᾽ αὐτῷ.

Textual Notes

5.a. P⁴⁶, some Western witnesses (D, F, G), and M switch the word order of τοῖς κατὰ σάρκα κυρίοις in the first colon* to τοῖς κυρίοις κατὰ σάρκα (woodenly, "your masters according to the flesh"). The meaning is unchanged by the variation of word order.

7.b. Vaticanus (B) has the singular ἀνθρώπῳ ("[not] for man") instead of the plural ἀνθρώποις ("[not] for men"), which matches the parallel singular κυρίῳ "as for the Lord and not for *man*." All of vv. 6–7 is missing at the bottom of this page of P⁴⁶, so we cannot check this important witness here, and the plural ἀνθρώποις (agreeing with pl. "masters" in v. 5) is the consensus reading otherwise.

8.c. Interestingly, the critical UBS/NA text adopts the reading at the end of the first colon* ἕκαστος ἐάν τι ποιήσῃ ἀγαθόν ("each one, if he does anything good") almost exclusively on the strength of Vaticanus (B). The first part is missing from P[46], but the latter agrees substantially with B, with ἐάν τι ποιῇ ἀγαθόν (see below for ποιῇ for ποιήσῃ). The readings in the other witnesses vary the word order or reading slightly (e.g., ἕκαστος ὃ [ἐ]άν ["each one, whatever"] in the major uncials). The various other readings in the MSS are a little smoother so that the reading accepted in the critical text is preferred as *lectio difficilior**.

8.d. P[46] reads the present tense ποιῇ instead of the aorist ποιήσῃ in the first colon* of v. 8, which is of interest for the study of tense forms and verbal aspect in Greek.

Translation

5 Slaves, obey[10] your human[11] masters with fear and trembling in sincerity of heart,[12] as to Christ, **6** not outwardly, as those who merely please people, but as slaves of Christ you must perform[13] the will of God willingly **7** with good intent,[14] and serve[15] as for the Lord and not for people, **8** for

10. For the pres.-tense form of ὑπακούετε ("obey") here see translation note on v. 1.
11. The κατά phrase in τοῖς κατὰ σάρκα κυρίοις has the same underlying semantics as an adj. gen.: τοῖς τοῦ σαρκὸς κυρίοις, "human masters." See the translation note on 1:15 for the phrase τὴν καθ' ὑμᾶς πίστιν, "your faith"; cf. BDF §224 (1).
12. The poss. pronoun in the phrase ἐν ἁπλότητι τῆς καρδίας **ὑμῶν** does not carry over smoothly into English; cf. BDAG, 104 (meaning 1); and ἐν ἁπλότητι καρδίας in Col 3:22. Hence, I have dropped the pronoun in my translation, as also NIV, "with sincerity of heart"; ESV, "with a sincere heart"; and NRSV, "in singleness of heart."
13. As seen several times already in Ephesians, this section consists of impvs. and parallel ptcs. functioning imperativally: ὑπακούετε ... ποιοῦντες ... δουλεύοντες ... ποιεῖτε ... ἀνιέντες; see translation notes on 3:17; 4:1–3; 5:15–21. The ptc. εἰδότες in vv. 8 and 9 is an exception, as explained under v. 8.
14. See the introduction and comment for defense of the punctuation here.
15. See note on v. 6 for the ptc. with impv. force because it parallels impv. ὑπακούετε ("obey") in v. 5.

you know[16] that whatever good each one does,[17] this will receive its reward[18] from the Lord, whether he is slave or free. **9** And masters, practice[19] the same things for them, and give up[20] threatening them, for you know[21] that both their and your Lord is in heaven, and there is no partiality with him.

Commentary

6:5 Οἱ δοῦλοι, ὑπακούετε τοῖς κατὰ σάρκα κυρίοις μετὰ φόβου καὶ τρόμου ἐν ἁπλότητι τῆς καρδίας ὑμῶν ὡς τῷ Χριστῷ, "Slaves, obey your human masters with fear and trembling in sincerity of heart, as to Christ." Some scholars estimate that slaves comprised about one-third of the population of a city like Ephesus.[22] Privately owned slaves were often considered to be a part of one's family, so Paul's instructions for slaves are natural for remarks dealing with family relationships alongside the others in 5:22–33 (wives and husbands)

---

16. The ptcs. ποιοῦντες, δουλεύοντες, and ἀνιέντες in vv. 5–9 function in parallel with impvs., but εἰδότες here and in v. 9 explains the reasons underlying the exhortations. This category could be described as "causal" (BDF §418 [1]; E. Burton, *Syntax of the Moods and Tenses in New Testament Greek* [Edinburgh: T&T Clark, 1898], §439), but more accurately it explains the *rationale* for an action.
17. This renders the phrase: ἕκαστος ἐάν τι ποιήσῃ ἀγαθόν ("whatever good each one does"), which more woodenly could be "each if he should do anything good." Cf. "whatever good thing each one does" (NASB) and "whatever good anyone does" (ESV). The aor. subjunctive ποιήσῃ focuses on the individual "good thing" (ἀγαθόν) practiced (as Matt 19:16; 20:32; 27:22; Mark 10:35; 1 Cor 6:18; etc.). The pres. subjunctive would have been used if the expression were pl.: ἐάν τινα ποιήσῃ ἀγαθά, "whatever good things each one practices" (as Mark 11:28; John 5:19; 15:14; Rom 2:14; Gal 5:17; etc.); cf. Col 3:17, 23.
18. For κομίζω where μισθός ("reward") may be implied; cf. 2 Cor 5:10; Col 3:25; BDAG, 557. Versions have: "the Lord will reward everyone" (NIV); " he will receive back" (ESV; NASB is similar); "we will receive the same again" (NRSV).
19. For the pres.-tense form of the impv. (ποιεῖτε), see the note on v. 1.
20. The ptc. ἀνιέντες is parallel with the impvs. in the passage; see note on v. 6.
21. See the note on εἰδότες in v. 8.
22. This is picked up in Lincoln, 417. The source of this estimate primarily derives from the second-century medical writer Galen, who estimated the slave population of Pergamum in his day; cf. Thomas Wiedemann, *Greek and Roman Slavery* (Baltimore: Johns Hopkins University Press, 1981; repr., New York: Routledge, 1994), 79. This high estimate has been challenged recently by Walter Scheidel, "The Comparative Economics of Slavery in the Greco-Roman World," version 1, *Princeton/Stanford Working Papers in Classics* (2005): 2–3.

and 6:1–4 (children and parents) in the ancient context (see "Excursus: Slavery at Ephesus").

One way to illustrate that slaves were members of the ancient household is their place in the family grave. Here is just one example from among many found at Ephesus:

> The Aurelii Menacrates and
> Metrodorus and Apollo-
> nius the sons of Metrodorus Sattys
> erected this tomb for th-
> emselves and (their) wife [see note] and children
> and their wives and descen-
> dants and (their) slaves (δούλοις).[23]

Another example is even more explicit about these members of the household: "In this tomb I desire to be placed my male slaves and freedmen and my female slaves" (*IvE* 2414).[24]

As noted in the introduction above, by giving slaves instructions to submit to their masters, Paul was not condoning slavery per se. In the ancient context, many people voluntarily submitted to slavery when faced with the alternative of starvation, while many other slaves originated as infants abandoned by their parents to die of exposure who were then picked up by slave dealers (e.g., Pliny, *Ep.* 10.65–66; see "Excursus: Slavery at Ephesus"). These were some of the harsh realities of antiquity that explain in part the prevalence of slavery.

Slavery slowly died out in antiquity; its demise and relation to serfdom in the medieval period in the West are still a matter of historical inquiry and interpretation.[25] Some scholars believe that Paul's teaching had an influence on manumission and treatment of slaves in the early church, and

---

23. *IvE* 3751. I have omitted the dating of the inscription from line 1 (AD 213/4) and the final lines assigning a fine for anyone who buries someone else in the tomb. The stone reads γυναιxί ("[their] wife") but is probably a simple spelling mistake for γυναιξί ("[their] wives"), as emended by Louis Robert, reported in a note in *IvE*.

24. Cf. Pliny, *Ep.* 8.16, who boasts of his liberal treatment of slaves by allowing them to "make a sort of will" and distribute their possessions "within the limits of the household: for the house provides a slave with a country and a sort of citizenship."

25. E.g., Kyle Harper, *Slavery in the Late Roman World, AD 275–425* (New York: Cambridge University Press, 2011).

especially on certain rulings of Constantine making manumission easier for Christian masters.[26]

As was noted on v. 1, Paul addresses exhortations to people who are not usually addressed in public literature: children and slaves, who are "fellow heirs, fellow body members, and fellow partakers of the promise in Christ Jesus through the gospel" (3:6; cf. 6:8; 1:14), as are adults and free persons. Hence, Paul has to specify that slaves are to obey their "*human* masters" (οἱ κατὰ σάρκα κύριοι) even though there is only one κύριος ("Lord," "Master") for both slave and master (so 4:5). Paul identifies himself as a "slave of Christ" (e.g., Rom 1:1; Gal 1:10; Phil 1:1).[27] And even Christ "took up the form of a slave" (Phil 2:7), especially by voluntarily accepting a shameful form of death usually reserved for slaves (Phil 2:8; cf. Heb 12:2). Paul's word to slaves comes in a context that puts their service to their human masters in a new perspective (vv. 6–8).

Paul himself knew "fear and trembling" (1 Cor 2:3; cf. 2 Cor 7:15; Phil 2:12; Hodge, 364), but the phrase here is explained by the phrase that follows: "in sincerity of heart" (ἐν ἁπλότητι τῆς καρδίας ὑμῶν). The noun ἁπλότης ("sincerity") refers here to openness and sincerity as opposed to duplicity and cunning (2 Cor 11:3), which is further explained as service ἐκ ψυχῆς ("willingly," "from the heart") in v. 6 and μετ' εὐνοίας ("with good intent") in v. 7 (cf. Col 3:22; 1 Pet 2:18). The insincere and duplicitous slave was a common theme in ancient Greek and Roman comedies. It would be natural for Christian slaves to despise their earthly masters in the name of their heavenly one; however, Paul says here and in vv. 6–7 that fulfilling their earthly obligations is, in fact, service to the Lord (cf. 1 Cor 7:22; 1 Tim 6:1; Titus 2:9).

6:6–7 μὴ κατ' ὀφθαλμοδουλίαν ὡς ἀνθρωπάρεσκοι ἀλλ' ὡς δοῦλοι Χριστοῦ ποιοῦντες τὸ θέλημα τοῦ θεοῦ ἐκ ψυχῆς μετ' εὐνοίας, δουλεύοντες ὡς τῷ κυρίῳ

26. Cf. J. Albert Harrill, *The Manumission of Slaves in Early Christianity*, HUT 32 (Tübingen: Mohr Siebeck, 1995); Reinhart Staats, "Kaiser Konstantin der Große und der Apostel Paul," *VC* 62 (2008): 334–70 (esp. 345–47).

27. See 1 Cor 9:19 examined particularly in Dale K. Martin, *Slavery as Salvation: The Metaphor of Slavery in Pauline Christianity* (New Haven, CT: Yale University Press, 1990), which also discusses Graeco-Roman slavery in general, particularly as it sometimes afforded upward mobility. Later Ephesian Christians adopted Paul's language: "The slave of God (ὁ δοῦλος τοῦ θεοῦ), Theodorus Domestikos" (*IvE* 2312B).

καὶ οὐκ ἀνθρώποις, "not outwardly, as those who merely please people, but as slaves of Christ you must perform the will of God willingly with good intent, and serve as for the Lord and not for people." See the introduction above for taking vv. 6–7 as one period and for the punctuation represented in my translation, which differs from the critical Greek edition. I take the phrase μετ' εὐνοίας ("with good intent") as an expansion of "from the heart" at the end of v. 6 and take the participle δουλεύοντες ("and serve") as parallel with the preceding participle ποιοῦντες ("perform") and as starting out the last colon* of the vv. 6–7 period.

The phrase κατ' ὀφθαλμοδουλίαν refers to obsequious service that is only performed in the presence of one's master (cf. Col 3:22; BDAG, 744). Pliny the Younger complained about just the opposite in his household, for "It is unconcerned to the point of indifference in the way it treats me. Slaves lose all fear of a considerate master once they are used to him, but they wake up at the sight of a new face and try to win his favour by giving his guests the service due to him" (Pliny, *Ep.* 1.4; LCL trans.). Paul expects his audience members who are slaves to cut through all this and seize the freedom they have in Christ to serve their earthly masters ἐκ ψυχῆς ("from the heart"; BDAG, 1099 [meaning 2c]), mirroring "from sincerity of heart" in v. 5. He adds the second prepositional phrase at the beginning of v. 7 to expand on "from the heart" with μετ' εὐνοίας ("with good intent"), which represents "a positive attitude exhibited in a relationship ... goodwill" (BDAG, 409).

Paul specifies that the service of slaves to earthly masters (κύριοι) should be "as to the Lord" (κύριος), which repeats what he has already said in v. 5 and is on analogy of how wives are to submit to their husbands (5:22, 24; cf. Col 3:24). This is indeed God's will for them, as Paul says. The submission of all members of the church to one another (5:21) is the good work for which God has created them by granting them entrance into newness of life (2:10; Rom 6:4). For slaves, this inaugurated new-creation reality puts their slave service in new perspective. Slaves in Christ are his freedmen in one sense (1 Cor 7:22). In quite another they are his brothers (Mark 3:33–34; Luke 8:21), who have a share in the Son of God's eternal inheritance (Rom 8:29). For now, all who are in service—today this would be primarily those who serve in the military or police forces—are in submission to authority even when it may cost life or limb. The next verse flows from here.

6:8 εἰδότες ὅτι ἕκαστος ἐάν τι ποιήσῃ ἀγαθόν, τοῦτο κομίσεται παρὰ κυρίου εἴτε δοῦλος εἴτε ἐλεύθερος, "for you know that whatever good each one does, this will receive its reward from the Lord, whether he is slave or free." The statement of v. 8 provides perspective and motivation for Christian slaves or others under orders to another for the sincere obedience they are obligated to perform. All who are in submission to proper authorities know that they and their selfless service—no matter how menial it appears in the world—are not ignored or forgotten by the Lord. "Why, even the hairs of your head are all numbered" (Luke 12:7).

The last part of v. 8 in particular expresses the Lord's absolute impartiality, which is expressed explicitly in the next verse (cf. Psa 62:12; Matt 16:27; 2 Cor 5:10; Col 3:24–25). Slaves do not live for this life but live now to show expressions of gratitude in this life for the full and free eternal reward already guaranteed to them in the next life (e.g., 1:13–14; 2:8). "But now that you have been set free from sin and have become slaves of God, the fruit you get leads to sanctification and its end, eternal life. For the wages of sin is death, but the free gift of God is eternal life in Christ Jesus our Lord" (Rom 6:22–23).

6:9 Καὶ οἱ κύριοι, τὰ αὐτὰ ποιεῖτε πρὸς αὐτούς, ἀνιέντες τὴν ἀπειλήν, εἰδότες ὅτι καὶ αὐτῶν καὶ ὑμῶν ὁ κύριός ἐστιν ἐν οὐρανοῖς καὶ προσωπολημψία οὐκ ἔστιν παρ' αὐτῷ, "And masters, practice the same things for them, and give up threatening them, for you know that both their and your Lord is in heaven, and there is no partiality with him." As Paul had done in the prior two household relationships in 5:22–33 and 6:1–4, he addresses both parties in the relationship with their mutual duties. In effect, masters are expressing their "submission in the fear of Christ" (5:21) by treating their slaves with respect and "practicing the same things for them." This latter does not mean that masters obey their slaves but points back to "performing the will of God" (v. 6) in relation to their slaves by treating them with respect as fellow creatures made in the divine image (Job 31:13–15). Christian masters and slaves have one κύριος ("Lord," "Master") in heaven (cf. Col 4:1).

Masters in antiquity theoretically had the power of life and death over their slaves.[28] Beatings, imprisonment, or sale into harsher servitude were more common punishments that masters meted out to their slaves. Yet Pliny the Younger's private moments reveal that slave owners often secretly feared their slaves, which may explain the harshness and threats Paul warns against. For instance, Pliny reports with horror the death of the "senator and ex-*praetor*" Larcius Macedo at the hands of his slaves.[29] Macedo, himself the son of a freedman, was "a cruel and overbearing master" (Pliny, *Ep.* 3.14), but he had the satisfaction of seeing his death avenged before succumbing to his injuries.[30] Masters were never completely safe at home, but when traveling they were particularly vulnerable, and Pliny suspects two of his acquaintances were murdered by their slaves on separate trips and were never seen again (*Ep.* 6.25). Domestic bliss with slaves in the house was never guaranteed in the ancient world.

In either case, Paul urges Christian slave owners to have the same kind of eternal perspective as their believing slaves, in the fear of the Lord (Lev 25:43), who shows no partiality whatsoever (Deut 10:17–18; 2 Chr 19:7; Acts 10:34; Rom 2:11; Col 3:25; 1 Pet 1:17; cf. Jas 2:1–5) and examines the heart and motive (e.g., 1 Sam 16:7; Prov 17:3; 1 Cor 4:5). This contributed eventually to the abolition of the ancient slave system.

Application and Devotional Implications

The principles articulated in this passage would apply today in submission to any lawfully constituted authority over us that does not fundamentally compromise our commitment to Christ. It is often interpreted as relating to the interrelations of workers to supervisors and employers in the workplace, but that needs careful qualification. Employees should certainly treat those over them with respect and work hard as they are asked, but "obedience"

28. Cf. Wiedemann, *Slavery*, 15–44, 167–87; esp. 184 (on Suetonius, *Claud.* 25) concerning how Claudius ruled that owners could be brought up on charge of murder for killing slaves who were sick or too worn out to work.

29. The office of praetor was a military command similar to a "governor-general"; Asia Minor had a proconsul, a civilian appointment.

30. The standard Roman punishment in this case was that all the slaves of the household and possibly the freedmen were executed (cf. Pliny, *Ep.* 8.14).

to employers has significant limits, and their relationship has significant differences from slavery—or at least it should have (cf. Jas 5:1–6).

A closer analogy today with ancient slavery relates to members of the military, who rarely get attention in scholarly biblical works (cf. Luke 3:14).[31] Soldiers, airmen, sailors, marines, and coast guardsmen obey orders from their superiors every day (cf. Matt 8:9; Luke 7:8). And they can only disobey an order—even when their lives are at grave risk—if it is clearly an illegal order, but even then there is significant pressure to obey. Ephesians 6:5–9, though, should give members of the military not just direction for obedience and for how to treat those under their command but a perspective for their lives that the Superior whom they actually obey takes note of their many, many sacrifices and willing service as those who "serve as for the Lord and not for people."

Selected Bibliography

Glancy, J. "Obstacles to Slaves' Participation in the Corinthian Church." *JBL* 117 (1998): 481–501.

Glancy, J. *Slavery in Early Christianity.* Minneapolis: Fortress, 2006; repr. of 2002 ed.

Harper, K. *Slavery in the Late Roman World, AD 275–425.* New York: Cambridge University Press, 2011.

Harrill, J. A. *The Manumission of Slaves in Early Christianity.* HUT 32. Tübingen: Mohr Siebeck, 1995.

———. *Slaves in the New Testament: Literary, Social, and Moral Dimensions.* Minneapolis: Fortress, 2006.

MacDonald, M. "Slavery, Sexuality and House Churches: A Reassessment of Colossians 3:18–4:1 in Light of New Research on the Roman Family." *NTS* 53 (2007): 94–113.

Scheidel, W. "The Comparative Economics of Slavery in the Greco-Roman World." Version 1. *Princeton/Stanford Working Papers in Classics.* 2005.

Staats, R. "Kaiser Konstantin der Große und der Apostel Paul." *VC* 62 (2008): 334–70.

Wiedemann, T. *Greek and Roman Slavery.* Baltimore: Johns Hopkins University Press, 1981. Repr., New York: Routledge, 1994.

31. Even though the next passage, Eph 6:10–20, has imagery drawn directly from the equipment of ancient warriors.

The Church Equipped for Its Struggle (6:10–20)

Introduction

In Ephesians 6:10–20 Paul urges the church to prayerfully persevere in this life against all spiritual opposition in reliance on the Lord's strong provisions. This is the longest section in this chapter and acts as the summary exhortation of the book. The chapter can easily be divided between vv. 10–17 (subdivisible between vv. 10–13 and 14–17), with their focus on the military imagery, and vv. 18–20, which have a concluding admonition to persistent prayers for the saints and for Paul specifically. This last component on prayer could easily be separated off from the preceding section thematically and was possibly written in Paul's own hand (see comment on v. 18), but it is retained here as an essential element in the larger vv. 10–20 passage since prayer is the church's most effective, real war implement in her fight.[1] The last section (vv. 18–20) is also linked grammatically with what precedes, with parallel participles as its main verbs (e.g., *προσευχόμενοι ... καὶ ... ἀγρυπνοῦντες*, "pray ... and ... be vigilant"; v. 18). To be truly freestanding, Paul would have used imperative mood verbs here.

Paul was in some ways in the position of Joshua.[2] As Moses departed, leaving Joshua, so Jesus ascended, leaving Paul to enter the Gentile area (Rom 11:13; 1 Tim 2:7). As Joshua set out on the other side of the Jordan to begin the conquest of the promised land, so Paul set out to launch an offensive campaign to take over the whole world. But the difference between

1. Many commentators treat vv. 10–20 together as a unit; e.g., Lincoln, 429; O'Brien, 456–57; Gnilka, 303; Best, 584–85; cf. NA[28].

2. And as Joshua was commanded to "be strong" before the conquest (Deut 31:6–7; Josh 1:6–9) then passed on the same exhortation to Israel to be strong (Josh 10:25), so Paul passes on this command to the church to be strong in the Lord.

the two is vital. Joshua was under orders to launch a theocratic invasion from the captain of the Lord's host with a drawn sword (Josh 5:13–15); Paul was under orders from the Prince of Peace (Isa 9:6; Eph 2:14–17), and his only offensive weapon for conquest of the world was the glad tidings of peace (v. 15), made effective through prayer in the Spirit (vv. 18–20). Paul set out to conquer a world that was already at the feet of its King (1:20–23), who said, *νενίκηκα τὸν κόσμον*, "I have conquered the world" (John 16:33). Therefore, the church Paul instructs in Eph 6:10–20 is not ordered to *advance* in battle array in theocratic conquest, but to *stand fast* and pray.

Paul brings the whole book together in a triumphant conclusion in the exhortations of vv. 10–20.[3] Lincoln analyzes this section in terms of a *peroratio* of an ancient speech, which served to bring the speech to a rousing conclusion with emphasis on the emotions (Lincoln, 432–33). Then he mentions connections between vv. 10–20 with ancient speeches given by generals on the eve of battle (Lincoln, 433).[4] (However, generals did not have to tell trained soldiers to put on their armor or to take up their swords; e.g., Scipio and Hannibal before their climactic battle [Polybius, *Hist.* 15.10–11].) Perhaps Ephesians 6:10–24 was the place where Paul wrote the final words of the epistle with his own hand, as was his custom (1 Cor 16:21; Gal 6:11–18; Col 4:1; 2 Thess 3:17; Phlm 19). Epistle writers often took over from their secretaries at the end of their letters to restate their main aims, which would fit the content of 6:10–24 but is not as clear as we could wish, since Paul does not explicitly tell us that he is writing these words in vv. 10–20 (see introduction to vv. 21–24 below).

The one prominent aspect of Eph 6:10–20 that is often observed is its connection with the Lord as a Divine Warrior.[5] The connections with Isaiah and the military equipment in 6:14–17 in particular are overt and

---

3. See esp. Thorsten Moritz, *A Profound Mystery: The Use of the Old Testament in Ephesians*, SNT 85 (New York: Brill, 1996), 181–83, and repetition of terms found in 6:10–20 from earlier in the epistle.

4. See also Lincoln, 436–38, for review of battle imagery in other ancient sources such as the Dead Sea Scrolls and contemporary Stoic authors; but, Lincoln correctly observes, "there can be no question of any direct dependency" (Lincoln, 437).

5. See above on 1:20 (and literature cited) and utilization of Psa 68 in 4:8–11; cf. Thomas R. Yoder Neufeld, *"Put on the Armour of God": The Divine Warrior from Isaiah to Ephesians*, JSNTSup 140 (Sheffield, UK: Sheffield Academic, 1997); Moritz, *Profound Mystery*, 178–212; Robert A. Wild, "The Warrior and the Prisoner: Some Reflections on Ephesians 6.10–20," *CBQ* 46 (1984): 284–89.

will be discussed below.[6] However, it should be underlined that the armor in Isaiah is the Lord's own, which he takes up to defeat his enemies for the sake of his people, who had no one in their ranks who was righteous to save:

> He saw that there was no man, and wondered that there was no one to intercede; then his own arm brought him salvation, and his righteousness upheld him. He put on righteousness as a breastplate, and a helmet of salvation on his head. (Isa 59:16–17)

Now that salvation has been decisively won by the Messianic King, his people are equipped in this very armor to defend themselves in this age.

One important question arises, which is periodically discussed: What constitutes the Christian's armor? Is it personal piety or virtue, that is, personal truth speaking and righteousness (v. 14), preparedness to share the gospel (v. 15), etc.?[7] Or is the armor objective aspects of Christ's victory in the divine armor he himself had put on to bring about salvation for his people (i.e., Isa 59:16–17 above)? In other words, the Christian puts on Christ's "armor of light" by putting on Christ (Rom 13:12–14; Gal 3:27; 1 Thess 5:8), and especially his imputed righteousness as one's breastplate armor (v. 14) because the believer's own "righteousness, integrity, or rectitude of mind ... cannot resist the accusations of conscience, the whispers of despondency, or the power of temptation, much less the severity of the law, or the assaults of Satan" (Hodge, 383).

> Christ is the "whole armor of God" so that "putting on the whole armour of God" is the same as "putting on the Lord Jesus

6. Some scholars see Paul using the Wisdom of Solomon rather than Isaiah directly in the passage (cf. Hoehner, 838, esp. n. 3), but there are key terminological differences and purposes between the two passages that make this unlikely: "The Lord will take his zeal as his whole armor, and will arm all creation to repel his enemies; he will put on righteousness as a breastplate, and wear impartial justice as a helmet (κόρυς); he will take holiness as an invincible shield (ἀσπίς), and sharpen stern wrath for a sword (ῥομφαία), and creation will join with him to fight against the madmen. Shafts of lightning will fly with true aim, and will leap to the target as from a well-drawn bow of clouds, and hailstones full of wrath will be hurled as from a catapult" (Wis 5:17–20 RSV). The helmet, shield, and sword (ῥομφαία is a calvary sword, something like a scimitar; Rev 19:11, 15) here are different from Paul's.

7. David H. Wenkel, "The 'Breastplate of Righteousness' in Ephesians 6:14: Imputation or Virtue?" *TynB* 58 (2007): 275–87; Calvin, 220.

> Christ" (Rom 13:14). … What other "whole armor of God" can one conceive to be meant, which one who will resist "the wiles of the devil" must put on, than the virtue which is Christ? (Origen in Origen and Jerome, 252–54)

A third view combines both of the previous two by adding an essential interpretive ingredient. Ephesians 6:10–20 does not treat Christians in isolation and call on them to act individually only, but treats them as members of a community in the same way that the individual soldier must be part of an army to stand fast against an enemy horde.[8] The exhortations of vv. 10–20 come to the church as a whole to *stand fast* in the panoply God supplies in Christ (see comments on vv. 11, 13), in which, naturally enough, individuals partake, but not on their own. Then the members of Christ's united people, clothed with Christ, in whom is all truth (4:21), can stand their ground clothed in truth (v. 14) and speak the truth to one another (4:25), maturing together to Christ's stature, produced by the word of God and its instruction (4:7–16; 6:17). God supplies the "armor of light," which Christians don by putting on Christ so they can stand firm in the steadily sanctified holy array:

> The night is far gone; the day is at hand. So then let us cast off the works of darkness and *put on the armor of light*. Let us walk properly as in the daytime, not in orgies and drunkenness, not in sexual immorality and sensuality, not in quarreling and jealousy. But *put on the Lord Jesus Christ*, and make no provision for the flesh, to gratify its desires. (Rom 13:12–14, emphasis added)

Ephesians 6:10–20 is deservedly the favorite part of this epistle—and perhaps of the Bible—for many Christians. It has been the subject of untold famous sermons, not least of which are 68 of the 232 sermons on Ephesians by D. Martyn Lloyd-Jones between 1954 and 1962. It displays the Christian life as one that is robust and requires courage and strength. And it gives a call to arms, combined with comfort and assurance of the Lord's provision and ultimate victory while not minimizing the dangers Christians face.

---

8. See esp. Donna R. Reinhard, "Ephesians 6:10–18: A Call to Personal Piety or Another Way of Describing Union with Christ?" *JETS* 48 (2005): 521–32.

For this reason, the preacher has pride of place in the exposition of this flower of the epistle.

The structure of Eph 6:10–20 is quite simple in broad terms (see outline below), but the details can be a little hard to follow with all the imperatives, participles, and subordinate clauses. For that reason, here are the verbs from the main statements of the passage, which are either imperatives or participles functioning as imperatives (see comment on v. 14):

10 ἐνδυναμοῦσθε	grow strong
11 ἐνδύσασθε	put on
13 διὰ τοῦτο ἀναλάβετε	for this reason, take up
14 στῆτε οὖν	so, stand fast
περιζωσάμενοι	(and) belt up
καὶ ἐνδυσάμενοι	and put on
15 καὶ ὑποδησάμενοι	and have (your feet) shod
16 ἀναλαβόντες	(and) take up
17 καὶ ... δέξασθε	and ... take up
18 προσευχόμενοι	pray
καὶ ... ἀγρυπνοῦντες	and ... be vigilant

The subordinate clauses are sprinkled throughout the passage to explain ideas such as purpose, result, or details through relative clauses. Here are the subordinate clauses all together from the passage, which will be explained where needed in the comments:

11 πρὸς τὸ δύνασθαι ὑμᾶς στῆναι ("so that you can stand"—result)
13 ἵνα δυνηθῆτε ἀντιστῆναι ("in order that you can hold your ground"—purpose)
καὶ ... κατεργασάμενοι ("and ... when you have done"—temporal adverb)
[καὶ ἵνα δυνηθῆτε] στῆναι ("[and in order that you can] stand"—purpose)
16 ἐν ᾧ δυνήσεσθε ... σβέσαι ("by which you will be able to extinguish"—means clause)
17 ὅ ἐστιν ("which is"—simple relative clause)
19 ἵνα ... δοθῇ ("that ... may be given"—content clause)
γνωρίσαι ("to make known"—result)

20 ὑπὲρ οὗ πρεσβεύω ("on behalf of which I am an emissary"—
relative clause)
ἵνα ... παρρησιάσωμαι ("that ... I may speak boldly"—purpose)
ὡς δεῖ με λαλῆσαι ("as I must so speak"—analogy in comparison)

The suggested division of the text into cola* and periods is as follows:

A 10 τοῦ λοιποῦ ἐνδυναμοῦσθε ἐν κυρίῳ
καὶ ἐν τῷ κράτει τῆς ἰσχύος αὐτοῦ

B 11 ἐνδύσασθε τὴν πανοπλίαν τοῦ θεοῦ
πρὸς τὸ δύνασθαι ὑμᾶς στῆναι
πρὸς τὰς μεθοδείας τοῦ διαβόλου

C 12 ὅτι οὐκ ἔστιν ἡμῖν ἡ πάλη
πρὸς αἷμα καὶ σάρκα ἀλλὰ πρὸς τὰς ἀρχάς
πρὸς τὰς ἐξουσίας
πρὸς τοὺς κοσμοκράτορας τοῦ σκότους τούτου
πρὸς τὰ πνευματικὰ τῆς πονηρίας ἐν τοῖς ἐπουρανίοις

D 13 διὰ τοῦτο ἀναλάβετε τὴν πανοπλίαν τοῦ θεοῦ
ἵνα δυνηθῆτε ἀντιστῆναι ἐν τῇ ἡμέρᾳ τῇ πονηρᾷ
καὶ ἅπαντα κατεργασάμενοι στῆναι

E 14 στῆτε οὖν περιζωσάμενοι τὴν ὀσφὺν ὑμῶν ἐν ἀληθείᾳ
καὶ ἐνδυσάμενοι τὸν θώρακα τῆς δικαιοσύνης
15 καὶ ὑποδησάμενοι τοὺς πόδας
ἐν ἑτοιμασίᾳ τοῦ εὐαγγελίου τῆς εἰρήνης

F 16 ἐν πᾶσιν ἀναλαβόντες τὸν θυρεὸν τῆς πίστεως
ἐν ᾧ δυνήσεσθε πάντα τὰ βέλη τοῦ πονηροῦ τὰ πεπυρωμένα σβέσαι

G 17 καὶ τὴν περικεφαλαίαν τοῦ σωτηρίου δέξασθε
καὶ τὴν μάχαιραν τοῦ πνεύματος
ὅ ἐστιν ῥῆμα θεοῦ

H 18 διὰ πάσης προσευχῆς καὶ δεήσεως
προσευχόμενοι ἐν παντὶ καιρῷ ἐν πνεύματι
καὶ εἰς αὐτὸ ἀγρυπνοῦντες

ἐν πάσῃ προσκαρτερήσει καὶ δεήσει
περὶ πάντων τῶν ἁγίων

I [19] καὶ ὑπὲρ ἐμοῦ
ἵνα μοι δοθῇ λόγος ἐν ἀνοίξει τοῦ στόματός μου
ἐν παρρησίᾳ γνωρίσαι τὸ μυστήριον τοῦ εὐαγγελίου
[20] ὑπὲρ οὗ πρεσβεύω ἐν ἁλύσει
ἵνα ἐν αὐτῷ παρρησιάσωμαι ὡς δεῖ με λαλῆσαι

As is clearly seen, there is an unusually large number of uses of the preposition πρός ("against") in vv. 11–12, with only one use of a conjunction between uses, in v. 12b (ἀλλὰ, "but"). This fits the style of Ephesians seen so far, especially in key places such as in 4:12 (see comment there). Interestingly, the whole series of phrases with πρός starts out with a different use of the preposition in the phrase πρὸς τὸ δύνασθαι ("so that you can") in v. 11. Furthermore, the end of v. 12 represents a feature of composition called "tricolon crescendo," in which each colon* builds to greater and greater length in a crescendo effect (noted above on 1:18–19). As it happens, each colon* in v. 12c–e is exactly six syllables longer than the previous one, as follows (with syllable counts in parentheses):

πρὸς τὰς ἐξουσίας (6)
πρὸς τοὺς κοσμοκράτορας τοῦ σκότους τούτου (12)
πρὸς τὰ πνευματικὰ τῆς πονηρίας ἐν τοῖς ἐπουρανίοις (18)

There are some other nice features to this powerful passage. The most noticeable is the repetition of the verb "stand" next to each other at the end of v. 13 and the beginning of v. 14 ("to stand. Stand fast …").

Outline

XVII. The Church Equipped for Its Struggle (6:10–20)
- A. Urged to stand fast in the spiritual struggle (6:10–13)
- B. Urged to stand fast in the Lord's battle armor (6:14–17)
- C. Urged to persevering prayer (6:18–20)

Original Text

10 Τοῦ λοιποῦ,[a, b] ἐνδυναμοῦσθε[c] ἐν κυρίῳ καὶ ἐν τῷ κράτει τῆς ἰσχύος αὐτοῦ.
11 ἐνδύσασθε τὴν πανοπλίαν τοῦ θεοῦ πρὸς τὸ δύνασθαι ὑμᾶς στῆναι πρὸς τὰς
μεθοδείας τοῦ διαβόλου· **12** ὅτι οὐκ ἔστιν ἡμῖν[d] ἡ πάλη πρὸς αἷμα καὶ σάρκα
ἀλλὰ πρὸς τὰς ἀρχάς, πρὸς τὰς ἐξουσίας,[e] πρὸς τοὺς κοσμοκράτορας τοῦ σκότους[f]
τούτου, πρὸς τὰ πνευματικὰ τῆς πονηρίας ἐν τοῖς ἐπουρανίοις. **13** διὰ τοῦτο
ἀναλάβετε τὴν πανοπλίαν τοῦ θεοῦ, ἵνα δυνηθῆτε[g] ἀντιστῆναι ἐν τῇ ἡμέρᾳ τῇ
πονηρᾷ καὶ ἅπαντα κατεργασάμενοι στῆναι. **14** στῆτε οὖν περιζωσάμενοι τὴν
ὀσφὺν ὑμῶν ἐν ἀληθείᾳ καὶ ἐνδυσάμενοι τὸν θώρακα τῆς δικαιοσύνης **15** καὶ
ὑποδησάμενοι τοὺς πόδας ἐν ἑτοιμασίᾳ τοῦ εὐαγγελίου τῆς εἰρήνης, **16** ἐν[h] πᾶσιν
ἀναλαβόντες τὸν θυρεὸν τῆς πίστεως, ἐν ᾧ δυνήσεσθε πάντα τὰ βέλη τοῦ πονηροῦ τὰ[i] πεπυρωμένα σβέσαι· **17** καὶ τὴν περικεφαλαίαν τοῦ σωτηρίου δέξασθε[j]
καὶ τὴν μάχαιραν τοῦ πνεύματος, ὅ ἐστιν ῥῆμα θεοῦ. **18** Διὰ πάσης προσευχῆς
καὶ δεήσεως προσευχόμενοι ἐν παντὶ καιρῷ ἐν πνεύματι, καὶ εἰς αὐτὸ ἀγρυπνοῦντες ἐν πάσῃ προσκαρτερήσει καὶ δεήσει περὶ πάντων τῶν ἁγίων **19** καὶ ὑπὲρ
ἐμοῦ, ἵνα μοι δοθῇ λόγος ἐν ἀνοίξει τοῦ στόματός μου, ἐν παρρησίᾳ γνωρίσαι τὸ
μυστήριον [k]τοῦ εὐαγγελίου, **20** ὑπὲρ οὗ πρεσβεύω ἐν ἁλύσει, ἵνα [l]ἐν αὐτῷ παρρησιάσωμαι ὡς δεῖ με λαλῆσαι.

Textual Notes

10.a. The genitive adverbial phrase τοῦ λοιποῦ, found in P^{46}, א*, A, B, 33, 81, 1175, 1739, 1881, and a few other witnesses, is difficult, since the meaning would be "from now on" or "henceforth" (as Gal 6:17, the only other NT occurrence). The idea is that the Ephesians are exhorted from this time forward to be strong in the Lord. This meaning, however, does seem a little curious in our context, hence the phrase was probably changed by scribes to the more friendly accusative form, τὸ λοιπόν, "Finally" (so KJV, NASB, NIV, ESV, NRSV; etc.), as found in the majority of extant MSS and a meaning suggested in BDAG, 602, though without any other examples of this meaning for the genitive phrase. The meaning "finally" would mark 6:10 as the beginning of the close of the epistle that leads into the final few points the apostle would write. While this latter meaning seems to fit the context well, we must take the more difficult genitive reading supported by our best and earliest MSS as original (*lectio difficilior**).[9]

10.b. The Western and later group of MSS include ἀδελφοί μου, "my brothers," after the opening adverbial phrase so that the reading in these witnesses mirrors Col 3:1: "Finally, my brothers ..." This seems to be an instance of scribal conformity of one passage to another.

10.c. Instead of the compound verb ἐνδυναμοῦσθε ἐν κυρίῳ ("be strong in the Lord"), P[46], B, and 33 have simply δυναμοῦσθε ("be enabled"), which is only found elsewhere in Col 1:11 and Heb 11:34. The more widely attested compound verb (ἐνδυναμοῦσθε; found in Acts 9:22; Rom 4:20; Phil 4:13; 1 Tim 1:12; 2 Tim 2:1; 4:17) seems most likely to be original.

12.d. There is a variant of the second-person pronoun "for you, your" (ὑμῖν) for the first-person pronoun "for us, our" (ἡμῖν) in the first colon* in P[46], B, D*, F, G, and Western witnesses. As Metzger reports, "the natural tendency of copyists would have been to alter ἡμῖν to ὑμῖν, since the rest of the paragraph involves the second person. A majority of the Committee preferred ἡμῖν as being perhaps the more difficult reading."[10]

12.e. The reading at the end of the second and the third cola is πρὸς τὰς ἀρχάς πρὸς τὰς ἐξουσίας, "against the rulers, against the authorities," but P[46] has only πρὸς τὰς μεθοδείας, "against the schemes." In isolation, this just looks like an inexplicable blunder, but the MS itself shows that the mistake was quite innocent. That the same phrase πρὸς τὰς μεθοδείας from v. 11 occurs two lines directly above the target phrase at the end of the line caused the misreading (note the same prep. and article as **πρὸς τὰς** ἀρχάς). Here is how the end of the three lines of vv. 11c–12b look in P[46]:

v. 11c	... ΠΡΟΣΤΑΣΜΕΘΟΔΙΑΣ	(πρὸς τὰς μεθοδείας)
v. 12a	... ΕΣΤΙΝΫΜΕΙΝΗΠΑΛΗ	(ἔστιν ἡμεῖν ἡ πάλη)
v. 12b	... ΠΡΟΣΤΑΣΜΕΘΟΔΙΑΣ	(πρὸς τὰς μεθοδείας; instead of ἀρχάς)

9. For the meanings of both τοῦ λοιποῦ and τὸ λοιπόν see LSJ, 1060, and BDAG, 602–3. LSJ suggest that τοῦ λοιποῦ comes from the fuller expression ἐκ τοῦ λοιποῦ χρόνου, "from the time remaining," "henceforward," or "hereafter."

10. Bruce M. Metzger, *A Textual Commentary on the Greek New Testament*, 2nd ed. (New York: United Bible Societies, 1994), 542.

Our scribe, undoubtedly anticipating the end of the book and possibly a moment's respite, simply looked at the end of the first line quoted above (v. 11c) when copying the end of the third line (v. 12b). The repetition of ΠΡΟΣΤΑΣ here threw him off.

12.f. Many MSS (e.g., corrector 2a of א, D[2], K, L, P, Ψ, 81, 104, 1505, 1881, M) add an interpretive phrase τοῦ αἰῶνος here, making the phrase read: "of the darkness of this age" (or "world"). There is early attestation to this phrase not being original (א*, A, B, D*, 33, 1175, 1739[txt], and some versions), which is preferred; cf. Christopher J. A. Lash, "Where Do Devils Live? A Problem in the Textual Criticism of Ephesians 6, 12," *VC* 30 (1976): 161–74 (esp. 161–62).

13.g. The aorist verb in the opening phrase of the second colon*, ἵνα δυνηθῆτε ("in order that you can"), is expressed in its present-tense form in P[46], yet as an active rather than as a passive (deponent) form (ἵνα δύνητε). This is a singular reading.

16.h. The opening prepositional phrase ἐν πᾶσιν ("in all circumstances") is supported by most early witnesses (e.g., P[46], א, B, 33, 1175, 1739, 1881), while M and other MSS mostly of Western origin (D, F, G, Ψ) but also A have the preposition ἐπί here, changing to "in addition to all [these]" (ἐπὶ πᾶσιν; cf. Col 3:14; BDF §235 [3]). Either preposition and meaning would fit the context, but the reading with ἐν has better external support.

16.i. The second article in the expression πάντα **τὰ** βέλη τοῦ πονηροῦ τὰ πεπυρωμένα ("all the flaming arrows of the evil one") in the second cola* is missing in P[46], B, D*, F, and G. This seems to be a simple omission, since the participle (πεπυρωμένα) must clearly be attributive here rather than adverbial, which would be the case were the second article not expressed.

17.j. The verb δέξασθε ("take up," "take") is missing in a few Western witnesses (e.g., D*, F, G), which would mean that the synonymous verb from v. 16 (ἀναλαβόντες, "take up") would be understood as repeated here. The attestation for dropping the verb is not strong (see also comment).

19.k. Some Western MSS (F, G, b, m*) along with Vaticanus (B) drop "of the gospel" in the phrase τὸ μυστήριον τοῦ εὐαγγελίου ("the mystery of the gospel"). As noted in the note above on 6:1, the testimony of B joined with such Western witnesses "should not be over evaluated."[11]

20.l. In the last colon*, P[46], B, 1739, and 1881 read *αὐτό* ("it") in place of ἐν αὐτῷ ("in it" or as KJV, "therein"). The antecedent of both forms of the pronoun is most likely "the mystery of the gospel" from the end of v. 19 (colon* 3), and either form of the pronoun makes good sense here: "that I may declare *it* (αὐτό) fearlessly" (NIV; cf. ESV; NRSV) or "that *therein* (ἐν αὐτῷ) I may speak boldly" (KJV). While αὐτό could be the original reading, with its good and early witnesses, it is more difficult to see how a scribe could change this easier reading to ἐν αὐτῷ, hence the latter is preferred as *lectio difficilior**. See comment on v. 20 for the possibility that ἐν αὐτῷ means "in him" (i.e., in Christ) and to reference Psa 12:5 (LXX 11:6).

Translation

10 Henceforth,[12] grow strong[13] in the Lord and in the strength of his might. **11** Put on the panoply[14] of God so that you can stand against the schemes of the Devil. **12** For our struggle[15] is not against flesh and blood,[16] but against the rulers, against the authorities, against the cosmic forces of this darkness, against the spiritual powers of evil[17] in the high-heavenlies.[18] **13** For

---

11. Ibid.
12. This is the expected meaning of the gen. adv. phrase τοῦ λοιποῦ; see textual note above and comment below.
13. While, as pointed out many times (see note on v. 1), the pres. tense is default for impvs. in general exhortations, the verb ἐνδυναμόω can itself communicate the idea of increasing in strength. I am not tying this progressive idea into the tense form itself, but to the lexeme*; so Acts 9:22; Rom 4:20; cf. BDAG, 333.
14. English has taken *panoply* from the Greek word, but not always with its original military association. See comment.
15. For πάλη (only here in the NT), which commonly refers to a wrestling match; cf. BDAG, 752; LSJ, 1291. See comment.
16. The Greek word order (αἷμα καὶ σάρκα) can be either "blood and flesh" as here (Heb 2:14; cf. John 1:13) or reversed like the English idiom, "flesh and blood" (Matt 16:11; 1 Cor 15:50; Gal 1:16).
17. Or "evil spiritual powers"; both take the gen. in the phrase τὰ πνευματικὰ τῆς πονηρίας as adj. (quality); BDF §165.
18. See note on 1:3 for this translation.

this reason, take up[19] the panoply[20] of God, in order that you can hold your ground in the evil day, and when you have done all you can,[21] to stand.
14 Stand fast then![22] And belt up[23] your waist[24] with truth, and put on the breastplate of righteousness, **15** and have your feet shod[25] with readiness from the gospel[26] of peace. **16** In all circumstances[27] take up the shield of faith, by which you will be able to extinguish all the flaming[28] arrows of

---

19. See comment on ἐνδύσασθε in v. 11.

20. See comment on v. 11 for πανοπλία as denoting both offensive and defensive military equipment taken over into English.

21. I am adding "you can" to convey the force of the emphatic form of "all" (πᾶς), ἁπᾶς, used only here and at 1 Tim 1:16 in Paul's writings (thirty-four total NT occurrences, compared with well over one thousand forms of πᾶς [over fifty in Ephesians]). The meaning of ἁπᾶς here is "all possible"; so LSJ, 181; not reported in BDAG, 98.

22. This is nearly the same as the NIV for στῆναι στῆτε οὖν ("to stand. Stand firm then, with ..."). See comment.

23. I am taking the ptc. περιζωσάμενοι ("belt up"; middle voice from περιζώννυμι/περιζωννύω; BDAG, 801) as well as the three to follow (ἐνδυσάμενοι ... ὑποδησάμενοι ... ἀναλαβόντες, "put on ... let your feet be shod ... take up," vv. 14–16) as parallel adv. ptcs. See comment.

24. The sg. ὀσφύς is distributive for "each one his waist"; cf. BDF §140.

25. Rendering this phrase into modern English requires a significant transformation of the Greek idiom ("and with your feet fitted with" [NIV]), which can also still be awkward: "and, as shoes for your feet, having put on" (ESV). The idea is that the readers put readiness on their feet as one puts on one's shoes. Hence, "have your feet shod" may sound pass., but I take the ptc. ὑποδησάμενοι as its middle-voice form with "feet" as its obj. (cf. Daniel B. Wallace, *Greek Grammar beyond the Basics* [Grand Rapids: Zondervan, 1997], 416–17; BDAG, 1037).

26. The phrase ἐν ἑτοιμασίᾳ τοῦ εὐαγγελίου (here "readiness from the gospel") is actually somewhat ambiguous because the word ἑτοιμασία is understood in different ways, which affects how it relates to the gen. εὐαγγελίου, "of," "from," or even "for the gospel." See comment.

27. This takes ἐν πᾶσιν ("in all circumstances"; cf. Phil 4:12; 2 Tim 4:5) as implying καιροῖς or χρόνοις ("seasons," "circumstances," or "times"; as ESV and footnote in NRSV). In other contexts the phrase means "in every way," "entirely" (as at 1:23; cf. 4:6 "in all"). Versions have less attractive "above all" (KJV), "in addition to all (this)" (NASB, NIV), or "with all these" (NRSV); cf. BDAG, 782–84 (esp. meaning 1dβ); cf. Lincoln, 449.

28. The perf. of the attributive ptc. πεπυρωμένα means "set alight," with the consequent state of "be burning"; cf. Rev 1:15; 3:18 for a similar meaning.

the evil one. **17** And take up[29] the helmet of salvation and the sword of the Spirit, which[30] is the word of God. **18** Pray[31] with all prayer and supplication[32] in every season[33] in the Spirit, and with this in mind[34] be vigilant in all persistent supplication[35] for all the saints, **19** and for me as well, that a message[36] may be given to me when I open my mouth, to boldly make the mystery of the gospel known, **20** on behalf of which I am an emissary[37] in chains, that therein[38] I may speak boldly as I must so speak.

Commentary

6:10 Τοῦ λοιποῦ, ἐνδυναμοῦσθε ἐν κυρίῳ καὶ ἐν τῷ κράτει τῆς ἰσχύος αὐτοῦ, "Henceforth, grow strong in the Lord and in the strength of his might."

---

29. The impv. δέξασθε both closes out the impv. sequence of impv. and ptcs. in vv. 13–17 and paves the way for a new sequence of parallel ptcs. (προσευχόμενοι and ἀγρυπνοῦντες, "pray" and "be vigilant") in v. 18, which also act as impvs. See comments on vv. 14 and 17.

30. The relative clause in v. 17c provides explanation of the antecedent; i.e., the sword of the Spirit is the word of God. Cf. E. Burton, *Syntax of the Moods and Tenses in New Testament Greek* (Edinburgh: T&T Clark, 1898), §295.

31. See comments on vv. 14 and 17 for impv. δέξασθε ("take up") in v. 17 and the parallel ptcs. προσευχόμενοι and ἀγρυπνοῦντες ("pray" and "be vigilant").

32. Προσευχή is the more general term for prayer, while δέησις refers more specifically to requests, especially when used together as also in Phil 4:6; 1 Tim 2:1; 5:5 (BDAG, 213, 878–79).

33. Or "on all occasions," as NIV for ἐν παντὶ καιρῷ; rendered "at all times" in NASB, ESV, NRSV.

34. As NIV for the phrase εἰς αὐτὸ ("to the same end"; cf. ESV and NRSV, "to that end"), which normally appears as εἰς αὐτὸ τοῦτο, "for this very reason" (6:22; cf. Rom 9:17; 13:6; 2 Cor 5:5; Col 4:8).

35. I am taking the two nouns in the phrase ἐν πάσῃ προσκαρτερήσει καὶ δεήσει ("in all persistence and supplication") as hendiadys*, in which one noun acts to qualify the other; cf. BDF §442 (16); A. T. Robertson, *A Grammar of the Greek New Testament in the Light of Historical Research*, 4th ed. (New York, 1923), 1179–83.

36. For the flexible word λόγος (BDAG, 598–601 [meaning 1aβ]).

37. For the verb πρεσβεύω ("to act as an emissary"; cf. BDAG, 861). This is often rendered "I am an ambassador" (e.g., ESV) but denotes a Greek envoy or emissary with a specific appeal or issue to bring before another nation rather than a permanent or semipermanent office of ambassador (like the Roman *legatus Augusti* [e.g., Pliny the Younger]) from the times of the Macedonian kings (e.g., *IvE* 1449) into the Roman imperial period (e.g., *IvE* 983). See comment.

38. "Therein" (as KJV). See comment.

As noted in the textual note, the genitive phrase τοῦ λοιποῦ ("henceforth"; as Gal 6:17) does not normally introduce concluding remarks, whereas accusative [τὸ] λοιπόν ("finally"; e.g., Phil 3:1; 4:8; 2 Thess 3:1) does.[39] Paul, however, is introducing his concluding and summarizing remarks to the Ephesians with a call to arms from this time forth.[40]

For Paul's focus on power and its background in Ephesians, see notes and commentary on 1:15–23, especially the phrase κατὰ τὴν ἐνέργειαν τοῦ κράτους τῆς ἰσχύος αὐτοῦ ("in accordance with the effectiveness of the strength of his might") in 1:19, which is virtually repeated here in 6:10. The overwhelming, divine strength made available to the church flows directly out of the exaltation of Christ to supremacy over every competing realm and power that can be named both in this age and in the next (again, see on 1:15–23; cf. 3:7, 16, 20). Hence, the audience is to be strong "in the Lord" and in *his* strength.[41] This is a particularly powerful message for those whose lives had been shackled by fear of unseen spiritual forces (v. 12), whose baneful effects were averted by amulets and invocation of powerful names, or through other magic practices that were part of the everyday life of pagans in Paul's day but particularly of the Ephesians, with their well-known fascination with the occult.[42] "Be watchful, stand firm in the faith, act like men, be strong. Let all that you do be done in love" (1 Cor 16:13–14; cf. 1 John 2:14).

39. See the discussion in the textual note above.

40. The pres. impv. for ἐνδυναμοῦσθε ("grow strong") or δυναμοῦσθε ("be strong") is default; see 2 Tim 2:1; cf. Psa 67:29 [68:28]. Cf. the aor. imperatival forms beginning in v. 11 with discussion there.

41. Cf. Mattathias Maccabeus's speech to his sons as his death approached: τέκνα ἀνδρίζεσθε καὶ ἰσχύσατε ἐν τῷ νόμῳ, "Children, be courageous and become strong *in the law*" (1 Macc 2:64; emphasis added).

42. So Clinton Arnold: "Paul has repeatedly prayed that they gain a heightened awareness of the vastness of God's power that is presently available through Christ for them (1:19). ... This power is not mediated through incantations, formulas, or shamanistic or magical rituals" (Arnold, 443). Cf. discussion and literature above on 1:15–23 and "Additional Exegetical Comments" there for specifically Ephesian material. For the application of this material to Eph 6:10–20 see esp. Clinton E. Arnold, *Ephesians: Power and Magic: The Concept of Power in Ephesians in Light of Its Historical Setting*, SNTSMS 63 (New York: Cambridge University Press, 1989), 103–22; cf. Moritz, *Profound Mystery*, 178–212.

6:11 ἐνδύσασθε τὴν πανοπλίαν τοῦ θεοῦ πρὸς τὸ δύνασθαι ὑμᾶς στῆναι πρὸς τὰς μεθοδείας τοῦ διαβόλου, "Put on the panoply of God so that you can stand against the schemes of the Devil." As already noted, the admonitions in vv. 10–20 in many ways reiterate and expand on what has been said earlier in the epistle. Here the "schemes" (μεθοδεία) the Ephesians are to stand against are said to originate from the devil, the father of lies (4:27; John 8:44; Acts 13:10; cf. Matt 38–39; 1 John 2:18, 22; 3:8–10; 4:3; 2 John 7), but they are manifested directly through human false teachers and their deceitful trickery (see Acts 13:8–10 and above on 4:14). There is also a moral and eschatological aspect to this fight: "The night is far gone; the day is at hand. So then let us cast off the works of darkness and put on the armor of light" (Rom 13:12).

Jeffrey Asher has recently made a compelling suggestion that classical and especially Homeric deceit and trickery lies behind v. 11.[43] Homer was memorized in the schools, chanted at the various festivals, and expanded on or imitated in countless other works (e.g., the *Aeneid*), and the Homeric myths, characters, and themes form the story lines of numerous plays in antiquity, including those put on in first-century Ephesus. One of the favorite Homeric characters was Odysseus, full of wit and guile (i.e., the Trojan horse and the deception of the Cyclops in his cave; *Od.* 8.487 and 9). Over against the deceiver Odysseus was the central hero, Achilles, "best of the Achaeans," who was godlike in battle strength with his divinely crafted, magically charmed armor (*Il.* 20.268). Asher's view is that in vv. 10–17 Paul is calling on the audience to imitate Achilles and the other Homeric heroes in strength and battle prowess, while through Paul's attribution of "schemes" (μεθοδεία) to the devil and his followers, he "labels the enemy of the believers as an unworthy foe."[44] This is illuminating background, though there is more to say in addition (below).

43. Jeffrey R. Asher, "An Unworthy Foe: Heroic Ἔθη, Trickery, and an Insult in Ephesians 6:11," *JBL* 130 (2011): 729–48. It should be noted that this classical Greek background to the weapons and armor in Eph 6:10–17 does not displace the OT background of the divine warrior (see below) but is offered in addition to it.

44. Asher, "Unworthy Foe," 731; and again, "By connecting the virtues of the saints metaphorically with the virtues of classical warfare, the author demonstrates that the followers of Jesus rightfully possess honor. The virtues of the opposition—the cosmic forces of evil and their human subjects—however, are of lower quality and shameful; they ultimately reflect the qualities of unworthy foes" (Asher,

The imperatives throughout Ephesians are predominantly expressed in their present-tense forms (see above on v. 1 and introduction). In 6:11–17 we encounter four of the six aorist imperative forms in Ephesians: ἐνδύσασθε ("put on"; v. 11), ἀναλάβετε ("take up"; v. 13), στῆτε ("stand fast"; v. 14), and δέξασθε ("take up"; v. 17).[45] Why shift to the aorist, after Paul opens the passage in v. 10 with a present imperative (ἐνδυναμοῦσθε, "grow strong")? While we may be tempted to take these aorist forms as conveying some nuance of aspect, the fact is that these verbs have simple telic meanings such that Greek speakers and writers tended to express them in their aorist-tense forms even in general exhortations like our context in vv. 10–20. The evidence for this is overwhelming, with eighty-six occurrences in the LXX and NT of these four verbs as aorist imperatives and only one present-tense form (for ἵστημι in Jer 28:50 [MT 51:50]).[46] In addition to these four imperative-mood forms, the same analysis bears on the (parallel) participles, which act as imperatives (these are discussed below on v. 14 and in "Additional Exegetical Comments").

The Greek word πανοπλία (here "panoply"), which the Christian is to put on, is a general term that refers to both the defensive ("armor") and offensive ("weapons") military equipment of an ancient soldier, sketched out by Paul in vv. 14 and 16–17 (cf. Luke 11:22; BDAG, 754).[47] Albrecht Oepke (*TDNT*, 5:295–315) takes this πανοπλία equipment and armor as corresponding "exactly" to the gear of contemporary Roman soldiers of Paul's day (301). Jeffrey Asher, though, adds: "This allusion to a Roman soldier, however, would not preclude additional and even more pronounced allusions to heroic characters such as Achilles and Odysseus. ... Achilles was an adaptable character who was often 'modernized' to meet the needs of a

---

"Unworthy Foe," 748); see 740–45 for discussion of the values of honor and shame in the ancient world (cf. above on 3:13 and 4:2).

45. Cf. ἀρθήτω ("must be removed"; 4:31) and ἀνάστα ("arise"; 5:14). See the translation note on v. 11 for the one (atelic) pres. impv. in vv. 10–20 (ἐνδυναμοῦσθε, "grow strong").

46. For example, see: Pss 34:26; 71:3; 108:29; Isa 51:9; 52:1, 4; Job 22:22; 40:10; Jer 13:20; 26:3; Luke 15:22; Rom 13:14; 2 Cor 11:16; Col 3:12; 4:10. See also Zeph 3:7: φοβεῖσθέ με καὶ δέξασθε παιδείαν, "fear me [an atelic meaning, hence pres.-tense form] and *accept* discipline."

47. The gen. "panoply *of God*" here in v. 11 and in the same phrase in v. 13 is either poss. ("God's own armor"; cf. Yoder Neufeld, *Armour of God*, 293) or, more likely, it denotes source as the panoply God supplies to his people (see Hoehner, 823).

new literary and artistic generation."[48] It should be noted that there were not very many Roman legionaries in first-century Ephesus, and most would have been in undress uniform rather than in their battle gear.[49] Ephesians more frequently saw classical Greek armor and warriors depicted in their art, architecture, and coins, which further supports Asher's insights.[50]

Paul expresses the purpose of donning the divine panoply as their being enabled "to stand."[51] Normally one does not think of ancient soldiers, whether Greek hoplites or Roman legionaries, as *standing*, but as *advancing* in their fight. Certainly the great battles in antiquity were won when the victorious army overran or encircled its enemy. In part, Paul's image is based on his metaphor of the Christian warfare as a "wrestling match" (πάλη; see v. 12 below), and the other part is that Christians are not engaged in a theocratic conquest of the world for geopolitical dominance, but in a spiritual fight for its existence:

> For though we walk in the flesh, we are not waging war according to the flesh. For the weapons of our warfare are not of the flesh but have divine power to destroy strongholds. We destroy arguments and every lofty opinion raised against the knowledge of God, and take every thought captive to obey Christ. (2 Cor 10:3–5)

"Standing" and "holding ground," then, occur throughout this passage as the goal of the church in its struggle (vv. 11–14), during which "the gates of

---

48. Asher, "Unworthy Foe," 730n3.

49. The Roman legions were mostly stationed on the borders of the empire or in trouble spots such as Galilee or Judaea (where Paul himself undoubtedly encountered soldiers in full armor). The proconsul of Asia Minor and other Roman officials (especially tax-collection officials) had a few soldiers as bodyguards, and one or two may have acted as guards at jails; see Pliny, *Ep.* 10.19–22, 27–28, 77–78.

50. For example, the frieze of a battle between classic Greek warriors and the mythical Amazons currently on display in the Ephesus museum; cf. the later ivory frieze with Trajan and Roman soldiers found in one of the Ephesian Terrace Houses; cf. Peter Scherrer, ed., *Ephesus: The New Guide* (Turkey: Zero, 2000), 205.

51. The expression πρὸς τὸ δύνασθαι ("so that you can") expresses the purpose (Burton, *Moods*, §414), while στῆναι ("to stand") is the inf. complement of δύνασθαι. Paul repeats πρὸς again ("against") to express that against which Christians stand in their fight ("against the schemes of the Devil").

hell" will not prevail against the holy temple and assembly of God's people, which Christ is building (Matt 16:18).

6:12 ὅτι οὐκ ἔστιν ἡμῖν ἡ πάλη πρὸς αἷμα καὶ σάρκα, "For our struggle is not against flesh and blood."[52] This verse starts out with "for" (ὅτι) to explain the reason Christians need divine armor and strength to withstand the devil's schemes. As also noted in the translation note above, the Greek word order is "blood and flesh" (αἷμα καὶ σάρκα), which I have swapped to "flesh and blood" in my translation to fit the English idiom.

The Greek word πάλη ("struggle") refers almost exclusively in Paul's writings and his audience's world to a "wrestling match" (BDAG, 752; LSJ, 1291).[53] Paul uses a boxing metaphor for his own ministry and Christian life elsewhere (1 Cor 9:24–27; with running), but this wrestling metaphor seems out of place in v. 12 in light of putting on armor and taking up a sword. Hence, μάχη ("battle," "combat"; LSJ, 1085), πόλεμος ("war" or "battle"; LSJ, 1432–33), or even ἀγών ("contest" or "fight"; LSJ, 18–19) would be more appropriate terms than πάλη for the armed combat typified in vv. 10–18 (cf. Gal 5:17; 1 Cor 14:8; 2 Cor 10:3–5; Col 2:1; 1 Tim 6:12; 2 Tim 4:7). Wrestling matches were conducted in the nude, not with armor and sword.[54]

The term πάλη is found several times on the Ephesian inscriptions for men who sometimes both wrestled and engaged in the *pankration* ("all-out fight"), a combination of wrestling and boxing.[55] The main aim of wrestlers was to throw the opponent off his feet through sheer strength and sometimes by feints and "guile" (v. 11–12).

> The Council and People honored Alexander, son of Menodorus son of Dionysius, the Ephesian who won victories (νεικήσαντα)

52. "In the early centuries of the Christian church, the degree of exegetical attention given this verse can only be described as amazing" (Wild, "Warrior and the Prisoner," 284).

53. "For we do not wrestle" (ESV; cf. KJV), but πάλη is rendered "struggle" in other modern English versions; cf. O'Brien, 465–66; Barth, 763–64; Best, 593.

54. See the wall painting of a (nude) wrestling match at Ephesus (possibly with Hercules) in a Terrace House at Ephesus; Scherrer, *Ephesus*, 41.

55. The danger to athletes in these contests was significant, since boxers wore leather thongs tied around their hands to protect the knuckles, not the opponent. In general see Victor C. Pfitzner, *Paul and the Agon Motif*, NovTSup 16 (Leiden: Brill, 1967).

> in the Ismian wrestling competition (πάλη), as well as the wrestling competition of the Koinon of Asia in Ephesus, the Great Ephesia (Games), and the Balbilleia of the Koinon of Asia in Smyrna, and the Smyrnean Koinon of Asia *pankration,* the wrestling competition of the Koinon of Galatia, the *pankration* of the Koinon of Lycia in Myra, and the wrestling competition of the Koinon of Asia in Sardis, and many other games, both wrestling competition (πάλην) and *pankration*. (*IvE* 1123)[56]

The possible connection between wrestling and the panoply of weapons and armor was that wrestling itself was traditionally a part of training for battle "under heavy arms" (ἐν ὅπλοις).[57] Furthermore, it is possibly more than a coincidence that the goal of wrestling was to *stand* (ἵστημι) and to not be thrown to the ground, so Paul focuses his exhortation on *standing* three times in vv. 11–14, with ἵστημι and once with related ἀντιστῆναι ("hold your ground") in v. 13.

In a brief essay, Michael Gudorf has very helpfully suggested that Paul's mixture of wrestling with armed combat in our passage reflects the reality of ancient battles that frequently devolved into hand-to-hand struggles between "heavily armed wrestlers" (οἱ ὁπλιτοπαλαί; LSJ, 1240).[58] He continues:

> Describing the "battle" being waged with the word πάλη in v. 12 rather than with what one would normally expect in the context, namely, μάχη (or even ἀγών [see above]), helps evoke in the reader's mind the concept not only of standing but also that of standing against a cunning opponent in a close-quarter struggle. …

56. This inscription is also translated in Arnold, 446. Clint Arnold and I began working on Ephesus as background to the NT around the same time in the 1980s. See also Arnold, 446–47, for a story of an Ephesian wrestler who utilized the magical Ephesian *grammata* ("letters," "sounds") to remain undefeated in his matches. For a thorough study of the Ephesian festivals and their competitions see Michael F. Lehner, "Die Agonistik im Ephesos der römischen Keiserzeit" (PhD diss., Ludwig-Maximilians-Universität, 2004). Cf. the two orations—including a funeral oration—for a boxer (possibly fictitious) named Melancomas by Dio Chrysostom (*Or.* 28–29) for an indication of how highly regarded these athletes were in antiquity.
57. So Lucian, *Anacharsis* 24 (put in the mouth of Solon).
58. Michael E. Gudorf, "The Use of ΠΑΛΗ in Ephesians 6:12," *JBL* 117 (1998): 331–35. For just one example of a "hand-to-hand" (ἐκ χειρός) battle between Romans and Celts in Polybius see *Hist.* 2.27–30.

> [While the armor and weapons detailed in vv. 10–17] serve the purpose rhetorically of further impressing upon the reader the dangerousness of the battle being waged.[59]

This danger of the Christian's hand-to-hand combat is exacerbated to the extreme by mention that it is not carried out "against flesh and blood," a notion that is elaborated on in the following statements in v. 12, which are rhetorically marked by parallel πρὸς ("against") clauses (picked up from v. 11c), arranged with only one (adversative) conjunction (ἀλλά, "but" in v. 12b): "not against ... but against ... against ... against ... against":

> [12] ὅτι οὐκ ἔστιν ἡμῖν ἡ πάλη
> **πρὸς** αἷμα καὶ σάρκα ἀλλὰ **πρὸς** τὰς ἀρχάς
> **πρὸς** τὰς ἐξουσίας
> **πρὸς** τοὺς κοσμοκράτορας τοῦ σκότους τούτου
> **πρὸς** τὰ πνευματικὰ τῆς πονηρίας ἐν τοῖς ἐπουρανίοις.[60]

ἀλλὰ πρὸς τὰς ἀρχάς, πρὸς τὰς ἐξουσίας, πρὸς τοὺς κοσμοκράτορας τοῦ σκότους τούτου, πρὸς τὰ πνευματικὰ τῆς πονηρίας ἐν τοῖς ἐπουρανίοις, "but against the rulers, against the authorities, against the cosmic forces of this darkness, against the spiritual powers of evil in the high-heavenlies." The danger of the wrestling match facing the Christian is now exacerbated by an enumeration of dark, unseen forces in terms of those that formerly held the Ephesians in thrall to sin and death (2:1–3).[61] It has generally been recognized in scholarship that Paul and church members in the first-century world believed that the unseen, spiritual realm contained such malignant, demonic forces. Ephesians 6:12 is one of the clear signs of this belief, so it came as a surprise when Wesley Carr challenged this widespread understanding by denying ancient belief in hostile demonic powers. Yet his only way of coping with Eph 6:12 is to posit, without any evidence, that this

---

59. Gudorf, "Use of ΠΑΛΗ," 334.
60. See the introduction above for "tricolon crescendo" in the last three cola* of v. 12.
61. See esp. Arnold, 447–48, for κοσμοοκράτωρ ("cosmic forces") used in magical texts and only here in the NT (cf. BDAG, 561).

verse was a later interpolation into the text of Ephesians.[62] Needless to say, Carr's view has not gained widespread acceptance.[63]

All previous uses of πνευματικός and ἐπουράνιος in Ephesians relate to the Holy Spirit and to the exalted heavens, to where Christ (and his people) ascended and from where Christ dispenses the fruits of his victory on the cross (cf. 1:3, 20; 2:2, 6; 3:10; 5:19).[64] The use of these two terms here in v. 13 is ironic and implies that, though the victory of Christ was a decisive triumph (Col 2:16), he rules in the midst of his enemies (Psa 110:2; Acts 2:35; 1 Cor 15:25; Eph 1:22; Heb 1:13, 10:13).[65] The world powers of darkness (cf. 5:8, 11; cf. Luke 22:53; Acts 26:18; Col 1:13) still have some hold in this age with its evil days (5:16; 6:13, 16) because the "kingdom of Christ and of God" (5:5) has been inaugurated but awaits consummation at the end of this age (1:21; see above on 5:5). Until then, those who put their faith in Christ experience true and lasting peace (2:14–16; 4:3; 6:15)—and war.

6:13 διὰ τοῦτο ἀναλάβετε τὴν πανοπλίαν τοῦ θεοῦ, ἵνα δυνηθῆτε ἀντιστῆναι ἐν τῇ ἡμέρᾳ τῇ πονηρᾷ καὶ ἅπαντα κατεργασάμενοι στῆναι, "For this reason, take up the panoply of God, in order that you can hold your ground in the evil day, and when you have done all you can, to stand." This verse forms a reprise of Paul's exhortation in vv. 10–12 and brings it to a conclusion with "for this reason" (διὰ τοῦτο) before he passes on to the details of the "panoply of God" (also v. 11) in vv. 14–17. The reason divine armor is needed is the spiritual nature of the Christian's foe (vv. 11–12; ; cf. 1 Pet 4:1; Jas 4:7), which requires the Lord's own armor.

In v. 11 Paul had told the audience to "put on" (ἐνδύσασθε) the panoply of God, while here they must "take it up" (ἀναλάβετε). There is not much

---

62. Wesley Carr, *Angels and Principalities: The Background, Meaning and Development of the Pauline Phrase* αἱ ἀρχαὶ καὶ αἱ ἐξουσίαι, SNTSMS 42 (Cambridge: Cambridge University Press, 1981), 110.
63. See esp. Clinton Arnold, "The 'Exorcism' of Ephesians 6.12," *JSNT* 30 (1987): 71–87; and Peter T. O'Brien, "Principalities and Powers: Opponents of the Church," in *Biblical Interpretation and the Church*, ed. D. A. Carson (Exeter, UK: Paternoster, 1984), 110–50; cf. Wild, "Warrior and the Prisoner," 285.
64. Cf. W. Hall Harris III, "'The Heavenlies' Reconsidered: Οὐρανός and Ἐπουράνιος in Ephesians," *BSac* 148 (1991): 72–89, esp. 86–87.
65. Cf. Christopher J. A. Lash, "Where Do Devils Live? A Problem in the Textual Criticism of Ephesians 6, 12," *VC* 30 (1976): 161–74, in the textual note above, and see discussion of 1:19–22 above.

difference between the two verbs, since one takes up armor and weapons in order to use them, as in the LXX of Jeremiah where ἀναλαμβάνω ("take up") also occurs with this meaning: ἀναλάβετε ὅπλα καὶ ἀσπίδας καὶ προσαγάγετε εἰς πόλεμον, "*Take up* your armor and shields and move off to battle" (Jer 26:3 LXX; MT 46:3).

Next we are told the purpose for this armament with God's panoply in terms again similar to v. 11: "in order that you can hold your ground in the evil day." The verb rendered "hold your ground" (ἀνθίστημι) is used frequently for "withstanding" an enemy in battle (LSJ, 140; BDAG, 80) and related to "stand" (ἵστημι), used three times in vv. 11, 13–14, for the main purpose of the church's wrestling match/military struggle. Here, "hold your ground" and "stand" are parallel infinitive complements: ἵνα δυνηθῆτε ἀντιστῆναι ... καὶ ... [ἵνα δυνηθῆτε] στῆναι, "in order that you can withstand ... and ... [you can] stand." The difficulty and energy of standing firm in this fight is expressed with the expression "when you have done all you can" (ἅπαντα κατεργασάμενοι), which then leads to the decisive *stand* (στῆναι).[66] And the difficulty of holding fast is further expressed by the fact that it is an "evil day" (cf. 5:16). Paul portrays the church as soldiers in a battle line holding forth against the enemy's vicious onslaught in the evil day of war and threatened disaster (see Pss 37:19; 41:1; 49:5; Jer 17:17–18). In the end, standing (στῆναι) receives the focus as the last word in the period and as that which opens the next with the imperative στῆτε, "Stand fast!" (v. 14; see below).

6:14 στῆτε οὖν περιζωσάμενοι τὴν ὀσφὺν ὑμῶν ἐν ἀληθείᾳ καὶ ἐνδυσάμενοι τὸν θώρακα τῆς δικαιοσύνης, "Stand fast then! And belt up your waist with truth, and put on the breastplate of righteousness." The larger section of vv. 10–17 can be subdivided here between vv. 10–13 and vv. 14–17. The first part has the general exhortation to stand fast and an enumeration of the church's spiritual enemies. The second part opens with an exhortation built on the

---

66. As explained in the translation note, ἅπας here has the sense of "all possible," leading to the translation "all you can" here, while the ptc. κατεργασάμενοι ("when you have done") is a simple aor. temporal ptc., referring to an event that precedes the inf. στῆναι ("[in order that you can] stand"); so more wooden "having done all" renderings in KJV, NASB, NRSV, ESV; and clearer NIV "after you have done everything." The ptc. could also very easily be taken as an expression of the means for accomplishing the later action: "*by doing* everything you can to stand."

end of v. 13. The word order brings this out, where "stand" (ἵστημι) is used twice alongside each other: ἵνα δυνηθῆτε … **στῆναι στῆτε** οὖν, "in order that you can … *stand. Stand fast* then!" The conjunction οὖν communicates that the imperative "stand fast" is a resulting inference from the previous statement (BDAG, 736–37, meaning 1b). "You can do this. *So do it!*" Rendering οὖν with a longer word like "therefore" (e.g., KJV, NASB, ESV, NRSV) makes the statement sound more like a calm, logical discussion than the impassioned battlefield utterance that it is. There then follows an enumeration of the components of the "panoply of God" (vv. 11, 13), inspired primarily from Isaiah, which allows Christians to hold their ground against attack.

The participle περιζωσάμενοι ("belt up") is the first of a sequence of four aorist participles that follow the opening imperative: στῆτε … περιζωσάμενοι … ἐνδυσάμενοι … ὑποδησάμενοι … ἀναλαβόντες ("Stand firm … belt up … put on … have your feet shod … take up"). Furthermore, the imperative δέξασθε ("take up") is followed by the participles προσευχόμενοι ("pray") and ἀγρυπνοῦντες ("be vigilant") in vv. 17–18. Here is how I have arranged these verbs in the introduction above:

14 στῆτε οὖν	so, stand fast
περιζωσάμενοι	(and) belt up
καὶ ἐνδυσάμενοι	and put on
15 καὶ ὑποδησάμενοι	and have (your feet) shod
16 ἀναλαβόντες	(and) take up
17 καὶ … δέξασθε	and … take up
18 προσευχόμενοι	pray
καὶ … ἀγρυπνοῦντες	and … be vigilant

How do these six participles in vv. 14–18 function?

Traditionally, English versions have often clumsily used English participial clauses to render the Greek participle phrases: "Stand therefore, *having fastened* … and *having put on* … (ESV; also KJV, NASB). This leaves the participle clauses uninterpreted, as some sort of adjunct actions. It is attractive to take the four aorist participles in vv. 14–16 as expressing the antecedent means that precede the imperative to stand and facilitate its accomplishment. This is hard to communicate in English but is probably behind "with" here: "Stand firm then, with the belt of truth buckled … with the breastplate of righteousness in place, and with your feet fitted …"

(NIV).[67] Yet even then, one can sense that the preceding actions are *enjoined* on the audience as necessary preparation for standing. Therefore, the second way to take the participles is one we have seen often in Ephesians and I have called the "parallel" use: They are virtual imperatives that parallel the main event (στῆτε).[68] The imperative verb ("stand fast") has prominence over the four participles in vv. 14–16 and is capped off by a terminating imperative, δέ ξεσθε ("put on"), in v. 17. The semantic value of the aorist and present-tense forms of the participles will be addressed in "Additional Exegetical Comments" below.

Verse 14 opens with a clarion call of defense in battle to "stand fast!" There are other examples of the military use of this imperative in the LXX: "Then Moses said to the people, 'Be courageous, stand fast (στῆτε), and you will see God's deliverance (σωτηρίαν)" (Exod 14:13); "Stand fast (στῆτε) now before our enemies and fight against them" (1 Macc 4:18). The same focus on standing fast has been the emphasis throughout vv. 10–13 to this point, so the imperative to stand fast forms its climax and leads into the exhortations to take up the individual elements of armor and the sword.

As mentioned in the introduction, the background to the military equipment Paul references in vv. 14–17 derives from various glimpses of the messianic divine warrior in Isaiah who would spring from the stump of Jesse (Isa 11:1) in the Spirit of the Lord (Isa 11:2) as a righteous judge of the poor and with equity for the meek and downcast (Isa 11:4), leading to Isa 11:5, which connects with Eph 6:14: "And his waist will be belted with righteousness (δικαιοσύνῃ) and his loins bound up with truth (ἀληθείᾳ; or 'fidelity')" (Isa 11:5 LXX; my trans.).[69] There has been much fruitful work

67. Cf. Hoehner, 837–38 (antecedent means or cause); Arnold, 440–41 (means). But then NIV takes ἀναλαβόντες in v. 16 as impv. "take up," as also the two ptcs. in v. 18 ("pray ... be alert").

68. This is how the NRSV takes all six ptcs. in vv. 14–18, and even the NASB takes the two in v. 18. For parallel ptcs. see excursus below. It is easy to see why this use of the ptc. was labeled "attendant circumstances" (e.g., Herbert Wier Smyth, *Greek Grammar*, rev. Gordon M. Messing [Cambridge, MA: Harvard University Press, 1956; original ed., 1920], §2054a; BDF §168 [2]), since these are ptc.-denoted events that "attend" the main impv.

69. See also: "But since we belong to the day, let us be sober, having put on the breastplate of faith and love, and for a helmet the hope of salvation" (1 Thess 5:8); and "I put on righteousness, and it clothed me; my justice was like a robe and a turban" (Job 29:14).

on this Isaiah connection with Ephesians.[70] One simple idea is key to keep in mind throughout the passage: The messianic warrior has won the battle decisively and risen to God's right hand in sovereign rule (1:19–22; 4:8–10; cf. 2:4–6). The armor and sword in Isaiah are his own, while in 6:14–17 he shares spoils of war for his people as they face their own "evil day" in the "strength of his might" (6:10; cf. 1:19–22; 3:16).

The wrapping of truth around one's waist derives from the Isa 11:5 text cited above.[71] It acts in 6:14 as a vivid metaphor to reiterate Paul's earlier reminder that they have embraced the truth found in Jesus (4:21) and his gospel (1:13). Then the church responds by speaking the truth (4:15, 25). The strength to do this is derived from the Lord (vv. 10–13) and his calling (1:4, 18; 4:1, 4), and inaugurated new-creation life in holiness and righteousness (1:4; 2:10; 4:20–24) through the purification in Christ (1:7; 5:26–27) and is the fruit of genuine saving faith (2:8–9; 5:5). Hence, the truth here is divine truth given to the church in the gospel, on which it stands.[72] Peter O'Brien states the point nicely: "As believers buckle on this piece of the Messiah's armour, they will be strengthened by God's truth revealed in the gospel, as a consequence of which they will display the characteristics of the Anointed One in their attitudes, language, and behaviour" (O'Brien, 474).

Likewise, the exhortation to "put on the breastplate of righteousness" should be understood in the same way. Righteousness acts as the material or content of the breastplate (BDF §167), as if Paul had said "put on righteousness as your breastplate" just as he said "belt your waist with truth" in the previous colon* (also 1 Thess 5:8; Rom 13:12; 2 Cor 6:7; cf. Hoehner, 840–41). Whose righteousness is it? It must be Christ's divine righteousness (Isa 11:5; 53:11) from his own messianic breastplate (Isa 59:17), granted to the believer in justification by faith alone as a gift (see esp. on 2:8–9; 4:20–24; cf. Rom 5:17; Heb 11:7). This righteousness produces its fruit as "a great honor and a heavy duty" (Barth, 797) in the church's own integrity

70. See works by Moritz, Neufeld, and Wild cited in the introduction above.

71. The long, loose clothing in the OT period was wrapped around one's waist and upper legs in preparation for wrestling (Job 38:3; 40:7) or battle.

72. See the introduction above on the alternatives of seeing the armor pieces in vv. 14–17 as the believer's "devout and holy life" (Calvin, 220; cf. Wenkel, "Breastplate"), or they are divine qualities and gifts (e.g., Hodge, 383–84). In fact, they are the latter, from which the former emerge in the lives of the saints and on which they stand firm against the enemy's onslaught.

and righteous lives (Calvin, 220; Lincoln, 447–48), with which they adorn their profession of Christ (cf. O'Brien, 474–75; Barth, 795–97). If believers have any righteousness and integrity, it springs up as fruit from the free gift of Christ's own righteousness sent from above: "Shower, O heavens, from above, and let the clouds rain down righteousness; let the earth open, that salvation and righteousness may bear fruit; let the earth cause them both to sprout; I the LORD have created it" (Isa 45:8).

6:15 *καὶ ὑποδησάμενοι τοὺς πόδας ἐν ἑτοιμασίᾳ τοῦ εὐαγγελίου τῆς εἰρήνης*, "and have your feet shod with readiness from the gospel of peace." Paul continues his elaboration on the exhortation to "stand fast" with the parallel participle ὑποδησάμενοι ("have your feet shod"; see above on v. 14). As explained in the translation note above, this participle is in the middle voice, so believers are exhorted to put on these shoes.

The phrase ἐν ἑτοιμασίᾳ τοῦ εὐαγγελίου ("with readiness from the gospel") is somewhat ambiguous because of ἑτοιμασία (occurring only here in the NT) and its relation to the genitive εὐαγγελίου ("gospel"). For example, the phrase is rendered "the readiness that comes from the gospel" (NIV; ESV is similar) or "whatever will make you ready to proclaim the gospel" (NRSV). The term ἑτοιμασία (related to ἑτοιμάζω, "make ready," "prepare") can simply refer to "readiness" or "preparation"; on the other hand, "equipment" or "boots" have been suggested in keeping with the other terms for military equipment in the context (so BDAG, 401; LSJ, 703). Heavy Roman hobnailed sandals for soldiers were called *caligae* in Latin, which was brought directly into Greek as τὰ καλίγια (LSJ, 867) or paraphrased as τὰ στρατιωτικὰ ὑποδήματα ("military shoes"; Dio Cassius, 48.12). Hence, we would expect either καλίγια or στρατιωτικὰ ὑποδήματα to have been used for "boots of the gospel," so "readiness" for ἑτοιμασία seems the better rendering here (cf. Hoehner, 842–43; Lincoln, 448–49).

This still leaves us to understand the two gens. in the whole phrase ἐν ἑτοιμασίᾳ τοῦ εὐαγγελίου τῆς εἰρήνης ("with readiness from the gospel of peace"). The second genitive, "gospel of peace," seems clear since the glad tidings of Christ are all about the peace he brings (see on 1:13; 2:14–16; 4:3; 6:23), hence peace is the content of the message, much like "gospel of your salvation" in 1:13 (cf. Hoehner, 843).[73] "Readiness" with connected genitive εὐαγγελίου could mean "being prepared to proclaim the gospel" (e.g., NRSV above), but better is to see "the gospel of peace" as a whole complex as the source of the believer's readiness, as Lincoln (449) expresses well as "the readiness or preparedness for combat and for standing in the battle that is bestowed by the gospel of peace" (Lincoln, 449; also Hoehner, 843).[74]

6:16 *ἐν πᾶσιν ἀναλαβόντες τὸν θυρεὸν τῆς πίστεως, ἐν ᾧ δυνήσεσθε πάντα τὰ βέλη τοῦ πονηροῦ τὰ πεπυρωμένα σβέσαι*, "In all circumstances take up the shield of faith, by which you will be able to extinguish all the flaming arrows of the evil one." As noted in v. 14, the participle ἀναλαβόντες ("take up") acts as an imperative here (see also impv. ἀναλάβετε in v. 13). Greek shields (ἀσπίς; cf. 1 Sam 17:45 LXX) tended to be round (as on the friezes from Ephesus mentioned on v. 11 above), but the larger shield (θυρεός) to which Paul refers in v. 16 was a large, heavy shield made from wood planks and covered on the outside with canvas and leather with metal trim on top and bottom.[75] The Lord is the shield of his people (e.g., Gen 15:1; Pss 3:3;

---

73. Isaiah 52:7 (quoted by Paul in Rom 10:15) is usually seen in the background here: "How beautiful upon the mountains are the feet of him who brings good news, who publishes peace, who brings good news of happiness, who publishes salvation, who says to Zion, 'Your God reigns.' " The LXX is similar but slightly different: "As an hour (ὥρα) on the mountains, as the feet of one who proclaims a glad message of peace (ὡς πόδες εὐαγγελιζομένου ἀκοὴν εἰρήνη), as one who proclaims glad tidings of good things, because I will make your salvation heard, saying to Zion, 'Your God shall reign!' " (my trans.). "As an hour" (or "time"; ὥρα) becomes "How timely are the feet" (ὡς ὡραῖοι οἱ πόδες) in Rom 10:15.

74. "Some expound it as an injunction to be prepared for the Gospel. But I interpret it as the effect of the Gospel, that we should lay aside every hindrance and be prepared both for journey and for battle" (Calvin, 220); cf. O'Brien, 476–78.

75. The θυρεός ("shield") from θύρα, "door" (BDAG, 462; LSJ, 811), used by the Roman legionaries (the *scutum*) versus the smaller ἀσπίς. As pointed out in Arnold, 436, 456, the various pieces of armor and armament of the Roman soldier are described by Polybius, *Hist.* 6.23, and see also Josephus, *Ant.* 3.93–97. Polybius says that this "barn-door" shield (θυρεός) was about two feet wide and four feet tall. A Roman shield of this type has been recovered and can be seen at: http://popular-archaeology.com/issue/june-2011/article/treasures-of-ancient-dura-europos-released-for-all-to-see (accessed January 2015, with thanks to Hall Harris for the link). Heavy military equipment was quite a load for men who probably averaged around five feet tall in antiquity; cf. G. R. Watson, *The Roman Soldier* (Ithaca, NY: Cornell University Press, 1969), 62–67, who discusses the extraordinary

28:7), but here τὸν θυρεὸν τῆς πίστεως ("the shield of faith") denotes the shield composed of the believer's solid faith in battle.[76]

In ancient warfare soldiers threw and slung rocks and lead weights as well as spears (*pila*), and various engines of war shot missiles (1 Macc 6:51, "fire and stones"), while bowmen shot arrows that were sometimes alight and therefore "fiery" (e.g., 2 Kgs 9:24; 2 Chr 26:14–15; Pss 7:13; 144:6).[77] Polybius says that the heavy shields (θυρεοί) were "serviceable for defense" (Polybius, *Hist.* 2.30) and were fitted with a metal iron boss in the middle, "which turns aside the more formidable blows of stones, pikes, and heavy missiles (βέλη) in general" (Polybius, *Hist.* 6.23). Even the smaller Greek shield from earlier times could turn away "missiles" (arrows, stones, spears, etc.). For example, Diodorus of Sicily describes a famous tyrant of Syracuse who had waded out during a city battle into some fierce hand-to-hand fighting such that "many missiles (βέλη) hurled at him fell upon his shield (ἀσπίς) and helmet, but he escaped these owing to the protection of his armor" (Diodorus Siculus, 16.12.4).

The ordinary military shield, then, can repulse ordinary missiles, including arrows shot from ordinary ("flesh and blood") enemies. But the enemies of Paul and of the church are not ordinary (vv. 11–13), and their arrows are "flaming."[78] One can only imagine a soldier on the battle line facing blazing arrows raining down on him and his mates. The leather covering on the shield would have been initially soaked with water to quench the flames (cf. Arnold, 458). But as the battle raged hour after hour, the leather on an ordinary shield would dry and then at best *turn aside* some of these

---

weights (sixty-six pounds or more) carried by Roman legionaries, nicknamed "Marius' Mules."

76. The gen. is similar to others in vv. 14–17, the content or material of the piece of armor (or "apposition"); cf. Best, 602; O'Brien, 479; Hoehner, 846.

77. The generic term τὸ βέλος for all these different kinds of "missiles" or "projectiles" became the common term for an "arrow" (BDAG, 174; LSJ, 313), which seems to be the meaning in Eph 6:15, since a shield could not hold up to fire thrown by a large machine, as in 1 Macc 6:51. Cf. Lucian, *Anach.* 31, where τὰ βέλη denotes both arrows and spears.

78. The perf. form of the attributive ptc. modifying the "arrows" (βέλη) is πεπυρωμένα (from πυρόω) and simply means something set alight, and therefore it is "flaming" or "blazing," as also in Rev 1:15. See Arnold, 457–58, for ancient descriptions of incendiary arrows and spears using a combination of tow and pitch.

missiles but no longer *extinguish* them.[79] Their shields would eventually burn and be useless, and they would then be uncovered, helpless, and soon dead.[80] In its struggle, then, the church needs the supernatural panoply of God, through which its members "will be able to extinguish *all* the flaming arrows of the evil one," not just some of them, and not just turn these blazing threats aside but quench them (cf. 4:27).

6:17 καὶ τὴν περικεφαλαίαν τοῦ σωτηρίου δέξασθε καὶ τὴν μάχαιραν τοῦ πνεύματος, ὅ ἐστιν ῥῆμα θεοῦ, "And take up the helmet of salvation and the sword of the Spirit, which is the word of God." The imperative verb in v. 17 serves to close out the imperative ideas dealing specifically with armor and the sword in vv. 13–17 before the two participles in vv. 18–20 turn away from the military metaphor to prayer. The outline is:

> [13] διὰ τοῦτο **ἀναλάβετε** τὴν πανοπλίαν τοῦ θεοῦ ... [14]**στῆτε** οὖν ... [17] καὶ τὴν περικεφαλαίαν τοῦ σωτηρίου **δέξασθε** καὶ τὴν μάχαιραν τοῦ πνεύματος
>
> *take up* the panoply of God. ... *Stand fast* then! ... And *take up* the helmet of salvation and the sword of the Spirit.

The one imperative verb, δέξασθε ("take up"), governs the two objects: the helmet and the sword.[81] That is probably why δέ χομαι ("take up," "take," or "grasp") was used: It would apply to both *taking up* one's helmet and *grasping* one's sword.

79. The aor. inf. for "extinguish" (σβέσαι) is default and therefore carries no aspectual nuance here. The aor. inf. of this verb (σβέννυμι) is found three times in the LXX (*4 Macc* 3:14; Song 8:7; Ezek 32:7) and various places in other ancient authors (e.g., Polybius, *Hist.* 8.28.4; Diodorus Siculus, 17.114.4; 20.65.1) for "to quench" or "extinguish" fire or flames.

80. Julius Caesar had developed the Roman spear (*pilum*) in such a way that it would plunge into the enemy's shield and bend, making it impossible to remove; the enemy soldier's shield would then be too unwieldy to use, leaving him "to fight with an exposed body" (*nudo corpore pugnare*; *Gallic Wars* 1.25); see Watson, *Roman Solider*, 58–59, and citation of Caesar on 173.

81. For δέχομαι ("take up" or simply "take," as all major English versions) see also Luke 16:6–7; 22:17; BDAG, 221. The aor. form in the impv. is default for δέχομαι, explaining why it is its only form used in the NT (Luke 16:6–7; Acts 7:59; 2 Cor 11:16; Col 4:10; Jas 1:21) and LXX (Gen 33:10; 50:17; Deut 33:11; Jdt 11:5; 1 Macc 2:51; Prov 4:10; Sir 2:4; Zeph 3:7; Jer 9:19).

The "helmet of salvation," like the "breastplate of righteousness" in v. 16, is derived directly from:

> καὶ ἐνεδύσατο δικαιοσύνην ὡς θώρακα καὶ περιέθετο περικεφαλαίαν σωτηρίου ἐπὶ τῆς κεφαλῆς καὶ περιεβάλετο ἱμάτιον ἐκδικήσεως καὶ τὸ περιβόλαιον
>
> And he put on righteousness as a breastplate, and placed the helmet of salvation on his head, and put on a cloak and a garment of vengeance. (Isa 59:17 LXX; cf. Isa 61:10)[82]

In the use of Isaiah in Eph 6:17, Paul shows how the messianic helmet used by Christ to accomplish his judgment on his enemies (cf. 1:19–22; 4:8–10) saved his people (2:5, 8; 5:23) and became for them the strength of salvation in the gospel (1:13), in which they can stand fast.[83]

The "sword of the Spirit" (μάχαιρα τοῦ πνεύματος) is the only weapon—versus pieces of body armor—Paul brings up as part of the church's divinely provided panoply. One thinks of a sword as an offensive weapon, but here it must still be part of the church's defense to fend off attack in its struggle in fulfillment of the repeated enjoinder to *stand* and *hold your ground* (vv. 11, 13–14).[84]

From earliest times (Origen), people who have read in Eph 6:17 that this "sword of the Spirit" is the "word of God" have had their minds leap instantly to Heb 4:12 (Origen and Jerome, 267): "For the word of God is living and active, sharper than any two-edged sword, piercing to the division of soul and of spirit, of joints and of marrow, and discerning the thoughts and intentions of the heart." This is a natural connection, but in fact the two passages are quite different. In Hebrews, the "word of God" mentioned is a word of warning for unbelief and disobedience leading to

---

82. Wis 5:18, 20, is similar: ἐνδύσεται θώρακα δικαιοσύνην καὶ περιθήσεται κόρυθα κρίσιν ἀνυπόκριτον ... ὀξυνεῖ δὲ ἀπότομον ὀργὴν εἰς ῥομφαίαν, "He will put on a breastplate, namely righteousness, and put on a helmet, namely impartial justice ... and he will sharpen relentless wrath as his broadsword." See above.

83. Cf. 1 Thess 5:8: "But since we belong to the day, let us be sober, having put on the breastplate of faith and love, and for a helmet the hope of salvation."

84. Both Polybius (*Hist.* 6.23) and Josephus (*Ant.* 3.93–97) note that Roman soldiers carried two swords, one longer than the other. The smaller μάχαιρα ("dagger") would be more useful in close-quarter fighting, such as is envisioned in Eph 6:10–17; cf. BDAG, 622.

apostasy, arising out of the citation of a word of warning and condemnation from Psa 95 (Heb 4:3, 7). Hence, Hebrews sees the penetrating acuity of God's word of judgment on faithless people, before which the whole of creation is "uncovered" (γυμνός) and prostrated before him with neck exposed (τετραχηλισμένος; Heb 4:13; cf. Isa 49:2; Hos 6:5; Rev 19:21; BDAG, 1014).

In Ephesians 6:17 the word of God is the prophetic, Spirit-uttered gospel, by which Christ's treasured people have been cleansed (5:26; cf. Heb 6:5), which gives the church the most solid ground on which to make its stand. It is not a word of warning and threat in the context, but the scriptural word, by which they can turn aside temptations and the attacks of Satan as did Jesus during his time on earth (Matt 4:1–11; Luke 4:1–10).

> In opposition to all error ... the sole, simple, and sufficient answer is the word of God. This puts to flight all the powers of darkness. The Christian finds this to be true in his individual experience. ... It is also the experience of the church collective. All her triumphs over sin and error have been effected by the word of God. ... *Hoc signo vinces*—the apostle may be understood to say to every believer and to the whole church. (Hodge, 389)[85]

The Latin motto may better be expressed in light of Eph 6:10–17 as *Hoc signo state*, "With this symbol stand fast!"

6:18 Διὰ πάσης προσευχῆς καὶ δεήσεως προσευχόμενοι ἐν παντὶ καιρῷ ἐν πνεύματι, καὶ εἰς αὐτὸ ἀγρυπνοῦντες ἐν πάσῃ προσκαρτερήσει καὶ δεήσει περὶ πάντων τῶν ἁγίων, "Pray with all prayer and supplication in every season in the Spirit, and with this in mind be vigilant in all persistent supplication for all the saints." As noted in the introduction, vv. 18–20 belong to the larger vv. 10–20 passage as the capstone. Interestingly, Codex Sinaiticus (א) attaches the first colon* of v. 18 to the end of v. 17 and starts a new paragraph with the participle "pray": "And take up the helmet of salvation and the sword of the Spirit ... with all prayer and supplication. Pray in every season in the Spirit."[86] A similar interpretation, curiously, is offered by the ESV, where the first participle phrase of v. 18 is attached to v. 17 and a new

85. *Hoc signo vinces* ("With this symbol conquer"), from the famous vision of Constantine at the Milvian Bridge.

86. Vaticanus (B) and Alexandrinus (A) treat vv. 14–20 as one unit.

sentence is begun with the participle ἀγρυπνοῦντες ("be vigilant") taken as an imperative.[87] The difficulty lies with a transition to a different kind of exhortation without the military metaphor that opens not with an imperative mood verb (as we may expect in English) but with two participles (προσευχόμενοι ... ἀγρυπνοῦντες, "pray ... be vigilant") used in parallel with imperatives and thus having imperatival force. As in 5:21, the parallel participle continues a line of exhortations (or other forms of speech) and can function more or less on its own with context governing its force and how it relates to other nearby events.[88]

In vv. 18–20 Paul turns from the military metaphors to the main defense and means for the church not just to stand fast but to advance in an inexorable, worldwide march fearful to her enemies—not through instruments of death but of life: prayer (v. 18) and the gospel proclamation (vv. 19–20). We are told in vv. 18–20 when, how, and for whom to pray. Everyone in the foxhole is a believer: "O God, get me out of this alive and I promise ..." Genuine believers pray inside and outside the foxhole even when the shelling stops because their mortal enemies never sleep (vv. 11–12). Paul accents this in v. 18 by urging the church to pray "with *all* prayer ... in *every* season ... be vigilant in *all* persistent supplication" and "for *all* the saints."[89]

---

87. So: "and take the helmet of salvation, and the sword of the Spirit, which is the word of God, praying at all times in the Spirit, with all prayer and supplication. To that end keep alert with all perseverance" (ESV). Even the NASB, which renders the four ptcs. in vv. 14–16 with English ptcs. (e.g., "having shod" v. 15), starts v. 18 as a new sentence and takes the ptcs. in v. 18 as impvs., "pray" and "be on the alert" (also NIV, NRSV).

88. Cf. discussions in O'Brien, 483; Lincoln, 451–52, where this function of the ptc. is not recognized in the same way and is connected to the impv. "stand" in v. 14 somehow. If it were an ordinary adv. ptc. it would merely have the force of two contemporary events: "stand fast ... while you pray." This could be a true statement, but it is not the best interpretation, since Paul is clearly *enjoining* prayer in the context, even if the ptc. events of prayer are supporting the main idea of standing (στῆτε), even as taking up one's armor and sword do (cf. Hoehner, 855). See the discussion and examples of parallel ptcs. in the excursus below.

89. Notice again, as in 1:22–23; 3:12; 4:6, the accumulation of five words (in addition to the four uses of πᾶς ["all"]) that begin with plosive π- in v. 18: διὰ **π**άσης **π**ροσευχῆς καὶ δεήσεως **π**ροσευχόμενοι ἐν **π**αντὶ καιρῷ ἐν **π**νεύματι καὶ εἰς αὐτὸ ἀγρυ**π**νοῦντες ἐν **π**άσῃ **π**ροσκαρτερήσει καὶ δεήσει **π**ερὶ **π**άντων τῶν ἁγίων. Authors and speakers do this to draw particular attention to arresting statements because the plosives catch the audience's ear.

Paul accents, then, that the church must be constant and persistent in prayer, much as he urges churches to do the same many times in his other epistles (e.g., Rom 12:12; Phil 4:6; Col 4:2; 1 Thess 5:17; 1 Tim 2:1–2; cf. O'Brien, 484) and as he himself practices (1:16; cf. 1 Thess 3:10; 2 Tim 3:1). Previously he urged the Ephesians to sing and express thanks to God (5:4, 19); now he presses his audience to be fervent in intercessory prayer (cf. Luke 18:1–8).[90] The fervency is stressed by three qualifying phrases that build on one another: διὰ πάσης προσευχῆς ... ἐν παντὶ καιρῷ ... ἐν πάσῃ προσκαρτερήσει καὶ δεήσει, "with all prayer ... in every season ... in all persistent supplication."[91] The adjective "all" in the last phrase is gratuitous and thus further stresses the fervency that the audience should be *entirely* or *wholeheartedly* persistent in their supplications (cf. BDAG, 782–84, meaning 3). The persistence and devotion to prayer is communicated not only by προσκαρτέρησις ("persistence") but with the second participle ἀγρυπνοῦντες, exhortation to "be vigilant" or "be on the alert" (BDAG, 16).

Attention to prayer is all the more appropriate because, just as the old-covenant temple was a house of prayer for God's people (e.g., Isa 56:7; Matt 21:13), so now the new-covenant people as a new priesthood and temple filled with the presence of God through the Spirit (1:3; 2:18–22; 3:12; 5:18–20) must be a house of prayer. This explains why Paul qualifies that prayer should be "in the Spirit" (cf. Jude 20). This does not mean prayer in Spirit-enabled foreign languages or "tongues."[92] But all genuine believers dwell in the Holy Spirit (so Rom 8:9) as the atmosphere of the inaugurated new creation (see above on 1:3; 2:21–22; 5:18–20). Paul points to prayer that relies on the Holy Spirit to convey and express one's desires and love (Phil 2:1; Col 1:8) while intervening for one's brothers and sisters in the

---

90. Intercession comes across clearly with δέησις ("supplication" or "intercession"; BDAG, 213) repeated twice in the verse, and that these prayers are interventions on behalf of "all the saints"; cf. Phil 4:6; 1 Tim 2:1–2; O'Brien, 484.

91. My rendering takes the two nouns in ἐν πάσῃ προσκαρτερήσει καὶ δεήσει, "in all persistence and supplication," as hendiadys*: "in all persistent supplication" (for hendiadys* see BDF §442 [16] or Robertson, *Grammar*, 1179–83). The noun προσκαρτέρησις is only used in v. 18 in the NT and denotes persistence or devotion to an undertaking (BDAG, 881).

92. As, for example, Gordon D. Fee, *God's Empowering Presence: The Holy Spirit in the Letters of Paul* (Peabody, MA: Hendrickson, 1994), 730–31.

Lord before the throne of grace (esp. Rom 8:15, 26–27), which is a form of worship (John 4:23–24).

6:19–20 καὶ ὑπὲρ ἐμοῦ, ἵνα μοι δοθῇ λόγος ἐν ἀνοίξει τοῦ στόματός μου, ἐν παρρησίᾳ γνωρίσαι τὸ μυστήριον τοῦ εὐαγγελίου, ὑπὲρ οὗ πρεσβεύω ἐν ἁλύσει, ἵνα ἐν αὐτῷ παρρησιάσωμαι ὡς δεῖ με λαλῆσαι, "and for me as well, that a message may be given to me when I open my mouth, to boldly make the mystery of the gospel known, on behalf of which I am an ambassador in chains, that therein I may speak boldly as I must so speak." These two verses are grammatically dependent on v. 18, where Paul's urging the audience to fervently pray (προσευχόμενοι … ἀγρυπνοῦντες, "pray … be vigilant") is implied again here: "and vigilantly pray for all the saints, and for me as well …" We have seen the same structure before in 5:21–22, where a parallel participle functioning as an imperative in 5:21 is implied as the controlling verb in 5:22 also: ὑποτασσόμενοι … αἱ γυναῖκες τοῖς ἰδίοις ἀνδράσιν, "Be subject to one another. … Wives, [be subject to] your own husbands." In that passage, 5:22 opens a new thematic section (5:22–33). This is, perhaps, why KJV and NIV treat 6:19 as starting a new paragraph even though it is grammatically dependent on v. 18 for its verb, as is also the case in 5:22, dependent on 5:21.[93]

Paul appears at first glance to be a superhero. He does not ask for prayer for his safety in custody or for kind treatment. He does not ask for his physical needs to be met or for health—or for his freedom. All he wants is *boldness* to proclaim the gospel. But in that request he shows just how real a human and not a superhero he really is. Paul asks for boldness because he is concerned about his lack of courage in the "evil day" (v. 13) that he had already faced before many times—"I was with you in weakness and in fear and much trembling" (1 Cor 2:3)—and, though not always (1 Thess 2:2), Paul did lack bold speech sometimes: "For they say, 'His letters are weighty and strong, but his bodily presence is weak, and his speech of no account' " (2 Cor 10:10).[94]

---

93. Contrast, for example, ESV, which has 6:19 as part of one English sentence spanning the middle of v. 18 to the end of v. 20.

94. See Stephen M. Pogoloff, *LOGOS AND SOPHIA: The Rhetorical Situation of 1 Corinthians*, SBLDS 134 (Atlanta: Scholars, 1992), for a persuasive case that Paul deliberately did not present elegant speech at Corinth because it was used by contemporaries there as a mark of elite social superiority that would have hampered his gospel reaching all kinds of people.

Paul does indeed ask for prayer for deliverance and for the advance of the gospel at the same time in other epistles:

> Finally, brothers, pray for us, that the word of the Lord may speed ahead and be honored, as happened among you, and that we may be delivered from wicked and evil men. (2 Thess 3:1–2)

> [F]or I know that through your prayers (διὰ τῆς ὑμῶν δεήσεως) and the help of the Spirit of Jesus Christ this will turn out for my deliverance, as it is my eager expectation and hope that I will not be at all ashamed, but that with full courage (ἐν πάσῃ παρρησίᾳ) now as always Christ will be honored in my body, whether by life or by death. (Phil 1:19–20)[95]

But in Ephesians 6:19–20 Paul is acutely aware of his office as *emissary* (see below), so that bold proclamation of the gospel is *required* of him ("as I must so speak"; cf. Acts 4:29; 2 Cor 3:12; 6:11). But he reveals his concerns about his preaching because he is in chains and needs divine help. Perhaps this explains why the previous strong and flowing Greek style now becomes awkward and halting in vv. 19–20.[96] Stanley Marrow helpfully concludes this point on boldness in Paul's prayer request: "*Parrhēsia* ["boldness"] is a gift granted the Christian for direct access to God in prayer, and for the untrammeled freedom to proclaim, 'in season and out of season,' the gospel of his Son."[97]

In 6:20 Paul says something that should shock anyone deeply, particularly in the ancient world: He is an emissary *in chains* (cf. 3:1; Acts 28:20; 2 Cor 5:18–20; Phil 1:7). Mistreatment of an emissary or ambassador in antiquity was not just a breach of political protocol or even, more seriously, a

95. Also: "At the same time, pray also for us (προσευχόμενοι ἅμα καὶ περὶ ἡμῶν), that God may open to us a door for the word, to declare the mystery of Christ, on account of which I am in prison—that I may make it clear, which is how I ought to speak (ὡς δεῖ με λαλῆσαι)" (Col 4:3–4); cf. Rom 15:30–32; 2 Cor 1:8–11.

96. The bulk of v. 19 is not smooth at all, with the pass. verb phrase (ἵνα μοι δοθῇ λόγος, "that a message may be given to me") and both following clauses "when I open my mouth" (ἐν ἀνοίξει τοῦ στόματός μου) and "boldly" (ἐν παρρησίᾳ) creating an awkward flow in the text.

97. Stanley B. Marrow, "*Parrhēsia* and the New Testament," *CBQ* 44 (1982): 431–46 (quote from 446).

cause of war or of its intensification among nations. It was an invitation for the gods to intervene with retribution against the offending nation.[98]

It is also heavy irony that Paul calls himself an emissary in chains, since "embassies" (πρεσβεῖαι) were frequently sent to Rome from the various cities like Ephesus and provincial associations (e.g., the "Koinon of Asia") throughout the empire. The emissaries gave speeches before the senate and/or emperor on behalf of these who sent them, and therefore they had to be proficient in (*bold!*) public speaking, since that was their main function as an emissary (πρεσβευτής [*IvE* 22] or ὁ πεσβεύων [*IvE* 1486]).[99] Though the apostle was brought to Rome in chains, he would appear before Nero to give a speech—not merely a personal defense, but a message of a disclosed mystery as an emissary from the risen and exalted messianic King (cf. Acts 26:1–32).[100] Thus he asks his audience to pray for his bold proclamation in vv. 19–20.

Paul's request is that bold speech may be granted to him to proclaim "the mystery of the gospel" (see esp. on 3:1–13 above for this "mystery"), and ἵνα ἐν αὐτῷ παρρησιάσωμαι, which I render as "that therein I may speak boldly" (as KJV; "in it," NKJV). The phrase ἐν αὐτῷ (here "therein") is taken

98. See the comprehensive study of Anthony Bash, *Ambassadors for Christ: An Exploration of Ambassadorial Language in the New Testament*, WUNT 2/92 (Tübingen: Mohr Siebeck, 1997); and the collection of essays on ancient diplomacy in Claude Eilers, ed., *Diplomats and Diplomacy in the Roman World*, Mnemosyne Supplements 304 (Boston: Brill, 2009); cf. Gene R. Smillie, "Ephesians 6:19–20: A Mystery for the Sake of Which the Apostle is an Ambassador in Chains," *TrinJ* 18 (1997): 199–222; and for a helpful treatment of παρρησία as expressing the freedom and free speech of free persons (cf. Lev 26:13) in contrast with the "emissary in chains" see Wild, "Warrior and the Prisoner," 291–94.

99. E.g., Julius Artemas the asiarch (Acts 19:31), who completed many other offices and services for Ephesus, including πρεσβείας πρὸς τοὺς αὐτοκράτορας Ἀντωνεῖνον Κόμοδον, "embassies to the emperors Antoninus (and) Commodus" (*IvE* 983; in AD 177–80). Pliny the Younger spent his early career prosecuting cases against former provincial governors for misgovernment at the instigation of such emissaries from cities and provincial leagues (e.g., Pliny, *Ep.* 2.11–12; 3.9).

100. See James B. Rives, "Diplomacy and Identity among Jews and Christians," in *Diplomats and Diplomacy*, 99–126. (He sees early apologists representing the Christians as an association or "assembly" [ἐκκλησία] without a particular national residence.)

as referring back to the "mystery of the gospel" and specifies the content of Paul's bold speech, concerning which he asks (cf. Hoehner, 864–66).[101]

Application and Devotional Implications

Christianity is not a stroll through the mall but a grim fight. Yet we are not engaged in earthly military forays, clumsily cutting off people's ears (Matt 26:51; John 18:10), but in a contest against supernatural foes. Because we cannot stand on our own against superhuman powers, we must rely on the strength of the Lord's own might, which he supplies chiefly through prayer (v. 18).

This divine strength is represented in the complete panoply of God from head to foot that consists of belt, breastplate, shoes, shield, helmet, and sword. These are metaphors for the spiritual resources given to us in Christ, namely, the truth, righteousness (v. 14), the gospel (v. 15), faith (v. 16), salvation, and the very word of God (v. 17). And as mentioned under v. 13, these are aspects of the Messiah's own divine character and work in Isaiah when he accomplishes the free and full salvation of his people in his life and work. Our connection with this armor is a vibrant trust in Christ based on the truth of the gospel. And it is "the mystery of the gospel" and its truth boldly disclosed in the word of God alone that forms the ground on which we can hold our own in the struggle. Any other truth people may set their hopes in, as Hodge states eloquently, is a breastplate of spiderwebs:

> Let not any one imagine that he is prepared to withstand the assaults of the powers of darkness, if his mind is stored with his own theories or with the speculations of other men. Nothing but the truth of God clearly understood and cordially embraced will enable him to keep his feet for a moment, before these celestial potentates. Reason, tradition, speculative conviction, dead orthodoxy, are a girdle of spider-webs. They give way at the first onset. Truth alone, as abiding in the mind of the form of divine knowledge, can give strength or confidence even in the ordinary

101. It is possible but not likely that ἐν αὐτῷ refers to Christ ("that I may speak boldly *in him*"); cf. BDAG, 782, on παρρησιάζομαι.

conflicts of the Christian life, much more in any really "evil day." (Hodge, 382–83)

Additional Exegetical Comments: Imperatives in 6:10–20

In "Additional Exegetical Comments" after 4:25–5:2, I briefly laid out why we can expect a predominance of present-tense infinitives in exhortations that seek to influence the lifestyle of the audience. This explains for the most part why there are thirty-four present imperative forms in Ephesians. In contrast, there are only six imperatives in their aorist forms in Ephesians, and, as was observed in the comment on v. 11, the four aorist imperatives in vv. 11–17 occur with verbs that by far predominate in their aorist forms in the NT and LXX (eighty-six aorists to one present-tense form). In other words, the meaning of the referent of the verb (either atelic or telic—see introduction to the commentary) may play a defining role in the choice of tense form for imperative-mood verbs in Greek.

In Ephesians 6:14–18 there are six participles, which I mentioned in comments on vv. 14 and 18 are functioning in parallel with the imperatives in the passage. Four of these are aorist in form: (στῆτε [the lead impv.]) ... περιζωσάμενοι ... ἐνδυσάμενοι ... ὑποδησάμενοι ... ἀναλαβόντες ... (δέξασθε [concluding impv.]), "Stand fast ... belt yourself ... put on ... put on shoes ... take up ... take up" (vv. 14–17). The final two imperative ideas are participles in v. 18: προσευχόμενοι ... ἀγρυπνοῦντες, "Pray ... be vigilant." When one learns NT Greek, the temporal relationship between adverbial participles like this and their main verbs with which they connect is their most important interrelation.[102] The present participle expresses an event contemporary with the main verb ("*while* PARTICIPLE EVENT, the MAIN VERB occurs"), and the aorist adverbial participle expresses an event prior to the main event ("*after* PARTICIPLE EVENT, the MAIN VERB occurs"). These ideas are certainly possible for all six participles in Eph 6:14–18, but there is another idea that is also not discussed in the literature that is worth mentioning.

102. Hence, I stress this for beginners in my *New Testament Greek Primer*, 3rd ed. (Phillipsburg, NJ: P&R, 2012), 90–91, 97.

It is my hypothesis that adverbial participles that operate in parallel with imperatives are controlled by the tense-form choice variables that control imperative mood verbs, not participles per se. This means that one could research *imperative* usage to see whether the tense forms of the participles acting in parallel with imperatives occur in their default forms—assuming they have a default form.[103] The following are preliminary results for imperative mood forms in both the NT and LXX for the four aorist parallel participle forms in vv. 14–16 (περιζωσάμενοι, ἐνδυσάμενοι, ὑποδησάμενοι, and ἀναλαβόντες) and the two present-tense participles in v. 18 (προσευχόμενοι and ἀγρυπνοῦντες).

Lexeme*	Present Imperatives	Aorist Imperatives[104]
περιζώννυμι/περιζωννύω	0	10
ἐνδύω	0	6
ὑποδέ ω	0	1
ἀναλαμβάνω	0	7
προσεύχομαι	18	12
ἀγρυπνέω	4	0

While the data is not as extensive as one could wish, five of these six lexemes* do seem to conform to regular patterns without exception. The four aorist participles have only corresponding aorist imperatives in the NT and LXX, while one of the present-tense form participles (ἀγρυπνέω) has only present imperatives in our literature.[105] Hence, it is probable that Paul chose these respective forms because they were default for those lexemes*. The exception is προσεύχομαι ("pray"), which is used as a present participle in v. 18

103. To be complete, further research would have to include results of other instances of the ptc. acting in parallel with impvs. and examination of the other moods that act like impvs. For the latter, specifically, the prohibitory subjunctive: καὶ **μὴ ἐνδύσησθε** δύο χιτῶνας, "And do not *put on* two tunics" (Mark 6:9); and the hortatory subjunctive: **ἐνδυσώμεθα** τὰ ὅπλα τοῦ φωτός, "*Let us put on* the armor of light" (Rom 13:12). But I do not believe the results would be significantly different, as these two aor. examples illustrate for ἐνδύω.

104. The one impv. form of ὑποδέω occurs in Acts 12:8 with another (telic) aor. impv.: **ζῶσαι** καὶ **ὑπόδησαι** τὰ σανδάλιά σου, "Get *dressed and put on your sandals.*"

105. It would be profitable for Greek literature outside the NT and LXX to be searched more systematically along these lines beyond the occasional attention I have given them in the course of reading various extrabiblical Greek works.

and has a high incidence of aorist imperative forms in biblical Greek literature. Why?

A comprehensive answer to this question is out of place here, but let me suggest a satisfactory answer for illumining the present participle form of προσεύχομαι in Eph 6:18 with an example from James. The passage reads (with all impv. forms highlighted):

> Κακοπαθεῖ τις ἐν ὑμῖν, **προσευχέσθω·** εὐθυμεῖ τις, **ψαλλέτω·** ἀσθενεῖ τις ἐν ὑμῖν, **προσκαλεσάσθω** τοὺς πρεσβυτέρους τῆς ἐκκλησίας καὶ **προσευξάσθωσαν** ἐπ' αὐτὸν **ἀλείψαντες** αὐτὸν ἐλαίῳ ἐν τῷ ὀνόματι τοῦ κυρίου
>
> Is anyone among you suffering? *Let him pray.* Is anyone cheerful? *Let him sing praise.* Is anyone among you sick? *Let him call for* the elders of the church, and *let them pray* over him, *anointing* him with oil in the name of the Lord. (Jas 5:13–14; emphasis added)[106]

There are two imperative forms of προσεύχομαι here, one present-tense form (προσευχέσθω) and one aorist form (προσευξάσθωσαν). From context we can see the present-tense form has an atelic referent for an activity in which one should engage whenever appropriate: engage in prayer (alongside ψαλλέτω, "sing songs"). The second aorist use refers to what the elders should do on a particular occasion—hence, the event is telic: They should offer prayer when someone calls on them (another aor. impv., προσκαλεσάσθω), and they should also anoint the sick person—not as a general behavior, but on this same occasion (with aor. ἀλείψαντες). Thus, προσεύχομαι switches tense forms when the activity shifts from a general behavior with the present-tense imperative (as in Eph 6:18) to the offering of prayer on a particular occasion with the aorist.

Selected Bibliography

Arnold, C. "The 'Exorcism' of Ephesians 6.12." *JSNT* 30 (1987): 71–87.

106. As an important aside, the ESV renders the final highlighted ptc. form (ἀλείψαντες) woodenly, with an English ptc. ("anointing"), but this is a classic case of the parallel ptc. use continuing the impv. idea, and it should be rendered as an impv.: "Let them offer prayer … (and) anoint him" (as NIV).

Asher, J. "An Unworthy Foe: Heroic Ἔθη, Trickery, and an Insult in Ephesians 6:11." *JBL* 130 (2011): 729–48.

Bash, A. *Ambassadors for Christ: An Exploration of Ambassadorial Language in the New Testament*. WUNT 2/92. Tübingen: Mohr Siebeck, 1997.

Carr, W. *Angels and Principalities: The Background, Meaning and Development of the Pauline Phrase* αἱ ἀρχαὶ καὶ αἱ ἐξουσίαι. SNTSMS 42. Cambridge: Cambridge University Press, 1981.

Eilers, C., ed. *Diplomats and Diplomacy in the Roman World*. Mnemosyne Supplement 304. Boston: Brill, 2009.

Gudorf, M. "The Use of ΠΑΛΗ in Ephesians 6:12." *JBL* 117 (1998): 331–35.

Lash, C. "Where Do Devils Live? A Problem in the Textual Criticism of Ephesians 6, 12." *VC* 30 (1976): 161–74.

Lehner, M. "Die Agonistik im Ephesos der römischen Keiserzeit." PhD diss. Ludwig-Maximilians-Universität, 2004.

Marrow, S. "*Parrhēsia* and the New Testament." *CBQ* 44 (1982): 431–46.

O'Brien, P. "Principalities and Powers: Opponents of the Church." In *Biblical Interpretation and the Church*, edited by D. A. Carson, 110–50. Exeter, UK: Paternoster, 1984.

Pfitzner, V. *Paul and the Agon Motif*. NovTSup 16. Leiden: Brill, 1967.

Reinhard, D. "Ephesians 6:10–18: A Call to Personal Piety or Another Way of Describing Union with Christ?" *JETS* 48 (2005): 521–32.

Smillie, G. "Ephesians 6:19–20: A Mystery for the Sake of Which the Apostle is an Ambassador in Chains." *TrinJ* 18 (1997): 199–222.

Watson, G. *The Roman Soldier*. Ithaca, NY: Cornell University Press, 1969.

Wenkel, D. "The 'Breastplate of Righteousness' in Ephesians 6:14: Imputation or Virtue?" *TynB* 58 (2007): 275–87.

Wild, R. "The Warrior and the Prisoner: Some Reflections on Ephesians 6.10–20." *CBQ* 46 (1984): 284–89.

Yoder Neufeld, T. *"Put on the Armour of God": The Divine Warrior from Isaiah to Ephesians*. JSNTSup 140. Sheffield: Sheffield Academic, 1997.

Concluding Thoughts and Benediction (6:21–24)

Introduction

In Ephesians 6:21–24 Paul concludes his epistle with notice of Tychicus' services for the audience on his behalf and with an apostolic blessing on the church. This is a relatively brief ending to a Pauline Epistle when compared with the others, yet it has a certain balance to it. The epistle opens as it began: with a brief pronunciation of blessing for God's grace and peace to rest on the letter's recipients (cf. 1:2 with 6:23–24). It is no accident that grace and peace are two themes that pervade this epistle as a whole (e.g., 2:8, 14–17).

As noted in the commentary introduction, mention of Tychicus in 6:21–22 is a very serious obstacle that rarely gets its due attention for those who believe that Ephesians is a post-Pauline forgery. The few real pseudepigraphical Pauline texts appear only in Latin MSS quite a bit after Paul's century and end quite differently from Ephesians. For example, the (Latin) pseudepigraphical letters of Paul (six letters) exchanged with Seneca (eight letters) contain short, rather banal exchanges of greetings and mutual good wishes that end most of the time simply with "greetings."[1] By mentioning Tychicus in Eph 6:21–22, the original recipients had a way to guarantee that what they were receiving was authentically from Paul. If Tychicus, an

1. In addition, two of the messages of Seneca express wishes that Paul would use better Latin style in his epistles! See J. K. Elliott, ed., *The Apocryphal New Testament* (Oxford: Clarendon, 1993), 547–54. Likewise, the supposed *Letter to the Laodiceans* (see Col 4:16), which is extant in the earliest MSS in Latin, consists of a series of short, mediocre statements derived mostly from Paul's Galatians and Philippians epistles. It has a general benediction at the end and the notice about reading the epistle at Colossae (Col 4:16) but no reference to the letter carrier (Elliott, *Apocryphal New Testament*, 543–46).

"Asian" from their province (Acts 20:4; cf. 2 Tim 4:12) whom they would undoubtedly have known, brought the epistle to them, it was genuine. He was himself the seal of authenticity. Forgeries could not provide this bona fide, and this was part of why Paul mentions Tychicus in vv. 21–22.[2]

A second manner of authenticating an epistle was to sign it with one's own hand (see esp. 2 Thess 3:17; cf. 1 Cor 16:21; Gal 6:11–18; Col 4:1; Phlm 19).[3] Hence, it is probable that Paul wrote at least vv. 21–24 himself as, for example, 1 Cor 16:21, where only the greetings were written by Paul (ὁ ἀσπασμὸς τῇ ἐμῇ χειρὶ Παύλου, "This greeting was written in my own hand, that of Paul."). This signature of an epistle is illustrated, interestingly, in an inscribed letter from Ephesus when Claudia Antonia Tatiane turned over to her brother ("his Excellency, Aemilius Aristides") a place in her tomb near the Magnesian Gate (at the southeast border of the city as now excavated) so that he could bury his wife there. Claudia Tatiane notes: *ἔγραψα τὴν ἐπιστολὴν διὰ δούλου μου Διονυσίου, ᾗ καὶ αὐτὴ ὑπέγραψα*, "I have written this letter through my slave, Dionysius, to which [letter] I have personally signed my name" (*IvE* 2121; late 2–early 3 AD). Her signature guaranteed the epistle's authenticity.[4]

In comparison with Paul's other epistles (e.g., Col 4:7–18), the epistolary closing of Ephesians is rather brief. Especially when compared with letters to churches rather than to individuals (1–2 Timothy, Titus, Philemon), it is notable that greetings from various people are not included in Ephesians, as, for example, the long greeting list in Romans (Rom 16:3–23).

---

2. See comments on vv. 21–22 below.

3. Cf. Jeffrey A. D. Weima, *Neglected Endings: The Significance of the Pauline Letter Closings* (Sheffield: JSOT, 1994); and more recently Weima, "Sincerely, Paul: The Significance of the Pauline Letter Closings," in *Paul and the Ancient Letter Form*, ed. Stanley E. Porter and Sean A. Adams (Boston: Brill, 2010), 307–45. For the authentication of signing letters see E. Randolph Richards, *The Secretary in the Letters of Paul*, WUNT 2.42 (Tübingen: Mohr Siebeck, 1991), 80–97. The final, signature part of the letter also served to summarize the letter's main concerns (as Gal 6:11–17; cf. Weima, "Sincerely, Paul," 337–40), but this does not seem to fit Ephesians unless 6:10–20 were included in the autograph part of the epistle.

4. Placing unauthorized bodies in family graves was usually subject to heavy fines, as often specified as part of the tomb's inscription. Usually the fine goes to the city treasury: "If anyone dares to put another body [here] or to excise its writing, he shall give to the treasury 2,500 [denarii]" *(IvE* 2222). The fine sometimes went to a group charged with supervision of the tomb's integrity, such as the silversmith guild (e.g., *IvE* 2212) or the Jewish community (*IvE* 1677).

This may simply be because none of those who remained with Paul at that time were known to the recipients, or personal greetings would have been conveyed by Tychicus.

The text can be divided as follows:

A [21] ἵνα δὲ εἰδῆτε καὶ ὑμεῖς τὰ κατʼ ἐμέ τί πράσσω
πάντα γνωρίσει ὑμῖν Τύχικος
ὁ ἀγαπητὸς ἀδελφὸς καὶ πιστὸς διάκονος ἐν κυρίῳ

B [22] ὃν ἔπεμψα πρὸς ὑμᾶς εἰς αὐτὸ τοῦτο
ἵνα γνῶτε τὰ περὶ ἡμῶν
καὶ παρακαλέσῃ τὰς καρδίας ὑμῶν

C [23] εἰρήνη τοῖς ἀδελφοῖς
καὶ ἀγάπη μετὰ πίστεως
ἀπὸ θεοῦ πατρὸς καὶ κυρίου Ἰησοῦ Χριστοῦ

D [24] ἡ χάρις μετὰ πάντων τῶν ἀγαπώντων
τὸν κύριον ἡμῶν Ἰησοῦν Χριστὸν ἐν ἀφθαρσίᾳ.

Unlike earlier sections of the epistle, this conversational closing is not a polished periodic composition. In fact, it has some awkward and repetitious parts to it (as also noted in vv. 19–20 above). For example, τί πράσσω ("what I am engaged in") is not necessary in v. 21; he switches in the circumstances from "me" (v. 21) to "us" (v. 22; probably Paul, Tychicus, and any other unnamed companion); and ἵνα γνῶτε … καὶ παρακαλέσῃ ("that you may learn … and to comfort") switches from second- to third-person verbs in a parallel construction, which is not polished. And v. 22b says essentially the same thing as v. 21a and is not really necessary. But this is how people speak in real communication rather than in edited compositions such as we find in the rest of the epistle. It could also differentiate Paul's style from that of his secretary (see comment).

Outline

XVIII. Concluding Thoughts and Benediction (6:21–24)
- A. The ministry of Tychicus (6:21–22)
- B. The closing apostolic blessing (6:23–24)

Original Text

21 Ἵνα δὲ εἰδῆτε, καὶ ὑμεῖς[a] τὰ κατ᾽ ἐμέ, τί πράσσω, πάντα γνωρίσει ὑμῖν
Τύχικος ὁ ἀγαπητὸς ἀδελφὸς καὶ πιστὸς διάκονος ἐν κυρίῳ, **22** ὃν ἔπεμψα πρὸς
ὑμᾶς εἰς αὐτὸ τοῦτο, ἵνα γνῶτε τὰ περὶ ἡμῶν καὶ παρακαλέσῃ τὰς καρδίας ὑμῶν.
23 Εἰρήνη τοῖς ἀδελφοῖς[b] καὶ ἀγάπη[c] μετὰ πίστεως ἀπὸ θεοῦ πατρὸς καὶ κυρίου Ἰησοῦ Χριστοῦ. **24** ἡ χάρις μετὰ πάντων τῶν ἀγαπώντων τὸν κύριον ἡμῶν
Ἰησοῦν Χριστὸν ἐν ἀφθαρσίᾳ.[d, e]

Textual Notes

21.a. The opening phrase (ἵνα δὲ) εἰδῆτε καὶ ὑμεῖς ("so that you as well may be informed") is expressed with a different word order in some early and good witnesses, along with later ones (καὶ ὑμεῖς εἰδῆτε; א, A, D, 33, 1739, 1881, and M), but the meaning is unchanged. The difference is merely stylistic, where καὶ ὑμεῖς would be expected to come before the verb so that a scribe may have intentionally or not expressed it in that word order (as, e.g., 1 Cor 5:2; 2 Cor 6:18; 1 Thess 1:6; cf. 2 Cor 6:13). (P[46] drops καὶ ὑμεῖς through apparent inattention; cf. the next note on v 23.)

23.b–c. Instead of ἀδελφοῖς ("to the brethren"), P[46] has ἁγίοις ("to the saints") in an apparently simple copying mistake. Similarly, instead of ἀγάπη ("love"), Alexandrinus (A) reads ἔλεος ("mercy"). Both are singular readings arising no doubt from tired scribes anticipating the end of a document when they may have earned a small respite from their labor.

24.d. The majority (M) of MSS add liturgical ἀμήν ("amen") to the end of the book (cf. Gal 6:18), but important early witnesses (P[46], א, A, B, F, G) and some early versions (it, vg, sy, bo) do not have this. Similar additions are found at the end of most of the other Pauline books as well.

Superscription.e. Our early uncial MSS Vaticanus (B), Sinaiticus (א), and Alexandrinus (A) have the superscription πρὸς Ἐφεσίους ("to the Ephesians"), while other, later texts and corrections (e.g., B[c]) have longer notes. The longest notation collects the fullest ancient opinions about the epistle: "This epistle was written to the Ephesians from Rome [and sent] through Tychicus" (Codex Angelicus [L]). We have no way to confirm the idea that this epistle was sent from Rome, but it is interesting and plausible nonetheless. Such ancient traditions may possibly preserve reliable historical information.

Translation

21 Tychicus, our beloved brother and faithful servant[5] in the Lord, will make everything known to you, so that you as well may be informed about my affairs, namely, what I am engaged in, **22** whom I have sent to you for this very reason, that you may learn about my condition and to comfort your hearts. **23** Peace be with the brothers[6] and love along with[7] faith from God the[8] Father and the[9] Lord Jesus Christ. **24** Grace be with all those who love our Lord Jesus Christ, who dwells in incorruptibility.[10]

Commentary

6:21–22 Ἵνα δὲ εἰδῆτε καὶ ὑμεῖς τὰ κατ᾽ ἐμέ, τί πράσσω, πάντα γνωρίσει ὑμῖν Τύχικος ὁ ἀγαπητὸς ἀδελφὸς καὶ πιστὸς διάκονος ἐν κυρίῳ, ὃν ἔπεμψα πρὸς ὑμᾶς εἰς αὐτὸ τοῦτο, ἵνα γνῶτε τὰ περὶ ἡμῶν καὶ παρακαλέσῃ τὰς καρδίας ὑμῶν, "Tychicus, our beloved brother and faithful servant in the Lord, will make everything known to you, so that you as well may be informed about my affairs, namely, what I am engaged in, whom I have sent to you for this very reason, that you may learn about my condition and to comfort your hearts." As noted in the introduction, this is not very polished prose as Paul closes his epistle with a personal note in more conversational style (see nearly the

---

5. BDAG, 230, takes διάκονος here and in the parallel at Col 4:7 as meaning more specifically "courier."

6. τοῖς ἀδελφοῖς ("with the brothers") refers to all Christians (i.e., male and female) as the members of one family (cf., e.g., 1:5; 2:19). The rendering"to the whole community"(NRSV) is similar but lacks the familial connection conveyed by ἀδελφοί. See also comment.

7. See translation notes on 4:2 for this associative meaning ("along with") for μετά. For faith and love added to grace see 1 Tim 1:14.

8. While both πατήρ ("Father") and κύριος ("Lord") are anarthrous here, they are definite as the objs. of the prep. ἀπό (so the majority of English versions; cf. ἀπ᾽ ἀρχῆς, "from *the* beginning," in 1 John 1:1).

9. See previous note.

10. Most English versions understand the phrase ἐν ἀφθαρσίᾳ as expanding on the love of those who love Christ: "with love incorruptible" (ESV) or "all who have an undying love" (NRSV); see comment.

same wording in Col 4:7–9).[11] It was also noted how important it was to mention the letter carrier of an ancient communication as a way to authenticate it as genuinely originating from the named sender(s).[12] It was also common to name the letter carrier if he was not known to the recipients to introduce him, though this does not seem to be the case with Tychicus, an Asian (Acts 20:4; cf. Col 4:7; 2 Tim 4:12; Titus 3:12) who was probably known by the recipients and a further aid to authentication of the epistle (cf. Acts 15:22, 25–27).[13]

A trusted colleague as a letter carrier often had a number of other roles to play in the correspondence, not least of which was to act as an intermediary of the communication. He could fill in the blanks, and, as Paul mentions in several ways in vv. 21–22, he could inform the recipients of his situation: "[He] will make everything known to you, so that you as well may be informed about my affairs, namely, what I am engaged in, whom I have sent to you for this very reason, that you may learn about my condition." Paul could not do this personally, so Tychicus could fill in during his absence. Paul particularly hopes Tychicus will dispel any doubts or fears they may have had at his circumstances (see on 3:1–13), so he adds that Tychicus would "comfort your hearts" (cf. Col 2:2; 4:8).[14]

We do not know if the "Asian" Tychicus was specifically from Ephesus or from one of the other cities. The name *Tychicus* was a fairly common name at Ephesus and around the Greek world, but in Colossians Paul adds to his mention of Tychicus that he had also sent "Onesimus ... who is one

---

11. Change of style like this can be used to mark the places where the author takes over from his secretary at the end of the composition; see Richards, *Secretary*, 92–97, 183–89.

12. *Contra* Schnackenburg, 288, 292. The only official postal service in the first century was reserved for Roman government correspondence and the military especially (e.g., Pliny, *Ep.* 10.45–46, 64, 120–21). Note that BDAG, 230, takes διάκονος in v. 21 and in the parallel at Col 4:7 as meaning more specifically "courier." This is an interesting suggestion but does not explain the qualification "faithful servant *in the Lord*." Cf. the διάκονος Burrhus, who acted as courier for Ignatius (*Phld.* 11.2; *Eph.* 2.1; *Smyrn.* 12.1).

13. Cf. E. Randolph Richards, "Silvanus Was Not Peter's Secretary: Theological Bias in Interpreting διὰ Σιλουανοῦ ... ἔγραψα in 1 Peter 5:12," *JETS* 43 (2000): 417–32.

14. See Richards, "Silvanus," 420–22; cf. Brian M. Rapske, "The Importance of Helpers to the Imprisoned Paul in the Book of Acts," *TynB* 42 (1991): 3–30, for the role of Tychicus and others as helpers in Paul's custody and why he calls Tychicus "our beloved brother and faithful servant in the Lord."

of your people" (Col 4:9; cf. Col 4:12) with that epistle.[15] Perhaps Paul did not have to specify to the Ephesians that Tychicus was one of theirs, but we do not know for certain.

We also cannot know for certain what role Tychicus had in the composition of the epistle. Was he the secretary who physically wrote it and polished part of it? More enticing is what role he may have had in the presentation or reading of the epistle at its destination. Ephesians is a manuscript that Paul himself never read in public as far as we can tell but could well have been written to be read initially by Tychicus as his deputy.[16] It is tantalizing to imagine Tychicus as a skilled reader and speaker who had a hand in the composition of Ephesians and of Colossians (along with Timothy) in order that he could use his particular skills in the presentation of these works. It could be that he was a skilled enough orator that the apostle knew he could handle the more subtle nuances of delivery that a more flowing periodic composition demanded. The journey from Paul, probably at Rome, to Ephesus would have taken many weeks, wherein Tychicus would have memorized the epistle to get it right, since written documents

15. Tychicus means "Lucky" (Latin *Fortunatus*; e.g., *1 Clem.* 65.1), and the name is found, for example, on *IvE* 2223, 2948a, 3818a.

16. Certainly ecclesiastical readers (ἀναγνῶσται) are known from a later period; see Harry Y. Gamble, *Books and Readers in the Early Church* (New Haven, CT: Yale University Press, 1995), 218–31; for an interesting instance see Malcolm Choat and Rachel Yuen-Collingridge, "A Church with No Books and a Reader Who Cannot Write: The Strange Case of *P.Oxy. 33.2673*," *Bulletin of the American Society of Papyrologists* 46 (2009): 109–38. LSJ, 101, defines "reader" (ἀναγνώστης) as a "reader" or "slave trained to read," and Pliny the Younger mentions several readers on his staff as well as belonging to the households of others of his acquaintance (e.g., *Ep.* 3.1; 5.19; 8.1; 9.20). It is conceivable that a Pauline-era church drew on a member with background and training in public reading for this task, since the ability to read privately does not mean that someone could read aloud fluently. This is especially the case with *scriptio continua*.

in antiquity acted as memory aids for the trained speaker.[17] It is at least possible, though not certain.[18]

6:23–24 Εἰρήνη τοῖς ἀδελφοῖς καὶ ἀγάπη μετὰ πίστεως ἀπὸ θεοῦ πατρὸς καὶ κυρίου Ἰησοῦ Χριστοῦ, ἡ χάρις μετὰ πάντων τῶν ἀγαπώντων τὸν κύριον ἡμῶν Ἰησοῦν Χριστὸν ἐν ἀφθαρσίᾳ, "Peace be with the brothers and love along with faith from God the Father and the Lord Jesus Christ. Grace be with all those who love our Lord Jesus Christ, who dwells in incorruptibility." The first phrase (εἰρήνη τοῖς ἀδελφοῖς, "peace be with the brothers") can be understood from context to mean: "May peace be with (all) our brothers and sisters."[19] Here, grammatically masculine ἀδελφοί refers to both men and women as the common gender, whom Paul has been addressing throughout along with their children (so 5:22–24 and 6:1–3). The same can be said of μετὰ πάντων τῶν ἀγαπώντων ("with all those who love") in v. 24. The second phrase in v. 23 (ἀγάπη μετὰ πίστεως ἀπὸ θεοῦ, "love along with faith from God ...") is also shorthand for the more expanded idea: "May God's own love rest on you in your believing."[20] Here, faith is seen as the sine qua non for love from the Father and from Jesus Christ. Saving faith then leads directly to love of the Lord Jesus Christ (v. 24).

Peace, love, faith, and grace are all central elements in the instruction of Ephesians—indeed, in all of Scripture—and recur here in Paul's benediction to convey from God increase and fullness in these things all the more.

---

17. See Pieter J. J. Botha, "New Testament Texts in the Context of Reading Practices of the Roman Period," *Scriptura* 90 (2005): 621–40; and Botha, "The Verbal Art of the Pauline Letters: Rhetoric, Performance and Presence," in *Rhetoric and the New Testament: Essays from the 1992 Heidelberg Conference*, ed. Stanley E. Porter and Thomas H. Olbricht (Sheffield: JSOT, 1993), 409–28.

18. Peter Head, after examining numerous papyri, believes that letter carriers like Tychicus would not have presented the epistles they carried; Peter M. Head, "Named Letter-Carriers among the Oxyrhynchus Papyri," *JSNT* 31 (2009): 279–99. However, the commonplace letters Head examines are quite different in both character and purpose from the more literary apostolic compositions that are addressed to groups rather than to an individual family member, a friend, a business associate, or to public officials, as in the papyri.

19. Cf. Luke 10:5, εἰρήνη τῷ οἴκῳ τούτῳ, "Peace be with this house." The dative conveys the person benefited in the benediction; i.e., the dative of advantage or disadvantage (BDF §188), hence "with" rather than more common "to" here.

20. The prep. μετά ("along with") simply associates faith with love in a general way that must be clarified by context; cf. 4:2 and BDAG, 637.

The blessing of grace and peace (vv. 23–24) is an increase in these things because all believers already have objective grace and peace in Christ. God's favor despite sin and guilt is how anyone comes to believe in the first place (see on 2:8). And all who come to faith through the gospel of peace (6:15) have peace objectively with God in Christ, who acquired that peace on the cross (see on 2:14–15; cf. Rom 5:1). The purpose of Paul's closing benediction is to call on God to increase that grace and peace throughout his people's lives: "Now may the Lord of peace himself give you peace at all times in every way" (2 Thess 3:16; cf. Rom 15:33; Gal 6:16; Phil 4:7, 9; 1 Pet 5:14).

As noted in the comment on the opening benediction ("grace to you and peace"; 1:2), the model of blessings like the one in vv. 23–24 is the great Aaronic benediction (Num 6:22–27), which is not a mere wish but conveyance of covenant blessing: "So shall they put my name upon the people of Israel, and I will bless them" (Num 6:27). This moves beyond the more common ending of an ordinary letter of the day, where the correspondent wished the recipient(s) good health: "I pray you farewell," or just "Farewell."[21] For example, the inscribed epistle in *IvE* 2121 cited in the introduction above has the following line: καὶ ἔρρωσθαι σε, κύριέ μου, εὔχομαι, "And I pray you farewell, my dear sir."

The closing Pauline benedictions are normally pronounced on second-person "you" rather than on the third-person "the brothers" or on "all who love," as in vv. 23–24. For example, "The grace of our Lord Jesus be with *you* (μεθ' ὑμῶν)" (Rom 16:23; 1 Thess 5:28; cf. 2 Thess 3:18), "The grace of our Lord Jesus Christ be with *your spirit*" (Gal 6:18; Phil 4:23), or more briefly, "Grace be with *you*" (Col 4:18).[22] Why, then, does Paul use the unique third-person reference in Eph 6:23–24? To express "a small amount of aloofness" (Barth, 815)? To be solemn or impersonal (see Best, 617)? The most attractive answer for why he used the third person is that Paul is keeping with the concerns of the epistle as a whole. By blessing

---

21. In the NT only in Acts 15:29, but "farewell" (ἔρρωσθε) is normal in Ignatius and many extrabiblical authors (and ten times in 2–3 Maccabees in the LXX). Cf. John L. White, *Light from Ancient Letters* (Philadelphia: Fortress, 1986), 200–202.

22. If Ephesians were a Pauline forgery, we would expect the author to have simply copied the closing benediction of Colossians or Romans verbatim. For example, the fourth-century pseudepigraphical *Epistle to the Laodiceans* copies the closing benediction from Gal 6:18 and Phil 4:23. This is another difficulty for the idea that Ephesians is pseudepigraphical.

"the brothers" (v. 23) and "all who love our Lord Jesus Christ" (v. 24; cf. 1 Cor 16:22), Paul calls on God to bless the church universal with his peace and grace. As a result, the whole church will grow solidly together in the "unity of the Spirit in the bond of peace" (4:3; see on 4:1–6). The benediction in vv. 23–24 certainly includes the Ephesians but helps them to see that they are part of a much larger group of saints brought together in "one body" through Christ's redemption (2:16). This has been Paul's concern in Ephesians all along.

Finally, most English versions understand the phrase ἐν ἀφθαρσίᾳ as connected to and expanding on the nature of the love of those identified as loving Christ: "with love incorruptible" (ESV) or "all who have an undying love" (NRSV). Yet this requires one to connect the last prepositional phrase with the participle phrase, skipping over the intervening five words (τὸν κύριον ἡμῶν Ἰησοῦν Χριστὸν, "our Lord Jesus Christ"). To be shown graphically, this would connect the words in bold together: μετὰ πάντων τῶν **ἀγαπώντων** τὸν κύριον ἡμῶν Ἰησοῦν Χριστὸν **ἐν ἀφθαρσίᾳ** ("with all those who *love* our Lord Jesus Christ *in incorruptibility*"). This is certainly possible, though it would have been clear and explicit if Paul had used another article connecting the two words.

In light of the word order, it seems best to take the final prepositional phrase "in incorruptibility" as qualifying the nearer phrase "our Lord Jesus Christ," as my suggested translation indicates: "our Lord Jesus Christ, who dwells in incorruptibility." This actually relates to Paul's teaching in that incorruptibility (ἀφθαρσία) characterizes the resurrection existence Christ has introduced by his resurrection as firstfruits of the harvest of his people in resurrection and Last Adam of a new creation (1 Cor 15:20–57; cf. Rom 2:7; 2 Tim 1:10). "For it is required that this corruptible (body) put on *incorruptibility* (ἀφθαρσία) and this mortal (body) must put on immortality. ... For I declare this, brothers, that flesh and blood cannot inherit the kingdom of God and neither can that which is corruptible inherit *incorruptibility* (ἀφθαρσία)" (1 Cor 15:53, 50; cf. vv. 42, 54; Rom 2:7; 2 Tim 1:10). This connects directly to the central message of Ephesians: that in Christ Jesus and the redemptive grace of the Triune God, believers experience now the inauguration of the new creation and will dwell with him in unified peace in an incorruptible new, resurrection existence. As he dwells in incorruptibility, so shall all his people dwell together evermore.

Application and Devotional Implications

The benediction at the end of the Christian worship service is its absolute high point. Due to our human weakness, it may be that we long for it to occur for the wrong reason. For parents it means no more dealing with fidgeting kids. For kids it means no more fidgeting in anticipation of a snack and play time. I challenge you, however, to see the concluding benediction as the crown jewel of our corporate worship with the Lord every week. Its origin at the end of the worship service is the apostolic benedictions at the end of the epistles. Its meaning goes back to the Israelite high priest's solemn covenant function: to put God's name on his people so that he can bless them. The benediction in our service is not a pious wish of the minister. What makes it so special is *what God is doing*. He puts his name on us and blesses us with his smile and with his peace:

> The LORD spoke to Moses, saying, "Speak to Aaron and his sons, saying, Thus you shall bless the people of Israel: you shall say to them, The LORD bless you and keep you; the LORD make his face to shine upon you and be gracious to you; the LORD lift up his countenance upon you and give you peace. So shall they put my name upon the people of Israel, and I will bless them." (Num 6:22–27)

To "lift up the countenance" means to smile. Next Sunday and thereafter, look up during the benediction and receive God's smile on you, and go in his peace.

Selected Bibliography

Botha, P. "New Testament Texts in the Context of Reading Practices of the Roman Period." *Scriptura* 90 (2005): 621–40.

———. "The Verbal Art of the Pauline Letters: Rhetoric, Performance and Presence." In *Rhetoric and the New Testament: Essays from the 1992 Heidelberg Conference*, edited by S. Porter and T. Olbricht, 409–28. Sheffield: JSOT Press, 1993.

Gamble, H. *Books and Readers in the Early Church.* New Haven, CT: Yale University Press, 1995.

Head, P. "Named Letter-Carriers among the Oxyrhynchus Papyri." *JSNT* 31 (2009): 279–99.

Rapske, B. "The Importance of Helpers to the Imprisoned Paul in the Book of Acts." *TynB* 42 (1991): 3–30.

Richards, E. R. "Silvanus was not Peter's Secretary: Theological Bias in Interpreting διὰ Σιλουανοῦ ... ἔγραψα in 1 Peter 5:12." *JETS* 43 (2000): 417–32.

Weima, J. *Neglected Endings: The Significance of the Pauline Letter Closings.* Sheffield: JSOT Press, 1994.

———. "Sincerely, Paul: The Significance of the Pauline Letter Closings." In *Paul and the Ancient Letter Form*, edited by S. Porter and S. Adams, 307–45. Boston: Brill, 2010.

White, J. *Light from Ancient Letters.* Philadelphia: Fortress, 1986.

Excursuses

Excursus: "Apostle"[1]

In the Greek world, a person who acted as an official representative or emissary would be called a "herald" (κῆρυξ; 1 Tim 2:7; 2 Tim 1:11), "ambassador" (πρεσβευτής; cf. Eph 6:20; 2 Cor 5:20), or "messenger" (ἄγγελος; cf. Gal 4:14), but not an "apostle" (ἀπόστολος).[2] While Paul does use some of these other terms for his office, he prefers "apostle," even though—as mentioned above on v. 1—he understands that God has given him special authorization to act in an official capacity. Add to this his use of other metaphors for himself: "teacher" (1 Tim 2:7; 2 Tim 1:11), "master building contractor" (1 Cor 3:10), "wet-nurse" (1 Thess 2:7), or a servant with a stewardship (esp. Eph 3:1–13) and with special appointment from Christ (Gal 1:1; cf. Mark 3:14; Luke 6:13; Acts 1:22–24), and one can see that the other terms such as "herald" or "messenger" would be too narrow to fit his understanding of the apostolate.[3] Apostles were "officers of Christ by whom

1. For review of literature and discussion of the apostolate see: Barnett, "Apostle," in *DPL*, 45–51; H. D. Betz, "Apostle," *ABD* 1:309–11; J.-A. Bühner, "*apostolos*," *EDNT*, 1:142–46; Rengstorf, *TDNT*, 1:407–46 (esp. 437–43); cf. Francis H. Agnew, "On the Origin of the Term *Apostolos*," *CBQ* 38 (1976): 49–53; and Agnew, "The Origin of the NT Apostle-Concept: A Review of Research," *JBL* 105 (1986): 75–96.

2. In later Judaism especially, the closely equivalent term שליח would be used for an emissary commissioned with some legal function and authority; see Rengstorf, *TDNT*, 1:414–20. Ernest Best, "Paul's Apostolic Authority—?" *JSNT* 27 (1986): 3–25, questions (unpersuasively) whether authority is associated with the apostolic office.

3. A "herald" was more of a mouthpiece in antiquity and probably fits something more like a media news announcer or a courier in today's world than someone with the broad range of functions captured by "apostle."

the church is built" (Rengstorf, *TDNT*, 1:423); they were commissioned by Christ "to preach the gospel and to found churches."[4]

By adopting the term "apostle," which could not be equated by his audience with limited, customary functions, Paul could freight this term with the broad range of functions that fit the office as he conceived it. Furthermore, the background for his understanding of his apostolic office comes from the OT prophets, not from Graeco-Roman emissaries (cf. on Eph 2:20; 3:5; 4:11).[5] Yet Paul did indeed see his office as having a central, word-based function: "Christ did not send me to baptize *but to proclaim the gospel*" (1 Cor 1:17; emphasis added). As James Dunn correctly observes, "Paul saw his apostleship as wholly subordinate to, or better, wholly in service of the gospel."[6] He was indeed a herald as an apostle, yet as an apostle he was so much more as one who helped lay the foundations of the worldwide church (Eph 2:20; 1 Cor 3:10; Rev 21:14).

Excursus: Articular Χριστός as Messianic Title

There are a number of verses in Ephesians where Χριστός ("Christ") appears with the article (ὁ Χριστός) and may not function as a proper name but as a royal title, "the Messiah," referencing Christ's kingship (*viz.* 1:10, 12, 20; 2:5; 3:17; 4:20; 5:2, 14, 23–25, 29; 6:5, 24). My rendering of the phrase ἐν τῷ Χριστῷ in 1:10, 12, 20 in particular represents this outlook and led to the translation "in the Messiah"—not "in Christ" throughout 1:3–14.

Ernest Best believes this is unwarranted: "AE's [= the author of Ephesians] use of the article with Christ seems quite haphazard and no significance should be attached to it" (Best, 143). He is joined in skepticism by Martin Hengel, who says that the article was sometimes used here "essentially at random."[7] Yet in my experience, elements of the Greek language

4. James D. G. Dunn, *The Theology of Paul the Apostle* (Grand Rapids: Eerdmans, 1998), 580; cf. also the paraphrase "apostolic missionary" and brief discussion offered by Thomas R. Schreiner, *Paul, Apostle of God's Glory in Christ: A Pauline Theology* (Downers Grove, IL: InterVarsity Press, 2001), 38–39.

5. See Karl Olav Sandnes, *Paul—One of the Prophets?* WUNT 2.43 (Tübingen: Mohr Siebeck, 1991).

6. Dunn, *Theology*, 572.

7. Martin Hengel, " 'Christos' in Paul," in *Between Jesus and Paul* (London: SCM, 1983), 69.

that appear random or haphazard to us are simply things we do not yet fully understand. In a recent monograph on Christ's kingship in Ephesians, Julien Smith says that the evidence of articular Χριστός should at least "give one pause," but he is properly more concerned with evaluating statements in Ephesians about Christ's actions and position as king rather than relying merely on grammatical tips such as the presence or absence of the Greek article.[8] Nevertheless, the discussion of the use of this name/title and its relation to the article is worthy of some further reflection.

To a Greek, the adjective Χριστός merely means something oil-based like a "salve" or even someone who has some sort of unguent or color agent rubbed on him ("oily," "smeared," "colored"; LSJ, 2007). But in a late Jewish context, Χριστός is the consistent term used to refer to the Messianic king (van der Woude, *TDNT*, 9:509–20), hence confusion over Jesus' use of the term "Son of Man" rather than the expected term ὁ Χριστός in John 12:34. Therefore, in the Gospels especially, ὁ Χριστός often carried the meaning of "the Messiah" (e.g., Matt 1:17; 2:4; Mark 8:29 and parallels; Luke 2:11, 26; John 1:20; 20:31), but at some point, especially in conjunction with the name "Jesus," the term seems to have become more of a proper name than a title: Ἰησοῦς Χριστός, "Jesus *Christ*."[9]

The main question, then, is whether the presence of the article in the prepositional phrase ἐν τῷ Χριστῷ in 1:10, 12, 20 alone indicates that the royal title is conveyed. It must be granted that there are many circumstances where the presence of the Greek article is caused by stylistic rather than semantic reasons.[10] But there are two other tendencies in Greek article usage that bear on our question.

---

8. Julien Smith, *Christ the Ideal King*, WUNT 2.313 (Tübingen: Mohr Siebeck, 2011); see esp. the section entitled "ὁ Χριστός: Messianic Title or Proper Name?" (176–82) and literature cited there; cf. Barth, 76; O'Brien, 111.

9. Yet it is pertinent to ask whether the titular nature of this word may still be conveyed even when used in this way. For example, in English, to say "Christ Jesus" seems to express a name only, but "Messiah Jesus" or "King Jesus" treats the first words as title and name as well. For example, Αὐτοκράτωρ Καίσαρ θεοῦ υἱὸς Σεβαστός is "Emperor Caesar Augustus, son of the deified" (*IvE* 252), where all of these names are essentially titles of the man originally named Gaius Octavian.

10. As, for example, the tendency in Greek article usage designated as "Apollonius' Canon"; cf. Daniel B. Wallace, *Greek Grammar beyond the Basics* (Grand Rapids: Zondervan, 1997), 239–40; Sanford D. Hull, "Exceptions to Apollonius' Canon in the New Testament: A Grammatical Study," *TrinJ* NS (1986): 3–16. For instance, τὸ

The first relevant rule of article usage is that proper names tend to be anarthrous (i.e., not modified by an article) in Greek. There are many exceptions to this, but, despite the exceptions, one does not expect a proper name to have the article without reason.[11] Three examples are found in Matt 1:1: Βίβλος γενέσεως Ἰησοῦ Χριστοῦ υἱοῦ Δαυὶδ υἱοῦ Ἀβραάμ, "The book of the genealogy of Jesus Christ, the son of David, the son of Abraham." Note that Apollonius' Canon is frequently not followed when a proper name is used *in regimen* with an articular noun; e.g., εἰς τὴν οἰκίαν Πέτρου ("into the house of Peter"; Matt 8:14) or εἰς τὸ ὄνομα Παύλου ("into the name of Paul"; 1 Cor 1:13). What this means for our question is that if Paul were treating Χριστός as a proper name in the phrase ἐν τῷ Χριστῷ (Eph 1:10, 12, 20), we would expect it to be anarthrous, not articular (ἐν Χριστῷ) as found over two dozen times in Paul's writings, including Eph 1:3; 4:32.

The second tendency in Greek article usage is that anarthrous nouns may be definite under various contextual circumstances—and, most relevant for our question, this is quite often the case when the noun is the object of a preposition. As just one example among many dozens we could cite from Paul's writings alone, in 5:20 we find ἐν **ὀνόματι** τοῦ κυρίου ἡμῶν Ἰησοῦ Χριστοῦ, "in *the* name of our Lord Jesus Christ," but not "in *a* name."[12]

σῶμα **τοῦ** Χριστοῦ (Eph 4:12; also Rom 7:4; 1 Cor 10:16; 12:27; Col 2:17) is ambiguous and does not necessarily mean "the body of *the Messiah*" (though it is possible), but more likely "the body ***of Christ.***" (Other examples in Ephesians of articular Χριστός *in regimen* are at 2:13; 3:1, 4, 8, 19; 4:7, 12–13; 5:5.)

11. One common place where an article is used with a proper name is in a gen. phrase (Apollonius' Canon in the previous note); e.g., **ἡ** μαρτυρία **τοῦ** Ἰωάννου ("the testimony of John"; John 1:19) or **ἡ** εὐλογία **τοῦ** Ἀβραὰμ ("the blessing of Abraham," Gal 3:14), where both nouns, including the proper names, have articles. A second reason is the use of a foreign, noninflected name where the article identifies the name's case, as in ἐν **τῷ** Ἀδὰμ ("in Adam"), found in 1 Cor 15:22. Interestingly, in the same 1 Cor 15:22, a parallel use of the article is found in the phrase ἐν **τῷ** Χριστῷ, which may be understood as "in *the* Messiah" (rather than "in Christ"), since Χριστός is inflected, even if it acts like a proper name and the article is not needed to identify its case. For survey of the article with proper names see Stanley E. Porter, *Idioms of the Greek New Testament*, Biblical Languages: Greek 2 (Sheffield, UK: JSOT, 1992), 2.2. In 4:21 we find one of the few times the name "Jesus" has an article in Paul's writings: ἐν **τῷ** Ἰησοῦ.

12. Cf. the next verse (Eph 5:21) for interesting ἐν φόβῳ Χριστοῦ, "in *the* fear of Christ"—or is it "in *the* fear of *the* Messiah"? Other Ephesian examples are: ἐν ἐπιγνώσει αὐτοῦ ("in *the* knowledge of him"; 1:17) and ἐν ματαιότητι τοῦ νοὸς αὐτῶν ("in *the* futility of their minds"; 4:17).

What this means is that the nouns in the phrases ἐν Χριστῷ and ἐν Χριστῷ Ἰησοῦ, which occur about seventy-five times in Paul's writings (in Eph at 1:1, 3; 2:6–7, 10, 13; 3:6, 21; 4:32), should be considered definite at least. Yet this does not solve the meaning of Χριστός here because it could be definite as a proper name ("in *Christ* [Jesus]") but not as a title ("in *the Messiah* [Jesus]").

To summarize to this point, if Χριστός in the phrase ἐν τῷ Χριστῷ were being expressed as a proper name, we would expect it to be anarthrous, as found many times in Paul's writings, not articular as found in 1:10, 12, 20. In fact, the articular phrase ἐν τῷ Χριστῷ is found only the three times in Ephesians and in 1 Cor 15:22; 2 Cor 2:14 (over against the seventy-five anarthrous occurrences already discussed).[13] While it is possible that anarthrous ἐν Χριστῷ could also be understood to mean "in *the Messiah*" in accordance with the second principle discussed, this leads us to see articular ἐν τῷ Χριστῷ as making the titular character of Χριστός explicit. How can we be sure?

At this stage, it seems best to look into the articular/anarthrous usage of other words that unambiguously denote a title with which to compare and to act as a test phrase for Χριστός. Our choice settles on κύριος ("Lord") because it is commonly used of Jesus and is not used as a name in Paul's writings.[14] What is remarkable is that anarthrous ἐν κυρίῳ ("in *the* Lord") occurs forty-three times in Paul's writings, and κύριος is both a title and definite here.[15] Furthermore, with other prepositions the article may or may not be expressed as, for example, ἀπὸ κυρίου (2 Cor 3:18; Col 3:24) and ἀπὸ **τοῦ** κυρίου (1 Cor 11:23; 2 Cor 5:6), which both mean "from *the* Lord," or πρὸς κύριον (2 Cor 3:16) and πρὸς **τὸν** κύριον (2 Cor 5:8; cf. Phlm 5), where both mean "to *the* Lord." Finally, the only occurrence of the article with this phrase (ἐν **τῷ** κυρίῳ Ἰησοῦ) is in Eph 1:15, where it is parallel in meaning

---

13. In those two Corinthian passages, "in the Messiah" may well also be the best rendering.

14. Κύριος may correspond to the enigmatic Hebrew name of God in the OT (YHWH), which is especially clear in the phrase κύριος ὁ θεός (YHWH God; e.g., Mark 12:29; Luke 20:37); this use is not found in Paul. As expected, κύριος occurs quite often in Paul with the article as it refers to "the Lord"; e.g., τῷ κυρίῳ as "pleasing *to the Lord*" (Eph 5:10), or "singing ... *to the Lord*" (Eph 5:20) or "as *to the Lord*" (Eph 5:22). This is clearly a title of Jesus, and the article seems to indicate it. Results from my research into other titles like σώτηρ, διδάσκαλος, and δεσπότης ("savior," "teacher," and "master") not reported here also confirm our conclusions.

15. The phrase ἐν κυρίῳ only occurs outside Paul at Rev 14:13.

with anarthrous ἐν κυρίῳ Ἰησοῦ (Rom 14:14; Phil 2:19; 1 Thess 4:1) and ἐν κυρίῳ Ἰησοῦ Χριστῷ (2 Thess 3:12), "in *the* Lord Jesus (Christ)."[16]

The outcome of our quick survey of κύριος usage is that with prepositions especially, where definite nouns may be anarthrous or articular, one should not jump to quick conclusions that an anarthrous use of Χριστός is necessarily used as a name and not as a title. Hence, just as we find ἐν κυρίῳ ("in *the* Lord") so often in Paul's writings, we find ἐν Χριστῷ, which itself may possibly mean "in *the* Messiah" if the usage between the two titles is truly analogous.

In conclusion, the articular phrase ἐν τῷ Χριστῷ in 1:10, 12, 20 undoubtedly refers to Christ's royal, messianic title rather than to a proper name and should be rendered "in the Messiah." This view is further substantiated by Paul's use of the phrase "kingdom of Christ and of God" (Eph 5:5) as sign that he uses Χριστός with reference to his messianic kingship (cf. esp. 1 Cor 15:20–28). The phrase only appears like this five times in Paul's writings. Furthermore, Χριστός in the much more common anarthrous prepositional phrase ἐν Χριστῷ—because of the common use of anarthrous definite nouns after the preposition and by analogy with definite ἐν κυρίῳ—*may* also refer to a title, but each case will depend on context to determine.

Excursus: The Mystery of Christ

Formerly, it was popular to understand Paul in Ephesians and elsewhere as adapting terms and concepts from pagan mystery religions.[17] Certainly when the Ephesians heard Paul speak of the "mystery" (μυστήριον; 1:9; 3:3–4, 9; 6:19; cf. 5:32; 1 Cor 2:1, 7; 4:1; Col 2:2; 4:3), they might hear it with two

---

16. Note that I am not counting here the frequent and distinctively Pauline articular phrase ὁ κύριος ἡμῶν ("*our* Lord") either before or after the name "Jesus Christ"; e.g., Eph 1:3, 17; 5:20; 6:24: τοῦ κυρίου ἡμῶν Ἰησοῦ Χριστοῦ; or 3:11: ἐν τῷ Χριστῷ Ἰησοῦ τῷ κυρίῳ ἡμῶν. The article is used with κύριος here because of the presence of the poss. personal pronoun (ἡμῶν, "our") in accordance with common Greek usage. This, of course, leads to the shorthand Greek idiom for the article itself functioning as a poss. pronoun; i.e., ὁ κύριος, "*our* Lord."

17. For broad surveys see Chrys C. Caragounis, *The Ephesian* Mysterion: *Meaning and Context*, ConBNT 8 (Lund: CWK Gleerup, 1977); Raymond E. Brown, *The Semitic Background of the Term "Mystery" in the New Testament* (Philadelphia: Fortress, 1968); Bornkamm, *TDNT*, 4:802–28. The excursus on "mystery" in Ephesians by Hoehner is helpful (Hoehner, 428–34).

common religious meanings in their context: public ceremonial rites associated with Artemis Ephesia (τὰ μυστήρια τῆς θεοῦ, "the mystic rites of the goddess" [Artemis Ephesia], *IvE* 3059; AD 2; or μυστήρια καὶ θυσίαι, "mystic rites and sacrifices," *IvE* 213; AD 88/9) and the classic mystery religions, especially the one connected with Dionysius.[18] Indeed, recent archaeological work in the "terrace houses" of Ephesus has yielded some interesting results, including the find of a chamber accessed only by crawling through a small passageway into a room with one small upper window. The chamber is understood as a place for conducting mystery rites for Dionysius in this home, which has other features of cult* practices.[19]

In the pagan mystery cults*, an initiate usually viewed a mysterious sacred object or participated in some other kind of secret experience. There is no more poignant example of this than Plutarch's consolation to his wife at the death of their infant daughter when he reminds her of the immortality of the soul as taught through "the mystic formulas (τὰ μυστικὰ σύμβολα) of Dionysiac rites, the knowledge of which we who are participants share with each other" (Plutarch, *Mor.* 611D [*Cons. ux.*,10]).

For Paul, though, *mystery* is a redemptive-historical term, not a secret experience or knowledge given to a select group of initiates. The "mystery of Christ" (3:4) *had* been hidden for long ages earlier, but specifically in the sense that Christ's cross work and ascension to all power (1:20–22; 2:6; etc.) had not yet been accomplished (esp. 3:11). There was *sufficient* revelation of Christ available for all the OT saints as their heritage, even if the particulars of God's redemptive accomplishment had been hidden: "The secret things belong to the LORD our God, but the things that are revealed belong to us and to our children forever, that we may do all the words of this law" (Deut 29:29).[20] But now God has openly disclosed this mystery in the "fullness of time" (1:10 above; Gal 4:4), and Paul and others have

18. For thorough treatment of the Artemis mysteries (and many other issues connected to ancient Ephesus) see Guy Maclean Rogers, *The Mysteries of Artemis of Ephesos: Cult, Polis, and Change in the Graeco-Roman World* (New Haven, CT: Yale University Press, 2012).

19. Described by Hilke Thür in "The House of C. Flavius Aptus in Ephesos: Club House of a Dionysic Community?" an unpublished paper given at the Ephesus conference at the Harding School of Theology in honor of Richard Oster, May 18–19, 2012.

20. Cf. W. Harold Mare, "Paul's Mystery in Ephesians 3," *BETS* 8 (1965): 77–84.

been entrusted with its open dissemination through the gospel (esp. 6:19). The mystery is a mystery no more. And God's wisdom regarding worldwide acceptance of anyone without discrimination by faith in Christ is openly proclaimed (3:10; cf. esp. Rom 16:25–27; 1 Cor 2:7; Col 1:25–27).

Excursus: Parallel Participles

It is unusual to have an excursus on Greek grammar in a commentary, yet it seems worthwhile to explain briefly the meaning of my term *parallel participle* and the rationale for this participle usage, which appears often in Ephesians (3:17; 4:2–3, 25; 5:15–21; 6:5–9). This is not the place to discuss this point of grammar and interact with other grammarians thoroughly; however, since this term is not used in NT grammars, a brief explanation may be helpful.[21] Put quite simply, a parallel participle is an adverbial participle that acts in parallel with another verb form and semantically replicates its function in the sentence. In the terminology one finds in the grammars on ancient Greek, this function is usually called a circumstantial (or adverbial) participle of "attendant circumstance," which "may often be rendered ... by a separate finite verb."[22]

In the NT it seems that many examples of this type of participle are employed in parallel with imperatives and have given rise to the category of

21. I first wrote about parallel ptcs. almost twenty years ago (S. M. Baugh, *A First John Reader: Intermediate Greek Reading Notes and Grammar* [Phillipsburg, NJ: P&R, 1999], 115–16). Happily, I have subsequently found the same ideas and term used in Guy L. Cooper III after K. W. Krüger, *Attic Greek Prose Syntax* (Ann Arbor: University of Michigan Press, 1998), 1:857–62.

22. Herbert Wier Smyth, *Greek Grammar*, rev. Gordon M. Messing (Cambridge, MA: Harvard University Press, 1956; original ed., 1920), §2054a; see also §§2068, 2147g; BDF §168 (2); MHT, 2:248–49; cf. G. Winer, *A Treatise on the Grammar of New Testament Greek* (Edinburgh: T&T Clark, 1882), 437–44 (who sees it as at least starting out as a periphrastic construction with copulative εἰμί that is elided or as ptcs. that are properly subordinate to the finite verb; cf. 716–17); Stanley E. Porter, *Idioms of the Greek New Testament*, Biblical Languages: Greek 2 (Sheffield, UK: JSOT, 1992), 183–86; Wallace, *Greek Grammar*, 640–45; A. T. Robertson, *A Grammar of the Greek New Testament in the Light of Historical Research*, 4th ed. (New York, 1923), 944–46.

the imperatival use of an independent participle.[23] In the context, though, these participles are replicating an expressed or implied imperative (or a different mood) in the context to which the participle is attached, albeit loosely.[24] For example, we have ἀνεχόμενοι and σπουδάζοντες (vv. 2–3a) attached to παρακαλῶ ... περιπατῆσαι (vv. 1–2) above, where the infinitive περιπατῆσαι has imperatival force in combination with παρακαλῶ (see comment). The semi-independent character of these parallel participles in 4:2–3 (and elsewhere) accounts for why the participles are expressed in their nominative case forms (i.e., ἀνεχόμενοι and σπουδάζοντες), whereas we would otherwise expect them to be accusative in agreement with the (implied) accusative case of the infinitive περιπατῆσαι.[25]

Grammars discussing syntax necessarily present examples in isolation from their surrounding contexts. Hence, I said earlier that the parallel participle *semantically* replicates another verb form's function because this looks at the syntactical function of the form only. The question now arises as to why an author would use one or more participle in parallel with another verb form; i.e., the pragmatics of the utterance. It is impossible to cover all the reasons and effects of this, but some things can be said to orient the reader on the issue.

---

23. The exceptions in Ephesians are 3:17; 4:1–3, where parallel ptcs. are connected with infs. As Wallace rightly notes (*Greek Grammar*, 642–44), this type of ptc. is frequent in NT narrative literature replicating the indic. (also true of its classical usage), and in some cases there may be Semitic influence from the LXX, especially with certain set impv. phrases (e.g., cf. LXX Gen 19:15; 21:18 with Matt 2:13, 20, and Luke 17:19 [cf. Acts 19:11; 22:10]). Yet he does not seem to be aware of the classical background and examples of this idiom, especially when he says that this ptc. is restricted in its word order as normally preceding its main verb.

24. Here is just one extrabiblical example: αὐτοὶ λαμβάνοντες πρὸ ὀφθαλμῶν ... οὕτως ἑαυτοὺς παραστήσεσθε πρὸς τὴν μάχην, "Fix your eyes ... and enter on this battle" (Polybius, *Hist.* 3.109.9; LCL trans.). W. R. Paton properly renders λαμβάνοντες as an impv. that is parallel with the juss. fut. indic. verb παραστήσεσθε (cf. Smyth, *Greek Grammar*, §1917, for the juss. fut.).

25. I.e., περιπατῆσαι ("to set out") is the (acc.) verbal obj. of παρακαλῶ ("I strongly urge"). The acc. case of such uses is clearer when the inf. obj. of a verb is copulative εἶναι; the subject and predicate are both in their acc. case forms as part of the obj. clause (e.g., 1:4 [εἶναι ἡμᾶς ἁγίους, "that we should be holy"] and 3:6 [εἶναι τὰ ἔθνη συγκληρονόμα, "that the Gentiles are fellow heirs"]).

Adverbial participles were put to a wide variety of uses and are very common forms in the NT and throughout ancient Greek.[26] The popularity of these participles is at least partly stylistic, as authors tried to vary their statements. A presentation that contained a string of imperatives joined by *καί* (e.g., Mark 2:9; 8:34; John 20:27) may be used by any author in a few places, but excessive use of them would seem "choppy" (i.e., *μονόκωλος*, "monocolon") and mark the author's style as unsophisticated.[27] When an author like Paul does use a string of finite imperative forms in parallel, as found in Ephesians, usually one is negated so that they are not precisely parallel.[28] The result is a certain strength to the statement, and one should take both cola* as equally prominent.

In contrast, when ideas were expressed with participles to replicate a central finite verb, there is a certain flow in the text that fits a more periodic style. And the event of the participle might be presented as either less or more prominent in the utterance than the controlling verb. For example, the controlling finite verb could be presented as either a more general or as the more central idea, while one or more parallel participles add specificity to it, elaborate on it, or they simply add coordinate events that accompany it that are important accessory elements.[29] These, at least, are general things one can say about this construction, while any further specifics must come from examination of concrete instances and their contexts.

Excursus: Hymns

Ephesus, like all ancient cities, was filled with religious music. Setting aside instrumental music, which proliferated in sacrificial and other pagan devotional contexts, the use of old and new songs was a common feature

26. There is on average one ptc. for every verse in the Greek NT.
27. As noted by Cooper that parallel ptcs. avoid "boringly repetitive parataxis of finite forms" (Cooper, *Attic Greek Prose Syntax*, 1:859).
28. For example, ὀργίζεσθε καὶ **μὴ** ἁμαρτάνετε ("Be angry, yet do not sin"; 4:26) and **μὴ** παροργίζετε τὰ τέκνα ὑμῶν **ἀλλὰ** ἐκτρέφετε αὐτὰ ("do not provoke your children to anger, but rear them"; 6:4).
29. An outstanding instance of this phenomenon outside Ephesians is Matt 28:19–20, with central *μαθητεύσατε* ("engage [or "enroll"] students") joined by three supporting, parallel ptcs.

of ancient religious life.[30] Rhapsodes, who sang or chanted the poems of Homer and other epics, would preface their performances at religious festivals with a hymn to the god of the festival.[31] These performers and others, especially the *citharodes* who were accompanied by the lyre (κιθάρα; 1 Cor 14:7; Rev 5:8; 14:2; 15:2), ended up as contestants in various municipal and regional festivals such as the Olympic, Great Epheseia, or provincial imperial festivals.[32]

But the singing of hymns was common in connection with ancient Greek cults*, so that we have record of Ephesian professionals who composed new hymns and performed both new and traditional hymns at public celebrations.[33] The following Ephesian inscription—which is suitably verbose and ornate for public performers—illustrates the international character and importance of these musical groups in Ephesus and throughout the empire:

> The motion was made by P. Aelius Pompeianus Paeon, citizen of Sidon, Tarsus, and Rhodes; a poet with many victories, a musical composer, and a rhapsode (of the temples) of the deified Hadrian, *theologos* of the temples in Pergamum; appointed as *Agonothete* of the Augustan Pythian (games);

30. Johannes Quasten believes that flutes (1 Cor 14:7), drums, cymbals (1 Cor 13:1), and other instruments were used in cultic* sacrifices and other venues because of a belief in music's magical powers to ward off hostile demons (*Music & Worship in Pagan & Christian Antiquity*, trans. Boniface Ramsey [Washington, D.C.: National Association of Pastoral Musicians, 1983], 15–16). Cf. Ignatius, *Eph.* 4.1.

31. These ended up in a collection of hymns attributed to Homer; so M. L. West, *Ancient Greek Music* (Oxford: Clarendon, 1992), 18–19; cf. the Homeric hymns bound with Hesiod in LCL 57 and Athanassakis, *The Orphic Hymns* (which are also dactylic hexameters).

32. Cf. S. R. F. Price, *Rituals and Power: The Roman Imperial Cult in Asia Minor* (Cambridge: Cambridge University Press, 1985), 101–32, for imperial festivals; Dio Chrysostom, *Or.* 27.5–6. One example of municipal festivals was the Balbilleia at Ephesus (*IvE* 1123), founded by Tib. Claudius Balbillus, a prefect under Claudius and court astrologer of Nero who was probably an Ephesian (*IvE* 3041–42).

33. These are the lyric musicians (μελοποιοί), hymn singers (ὑμνῳδοί [very frequent references] and ὑμνολόγοι [*IvE* 973 only]), and hymn composers (ὑμνογράφοι [*IvE* 1149 only]), as well as the guild of Dionysian artists mentioned in many epigraphical remains from Ephesus (see above introduction to 1:3–14 for some of the references).

Put to the vote by P. Aelius [...] the Admirable, citizen of Cyzicos, *Citharode*, victor of the Capitolinian and Olympic games;

Since Aelius Alcibiades, a man excelling in culture, magnanimity, and adorned with the other excellences of virtue; conti[nuing] for some time, even for 12 years, to provide benefactions in every way for the musicians, and offering help to the guild for the sake of honor and magnificence and for many acts of self-generosity to us and to the province; and further, he adorned the temple precinct of Roma of the Artisans of the [whole] world with sacred books and he furnished magnificent gifts of estates[34] supplied with a stable, from which we shall perpetually enjoy eternal revenue—we shall distribute the revenues annually among ourselves on each birthday of the deified Hadrian—for which the craftsmen in Rome, repaying the favor, voted other fitting honors for him and appointed him as high-priest for all time, and that he shall be preferred in honor, and they deemed that he be enrolled first in double (?) rank above other high-priests; wherefore he adorned the eternal memory of Hadrian, and he made the guild all the more esteemed through gifts by magnificently putting on solemn processions and funding lavish sacred-month festivals;

Because of these things, and now, to good fortune,

The craftsmen from the world under the aegis of Dionysus and of Caesar T. (Aelius) Hadrian Antoninus Augustus Pius, and the sacred victors, crown-bearers and their candidates (?) (who take part) in the pent-annual contest of the Great Epheseia in the greatest and first metropolis of Asia and twice-neocorate city of the Ephesian Augustean;

And they voted as honors resolved upon by us for this man to be devised as a just expression of thanks as recompense, to erect images overlaid with gold and statuettes both in the sacred temples of Asia for the emperors and in Nysa, the emperor-loving fatherland of Alcibiades; and to inscribe a plaque of the

34. The word here is χωρία ("estates"), used for investment estates, which draw an income for absentee owners such as those sold in the early church in Acts 4:34.

> decrees in the temple of Apollo and in his remaining buildings even in all the cities; in order that the double memorial might be fitting for both the magnanimity of Alcibiades and for the expression of thanks of those who have benefited (by him); and that he should be honored by being publicly singled out with a gold crown in the sacrifices and drink-offerings of the common game(s), and also to be publicly singled out and honored above all at every meeting; let copies of the decrees be sent out to him and to Nysa, his most illustrious fatherland-city, through the emissaries, P. Aelius Pompeianus Paeon, citizen of Sidon, Tarsus, and Rhodes; a poet with many victories, a musical composer, and a rhapsode (of the temples) of the deified Hadrian, sacred orator of the temples in Pergamum; appointed as Agonothete of the Augustan Pythian (games); and Aristides the Admirable, son of Aristides, citizen of Perga and Pergamum, the poet; and let a delegation be sent also to the greatest emperor, and to the guild in Rome which should make public the (thanks) for the actions (belonging to) the benefactor, Alcibiades. (*IvE* 22; mid-2 AD)

Given this background, it seems to me natural to suppose that if the Ephesians were to sing "hymns," and not only the Psalms and other biblical types of songs, that these Greek speakers with their rich heritage and experienced musical life would compose songs in the forms of Greek rather than in Semitic hymnody.[35] And that means that they would be metrical.[36]

One example of such hymns was the *Hymn to Zeus* by Callimachus in dactylic hexameter, which contains the following:

> Κρῆτες ἀεὶ ψεῦσται καὶ γὰρ τάφον ὦ ἄνα σεῖο
> Κρῆτες ἐτεκτάναντο σὺ δ' οὐ θάνες ἐσσὶ γὰρ αἰεί.[37]

---

35. Cf. Allen Cabaniss, "The Background of Metrical Psalmody," *CTJ* 20 (1985): 191–206.

36. See West, *Ancient Greek Music*, 129–59, for common musical rhythms in Greek hymnody for dactyls (¯ ˘ ˘), anapests (˘ ˘ ¯), iambics (˘ ¯), and other meters in all their rich variety and complex exceptions.

37. " 'Cretans are ever liars.' Yea, a tomb, O Lord, for thee the Cretans builded; but thou didst not die, for thou art for ever" (LCL trans.).

The dactylic hexameter contains six metrical feet with dactyls (¯ ˘ ˘), while spondees (¯ ¯) are allowed in places where its second long substitutes for the dactyl's two short syllables. The first line above scans as: ¯ ˘ ˘ | ¯ ¯ | ¯ ¯ | ¯ ˘ ˘ | ¯ ˘ ˘ | ¯ ¯. In Titus 1:12, Paul quotes a source used by Callimachus for his lines above (thought to have originated with Epimenides in a lost work) as follows:

> Κρῆτες ἀεὶ ψεῦσται κακὰ θηρία γαστέρες ἀργαί.[38]

Though the last part of the line is different from Callimachus, Paul quotes a whole hexameter in Titus, which scans properly: ¯ ˘ ˘ | ¯ ¯ | ¯ ˘ ˘ | ¯ ˘ ˘ | ¯ ˘ ˘ | ¯ ¯. In other words, where Paul quotes a Greek poetic text, he is able to preserve the meter properly, for meter was a central feature of Greek hymns.

Indeed, one of the first extrabiblical Christian hymns we possess (P.Oxy. 1786) is metrical. This scrap of papyrus from Oxyrhynchus contains just a snippet of a bicola composition with a generally anapaestic meter (˘ ˘ ¯), but it also contains ancient musical notation.[39] The translation of M. L. West fills in gaps but gives a sense of the content of this hymn:

> Let it be silent, let the luminous stars not shine, let the winds (?) and all the noisy rivers die down; and as we hymn the Father, the Son, and the Holy Spirit, let all the powers (πᾶσαι δυνάμεις) add "Amen, amen." Empire (κράτος), praise always, and glory to God, the sole giver of all good things. Amen, amen.[40]

The use of "amen" here, and focus on light and power, seems compatible with Ephesians (e.g., 1:20–23; 5:8) and its focus on God's supremacy over all

---

38. "Cretans are ever liars, evil beasts, lazy gluttons ['stomachs']."

39. For metrical analysis (including the many exceptions *metri gratia*) see the *editio princeps:* Bernard P. Grenfell and Arthur S. Hunt, eds., *The Oxyrhynchus Papyri* (London: Egypt Exploration Society, 1922), 15:21–25; and West, *Ancient Greek Music*, 324–26. The papyrus is dated to the third century AD, and it is important to note that the meter is "purely quantitative and uninfluenced by accent" (22), since accent was displacing the old syllable length for poetic measurement sometime in the first centuries after Christ. This hymn competes with another ancient hymn, Φῶς Ἱλαρόν ("O Gladsome Light"), as the earliest Christian hymn. The latter is still sung today in many communions; cf. Antonia Tripolitis, "ΦΩΣ ΙΛΑΡΟΝ: Ancient Hymn and Modern Enigma," *VC* 24 (1970): 189–96, who dates its origin to the late second to early third century.

40. West, *Ancient Greek Music*, 325.

competing powers and might in Christ. It is a hymn befitting an Ephesian at the least.

Excursus: Boys and Girls at Ephesus

In the comment on 6:1 above, I maintained that Paul's address to τέκνα ("children") denotes both sons and daughters in context, and I mentioned some evidence exists to substantiate this for the Ephesian audience. It is a difficult thing to read the minds of ancient peoples from whom we have no literature explaining their ideas in detail. However, we do have around six thousand epigraphical remains from ancient Ephesus that can inform us on some of these questions quite adequately.

One pertinent piece of evidence on the question of the referent of τέκνα ("children") as both sons and daughters is the donation list of Ephesian "fishermen and fish sellers" for building a toll office for their industry at Ephesus in AD 54–59 (*IvE* 20).[41] This is an important inscription for a number of issues, ranging from the local economy and taxation to Roman citizenship in the provinces. For our purposes, in addition to listing their individual donations (e.g., "2,000 bricks," "20 denarii"), the donors list their names and often their family members. Here is just one example from the first name listed, representing an important Ephesian family:

> Πόπλιος Ὁρδεώνιος
> Λολλιανὸς σὺν γυναικὶ
> καὶ τοῖς τέκνοις κίον(ας) δ›
>
> Publius Hordeonius Lollianus with (his) wife and his children (gave) 4 columns.

The (male) fishermen and fish sellers often list various family members on this inscription (which is extensive though incomplete because it is broken at the end and has some lacunae) as follows:

mother	2
wife	5
brothers	1

41. See also note above on 5:25. We could also study the various funerary inscriptions on this question, but the results would be the same as with *IvE* 20.

son	14	
sons	8	
daughter	2	
children:		
	τέκνα	5
	παιδία	1
	θρεπτοί	1

Granted that most of those mentioned are sons, it is possible that the children are mentioned because they worked in the family fishing business.[42] For our purposes, though, it seems plausible to read τέκνα (and synonyms) as referring to *both* sons and daughters, who are otherwise specifically referenced on this list. In other words, if τέκνον would automatically mean "son" or "sons," why did twenty-four Ephesians specifically mention their "son," "sons," or "daughter" rather than just "children"? Paul's reference to τέκνα in Eph 6:1, then, probably also refers to both daughters and sons.

Excursus: Slavery at Ephesus

There are a number of helpful and easily obtainable resources on ancient slavery that bear on Eph 6:5–9.[43] Yet there are some specifics from Ephesus that are not always mentioned that deserve brief notice (see also above on 3:6 for the imperial freemen Mazaeus and Mithridates).

42. The fishing took place on nearby "sacred" salt pan ponds and lakes—i.e., controlled by the Artemisium (*IvE* 17–19), which explains the taxes. Fishermen rarely went out into the ocean to fish at that time. These tolls had earlier been usurped by Roman *publicani* ("tax-gatherers"), but had been returned to Artemis when the city protested through an embassy to Rome by one of its leading men, Artemidorus (Strabo, 14.1.26). See below on v. 20 for Paul as an "emissary in chains."

43. For slavery in our time period see E. Ferguson, *Backgrounds of Early Christianity*, 3rd ed. (Grand Rapids: Eerdmans, 2003), 59–62, and works cited there, including the source anthology by Thomas Wiedemann, *Greek and Roman Slavery* (Baltimore: Johns Hopkins University Press, 1981; repr., New York: Routledge, 1994); cf. *New Docs*, 7:163–96; 8:1–46; Henrik Mouritsen, *The Freedman in the Roman World* (Cambridge: Cambridge University Press, 2011). Both Hoehner, 800–804, and Lincoln, 415–20, have substantial excursuses on ancient slavery, which focus on the standard literature and legal relations.

First, it should be noted that Ephesus housed an important wholesale slave market for distribution of slaves to the western Roman districts.[44] This is evidenced by a honorary statue of C. Sallustius Crispus Passienus, Roman proconsul ("governor") of Asia in AD 42/3 as the patron of "those who do business in the slave market" (*qui in statario negotiantur*; *IvE* 3025). Another similar inscription is made out "to the benefactor of Ephesian citizens who do business in the slave market" (*IvE* 646; under Trajan). Most honorary inscriptions to Roman dignitaries from the imperial period were written either in Greek or in both Greek and Latin. However, both inscriptions in *IvE* 3025 and 646 dealing with the slave market were written only in Latin, which suggests that this Ephesian market was controlled by the Romans and specially sanctioned by the provincial Roman power. They apparently served primarily Roman interests.[45]

The source of these slaves at market is of interest. In previous eras, the bulk of their ranks were filled in time of war with surviving enemy combatants and their households (i.e., their own families and their own slaves). But there was no warfare in Paul's day in Asia Minor or in the near vicinity. The second source was the children of slaves, the so-called house-born, but these usually stayed in the household to fill out the ranks of those who died prematurely (Pliny, *Ep.* 8.16; cf. *Ep.* 5.19; cf. comment on Eph 3:7). The last three sources of slaves would be the most common in our period in Ephesus: debt bondage (that is, the sale of oneself or one's children into slavery, usually out of extreme poverty), rearing foundlings into slavery, and illegal kidnapping of free persons by brigands and pirates.[46]

---

44. Especially for the large Roman "plantations" (*latifundia*) in Italy and Sardinia, with the few who showed intellectual promise going into domestic service for various functions on the staff of wealthy Romans. For example, the readers and secretarial staff of Pliny the Younger (*Ep.* 5.19; 8.1; 9.20, 36).

45. In line with this statement is a passage in Varro cited in Wiedemann (*Greek and Roman Slavery*, 34) discussing how people named slaves, using a hypothetical example of one purchased at Ephesus.

46. Foundlings were children "exposed" (i.e., thrown out to die) by their parents and picked up by someone to be raised as their slaves. The papyrus finds from Egypt contain a number of business contracts with wet nurses who were given charge of such foundlings for their first few years (as well as a famous, pathetic letter of a soldier to his pregnant wife saying, "if it is a girl, throw her out" [*P.Oxy.* 744]). An early Greek romantic novel has its hero and heroine discover that they

"Slave traders" or "kidnappers" (1 Tim 1:10) appear often in the literature of the period, for example, in the romantic novel called the *Ephesiaca* by someone known as Xenophon of Ephesus.[47] More pointedly, Paul himself often faced the real threat of kidnapping during his missionary trips through inland Asia Minor (2 Cor 11:26), especially during his trips through the narrow pass of the Taurus Mountains (the "Cilician gates") northwest of Tarsus. This pass was a notorious place for ambush by bands of cutthroats. There were strict laws against the sale of free persons against their will, of course, but it happened with sometimes widespread regularity, as well as the rearing of free-born foundlings into slavery, causing discussions in the Roman imperial circles about their status (Pliny, *Ep.* 10.65–66).

On the issue of foundlings, we come to one of the more interesting inscriptions from Ephesus, dating from around two decades before Ephesians was written. It is a long edict from the provincial governor of Asia Minor, Paullus Fabius Persicus (*IvE* 17–19; AD 44), who intervened in several financial matters related to the revenues of the state goddess, Artemis Ephesia. Part of the decree reads as follows:

> Likewise there are free persons who are supplying the service (ὑπηρεσία) of public slaves and burdening the state with extraordinary expense, these must be dismissed and public slaves substituted in their positions of service. Likewise public slaves, who, it is reported, are purchasing babies at the normal cost to devote them to Artemis that their slaves may be reared (τρέφω; cf. Eph 6:4) from her revenues, it is resolved that they must provision nurses for their slaves themselves. (*IvE* 18c; my trans.)

Lincoln (417) notes that slaves could own their own slaves, yet what is happening at Ephesus is that these public slaves were billing Artemis for their own surrogate workers. It was a nice deal. It should be noted that public slaves in the cities of the eastern empire were often criminals committed over to this slave service (cf. Pliny, *Ep.* 10.31–32). It should also be noted that we do not know how many, if any, of Persicus' decisions were ever

were (freeborn) foundlings when both sets of natural parents miraculously appear on the scene, and they all live happily ever after (Longus, *Daphnis and Chloe*).

47. Cf. B. P. Reardon, ed., *Collected Ancient Greek Novels* (Berkeley and Los Angeles: University of California, 2008).

actually fully implemented. Provincial governors came and went, but city bureaucrats always had nephews and other relations who could use a lucrative state job, even if these positions did properly belong to cheaper public slaves. And public slaves were probably not the only ones profiting from the rearing of slaves from the revenues of Artemis.

List of Foreign and Technical Words

anaphoric: From the Latin noun *anaphora*. Indicates a reference back to a previous context by the repetition of a word or phrase.

asyndeton: A figure of speech where a word is left out for emphasis.

chiasm: A literary structure where parallel elements correspond in an inverted order (i.e., A-B-C-C′-B′-A′).

colon: (pl. "cola") A single line of poetry; also called a stich. A line of poetry may consist of one colon (monocolon), two cola (bicolon), three cola (tricolon), or four cola (tetracolon).

conative: Denotes verbal action that is intended, attempted, or about to occur.

cult/cultic: A system of religious worship, especially with reference to its rituals and ceremonies. This definition is to be distinguished from the more specific and common modern usage of the word in the sense of "a religion regarded as unorthodox or false."

genitive absolute: A grammatically independent word or clause in the genitive case.

hendiadys: A figure of speech in which two related nouns or verbs are used to communicate a single idea, often heightening its meaning (e.g., "signs and wonders").

inclusio: A literary framing device by which the same word or phrase occurs at both the beginning and the end of a linguistic unit.

***lectio difficilior*:** A principle of textual criticism whereby the more difficult reading is to be preferred, since scribes are more likely to have altered a difficult reading than an easy one.

***nomina sacra*:** "Sacred names" that occur in manuscripts with an abbreviated form and a line above the word.

stanza: The main subunit of an entire poem, consisting of multiple strophes.

strophe: Poetry units of one or more cola. Multiple strophes comprise a stanza.

synecdoche: A figure of speech in which one idea is exchanged for another; for example, the whole for the part or the part for the whole.

***Vorlage*:** An original document; the manuscript from which a scribe copied a text.

General Bibliography

Technical Monographs

Arnold, C. *Ephesians: Power and Magic: The Concept of Power in Ephesians in Light of Its Historical Setting.* SNTSMS 63. New York: Cambridge University Press, 1989.

Barth, M. *The Broken Wall: A Study of the Epistle to the Ephesians.* Valley Forge, PA: Judson, 1959.

Brannon, M. *The Heavenlies in Ephesians: A Lexical, Exegetical, and Conceptual Analysis.* LNTS. London: T&T Clark, 2011.

Caragounis, C. C. *The Ephesian* Mysterion: *Meaning and Context.* Lund: CWK Gleerup, 1977.

Dahl, N. *Studies in Ephesians: Introductory Questions, Text-Critical Issues, Interpretation of Texts and Themes.* WUNT 131. Tübingen: Mohr Siebeck, 2000.

Darko, D. *No Longer Living as the Gentiles: Differentiation and Shared Ethical Values in Ephesians* 4.17–6.9. New York: T&T Clark, 2008.

Dawes, G. *The Body in Question: Metaphor and Meaning in the Interpretation of Ephesians 5:21–33.* Boston: Brill, 1998.

Fleckenstein, K.-H. *Ordnet euch einander unter in der Furcht Christi: Die Eheperikope in Eph 5,21–33: Geschichte der Interpretation, Analyse und Aktualisierung des Textes.* Würzburg: Echter, 1994.

Gese, M. *Das Vermächtnis des Apostels: Die Rezeption der paulinischen Theologie im Epheserbrief.* WUNT 99. Tübingen: Mohr Siebeck, 1997.

Gombis, T. *The Drama of Ephesians: Participating in the Triumph of God.* Downers Grove, IL: InterVarsity Press, 2010.

Harris, H., III. *The Descent of Christ: Ephesians 4:7–11 and Traditional Hebrew Imagery.* AGJU 32. Grand Rapids: Baker, 1998.

Kreitzer, L. *Hierapolis in the Heavens: Studies in the Letter to the Ephesians.* London: T&T Clark, 2007.

Lau, T.-L. *The Politics of Peace: Ephesians, Dio Chrysostom, and the Confucian Four Books.* Boston: Brill, 2010.

Lindemann, A. *Die Aufhebung der Zeit: Geschichtsverständnis und Eschatologieim Epheserbrief.* Gütersloh: Mohn, 1975.

Merklein, H. *Christus und die Kirche: Die theologische Grundstruktur des Epheserbriefe nach Eph 2,11–18*. Stuttgart: KBW Verlag, 1973.

———. *Die kirchliche Amt nach den Epheserbrief.* StANT 33. Munich: Kösel, 1973.

Miletic, S. *"One Flesh": Eph. 5.22–24, 5.31, Marriage and the New Creation.* AnBib 115. Rome: Pontifical Biblical Institute, 1988.

Mitton, C. L. *The Epistle to the Ephesians: Its Authorship, Origin and Purpose.* Oxford: Clarendon, 1951.

Moritz, T. *A Profound Mystery: The Use of the Old Testament in Ephesians*. SNT 85. New York: Brill, 1996.

Murphy-O'Connor, J. *St. Paul's Ephesus: Texts and Archaeology*. Collegeville, MN: Liturgical, 2008.

Petrenko, E. *Created in Christ Jesus for Good Works: The Integration of Soteriology and Ethics in Ephesians*. PBM. Milton Keynes, UK: Paternoster, 2011.

Rader, W. *The Church and Racial Hostility: A History of Interpretation of Ephesians 2,11–22*. Tübingen: Mohr, 1978.

Sampley, J. P. *"And the Two Shall Become One Flesh": A Study of Traditions in Ephesians 5:21–33*. Cambridge: Cambridge University Press, 1971.

Schlier, H. *Christus und die Kirche im Epheserbrief.* BHT 6. Tübingen: Mohr Siebeck, 1930.

Sellin, G., and D. Sänger. *Studien zu Paulus und zum Epheserbrief.* FRLANT 228. Göttingen: Vandenhoeck & Ruprecht, 2009.

Thiessen, W. *Christen in Ephesus.* TANTZ 12. Tübingen: Francke, 1995.

van Roon, A. *The Authenticity of Ephesians.* NovTSup 39. Leiden: Brill, 1974.

Yee, T.-L. *Jews, Gentiles and Ethnic Reconciliation: Paul's Jewish Identity and Ephesians*. SNTSMS 130. Cambridge: Cambridge University Press, 2005.

Articles and Essays

Abasciano, B. "Clearing Up Misconceptions about Corporate Election." *ATJ* 41 (2009): 59–90.

Agnew, F. "On the Origin of the Term *Apostolos.*" *CBQ* 38 (1976): 49–53.

———. "The Origin of the NT Apostle-Concept: A Review of Research." *JBL* 105 (1986): 75–96.

Ahern, B. "The Indwelling Spirit, Pledge of Our Inheritance (Eph 1:14)." *CBQ* 9 (1947): 179–89.

Alexander, L. "Chronology of Paul." In *DPL*, 115–23.

Allen, T. "Exaltation and Solidarity with Christ. Ephesians 1:20 and 2:6." *JSNT* 28 (1986): 103–20.

Arnold, C. "Ephesians, Letter to the." In *DPL*, 238–49.

———. "The 'Exorcism' of Ephesians 6.12." *JSNT* 30 (1987): 71–87.

Asher, J. "An Unworthy Foe: Heroic Ἔθη, Trickery, and an Insult in Ephesians 6:11." *JBL* 130 (2011): 729–48.

Barkhuizen, J. H. "The Strophic Structure of the Eulogy of Ephesians 1:3–14." *Hormormde Teologiese Studies* 46 (1990): 390–413.

Barton, S., and G. Horsley. "A Hellenistic Cult Group and the New Testament Churches." *JAC* 24 (1981): 7–41.

Bauckham, R. "Pseudo-Apostolic Letters." *JBL* 107 (1988): 469–94.

Baugh, S. M. "A Foreign World: Ephesus in the First Century." In *Women in the Church*, edited by A. Kostenberger and T. Schreiner, 13–38. 2nd ed. Grand Rapids: Baker, 2005.

———. "Galatians 5:1–6 and Personal Obligation: Reflections on Paul and the Law." In *The Law Is Not of Faith: Essays on Works and Grace in the Mosaic Covenant,* ed. B. Estelle, J. V. Fesko, and D. VanDrunen, 265–70. Phillipsburg, NJ: P&R, 2009.

———. "Marriage and Family in Ancient Greek Society." In *Marriage and Family in the Biblical World*, edited by K. M. Campbell, 103–31. Downers Grove, IL: InterVarsity Press, 2003.

———. "The Poetic Form of Col 1:15–20." *WTJ* 47 (1985): 227–44.

———. " 'Savior of All People': 1 Tim 4:10 in Context," *WTJ* 54 (1992): 331–40.

Benoit, P. "Pauline Angelology and Demonology: Reflexions on Designations of Heavenly Powers and on Origin of Angelic Evil according to Paul." *RelSBul* 3 (1983): 1–18.

Berger, K. "Apostelbrief und apostolische Rede / zum Formulae frühchristlicher Briefe." *ZNW* 65 (1975): 190–231.

Best, E. "Ephesians i.1 Again." In *Paul and Paulinism*, edited by M. D. Hooker and S. G. Wilson, 273–79. London: SPCK, 1982.

———. "Paul's Apostolic Authority—?" *JSNT* 27 (1986): 3–25.

Betz, H. "Secrecy in the Greek Magical Papyri." In *Antike und Christentum*, 4:152–74. Tübingen: Mohr Siebeck, 1998.

Bickerman, E. "The Warning Inscriptions of Herod's Temple." *JQR* 37 (1947): 387–405.

Black, D. "The Peculiarities of Ephesians and the Ephesian Address." *GTJ* 2 (1981): 59–73.

Boyer, J. "A Classification of Imperatives: A Statistical Study." *GTJ* 8 (1987): 35–54.

Burn, A. "*Hic Breve Vivitur:* A Study of the Expectation of Life in the Roman Empire." *Past and Present* 4 (1953): 2–31.

Byrskog, S. "Co-Senders, Co-Authors and Paul's Use of the First Person Plural." *ZNW* 87 (1996): 230–50.

Cabaniss, A. "The Background of Metrical Psalmody." *CTJ* 20 (1985): 191–206.

Cambier, J. "La Bénédiction D'Eph 1 3–14." *ZNW* 54 (1963): 58–104.

Campbell-Reed, E. "Should Wives 'Submit Graciously'? A Feminist Approach to Interpreting Ephesians 5:21–33." *RevExp* 98 (2001): 263–76.

Cervin, R. "Does Κεφαλή Mean 'Source' or 'Authority Over' in Greek Literature? A Rebuttal." *TrinJ* 10 (1989): 85–112.

Cirafesi, W. "ἔχειν πίστιν in Hellenistic Greek and Its Contribution to the πίστις Χριστοῦ Debate." *BAGL* 1 (2012): 5–37.

Clarke, A. " 'Be Imitators of Me': Paul's Model of Leadership." *TynB* 49 (1998): 329–60.

Collins, J. "Ephesians 5:18: What Does πληροῦσθε ἐν πνεύματι Mean?" *Presb* (2007): 12–30.

Coutts, J. "Ephesians 1:3–14 and 1 Peter 1:3–12." *NTS* 3 (1957): 115–27.

Denton, D. "Inheritance in Paul and Ephesians." *EvQ* 54 (1982): 157–62.

Dillon, J. "*Pleroma* and Noetic Cosmos: A Comparative Study." In *Neoplatonism and Gnosticism*, 99–110. Albany: State University of New York Press, 1992.

Dunning, B. "Strangers and Aliens No Longer: Negotiating Identity and Difference in Ephesians 2." *HTR* 99 (2006): 1–16.

Easley, K. "The Pauline Usage of *Pneumati* as a Reference to the Spirit of God." *JETS* 27 (1984): 299–313.

Easton, B. "New Testament Ethical Lists." *JBL* 51 (1932): 1–12.

Elmer, I. "I, Tertius: Secretary or Co-author of Romans." *ABR* 56 (2008): 45–60.

Evans, C. "The Meaning of *Pleroma* in Nag Hammadi." *Bib* 65 (1984): 254–65.

Fenik, J. "Enthroned with Christ: An Exegetical and Theological Study of Eph 1:20–23 and 2:5–6." STD diss. Catholic University of America, 2008.

Fitzmyer, J. "*Kephalê* in I Corinthians 11:3." *Int* 47 (1993): 52–59.

Fong, B. "Addressing the Issue of Racial Reconciliation according to the Principles of Eph 2:11–22." *JETS* 38 (1995): 565–80.

Forbes, C. "Paul's Principalities and Powers: Demythologizing Apocalyptic?" *JSNT* 82 (2001): 61–88.

Foster, P. "The First Contribution to the πίστις Χριστοῦ Debate: A Study of Ephesians 3.12." *JSNT* 85 (2002): 75–96 .

Foster, R. " 'A Temple in the Lord Filled to the Fullness of God': Context and Intertextuality (Eph. 3:19)." *NovT* 49 (2007): 85–96.

Gibson, J. "Ephesians 5:21–33 and the Lack of Marital Unity in the Roman Empire." *BSac* 168 (2011): 162–77.

Glancy, J. "Obstacles to Slaves' Participation in the Corinthian Church." *JBL* 117 (1998): 481–501.

Gombis, T. "Being the Fullness of God in Christ by the Spirit: Ephesians 5:18 in Its Epistolary Setting." *TynB* 53 (2002): 259–71.

———. "Cosmic Lordship and Divine Gift-Giving: Psalm 68 in Ephesians 4:8." *NovT* 47 (2005): 367–80.

———. "Ephesians 2 as a Narrative of Divine Warfare." *JSNT* 26 (2004): 403–18.
———. "Ephesians 3:2–13: Pointless Digression, or Epitome of the Triumph of God in Christ?" *WTJ* 66 (2004): 313–23.
———. "A Radically New Humanity: The Function of the *Haustafel* in Ephesians." *JETS* 48 (2005): 317–30.
Goodrich, J. "Paul, the *Oikonomos* of God: Paul's Apostolic Metaphor in 1 Corinithians and Its Greco-Roman Context." PhD diss. Durham University, 2010.
Gordon, D. " 'Equipping' Ministry in Ephesians 4?" *JETS* 37 (1994): 69–78.
Gosnell, P. "Ephesians 5:18–20 and Mealtime Propriety." *TynB* 44 (1993): 363–71.
———. "Honor and Shame Rhetoric as a Unifying Motif in Ephesians." *BBR* 16 (2006): 105–28.
Grudem, W. "Does ΚΕΦΑΛΗ ('Head') Mean 'Source' or 'Authority Over' in Greek Literature?" *TrinJ* 6 (1985): 38–59.
———. "The Meaning of Κεφαλή ('Head'): A Response to Recent Studies." *TrinJ* 11 (1990): 3–72.
———. "The Meaning of Κεφαλή ('Head'): An Evaluation of New Evidence, Real and Alleged." *JETS* 44 (2001): 25–65.
Gudorf, M. "The Use of ΠΑΛΗ in Ephesians 6:12." *JBL* 117 (1998): 331–35.
Gupta, N., and F. Long. "The Politics of Ephesians and the Empire: Accommodation or Resistance?" *JGRChJ* 7 (2010): 112–36.
Hamann, H. "The Translation of Ephesians 4:12—A Necessary Revision." *Concordia Journal* 14 (1988): 42–49.
Hammer, P. "A Comparison of *KLĒRONOMIA* in Paul and Ephesians." *JBL* 79 (1960): 267–72.
Harris, H., III. "The Ascent and Descent of Christ in Ephesians 4:9–10." *BSac* 151 (1994): 198–214.
———. " 'The Heavenlies' Reconsidered: Οὐρανός and Ἐπουράνιος in Ephesians." *BSac* 148 (1991): 72–89.
Harrisville, R. "Before ΠΙΣΤΙΣ ΧΡΙΣΤΟΥ: The Objective Genitive as Good Greek." *NovT* 48 (2006): 353–58.
———. "The Concept of Newness in the New Testament." *JBL* 74 (1955): 69–79.
Head, P. M. "Named Letter-Carriers among the Oxyrhynchus Papyri." *JSNT* 31 (2009): 279–99.
Heil, J. "Ephesians 5:18b: 'But Be Filled in the Spirit.' " *CBQ* 69 (2007): 506–16.
Heinzel, E. "Zum Kult der Artemis von Ephesos." *JAÖI* 50 (1970): 243–51.
Hemer, C. "The Name of Paul." *TynB* 36 (1985): 179–83.
Hoch, C. "The Significance of the *Syn-* Compounds for Jew-Gentile Relationships in the Body of Christ." *JETS* 25 (1982): 175–83.
Horsley, G. "The Inscriptions of Ephesus and the New Testament." *NovT* 34 (1992): 105–68.
Howard, G. "The Head/Body Metaphors of Ephesians." *NTS* 20 (1974): 350–56.

Hultgren, A. "The *Pistis Christou* Formulation in Paul." *NovT* 22 (1980): 248–63.

Iwry, S. "Notes on Psalm 68." *JBL* 71 (1952): 161–65.

Jeal, R. "A Strange Style of Expression: Ephesians 1:23." *Filologia Neotestamentaria* 10 (1997): 129–38.

Jolivet, I. "The Ethical Instructions in Ephesians as the Unwritten Statutes and Ordinances of God's New Temple in Ezekiel." *ResQ* 48 (2006): 193–210.

Kearsley, R. "Women in Public Life in the Roman East: Iunia Theodora, Claudia Metrodora and Phoebe, Benefactress of Paul." *TynB* 50 (1999): 189–211.

Kerr, A. J. "*ARRABŌN*." *JTS* 39 (1988): 92–97.

Kienast, D. "Zu den Homonoia-Vereinbarungen Keiserzeit in der Römischen Kaiserzeit." *ZPE* 109 (1995): 267–82.

Klingbeil, G. "Metaphors and Pragmatics: An Introduction to the Hermeneutics of Metaphors in the Epistle to the Ephesians." *BBR* 16 (2006): 273–93.

Knibbe, D., H. Engelmann, and B. Iplikçioglu. "Neue Inschriften aus Ephesos XII." *JAÖI* 62 (1993): Hauptblatt 113–50.

Kostenberger, A. "The Mystery of Christ and the Church: Head and Body, 'One Flesh.' " *TrinJ* 12 (1991): 79–94.

———. "What Does It Mean to Be Filled with the Spirit? A Biblical Investigation." *JETS* 40 (1997): 229–40.

Kreitzer, L. " 'Crude Language' and 'Shameful Things Done in Secret' (Ephesians 5.4, 12): Allusions to the Cult of Demeter/Cybele in Hierapolis?" *JSNT* 71 (1998): 51–77.

Krentz, E. "Epideiktik and Hymnody: The New Testament and Its World." *BR* 40 (1995): 50–97.

Lash, C. "Where Do Devils Live? A Problem in the Textual Criticism of Ephesians 6, 12." *VC* 30 (1976): 161–74.

Lehner, M. "Die Agonistik im Ephesos der römischen Keiserzeit." PhD diss. Ludwig-Maximilians-Universität, 2004.

Lincoln, A. "The Use of the OT in Ephesians." *JSNT* 14 (1982): 16–57.

Lindemann, A. "… ἐκτρέφετε αὐτὰ ἐν παιδείᾳ καὶ νουθεσίᾳ κυρίου (Eph 6:4): Kinder in der Welt des frühen Christentums." *NTS* 56 (2010): 169–90.

Longman, T. "The Divine Warrior: The New Testament Use of an Old Testament Motif." *WTJ* 44 (1982): 290–307.

López, R. "Paul's Vice List in Ephesians 5:3–5." *BSac* 169 (2012): 203–18.

———. "Vice Lists in Non-Pauline Sources." *BSac* 168 (2011): 178–95.

Lotz, J. "The Homonoia Coins of Asia Minor and Ephesians 1:21." *TynB* 50 (1999): 173–88.

Lunde, J., and J. Dunne. "Paul's Creative and Contextual Use of Isaiah in Ephesians 5:14." *JETS* 55 (2012): 87–110.

———. "Paul's Creative and Contextual Use of Psalm 68 in Ephesians 4:8." *WTJ* 74 (2012): 99–117.

MacDonald, M. "The Politics of Identity in Ephesians." *JSNT* 26 (2004): 419–44.

———. "Slavery, Sexuality and House Churches: A Reassessment of Colossians 3:18–4:1 in Light of New Research on the Roman Family." *NTS* 53 (2007): 94–113.

Mare, W. "Paul's Mystery in Ephesians 3." *BETS* 8 (1965): 77–84.

Marrow, S. "*Parrhēsia* and the New Testament." *CBQ* 44 (1982): 431–46.

Martin, R. "Aspects of Worship in the New Testament Church." *VE* 2 (1963) 6–32.

McGrath, B. " 'SYN' Words in Saint Paul." *CBQ* 14 (1952): 219–26.

McKelvey, R. "Christ the Cornerstone." *NTS* 8 (1962): 352–59.

Moule, C. " 'Fulness' and 'Fill' in the New Testament." *SJT* 4 (1951): 79–86.

Oster, R. "The Ephesian Artemis as an Opponent of Early Christianity." *JAC* 19 (1976): 24–44.

———. "Ephesus as a Religious Center under the Principate." *ANRW* 2.18.3 (1990): 1661–1728.

Overfield, P. "Pleroma: A Study in Context and Content." *NTS* 25 (1979): 384–96.

Page, S. "Whose Ministry? A Re-Appraisal of Ephesians 4:12." *NovT* 47 (2005): 26–46.

Pelser, G. "Once More the Body of Christ in Paul." *Neot* 32 (1998): 525–45.

Peppard, M. " 'Poetry', 'Hymns' and 'Traditional Material' in New Testament Epistles or How to Do Things with Indentations." *JSNT* 30 (2008): 319–42.

Perriman, A. "The Corporate Christ: Re-Assessing the Jewish Background." *TynB* 50 (1999): 239–63.

Peterman, G. "Marriage and Sexual Fidelity in the Papyri, Plutarch and Paul." *TynB* 50 (1999): 163–72.

Pickup, M. "New Testament Interpretation of the Old Testament: The Theological Rationale of Midrashic Exegesis." *JETS* 51 (2008): 353–81.

Poythress, V. "Why Lying Is Always Wrong: The Uniqueness of Verbal Deceit." *WTJ* 75 (2013): 83–95.

Qualls, P., and J. Watts. "Isaiah in Ephesians." *RevExp* 93 (1996): 249–59.

Rapske, B. "The Importance of Helpers to the Imprisoned Paul in the Book of Acts." *TynB* 42 (1991): 3–30.

Reinhard, D. "Ephesians 6:10–18: A Call to Personal Piety or Another Way of Describing Union with Christ?" *JETS* 48 (2005): 521–32.

Rese, M. "Die Vorzüge Israels in Röm 9,4f und Eph 2,12: exegetische Anmerkungen zum Thema Kirche und Israel." *TheolZeit* 31 (1975): 211–22.

Reumann, J. "OIKONOMIA = 'COVENANT'; Terms for *Heilsgeschichte* in Early Christian Usage." *NovT* 3 (1959): 282–92.

———. "Οἰκονομία-Terms in Paul in Comparison with Lucan *Heilsgeschichte*." *NTS* 13 (1967): 147–67.

Richards, E. R. "Silvanus Was Not Peter's Secretary: Theological Bias in Interpreting διὰ Σιλουανοῦ ... ἔγραψα in 1 Peter 5:12." *JETS* 43 (2000): 417–32.

Robbins, C. J. "The Composition of Eph. 1:3–14." *JBL* 105 (1986): 677–87.

Rogers, C. "The Dionysian Background of Ephesians 5:18." *BSac* 136 (1979): 249–57.

Rojas, J. "Ephesians 4,12. A Revised Reading." *Bib* 92 (2011): 81–96.

Rubinkiewicz, R. "Ps LXVIII 19 (= Eph IV 8) Another Textual Tradition or Targum?" *NovT* 17 (1975): 219–24.

Scheidel, W. "The Comparative Economics of Slavery in the Greco-Roman World." Version 1. *Princeton/Stanford Working Papers in Classics.* 2005.

Sherwood, A. "Paul's Imprisonment as the Glory of the Ethnē: A Discourse Analysis of Ephesians 3:1–13." *BBR* 22 (2012): 97–112.

Sicking, C., and P. Stork. "The Synthetic Perfect in Classical Greek." In *Two Studies in the Semantics of the Verb in Classical Greek*, 119–298. New York: Brill, 1996.

Smillie, G. "Ephesians 6:19–20: A Mystery for the Sake of Which the Apostle is an Ambassador in Chains." *TrinJ* 18 (1997): 199–222.

Smith, D. "Cultic Language in Ephesians 2:19–22: A Test Case." *ResQ* 34 (1989): 207–17.

Smith, G. "Paul's Use of Psalm 68:18 in Ephesians 4:8." *JETS* 18 (1975): 181–89.

Staats, R. "Kaiser Konstantin der Große und der Apostel Paul." *VC* 62 (2008): 334–70.

Still, T. "Did Paul Loathe Manual Labor? Revisiting the Work of Ronald F. Hock on the Apostle's Tentmaking and Social Class." *JBL* 125 (2006): 781–95.

Stuhlmacher, P. " 'He Is Our Peace' (Eph 2:14)—On the Exegesis and Significance of Eph 2:14–18." In *Reconciliation, Law, & Righteousness: Essays in Biblical Theology*, 182–200. Philadelphia: Fortress, 1986.

Suh, R. "The Use of Ezekiel 37 in Ephesians 2." *JETS* 50 (2007): 715–33.

Tan, K. "The Shema and Early Christianity." *TynB* 59 (2008): 181–206.

Taylor, R. "The Use of Psalm 68:18 in Ephesians 4:8 in Light of the Ancient Versions." *BSac* 148 (1991): 319–36.

Thomas, R. "The Seal of the Spirit and the Religious Climate of Ephesus." *ResQ* 43 (2001): 155–66.

Tonstad, S. "Πιστις Χριστου: Reading Paul in a New Paradigm." *AUSS* 40 (2002): 37–59.

Wallace, D. "Ὀργίζεσθε in Ephesians 4:26: Command or Condition?" *CTR* 3 (1989): 353–72.

Walter, N. "Nikolaos, Proselyt aus Antiochien, und die Nikolaiten in Ephesus und Pergamon: Ein Beitrag auch zum Thema: Paulus und Ephesus." *ZNW* 93 (2002): 200–226.

Warden, P., and Bagnall, R. "The Forty Thousand Citizens of Ephesus." *CPhil* 83 (1988): 220–23.

Wenkel, D. "The 'Breastplate of Righteousness' in Ephesians 6:14: Imputation or Virtue?" *TynB* 58 (2007): 275–87.
White, R. "Gaffin and Grudem on Eph 2:20: in Defense of Gaffin's Cessationist Exegesis." *WTJ* 54 (1992): 303–20.
Wild, R. "The Warrior and the Prisoner: Some Reflections on Ephesians 6.10–20." *CBQ* 46 (1984): 284–89.
Wilder, W. "The Use (or Abuse) of Power in High Places: Gifts Given and Received in Isaiah, Psalm 68, and Ephesians 4:8." *BBR* 20 (2010): 185–200.
Wold, B. "Family Ethics in *4QInstruction* and the New Testament." *NovT* 50 (2008): 286–300.
Wolter, M. "Verborgene Weisheit und Heil für die Heiden. Zur Traditionsgeschichte und Intention des 'Revelationsschemas.'" *ZTK* 84 (1987): 297–319.
Woodcock, E. "The Seal of the Holy Spirit." *BSac* 155 (1998): 139–63.
Yorke, G. "Hearing the Politics of Peace in Ephesians: A Proposal from an African Postcolonial Perspective." *JSNT* 30 (2007): 113–27.

General Books

Alford, Henry. *The Greek New Testament: With a Critically Revised Text: A Digest of Various Readings: Marginal References to Verbal and Idiomatic Usage: Prolegomena: and a Critical and Exegetical Commentary*. 3 vols. 5th ed. London: Rivingtons, 1871.
Arnold, C. *Powers of Darkness : Principalities & Powers in Paul's Letters*. Downers Grove, IL: InterVarsity Press, 1992.
Aune, D. *Prophecy in Early Christianity and the Ancient Mediterranean World*. Grand Rapids: Eerdmans, 1983.
Bammer, A. *Das Heiligtum der Artemis von Ephesos*. Graz: Akademische, 1984.
Barnett, P. *Paul: Missionary of Jesus*. Grand Rapids: Eerdmans, 2008.
Barrett, C. *From First Adam to Last: A Study in Pauline Theology*. London: Adam & Charles Black, 1962.
Bash, A. *Ambassadors for Christ: An Exploration of Ambassadorial Language in the New Testament*. WUNT 2/92. Tübingen: Mohr Siebeck, 1997.
Bauckham, R. *Jesus and the God of Israel: God Crucified and Other Studies on the New Testament's Christology of Divine Identity*. Grand Rapids: Eerdmans, 2008.
Baugh, S. M. *A New Testament Greek Primer.* 3rd ed. Phillipsburg, NJ: P&R, 2012.
Beale, G. K. *A New Testament Biblical Theology: The Unfolding of the Old Testament in the New*. Grand Rapids: Baker Academic, 2011.
———. *The Temple and the Church's Mission*. NSBT 17. Downers Grove, IL: InterVarsity Press, 2004.

Beale, G. K., and D. A. Carson, eds. *Commentary on the New Testament Use of the Old Testament*. Grand Rapids: Baker, 2007.

Beasley-Murray, G. *Baptism in the New Testament.* 2nd ed. Carlisle, UK: Paternoster, 1997.

Best, E. *One Body in Christ.* London: SPCK, 1955.

Best, E., and R. McL. Wilson, eds. *Text and Interpretation.* Cambridge: Cambridge University Press, 1979.

Bird, M., and P. Sprinkle, eds. *The Faith of Jesus Christ: Exegetical, Biblical, and Theological Studies*. Peabody, MA: Hendrickson, 2009.

Blocher, H. *Original Sin: Illuminating the Riddle.* NSBT 5. Downers Grove, IL: InterVarsity Press, 1997.

Bockmuehl, M. *Revelation and Mystery in Ancient Judaism and Pauline Christianity*. Grand Rapids: Eerdmans, 1997. Reprint of 1990 ed.

Bowersock, G. *Greek Sophists in the Roman Empire.* Oxford: Clarendon, 1969.

Breytenbach, C. *Grace, Reconciliation, Concord: The Death of Christ in Graeco-Roman Metaphors*. NovTSup 135. Leiden: Brill, 2010.

Brown, R. *The Semitic Background of the Term "Mystery" in the New Testament.* Philadelphia: Fortress, 1968.

Burke, T. J. *Adopted into God's Family.* NSBT 22. Downers Grove, IL: InterVarsity Press, 2006.

Burkert, W. *Greek Religion.* Cambridge, MA: Harvard University Press, 1985.

Burtchaell, J. *From Synagogue to Church: Public Services and Offices in the Earliest Christian Communities*. Cambridge: Cambridge University Press, 1992.

Burton, E. D. *Syntax of the Moods and Tenses in New Testament Greek.* Edinburgh: T&T Clark, 1898.

Caird, G. *Principalities and Powers: A Study in Pauline Theology.* New York: Oxford University Press, 1956.

Calvin, J. *Institutes of the Christian Religion.* Translated by L. F. Battles. 2 vols. Philadelphia: Westminster, 1960.

———. *Sermons on Ephesians.* London: Banner of Truth, 1973.

Campbell, C. *Paul and Union with Christ: An Exegetical and Theological Study*. Grand Rapids: Zondervan, 2012.

Campbell, K., ed. *Marriage and Family in the Biblical World.* Downers Grove, IL: InterVarsity Press, 2003.

Carr, W. *Angels and Principalities: The Background, Meaning and Development of the Pauline Phrase* αἱ ἀρχαὶ καὶ αἱ ἐξουσίαι. SNTSMS 42. Cambridge: Cambridge University Press, 1981.

Carson, D., ed. *Biblical Interpretation and the Church.* Exeter, UK: Paternoster, 1984.

Carson, D., and D. Moo. *An Introduction to the New Testament.* 2nd ed. Grand Rapids: Zondervan, 2005.

Carson, D., P. O'Brien, and M. Seifrid, eds. *Justification and Variegated Nomism.* Vol. 1. Grand Rapids: Baker, 2001.

Charlesworth, J., ed. *The Old Testament Pseudepigrapha.* 2 vols. New York: Doubleday, 1983, 1985.

Clark, R. S., ed. *Covenant, Justification and Pastoral Ministry: Essays by the Faculty of Westminster Seminary California.* Phillipsburg, NJ: P&R, 2007.

———. *Recovering the Reformed Confession: Our Theology, Piety, and Practice.* Phillipsburg, NJ: P&R, 2008.

Clowney, E. *The Church.* Downers Grove, IL: InterVarsity Press, 1995.

———. *The Unfolding Mystery: Discovering Christ in the Old Testament.* Phillipsburg, NJ: P&R, 1989.

Collins, J. *Diakonia: Re-interpreting the Ancient Sources.* Oxford: Oxford University Press, 1990.

Cooper, G. after Küger, K. *Attic Greek Prose Syntax.* 4 Vols. Ann Arbor: University of Michigan Press, 1998.

Cribiore, R. *Gymnastics of the Mind: Greek Education in Hellenistic and Roman Egyp*t. Princeton, NJ: Princeton University Press, 2001.

Danker, F. *Benefactor: Epigraphic Study of a Graeco-Roman and New Testament Semantic Field.* St. Louis: Clayton, 1982.

Deichgraber, R. *Gotteshymnus und Christushymnus in der Frühen Christenheit: Untersuchungen zu Form, Sprache und Stil der frühchristlichen Hymnen.* SUNT. Göttingen: Vandenhoeck & Ruprecht, 1967.

deSilva, D. *Honor, Patronage, Kinship & Purity: Unlocking New Testament Culture.* Downers Grove, IL: InterVarsity Press, 2000.

Dibelius, M. *Die Geisterwelt im Glauben des Paulus.* Göttingen: Vandenhoeck & Ruprecht, 1909.

Dignas, B. *Economy of the Sacred in Hellenistic and Roman Asia Minor.* New York: Oxford University Press, 2002.

Dunn, J. *The Theology of Paul the Apostle.* Grand Rapids: Eerdmans, 1998.

Eilers, C., ed., *Diplomats and Diplomacy in the Roman World.* Mnemosyne Supplement 304. Boston: Brill, 2009.

Elliger, W. *Ephesos: Geschichte einer antiken Weltstadt.* Stuttgart, Berlin, Cologne, and Mainz: Kohlhammer, 1985.

Ernst, J. *Pleroma und Pleroma Christi: Geschichte und Deutung eines Begriffs der paulinischen Antilegomena.* BU 5. Regensburg: Pustet, 1970.

Fanning, B. *Verbal Aspect in New Testament Greek.* Oxford: Clarendon, 1990.

Fantin, J. *The Greek Imperative Mood in the New Testament: A Cognitive and Communicative Approach.* SBG 12. New York: Peter Lang, 2010.

Faraone, C., and D. Obbink, eds. *Magika Hiera: Ancient Greek Magic and Religion.* New York: Oxford University Press, 1991.

Fee, G. *God's Empowering Presence: The Holy Spirit in the Letters of Paul.* Peabody, MA: Hendrickson, 1994.

Ferguson, E. *Backgrounds of Early Christianity.* 3rd ed. Grand Rapids: Eerdmans, 2003.

Ferguson, S. *The Holy Spirit.* Downers Grove, IL: InterVarsity Press, 1996.

Fesko, J. *Beyond Calvin: Union with Christ and Justification in Early Modern Reformed Theology (1517–1700).* Bristol, CT: Vandenhoeck & Ruprecht, 2012.

Frank, T. *An Economic Survey of Ancient Rome.* 4 vols. Baltimore: Johns Hopkins University Press, 1938.

Friesen, S. *Twice Neokoros: Ephesus, Asia, and the Cult of the Flavian Imperial Family.* Leiden: Brill, 1993.

Gamble, H. *Books and Readers in the Early Church.* New Haven, CT: Yale University Press, 1995.

Gardner, J. *Family and* Familia *in Roman Law and Life.* Oxford: Clarendon, 1998.

———. *Women in Roman Law and Society.* Bloomington: Indiana University Press, 1991.

Glancy, J. *Slavery in Early Christianity.* Minneapolis: Fortress, 2006.

Gordley, M. *Teaching through Song in Antiquity.* WUNT 2.302. Tübingen: Mohr Siebeck, 2011.

Graf, F. *Magic in the Ancient World.* Cambridge, MA: Harvard University Press, 1999.

Gundry, R. *Soma in Biblical Theology, with Emphasis on Pauline Anthropology.* Cambridge: Cambridge University Press, 1976.

Gundry, S., ed. *Three Views of the Millennium and Beyond.* Grand Rapids: Zondervan, 1999.

Harper, K. *Slavery in the Late Roman World, AD 275–425.* New York: Cambridge University Press, 2011.

Harrill, J. A. *The Manumission of Slaves in Early Christianity.* HUT 32. Tübingen: Mohr Siebeck, 1995.

———. *Slaves in the New Testament: Literary, Social, and Moral Dimensions.* Minneapolis: Fortress, 2006.

Harrison, J. *Paul's Language of Grace in Its Graeco-Roman Context.* WUNT 2.172. Tübingen: Mohr Siebeck, 2003.

Harrisville, R. *The Concept of Newness in the New Testament.* Minneapolis: Augsburg, 1960.

Harvey, J. *Listening to the Text: Oral Patterning in Paul's Letters.* Grand Rapids: Baker, 1998.

Hays, R. *The Faith of Jesus Christ: The Narrative Substructure of Galatians 3:1–4:11.* BRS. 2nd ed. Grand Rapids: Eerdmans, 2002.

Head, B. *Historia Numorum: A Manual of Greek Numismatics.* 2nd ed. Oxford: Clarendon, 1911.

Hengel, M. *The Pre-Christian Paul*. Philadelphia: Trinity Press International, 1991.

Hester, J. *Paul's Concept of Inheritance: A Contribution to the Understanding of Heilsgeschichte*. Edinburgh and London: Oliver & Boyd, 1968.

Hoch, C. *All Things New: The Significance of Newness for Biblical Theology*. Grand Rapids: Baker, 1995.

Hock, R. *The Social Context of Paul's Ministry: Tentmaking and Apostleship*. Philadelphia: Fortress, 1980.

Horton, M. *The Christian Faith: A Systematic Theology for Pilgrims On the Way*. Grand Rapids: Zondervan, 2011.

———. *Covenant and Eschatology: The Divine Drama*. Louisville: Westminster John Knox, 2002.

———. *Covenant and Salvation: Union with Christ*. Louisville: Westminster John Knox, 2007.

Hubbard, M. *New Creation in Paul's Letters and Thought*. SNTSMS 119. Cambridge: Cambridge University Press, 2002.

Hultin, J. *The Ethics of Obscene Speech in Early Christianity and Its Environment*. SNT 128. Leiden: Brill, 2008.

Hurtado, L. *One God, One Lord: Early Christian Devotion and Ancient Jewish Monotheism*. Philadelphia: Fortress, 1988.

Jackson, T. *New Creation in Paul's Letters: A Study of the Historical and Social Setting of a Pauline Concept*. WUNT 2.272. Tübingen: Mohr Siebeck, 2010.

Jaeger, W. *Early Christianity and Greek Paideia*. Cambridge, MA: Harvard University Press, 1965.

Jewett, R. *A Chronology of Paul's Life*. Philadelphia: Fortress, 1979.

Karwiese, S. *Groß ist die Artemis von Ephesos: die Geschichte einer der großen Städt der Antike*. Vienna: Phoibos, 1995.

Kelly, J. *Early Christian Creeds*. 3rd ed. New York: Continuum, 1972.

Kennedy, G. *New Testament Interpretation through Rhetorical Criticism*. Chapel Hill: University of North Carolina Press, 1984.

Kenny, A. *A Stylometric Study of the New Testament*. Oxford: Clarendon, 1986.

Kim, S. *The Origin of Paul's Gospel*. Eugene, OR: Wipf & Stock, 2007.

Kirk, J. R. D. *Unlocking Romans: Resurrection and the Justification of God*. Grand Rapids: Eerdmans, 2008.

Klauck, H.-J. *Ancient Letters and the New Testament: A Guide to Context and Exegesis*. Waco, TX: Baylor University Press, 2006.

Klein, W. *The New Chosen People: A Corporate View of Election*. Grand Rapids: Zondervan, 1990.

Kline, M. *The Structure of Biblical Authority*. 2nd ed. Grand Rapids: Eerdmans, 1975.

Knibbe, D. *Ephesus = Ephesos: Geschichte einer bedeutenden antiken Stadt und Portrait einer modernen Großgrabung im 102. Jahr der Wiederkehr des*

Beginnes österreichischer Forschungen (1895–1997). New York: Peter Lang, 1998.

Knibbe, D., and B. Iplikçioglu. *Ephesos im Spiegel seiner Inschriften.* Vienna: Schindler, 1984.

Koester, H., ed. *Ephesos, Metropolis of Asia.* Valley Forge, PA: Harvard Divinity School Press, 1995.

Kostenberger, A., and T. Schreiner, eds. *Women in the Church.* 2nd ed. Grand Rapids: Baker, 2005.

Lampe, G. W. H. *The Seal of the Spirit.* New York: Longmans, Green, 1951.

Lausberg, H. *Handbook of Literary Rhetoric: A Foundation for Literary Study.* Edited by D. Orton and R. D. Anderson. Boston: Brill, 1998.

Lelis, A., W. Percy, and B. Verstraete. *The Age of Marriage in Ancient Rome.* Studies in Classics 26. Lewiston, NY: Edwin Mellen, 2003.

Letham, R. *Union with Christ: In Scripture, History, and Theology*. Phillipsburg, NJ: P&R, 2011.

Lincoln, A. T. *Paradise Now and Not Yet.* SNTSMS. Cambridge, Cambridge University Press, 1981.

Lincoln, A., and A. Wedderburn. *The Theology of the Later Pauline Letters*. New York: Cambridge University Press, 1993.

Lindsay, H. *Adoption in the Roman World.* Cambridge: Cambridge University Press, 2009.

Longenecker, R. *Biblical Exegesis in the Apostolic Period*. Grand Rapids: Eerdmans, 1975.

Lotz, J. *Ignatius and Concord: The Background and Use of the Language of Concord in the Letters of Ignatius of Antioch*. New York: Peter Lang, 2007.

Luck, G. *Arcana Mundi: Magic and the Occult in the Greek and Roman Worlds*. Baltimore: Johns Hopkins University Press, 1985.

Lyall, F. *Slaves, Citizens, Sons: Legal Metaphors in the Epistles*. Grand Rapids: Zondervan, 1984.

Malherbe, A., F. Norris, and J. Thompson, eds. *The Early Church in Its Context.* Leiden: Brill, 1998.

Marcel, P. *The Biblical Doctrine of Infant Baptism: Sacrament of the Covenant of Grace*. Translated by P. E. Hughes. Cambridge: James Clarke, 1953.

Martin, D. *Slavery as Salvation: The Metaphor of Slavery in Pauline Christianity*. New Haven, CT: Yale University Press, 1990.

Martin, R. *Reconciliation: A Study of Paul's Theology*. Atlanta: John Knox, 1981.

McGrath, J. *The Only True God: Early Christian Monotheism in Its Jewish Context*. Urbana and Chicago: University of Illinois Press, 2009.

McKay, K. L. *A New Syntax of the Verb in New Testament Greek*. SBG 5. New York: Peter Lang, 1994.

McKelvey, R. *The New Temple: The Church in the New Testament.* New York: Oxford University Press, 1969.

Meade, D. *Pseudonymity and Canon: An Investigation into the Relationship of Authorship and Authority in Jewish and Earliest Christian Tradition.* Grand Rapids: Eerdmans, 1987.

Meli, U. *Neue Schöpfung: Eine traditionsgeschichtliche und exegetische Studie zu einem soteriologischen Grundsatz paulinischer Theologie.* BZNW 56. New York: de Gruyter, 1989.

Metzger, B. *A Textual Commentary on the Greek New Testament.* 2nd ed. New York: United Bible Societies, 1994.

Meyer, M., and P. Mirecki, eds. *Ancient Magic and Ritual Power.* RGRW 129. Leiden: Brill, 1995.

Meyer, M., and R. Smith, eds. *Ancient Christian Magic: Coptic Texts of Ritual Power.* San Francisco: HarperCollins, 1994.

Mickelsen, A., ed. *Women, Authority and the Bible.* Downers Grove, IL: InterVarsity Press, 1986.

Minear, P. *Christians and the New Creation: Genesis Motifs in the New Testament.* Louisville: Westminster John Knox, 1994.

Mitchell, S. *Anatolia.* Oxford: Clarendon, 1993.

Morales, L. *The Tabernacle Pre-Figured: Cosmic Mountain Ideology in Genesis and Exodus.* BTS 15. Leuven: Peeters, 2012.

Morales, R. *The Spirit and the Restoration of Israel: New Exodus and New Creation Motifs in Galatians.* WUNT 2.282. Tübingen: Mohr Siebeck, 2010.

Morgan, T. *Literate Education in the Hellenistic and Roman Worlds.* Cambridge: Cambridge University Press, 1998.

Morris, L. *The Apostolic Preaching of the Cross.* 3rd ed. London: Tyndale, 1965.

Mouritsen, H. *The Freedman in the Roman World.* New York: Cambridge University Press, 2011.

Murphy-O'Connor, J. *Paul the Letter-Writer: His World, His Options, His Skills.* GNS 41. Collegeville, MN: Liturgical, 1995.

Murray, J. *Christian Baptism.* Philadelphia: P&R, 1974.

———. *Principles of Conduct.* Grand Rapids: Eerdmans, 1957.

Neumann, K. *The Authenticity of the Pauline Epistles in the Light of Stylostatistical Analysis.* SBLDS 120. Atlanta: Scholars Press, 1990.

Neyrey, J. *Give God the Glory: Ancient Prayer and Worship in Cultural Perspective.* Grand Rapids: Eerdmans, 2007.

Norden, E. *Agnostos Theos: Untersuchungen zur Formengeschichte religiöser Rede.* Leipzig and Berlin: Tuebner, 1913.

Pfitzner, V. *Paul and the Agon Motif.* NovTSup 16. Leiden: Brill, 1967.

Piper, J., and W. Grudem, eds. *Recovering Biblical Manhood and Womanhood: A Response to Evangelical Feminism.* Wheaton, IL: Crossway, 1991.

Porter, S., ed. *Paul's World.* Boston: Brill, 2008.

———. *Verbal Aspect in the Greek of the New Testament.* SBG 1. New York: Peter Lang, 1989.

Porter, S., and S. Adams, eds. *Paul and the Ancient Letter Form.* Boston: Brill, 2010.

Porter, S., and T. Olbricht, eds. *Rhetoric and the New Testament: Essays from the 1992 Heidelberg Conference.* Sheffield: JSOT Press, 1993.

Porter, S., and A. Pitts, eds. *Christian Origins and Greco-Roman Culture: Social and Literary Contexts for the New Testament.* Boston: Brill, 2013.

Price, S. *Rituals and Power: The Roman Imperial Cult in Asia Minor.* Cambridge: Cambridge University Press, 1984.

Purvo, R. I. *The Making of Paul: Constructions of the Apostle in Early Christianity.* Minneapolis: Fortress, 2010.

Rapske, B. *Paul in Roman Custody.* Grand Rapids: Eerdmans, 1994.

Rawson, B., ed. *The Family in Ancient Rome.* Ithaca, NY: Cornell University Press, 1986.

Richards, E. R. *Paul and First-Century Letter Writing: Secretaries, Composition and Collection.* Downers Grove, IL: InterVarsity Press, 2004.

———. *The Secretary in the Letters of Paul.* WUNT 2.42. Tübingen: Mohr Siebeck, 1991.

Ridderbos, H. *The Coming of the Kingdom.* Phillipsburg, NJ: P&R, 1962.

Riddlebarger, K. *A Case for Amillennialism: Understanding the End Times.* Grand Rapids: Baker, 2003.

Rijksbaron, A. *The Syntax and Semantics of the Verb in Classical Greek: An Introduction.* 2nd ed. Amsterdam: J. C. Gieben, 1994.

Robertson, A. T. *A Grammar of the Greek New Testament in the Light of Historical Research.* 4th ed. New York, 1923.

Robinson, H. W. *Corporate Personality in Ancient Israel.* Philadelphia: Fortress, 1964.

Rogers, G. M. *The Mysteries of Artemus of Ephesos: Cult, Polis, and Change in the Graeco-Roman World.* New Haven, CT: Yale University Press, 2012.

———. *The Sacred Identity of Ephesos.* New York: Routledge, 1991.

Şahin, S., E. Schwertheim, and J. Wagner, eds. *Studien zur Religion und Kultur Kleinasiens II. Festschrift für Friedrich Karl Dörner zum 65. Geburtstag am 28. Februar 1976.* Leiden: Brill, 1978.

Sanders, E. *Paul and Palestinian Judaism.* Philadelphia: Fortress, 1977.

Sandnes, K. *Paul, One of the Prophets? A Contribution to the Apostle's Self-Understanding.* Tübingen: Mohr Siebeck, 1991.

Scaglione, A. *The Classical Theory of Composition from Its Origins to the Present.* Chapel Hill: University of North Carolina Press, 1972.

Scherrer, P. *Ephesus: The New Guide.* Turkey: Zero, 2000.

Schreiner, T. *Paul, Apostle of God's Glory in Christ: A Pauline Theology.* Downers Grove, IL: InterVarsity Press, 2001.

Schreiner, T., and S. Wright, eds. *Believer's Baptism: Sign of the New Covenant in Christ.* Nashville: Broadman and Holman, 2006.

Schüssler Fiorenza, E. *In Memory of Her: A Feminist Theological Reconstruction of Christian Origins*. New York: Crossroad, 1989.

Schweitzer, A. *The Mysticism of Paul the Apostle.* Translated by W. Montgomery. London: A&C Black, 1931. Repr., Baltimore: Johns Hopkins University Press, 1998.

Scott, J. M. *Adoption as Sons of God: An Exegetical Investigation into the Background of Huiothesia in the Pauline Corpus*. WUNT 2.48. Tübingen: Mohr Siebeck, 1992.

Scroggs, R. *The Last Adam: A Study in Pauline Anthropology*. Philadelphia: Fortress, 1966.

Segovia, F., ed. *Discipleship in the New Testament.* Philadelphia: Fortress, 1985.

Sherwin-White, A. *Roman Citizenship.* 2nd ed. Oxford: Oxford University Press, 1973.

Smith, J. *Christ the Ideal King.* WUNT 2.313. Tübingen: Mohr Siebeck, 2011.

Stork, P. *The Aspectual Usage of the Dynamic Infinitive in Herodotus*. Groningen: Bouma's Boekhuis, 1982.

Strelan, R. *Paul, Artemis, and the Jews in Ephesus.* BZNTW 80. New York: de Gruyter, 1996.

Tajra, H. *The Martyrdom of St. Paul.* WUNT 2.67. Tübingen: Mohr Siebeck, 1994.

———. *The Trial of St. Paul: A Judicial Exegesis of the Second Half of the Acts of the Apostles*. WUNT 2.35. Tübingen: Mohr Siebeck, 1989.

Trebilco, P. *The Early Christians in Ephesus from Paul to Ignatius*. Grand Rapids: Eerdmans, 2008.

———. *Jewish Communities in Asia Minor.* Cambridge: Cambridge University Press, 1991.

Turner, N. *Grammatical Insights Into the New Testament*. Edinburgh: T&T Clark, 1965.

Usami, K. *Somatic Comprehension of Unity: The Church in Ephesus*. Rome: Biblical Institute, 1983.

van Kooten, G. *Paul's Anthropology in Context: The Image of God, Assimilation to God, and Tripartite Man in Ancient Judaism, Ancient Philosophy and Early Christianity*. WUNT 1.232. Tübingen: Mohr Siebeck, 2008.

VanDrunen, D. *Divine Covenants and Moral Order: A Biblical Theology of Natural Law*. Grand Rapids: Eerdmans, 2014.

Vickers, B. *Jesus' Blood and Righteousness: Paul's Theology of Imputation*. Wheaton, IL: Crossway, 2006.

Vos, G. *Biblical Theology: Old and New Testaments*. Grand Rapids: Eerdmans, 1948.

———. *The Pauline Eschatology.* Grand Rapids: Eerdmans, 1953.

———. *Redemptive History and Biblical Interpretation: The Shorter Writings of Geerhardus Vos*. Edited by R. Gaffin Jr. Phillipsburg, NJ: P&R, 1980.

Wallace, D. *Granville Sharp's Canon and Its Kin: Semantics and Significance*. SBG 14. New York: Peter Lang, 2009.

Wansink, C. *Chained in Christ: The Experience and Rhetoric of Paul's Imprisonments*. JSNTSup 130. Sheffield: Sheffield Academic, 1996.

Watson, G. *The Roman Soldier.* Ithaca, NY: Cornell University Press, 1969.

Weima, J. *Neglected Endings: The Significance of the Pauline Letter Closings*. Sheffield: JSOT Press, 1994.

West, M. *Introduction to Greek Metre.* Oxford: Clarendon, 1987.

White, J. *Light from Ancient Letters.* Philadelphia: Fortress, 1986.

Wiedemann, T. *Greek and Roman Slavery.* New York: Routledge, 1994.

Wilder, T. *Pseudonymity, the New Testament, and Deception: An Inquiry into Intention and Reception*. Lanham, MD: University Press of America, 2004.

Wiles, G. *Paul's Intercessory Prayers: The Significance of the Intercessory Prayer Passages in the Letters of Paul*. SNTSMS 24. Cambridge: Cambridge University Press, 1974.

Winer, G. B. *A Treatise on the Grammar of New Testament Greek: Regarded as a Sure Basis for New Testament Exegesis.* Edinburgh: T&T Clark, 1882.

Wink, W. *Engaging the Powers: Discernment and Resistance in a World of Domination*. Minneapolis: Fortress, 1992.

———. *Naming the Powers: The Language of Power in the New Testament*. Philadelphia: Fortress, 1984.

———. *Unmasking the Powers: The Invisible Forces That Determine Human Existence*. Philadelphia: Fortress, 1986.

Winter, B. *Roman Wives, Roman Widows: The Appearance of New Women and the Pauline Communities*. Grand Rapids: Eerdmans, 2003.

———. *Seek the Welfare of the City: Christians as Benefactors and Citizens*. Grand Rapids: Eerdmans, 1994.

Wright, D., ed. *Baptism: Three Views.* Downers Grove, IL: InterVarsity Press, 2009.

———. *Infant Baptism in Historical Perspective: Collected Studies*. SCHT. Eugene, OR: Wipf & Stock, 2007.

Wright, N. T. *The New Testament and the People of God.* Minneapolis: Fortress, 1992.

———. *The Resurrection of the Son of God.* Minneapolis: Fortress, 2003.

Yoder Neufeld, T. *"Put on the Armour of God": The Divine Warrior from Isaiah to Ephesians.* JSNTSup 140. Sheffield: Sheffield Academic, 1997.

Ancient Sources

Augustine. "The Predestination of the Saints." In *The Works of Saint Augustine: A Translation for the 21st Century*, 149–90. 1/26. Translated by R. Teske. New York: New City, 1999.

Ehrenberg, V., and A. Jones, eds. *Documents Illustrating the Reigns of Augustus and Tiberius.* 2nd ed. Oxford: Clarendon, 1976.

Grenfell, B. P., and A. S. Hunt, eds. *The Oxyrhynchus Papyri.* London: Egypt Exploration Society, 1922.

Pomeroy, S. *Xenophon Oeconomicus: A Social and Historical Commentary*. Oxford: Clarendon, 1994.

Index of Biblical Verses

Old Testament

2 Samuel

1 Kings

2 Kings

1 Chronicles

2 Chronicles

Ezra

Nehemiah

Esther

Job

Psalms

New Testament

John

Acts

Romans

Ephesians

Philippians

James

1 Peter

Apocrypha and Pseudepigrapha